Global Health

The Library of Essays in Global Governance

Titles in the Series:

Global Health
John J. Kirton

Global Law
John J. Kirton with Jelena Madunic

Global Trade
John J. Kirton

International Finance
John J. Kirton

International Organization
John J. Kirton

Global Health

Edited by

John J. Kirton
University of Toronto, Canada

ASHGATE

Wherever possible, these reprints are made from a copy of the original printing, but these can themselves be of very variable quality. Whilst the publisher has made every effort to ensure the quality of the reprint, some variability may inevitably remain.

Published by
Ashgate Publishing Limited
Wey Court East
Union Road
Farnham
Surrey GU9 7PT
England

Ashgate Publishing Company
Suite 420
101 Cherry Street
Burlington, VT 05401-4405
USA

Ashgate website: http://www.ashgate.com

British Library Cataloguing in Publication Data
Global health. – (The library of essays in global governance)
   1. World health 2. Public health – International
   cooperation 3. Globalization – Health aspects
   I. Kirton, John J.
   362.1

Library of Congress Control Number: 2008924591

ISBN: 978-0-7546-2665-7

Printed and bound in Great Britain by
TJ International Ltd, Padstow, Cornwall

Contents

PART III COMMUNICABLE DISEASE

PART IV HEALTH AND TRADE

PART V   GLOBAL HEALTH GOVERNANCE

Acknowledgements

The editor and publishers wish to thank the following for permission to use copyright material.

American Society for Clinical Investigation for the essay: David P. Fidler (2004), 'Germs, Governance, and Global Public Health in the Wake of SARS', *The Journal of Clinical Investigation*, **113**, pp. 799–804. Copyright © 2004 American Society for Clinical Investigation.

American Society of International Law for the essay: Walter R. Sharp (1947), 'The New World Health Organization', *The American Journal of International Law*, **41**, pp. 509–30. Copyright © 1947 American Society of International Law.

Blackwell Publishing Ltd for the essays: Daniele Archibugi and Kim Bizzarri (2005), 'The Global Governance of Communicable Diseases: The Case for Vaccine R&D', *Law & Policy*, **27**, pp. 33–51. Copyright © 2005 Blackwell Publishing Ltd; Stefan Elbe (2006), 'Should HIV/AIDS Be Securitized? The Ethical Dilemmas of Linking HIV/AIDS and Security', *International Studies Quarterly*, **50**, 119–44. Copyright © 2006 Blackwell Publishing Ltd; Jillian Clare Cohen and Patricia Illingworth (2003), 'The Dilemma of Intellectual Property Rights for Pharmaceuticals: The Tension Between Ensuring Access of the Poor to Medicines and Committing to International Agreements', *Developing World Bioethics*, **3**, pp. 27–48. Copyright © 2003 Blackwell Publishing Ltd; Allyn L. Taylor (2004), 'Governing the Globalization of Public Health', *The Journal of Law, Medicine & Ethics*, **32**, pp. 500–508. Copyright © 2004 Blackwell Publishing Ltd; David P. Fidler and Lawrence O. Gostin (2006), 'The New International Health Regulations: An Historic Development for International Law and Public Health', *Journal of Law, Medicine & Ethics*, pp. 85–94. Copyright © 2006 Blackwell Publishing Ltd.

British Medical Journal Publishing Group Ltd for the essays: N. Howard-Jones (1950), 'Origins of International Health Work', *British Medical Journal*, **12**, pp. 1032–37. Copyright © 1950 British Medical Journal Publishing Group Ltd; Fiona Godlee (1994), 'The World Health Organization: WHO in Crisis', *British Medical Journal*, **309**, pp. 1424–28. Copyright © 1994 British Medical Journal Publishing Group Ltd.

Cambridge University Press for the essay: Mark Harrison (2006), 'Disease, Diplomacy and International Commerce: The Origins of International Sanitary Regulation in the Nineteenth Century', *Journal of Global History*, **1**, pp. 197–217. Copyright © 2006 Cambridge University Press.

Elsevier Ltd for the essays: Robert Beaglehole and Derek Yach (2003), 'Globalization and the Prevention and Control of Non-Communicable Disease: The Neglected Chronic Diseases

Editor's Preface

This volume on global health is one of five works prepared for the International Library series on global governance in the major fields of international relations today. As with the other volumes, it assembles in one easily accessible collection the most important articles that have shaped scholarship in the field in the post-Second World War years.

Scholarship in global health has been importantly driven by theory, research, reviews and commentaries published in books, edited volumes, research reports, working papers from research institutions, reports from national governments and international organizations, and increasingly from pieces made available directly on the internet. However, this collection contains only those works published in scholarly journals or university-based equivalents, above all in those peer reviewed, English-language journals that stand at the centre of the key disciplines that serve the field. The focal point is those essays that have defined and driven the debates, theories and research in political science, while recognizing that there is a great diversity of important scholarship within this discipline and in the many subfields and approaches which now make it up. Thus this collection is deliberately interdisciplinary. It encompasses works from and inspired by the major social sciences disciplines of economics, management studies and sociology, from the humanities disciplines history, philosophy and ethics, and, critically, from the natural science disciplines and professions of medicine, biology, pharmacy, nursing and public health.

To select the most important pieces of enduring value from this rich repertoire required a systematic review comprising several stages. The first was to compile a list of the classic essays most used in reading lists in relevant courses as I encountered them from my undergraduate through graduate school years, and then as a teacher in my own courses in international relations and global governance taught over a period of thirty years at the University of Toronto, from the sophomore to the Ph.D. level. The second step was to check this list against the essays most cited and actively used in the major textbooks and monographs on global health and international relations. The third step was to undertake a thorough review of the major journals in the field and in the discipline more generally to ensure that key works were not overlooked and to see which have endured as the most referenced and referred to over many years. The fourth step was to check several composite citation indexes and databases to identify the works most cited by scholars today. The fifth and final step was to send the resulting list out to several trusted scholarly colleagues who are experts in global health, asking them to confirm the selections or adjust them with additions or deletions they might propose.

Even with these procedures, I was left with far too many attractive, indeed compelling, candidates than the 500-page limit for this book allowed. A little relief came from sending some pieces for consideration in the parallel volumes I was producing on Global Trade, International Finance, International Organization and Global Law. Further exclusions arose at the margins as I adjusted the contents to provide as comprehensive and balanced a treatment of the overall field as I could. Finally, many strong candidates had to be excluded due to the need to focus on the works of most value to political scientists, especially those written by political scientists and published in political science journals, even while fully cognisant of the enormous contribution made by scholars and practitioners in the many closely related fields. The excluded pieces with the strongest claim have been noted, and where possible highlighted, in the Introduction to this volume.

In preparing this volume, I have been assisted by several individuals whose contribution I gratefully acknowledge here. I am indebted to Kirstin Howgate at Ashgate, who first proposed this project, and to Dymphna Evans for her support in my decision to go ahead. I acknowledge the important role of Madeline Koch, Managing Director of the G8 Research Group, in securing essays and providing editorial assistance, and of Laura Sunderland, Senior Researcher of the G8 Research Group, in scanning journals and books, obtaining the candidate essays and otherwise helping me assess and select them. I am also crateful to my co-authors and students who have worked with me on global health issues over the past several years: Hana Dhanji, Klaudia Dmitrienko, Safina Kahn, Ella Kokotsis, Jenilee Guebert and Jenevieve Mannell

I acknowledge with particular pleasure the intellectual contribution of professors Harriet Friedmann and Rima Berns-McGown with whom I have taught a graduate seminar on 'Global Governance' at the University of Toronto for many years, and our many exceptional students in that class.

I owe much to the many fine scholars and policy practitioners I have had the pleasure of working with as collaborators in my ongoing project and recent book with Ashgate on 'Governing Global Health': Obijiofor Aginam, Chantal Blouin, Colin Bradford, Andrew Fenton Cooper, Nick Drager, David Fidler, Lee-Nah Hsu, Ella Kokotsis, Ronald Labonte, Jenevieve Mannell, Colleen O'Manique, James Orbinski, Laura Sunderland, Jessica White, Ted Schrecker, David Sanders and Mark Zacher. I am particularly indebted to Andrew Cooper, associate director, John English, executive director, and Jim Balsillie, chair of the operational board of directors, of the Centre for International Governance Innovation under whose critical co-sponsorship we have conducted this work.

I am above all especially grateful to my colleagues, Obijiofor Aginam, Nick Drager, David Fidler, Lisa Forman, Adam Kamradt-Scott, Ronald Labonte, Ted Schrecker, Jillian Claire Cohen and Mark Zacher for responding so fast and fully to my request to review my preliminary list of essays for inclusion and to do so with many thoughtful and valuable suggestions. I have done my best to incorporate them in this final version of the work. Any shortcomings, of course, remain entirely my own.

In conclusion, I owe a special debt to several individuals. Janet Gordon graciously provided the retreat, founded by Dr Roderick Angus Gordon, where the final composition of the Introduction could be completed with minimum distraction and maximum care. Mary Kirton, Sandra Larmour, Laura Mayrand and Emily Gordon helped develop my awareness and knowledge of the AIDS epidemic afflicting Africa.

Above all, I began to learn of the formidable complex challenges facing Africa from infectious disease, as they unfolded on the front lines in the field in various forms, from my daughter, Joanna Kirton, as she embarked upon her career working with orphaned and vulnerable children in Malawi and now with AIDS awareness programmes in Botswana. It is to her that I proudly and gratefully dedicate this book.

JOHN J. KIRTON
University of Toronto, Canada

Introduction

Global health commands centre stage in the concerns of scholars, policy-makers and publics today. Around the world, people are dying each day in large numbers from largely preventable, curable or treatable disease. Each year an estimated four million people die from tobacco-related illnesses, almost three million from HIV/AIDS, over two million from tuberculosis, more than one million from malaria and many more from other chronic illnesses and emerging and re-emerging infectious disease (Osterholm, Chapter 16). The body count far surpasses, as it has throughout history, that from interstate war and civil conflict – the traditional core of the international politics field. To be sure, the world has responded with a rich legacy of institutionalized intergovernmental co-operation on health dating back to 1851, continuing with the World Health Organization (WHO) created in 1948 and culminating in the new institutional innovations of the twenty-first-century globalized world. But the repertoire of actors, instruments, ideas, institutions and processes that constitute contemporary global health governance remain manifestly inadequate to meet the many challenges of the real world. The gap between physical disease and political response is great and growing. The result is death on a massive scale.

This deadly crisis of global health, the dramatic failure of global health governance and the ways they can be controlled and corrected are the central concerns of the scholarly field of global health. To be sure, scholars of international politics and their colleagues in cognate disciplines such as law, economics, sociology and history have long had a serious interest in issues of international public health. But only since the mid-1990s has this interest acquired the intensity, concern with conceptual and theoretical development, internal debates and inventory of empirical research to create the diverse dynamic, fast growing field of global health that has now emerged.

The Field of Global Health

The first generation of global health scholarship arose at the start of the post-Second World War period (Sharp, Chapter 3; Chisholm, 1950; Mackenzie, 1950). In response to dramatic real world developments, this work focused heavily on the revolutionary institutional creation of the new order – above all on the WHO as a great leap forward from what had gone before. As the first self-generated, model specialized agency of the new United Nations (UN) galaxy, the WHO was an attractive focus for students of international politics and organization. Interest was infused with the optimism of the time that a new, much improved world order was being born through the UN. The overwhelmingly Anglo-American scholarship that told this story was guided by the legal-institutional approach that then dominated the study of political science in general. And understandably for a field with a direct, immediate impact on the life and death of people, both in their overall millions and in their readily comprehensible individuality, the field from the start was strongly normative in nature, problem-solving in orientation, and policy prescriptive in aim. Its concern with, and contribution to, theoretical development in international relations and any reciprocal enrichment was then, and for several decades after, very weak.

Yet even at the start there were early signs of the conceptual development, competing approaches and concentrated debates among them that were to flourish later, to help define the field of global health and contribute to scholarship on international politics as a whole. At the very dawn of the new post-war order, the pioneering theoretician of international politics David Mitrany identified health as a suitable, indeed ideal, subject for his 'functional' approach to developing the post-Second World War institutions of a 'working peace' (Mitrany, 1944, 1953, 1966). Somewhat later Ernst Haas used the WHO as empirical material for his landmark book which outlined the neo-functional approach to integration that would take global governance 'beyond the nation state' (Haas, 1964; Haas and Ruggie, 1982). And as the idealistic enthusiasm of the wartime victory and creation of a new institutionalized order gave way to the geo-political and ideological strains of the rapidly coming Cold War, the realists arose to shift attention to how and how much the world's fundamental functional needs for health and the design of the new international organizations centred on the WHO could actually withstand the pressures which these realities of interstate rivalry in an anarchic international system so strongly brought back (Allen, 1950).

This debate was soon won decisively by the realists, especially when the USSR and its fellow Soviet republics withdrew from the new WHO in February 1949. International health as a field and the WHO as a focal point soon faded from sustained scholarly concern in political science, in its law and economics cousins, and in their respective international relations fields. In the broader public, the earlier idealist if inaccurate image of the WHO's white hospital ships sailing anywhere in the world to end disease quickly died. Even Haas' landmark work in 1964 had as its primary empirical focus labour and the International Labour Organization (ILO), rather than health and the WHO. The latter were largely irrelevant to the realist thinking that rapidly arose to dominate scholarship in the Anglo-American world during the 1950s and 1960s.

During the 1950s, 1960s and early 1970s concern with the WHO and the many specific health problems continued (Goodman, 1971; Howard-Jones, 1975). But it was driven overwhelmingly by work in the health sciences of medicine, pharmacy, nursing and public health. Political scientists, legal scholars and even economists focused on national security, national interest and national power, and the rivalry, balance and conflict they bred. Very few ventured beyond to employ human security, human rights, international co-operation and similar concepts that would lead them to global health. In the prevailing realist tradition, health as a recognized subject of any importance was reduced to passing references, such as one of the 'mileu goals' that Arnold Wolfers added to the 'possession goals' then reigning in the realist repertoire (Wolfers, 1962, p. 75).

Liberal-internationalist theorizing, infused by the early functionalist and neo-functionalist insights, did come back in some force to international relations theory in the 1970s. But health did not return with it as a subject then. The new work on transnational relations, complex interdependence and then international regimes was founded on and applied to many issue areas other than public health (Keohane and Nye, 1977). Rare indeed were the exceptions, such as the use of the growth of international quarantine regulations to illustrate how changing understanding and knowledge transformed state interests and thus created regimes (Stein,

1983, pp. 136–37). Even here it took an economist, Richard Cooper, showing how slowly an effective international regime formed in such an obvious knowledge-driven field, to bring health back towards the central theoretical development in the international politics field (Cooper, 1989).

Only in the 1990s did interest in global health return to scholarship on international politics, this time with a proliferating intensity that endures to this day. As in the first generation in the 1940s this scholarly interest was a direct response to dangerous and deadly developments in the real world (Garrett, Chapter 5). The dominant driver was the advent of post-Cold War globalization, and with it the freedom and need to turn from traditional state-centric concepts and concerns with national security and intergovernmental co-operation to newer ones such as threats and vulnerabilities to human security and broader forms of now multi-centred global governance writ large (Kirton, 1993). While problems such as the polluted natural environment quickly arose to occupy this new space, scholars from the many health disciplines highlighted the deadly shocks from emerging and re-emerging infectious disease. Even amidst the earlier Cold War that had pre-occupied political scientists, those in the health disciplines, with their largely biomedical models, had been able to sustain some of the 1940s optimism, through to the eradication of smallpox from the world in 1979. But then came the HIV/AIDS epidemic, first diagnosed in 1981, hitting the developed world hard and then the developing world much harder still. The 1990s brought a further succession of shocks from the Ebola virus, Marburg and many more. Infectious disease emerged as one of the world's greatest killers, surpassing interstate war as it had in 1918 owing to the pandemic flu at the First World War's end. Now the world was equipped with the WHO to defend it. But the WHO seemed increasingly incapable of providing human security in the new age.

Thus global health burst onto the scene as a major subject for political scientists. It has maintained that place ever since. Yet no single political scientist or group of established scholars has been responsible for forming and fuelling this new field. Rather the work has come from a disparate array of largely emerging scholars studying globalization in general and health in particular from a wide array of disciplines. These have included economics, law, sociology, history, management studies, ethics, biology, public health, medicine, pharmacy and nursing too. Far more than most fields in international politics, global health has been born as, and has grown as, a genuinely interdisciplinary concern. The recent collections of works on governing global health well reflect this essential multidisciplinary base (Cooper, Kirton and Schrecker, 2007; Cooper and Kirton, 2009).

At the same time, the field has begun to acquire coherence in ways that scholars of international politics can easily recognize. The concepts, theories and research programmes of globalization and global governance are now central. The relevant major offerings from political science are now applied directly to global health. The same is true for particular theories such as the global commons and global public goods (Kaul, Grunberg and Stern, 1999). The broader traditions of realism, liberal institutionalism, political economy and constructivism in their many variants are also starting to have direct application to global health. And the empirical concern with North–South inequalities and the work of international institutions and actors in their kaleidoscopic complexity further connect the field of global health to that of international politics as a whole.

Defining the Field of Global Health

In large part, the ecumenical nature of the scholarship reflects a comprehensive conception of what the field of global health contains. At the start, the core conception of the field came from the definition contained in the charter of the WHO. Here health was defined not negatively as the absence of illness, but positively, proactively and expansively as 'a state of complete physical, mental and social well-being without distinction of race, religion, political belief, or economic and social conditions, which is essential for peace and social security in order that man may live harmoniously with his fellow man' (as cited in Mackenzie, 1950, p. 516). While the definition may have excluded the important gender and environmental dimensions of the current conception, it included the central human rights, social, economic, and peace and security concerns that structure the field today.

If health itself had such *globalite* from the beginning, the instruments and actors through which it was to be achieved did not. With a definition taken from the charter of an intergovernmental organization, it was easy for scholars, analysts, advocates and practitioners to explore the field with a focus on how national governments, vertically responsible for providing health in their domain of hierarchical sovereign authority at home, would and could co-operate horizontally with one another for limited degrees and purposes in the anarchic international domain. The resulting field of 'international health', as with most theory and research in international politics during the first few post-war decades, had an almost exclusive concern with national governments as the only actors, international co-operation as the only subject, managing transborder flows of pathogens, pests, people and products as the only problems, and the WHO, and its supporting cast of institutions such as the Food and Agriculture Organization (FAO), as the only focal point for research.

Several real world forces transformed the traditional 'international' health into today's 'global' health. One was the agency of the WHO, whose programmes on 'health for all' and on the social and economic determinants of health, brought the individual alongside the nation-state as a value and actor, and human rights and economics as matters integrally linked to health. The second was post-war globalization, which gave rise to a focus on human security and on newer types of intergovernmental bodies, such as the Group of Eight (G8) major market democracies, now increasingly moving into the global health governance game. The third was the failure of the old international organizations in the face of the new shocks from infectious disease. This failure brought new actors, notably corporations, NGOs and philanthropists into the mix, and new forms, notably public–private partnerships and networks, through which they were mixed.

From this has emerged today's dominant definition of the field of 'global health governance'. As scholars unaffiliated with and indeed critical of the WHO insist, it is an open-ended, fluid and contested conception in which different actors, with different political projects, seek to have their preferred understanding prevail (Thomas and Weber, Chapter 7). However, central to it is the way multiple actors, through multiple instruments and multiple forms of associations, politically interact to affect human health outcomes within the human rights, socioeconomic, ecological and security context in which health is embedded on a global scale. One prominent formal definition conceives of global public health as 'the collective ability to conduct healthy public policy at a global level through a network of public, private, non-governmental, national, regional and international organizations by regime formation'

(Kickbusch and Leeuw, Chapter 9, p. 135, this volume). It is this current definition which forms the foundation for the conception of 'global health' in this book.

Aim and Approach

This volume addresses the central questions in the rich and rapidly expanding field of global health. It assembles in one conveniently available collection the most important journal articles that have anchored and defined the agenda, concepts, debates and direction of the field since its emergence within political science as a subject of interest in the 1940s and its re-emergence as a self-contained field in the 1990s. It is based on a careful selection of the classic and contemporary journal articles of enduring value that are central to the scholarship on global health today and will be in the years ahead.

The selections are those essential to the work of, and where possible from, political scientists specializing in their discipline's fields of international relations and development studies. Yet given the highly multidisciplinary character of the field, this collection relies heavily on offerings from similar fields within the disciplines of economics, management studies, sociology, history and the health sciences, whose research remains integrally intertwined. It places the selected essays in the context of evolving debates and real world developments, highlights their distinctive character and contributions to the field of global health, and indicates where they relate to the evolving area of international relations in political science as a whole. Beyond that it lets them speak for themselves, without adding any independent critique of their content or value.

The selection has been guided by a desire for comprehensiveness and balance across successive generations of scholars, and from several leading theoretical traditions in political science, as these have been adapted for and applied to global health. It has not flowed from any particular preferred philosophy or approach to the field. An emphasis has been placed on contributions dealing with core concepts of comprehensive application, and of cumulative, continuing relevance in defining the research and debates of today, together with essays that have helped pioneer new areas of study of this richly textured, complex and constantly changing field.

This collection appropriately reflects the particular character of the field in several ways. While its opening section highlights contributions from political scientists writing in leading political science journals, the volume encompasses a wide range of disciplines and journals, with many coming from the various public health fields. Moreover, while its opening section offers key essays from the origins of the field in the 1940s, there is a great gap during the dark ages of subsequent decades and a heavy concentration on the field as it has rapidly developed from the 1990s on. Finally, while the collection features essays driven by and driving theory, and those theories recognizable to scholars of international politics today, the heavily problem-solving and policy-oriented nature of the field shines through.

The Foundations and Evolution of the Field

The scholarly study of global health in political science is overwhelmingly a post-Second World War project, even if earlier scholars studied subjects that remain central to the subject to this day. Indeed, disease and its relationship to war figure prominently in the first major book on international politics ever written – that by Thucydides on the Peloponnesian War (*c*.420 BC (1998)). Prior to the Second World War, scholars traced the various international health regulations and conferences, and the work of the League of Nations in this field (Woodworth, 1875; Cabell, 1881; Popkin, 1928; Greaves, 1931; Barkhuus, 1943). They also produced a few great debates, such as the great dissent from a leading medical pioneer that international co-operation on health was dangerous as it diverted attention and resources from the far more important task of producing proper public health systems and regulations by national governments at home.

After the war, scholars continued to focus on the intergovernmental health institutions, including through works that looked back to examine in greater rigour and detail what had gone before (Goodman, 1971; Brockington, 1975; Howard-Jones, 1975, 1981; Pannenborg, 1979; Reich and Marui, 1989; Dubin, 1995; Weindling, 1995). They also dealt to a lesser degree with the defining debate about the balance and relationship between international and domestic health governance. Here the compromise of embedded liberalism in the post-Second World War order offered a compelling answer and a firewall in the scholarly as well as the policy world (Ruggie, 1983). The new field was thus easily driven by enthusiasm about the new United Nations order, faith in intergovernmental functionalism and the disappointment and then despair that arrived when the Cold War came.

After many decades of Cold War exclusion, the field re-emerged in ever greater vibrancy in the mid-1990s, again driven very much by real world concerns. The great Cold War victory, and the intensifying globalization that followed brought global health problems to physical and political prominence, and thus to the attention of public policy commentators, social science scholars and finally political scientists as well. From that starting point, the field has been progressively shaped by the dynamics, concepts and debates over globalization, by the course of deadly infectious disease itself, by the links health has with socieconomic, political security and human rights concepts, causes and consequences, and by global governance writ large. The anthrax attacks on the USA in the autumn of 2001 spurred a renewed concern with the old subject of security and health (Price-Smith, 2001, 2002; Brundtland, 2003). Part I captures this cadence, from the foundations of the field in the 1940s through to the progression in the years after post-Cold War globalization began.

In Chapter 1, 'Disease, Diplomacy and International Commerce: The Origins of International Sanitary Regulation in the Nineteenth Century', historian Mark Harrison explores the early nineteenth-century move of European nations towards international health co-operation, through a succession of international sanitary conferences starting in 1851 and culminating in conventions by the century's end. Noting that commercial pressures were the main catalyst for reform of the unilateral quarantine laws used by states, Harrison argues that most European countries came to co-operate because of the broader diplomatic context. Above all the key causes were the 1815 settlement, the resulting Concert of Europe and its common thrust towards a more systematic, and more liberal, international sanitary regime. Here the realists' high politics of health diplomacy dominated and drove the functional need for health co-operation itself.

Norman Howard-Jones, in Chapter 2, 'Origins of International Health Work', places the causal emphasis more on the early absence of scientific consensus and the later emergence of formal international organization in the League of Nations. He reviews intergovernmental activity on health problems from the start of unilateral national quarantine measures in Europe in 1377 through to the creation of the WHO in 1948. He identifies four phases: the use of national quarantines from 1377 to 1851; the emergence of plurilateral sanitary conferences, conventions and an organization at French and European initiative, and regionally at American initiative from 1851 to 1918; the League of Nation's health work from 1923 to 1939; and the emergence of the UN's health activity through the United Nations Relief and Rehabilitation Agency (UNRRA) during the Second World War and then with the new WHO in 1948. He attributes the slowness of the first two phases to the absence of a scientific consensus on what caused the major infectious diseases of the time, on a predominant British protection of its maritime interests, and on an increasing European desire for self-protection from diseases coming in from the developing world. However, with the birth of the League of Nations, a multilateral organization, even without the United States, was able to expand international health co-operation, keep it alive through the Second World War and have it flourish in the WHO's regard for the health of the world as a whole as the post-Second World War years began.

In Chapter 3, 'The New World Health Organization', legal scholar Walter Sharp captures much of this optimism surrounding the unfolding creation of the WHO – a revolutionary institution whose charter constitutes the 'Magna Carta' of global health law. Using the then dominant legal-institutional approach, he explores in turn the importance, institutional structure, controversial features, range of activity and place in the UN system of the prospective body, based on its just-concluded constitution. By discussing the negotiating history and controversies, he launches the subject of global health diplomacy. He further focuses on several controversies central to the WHO and international organizations, institutions and regimes in general: universalism in membership; multilateralism versus regionalism; financing; and control of and by the executive board, the secretariat and its head. He argues that the WHO is a landmark as a single agency for health, embracing all nations in membership and a few NGOs in the negotiation, with a far wider scope and function than before. It is based on the recent revolutionary advances in medicine, and serves as the 'first born child', or first specialized agency of the UN. He concludes hopefully if conditionally that the WHO should serve as a 'powerful impetus for progress' (p. 52) in the medical and social field, if it avoids bureaucratic timidity, is supported by the major countries, and if the world remains at peace.

Charles Allen, in Chapter 4, 'World Health and World Politics', brings in the political dimension more explicitly and actively. He offers a clear casual model of global health governance, explaining how the growth of transportation, national health services and medical knowledge drove increasingly intense and institutionalized international health co-operation from 1851, with the WHO as the culminating crown. He explores national behaviour within the WHO and like bodies, as driven by the general forces of world politics. He concludes, optimistically and in terms welcome to today's liberal institutionalist regime theorists, that 'the common will to meet world health problems has become strong enough to withstand and even to modify at times some of the forces of world politics' (p. 61). While showing how America adjusts to the preferences of lesser powers within the WHO, he identifies the then recent withdrawal of the Soviet Union and its fellow Soviet republics as the greatest threat to the body thus far. But even if the WHO, with its state-centric decision-making and sovereignty, remains vulnerable to the deep ideological and political cleavages of international politics, most nations have willingly subordinated their national, regional and ideological interests to the work of world health. Every advance in technology will make such co-operation more imperative still.

In Chapter 5, 'The Return of Infectious Disease', policy analyst Laurie Garrett discusses global health governance as it emerged from its decades-long Cold War freeze. Gone for good is the technological determinism and optimism of the earlier literature. In its place the grim world of germs, geographic globalization and ineffective intergovernmental institutions takes centre stage. While the WHO had proudly proclaimed the end of smallpox in 1979, the world now realized that germs and other microbes mutated and could not be geographically confined. With human mobility, transparency and interstate tensions now the dominant drivers, the 1994 pneumonic plague in India, the 1995 terrorist attacks on the Tokyo subway, the 1995 Ebola epidemic, Iraq's threat to use bio-weapons in the 1990–91 Gulf War, the eruption of the Marburg virus in Germany and above all the proliferating HIV/AIDS pandemic showed that global health had become a new dominant national security concern. National governments lacked the laboratories and the WHO the powers to mount an effective defence against this new deadly human security threat. Global health thus leapt back on the agenda of scholars of international relations and did so as a national security concern in a globalizing age.

In Chapter 6, 'Ghosts of Kigali: Infectious Disease and Global Stability at the Turn of the Century', Andrew Price-Smith, as a new scholar of international politics, took up the task of framing the new global problem in the discipline's core concepts both old and new. He argues that 'The global resurgence of infectious disease has significant implications for state survival, stability, and prosperity, as well as ramifications for interstate relations' (p. 99). It is thus central to international politics, long focused on the physical protection by the state of its citizens, in a world where disease more than war has long importantly determined the outcomes of war, empire, the feudal order and the relative capability of states. This classic realist case, he argues, now requires an interdisciplinary effort, embracing natural and social scientists, to understand and address the onslaught of emerging and re-emerging infectious disease starting with HIV/AIDS. Price-Smith presents such a model, with pathogens as the independent variable, many disease amplifiers as intervening variables, state capacity, adaptive resilience and ingenuity as critical components, and the impacts on economic, governance and national security at the state and system level as the dependent variable that results. He concludes by noting how these developments make the WHO increasingly ineffective, and how, in response, global health governance is migrating to other institutions such as the Group of Seven (G7) major market democracies and private sector networks such as Pro-Med.

Writing five years after Price-Smith, Caroline Thomas and Martin Weber, in Chapter 7, 'The Politics of Global Health Governance: Whatever Happened to "Health for All by the Year 2000"?', evaluate how well international relations scholarship has embraced the new global health realities, and systematically assess how the world's dominant ideas and institutions have guided a governance response. Arguing that international relations scholarship has been slow to respond, they trace how the 1970s global governance emphasis on global social democracy, multilateralism, the WHO and the UN has been replaced by the dominant disciplinary neo-liberalism of the World Bank and G7. Yet an analysis of states, organizations and social movements as agents of change leads them to conclude that the tide may have turned, and can turn more, towards social justice integrated with wider social concerns, as the dominant approach to governing global health.

Globalization and Global Health

Certainly the dominant driver of the revival and dynamism of, and debates about global health in international relations has been the advent of post-Cold War globalization in its many conceptions and forms. Globalization burst onto the agenda as a defining concept and research problem of international relations scholars, public health analysts and the WHO itself as the twenty-first century began (Fidler, 1997; Drager and Beaglehole, 2001, Woodward *et al.*, 2001; Taylor, Chapter 30). It has inspired a great debate about health, especially its impact on health in the developing world (Fidler, 1999; Aginam, 2000, 2002a, 2002b, 2004, 2005). It has guided the relevant scholarship on health–trade linkages and global health governance as well. What globalization is, how new and different it is, and how it can help global and domestic health were the starting questions for this generation of work in the global health field. Then came a particular concern with globalization's unequal deadly impact on poor countries and poor people in particular, the broader socioeconomic and political-security drivers, human rights and human security as defining concepts for corrective action, and a concern with how globalization could be controlled to generate 'health for all' (Parker, 2002).

Part II explores the dual dynamic of how globalization as a physical process has been discovered by those concerned with health and how globalization as a political concern and concept in international relations has been applied to and enriched by scholarship in the global health field. It includes the major essays that address how globalization has affected global health and its governance, and how they in turn have affected the course and the consequences of globalization.

This section begins with reviews covering 150 years of global health and its governance to see what, if anything, has fundamentally changed (Fidler, Chapter 8). It then explores whether the old concept of interdependence, now with new players and partnerships, can continue to capture the health risks and governance responses of the real world (Lee, 1998; Yach and Bettcher, 1998). The initial judgements were that continuity had prevailed and that the old concepts thus worked well. But immediately after came powerful arguments that things had fundamentally changed as globalization arrived in the health field (Kickbusch and Quick, 1998; Kickbusch, 1999; Kickbusch and Leeuw, Chapter 9).

In Chapter 8, 'The Globalization of Public Health: The First 100 Years of International Health Diplomacy', legal scholar David Fidler reviews what lessons the records of health risks, government responses and resulting global health regimes from 1851 to 1951 offer for global health governance in today's globalized world. Surveying a wide range of health regimes, he concludes that international commerce made health risks global, led states to co-operate through international law and to involve multinational corporations (MNCs) and NGOs in the process, but with decidedly mixed results. Above all these 100 years have shown how great power rivalry and diplomacy have undermined health governance, which still lags behinds the capacity of humans to create and spread disease. Even with the greater involvement of MNCs and NGOs, making health governance global rather than international, and with new technological tools such as the internet and genetic engineering, the prospects for global health governance in the twenty-first century are largely unchanged from the nineteenth century, unless states internalize public health as an interest, value and fundamental human right.

In Chapter 9, 'Global Public Health: Revisiting Healthy Public Policy at the Global Level', Ilona Kickbusch and Evelyne de Leeuw counter that globalization, far more than increased interdependence and interconnectedness, challenges the internal sovereignty and restricts the policy autonomy of states. This is because their instruments do not reach into the global sphere of those they need to affect. In practice states continue to defend their sovereignty over health care even as they lose it over the determinants of health. A new framework is needed to understand how health sovereignty can be balanced with globalization. Allowing non-government actors into new networks, as in HIV/AIDS, is a key start. Drawing on the concepts of the global commons and global public goods, and a heightening concern with non-compliance with international commitments, schools of public health should be in the vanguard of this new and urgent interdisciplinary task.

Robert Beaglehole and Derek Yach address the growth of non-communicable diseases among poor people in poor countries and their relative neglect by the scholarly and policy world in Chapter 10, 'Globalization and the Prevention and Control of Non-Communicable Disease: The Neglected Chronic Diseases of Adults'. Globalization importantly causes such epidemics, which directly impose risks on vulnerable populations and indirectly harm national health systems and economies as a whole. The globalized production and marketing of the tobacco and alcohol industries highlight the harm to health and the policy challenge. While the intergovernmental control of tobacco inspires some hope, much more needs to be done on a much wider front.

In Chapter 11, 'Epidemic Disease and National Security', Susan Peterson explores whether, when and how epidemic disease harms national security, defined as the preservation of the territorial integrity, political institutions and national sovereignty of the state in the face of physical threat. She claims that disease can do so by changing the balance of power, fuelling foreign policy conflicts, creating political-economic instability and thus fostering violent conflicts, and altering their outcome consciously through biological warfare or inadvertently by lessening military readiness. She concludes that epidemic disease may pose a national security threat to Russia but not to the United States, apart from the latter's vulnerability to biological attack as in the anthrax assaults in the autumn of 2001. Thus turning epidemic disease into a national security threat for America is likely to fail and lead to other outcomes that public health advocates would not want.

Communicable Disease

The most visible manifestation of globalization's impact on and importance for global health was the sudden sharp arrival of deadly infectious diseases to citizens behind the long well-guarded borders of countries in the developed world. To be sure, the globalization generated in the North may have silently been killing many more people in the South, and the chronic killers partly bred by affluence may have been killing more people in the North. But the shocks from infectious disease travelling from South to North stood out with particular visibility and force. The HIV/AIDS pandemic that was born in Africa and arrived in America in the 1980s started a trend that reached new levels when Marburg and other such diseases struck. And when attention in the North globalized to embrace the common cause between North and South, it became apparent that, even though illnesses related to tobacco, heart disease and obesity were spreading North to South, the infectious diseases that the South and North shared could claim to be among the leading killers of people in the world today.

Part III moves from globalization's role in global health in general to its particular impact on infectious disease creation and control. It looks in turn at how infectious disease was initially dealt with internationally, at the response when it hit in the globalizing 1990s, and what might lie ahead when it strikes again in the tightly wired twenty-first-century world.

In Chapter 12, 'The Lessons of the Pandemic', George Soper looks at the 1918–19 influenza pandemic that killed tens of millions of people around the world. Writing in 1919 as the world was still coping with this unprecedented pandemic, he emphasizes the challenge of dealing with a disease when no one knew what it was, where it came from, how to halt it or when, where and why it would come again. He notes that prevention had been inhibited by public indifference, the personal character of the measures that must be used in response and the highly infectious nature of a disease with a very short incubation period. There was also uncertainty about its causes, reminiscent of an earlier age, with those claiming human contagion competing with those countering with global environmental conditions or forces unleashed by the Great War. With the evidence pointing to human contagion, what scholars today would call 'globalization' led it to quickly spread around the globe. The concluding prescription is better personal health, through a series of specific measures that individuals are advised to voluntarily undertake on their own.

In Chapter 13, 'Communicable Disease Control: A "Global Public Good" Perspective', Richard Smith, David Woodward, Arnab Acharya, Robert Beaglehole and Nick Drager assess the concept of global public goods (GPG) as a way of addressing the mismatch between increasingly globalized health problems and still national responsibility for dealing with them in the area of communicable disease control (CDC). They conclude that few areas of CDC qualify as GPGs and that elsewhere it may be unnecessary to provide for all that do. Thus a focus on collective action failure can show where the GPG concept offers a rationale to raise money and investment and establish the mechanisms for CDC.

Daniele Archibugi and Kim Bizzarri, in Chapter 14, 'The Global Governance of Communicable Diseases: The Case for Vaccine R&D', focus on the importance of vaccines in infectious disease control and the failure of public and private researchers to respond on a scale commensurate with the size of the global health crisis caused by the HIV/AIDS, tuberculosis and malaria pandemics. They argue that the current emphasis on 'research pull' mechanisms to stimulate private investment through market competition produces socially suboptimal results. Using the economics of innovation and global public goods theory, they conclude that direct public intervention in vaccine development is far socially superior and justified in policy terms. They thus call for a Global Health Research Fund to manage the effort and an International Health Treaty to enshrine countries' commitments.

'Germs, Governance, and Global Public Health in the Wake of SARS' is the subject of Chapter 15 by David Fidler. Fidler addresses the most recent deadly infectious disease to assault Asia and North America – the SARS epidemic of 2003. He explores how earlier trends in the governance of global infectious disease were affected by the SARS outbreak and traces the resulting revolution in governance that is now taking place. He concludes that 'germ governance' has now become a core criterion of 'good governance' in global affairs.

In Chapter 16, 'Preparing for the Next Pandemic', Michael Osterholm takes up the more recent threat of avian flu. Starting with a reminder that deadly influenza pandemics have regularly afflicted the global community in successive waves, Osterholm identifies the unique characteristics of today's H5N1 avian flu virus that give it a priority claim for public concern amidst the many other infectious diseases destroying lives on a large scale today. Using the 2003 SARS attack as a precursor case and a warning, he identifies what must be done were the next influenza pandemic to strike tonight, in one year, in three years or in ten years. He calls on the G8 to take as a top priority an international project to radically transform the present system of producing influenza vaccines, so that the world might be prepared when, not if, the next pandemic strikes.

Stefan Elbe asks if the global AIDS pandemic should be framed as an international security issue, from an ethical concern, in Chapter 17, 'Should HIV/AIDS be Securitized? The Ethical Dilemmas of Linking HIV/AIDS and Security'. Using securitization theory, he argues that there is an ethical dilemma in doing so. Such a move may mobilize awareness, action and resources. But it could move responsibility away from civil society to military and intelligence actors, stigmatize and harm the civil liberties of those living with HIV/AIDS, create a threat-defence logic that inhibits international co-operation, lead narrow national interests to trump humanitarian altruism and divert AIDS resources to military and governmental elites. Securitization theory, by drawing on the many links between security and AIDS, can help policy-makers minimize the dangers of making such a move.

Health and Trade

Part IV, on health and trade, addresses another defining feature of global health governance (Labonte, 1998; Baris and McLeod, 2000). As the history of the International Sanitary Conferences and International Health Regulations (IHRs) show, and as the early post-Second World War causal models of global health governance highlight, trade has been central in transmitting infectious disease internationally and in defining the need for and place of its control through international regimes. Globalization has added an exponential increase in the volume, speed and reach of trade in goods and services, including humans on the move. It has also inspired a far more legally powerful trade regime, embedded in the WTO and its agreement on trade related intellectual property (TRIPS) (Sell, 2002). Many see the latter overtaking the classic IHR-based global health regime and constraining the ability of states to govern vertically for the public health good. In the control of infectious disease, access to essential medicines, combating chronic killers such as tobacco-related diseases and almost everywhere else, trade and health, and their respective governance regimes, are integrally linked on a global scale.

In Chapter 18, 'Drug Development for Neglected Diseases: A Deficient Market and a Public-Health Policy Failure, Patrice Trouiller, Piero Olliaro, Els Torreele, James Orbinski, Richard Laing and Nathan Ford provide the empirical evidence for a major market failure in public health – the virtual absence of research and development in the private sector on drugs for diseases that occur mainly in the developing world. They find that only sixteen of the 1,393 new chemical entities marketed between 1975 and 1999 were for tropical disease and tuberculosis. Neither the trade regime in pharmaceuticals nor public–private partnerships provide a solution to developing drugs for the diseases of the poor. An international pharmaceutical policy is needed to treat all neglected diseases.

Caroline Thomas, in Chapter 19, 'Trade Policy and the Politics of Access to Drugs', deals with the links between trade policy and access to drugs, especially the anti-retroviral drugs essential for treating HIV/AIDS. Starting with the moral problem posed by the inequality in access between the rich, well-equipped North and the poor South, she examines what is legally allowable under WTO rules for national governments to ensure affordable access for their citizens. She then identifies what is allowable and desirable from the standpoint of American trade policy. She concludes that the predominant global market system for access to drugs creates problems of credibility for global health governance. She calls on the WHO, health activists and scholars to respond.

In Chapter 20, 'The Dilemma of Intellectual Property Rights for Pharmaceuticals: The Tension Between Ensuring Access of the Poor to Medicines and Committing to International Agreements', Jillian Clare Cohen and Patricia Illingworth first review how the Uruguay Round that gave rise to the WTO and the TRIPS agreement altered the global application of intellectual property rights for pharmaceuticals. Drawing on theories of the firm from management studies and from ethical arguments, they then identify how developing countries can use pharmaceutical policy tools to reduce the negative impacts of the TRIPS agreement, how the World Bank can inspire research and development on innovative medicines and increase access to medicines for the poor, and how ethical pricing provides a morally preferable policy guide.

In Chapter 21, 'TRIPS, Pharmaceutical Patents and Access to Essential Medicines: A Long Way from Seattle to Doha', Ellen 't Hoen explores the problem of access to affordable, effective medicines for the poor and the process of NGO, international organizational and developing country activism that led to the WTO's 2001 Doha Declaration affirming the primacy of public health over private intellectual property. She attributes this breakthrough to the strong preparations of developing countries operating as a single bloc, the 2001 anthrax scare that led the USA and Canada to understand the need to set aside private patents in the face of public health emergencies, and an increasingly active NGO movement. However, she notes that important barriers remain. These begin with allowing production for export to a country issuing a compulsory licence, the absence of needed research and development for drugs for neglected diseases of the poor, and the need for an international treaty on research and development for essential heath needs.

Susan Sell examines the campaign to modify the TRIPS agreement to allow greater access to affordable medicines in Chapter 22, 'The Quest for Global Governance in Intellectual Property and Public Health: Structural, Discursive and Institutional Dimensions'. She focuses on how the realist asymmetries in power between the North and South have been and can be offset by developing countries taking advantage of strategic forum shopping among the many competing international institutions involved in intellectual property, and by using hard and soft law and discursive reframing strategies in their favourite forums to offset the power of the WTO. On this basis she calls for institutionalizing support for developing country delegations at WTO headquarters and for developing countries to pursue strong competition policies at home.

How tobacco control challenges global health governance in a globalizing age is examined by Jeff Collin, Kelley Lee and Karen Bissell in Chapter 23, 'The Framework Convention on Tobacco Control: The Politics of Global Health Governance'. While health systems and regulation have long been national and vertical, the growing global character of the tobacco industry and the resulting of tobacco-related disease require transnational regulation. This need has been recognized by the WHO in its negotiation of a Framework Convention on Tobacco Control (FCTC). Here the WHO has explicitly sought to counter the imbalance generated by globalization, and has included a wide range of interests, including civil society, in various ways and with varying effects. The FCTC represents a major innovation in global health governance. But the involvement of NGOs in its governance remains too weak and that of the tobacco industry too strong.

Global Health Governance

Just as the WHO and its work served as the catalyst and centre piece for the first generation of scholarship on global health in the immediate post-Second World War period, so it has continued to serve as a subject of commentary, concern and, increasingly, criticism ever since. The decades following the 1940s were filled with works, largely from the health science disciplines, about the WHO, its successes such as the eradication of smallpox around its 30th anniversary in 1978 and its shortcomings on much else (Bryant, 1980; Justice, 1987; Reich, 1987). Slowly the WHO became a subject where the theories and tools of a wide range of social science disciplines, including anthropology, were put to work (Foster, 1987). And in the 1990s, as globalization arrived in full force to generate new demands for global governance well beyond that easily delivered by the intergovernmental organizations of the 1940s edifice, scholarship on the WHO erupted from many fronts (Godlee, 1994; Zacher, 1999; Gostin, 2004).

During this most recent generation, other intergovernmental institutions had arisen. They received recognition for their relevance in governing the socioeconomic determinants of health, intruded directly into the health policy domain and attracted increasing attention from scholars of global health as a result. At the very beginning of the WHO, its relationship with and the relevance of its sister organizations in the UN family, notably the FAO, UNRRA, UNICEF and the ILO, were acknowledged and briefly explored by scholars still firmly focused on the central WHO. But increasingly the major economic organizations entered, beginning with the Bretton Woods bodies of the World Bank and IMF and the GATT, especially after the GATT took full flight as the new WTO in 1995 (Stott, 1999).

This cumulative crowding of and competition among intergovernmental organizations on the playing field generated a growing concern with the comprehensiveness, coherence, co-ordination and balance of what was coming to be conceived of as the global health governance system as a whole. Similar subjects for scholarship arose in regard to the instrument of international health law, whether taking the form of hard or soft law, and whether created by and embedded in intergovernmental organizations or not (Fidler, 2002; Kirton and Trebilcock, 2004). Further complicating the policy and analytical challenge of global health governance, and enriching the scholarship on it, was the rapid emergence of old and new international environmental institutions and laws that were relevant to health, such as the Codex Alimentarius and the United Nations Framework Convention on Biodiversity and its Secretariat (Le Prestre, 2004; Mills, 2004). Not surprisingly, scholars of global health turned to their colleagues in global environmental governance for analytic inspiration, guidance and a convenient empirical comparison. This work often began with the striking contrast between the field of health where there had been a central comprehensive organization – the WHO – since the start, and that of the environment, where there is none to this day (Biermann and Bauer, 2005).

The policy frustration and analytical concern with this agenda of inter-institutional competition and coherence among the UN-based intergovernmental organizations increasingly led scholars to look beyond it in several ways. The first extension, building on a few classic works, was to the non-state actors, both for and not for profit, soft law and the networks rapidly taking shape. The second was the new relationship between the old international organizations and the new non-state actors and networks, above all the many public–private partnerships such as the Global Fund in which the WHO was increasingly involved (Buse and Waxman, 2001; Brugha *et al.*, 2004). And the third was the G7 and after 1997 the G8 summit-centred system of the major market democracies which had taken up health in the late 1980s and had made it a central priority by 2006 (Kirton and Mannell, 2007).

The G7/G8 had entered the consciousness and commentary and become part of the call for action of scholars of global health as a consequence of its emerging status as a centre of comprehensive, integrated, effective global governance and of the continuing strong normative commitments and policy prescriptions that were usually an integral part of these scholars' work (Fidler, 2003c; Labonte *et al.*, 2004; Labonte and Schrecker, 2007). Most writings on the G8 and other international institutions in this most recent generation flowed seamlessly from an analysis of the international institutional architecture and action into usually explicit normative assessments and sometimes detailed prescriptions about how their policies, programmes, operations and overall configuration could be improved.

Part V reflects this evolution in the current generation in global health scholarship on governance issues. It begins with an assessment of the WHO as it entered the era of intense post-Cold War globalization. It proceeds to deal with accountability, public–private partnerships and the role of law. It ends with works on the G8, including a critique of its members' compliance with their health commitments and an analysis of how their compliance could be improved – notably by returning to where modern global health governance began and relying more on the WHO.

In Chapter 24, 'The World Health Organization: WHO in Crisis', Fiona Godlee examines the criticisms, goals and strategy of the WHO amidst the crisis that it faced as the 1990s arrived. She argues that its problems relate not merely to its leadership, but more deeply to its structure, priorities, methods and management. She concludes that in the face of this crisis of confidence and calls for radical reform, it remains an open question whether the WHO is capable of change or doomed to irrelevance like much of the rest of the UN.

Ilona Kickbusch notes, in Chapter 25, 'The Development of International Health Policies – Accountability Intact?', how globalization, the growing transfer of international health risks and increasing global health inequalities create a structural challenge for international health governance and weaken the ability of the nation-state to shape health determinants and ensure health for its citizens. The increasing intersection of domestic and foreign policy, national and international interest, bilateral and multilateral strategies, and involvement of new players engender a new organizational form for global health governance based on networks, shifting alliances and unclear responsibility. It is thus necessary to pool state sovereignty and structure the networks, with the WHO playing a critical role. An international relations framework shows how states are socialized into adopting new norms, values and conceptions of their interest in health on a national and international level. It also shows the obstacles the WHO will face in inventing global, rather than international, health policy.

In Chapter 26, 'Globalization and Cholera: Implications for Global Governance', Kelley Lee and Richard Dodgson mobilize the international relations and international political economy literature on globalization to explore the latter's impact on health and its governance. They do so with reference to the cholera epidemic from the nineteenth century to the present. They conclude by considering the functions and forms of a new system of global governance for the age of globalized health.

The large number and variety of public–private partnerships for global health that have arisen among firms, NGOs, other civil society actors and, at times, international organizations are reviewed by Roy Widdus in Chapter 27, 'Public–Private Partnerships for Health'. He concludes that these social experiments are not a panacea. They have proven valuable in areas where the public sector lacks skills and resources, such as those relating to product and production process development, manufacturing, marketing and distribution. But they are not appropriate for policy-making and regulatory approval. They thus need to be carefully crafted for the particular, well-specified, synergistic purpose at hand.

In Chapter 28, 'Global Health Governance: A Conceptual Review', Richard Dodgson, Kelley Lee and Nick Drager first consider the concept of global health governance (GHG), identify globalization's impacts on individuals and states, and note the problems this poses for health. They then review the history of international health governance, centred on the WHO, and what is needed for a move to global health governance in a globalizing world. They conclude with five challenges: creating consensus on a new normative framework for GHG; defining leadership and authority in it; generating adequate resources; creating effective compliance; and securing a more pluralistic but still cohesive system.

Obijiofor Aginam, in Chapter 29, 'Between Isolationism and Mutual Vulnerability: A South-North Perspective on Global Governance of Epidemics in an Age of Globalization', uses the SARS crisis to consider two competing approaches to global health governance. These are isolationism based on Westphalian nation-state sovereignty and mutual vulnerability leading to transnational structures for an inclusive human globalism. He argues that isolationism, which sees the developing South as a reservoir of disease attacking the North, has been the foundation of the historic approaches of quarantine and cordons sanitaires since the fourteenth century. It has a legacy that lives on to this day. He calls for a move to a post-Westphalian approach based on the 'law of humanity' and 'cosmopolitan social democracy'. But he concludes that the prospects for such a move remain uncertain.

In Chapter 30, 'Governing the Globalization of Public Health', Allyn Taylor observes that conventional international health law, already encompassing, will continue to embrace ever more diverse and complex matters and will create a co-ordinative framework for states in a globalized world. She examines the causes of this expansion and the resulting challenges for the many actors involved in law-making. She concludes that the WHO should serve as a co-ordinator, catalyst and platform for codifying health law, in order to improve co-ordination, coherence and implementation, even though full consolidation of activity under the WHO is neither possible nor desirable.

The 1995–2005 process of revising the International Health Regulations is charted by David Fidler and Lawrence Gostin in Chapter 31, 'The New International Health Regulations: An Historic Development for International Law and Public Health'. They analyse why the adoption of a new version on 23 May 2005 constitutes a historic advance in global public health and international law, and assess the implications of the new regulations for health and security in the twenty-first century. They describe how the negotiation process was bedeviled by disagreements over the conflict with other international laws, bioterrorism and Taiwan, and chart the advances made and the shortcomings that remain in regard to several matters. These are the scope of IHR coverage, human rights, national surveillance and response, notification obligations, data and verification, WHO declaration and recommendation powers, and limits on national measures. They conclude that if the high potential of the new IHRs is to be realized, implementation will be key.

In Chapter 32, 'Committed to Health for All? How the G7/G8 Rate', Ronald Labonte and Ted Schrecker directly address the G8, the many commitments related to health made by its leaders at their annual summits, and how well they have complied with them in the following years. Focusing on the 1999, 2000 and 2001 summits, the commitments relating to the socioeconomic determinants of health, and the impact of G8 compliance on the developing world, they find a considerable commitment–compliance gap. They conclude that 'health for all' will not come without a strong commitment by G8 leaders to promise and deliver policies that redistribute resources from the rich to the poor.

The G8 summit's commitment and compliance record in the field of health is also addressed by John Kirton, Nikolai Roudev and Laura Sunderland in Chapter 33, 'Making G8 Leaders Deliver: An Analysis of Compliance and Health Commitments, 1996–2006'. They focus not on compliance's consequences but on its causes and possible paths to improvement. They present a more hopeful portrait of G8 health governance, finding that on both commitment and compliance the G8 has considerably improved its performance since 1996. But as compliance varies across G8 countries and particular health subjects, there is room for greater improvement still. Higher compliance comes when leaders embed into their commitments a one year deadline for delivery and rely on the WHO to do the implementing work. Thus G8 leaders should craft their health commitments in this way and create a health ministers' institution of their own to help.

In Chapter 34, 'The Challenge of Global Health', Laurie Garrett argues that the greatest problem in global health is no longer the lack of money but its uncoordinated, bureaucratic and corrupt disbursement, its 'stove-piped' focus on a few specific high profile diseases and short-term numerical targets, and the neglect of underlying long-term health care systems in poor countries that have deteriorated badly in the last decades. Moreover, health care professionals are migrating from the poor, young, disease-ridden South to the rich, ageing, relatively healthy North. Meanwhile visionary leadership, appropriate strategies and a sense of responsibility are lacking at the WHO and the Global Fund. Few projects contain monitoring mechanisms and participation by the poor. OECD nations should thus become self-sufficient in training the medical personnel they need, shift the OECD and G8 focus to the two basic goals of maternal survival and life expectancy, remove current disease-specific targeting requirements in major donor countries, and have donors and the UN system integrate infectious disease programmes into general public health systems.

References

Aginam, Obijiofor (2000), 'Global Village, Divided World: South–North Gap and Global Health Challenges at Century's Dawn', *Indiana Journal of Global Legal Studies*, **7**, pp. 603–28.

Aginam, Obijiofor (2002a), 'From the Core to the Peripheries: Multilateral Governance of Malaria in a Multi-Cultural World', *Chicago Journal of International Law*, **3**, no. 1, pp. 87–104.

Aginam, Obijiofor (2002b), 'International Law and Communicable Diseases', *Bulletin of the World Health Organization*, **80**, no. 12, pp. 946–51.

Aginam, Obijifor (2004), 'Salvaging Our Global Neighbourhood: Critical Reflections on the G8 Summit and Global Health Governance in an Interdependent World', *Law, Social Justice, and Global Development Journal (LGD)*, **1** (June). Available from: http://ejl.warwick.ac.uk/global/04-1/aginam. html

Aginam, Obijifor (2005), *Global Health Governance: International Law and Public Health in a Divided World*, Toronto: University of Toronto Press.

Baris, Enis and McLeod, Kari (2000), 'Globalization and International Trade in the Twenty-First Century: Opportunities for and Threats to the Health Sector in the South', *International Journal of Health Services*, **30**, no. 1, pp. 187–210.

Barkhuus, Arne (1943), 'The Dawn of International Cooperation in Medicine', *Ciba Symposia*, **5**, no. 7, pp. 1554–62.

Biermann, Frank and Bauer, Steffen (2005), *A World Environment Organization: Solution or Threat for Effective International Environmental Governance*, Aldershot: Ashgate.

Brockington, Fraser (1975), *World Health*, London: Churchill Livingston.

Brugha, Ruairi, Donoghue, Martine, Starling, Mary, Ndubani, Phillimon, Ssengooba, Freddie, Fernandes, Benedita and Walt, Gill (2004), 'The Global Fund: Managing Great Expectations', *The Lancet*, **364**, no. 9428, pp. 95–100.

Brundtland, Gro Harlem (2003), 'Global Health and International Security', *Global Governance*, **9**, no. 4, pp. 417–23.

Bryant, John H. (1980), 'WHO's Program of Health for All by the Year 2000: A Macrosystem for Health Policy Making—A Challenge to Social Science Research', *Social Science & Medicine*, **14A**, pp. 381–86.

Buse, Kent and Waxman, Amalia (2001), 'Public–Private Health Partnerships: A Strategy for WHO', *Bulletin of the World Health Organization*, **79**, no. 8, pp. 748–54.

Cabell, John L. (1881), 'The National Board of Health and the International Sanitary Conference of Washington', *Transactions of the American Medical Association*, **32**, pp. 321–39.

Chisholm, Brock (1950), 'The World Health Organization', *British Medical Journal*, **12**, (6 May), pp. 1021–27.

Cooper, Andrew F. and Kirton, John J. (eds) (2009), *Innovation in Global Health Governance: Critical Cases*, Aldershot: Ashgate.

Cooper, Andrew F., Kirton, John J. and Schrecker, Ted (eds) (2007), *Governing Global Health: Challenge, Response, Innovation*, Aldershot: Ashgate.

Cooper, Richard (1989), 'International Co-operation in Public Health as a Prologue to Macroeconomic Co-operation', in Richard N. Cooper, Barry Eichengreen, C. Randal Henning, Gerald Holtham and Robert D. Putnam, *Can Nations Agree? Issues in International Co-operation*, Washington, DC: Brookings Institution, pp. 178–254.

Drager, Nick and Beaglehole, Robert (2001), 'Globalization: Changing the Public Health Landscape', *Bulletin of the World Health Organization*, **79**, no. 9, p. 803.

Dubin, Martin David (1995), 'The League of Nations Health Organisation', in Paul Weinding (ed.), *International Health Organisations and Movements, 1918–1939*, Oxford: Oxford University Press.

Fidler, David (1997), 'The Globalization of Public Health: Emerging Infectious Diseases and International Relations', *Indiana Journal of Legal Studies*, **5**, no. 11, pp. 11–51.

Fidler, David (1999), *International Law and Infectious Disease*, Oxford: Oxford University Press.

Fidler, David (2002), 'Global Health Governance: Overview of the Role of International Law in Protecting and Promoting Global Public Health', Discussion Paper No. 3, World Health Organization and London School of Hygiene and Tropical Medicine, Geneva.

Fidler, David (2003a), 'Emerging Trends in International Law Concerning Global Infectious Disease Control', *Emerging Infectious Diseases*, **9**, no. 3, pp. 285–90.

Fidler, David (2003b), 'Racism or *Realpolitik?* U.S. Foreign Policy and the HIV/AIDS Catastrophe in Sub-Saharan Africa', *Journal of Gender, Race & Justice*, **7**, pp. 97–146.

Fidler, David (2003c), *SARS, Governance, and the Globalization of Disease*, London: Palgrave Macmillan.

Foster, George M. (1987), 'Bureaucratic Aspects of International Health Agencies', *Social Science and Medicine*, **25**, no. 2, pp. 1039–48.

Godlee, Fiona (1994), 'WHO in Retreat: Is it Losing its Influence?', *British Medical Journal*, **309**, pp. 1491–95.

Goodman, Neville M. (1971), *International Health Organizations and Their Work* (2nd edn), Baltimore: Williams & Wilkins.

Gostin, Lawrence (2004), 'Revision of the World Health Organization's International Health Regulations', *International Infectious Disease Law*, **291**, no. 21, pp. 2623–27.

Greaves, H.R.G. (1931), *The League Committees and the World Order*, London: Oxford University Press.

Haas, Ernst (1964), *Beyond the Nation State: Functionalism and International Organization*, Stanford: University of California Press.

Haas, Ernst B. and Ruggie, John Gerard (1982), 'What Message in the Medium of International Systems?', *International Studies Quarterly*, **26**, no. 2, pp. 190–219.

Howard-Jones, Norman (1975), *The Scientific Background of the International Sanitary Conferences 1851–1938*, Geneva: World Health Organization.

Howard-Jones, Norman (1981), *The Pan American Health Organization, Origins and Evolution*, Geneva: World Health Organization.

Justice, Judith (1987), 'The Bureaucratic Context of International Health: A Social Scientist's View', *Social Science and Medicine*, **25**, No. 12, pp. 1301–306.

Kaul, Inge, Grunberg, Isabelle and Stern, Marc (eds) (1999), *Global Public Goods: International Co-operation in the 21ˢᵗ Century*, Oxford: Oxford University Press.

Keohane, Robert and Nye, Joseph (1977), *Power and Interdependence: World Politics in Transition*, Boston: Little, Brown.

Kickbusch, Ilona (1999), 'Global + Local = Global Public Health', *Journal of Epidemiological Community Health*, **53**, no. 8, pp. 451–52.

Kickbusch, Ilona and Quick, J. (1998), 'Partnerships for Health in the 21st Century', *World Statistics Quarterly*, **51**, no. 1, pp. 68–74.

Kirton, John (1993), 'The Seven Power Summit as a New Security Institution', in David Dewitt, David Haglund and John Kirton (eds), *Building a New Global Order: Emerging Trends in International Security*, Toronto: Oxford University Press, pp. 335–57.

Kirton, John and Mannell, Jenevieve (2007) 'The G8 and Global Health Governance', in Andrew F. Cooper, John J. Kirton and Ted Schrecker (eds), *Governing Global Health: Challenge, Response, Innovation*, Aldershot: Ashgate, pp. 115–46.

Kirton, John and Trebilcock, Michael (eds) (2004), *Hard Choices, Soft Law: Voluntary Standards in Global Trade, Environment and Social Governance*, Aldershot: Ashgate.

Labonte, Ronald (1998), 'Health Public Policy and the WTO: A Proposal for an International Presence in Future Trade/Investment Talks', *Health Promotion International*, **13**, no. 3, pp. 245–56.

Labonte, Ronald and Schrecker, Ted (2007), 'Foreign Policy Matters: A Normative View of the G8 and Population Health', *Bulletin of the World Health Organization*, **85**, no. 3, pp. 185–91.

Labonte, Ronald, Schrecker, Ted, Sanders, David and Mieeus, Wilma (2004), *Fatal Indifference: The G8, Africa and Global Health*, Ottawa: International Development Research Centre.

Le Prestre, Philippe (ed.) (2004), *Governing Global Biodiversity: The Evolution and Implementation of the Convention on Biological Diversity*, Aldershot: Ashgate.

Lee, Kelly (1998), 'Globalization and Health Policy', Discussion Paper No. 1, London School of Hygiene and Tropical Medicine, London.

Mackenzie, Melville (1950), 'International Collaboration in Health', *International Affairs*, **26**, no. 4, pp. 515–21.

Mills, Lisa (2004), 'Terminating Agricultural Biotechnology? Hard Law, Voluntary Measures and the Life Sciences Industry', in John Kirton and Michael Trebilcock (eds), *Hard Choices, Soft Law: Voluntary Standards in Global Trade, Environment and Social Governance*, Aldershot: Ashgate, pp. 329–46.

Mitrany, David (1944), *A Working Peace System*, London: Royal Institute of International Affairs (reprinted Chicago: Quadrangle Books, 1966).

Mitrany, David (1953), 'The International Technical Assistance Program', *Proceedings of the Academy of Political Science*, **25**, no. 2, pp. 13–24.

Mitrany, David (1966), 'The Functional Approach in Historical Perspective', *International Affairs*, **47**, No. 3, pp. 532–43.

Pannenborg, Charles O. (1979), *A New International Health Order: An Inquiry into the International Relations of World Health and Medical Care*, Germantown: Sihthoff & Noordhoff.

Parker, Richard (2002), 'The Global HIV/AIDS Pandemic: Structural Inequalities and the Politics of International Health', *American Public Health Association*, **92**, no. 3, pp. 343–47.

Popkin, Charles W. (1928), 'The Interchange of Public Health Personnel under the Health Organization of the League of Nations: A Study of the Creation of an International Standard of Public Health Administration', Geneva: League of Nations Non-Partisan Association.

Price-Smith, Andrew (2001), *Plagues and Politics: Infectious Disease and International Policy*, New York: Palgrave.

Price-Smith, Andrew (2002), *The Health of Nations: Infectious Disease, Environmental Change, and Their Effects on National Security and Development*, Cambridge, MA: MIT Press.

Reich, Michael R. (1987), 'Essential Drugs: Economics and Politics in International Health', *Health Policy*, **8**, pp. 39–57.

Reich, Michael R. and Marui, Eiji (1989), *International Cooperation for Health: Problems, Prospects and Priorities*, Dover: Auburn House Publishing.

Ruggie, John G. (1983), 'International Regimes, Transactions, and Change: Embedded Liberalism in the Postwar Economic Order', *International Organization*, **36** (Spring), pp. 379–415.

Sell, Susan (2002), 'TRIPS and the Access to Medicines Campaign', *Wisconsin International Law Journal*, **20**, no. 3, pp. 481–522.

Stein, Arthur (1983), 'Coordination and Collaboration: Regimes in an Anarchic World', in Stephen Krasner (ed.), *International Regimes*, Ithaca: Cornell University Press, pp. 115–40.

Stott, Robin (1999), 'The World Bank: Friend or Foe?', *British Medical Journal*, **318**, pp. 822–23.

Thucydides (1998), *The Peloponnesian War*, trans. Steven Lattimore, Indianapolis: Hackett.

Weindling, Paul (1995), *International Health Organizations and Movements, 1918–1939*, Cambridge: Cambridge University Press.

Woodward, David, Drager, Nick, Beaglehold, Robert and Lipson, Debra (2001), 'Globalization and Health: A Framework for Analysis and Action', *Bulletin of the World Health Organization*, **79**, no. 9, pp. 875–81.

Woodworth, John M. (1875), *The Cholera Epidemic of 1873 in the United States*, Washington: Government Printing Office.

Wolfers, Arnold (1962), *Discord and Collaboration: Essays on International Politics*, Baltimore: Johns Hopkins Press.

Yach, Derek and Bettcher, Douglas (1998), 'The Globalization of Public Health I and II', *American Journal of Public Health*, **88**, pp. 735–41.

Zacher, Mark (1999), 'Global Epidemiological Surveillance: International Cooperation in Monitoring Infectious Diseases', in Inge Kaul, Isabelle Grunberg and Marc Stern (eds), *Global Public Goods: International Cooperation in the 21st Century*, Oxford: Oxford University Press, pp. 266–83.

Part I
The Foundations and
Evolution of the Field

[1]

Disease, diplomacy and international commerce: the origins of international sanitary regulation in the nineteenth century

Mark Harrison
Wellcome Unit for the History of Medicine, University of Oxford, 45–47 Banbury Road, Oxford OX2 6PE, UK
E-mail: mark.harrison@wuhmo.ox.ac.uk

Abstract

During the early nineteenth century, European nations began to contemplate cooperation in sanitary matters, starting a diplomatic process that culminated in the International Sanitary Conferences and the first laws on the control of infectious disease. This article examines the origins of these conferences and highlights certain features that have been neglected in existing scholarship. It argues that while commercial pressures were the main stimuli to the reform of quarantine, these were insufficient in themselves to explain why most European nations came to see greater cooperation as desirable. It places special emphasis on the diplomatic context and shows that the peace of 1815 produced a climate in which many European nations envisaged a more systematic and liberal sanitary regime.

The first International Sanitary Conference, held in Paris, in 1851, is generally regarded as a milestone in international sanitary cooperation. Although there was little agreement among the twelve nations that sent delegates to the conference, it established the principle that quarantine and similar sanitary measures ought to be fixed by international agreement, so as to minimize the expense and inconvenience arising from a multiplicity of practices. The Paris conference applied only to the Mediterranean but all subsequent international forums and laws on the control of infectious diseases stemmed from these tentative steps towards international sanitary collaboration, more than 150 years ago. Yet historians have shown comparatively little interest in the origins of the Paris conference or in attempts to control the spread of diseases across borders prior to 1851. Above all, we have little idea of why the idea of international collaboration suddenly became attractive to many countries in

The author wishes to thank the editors and referees, together with those who commented on earlier versions of this paper at Johns Hopkins University, the London School of Tropical Medicine and Hygiene, the University of Geneva, and the University of Valencia. The author is especially grateful to Professors Harry Marks, Graham Mooney and Josep Barona.

the decades before 1851: it was by no means an easy or natural evolution, as quarantine had typically been regarded as an instrument of foreign policy, to be used aggressively in further-ance of national interests.

In so far as an explanation has been attempted, it has stressed the growth of international commerce and particularly the trading interests of Britain and France.[1] The fact that these countries took the initiative would appear to suggest that they saw international agree-ment as a means of diminishing impediments to their maritime trade. Other factors, such as the growth of political liberalism have also been suggested as reasons why certain states sought to reduce the burden of quarantine, although there is little agreement about how far ideology had a consistent bearing upon sanitary policies.[2] Yet neither explanation seems sufficient in itself to account for the radical shift that was needed for states to contemplate cooperation in sanitary matters. As Peter Baldwin has noted, mercantile interests were far from uniform and tended to be regarded as having a rather narrow view, sometimes incom-patible with the national good. Two important questions therefore arise. First, how and with what degree of success did mercantile groups enlist the support of others in their campaign to reform quarantine regulations? Second, how did the reform of quarantine come to be identified, not only with national interests, but with the welfare of humanity in general?

It is not possible here to reconstruct the process whereby the critics of quarantine were able to forge coalitions in their respective countries, but it is possible to examine the international context from which the desire for sanitary cooperation developed. As is well known, the Congress of Vienna (1815) brought to an end an atomized system of international relations in which armed conflict had been common. The system of diplomacy inaugurated at Vienna recognized the existence of different national interests but sought agreements that transcended them. Although this system fell into disarray in 1823, con-gresses were replaced by smaller conferences on specific topics, and these often proved to be more effective than the rather grandiose gatherings they replaced. It was in this context that the concept of international sanitary cooperation was first articulated, marking a fun-damental shift from the state of affairs prior to 1815. While the growth of international trade loomed large in these discussions, other considerations were also important, not least the balance of power and the avoidance of war. Both within individual countries and in the international arena, the proponents of quarantine reform grew in support and stature as their campaign became enmeshed with these broader political and humanitarian concerns.

Quarantine's *ancien régime*

By the middle of the fifteenth century, legislation banning commerce with infected places was common in many Mediterranean countries, particularly those closest to reservoirs of

---

1   N. M. Goodman, *International health organizations and their work*, London: J. & A. Churchill, 1952, pp. 34–6; Howard-Jones, *The scientific background of the international sanitary conferences*, Geneva: WHO, 1975, p. 11; David P. Fidler, *International law and infectious diseases*, Oxford: Clarendon Press, 1999, pp. 21–37.

2   The classic statement of the relationship between ideology and sanitary policy is Erwin Ackerknecht's essay, 'Anticontagionism between 1821 and 1867', *Bulletin of the History of Medicine*, 22, 1948, pp. 562–93. However, as Peter Baldwin has recently pointed out, the connection between politics and policy is far more complex than Ackerknecht's formulation suggests. See Peter Baldwin, *Contagion and the state in Europe 1830–1930*, Cambridge: Cambridge University Press, 1999.

plague in Central Asia. Although the plague was still regarded as a 'blight of God', prayer and penitence – formerly 'the first and sovereign remedy' – were gradually supplemented by more secular interventions.[3] Some countries, especially the Italian states, also began to develop permanent bureaucracies to administer quarantine and lazarettos, in the belief that plague was a contagious disease that could be prevented by thwarting its transmission.[4] This belief rested on two related observations. First, of all the maladies afflicting Europe, plague alone originated outside the continent; second, it appeared to be a specific disease, with easily recognizable symptoms that could be differentiated from common fevers. Quarantine was invariably imposed whenever the disease was reported in the Levant, which had long been regarded as the conduit of plague into Europe. It was also sometimes imposed against ships from the West Indies, when epidemic disease (most likely yellow fever) was known to be prevalent.[5] In the seventeenth century, these measures were usually *ad hoc* in nature rather than the subject of specific statutes.[6] Even in the Mediterranean, more vulnerable to plague than northern Europe because of its proximity to the Levant, quarantine stations were isolated and their practices irregular. In France, for instance, there were only two quarantine stations along the Mediterranean Sea, at Toulon and Marseilles. Contemporaries were struck by the lack of coordination between these stations and also by the fact that quarantine often continued to be imposed at the ports when the plague was ravaging the interior. This situation led, in 1683, to the first statute relating to quarantine, which began to standardize practices across the country.[7]

In many Mediterranean countries, quarantines came to enjoy a good measure of popular support and were widely credited with the freedom of certain countries from plague. Liberal quarantine regimes like those at Marseilles, however, were generally the exception rather than the rule, and other Mediterranean stations, such as those along the Barbary Coast, became notorious for malpractice and exorbitant charges. But in some European countries, most notably France and Britain, the eighteenth century saw increasing divergence of opinion on quarantine. While such measures continued to command popular support, the medical profession began to divide sharply over the utility of quarantine and the theory of contagion that underpinned it. At the same time, merchants involved in the export trade with the Levant grew increasingly critical of quarantine restrictions, which cost them a great deal through delays, charges and the destruction or damage of goods by fumigation in quarantine houses. Arrangements in the Mediterranean were the main cause of complaint but the

---

3   *L' ordre public pour la ville de Lyon, pendant la maladie contagieuse*, Lyon: A. Valancol, 1670.

4   Ann G. Carmichael, *Plague and the poor in Renaissance Florence*, Cambridge: Cambridge University Press, 1986, pp. 110–21.

5   Paul Slack, *The impact of plague in Tudor and Stuart England*, Oxford: Clarendon Press, 1985, p. 324. Those who believed that yellow fever was a contagious disease often likened it to plague, some claiming it was different from plague only in degree rather than in kind. For example, Henry Warren, *A treatise concerning the malignant fever in Barbados, and the neighbouring islands: with an account of the seasons there, from the year 1734 to 1738, in a letter to Dr. Mead*, London: Fletcher Gyles, 1740.

6   In England, for example, quarantine was imposed by orders in council, which were to be implemented by the corporations governing ports. See Wellcome Library for the History and Understanding of Medicine, London (henceforth WLHUM), Western MS.3109, Thursday meeting book, Kingston-upon-Hull Corporation, 8 September 1668.

7   'Quarantaines', *Dictionnaire encyclopédique des sciences médicales*, Paris: P. Asselin & G. Masson, 1874, p. 24.

enactment of quarantine statutes in northern countries during the eighteenth century constituted an additional burden.[8]

Perhaps the clearest example of this polarization of opinion was the response to the plague in Marseilles in 1720. The outbreak was immediately traced to a merchant vessel that had arrived from Syria, and neighbouring countries lost no time in imposing quarantine against French shipping; a sanitary cordon was also imposed around Marseilles and other infected provinces. The cordons appeared to prevent plague from spreading beyond southern France but some medical practitioners questioned the contagious nature of the disease. If plague were contagious, why did it appear only at certain times of the year? Might not epidemics be related to other factors, such as seasonal climatic changes and states of the atmosphere? Such ideas had steadily gained ground since the revival of Hippocratic medicine in the Renaissance, and by the late seventeenth century they were being clearly articulated by the English physician Thomas Sydenham (1624–89), amongst others.[9] Many of the medical practitioners who commented on the epidemic in southern France employed such explanations as an alternative or supplement to contagion. The fact that the Levant was afflicted more often than Europe was explained by the fact that it was subject to great heat, the plague 'poison' arising from the rapid putrefaction of dead animals and plants; likewise, plague tended to occur in Europe during the summer, when conditions approximated to those in the East. Quarantine therefore seemed to be unnecessary, as well as injurious to trade.[10]

In Britain, the incorporation of quarantine into statute law provoked similar debates. The first act was passed in 1710, and further legislation followed the arrival of plague in Marseilles, creating a quarantine station in the Medway and elevating the maximum penalty for evasion to death.[11] However, the draconian powers of the 1721 Act were modified as the threat from the Mediterranean diminished.[12] As in France, the broad consensus over preventative measures that had existed in the 1600s was beginning to break down: medical opinion was diverging and exporters were growing increasingly impatient of restrictions on trade. Critics claimed that quarantine in Britain was unnecessary if men boarding ships in the Levant were healthy, as the voyage of seven or eight weeks was long enough to ensure that plague was not present.[13]

Some critics went further and suggested that quarantine in Europe could be relaxed in view of the fact that ships leaving the Levant with foul bills of health were required to perform quarantine at Malta, Leghorn and Venice. But quarantine was far from infallible. In Spain, for instance, the authorities experienced great problems in imposing an embargo against ships from Marseilles, despite posting guards along the Mediterranean

---

8   *Ibid.*, pp. 26–30.

9   David Cantor, ed., *Reinventing Hippocrates*, Aldershot: Ashgate, 2002.

10   Jean Baptiste Senac, *Traité des causes des accidens, et de la cure de la peste*, Paris: P-J. Mariette, 1744.

11   Arnold Zuckerman, 'Plague and contagionism in eighteenth-century England: the role of Richard Mead', *Bulletin of the History of Medicine*, 78, 2004, pp. 273–308.

12   Slack, *Impact*, pp. 330–2.

13   'Extracts of several letters of Mordach Mackenzie, M.D. concerning the plague at Constantinople', trans. 93, *Philosophical Transactions of the Royal Society*, 47, 1752, pp. 384–95; 'A further account of the late plague at Constantinople, in a letter of Dr Mackenzie from thence', trans. 87, *ibid.*, pp. 514–16.

coast. Ships also attempted to dock in Spanish ports with fraudulent bills of health, which falsely claimed that the ships had sailed from non-infected ports. Cordons imposed along land borders were even more porous,[14] and plague epidemics were often blamed on illicit traders who stealthily crossed borders to evade customs duties and quarantine.[15]

Even supporters of quarantine admitted that this was a problem and some concluded that the answer lay in more efficient systems of disease notification, which would mean that quarantine could be resorted to selectively. The British physician William Brownrigg, for example, conceded that less resort need be had to quarantine if the bills of health issued from plague-infected countries were more reliable.[16] By the 1770s, bills were issued routinely by some of the Italian states and by foreign consuls in the Ottoman dominions. Bills normally declared the time and place from which they were granted, the names and numbers of crew and passengers, and indicated the health status of the vessel. They also recorded whether or not quarantine had been performed and the nature of any merchandise carried.[17]

One of the problems with the system was that consuls had to depend on unreliable sources of information. All it took for a consul to issue a foul bill of health was a single reported case in a Levantine city or its environs, and some British merchants suspected that consuls were deliberately fed false reports by their commercial rivals. 'The Greeks carry on three-fourths of the Dutch as well as the Italian trade', protested a group of Smyrna merchants, 'it is therefore their interest (and unfortunately that of every other nation) to depress ours as much as possible.' For this reason, the merchants, championed by the prison-reformer John Howard, advocated the construction of a model lazaretto in Britain, thereby dispensing with the need to quarantine ships in the Mediterranean. In view of the distance from the Levant, Howard proposed that a quarantine of no longer than forty-eight hours need be performed, if no cases of sickness developed among crew or passengers. Although the British government had hitherto rejected the idea on grounds of cost, the Levantine merchants claimed that a boom in trade with Turkey would more than repay it.[18]

Despite its obvious flaws, quarantine remained firmly entrenched for the rest of the century, both in the Catholic Mediterranean and in the Protestant North.[19] Quarantine was imperfect but it was the art of the possible, and to abandon any form of protection was incompatible with contemporary theories of statecraft, which viewed population as a source of wealth and power. Johann Peter Frank's multi-volume treatise, *A system of complete medical police*, exemplified this line of thinking. An exponent of enlightened absolutism, Frank proposed a comprehensive system to protect and improve the health of all persons through generous state provisions and the regulation of social relations. In this system, quarantine played an important part in protecting enlightened states – like that of his

---

14   WLHUM, Western MS.963, Balthasar de Aperregui, 'Ordenes relativos a sanidad y lazarettos en el Puerto de Barcelona, con motivo de la peste, en el año de 1714, y siguientes', Barcelona, 1752.

15   William Brownrigg, *Considerations on the means of preventing the communication of pestilential contagion and of eradicating it in infected places*, London: Lockyer Davis, 1771, p. 4.

16   Brownrigg, *Considerations*.

17   *Ibid.*, pp. 5–6.

18   John Howard, *An account of the principal lazarettos in Europe*, Warrington: William Eyres, 1789, pp. 25–7.

19   E.g. *Della peste ossia della cura per preservarsene, e guarire da questo fatalismo morbo*, Venice: Leonardo & Giammaria, 1784.

emperor, Joseph II of Austria – against the ingress of disease from their less diligent neighbours. 'It is one of the foremost tasks of the state to prevent persons or animals, goods, and all objects to which or whom contagions cling, from entering the country', he proclaimed, 'and there is no doubt that governments are entitled to use all suitable means that do not contravene international law in order to achieve this.'[20] Indeed, some writers advocated quarantine explicitly on mercantilist grounds, contrasting the absence of such measures in the plague-ravaged Ottoman provinces with more 'enlightened' regimes that were free from the disease.[21] However, writers such as Paskal von Ferro and Martin Lange argued that quarantine measures ought to be brought into conformity with enlightened government, minimizing inconvenience and disruption of trade.[22]

Despite calls for moderation, quarantine was often employed as a form of commercial protection or was used to sever the economic arteries of rival countries;[23] sanitary cordons were also attractive to states because they could be used to strengthen national and imperial borders. It was partly for this reason that the Venetian republic maintained a sanitary cordon against the adjacent Ottoman provinces of Istria and Dalmatia, but the most striking example is the 1,600 km cordon established by Austria-Hungary along its borders with the Ottoman Empire. The cordon was policed by watchtowers and roving bands of soldiers, ordered to shoot on sight those who crossed the border without performing quarantine. The sanitary functions of the cordon developed gradually from 1710, having originated in the Military Border established to defend against Ottoman invasion. This military and sanitary cordon constituted an important additional source of manpower for the Hapsburg Empire and troops raised in the border provinces to form the cordon were sometimes deployed elsewhere for purely military purposes.[24] Indeed, sanitary cordons were sometimes used to cloak the aggressive intentions of predatory nations. During the plague epidemics in Eastern Europe in 1770, for example, Prussia established a sanitary cordon that encroached upon Polish territory, its ostensibly defensive nature concealing Prussia's predatory intentions.[25]

For these reasons, sanitary matters began to figure prominently in international diplomacy by the 1770s, providing an early indication that some form of dialogue was necessary if damaging disputes and even conflict were to be averted. As the system of diplomacy became more professional,[26] decisions over whether or not to impose quarantine became more difficult and those responsible rarely took action without carefully considering the likely reactions of other states. For instance, when plague appeared in western Russia in 1771, threatening the port of St Petersburg, quarantine was imposed upon all goods brought

---

20   Johann Peter Frank, *A system of complete medical police*, ed. E. Lesky, Baltimore: J. H. V. Press, 1976, trans. by E. Vlim from 3rd edn., Vienna, 1786, p. 446.

21   Paskal Joseph Ferro, *Untersuchung der Pestanstekung, nebst zwei Aufsätzen von der Glaubwürdigkeit der meisten Pestberichte aus der Moldau und Wallachey, und der Schädlichkeit der bisherigen Contumazen von D. Lange und Fronius*, Vienna: Joseph Edlen, 1787.

22   Martin Lange, *Rudimenta doctrinae de peste*, Vienna: Rudolph Graeffer, 1784.

23   Mark Harrison, *Disease and the modern world: 1500 to the present day*, Cambridge: Polity, 2004, pp. 58–68.

24   Gunther E. Rothenberg, 'The Austrian sanitary cordon and the control of bubonic plague: 1710–1871', *Journal of the History of Medicine and Allied Sciences*, 28, 1973, pp. 15–23.

25   Herbert H. Kaplan, *The first partition of Poland*, New York and London: Columbia University Press, 1969, pp. 129–30.

26   D. McKay and H. M. Scott, *The rise of the great powers 1645–1815*, London: Longman, 1983.

to the city for export, in the hope that this would deter other countries from imposing embargos or quarantines against Russian shipping. But despite active diplomacy, fear of plague and commercial ostracism led most northern European countries to impose quarantine against Russia, much to the disappointment of the British mercantile community in St Petersburg.[27]

Nevertheless, mercantile opposition to quarantine was growing and was becoming quite influential in some regions that depended heavily on international commerce, such as the eastern seaboard of North America. Here, among Republicans such as Dr Benjamin Rush, a signatory of the Declaration of Independence, quarantine had also come to be identified with tyranny.[28] Free trade had long been associated with political liberty,[29] and the growing influence of such doctrines in the Anglophone world led a number of writers to equate quarantine with authoritarian regimes. For Protestant writers such as Dale Ingram and Sir Richard Manningham, the doctrine of contagion was merely a Popish fabrication, originally calculated to exclude certain delegates from the Council of Trent.[30] Yet, opposition to quarantine was not confined to mercantile groups and the doctors with whom they associated: those who travelled regularly by sea also came to resent the costs and delays occasioned by quarantine. The French explorer Corneille le Brun was one of many who complained of the great inconvenience of being detained in Mediterranean lazarettos while returning from the Levant to Europe.[31]

One of the chief problems facing merchants and travellers was the great variety of regulations imposed at ports in the Mediterranean: some maintained forty-day quarantines against all vessels from the Levant, regardless of their bills of health, while others settled for a period of only eighteen days. Irregularities in ships' manifests could also result in the impounding of vessels when there was no disease on board, and for this reason travellers from the Levant often purchased bills of health separately from those of the crew.[32] It was not sufficient, however, to oppose quarantine solely on grounds of inconvenience or even for commercial reasons; its opponents had to attack the doctrine of contagion on which quarantine was based and, even if they did not deny the possibility of contagion, they stressed the vital role of climate and meteorological conditions in epidemic disease. Colonial experience was crucial here, for the seemingly distinctive disease environments of

27　John T. Alexander, *Bubonic plague in early modern Russia: public health and urban disaster*, Oxford: Oxford University Press, 2003, pp. 249–51.

28　Benjamin Rush, *An account of the bilious remitting yellow fever*, Philadelphia: Thomas Dobson, 1794; J. H. Powell, *Bring out your dead: the great plague of yellow fever in Philadelphia in 1793*, Philadelphia: University of Pennsylvania Press, 1949; William Coleman, *Yellow fever in the north: the methods of early epidemiology*, Madison: University of Wisconsin Press, 1987; Martin S. Pernick, 'Politics, parties and pestilence: epidemic yellow fever in Philadelphia and the rise of the first party system', in J. Walzer Leavitt and R. L. Numbers, eds., *Sickness and health in America: readings in the history of medicine and public health*, Madison: University of Wisconsin Press, 1985, pp. 356–71.

29　Carla G. Pestana, *The English Atlantic in an age of revolution 1640–1661*, Cambridge, MA: Harvard University Press, 2004.

30　Dale Ingram, *An historical account of the several plagues that have appeared in the world since the year 1346*, London: R. Baldwin, 1755; Richard Manningham, *A discourse concerning the plague and pestilential fevers*, London: Robinson, 1758.

31　Corneille le Brun, *Voyages de Corneille le Brun au Levant, c'est-à-dire, dans les principaux endroits de l'Asie Mineure, dans les Isles de Chio, Rhodes, Chypres, etc.*, Paris: P. Gosse & J. Neautme, 1732, p. 554.

32　John Taylor, *Travels from England to India, in the year 1789*, London: S. Low, 1799, vol. 1, pp. 114–5.

Asia, Africa, and the Americas made a profound impression upon medical practitioners. Colonial practitioners worked consciously in the tradition of Sydenham and were increasingly vocal in their opposition to simplistic notions of contagion.[33] The surgeon John Wade, employed by the East India Company, declared that he had not encountered a 'single instance of contagion' during his service and added that most epidemics in hot climates were the product of miasma.[34]

Yet opposition to contagion and quarantine was by no means universal among medical practitioners with overseas experience. Senior military and naval medical officers, for example, tended to reaffirm official views on the control of diseases like plague and yellow fever.[35] Support for quarantine was also to be found among those practitioners working for trading concerns such as the English Levant Company. The physician Patrick Russell, who had experienced plague epidemics while working at Aleppo, acknowledged that it was affected by seasonal factors, but he also believed that plague could be communicated through contact between persons and through certain kinds of merchandise, such as clothing. It was therefore wise to maintain the precautions that had served Britain well, cautioned Russell, as the inconvenience caused by quarantine was preferable to the massive disruption that would be caused by an epidemic at home.[36]

Nevertheless, the revolutionary and Napoleonic wars tilted the balance of medical opinion towards those who sought to abolish or, more commonly, to reform quarantine. This may seem counter-intuitive in view of the fact that European armies suffered gravely from both plague and yellow fever,[37] yet overseas campaigns provided practitioners with the opportunity of studying these diseases at first hand, to observe how they spread, under what conditions they seemed to occur, and what effects they had on the human body. Plague and yellow fever were thus demystified and some medical practitioners came to regard them, not as separate diseases, but merely as varieties of common or garden 'epidemic fever'.[38] A growing number of practitioners claimed that these diseases were not contagious

33 Some of the best examples are: James Lind, *An essay on diseases incidental to Europeans in hot climates*, London: T. Beckett & P. A. De Hondt, 1768; John Clark, *Observations on the diseases in long voyages to hot countries, and particularly to those which prevail in the East Indies*, London: D. Wilson and G. Nicol, 1773; Charles Curtis, *An account of the diseases of India*, Edinburgh: W. Laing, 1807. For a discussion of this literature, see W. F. Bynum, 'Cullen and the study of fevers in Britain, 1760–1820', in W. F. Bynum and V. Nutton, eds., *Theories of fever from antiquity to the enlightenment, Medical History* supplement no. 1, London: Wellcome Institute for the History of Medicine, 1981; Richard B. Sheridan, *Doctors and slaves: a medical and demographic history of slavery in the British West Indies, 1680–1834*, New York: Cambridge University Press, 1985; Mark Harrison, *Climates and constitutions: health, race, environment and British imperialism in India 1600–1850*, Delhi: Oxford University Press, 1999.

34 John P. Wade, *A paper on the prevention and treatment of the disorders of seamen and soldiers in Bengal*, London: J. Murray, 1793, pp. 5, 9.

35 Gilbert Blane, *Observations on the diseases incident to seamen*, London: Joseph Cooper, 1785, p. 128.

36 Patrick Russell, *A treatise of the plague*, London: G. G. J. & J. Robinson, 1791.

37 John R. McNeill, 'The ecological basis of warfare in the Caribbean, 1700–1804', in M. Utlee, ed., *Adapting to conditions: war and society in the eighteenth century*, Tuscaloosa: University of Alabama Press, 1982; David Geggus, *Slavery, war, and revolution: the British occupation of Saint Domingue, 1793–1798*, Oxford: Clarendon Press, 1982; Roger N. Buckley, *The British army in the West Indies: society and the military in the revolutionary age*, Gainesville: University Press of Florida, 1998.

38 P. Assalini, *Observations on the disease called the plague, on the dysentery, the opthalmy of Egypt, and on the means of prevention, with some remarks on the yellow fever of Cadiz*, trans. A. Neale, New York: T. J. Swords, 1806.

in any sense other than they could be conveyed in the breath of the sick,[39] and they placed more emphasis on the climatic and sanitary conditions necessary to produce the diseases in epidemic form.[40] The opponents of quarantine looked back at its chequered history, the frequent abuses of sanitary regulations for political ends, and portrayed it as a vestige of a less enlightened era.

Towards an international sanitary system

An additional impetus to the reform of sanitary legislation was provided by the recovery of international trade following the disruption of the French wars. The dynamic force behind the recovery was Britain, now the predominant sea power, although non-European states such as Egypt also played a significant part,[41] ushering in what some historians have referred to as a new wave of globalization.[42]

It is questionable whether the concept of globalization accurately describes the fractured nature of international trade at this time,[43] but the expansion of international commerce undoubtedly became more prominent in discussions over sanitary regulation. On the one hand, certain mercantile interests – particularly those involved in the booming cotton trade with Egypt – increased their demands for the relaxation of quarantine.[44] On the other, there was a heightened sense of the danger posed by infectious diseases originating outside Europe. Although many medical practitioners declared that these diseases were not contagious, epidemics caused alarm among the lay public, dispelling the complacency that followed the retreat of plague. The outbreak of yellow fever in the West Indies during the 1790s, for instance, aroused fears that troops and prisoners sent back to Europe would carry the disease,[45] and vessels were sometimes impounded, much to the frustration of naval authorities.[46]

---

39   Margaret Pelling, 'The meaning of contagion: reproduction, medicine and metaphor', in A. Bashford and C. Hooker, eds., *Contagion: historical and cultural studies*, London: Routledge, 2001, pp. 15–38.

40   E.g. Hector M'Lean, *An enquiry into the nature, and causes of the great mortality among the troops at St. Domingo*, London: T. Cadell, 1797; James Clark, *A treatise on the yellow fever, as it appeared in the island of Dominica, in the years 1793–4–5*, London: J. Murray and S. Highley, 1797; J. Mabit, *Essai sur les maladies de l'armée de St.-Domingue en l'an XI, et principalement sur la fièvre jaune*, Paris: École de Médecine, 1804; Victor Bally, *Du typhus d'Amérique ou fièvre jaune*, Paris: Smith, 1814.

41   See A. G. Hopkins, ed., *Globalization in world history*, London: Pimlico, 2002; C. A. Bayly, *The birth of the modern world 1780–1914*, Oxford: Blackwell, 2004.

42   Robbie Robertson, *The three waves of globalization*, London: Zed Books, 2003; Rondo Cameron and Larry Neal, *A concise economic history of the world*, New York and Oxford: Oxford University Press, 2003.

43   See 'Globalization', in Frederick Cooper, *Colonialism in question: theory, knowledge, history*, Berkeley: University of California Press, 2005.

44   *Second report of the select committee appointed to consider the means of improving and maintaining the foreign trade of the country*, PP 1824.

45   National Maritime Museum ADM/F/27, letter from Office of Sick and Wounded Seamen to Admiralty Board, 19 August 1797.

46   In 1794, for instance, the British navy was irked by the prolonged quarantine in Lisbon of a captured French vessel containing valuable merchandise from Saragossa. The seemingly arbitrary extension of the quarantine led to protracted negotiations with the Portuguese secretary of state and other officials. See WLHUM, Western MS.7313, Thomas Mayne, Lisbon, 8 November 1794, to Sir Charles Hamilton, commander, HMS *Rodney*, Portsmouth.

Epidemics of yellow fever in some Mediterranean ports in the early 1800s showed that these fears were justified,[47] while the appearance of plague on Corfu in 1816 caused great alarm because of the enlargement of trade between the northern Atlantic countries and the eastern Mediterranean.[48] Alien epidemics now stood alongside a host of other seemingly new diseases – principally nervous and digestive disorders – that were attributed to the luxurious and frenetic lifestyles produced by commercial and colonial expansion.[49]

This sense of vulnerability meant that most nations – especially those closest to the presumed sources of epidemics – were reluctant to abandon quarantine, their traditional defence against epidemic disease.[50] This was clearly illustrated by the response to the appearance of cholera in European Russia, in 1830, which led most states to fall back on quarantine, despite the lack of consensus about its causation and spread. As with plague and yellow fever, there was little agreement among medical practitioners about whether the disease was contagious or whether quarantine was of any use. For some, the slow and uneven spread of the disease provided evidence that quarantine did not work,[51] while for others it was proof that it had not been sufficiently enforced.[52] Likewise, the spread of the disease from East to West was enough to persuade many that it was in some sense contagious, while the fact that it spread very unevenly – geographically and socially – suggested that other factors were involved.[53] In general, the severity of quarantine and similar measures imposed against cholera depended on the extent to which commercial and manufacturing interests held sway. As Richard Evans has shown, authorities in Hamburg took little action in the fight against cholera during the epidemics of 1832 and 1848, while the Prussian authorities, less dependent upon commerce, insisted on the contagiousness of cholera and the need for restrictions of trade and population movement.[54] However, commercial interests – like the medical profession – were still divided on the issue

---

47 See for example, J. Tommasini, *Recherches pathologiques sur la fièvre de Livorne de 1804, sur la fièvre jaune d' Amérique*, Paris: Arthus-Bertrand, 1812.

48 WLHUM, Western MS.3883, Maj.-Gen. Sir Charles Phillips, 'Letters and instructions to the officers during the plague at Corfu, 1816'.

49 E.g. Hugh Smith, *An essay on the nerves...to which is added an essay on foreign teas*, London: P. Norman, 1799; Thomas Trotter, *Medicina nautica: an essay on the diseases of seamen*, London: T. Cadell and W. Davies, 1797, pp. 9–10; Thomas Trotter, *A view of the nervous temperament*, London: Longman et al., 1807; James Johnson, *An essay on the morbid sensibility of the stomach and bowels*, London: T. & G. Underwood, 1827.

50 James McGrigor, *Medical sketches of the expedition to Egypt, from India*, London: J. Murray, 1804.

51 E.g. James McCabe, *Observations on the epidemic cholera of Asia and Europe*, Cheltenham: G. A. Williams, 1832, pp. 1–4.

52 West Sussex Record Office, Goodwood Papers, MS.1451, Sir Gilbert Blane to the Duke of Richmond, 28 November 1831, 30 November 1831; Richmond to Blane, 17 October 1831, 18 October 1831, 18 January 1832.

53 McCabe, *Observations*, pp. 5–6; William White, *The evils of quarantine laws, and non-existence of pestilential contagion*, London: Effingham Wilson, 1837. See also Pelling, *Cholera*, pp. 24–5; Michael Durey, *Return of the plague: British society and the cholera of 1831–2*, London: Macmillan, 1979; Harrison, *Climates*, chap. 4.

54 Richard Evans, 'Epidemics and revolutions: cholera in nineteenth-century Europe', in P. Slack and T. Ranger, eds., *Epidemics and ideas*, Cambridge: Cambridge University Press, 1992, pp. 167–8; Richard Evans, *Death in Hamburg: society and politics in the cholera years 1830–1910*, Oxford: Clarendon Press, 1987.

of quarantine, and some thought moderate measures indispensable in preventing more damaging restrictions.[55]

It is perhaps surprising that cholera did not figure prominently in debates over quarantine in the 1830s and 1840s. The most important reason for this was that almost all the quarantine establishments in the Mediterranean had been created to deal with plague and it was not yet clear that cholera would become a perpetual threat. Cholera remained marginal to international discussions of quarantine until the late 1840s, following its second epidemic visitation in Europe, after which time it grew in importance in debates over sanitary regulation. However, at the first international sanitary conference in 1851, it was still less important than plague, and some states, such as that of Austria, had even requested that it be excluded from discussions.

The first suggestion that quarantine might be regulated on an international basis came from France, which entered a more liberal phase of government under Louis Philippe. The Orleanist regime enjoyed a relatively harmonious relationship with the Academy of Medicine, which had become increasingly hostile to contagion and quarantine. The abuse of sanitary cordons by the Bourbon monarchy had led to widespread criticism and had turned many away from quarantine to consider more liberal alternatives. In 1823, for example, a sanitary cordon assembled along the border with Spain to protect against yellow fever was used to restore the Spanish Bourbon monarch to power following a liberal revolt.[56] French merchants and diplomats in the Eastern Mediterranean were also protesting against the disruption caused by quarantine during outbreaks of plague and the high cost of detaining goods and persons in lazarettos.[57] The main causes of complaint were the quarantines imposed against plague after Muhammed Ali became Pasha (Ottoman viceroy) of Egypt in 1805. As part of his programme of modernization, Muhammed Ali began to impose quarantine against shipping from infected ports and took strict measures within his own territories to deal with epidemics.[58] The situation became more serious in 1831, when his army invaded the Ottoman province of Syria, engendering nearly two years of war and political tension between Russia, and France and Britain. In 1833, however, Muhammed Ali established a sanitary board with a consular commission that represented the interests of several foreign powers, arousing cautious optimism about the prospect of more extensive international cooperation.

It was in these circumstances that M. de Ségur Dupeyron, Secretary to the Supreme Council of Health in France, was charged by the Minister of Commerce with investigating the different modes of quarantine operating in the Mediterranean. He examined a number of lazarettos personally and took note of their rules for fixing the length of quarantine.

---

55 Baldwin, *Contagion*, pp. 97–8.

56 On the rise of anticontagionist sentiment in France see Ackerknecht, 'Anticontagionism'; Ann F. La Berge, *Mission and method: the early nineteenth-century French public health movement*, Cambridge: Cambridge University Press, 1992, pp. 90–4; E. A. Heaman, 'The rise and fall of anticontagionism in France', *Canadian Bulletin of the History of Medicine*, 12, 1995, pp. 3–25.

57 See WLHUM, Western MS.4911, A. D. Vasse St. Ouen, French consul at Larnaca, Cyprus, to A. R. Roussin, French ambassador at Constantinople, 27 November 1834 to 26 April 1836.

58 La Verne Kuhnke, *Lives at risk: public health in nineteenth-century Egypt*, Berkeley: University of California Press, 1990; Sheldon Watts, *Epidemics and history: disease, power, and imperialism*, New Haven: Yale University Press, 1997, pp. 35–9.

Eschewing the speculation which he felt had been characteristic of medical works, Dupeyron adopted an historical approach, seeing present arrangements in the light of epidemics and quarantine arrangements over several centuries. He concluded that there was a close link between commerce and plague, pointing to the fact that the disease never seemed to occur in those countries whose commerce had been disrupted by war. All epidemics of plague in Europe also appeared to have spread outwards from the Levant, suggesting that the disease was contagious. Although sanitary precautions had been effective in some cases, he felt they were unnecessarily oppressive because they were imposed in an unsystematic way. In view of this, he made a number of suggestions to establish what he termed a 'reasonable and uniform system'. This included quarantines of shorter duration; abolition of quarantines of observation against vessels coming from the West Indies and the USA with clean bills of health; and, most importantly, forbidding arbitrary increases in the duration of quarantine.[59]

When Dupeyron's report was published, the diplomatic climate was not especially conducive to international cooperation. Although Britain and France had been ideologically aligned, in principle, since 1830, the so-called 'liberal alliance' was experiencing difficulties and in 1834–5 France was moving away from Britain in an effort to heal the diplomatic breach that had arisen between the Eastern and Western powers; by 1836, France was far closer to Austria than its erstwhile partner.[60] In 1838, however, the French government, which accepted the thrust of Dupeyron's report, proposed a conference of delegates from various European countries with ports on the Mediterranean, the aim being to agree upon a system of uniform quarantine arrangements. Contemporaneously, in Britain, free-trade agitators in parliament, such as the Benthamite MP Dr John Bowring, kept up the pressure with speeches and publications designed to demonstrate the non-contagiousness of plague and the uselessness of quarantine.[61] In November that year, the British government, along with other nations, agreed in principle to the French proposal.[62]

The most significant of these other powers was Austria, which had numerous quarantine stations along its borders with the Ottoman Empire and along the Danube, as well as substantial commercial interests in the eastern Mediterranean. The Austrians had been protesting for some years about 'impediments thrown in the way of navigation' in the Ionian Sea. The British administration of the Ionian islands appears to have imposed quarantines against vessels from the Levant that sometimes exceeded the fourteen-day period prescribed.[63] For its part, Britain was anxious to secure a reduction in quarantine, not only

59   De Ségur Dupeyron, *Rapport adressé a son exc. le ministre du commerce, chargé de procéder a une enquête sur les divers régimes sanitaires de la Méditerranée*, Paris: L'Imprimerie Royale, 1834.

60   C. K. Webster, *Palmerston, Metternich and the European system 1830–1841*, London: The British Academy, 1934, pp. 19–21.

61   John Bowring, *Observations on the oriental plague, and on quarantine as a means of arresting its progress*, Edinburgh: W. Tait, 1838.

62   Earl of Aberdeen, to Lord Cowley, British Ambassador to France, 27 June 1843, *Correspondence respecting the quarantine laws since the correspondence last presented to parliament*, London: T. R. Harrison, 1846, PP 1846 [718], 45.

63   Prince Esterhazy, Austrian ambassador to Britain, to Palmerston, 19 November 1936, *Correspondence relative to the contagion of plague and the quarantine regulations of foreign countries, 1836–1943*, London: T. R. Harrison, 1843, PP 1843 [475], 54.

for commercial reasons, but because its naval vessels and mail ships were often subjected to long delays at quarantine stations in the Mediterranean.[64]

These tentative steps towards an agreement on quarantine exemplified the system of international relations inaugurated by the Congress of Vienna and which prevailed until the Crimean War.[65] It was fundamentally different to that which existed before 1815, when colonial rivalry between the Atlantic nations intermingled with the continental struggles of the Great Powers. The defeat of France brought to an end any hopes of regaining lost territory in India and North America and, although it was to colonize Algeria between 1829 and 1848, France did not see itself as an imperial rival of Britain until the last quarter of the nineteenth century. Indeed, its interests in Algeria gave France a greater incentive to work with Britain in order to moderate quarantine in Mediterranean ports.[66]

In the forty years after the Vienna congress, the Great Powers sought to work out their differences at the conference table rather than on the battlefield and, in such a system, there was less need or scope for the use of quarantine as a political weapon. Although abuses of quarantine continued to occur, they were increasingly seen as potential causes of discord between nations. Although there was no mention of quarantine in the Vienna settlement, the congress did agree on some related matters, such as freedom of navigation on the Rhine. Like subsequent agreements on traffic on the Danube, this was concluded partly to satisfy economic interests but also because economic cooperation was seen as conducive to peaceful coexistence.[67]

The 'conference system' that evolved following the failure of congress diplomacy remained dedicated to the peaceful solution of political problems. It was also more pragmatic and, in many respects, more successful, involving smaller gatherings of states which aimed to reach agreement on specific matters.[68] Although predominantly driven by the commercial and colonial interests of Britain and France, agreement over such issues as quarantine must be seen in the light of other considerations, with which they became increasingly intertwined, not least the desire to remove potential sources of tension between nations. In this sense, the effort to reach agreement on quarantine closely resembled previous and parallel discussions over navigation. The fact that the focus of sanitary discussions was the eastern Mediterranean made such an agreement all the more desirable, in view of the fact that the Levant had become a potential flash-point in international relations.

---

64 Palmerston to Sir Frederick Lamb, British ambassador to Austria, 11 June 1838, *ibid.*

65 Harold Nicolson, *The congress of Vienna: a study in allied unity 1812–1822*, London: Constable and Co., 1946; Henry A. Kissinger, *A world restored: Metternich, Castlereagh and the problems of peace 1812–22*, London: Weidenfeld and Nicolson, 1957; Charles Webster, *The congress of Vienna 1814–1815*, London: Thames and Hudson, 1963; Tim Chapman, *The congress of Vienna: origins, processes and results*, London: Routledge, 1998.

66 These efforts were grounded on a report on quarantine in the Mediterranean by the French academy of medicine chaired by Dr R. C. Prus and published in 1846. See George Weisz, *The medical mandarins: the French academy of medicine in the nineteenth and early twentieth centuries*, New York: 1995, p. 77.

67 F. S. L. Lyons, *Internationalism in Europe 1815–1914*, Leyden: A. W. Sijthoff, 1963, pp. 56–64.

68 F. R. Bridge and Roger Bullen, *The great powers and the European states system 1815–1914*, London: Longman, 1980, pp. 41–2.

It is perhaps significant that attempts to convene an international conference coincided with rising tension sparked by another war between the Ottoman sultan and the rebellious province of Egypt, which again raised the spectre of Russian influence in Istanbul. Tension also rose between Britain and France because of French support for Muhammed Ali, but the French were unwilling to risk war with the Austrians and British, who had sent an expeditionary force to the Levant. The situation was defused after Egyptian forces retreated and by the Treaty of London (1840), in which the four principal European powers (Austria, Britain, Prussia and Russia) jointly guaranteed the security of the Ottoman Empire. As the British foreign secretary Lord Palmerston put it, the aim of all governments concerned was to 'agree upon a common course of policy, which may be calculated to accomplish purposes [i.e. the preservation of peace in the Levant] so essential for the general interests of Europe'.[69] The Straits Convention of the following year also made the prohibition of foreign naval traffic through the Bosphorous and Dardanelles a matter of international agreement rather than simply an Ottoman policy, as it had been before.[70] At the same time, there was an improvement in relations between Britain and France, following the dismissal of Thiers in 1840, and the subsequent fall from power of Palmerston and the Whig government. The two countries once again sought to work together amicably to resolve conflicts of interest, and this gave added momentum to discussions over quarantine.[71] According to the quarantine reformer Dr Gavin Milroy, everyone who had studied the subject – statesmen, travellers, merchants and physicians – had come to the conclusion that an international agreement on quarantine was vital to their 'common welfare'.[72]

Metternich claimed that it was now possible to relax quarantine in the Mediterranean because Egyptian measures against plague made its spread westwards less likely. The prospect of similar regulations being introduced in the Ottoman Empire also gave grounds for optimism. In 1838 the sultan asked the Austrian government to send him several experienced quarantine officials to assist in establishing quarantine stations throughout the Ottoman provinces. Most parts of the Empire had been severely affected by plague during the late eighteenth and early nineteenth centuries: in 1812 an estimated 300,000 people died during an outbreak in the greater Istanbul area and, as late as 1836, the disease had claimed the lives of 30,000 people in the Ottoman capital. Although its virulence was decreasing, plague continued to visit Istanbul and the Balkan provinces almost annually through to the middle of the century; moreover, the Empire faced a new threat in the form of cholera, which arrived from Russia in 1821. In the next three decades, seven epidemics of cholera spread through the Ottoman world, having arrived with pilgrims to the Holy cities of Mecca

---

69   Palmerston to Marquess of Clanricarde, 9 July 1839, correspondence relative to the affairs of the Levant, PP 1841 [304], 8, Session 2.

70   Coleman Phillipson and Noel Buxton, *The question of the Bosphorous and Dardanelles*, London: Stevens and Hayes, 1917, pp. 74–80.

71   Roger Bullen, *Palmerston, Guizot and the collapse of the entente cordial*, London: The Athlone Press, 1974, p. 334.

72   Gavin Milroy, *Quarantine and the plague: being a summary of the report on these subjects recently addressed to the royal academy of medicine in France*, London: Samuel Highley, 1846, p. 5.

DISEASE, DIPLOMACY AND INTERNATIONAL COMMERCE 211

and Medina.[73] This new threat from the East presented a great challenge to successive administrations which were attempting to modernize the Empire; they stunted population growth and disrupted the flourishing international trade promoted by railways and steam navigation.[74]

In seeking European expertise, the administrations of Mahmut II (1808–39) and Abdlmecit I (1839–61) were following precedents set in other branches of state, not least in the army. Moreover, the attempt to construct a sanitary infrastructure across the empire was in line with the rapid growth of the Ottoman state during the nineteenth century, with regulations in all ports expected to conform to instructions issued in the Ottoman capital.[75] However, the European powers saw the creation of a 'Commission of Public Health' in Istanbul as another means of exercising influence over the sultan and of securing concessions beneficial to European navigation.[76] Although the influence of foreign representatives on the Constantinople Council of Health,[77] as it became known, was rather less than the European powers had hoped, their representation, like the Straits Settlement of the following year, was symbolic of the sultan's waning independence.[78]

The establishment of the Constantinople Council showed heightened awareness of the need for international cooperation in sanitary matters, which had the effect of bringing Austria into closer cooperation with Britain and France.[79] But despite his initial support for a conference to discuss quarantine, Metternich and other foreign ministers were unable to agree about where to hold the meeting. These wrangles were in no sense untypical, as both Metternich and Palmerston tended to favour conferences over which they could exert control.[80] Talks resumed in 1843, again as a result of French initiative and the British foreign secretary Lord Aberdeen, one of the architects of the new *entente cordiale*, responded enthusiastically, declaring that 'great benefits would result from it to Mediterranean commerce and communications'. However, he felt that prior to offering an invitation to Russia and the Italian states, it would be wise for Britain, France and Austria to first reach agreement between themselves on key issues. He then hoped that Austria would exert its influence on the Italian states to induce them to cooperate. Aberdeen was keen that Russia be involved in the conference because it was a major regional power and any agreement was unlikely to be workable without it. He proposed the neutral port of

---

73 Donald Quataert, 'Population', in H. Inalcik and D. Quataert, eds., *An economic and social history of the Ottoman empire*, vol. 2, Cambridge: Cambridge University Press, 1994, pp. 787–9.

74 Donald Quataert, *The Ottoman empire: 1700–1922*, Cambridge: Cambridge University Press, 2005, pp. 127–8.

75 The regulations were approved in May 1841 and were accompanied by detailed guidelines for all doctors in the sanitary service of the Ottoman empire. See *Papers respecting quarantine in the Mediterranean*, London: Harrison & Sons, 1860, pp. 81–7.

76 Metternich to Baron Langsdorff, French chargé d'affaires at Vienna, 13 July 1838, PP 1843 [475], 54.

77 The council consisted of sixteen members, with an Ottoman official as president; around half were sent by foreign powers, principally Britain, France and Austria-Hungary. See *Papers respecting quarantine*, p. 94.

78 Convention between Great Britain, Austria, France, Prussia, Russia, and Turkey respecting the straits of the Dardanelles and of the Bosphorous, PP 1842 [350], 44.

79 Webster, *Palmerston*, p. 24.

80 *Ibid.*, pp. 6–7.

Genoa as a venue.[81] Other departments of the British government were equally enthusiastic, noting that the mood internationally seemed more conducive to progress than ever before. Mr J. MacGregor of the Office of the Privy Council for Trade declared that 'A very decided tendency has been manifested on the part of the principal Powers, to assimilate in some degree the periods of detention, and at all events to relax very considerably the severity of the restrictions on merchandise and vessels'. He noted that 'the general good understanding which now prevails between this country and foreign Powers... encourage[s] the hope that the deliberations of such a conference... would result in the adoption of that general system of Quarantine which is so desired'.[82] It is therefore clear that the system of international diplomacy that developed after 1815 – with its overriding objective of preventing war in Europe – was a vital precondition to any agreement on international sanitary regulation. By contrast, the atomized nature of international relations that had existed before the French wars had meant that all attempts to mitigate the effects of quarantine through diplomacy were doomed to failure.

All the signs were, indeed, encouraging, with Britain and France showing their willingness to participate in a conference if it were convened in one of a number of neutral cities. The Austrians, however, were slow to respond and when they did, they did so with less enthusiasm than expected. Metternich considered a conference premature and insisted that the three principal parties first reach an agreement over technical matters such as the minimum and maximum terms of quarantine necessary for humans, the terms for various types of merchandise, and the best methods of disinfecting objects thought susceptible of contagion. This was not unlike Aberdeen's proposal, but the Austrians stated that they required a period of six months in which to consider the matter by themselves; Metternich also stated his preference for any such conference to be held in Vienna.[83]

While France awaited a response from Vienna, the British government commissioned its own investigation of quarantine in the Mediterranean from a former naval officer, Sir William Pym, the Superintendent of Quarantine at the Privy Council. In 1845 he made a detailed report on the numbers of persons and vessels quarantined at different stations, procedures for the handling of goods, charges levied, and so forth. Pym reached a similar conclusion to that of Dupeyron: that quarantine was necessary in some form but that it operated unsystematically. It was this arbitrariness, rather than quarantine *per se*, that posed the chief obstacle to trade in the Mediterranean.[84] On the basis of his investigation, Pym drafted a response to the issues raised by Metternich,[85] but the latter continued to procrastinate, telling British and French officials that he would only consider the matter once he had received information from the Austrian departments of the Interior and of Finance.[86]

---

81   Aberdeen to Lord Cowley, 27 June 1843, PP 1846 [318], 45.

82   J. Macgregor to Viscount Canning, 2 March 1844, PP 1846 [718], 45.

83   Metternich to Sir Robert Gordon, British ambassador to Austria, 24 May 1844; Gordon to Aberdeen, 31 May 1844; Canning to M. Lefevre, 17 April 1845; Canning to Lefevre, 12 September 1845, PP 1846 [718], 45.

84   Pym to the Earl of Dalhousie, 5 June 1845; Pym to Lefevre, 6 June 1845, PP 1846 [718], 45.

85   Pym to Lefevre, 22 September 1845, PP 1846 [718], 45.

86   Mr Magenis, Austrian ambassador to Britain, to Aberdeen, 15 December 1845, PP 1846 [718], 45.

How is one to explain the apparently contradictory position of the Austrian government? It does seem that there was a genuine desire on the part of Metternich to conclude an international agreement that would be potentially of great benefit to Austrian commerce. The records kept by quarantine stations in the Eastern Mediterranean show that Austrian ships were among those most commonly inconvenienced by quarantine.[87] Steam navigation had led to an increasing volume of trade with the East and there was also increasing pressure from within Austria to relax quarantine regulations along the border of the Hapsburg Empire, for both commercial and humanitarian reasons. Some prominent medical men, such as Professor Sigmund of Vienna, recommended that Austria rely more on sanitary measures than quarantine.[88] The Austrian Ambassador to Britain also told Lord Aberdeen in 1845 that a commission had been established 'with the desire to diminish the expenses of the Cordon Sanitaire, which it is said has completely failed in preventing intercourse across the frontier, and which offers unnecessary interruption to traffic'.[89] Metternich was similarly inclined but Austria's long boundary with the formerly plague-ridden Ottoman Empire meant that others were reluctant to abandon 'tried and tested' sanitary measures. The extent to which other foreign policy objectives affected Metternich's thinking is unclear, except in so far as an agreement between the various powers with interests in the Mediterranean was consonant with his broader aim to reach an accord with Russia as well as the Western powers. His diplomatic correspondence with Britain and France similarly stressed the need to ensure that a conference on quarantine included Russia simply because of its status as a power in the region.[90]

For Britain and France, the chief motives in seeking international agreement were of course related to their commercial and imperial interests. Growing French involvement in Algeria and its trade with the Eastern Mediterranean provided an obvious incentive to reform quarantine and, in the 1840s it took measures unilaterally to reduce quarantine in its Mediterranean ports. Medical opinion, too, was moving increasingly in support of the relaxation or abolition of quarantine. In Britain commercial interests were also becoming more influential and the repeal of the protectionist Corn Laws in 1846 encouraged free traders to seek reductions in other restrictions on trade. Critics of quarantine estimated that its annual cost to Britain amounted to between two and three millions pounds, with similar losses incurred by merchants in the Mediterranean.[91] In the late 1830s, Britain and other nations had also concluded a series of commercial and navigation treaties with the Ottoman Empire, with the aim of opening up areas of trade formerly prohibited to foreign merchants and of agreeing a moderate tariff on imports into the Ottoman dominions.[92] The attempt to

---

87   See tables of vessels subjected to quarantine at Rhodes, *Papers respecting quarantine*, pp. 66–70.

88   General Board of Health, *Report on quarantine*, London: W. Clowes & Sons, 1849, pp. 78–9.

89   Magenis to Aberdeen, 15 November 1845, PP 1846 [718], 45.

90   Metternich to Langsdorff, 13 July 1838, PP 1843 [475], 54.

91   Speech by Bowring, 15 March 1842, Hansard, *Parl. debates*, col. 610.

92   See 'Copy of the tariff agreed upon by the commissioners appointed under the seventh article of the convention of commerce and navigation between Turkey and England', PP 1839 [549], 47; *Convention of commerce and navigation between her majesty, and the sultan of the Ottoman empire*, London: J. Harrison, 1839, PP 1839 [157], 50; Correspondence respecting the operation of the commercial treaty with Turkey, of August 16, 1838, PP [341], session 2, 8.

reach an agreement on quarantine that involved the sultan was thus part of a more general process, whereby foreign powers were attempting to exploit Ottoman weakness in order to secure concessions on trade and navigation.[93]

But commercial interests were not the only factors that induced Britain to seek international agreement over quarantine. Quarantine was becoming a great inconvenience to the growing number of Britons who travelled to and from India by way of the Levant and there were increasing complaints about the 'absurdities' and 'irregularities' of quarantine in Mediterranean stations, particularly Alexandria.[94] Since quarantines and sanitary cordons had been established in Egypt in the early 1830s, European merchants and diplomatic staff had complained that they had been enforced selectively and that the system was inefficient;[95] the severe plague epidemic that affected Egypt in 1835 was sometimes used in support of these arguments. The tense relationship that existed between the British and Egyptian governments since the early 1830s continued to arouse suspicions that quarantine was being used to damage British interests. Muhammed Ali was deeply suspicious of the East India Company's establishment of a base in Aden and resented the presence of a British garrison adjacent to his territories.[96] The combined European force sent to assist the Ottomans in 1839 had also thwarted his ambitions in Syria.

In view of this, it is hardly surprising that the Egyptian authorities made use of one of the best opportunities they had to monitor the intentions of what they regarded as a hostile power. The advent of steam navigation led to an increasing volume of mail being sent through Egypt, to and from Britain and India, and packet agents in Alexandria and Cairo frequently complained that sanitary fumigation was used as a pretext to intercept, delay or destroy diplomatic communiqués.[97] Dr John Bowring also told the House of Commons in 1842 that 'Official dispatches were opened, perforated with awls, incised by chisels, dipped in vinegar ... and at length transmitted to their destination in a mutilated, and scarcely legible condition.' He continued that: 'There was no doubt that political objects were sought for in the maintenance of quarantine in the east; and it was equally certain that political interests were promoted by them, and that these, and not the health of nations, were the principal motives for the great severity with which the regulations were enforced abroad.' It was not only the Egyptians who used quarantine in this way, he insisted, but also – to his shame – British consular officials. Yet there was no country that used quarantine for political ends so routinely as Russia. Bowring claimed that its quarantine officials were merely 'political functionaries' that 'arrested and released travellers at will. They took possession of all correspondence ... they checked or facilitated commerce according

---

93   Note of the representatives of Austria, France, Great Britain, Prussia, and Russia at Constantinople, to the Porte, 27 July 1839, PP 1839 [205], 50; Correspondence relative to the affairs of the Levant, Part 3, PP 1841 [337], session 2, 8.

94   E.g. Arthur T. Holroyd, *The quarantine laws, their abuses and inconsistencies*, London: Simpkin, Marshall & Co., 1839.

95   *Papers respecting quarantine*, p. 26.

96   Campbell to Lord Palmerston, 27 March 1838, G/17/10, OIOC, British Library.

97   Lt.-Col. P. Campbell, East India Company agent, Cairo, to Peter Amber, 14 July 1835; Campbell to James Melville, 14 July 1837; Alexander Waghorn, EIC agent, Alexandria, to French post office, Alexandria, 18 July 1837, G/17/10, OIOC.

to the passing interests of the moment... and in the name of public health', he declared, 'they had introduced a system of universal police and espionage.' In view of this, he insisted, the government ought to do all in its power to ensure that an international agreement was reached. His motion was enthusiastically supported by members of the government, including the Prime Minister, Sir Robert Peel.[98]

The revolutions of 1848 distracted attention from efforts to bring about an international conference on sanitary regulation. However, the French reopened negotiations with renewed vigour and were successful in persuading eleven other states with interests in the Mediterranean (including the Ottoman Empire) to agree to a conference in Paris in 1851. Most countries sent two delegates, a diplomat and a physician, the former in order to ensure that political and commercial matters were given due consideration. As the French Minister of Foreign Affairs insisted, it was necessary to find a *modus operandi* befitting an age of technical and industrial progress, and to strike a mutually beneficial balance between the needs of commerce and of public health. Just as new modes of communication were erasing the tyranny of distance, he argued, it was now time to remove political and commercial impediments that stood in the way of international harmony.[99] The mood internationally was receptive, too. Tension between Britain and France over the Spanish succession evaporated following the removal of the Orleans monarchy in 1848,[100] while the triumph of reaction elsewhere brought stability and a desire to avoid conflict.[101]

The Paris conference is usually considered a failure because its proceedings were marked by disagreement over key issues such as the transmissibility of cholera and because the resulting convention was signed by only three states – France, Sardinia and Portugal – and ratified by Sardinia alone.[102] Although the divisions were primarily between the Mediterranean countries, which were more reluctant to abandon quarantine, and Britain and France, which were eager for commercial and colonial reasons to liberalize it, the fault lines were numerous and often cut across each other. Despite Metternich's earlier optimism, Austrian delegates opposed any attempt to modify maritime quarantine and disinfection regimes in times of plague, and were particularly hostile to British proposals to reclassify susceptible merchandise so as to downgrade the threat from cotton, long regarded as a carrier of plague. Together with Russian delegates, they also opposed British proposals to abandon land-based cordons, which, however imperfect, were regarded as the only means of defending their empires against plague from the Levant. Yet Austrian (but not Russian) delegates backed the French and British position that cholera was not contagious in the same way as plague, and opposed the use of quarantines and sanitary cordons to control it.[103] As Baldwin has noted, public opinion was also important in affecting positions at the conference, often to the detriment of liberalization as in the case of most Italian

---

98   Hansard, *Parl. debates*, 15 March 1842, cols. 608–18.

99   *Procés-verbaux de la conférence sanitaire internationale, ouverte à Paris le 27 Juillet 1851*, vol. 1, 5 August 1851, pp. 3–4.

100   Bullen, *Palmerston*, pp. 337–8.

101   A. J. P. Taylor, *The struggle for mastery in Europe 1848–1918*, Oxford: Clarendon, 1954, p. 46.

102   Howard-Jones, *Scientific background*, pp. 15–16.

103   *Conférence sanitaire internationale*, 24 October 1851, pp. 23–25; 4 October 1851, pp. 8–9; 18 September 1851, pp. 3–12.

states.[104] Yet the conference agreed in principle upon the basic aim of achieving agreement internationally over sanitary regulations, as well as the desirability of some specific measures, including the strengthening of sanitary surveillance in Egypt and the Ottoman Empire.[105]

Even this limited degree of consensus would have been unthinkable before 1815 but the nature of international relations in the four decades following the Vienna congress was such that it became less acceptable to use quarantines and sanitary cordons for overtly political purposes. From 1815, matters such as navigation and quarantine were considered partly with conflict avoidance in mind, especially in potential trouble spots like the Levant. And, from 1851, the attempt to reach an international consensus gathered momentum, with ten further international sanitary conferences being convened over the next half century, most of which were widely ratified. Unlike 1851, the primary concern at most of these conferences (1881 and 1897 excepted) was to devise an effective but not too disruptive means of preventing incursions of cholera from Asia. Until 1881, the conferences were attended and hosted by European countries only, but, in that year, a conference was held in Washington DC. The USA continued to be involved in European conferences but it simultaneously attempted to develop and lead international sanitary discussions in its own sphere of influence. A conference of South American states had already been held at Rio de Janeiro in 1887, but this was followed in 1902 by a Pan-American Conference at Washington DC, which resulted in the establishment of the Pan-American Sanitary Bureau. A few years later, in 1907, the first European international health organization, the Office International d'Hygiène Publique, was established in Paris.[106]

These measures and those that developed subsequently were the fruit of an evolving international consciousness, of which we see the first signs in the 1830s and 1840s. It is ironic that the growth of such institutions came at a time of mounting international tension. Although the idea of international sanitary cooperation was a brainchild of conference diplomacy, this system broke down with the outbreak of the Crimean War. Indeed, the first conference at Paris, in 1851, was as much the end of an era as the beginning of a new one. In the years that followed, disputes over quarantine escalated in tandem with rivalry between the imperial powers. For instance, after Britain's unilateral ending of the system of Dual Control of the Egyptian debt in 1882, France, its former partner in Egypt, sought every opportunity at international sanitary conferences to oppose British interests, by insisting on strict quarantine for vessels at Suez. As the Suez Canal, which opened in 1869, was a vital conduit for British eastern trade and for communications with India, quarantine measures at Suez affected Britain disproportionately. However the emergence of a united Germany and the formation of the Triple Alliance with Italy and Austria served as a counterweight to French demands. From 1885, after it had become a colonial power in East Africa, Germany and its partners sided with Britain in seeking relaxation of quarantine at Suez.[107] Quarantine was also the subject of contention between Britain and Russia, where

---

104   Baldwin, *Contagion*, p. 198.

105   *Conférence sanitaire internationale*, vol. 2, Annex to Proc. 29, 11 November 1851.

106   Fidler, *International law*, chap. 2.

107   Mark Harrison, *Public health in British India: Anglo-Indian preventive medicine 1859–1914*, Cambridge: Cambridge University Press, 1994, chap. 5.

it was used by both powers in their attempt to gain territorial and commercial influence in Central Asia.[108] Nevertheless, the foundations of an international sanitary order had been established and the sanitary conferences of the late nineteenth century provided a context in which such disputes could be moderated and their political impact blunted by international consensus.

> *Mark Harrison is Director of the Wellcome Unit for the History of Medicine, University of Oxford.*

---

108 E.g. Amir A. Afkhami, 'Defending the guarded domain: epidemics and the emergence of an international sanitary policy in Iran', *Comparative Studies of South Asia, Africa and the Middle East*, 19, 1999, pp. 122–34.

[2]

ORIGINS OF INTERNATIONAL HEALTH WORK

BY

N. HOWARD-JONES, O.B.E., M.R.C.S., L.R.C.P.

*Director, Division of Editorial and Reference Services,
World Health Organization, Geneva*

The subject of this article is international health work in the restricted sense of intergovernmental action on health problems.   As Sir George Buchanan (1943a) remarked some years ago in his Milroy Lectures : " Any suggestion that medicine, always amongst the most international of the learned professions, should henceforth first look to the League of Nations or any other intergovernmental office in order to maintain its proud tradition of internationalism would indeed be retrograde."   In any complete account of international health work reference would also have to be made to the International Red Cross Organization, the International Health Division of the Rockefeller Foundation, and the various international medical congresses.

Nevertheless, in spite of technical improvements in facilities for communication, the last century has seen the growth of many obstacles to non-governmental internationalism in medicine. Latin no longer provides a common scientific language for physicians, and the excessive proliferation of periodical medical literature not only creates difficulties for the individual worker but makes it impossible for medical libraries in all but a few wealthy countries to maintain collections which are representative of the world's output.*

The rise of political and economic nationalism has seriously limited the individual's freedom to travel and study abroad, and the increasing responsibilities for health services undertaken by governments cannot be without effect on the fruitfulness of unofficial international relations in medicine. These factors, and the widening gap between the level of development of science and technology in the advanced and that in the less-advanced countries, necessarily increase the potential usefulness and range of activities of an intergovernmental health organization.

Early Quarantine Measures

The first intergovernmental health measures depended upon the theory of the contagiousness of certain diseases, and originated with precautions, often excessive, designed to restrict the importation of such diseases from one country into another. Although the segregation of lepers had long been common, maritime quarantine measures were first instituted when the pandemic of bubonic plague—the Black Death—devastated Europe in the fourteenth century. There is little agreement among writers concerning the date and place of the first introduction of maritime quarantine, and such agreement as exists is probably more correctly regarded as the product of faithful emulation than as the weight of cumulative testimony.

Some writers attribute this distinction to the Republic of Ragusa, on the eastern shore of the Adriatic, in 1377. It is said that seafarers suspected of being affected by plague were isolated for 30 days at a place distant from the

---

*As late as 1834, William McMichael, in his evidence to the Select Committee on Medical Education, said : " Most of our best treatises on physic are written in Latin; it is not possible to read them without a knowledge of this language." McMichael also said : " The science [of medicine] is advanced so much, that it is not expected that we should have voluminous publications."

harbour. Other writers credit the Republic of Venice with the introduction of maritime quarantine, but, as Beckmann (1846) showed, the accounts contained in earlier histories are completely at variance. Nevertheless, all are agreed that a 40-day period, or *quarantenaria,* became established as the usual period of isolation of suspected seafarers and sea-borne merchandise. As Beckmann points out, this period was probably chosen because the fortieth day of many diseases was held to be critical, and was also related to " various astrological conceits."

The first English quarantine regulations were drawn up in 1663, and provided for the isolation of suspected ships and their crews for 40 days in the Thames estuary (Simon, 1897). These measures did not, however, suffice to prevent the last and worst visitation in the form of the Great Plague of 1665–6, which is vividly recorded in the diary of Samuel Pepys and elsewhere.

The epidemic of plague which broke out in 1720 in Marseilles and ravaged the Mediterranean seaboard of France caused considerable apprehension in England, and the Government called upon Richard Mead (1673–1754) for advice, which he published as *A short discourse concerning the Pestilential Contagion and the methods used to prevent it* (1720). Mead declared his opinion that plague was contagious, as a result of which quarantine measures were prescribed.

To the modern mind it seems strange that the communicable nature of plague (and later of cholera) was ever in doubt. But until almost the end of the nineteenth century this question was the subject of lively controversy. Schools of thought were broadly divided into : (*a*) contagionists, who believed that epidemic diseases were spread by absorption of a morbific principle (not necessarily living) following contact with persons or fomites ; (*b*) miasmatists, who believed in a neo-hippocratic mixture of cosmo-telluric and atmospheric causes, to which were added, by the English sanitarians of the nineteenth century, " dirt " and " filth " ; and (*c*) the theurgists, who were content to regard Divine Providence as the principal aetiological agent, and the Old Testament as an appropriate technical reference work.

John Quincy, who in 1720 exploited the prevailing fear of plague by publishing an annotated translation into English of Nathaniel Hodges's *Loimologia* (first published in Latin in 1672), makes the following comment on the last-mentioned school : " Although too great a regard cannot be had to the Author of our Beings, yet care should likewise be taken, not to ascribe every Calamity to the immediate Exertion of the Almighty Power."

Cholera Reaches Europe

Fortunately, the plague epidemic in France did not extend to Britain. But in October, 1831, a new menace made its first appearance in the form of Asiatic cholera, which was imported into Sunderland by a ship from Hamburg (Hirsch, 1883). In the course of 1832 it spread over a great part of Britain, following commercial highways, coast routes, and rivers. Cholera had previously been known as a disease which was endemic in a few regions of India, but in the years of the first cholera pandemic (1817–23) it had spread far beyond India's frontiers. The second pandemic (1826–37) involved most of Europe, and in 1832 emigrants carried it to Canada and the U.S.A. The third pandemic (1846–63) reached Britain in 1848, and again in 1853, and there were further but limited outbreaks in Britain in later years. The extensive diffusion of cholera in Europe was one of the consequences of the increased speed of communication.

Koch's announcement of his discovery of the cholera vibrio was not to come until 1884, and there was within the medical profession no agreement on the means by which the disease was contracted or could be prevented. Contagionists and miasmatists represented completely opposing points of view, and there were eclectics, among them Hirsch (1883), who took the middle course of combining elements of both schools.

The appearance in Europe of this new and frightening visitation prompted some international exchanges of experience. Early in 1831, when fears arose that cholera might invade Britain, the Government sent Dr. William Russell and Dr. David Barry to St. Petersburg to study the manifestations of the disease. Later in the year, when these fears were realized, the great French physiologist, François Magendie, asked the Académie des Sciences to send him to Britain to study the epidemic.* The Academy assented, and Magendie arrived in Sunderland on December 2, 1831. On his return he deprecated the value of quarantine measures, and, when cholera struck Paris, proposed that samples of air from different parts of the city should be analysed. Later, a committee of Italian physicians arrived from Rome to study cholera in Paris. All these visits of investigation were fruitless.

The official British standpoint was unswervingly miasmatist and anti-quarantine. In a *Report on Quarantine,* published by the General Board of Health in 1849, the specificity of epidemic diseases was discredited and the conclusion was reached (Masters, 1947) that " the only real security against epidemic disease is an abundant and constant supply of pure air." Typical also of the British point of view was the comment of the joint editors of the fourth edition of Beckmann's *History of Inventions* (Beckmann, 1846), Dr. William Francis, editor of the *Chemical Gazette,* and Dr. J. W. Griffith, a physician :

" It is a disputed point whether the plague is *even* contagious ; and the mass of evidence is in favour of its being so occasionally, but that the plague is usually not propagated in this manner. The disappearance of this pest from our own and most other countries of Europe is undoubtedly owing to the much greater attention paid to drainage, ventilation, and the prevention of the accumulation of filth in the streets, etc. When the peculiar atmospheric conditions upon which its diffusion depends are present, quarantine has proved insufficient to prevent its propagation."

In the report referred to above, the General Board of Health, which at the time included no medical member, expressed the view that the effectiveness of quarantine was " not a technical question, but one of evidence, on which a person capable of observation is as competent a judge as any physician." Considering the complete absence of scientifically based information on the aetiology of cholera at the time, this last contention was doubtless amply justified. In fact, the views of medical experts on cholera and other epidemic diseases were hardly more consistent than the present-day testimony of medical witnesses called by rival parties to a lawsuit.

Two circumstances had an important influence on the British tradition of opposition to quarantine measures. The first was the influence of the English sanitarian movement, which focused attention on the relation of poverty and squalor to the spread of disease. The second was the natural reluctance of a great maritime nation to countenance precautionary measures which imposed a severe handicap on shipping. In a study commissioned by the Fabian Society, Woolf (1916) said : " It became a plank in British foreign policy that her national interests required an

*Olmstead, J. M. D. (1944). *François Magendie.* New York.

unbending resistance to any interference with shipping:" But he also pointed out that " cholera entered equally the closed ports of Greece and the open ports of Britain." Although the theoretical views of the contagionists have now been largely vindicated, it is also true that the practical quarantine measures adopted were often both onerous and futile.

International Sanitary Conferences and Conventions

The complete lack of agreement on the mode by which cholera and other epidemic diseases were contracted entailed a corresponding lack of agreement on means of prevention. There was no consistency in the different quarantine requirements—or lack of them—of the different nations, or even of different ports of the same nation, and in some cases the restrictions imposed constituted an intolerable hindrance to international communications and commerce.

It was in these circumstances that the French Government convened the first International Sanitary Conference, which was held in Paris in 1851 and was attended by one diplomatic and one medical delegate from each of twelve nations. The immediate object of the conference was to reach agreement on prophylactic measures against cholera, plague, and yellow fever, particularly in regard to maritime communications in the Mediterranean and the Black Sea. An international convention was drawn up, but only France, Portugal, and Sardinia ratified it, and the two latter powers denounced it 14 years later. A second International Sanitary Conference, consisting only of diplomats, was convened in Paris by the French Government in 1859, but was barren of results. During the nineteenth century a third International Sanitary Conference was held in Constantinople (1866), a fourth in Vienna (1874), a fifth in Washington (1881), a sixth in Rome (1885), a seventh in Venice (1892), an eighth in Dresden (1893), a ninth in Paris (1894), and a tenth in Venice (1897). These conferences were, however, of an essentially diplomatic character, and at all but the most recent of them such medical testimony as was available was so conflicting as to be an obstacle rather than an aid to international agreement.

The first International Sanitary Convention was not signed until 1892, by which time seven conferences had been held and 40 years had elapsed. This convention, which was unanimously ratified in the following year by the 14 signatory Powers, provided for protection against the introduction of cholera via the Suez Canal, which had been opened in 1869. The eighth conference resulted in a convention designed to limit the spread of cholera by land, the ninth in a convention for the sanitary regulation of the Mecca pilgrimage, and the tenth in a convention to guard against the introduction of plague.

In 1903, on the initiative of the Italian Government, an eleventh International Sanitary Conference was convened in Paris. One of the main achievements of this conference was the unification of earlier conventions (1892, 1893, 1894, 1897) in the light of contemporary scientific knowledge, and the result was the International Sanitary Convention of 1903, which was ratified by most of the participating States in 1907. This was the first convention to introduce some measure of international uniformity against the importation of cholera and plague. It was superseded by the conventions relating to maritime traffic of 1912 and 1926, and the latter was modified in 1938 and again in 1944. In 1933 the International Sanitary Convention for Aerial Navigation was signed at The Hague, and this was amended by a new convention in 1944.

In addition to the international sanitary conferences described above there were several national or regional health councils, which included diplomatic representatives of foreign powers. These were the Conseil Supérieur de Santé de Constantinople, which dated from 1839 ; the Conseil Sanitaire, Maritime et Quarantinaire d'Egypte, created in Alexandria in 1831 ; the Conseil Sanitaire International de Tanger, which had its beginnings in 1792 but was not constituted until 1840 ; and the Conseil Sanitaire de Teheran, created in 1867. The origins and functions of these regional bodies have been well summarized by Faivre (1908).

The history of the earlier international sanitary conferences is one of nations driven to international negotiation by a common danger but completely unable to reach agreement because of the limitations of scientific knowledge. As Sir Edward Mellanby* wrote : " The work of Government departments . . . in controlling disease can only be as good as knowledge allows it to be, and this knowledge has come, and can only come, by medical research."

It is amusing to read in the proceedings of the earlier conferences accounts of the voting taken on purely scientific questions—for example, whether cholera could be conveyed by water and foodstuffs.   Beliefs are commonly most strongly held about matters on which the least information is available, and delegates who came to a conference with strong but unverifiable views on scientific questions were hardly likely to be influenced by a majority vote against them.

The difficulties and the failures of these earlier attempts of nations to reach agreement on health matters throw into relief the significance of the international health work in many fields that has been accomplished in later years and is now largely taken for granted.   Yet the present International Sanitary Conventions are widely recognized as being imperfect instruments for the control of communicable diseases, especially as their signatories may delay ratification of their signatures for periods of years.   On the authority of Articles 21 and 22 of its Constitution, much work has been done by the World Health Organization, and especially by its Expert Committee on International Epidemiology and Quarantine, on the replacement of the present conventions by International Sanitary Regulations which will automatically come into force for all Member States of W.H.O. after due notice of their adoption by the World Health Assembly (States may notify W.H.O. in writing of any reservations that they may wish to make).

The opposition of the English sanitarians to quarantine measures was based on speculative conceptions of the aetiology of epidemic diseases which were later shown to be false.   But it is no uncommon happening in science for the right conclusions to be drawn for the wrong reasons, and the present tendency is to reduce quarantine measures to a minimum.   In a paper presented at a recent session of the Expert Committee on International Epidemiology and Quarantine of W.H.O., the South African member, Dr. H. S. Gear, was repeating substantially what had been said by the English sanitarians more than a century ago when he commented that " quarantine barrier methods are of very limited value and . . . resistance of a community to infection is dependent upon its internal conditions."

Towards an International Health Agency

The idea of a permanent international agency to deal with health questions was seriously discussed for the first time at the fourth International Sanitary Conference at Vienna in 1874.   Dr. A. Proust, a member of the French delegation, presented to the conference a plan drawn up

*Mellanby, E. (1943). *British Medical Journal*, 2, 351.

by a drafting committee for an international Permanent Commission on Epidemics (Commission Permanent des Epidémies). The responsibilities of this committee were to be " purely scientific," and its main task was to be the study of the aetiology and prophylaxis of cholera, although it would also pay attention to other epidemic diseases. Vienna was proposed as the seat of the commission, which would be composed of physicians appointed by participating governments. All these recommendations were adopted by the conference, which also endorsed as the first objects of research of the commission the study of the rainfall and telluric conditions in the Eastern Mediterranean and Black Sea regions, the epidemiology of cholera in ships and ports, and the period of incubation of cholera.

At the fifth International Sanitary Conference (Washington, 1881) the proposal for an international health agency was revived in a modified form. As a result of this conference the idea of a single international agency for studying epidemic diseases fell entirely into the background, and instead there emerged a proposal for " a permanent international Sanitary Agency of Notification," with offices in Vienna and Havana. The former office was to collect and distribute information from Europe, Asia, and Africa, and the latter was to do the same for the Americas. The possibility of a third office in Asia was also mentioned. The governments of Spain (Cuba then being a Spanish possession) and Austria-Hungary were to fix the annual budget of the agency and notify participating governments of their share of the expenses. However, at subsequent international sanitary conferences no enthusiasm for an international health agency was manifested, and it was not until the conference of 1903 in Paris that the project was again—and finally—endorsed. Proust, who had taken the initiative at the conference of 1874, was still pressing in 1896 for the creation of a " Bureau International de Santé," which would be the organ (without any executive powers) of a " Union Sanitaire." The main object of the sanitary union as advocated by Proust was to protect the public health of Europe.

Implicit in all these strivings towards the foundation of an international health agency was, not a wish for the general betterment of the health of the world, but the desire to protect certain favoured (especially European) nations from contamination by their less-favoured (especially Eastern) fellows. Half a century later the Constitution of the World Health Organization is a measure of the tremendous moral evolution which has made it impossible to accept as part of the natural order the existence of preventable disease and suffering over a large part of the habitable globe.

Office International d'Hygiène Publique

At the eleventh International Sanitary Conference (Paris, 1903) the creation of an international health office was agreed upon, and at the Rome Conference of 1907, at which thirteen governments* were represented, the French Government submitted a definite plan for its establishment. The conference resulted in the Rome Agreement of 1907, which determined Paris as the seat of the new office—the Office International d'Hygiène Publique (O.I.H.P.). The Agreement admonished the office not to interfere in any way in the administration of different States, and defined its principal functions as the collection and distribution of facts and documents of general public health interest, especially those which related to infectious diseases—in particular, cholera, plague, and yellow fever. The O.I.H.P. was also obliged to publish a monthly bulletin—well known

*Belgium, Brazil, Egypt, France, Great Britain, Italy, the Netherlands, Portugal, Roumania, Russia, Spain, Switzerland, and the U.S.A.

during the 40 years of its existence as the *Bulletin mensuel de l'Office international d'Hygiène publique*—which was to contain (i) legislation on communicable diseases, (ii) information on the spread of diseases, (iii) information on measures taken for environmental sanitation, (iv) public health statistics, (v) bibliographical notes. The number of governments adhering to the Rome Agreement increased until 55 were represented on its governing body—the Comité Permanent—which usually met twice a year.

The O.I.H.P. was not the first international health agency to represent many different governments, as the first Pan-American Sanitary Conference in 1902 resulted in the establishment of the Pan-American Sanitary Bureau (these conferences, and the Bureau, were originally designated " international " instead of " Pan-American "), but it was the first to acquire a truly international character. The O.I.H.P. was finally constituted in 1908, and in 1909 its seat and its secretariat were established in Paris.

However, even the long-delayed establishment of an international health office did not symbolize the desire of nations to unite in a common effort against disease. When Sir George Buchanan was nominated in 1914 to be the British delegate to the Permanent Committee of O.I.H.P., " its importance in British eyes was . . . mainly diplomatic."

The achievements of the O.I.H.P. during its first 25 years have been ably summarized by its former director, Dr. G. Abt (Office International d'Hygiène Publique, 1933). Its main preoccupation was with the administration and revision of the International Sanitary Conventions, and as a result of its efforts a new convention, replacing that of 1903, and including cholera, plague, and yellow fever within its provisions, was signed by 41 Member States. However, the outbreak of the 1914–18 war delayed the coming into force of the convention, and it was not until 1920 that 16 of the signatory governments ratified their signatures, other Powers adhering in later years.

The International Sanitary Convention of 1926, which replaced the 1912 convention, brought typhus and smallpox within its provisions and also made possible improvements in epidemiological reporting. It also established an international system for the control of rat-infestation of ships. Another important international convention for which O.I.H.P. was responsible was the Brussels Agreement of 1924, which dealt with facilities for the free treatment of venereal diseases in merchant seamen at sea- and riverports.

Health Organization of the League of Nations

The disruption of life in Eastern Europe as a result of the 1914–18 war was accompanied by widespread epidemics, especially of typhus in Russia, which threatened to spread through Poland to Western Europe. The newly created League of Nations was empowered by Article 23f of the Covenant to " take steps in matters of concern for the prevention and control of disease," and in May, 1920, it established a temporary Epidemic Commission, which coordinated and helped to direct the work of health administrations in afflicted countries, and provided much-needed funds and medical supplies.

In the meantime discussions had been initiated on the creation of a single international health agency, under the League of Nations, and a plan for such an agency was accepted by the first Assembly of the League on December 10, 1920. Unfortunately, this ideal did not materialize until after a quarter of a century and another world war. Several signatories of the Rome Agreement of 1907—notably the U.S.A.—were not members of the

League, and this was the main reason for the continued independent existence of O.I.H.P. after the definitive establishment in 1923 of the Health Organization of the League of Nations. This organization consisted of (i) a Health Committee of 15 members ; (ii) as an Advisory Council, the Permanent Committee of O.I.H.P., which appointed a proportion of the members of the Health Committee and was asked to advise on certain health problems ; and (iii) the Health Section of the League of Nations secretariat, consisting of public health specialists assisted by auxiliary staff. The fact that the Permanent Committee of O.I.H.P. was at the same time the Advisory Council of the Health Organization ensured co-ordination of the work of these two international health agencies. In 1925 the Health Organization established an Eastern Bureau at Singapore— a development which had been foreshadowed in the plan for an international health agency adopted at the International Sanitary Conference of 1881.

The earlier activities of the Health Organization were characterized by a traditional preoccupation with the limitation of the spread of epidemic diseases, of which the epidemiological intelligence centres at Geneva and Singapore were a product. As the post-war wave of epidemics subsided, attention was turned also to methods of active immunization against communicable diseases and to the improvement of serodiagnostic tests, and later to wider aspects of the biological standardization of diagnostic, prophylactic, and therapeutic agents.

In 1934 the Health Committee decided to take up the study of nutrition, housing, and physical culture, and the work of the Technical Commission on Nutrition is perhaps one of the most widely known and understood examples of the health work of the League. Among the other Technical Commissions established were those on malaria and biological standardization (both of these permanent) and on cancer, housing, physical fitness, typhus, leprosy, medical and public health training, rural hygiene, and unification of pharmacopoeias.

The Health Organization marked a new departure in international health work, which was no longer concerned merely with the erection of sanitary barriers, but embraced a wide and ever-growing range of medical subjects upon which international agreement was desirable or in relation to which the more advanced countries could, through an international agency, confer benefits upon countries whose technical resources were more limited. The volume and range of the work can best be gauged by reference to the *Bibliography of the Technical Work of the Health Organization of the League of Nations, 1920–45* (League of Nations, 1945a). An especially valuable feature of the League's work was the award of travelling fellowships and the organization of collective study-tours.

World War II and After

On the outbreak of war in 1939 many of the activities of the Health Organization had to be suspended, although some—including the publication of the *Weekly Epidemiological Record*—were maintained in spite of great difficulties. The Health Committee appointed an emergency subcommittee, consisting of its chairman (Professor J. Parisot, France) and four members (Professor J. Balteanu, Roumania ; Dr. N. M. Goodman, United Kingdom ; Dr. B. Johan, Hungary ; and Professor R. Sand, Belgium), and this subcommittee met in March, 1940.

By June, 1940, the staff of the Health Section had been so depleted by resignations and departures for national service that it included only two medically qualified members—Dr. R. Gautier, the officer in charge of the Health

Section, and Dr. Y. Biraud,* head of the Epidemiological Intelligence Service. During the war Dr. Gautier visited both London and Washington to advise on plans for the post-war relief of occupied countries. In March, 1944, the Director-General of Unrra proposed that the Health Section should establish an epidemiological " research unit " in Washington, and in May, 1944, such a unit began work under the direction of Dr. Gautier, assisted by Mr. Z. Deutschman,† a former member of the Health Section of the League at the Eastern Bureau (the activities of which were suspended owing to the Japanese occupation), and later at Geneva. On January 1, 1945, this " research unit " was transferred to the staff of the Health Division of Unrra to form the nucleus of its epidemiological intelligence service. At the same time, duties relating to the administration of the International Sanitary Conventions which O.I.H.P. was now unable to perform were also transferred to Unrra. In October, 1944, Dr. Gautier had again visited London to participate in the International Conference on the Standardization of Penicillin, which was convened on the initiative of the Health Section.

Thus was the continuity of the Health Organization's work preserved under conditions of extraordinary difficulty, which included the deportation to Germany of Professor J. Parisot, the chairman of the Health Committee, and of one of its members, Professor René Sand.

In 1945 the San Francisco Conference, which led to the establishment of the United Nations Organization, approved the declaration calling for the creation of an international health agency, and the Economic and Social Council of the U.N. at its first session established a Technical Preparatory Committee, which met in Paris from March 18 to April 5, 1946, to prepare plans for an International Health Conference. The conference opened in New York on June 19, 1946, and on July 22 representatives of 61 States signed the Constitution of the World Health Organization. By its Constitution W.H.O. is the single international health agency, which not only inherits the functions of its precursors—including O.I.H.P.—but also has new responsibilities.

Only two of the States participating in the International Health Conference—China and the United Kingdom— signed the Constitution without reservation, and, as it could not come into force until a total of 26 Member States of United Nations had ratified their signatures, an Arrangement was concluded establishing an Interim Commission to continue essential international health functions and to prepare for the First World Health Assembly.

On April 7, 1948, the Constitution came into force, the First World Health Assembly opened on June 24, 1948, and the World Health Organization was established in its definitive form on September 1, 1948.

Note on W.H.O. Publications

For the general reader the best source of information on W.H.O. activities is the *Chronicle of the World Health Organization*, which has been published monthly since the beginning of 1947 and gives short accounts of conferences, meetings of expert committees, and field activities.

Full accounts of the proceedings of conferences, and especially of the annual World Health Assembly, are published in the series *Official Records of the World Health Organization*, which includes also the annual report of the director-general. The series was started during the time of the Interim Commission of W.H.O., and No. 1 contains the proceedings of the

---

*Secretary of the International Health Conference, New York, 1946.

†Assistant secretary of the International Health Conference, New York, 1946.

MAY 6, 1950   ORIGINS OF INTERNATIONAL HEALTH WORK   BRITISH MEDICAL JOURNAL   1037

Technical Preparatory Committee ; No. 2 is the proceedings of the International Health Conference ; and Nos. 3 to 7 inclusive contain the proceedings of the five sessions of the Interim Commission. No. 9 is Part I of the Interim Commission's Report to the First World Health Assembly, and contains a detailed account of the work of the Commission from the date of its establishment in 1946 to the end of April, 1948. A Supplementary Report, including information on the later phases of the Commission's work, was issued as No. 12. No. 10 was the Provisional Agenda, with recommendations for programme activities, presented by the Commission to the First World Health Assembly. The proceedings of the First and Second World Health Assemblies are printed as Nos. 13 and 21 of the series, and the reports of the first five sessions of the executive board appear in Nos. 14, 17, 22, 25, and 26. No. 16 is the *Annual Report of the Director-General to the World Health Assembly to the United Nations, 1948,* and covers the first four months' (September to December, 1948) work of the permanent Organization. The annual report for 1949 is No. 24.

Reports of expert committees and other advisory bodies were until the end of 1949 also published in the *Official Records* series (Nos. 8, 11, 15, and 19). At the beginning of 1950 these technical reports were published in a new series—*World Health Organization : Technical Report Series*—of which twenty-one have now either been printed or are being prepared for press.

Scientific papers relating to the work of the Organization are published in the *Bulletin of the World Health Organization,* and laws and regulations relating to health are reproduced, abstracted, or indexed in a separate publication—the *International Digest of Health Legislation.*

The *Weekly Epidemiological Record* contains notifications of first cases of pestilential diseases and other information of interest principally to quarantine authorities. The *Epidemiological and Vital Statistics Report,* which is published monthly, contains epidemiological and statistical information of wider interest. Non-serial publications, such as the *Manual of the International Statistical Classification of Diseases, Injuries, and Causes of Death* and the *International Pharmacopoeia,* are also published. All W.H.O. publications are published in the English and French languages, and there are also Chinese, Russian, and Spanish editions of the *Chronicle.*

The Public Information Division issues a monthly *W.H.O. Newsletter,* an occasional Special Features series, and numerous Press Releases.

SELECTED LIST OF WORKS CONSULTED

Barkhuus, A. (1943). *Ciba Symposia,* **5**, 1554.
Beckmann, J. (1846). *A History of Inventions, Discoveries, and Origins,* 4th ed. revised and enlarged by William Francis and J. W. Griffith, vol. 1, London. Art. " Quarantine," p. 373.
Buchanan, G. S. (1934a). *Lancet,* **1**, 879, 935, 992.
—— (1934b). *British Medical Journal,* **2**, 977.
Clerc, M., Bohec, J., Villejean, A., Navarre, Ph., and Tanon, L. (1933). *Hygiène maritime et prophylaxie internationale.* Paris.
Dujarric de la Rivière, R. (1948). *Prophylaxie nationale et internationale des maladies épidémiques.* Paris.
Faivre, P. (1908). *Prophylaxie internationale et nationale.* Paris.
Gerlitt, J. (1935). *Ciba Z.,* **2**, 810.
Hirsch, A. (1883). *Handbook of Geographical and Historical Pathology,* vol. 1. Acute Infectious Diseases. Translated from the second German edition by Charles Creighton. The New Sydenham Society, London.
Kramer, M. A., Maylott, M., and Foley, J. W. (1947). *International Health Security in the Modern World.* (Reprint from the *Department of State Bulletin,* 1947, 953.)
League of Nations (1939–45). *Chronicle of the Health Organisation,* vols. 1 and 2, and three special numbers issued between October, 1943, and December, 1945.
—— (1945a). *Bull. Hlth Org. L. o. N.,* **11**, 1.
—— (1945b). *Report on the Work of the League During the War.* Geneva.
Mackenzie, M. D. (1944). *J. R. Inst. publ. Hlth,* **7**, 66, 90, 117.
Masters, R. D. (1947). *International Organization in the Field of Public Health.* Washington. (Advance print of a chapter on public health in the forthcoming *Manual of International Organization* of the division of international laws of the Carnegie Endowment for International Peace.)
Office International d'Hygiène Publique (1933). *Vingt-cinq ans d'activité de l'Office international d'Hygiène publique, 1909–1933.* Paris.
Proceedings of the International Sanitary Conference provided for by joint resolution of the Senate and House of Representatives in the early part of 1881. Washington, 1881.
Procès-verbaux de la conférence sanitaire internationale ouverte à Vienne le 1 juillet, 1874. Vienna, 1874.
Proust, A. (1896). *L'orientation nouvelle de la politique sanitaire.* Paris.
Quincy, J. (1720). Translation of N. Hodges's *Loimologia . . . To which is added, an essay on the different causes of Pestilential diseases, and how they become contagious. . . .* London, E. Bell.
Simon, J. (1897). *English sanitary institutions, reviewed in their course of development, and in some of their political and social relations,* 2nd ed. London.
Woolf, L. S. (1916). *International Government.* New York.

[3]

THE NEW WORLD HEALTH ORGANIZATION

By Walter R. Sharp *

The signing of the Constitution for a World Health Organization, on 22 July 1946 in New York City, is likely to be a landmark in the history of international coöperation for public health and medicine. At this ceremony the representatives of sixty-one nations affirmed their intention of bringing all inter-governmental health action under the aegis of a single agency which, it is hoped, will soon embrace the entire family of states. The new "Magna Carta" of health envisages an organization far wider in scope and function than any previous undertaking in this sphere of international collaboration. Still more significant is the new approach to the problem of disease embodied in the WHO Constitution—an approach which takes full cognizance of the revolutionary advances of the past decade in preventive and curative medicine.

The steps leading to the International Health Conference at Hunter College last summer constitute equally a landmark in the development of the United Nations system. The idea of creating a new world-wide health agency had its inception at the San Francisco Conference. At the instance of the Brazilian and Chinese delegations a resolution was unanimously adopted requesting the United Nations to call as soon as possible a conference with this end in view. The following February the Economic and Social Council initiated action to this effect by establishing a Technical Preparatory Committee of Experts to formulate draft constitutional proposals for the new organization and instructing the Secretary-General to convene an International Health Conference in New York not later than 20 June. WHO, when it comes into being, will therefore be "the first-born child" of the United Nations in the sense of Article 62 of the Charter; and once WHO is brought into formal relationship with the UN, it will be the first "specialized agency" to materialize as a result of direct UN sponsorship.

In the birth of WHO there was a further innovation. For the first time since the end of hostilities against the Axis representatives of neutral and ex-enemy states were permitted not only to participate in a meeting held under official United Nations auspices but also to affix their signatures to the formal instruments adopted by the Conference. Sixteen countries not members of the UN were invited to send observers to Hunter College and

* Chairman, Department of Government, College of the City of, New York. The opinions expressed in this article are those of the author in his private capacity and not as a staff official of the International Health Conference or as Administrative Consultant to the Interim Commission of WHO.

thirteen of them accepted.[1]   There were also present observers from the Allied Control Authorities for Germany, Japan, and Korea, as well as from seven inter-governmental organizations namely FAO, ILO, PICAO, UNESCO, UNRRA, the *Office international d'Hygiène publique,* the Pan-American Sanitary Bureau, and from three private organizations namely the League of Red Cross Societies, the World Federation òf Trade Unions, and the Rockefeller Foundation.   These observers, together with voting delegations from all the then fifty-one members of UN, made up the largest and most representative gathering of public health officials ever to assemble under the same roof.   All the world but Spain took part (or was invited to take part) in the historic meeting.

In addition to the Constitution of WHO three other instruments were signed at the conclusion of the Conference : the Final Act, an Arrangement for the immediate establishment of an Interim Commission, and a Protocol providing for the gradual liquidation of the *Office international d'Hygiène publique.*[2]   In accordance with Chapter XIX of the WHO Constitution the latter will come into force as soon as twenty-six states members of the United Nations formally accept the instrument.[3]   Under the Arrangement setting up the Interim Commission, the inaugural session of the World Health Assembly (the general policy-determining organ of WHO) must be convened not later than six months after the Constitution becomes effective.

Pending the establishment of the permanent Organization, the Interim Commission is instructed by the Arrangement to formulate detailed plans for its initial administrative set-up and working program.[4]   The Commission is also entrusted with the task of expediting the transfer of the functions of the League of Nations Health Organization, the *Office,* and the

[1] Countries accepting were: Albania, Austria, Bulgaria, Eire, Finland, Hungary, Iceland, Italy, Portugal, Siam, Sweden, Switzerland, and Transjordan.   Only Afghanistan, Rumania, and Yemen failed to respond.

[2] The Final Act, WHO Constitution, and Arrangement were signed on behalf of sixty-one states; the Protocol on behalf of sixty.   Among the signatories to all four instruments were the U.S.S.R., Byelorussia, and the Ukraine—subject to subsequent approval.

[3] By 1 June 1947 fourteen states had indicated acceptance: China and the United Kingdom (by signature without reservation as to approval), and Albania, Canada, Ethiopia, Iran, Italy, Liberia, Netherlands, New Zealand, Saudi Arabia, Switzerland, Syria, and Transjordan (by deposit of instruments of acceptance with the Secretary-General of the United Nations).

[4] The Commission consists of "eighteen states entitled to designate persons to serve on it," these states having been elected by the Conference.   They are: Australia, Brazil, Canada, China, Egypt, France, India, Liberia, Mexico, Netherlands, Norway, Peru, Ukraine, United Kingdom, United States, U.S.S.R., Venezuela, and Yugoslavia. In making the selection the Conference gave special regard to the desirability of a broad geographical representation, particularly since the members of the Interim Commission are expected to act collectively for all the signatories to the WHO Constitution.

UNRRA Health Division, as well as the initiation of negotiations with the Pan-American Sanitary organization looking toward its eventual merger with WHO. The Interim Commission has established its headquarters office in New York (Empire State Building) and a working center in the *Palais des Nations* at Geneva.

At its first session in New York (July 1946) the Commission appointed Dr. Brock Chisholm, formerly Canadian Deputy Minister of Health and an internationally known psychiatrist, as its Executive Secretary. A small technical and administrative staff was promptly assembled, consisting largely of personnel transferred from the League Health Section, the *Office*, and the UNRRA Health Division. Desirous of avoiding any break in the continuity of international health coöperation, the Commission, at its second and third sessions in Geneva (November 1946 and March–April 1947), set up a number of expert committees to develop programs of disease control and biological standardization work and to draft proposals for revising existing International Sanitary Conventions. Early in 1947 the responsibility for continuing through the year the peace-time phases of the UNRRA program of emergency assistance to the health services of of war-devastated European countries, Ethiopia, and China was assumed by the Commission's staff, a grant of $1,500,000 from UNRRA funds being made for this purpose. Other committees of the Commission are now actively engaged in the initiation of negotiations with a view to the eventual conclusion by WHO of coöperative agreements with the United Nations and with those specialized agencies (ILO, FAO, UNESCO, and ICAO) whose activities overlap the field of WHO's competence. When the World Health Assembly meets, probably during the early part of 1948, the transition to the permanent Organization should accordingly be effected with a minimum of lost motion.

The Central Institutional Structure of WHO

If the United Nations may be considered the "constitutional father" of WHO, the League of Nations Health Organization is clearly its "organic grandfather." The Report of the Technical Preparatory Committee of Experts, which served as "the bible" for the deliberations of the International Health Conference, borrowed extensively from the experience of the League in health matters.[5] It will be recalled that the health work of

[5] This Report is reproduced in the *Journal of the Economic and Social Council*, No. 13, 22 May 1946. The Technical Preparatory Committee consisted of sixteen public health experts designated by the Council from the following countries: Argentina, Belgium, Brazil, Canada, China, Czechoslovakia, Egypt, France, Greece, India, Mexico, Norway, Poland, United Kingdom, United States, and Yugoslavia. The U.S.S.R. was invited to send an expert but did not do so. Representatives of the *Office*, the League Health Organization, UNRRA, and the Pan-American Sanitary Bureau attend the sessions of the Committee in a consultative capacity. The Committee met in Paris for three weeks during March–April 1946.

the League was conducted by means of three principal bodies: (1) a General Advisory Health Council, whose functions were entrusted to the Permanent Committee of the *Office,* (2) a Standing Health Committee of twelve medical experts, and (3) the Health Section of the Geneva Secretariat. Flanking these three bodies was a cluster of expert commissions and committees set up as circumstances required to study and report on methods of coping with specific diseases and miscellaneous health problems.[6] The Advisory Council met annually as a central planning and policy body while the Health Committee, convening four times a year, supervised the work of the Secretariat and the expert committees.

In the new agency these three organs substantially reappear in expanded form as the World Health Assembly, the Executive Board, and the Secretariat, respectively.[7] As the general policy-determining organ of WHO, the Health Assembly is given the specific functions of appointing the Director-General, approving the budget, electing the Executive Board, sponsoring special health conferences, establishing technical committees, making recommendations to Member states, and adopting conventions and regulations on a wide variety of subjects.[8]

While the Executive Board is analogous in size and function to the Standing Health Committee of the League, the expert character of its membership is less firmly assured. The Board will "consist of eighteen persons designated by as many Members" (member states) for overlapping terms of three years. Such states will be chosen by the Health Assembly, due account being taken of the desirability of "an equitable geographic distribution." While the persons designated by these eighteen states "should be technically qualified in the field of health," they will serve as government representatives and not as experts in their personal capacities. As such, they may be changed at the will of the appointing governments.[9]

[6] Accounts of the League's activities in the health field may be found in Mander, L. A., *Foundations of Modern World Society,* Stanford, 1941, Chap. I; Davis, H. E., ed., *Pioneers in World Order.* New York, 1944, pp. 193–208 (by Frank G. Boudreau); de Huszar, G. B., ed., *Persistent International Issues,* New York, 1947, Chap. 4 (by George K. Strode); and Winslow, C. E. A., "International Organization for Health," in *Report of the Commission to Study the Organization for Peace,* New York, 1944.

[7] Art. 9 of the WHO Constitution. The Technical Preparatory Committee proposed "Conference" as the name for the deliberative organ of WHO—a term which would have better conformed to the terminology employed in similar UN specialized agencies; curiously enough, the delegates at Hunter College insisted on adopting the term "Assembly" because, in their view, it connoted a more representative type of organ.

[8] Arts. 13, 14, 18. The provisions dealing with conventions and regulations are discussed below.

[9] Arts. 24–25. A proposal introduced by the Ukraine to have the "Big Five" permanently represented on the Board received the support of only one other delegation.

Some difference of opinion developed in the Conference regarding the powers of the Board. The United States delegation sponsored an amendment to the Paris Draft Proposals which would have in effect limited the Board's role to that of a "standing committee" of the Assembly. This amendment, seconded by Canada, China, and a number of other delegations, met with strong opposition from the Soviet and many European and Latin-American representatives. Accordingly, in the final text of the Constitution, not only is the Board designated as "the executive organ of the Health Assembly," but it is authorized to submit program-proposals on its own initiative, to convene special conferences, to establish standing committees, and "to take emergency measures within the functions and financial resources of the Organization to deal with events requiring immediate action." The Board, in addition, nominates the Director-General to the Assembly and submits to the Assembly recommendations regarding his budget. The Constitution further stipulates that the Director-General shall be "subject to the authority of the Board" when exercising his duties as "chief technical and administrative officer of the Organization."

It is apparent that in a fairly wide sphere of activity the functions of the Assembly and Board will overlap. Although this overlapping of authority has the virtue of flexibility it may possibly give rise to some friction and confusion. Moreover, the Board's broad powers of supervision over the Director-General could be so exercised as to compel him to secure its prior consent not merely to the appointment of staff but to current decisions on organizational and technical matters. To be sure, no such tight control is likely to develop, but the fact remains that the executive head of the Organization may find himself in a position where he may be obliged to consult the Board far more often than will be found consistent with vigorous and progressive administration. The "doctors" at Hunter College, not unlike certain American judges and constitutional lawyers, evinced a marked aversion to "executive discretion."

There is little that is novel in the provisions of the WHO Constitution dealing with the permanent Secretariat, which will comprise "the Director-General and such technical and administrative staff as the Organization may require" (Art. 30). The Paris Draft proposed a five year term for the Director-General but the Conference wisely left to the Health Assembly the power to fix the tenure and other conditions of his appointment. The conditions governing the selection of staff substantially duplicate the provisions of Art. 101 of the United Nations Charter, the parentage of which, incidentally, may be traced back through the UNESCO and FAO Constitutions to the practice of the League and the ILO. Individual integrity, efficiency, and competence are laid down as "the paramount consideration in the employment of staff," with due regard also the importance of its recruitment "on as wide a geographical basis as possible" (Arts. 35–37).

514   THE AMERICAN JOURNAL OF INTERNATIONAL LAW

Controversial Features of the WHO Constitution

There were two major areas of dispute in the framing of WHO's fundamental charter. These had to do (1) with the basis of membership in the Organization and (2) with arrangements for operations at the regional level.

(1) *Membership.* The note of universality recurred time and again in the discussion of the conditions which should govern admission to membership in WHO. "Germs know no frontiers," "health is indivisible" and "germs carry no passports"—these were the action slogans of the Conference. Every delegation readily approved the general principle that "membership in the Organization shall be open to all States" (Art. 3). Nor was there any appreciable dissent from the view that those neutral and ex-enemy states invited to send observers to the Conference should be permitted to become members merely by accpting the Constitution (provided such acceptance is effected before the first session of the World Health Assembly).[10] Political considerations nevertheless intruded when it came to determining the requirement for the admission of states *not* represented at the Conference. It was the Spanish question that precipitated the controversy—and the closest vote taken during the entire Conference.

Here the point at issue, concretely, was whether the Health Assembly should be granted power to approve applications for membership by a simple majority or a two-thirds vote. The three Soviet delegations vehemently argued in favor of the latter provision, and the Legal Committee incorporated this view in its Report to the full Conference. However, when the Conference in plenary session proceeded to consider the Report, the Chilean delegate moved an amendment providing for simple majority action by the Health Assembly on future membership applications. This amendment was supported with lavish oratory by a solid Latin-American bloc, effectively aided by Canada. The Canadian delegate explained in moving terms the position of the advocates of easy admission: "We cannot afford to have gaps in the fence against disease; and any country, no matter what its political attitudes or affiliations are, can be a serious detriment to the effectiveness of the World Health Organization if it is left outside. It is important that health should be regarded as a world-wide question, quite independent of political attitudes in any country in the world."

The chief of the U.S.S.R. delegation led the onslaught on the Chilean amendment. Its purpose, in his opinion, was clearly to "open the doors to Spain"; but there "are other countries. What about Japan? What about Germany? . . . Our charter does not have in view separate states. It

---

[10] Art. 5. States members of the United Nations are not bound by this time restriction (Art. 4).

has in view the World Health Organization. It is not written to preserve health in any particular state. . . . It is written to preserve health internationally, in the whole world. . . . If Spain asks to become a member of this organization, I will be the first to accept such a request, but on condition that this request be made by a democratic Spain." Thus drawn, the issue provoked several hours of spirited argument before it was settled. The Chilean amendment was finally adopted by a vote of 25 to 22, the Ukraine insisted upon a roll call so that every delegation's position might be on record. Aside from the Latin-American and Arab League states, which unanimously supported the amendment, only Canada and the Philippines cast their ballots with the majority. All the "Big Five" but China, which abstained, voted against the amendment.

Associate Members. A second question affecting membership which gave rise to considerable debate concerned arrangements for the participation of dependencies, protectorates, and trust territories in the Organization. At the instance of the Chinese delegation, a proposal was introduced in the Legal Committee of the Conference for the admission as "associate members," with all rights and privileges except voting and holding office, of all such territories "ineligible to separate membership in the United Nations, whose areas and populations are large enough, whose health problems are of world concern, and which have indigenous health administrations." The United States countered with the suggestion that provision be made for direct relationships with these categories of territories "through special agreements with the responsible governments." Still a third solution of the problem, brought forward by the United Kingdom and supported by France, Canada, Mexico, New Zealand, and South Africa (all but two of them states having colonies or mandates), would have limited the participation of non-self-governing territories to the regional branches of the Organization.

As the discussion progressed, the United Kingdom delegation indicated its willingness to accept the principle of associate membership at the central level provided such members be limited in number to a fixed maximum of twenty. China lent its support to this solution and agreed with the United States that participation by such territories in the central organs of WHO should require the consent of the governments responsible for the foreign relations of the territories concerned.

After reference of the issue to a special drafting sub-committee, a generally acceptable formula was evolved. The text embodying this formula authorizes the Health Assembly by simple majority vote to admit to associate membership "territories or groups of territories which are not responsible for the conduct of their international relations" . . . "upon application on behalf of such territories or groups of territories by the Member or other authority having responsibility for their international relations." The purpose of the revised wording was to make it possible for trust territories, whether under single-power or United Nations administration, to be admitted to WHO as associate members. As adopted the text leaves to the Health Assembly the discretionary duty of determining "the nature and extent of the rights and obligations of associate members." But there is no constitutional limit on the number of such members.

(2) *Regional Arrangements*. By far the most contentious question before the Conference was the problem of regionalism. The practical solution of this problem was complicated by reason of the existence of the Pan-American Sanitary organization and the vigorous support for its continued identity which came from the American Republics. Before the issue was ironed out, a special "harmonizing" subcommittee had to labor long and arduously in the search for a formula satisfactory both to the "federalists" and the "autonomists."

Spearheading the "bloc" which urged immediately and complete adsorption of the PASB by WHO were the three Soviet delegations. Early in the debate they introduced a resolution which would have empowered the World Health Assembly, by unilateral act, to transform all existing regional inter-governmental health organizations into "regional committees subordinated to the World Health Organization." No such drastic solution as this was acceptable to the United States, let alone the Latin-Americans. The Peruvian delegate pointedly called attention to the fact that the Mexico City Conference of 1945 had resolved that the Pan-American Sanitary Bureau should continue to act as "the general coördinating sanitary agency of the American Republics." The PASB, in the view of the Latin-Americans, constituted the oldest and most successful example of international health coöperation—from which, incidentally, they have enjoyed substantial subsidies largely made possible by funds contributed to the PASB by the United States government. While the PASB should obviously work in the closest harmony with WHO, its operating autonomy must be preserved.

As a concrete basis for discussion, a draft resolution was submitted by the Chairman of the United States delegation, Dr. Thomas Perran,[11] to the effect that regional health agencies should be integrated or brought into relationship with WHO through special agreements providing either that such agencies be transformed into regional offices or that their facilities and services be utilized by WHO pending their progressive merger as circumstances permitted. Meanwhile, the PASB would be expressly recognized "as the appropriate body both to promote programs and undertakings among the American Republics on regional health problems of common interest in continuation of its present work and in harmony with the general policies of the World Health Organization, and in addition to act, when necessary, as the Regional Committee for the Organization."

[11] Dr. Parran also served as President of the Conference.

Within six months after the coming into force of the WHO Constitution the Director-General would be directed to enter into negotiations with the appropriate authorities of PASB for the purpose of bringing it into formal relationship with WHO.

To the Latin-American bloc this United States proposal appeared to provide adequate safeguards for the continuance of a quasi-autonomous status for the PASB. Various other delegations, among them China, the United Kingdom, and Norway, nevertheless pressed for an arrangement which would ensure its consolidation with WHO as rapidly as possible, and Egypt contended that the nascent health bureau of the Arab League should be given equal treatment in case the PASB were allowed to maintain its identity.

After prolonged argument the principle of "progressive and ultimate merger" was approved. Even so, the language embodying this principle is studiously vague and it may require tedious and complicated negotiations before consolidation is completely effected. Accordingly to the "harmonizing" formula the PASB and all other inter-governmental regional health organizations in existence prior to the signing of the WHO Constitution are "in due course" to be "integrated with" (not into) the WHO. This integration will be effected "as soon as practicable through common action based on mutual consent of the competent authorities expressed through the organizations concerned." [12] Clearly a wide area of adjustment will be open to the negotiators as a result of these very elastic provisions.

Once the future status of the Pan American Sanitary Bureau was resolved, the other problems relating to arrangements for regional action were adjusted without too much difficulty. It was agreed that the Health Assembly might from time to time define the geographical areas in which it seemed desirable to establish regional committees and offices. With the consent of a majority of the Member states located within an area thus defined, the Assembly is authorized to set up a regional branch of WHO consisting (a) of a regional committee composed of representatives of all Members and Associate Members from the area, and (b) of a regional office to reserve as "the administrative organ" of the regional committee (Arts. 44-51). Non-self-governing territories within the region which have not been admitted to WHO as Associate Members may, with the consent of the controlling governments or authorities, participate in the regional

---

[12] Art. 53. The Interim Commission ran into certain snags in its initial conversations with the Pan American Sanitary Bureau, though there is no reason to suppose that, given a spirit of conciliation and good will on both sides, mutually satisfactory arrangements cannot eventually be worked out. The Twelfth Pan American Sanitary Conference at Caracas (January 1947), in authorizing the negotiation of a working agreement with WHO, took the position that the PASB should retain its present name with the subtitle "Regional Office of the WHO."

committee in such manner as may be determined by the Health Assembly after consultation with the governments or authorities concerned.

The definition of the functions to be performed by a regional committee provoked some difference of opinion. The advocates of "centralization," led by the United Kingdom and Soviet delegations, took the position that action by a regional committee should be "subject to the general authority" of the central policy-making organ of the Organization. This group was eventually persuaded to accept a milder statement to the effect that the regional committee should be designated as "an integral part of the Organization" in accordance with the Constitution (Art. 45). The attributions of the regional committee were nevertheless spelled out with some precision. These attributions will encompass: (a) intra-regional activities, including the determination of policies on "exclusively regional" matters, the supervision of the regional office, and the calling of technical conferences on regional problems; (b) the tendering of advice to the central organization, including, in particular, the recommendation of additional regional appropriations by the regional Members of WHO "if the proportion of the central budget of the Organization allotted to that region is insufficient for the carrying out of the regional functions"; and (3) the exercise of any additional functions delegated to the committee by the Health Assembly, the Executive Board, or the Director-General (Art. 50).

The final problem to be resolved was that of how the head of a regional office and its staff should be appointed. On one side various proposals were submitted which in effect would have given either to the Director-General or to the Executive Board the power to select the regional director. This procedure, it was observed by the Canadian delegate, would "permit interchange of regional directors" and "protect regional committees against undue political influence." But because this arrangement was objectable to the Pan American bloc an intermediate solution was proposed whereby the Executive Board's approval of the regional committee's nomination would be necessary. In the end, on the suggestion of the United States and Mexico, it was decided that the appointment of the regional director should rest with the Board "in agreement with the Regional Committee" (Art. 52). Under this formula the initiative in nominating a regional director will presumably be taken by the Board but the Regional Committee may force the Board to submit an alternative name (or names) if it objects to the original nomination. There is nothing in the Constitution to prevent the appointment of a regional director from outside the regional area in question, nor his subsequent assignment to another regional office or even to the central headquarters office, or *vice versa*. An analogous compromise was reached as to the appointment of the staffs of regional offices, with a similar alignment of views, the text adopted providing for their appointment "in a manner to be determined by agreement between the Director-General and the Regional Director." [13]

Although the prolonged and often heated discussion of thé regional issue did not yield complete unanimity the final solutions reflect the overwhelming opinion of the Conference that WHO should have world-wide paramountcy in the future development of inter-governmental coöperation on health problems. At the same time it was generally accepted that considerable freedom of action on regional matters should be left to regional units functioning as organic parts of the general organization. Accordingly the provisions dealing with regional arrangements in the WHO charter are more elaborate and detailed than are to be found in the basic instrument of any of the other specialized agencies to date. The successful operation of the WHO framework of central-regional relationships will obviously depend upon the wisdom and skill with which the leadership of the Organization utilizes its policy-shaping and administrative prerogatives. At the least the plan should make for a much more effective coördination of effort in the international health field than heretofore especially since there will henceforth be only one inter-governmental agency of global scope with general jurisdiction over health matters.

The Ambit of WHO Activity

The architects of the WHO Consitution were not content merely to carry forward the not inconsiderable accomplishments of previous undertakings in public health involving international collaboration. On the contrary, their conception of the field of action which WHO should encompass was a broad and progressive one. In the Preamble of the charter health is defined not negatively as the absence of disease or infirmity but positively as "a state of complete physical, mental, and social well-being," the enjoyment of which is "one of the fundamental rights of every human being without distinction of race, religion, political belief, economic or social condition." The attainment "by all peoples of the highest possible level of health," is set forth as the over-all objective of the Organization.[14]

Among the fundamental principles upon which an effective international health program should be based the "healthy development of the child," in order that he may "live harmoniously in changing total environment," has an important place in the WHO charter. The introduction

[13] Art. 53. Only the Arab states, Paraguay, and the Dominican Republic refused to cast their votes for adoption of the two compromise formulas governing the appointment of regional directors and regional staffs.

[14] Art. 1. The Draft Proposals submitted by the Technical Preparatory Committee listed seven different ways by which this broad aim might be furthered, but the Conference Committee on Scope and Functions felt that there would be a signal advantage, from the psychological standpoint, if a single, all-inclusive objective were put forward at the beginning of the Constitution.

of psychiatric techniques into public educational systems is clearly implied by this statement. The Preamble of the Constitution further recognizes that the realization of high levels of health the world over may have a vital bearing on the quest for peace and security and to this end "the extension to all peoples of the benefits of medical, psychological, and related knowledge" will be sought in every practicable manner. It was also the consensus at Hunter College that the only effective means of controlling the international spread of pestilential disease in our day is to strengthen national health services everywhere, because the glaringly low standards of sanitation and hygiene which still prevail over two-thirds of the globe constitute "a common danger" to all peoples. For the eradication of communicable disease, it must be attacked at the source. The older techniques of quarantine, while still necessary, were considered no longer adequate for an age in which air transport may carry bubonic plague or typhus fever to the ends of the earth in a few hours.

Such are the basic concepts underlying the formulation of WHO's aims and purposes. It cannot be denied that they are ambitious and sweeping in their implications. How are they to be implemented concretely? No more than its predecessors among international health agencies is WHO endowed with independent legislative or executive power. The positive obligations assumed by its Members are limited indeed. Aside from agreeing to contribute to its annual budget whatever quota is set by the Health Assembly no participating state is constitutionally bound to do more than (a) submit to the Organization an annual report "on the action taken and progress achieved in improving the health of its people," including measures it may have put into effect with respect to recommendations, conventions, agreements, and regulations adopted by the Assembly; and (b) communicate promptly such statistical and epidemiological information as may be requested by that body (Arts. 61–65). Although these obligations admittedly represent some advance beyond the pre-war stage of international health organization, their net effectiveness will be conditioned by the impact of comparative analysis, research, publicity, and demonstration upon national health policies.

In realistic terms it may be said that WHO will be able to move toward its central objective only insofar as it can prod governments and private groups to provide services and initiate programs they might not otherwise undertake. The financial and technical resources essential to its work will be forthcoming only in the degree that Member states, chiefly a few of the richer ones, are willing to supply them. During the earlier phases of its life the new Organization will probably not have either the means or the authority to conduct extensive field activities comparable to those of an advanced national health administration though such developments may come later. The role of WHO will be primarily that of a catalytic agent.

It is within this context that the various functions conferred upon the Organization by its Constitution should be assessed. For convenience, these functions may be grouped as follows: (1) administrative and coördinative, (2) technical and research services, (3) informational, (4) assistance and promotion, and (5) quasi-legislative.

(1) *Administrative and coördinative.* In the language of its Constitution WHO is designated as the "directing and coördinating authority on international health work." Specifically it will administer the duties previously assigned to the *Office international d'Hygiène publique,* and since 1944 to UNRRA, by existing international sanitary conventions. As a continuing part of this task the permanent staff and expert committees of WHO will have the obligation of formulating draft proposals for unifying, strengthening, and extending such conventions, concerning which more will be said below. Secondly the Constitution enjoins the Organization to establish coöperative relations with other organizations, both inter- and non-governmental, international and national, which are concerned with any phase of WHO's work.[15] All of this implies that international coöperation for health cannot effectively be conducted today, so to speak, "functional isolation" from the surrounding social and economic environment. It is wisely recognized that WHO will need to collaborate closely with cognate "specialized agencies," such as ILO, FAO, UNESCO, and ICAO, not only in order to deal effectively with "borderland" problems like industrial hygiene, health insurance, nutrition, rural hygiene, research in the biological and physical sciences, and the sanitary aspects of aerial navigation, but also with a view to minimizing as far as possible duplication of effort and jurisdictional friction. This will be equally true of the relations of WHO with various commissions of the Economic and Social Council, notably the Social, Narcotic Drugs, Population, and Statistical Commissions, as well as with the Trusteeship Council and the recently created International Children's Emergency Fund.[16] Some of these coöperative arrangements will doubtless be spelled out more fully in formal agreements concluded between WHO and the United Nations and other specialized agencies.

---

[15] Arts. 70 and 71, as part of the Chapter entitled "Relations with Other Organizations," stipulate that any formal agreements entered into with other inter-governmental agencies shall be subject to approval by a two-thirds vote of the Health Assembly. Consultative arrangements with non-governmental agencies, on the other hand, may be worked out at the staff level, although, in the case of national organizations, the consent of the government concerned must be obtained.

[16] In the enumeration of "Functions" in Article 2 of the Constitution, reference is made three times to "coöperation with other specialized agencies where necessary." Arrangements have already been initiated by the Interim Commission for the setting up of joint WHO–ILO expert committees on industrial hygiene and medical care and a similarly constituted joint WHO–FAO committee on nutrition.

522 THE AMERICAN JOURNAL OF INTERNATIONAL LAW

(2) *Technical and research services.* Under this head a variety of activities are envisaged. First and most immediate is the continuation of two services performed by the League Health Section: epidemiological intelligence and the administration of work in biological standardization. The Geneva office of the Interim Commission has already taken over the publication of the *Weekly Epidemiological Record* formerly issued by the League, and provision has been made in the 1947 budget of the Commission to maintain the pre-war system of grants-in-aid to the biological laboratories at Copenhagen and Hampstead (London). The Organization, once firmly established, may, within the limits of its budgetary resources, establish such other statistical and research services as it considers appropriate, undertake the technical work involved in the preparation of proposals for standardizing diagnostic procedures and revising as necessary the international nomenclature of diseases, causes of death, and public health practices, and assist in developing international standards with respect to food, biological and pharmaceutical products.

A sharp division of opinion emerged at the Conference as to whether WHO should directly concern itself with health insurance. Although the importance of improving the quality of medical care available to low income groups was not challenged, certain delegations believed it unwise for the new Organization to get entangled in the highly explosive subject of "state medicine." As a compromise the Constitution provides merely that WHO may "study and report on . . . administrative and social techniques affecting public health and medical care from preventive and curative points of view, including hospital and social security." [17] Considerable caution will no doubt be exercised in launching any program of fact-finding and analysis in this field.

(3) *Informational.* Not only can WHO, like its Geneva predecessor, do much to facilitate the international exchange of technical information, but its charter places special emphasis on popular health education. The development of "an informed public opinion among all peoples on matters of health" appears conspicuously in the impressive list of functions set forth in Chapter II of the Constitution. To this end an ambitious publications program aimed at the general public is contemplated. In addition—and potentially even more important—the radio and film are to be employed as instruments for explaining to the world's population in simple and graphic terms the implications of preventive medicine and social hygiene. These informal activities will be articulated closely with the overall public relations work of the United Nations Secretariat, particularly in the field of films and broadcasting. While opportunities for this kind of experimentation are almost unlimited, the long-range results will

[17] Art. 2 (p). .Belgium, the Netherlands, and Sweden contended that health insurance properly belonged to the International Labor Organization.

obviously depend upon the extent to which the leadership of WHO succeeds in mobilizing the resources of private as well as public groups in scores of countries for a concerted and vigorous attack on superstition and ignorance.

(4) *Assistance and promotion.* Under these two rubrics the ambit of possible operations is equally wide. The Organization is directed to furnish assistance to governments upon request for the strengthening of their health services—by giving technical advice, lending experts, and organizing field missions. In emergencies, such as the threat or outbreak of an epidemic, it may be called upon for whatever aid it can render within the limits of its facilities. The long and fruitful experience of the League and the Pan American Sanitary Bureau in furnishing assistance to countries whose health standards are backward affords a solid base upon which to build this type of work, embracing, *inter alia,* the sponsoring of fellowships, travel grants, and supervised study tours for public health personnel.

The beneficiaries of technical aid are not confined to the governments of Member states. Whenever requested by the United Nations the Organization is also directed to assist in improving health services for "the peoples of trust territories." Since the source of such requests will presumably be the Trusteeship Council, the maintenance of close working relations between it and the Health Organization should contribute materially to the development of the social welfare aspects of the trusteeship system.[18]

Over and beyond action in response to direct appeals for aid in specific situations the Organization is authorized to promote on its own initiative improved standards of teaching in the "health, medical, and related professions." Further, it is expected to foster the advancement of "maternal and child health and welfare," and, in coöperation with such agencies as the ILO and FAO, it may participate in promotional efforts reaching into the broad domain of social legislation—housing, recreation, working conditions, the prevention of accidental (chiefly household) injuries, and related aspects of environmental hygiene. Finally, it may, in collaboration with UNESCO, undertake such activities as it deems advisable in the field of mental health, "especially those affecting the harmony of human relations"—and presumably calling for the encouragement of psychiatric methods in treating the ills of international society.

(5) *Quasi-legislative.* Although WHO is not granted by its Constitution any legislative authority *per se,* it may nevertheless engage in three types of operations of a quasi-legislative character for which partial prece-

---

[18] Among the delegates at the Conference there was strong support for including specific mention of "displaced persons" in the section of the Constitution covering forms of assistance which might be requested by the United Nations. Because of the insistent opposition of the Soviet representatives, however, it was finally decided to adopt a more general phraseology referring to "special groups, such as the peoples of trust territories."

dents exist in other fields of international organization, notably labor and
civil aviation. The first of these quasi-legislative functions consists of
formal recommendations which the Health Assembly may submit to Member
governments "with respect to any matter within the competence of
the Organization." [19] The Paris Draft Proposals did not include any
provision for recommendations, but the Conference, after some hesitancy,
voted to accept the substance of a Belgian amendment to this effect, based
largely upon the practice of the ILO during the last twenty-five years.
There is one difference, however, between the WHO procedure as to recommendations and that of the ILO: unlike the Members of the latter Organization, the Members of WHO will not be constitutionally obligated
to bring such proposals to the attention of their competent national authorities, within a specified period, for the purpose of making appropriate
legislative or administrative arrangements for their application. An explicit requirement covering this point was not believed to be necessary in
the light of the obligation of every Member government to render an annual
report to the Organization on the action taken not only in respect of
recommendations but also as to conventions and regulations.

The second type of quasi-legislative action includes conventions and
agreements dealing with any matter within WHO's jurisdiction. Such
instruments, if approved by a two-thirds majority of the Health Assembly,
become legally binding on a Member of the Organization "when accepted
by it in accordance with its constitutional processes." Concerning the
obligation of Member states to effect such acceptance, a procedure closely
resembling ILO practice was embodied in the WHO charter. Within
eighteen months each Member must notify the Director-General of the action it has taken, and if it has not accepted the instrument in question it
is required to "furnish a statement of the reasons for non-acceptance."
Once the convention (or agreement) has been accepted, an annual report on
its application must thereafter be made to WHO headquarters (Arts.
19–20).

The import of the foregoing provisions for the development of an effective international health code may be far-reaching. In the past, as the
Report of the United States Delegation on the International Health Conference pertinently observes, it has been necessary for governments interested in a particular phase of international health legislation to convene
special conferences for the purpose of formulating new or revised conventions. "Such conferences have been held at long and irregular intervals
to deal only with particularly pressing problems," with the result that
"sanitary conventions have remained unmodified for long periods during
which scientific advance has often made their provisions archaic." [20] In

---

[19] Art. 23. Such recommendations may be adopted by simple majority vote of the
Assembly.

[20] *Dept. of State Publication 2703, Conference Series 91,* p. 16.

the future there will be a permanent mechanism through which steps can be taken periodically with a view to broadening the scope and strengthening the provisions of world health law. This represents a distinct advance in international legislative technique for the health field.

Still more significant are the provisions of the WHO charter governing regulations. By simple majority vote the Health Assembly is empowered to formulate regulations on five classes of subjects:

> sanitary and quarantine requirements;
> nomenclatures as to diseases, causes of death, and public health practices;
> standards as to diagnostic procedures for international use;
> standards affecting the safety, purity and potency of biological, pharmaceutical and similar products in international commerce; and the
> advertizing and labelling of such products.

The range of this regulatory action was extended by the Conference beyond the Draft Proposals presented by the Technical Preparatory Committee so as to include not merely "drugs in official pharmacopoeia and biological products," but "similar products" as well. Concurrently, "advertizing" was added to "labelling" in connection with the regulation of all such products in international trade.[21]

On the enforceability of regulations the Conference accepted the comparatively novel principle known as "contracting out." Accordingly regulations voted by the Health Assembly become binding on all Member states which do not notify the Director-General of their rejection or reservations within the period stated in the notice given of the Assembly's action (Art. 22). This procedure, which places on each Member the burden of declaring its refusal to accept a regulation, was the subject of warm debate. The Ukraine and Belgium spearheaded the opposition to what was branded "an infringement on sovereignty," or, in milder terms, an arrangement by which a state might be bound "through oversight." In the special subcommittee to which the question was referred, the procedure for modifying the International Sanitary Convention for Aerial Navigation of 1933 was cited as a precedent, while certain delegates argued with some justification that the Chicago Convention on International Civil Aviation establishing ICAO contained comparable provisions.[22]

After the Ukraine had indicated its willingness to accept the proposed procedure provided its application "were limited, on a temporary basis

[21] Art. 21. On the other hand, the Conference yielded to the views of the Soviet and Latin-American delegations in refusing to include in the regulatory powers of WHO the prevention of the importation of products "not conforming to standards adopted by the Health Assembly."

[22] Under the 1933 Convention for Aerial Navigation, the *Office international d'Hygiène publique* could submit to the contracting parties a proposal of amendment suggested by any one of them and a government's approval could either be expressly given

pending later positive action by governments,'' to the employment of new techniques for controlling the international spread of disease, a number of complicated amendments were evolved by the subcommittee as substitutes for the original proposal. In the end all of these were rejected and the original proposal was adopted by unanimous vote of the full Conference.

The American government played a leading role in developing the ''contracting out'' concept before the Technical Preparatory Committee. To quote again from the Report of the United States Delegation: ''This was done in pursuance of a suggestion made in the Senate Foreign Relations Committee that some way be found'' [to permit the rapid application of new scientific techniques] ''without requiring that Committee to consider highly specialized technical matters. It is felt that the mechanism incorporated in the Constitution can accomplish this result. In most cases it will only be necessary to modify existing domestic regulations, within the scope of the executive branch of the Government, to meet the requirements of international health regulations. When more is required the Government can reserve its position pending necessary reference to Congress.'' [23]

The WHO charter does not attempt to define in substantive terms the difference between a regulation and a convention (or an agreement). This lacuna may conceivably be a subject of dispute which may some day have to be referred for settlement to the International Court of Justice in pursuance of Article 75 of the Constitution.[24] Nor is there any constitutional sanction in case a Member state is charged by another Member with failure to enforce an international regulation which has duly come into effect. The only way in which a Member may be penalized directly by the Organization for non-fulfilment of its obligations lies in the discretionary right of the Health Assembly to suspend the voting privileges and services to which such Member is entitled in the event it ''fails to meet its financial obligations or in other exceptional circumstances.'' [25] In the last analysis

---

or implied ''from the fact that it refrains from notifying the latter of any objections within twelve months.'' The Chicago Civil Aviation Convention authorizes the Council of ICAO, by two-thirds vote, to adopt ''annexes'' (recommended international technical standards and practices) which become effective within three months, or such longer period as the Council may prescribe, ''unless in the meantime a majority of the contracting States register their disapproval with the Council.''

[23] Work cited, p. 17.

[24] Article 76 provides further that the Organization, upon authorization by the General Assembly or in accordance with any agreement between WHO and the United Nations, may request the Court for an advisory opinion ''on any legal question arising within the competence of the Constitution.''

[25] Art. 7. The point was made by the Canadian delegate that in the remote contingency of resort by a Member state to bacteriological warfare it would be essential to withhold from such Member epidemiological information which might reveal the effectiveness of its action.

the principal enforcement sanction in the hand of WHO will be the mutuality of interest of its Members in the world-wide observance of agreed *minimum* protective standards.

WHO Within the United Nations System

The Constitution of the World Health Organization bears the imprint of the United Nations specialized agency pattern of inter-relationship more fully than is the case with the basic charter of any of the other functional institutions thus far affiliated with the central UN machinery. The term "United Nations" occurs twenty-three times in the WHO charter and there are seven different references to the Secretary-General. In the introduction to the Preamble the contracting states proclaim its basic principles to be "in conformity with the Charter of the United Nations," and the Preamble closes with the declaration that they "hereby establish the World Health Organization as a specialized agency of the United Nations."

Many of the procedural provisions of the Constitution were reproduced from the UN Charter with little variation. Two instances of this have been cited earlier in these pages—relative to the appointment and status of staff and the suspension of Members' voting privileges. A further example is to be found in the section governing voting procedure in the Health Assembly and Executive Board. At the end of long and snarled discussion of this problem the Canadian delegation brought forward a compromise formula which was frankly lifted from Article 18 of the Charter. Thus in WHO such questions as the adoption of conventions, the approval of formal agreements with the UN and other inter-governmental organizations, and amendments to the Constitution will require a two-thirds majority vote of the Members present and voting, whereas decisions on less fundamental matters, "including the determination of additional categories of questions to be decided by a two-thirds majority," will need only a simple majority (Art. 60). Except for the absence of the "Big Five" veto, the provision of the WHO Constitution (Art. 73) governing the coming into force of amendments conforms to that laid down in Art. 108 of the UN Charter for the "parent" organization. Again, while the WHO, like the UN, does not constitutionally recognize the right of members to withdraw from the Organization, the Health Conference, following the example set at San Francisco, inserted into the record of its proceedings a "declaratory statement" that "a Member is not bound to remain in the Organization if its rights and obligations as such are changed by an amendment to the Constitution in which it has not concurred and which it finds itself unable to accept."

It is further provided that the Secretary-General, or the United Nations in an organic sense, shall be consulted before the Health Assembly may make certain procedural and organizational arrangements. Such consultation is mandatory with regard to fixing the date of the sessions of the Assembly (Art. 15), determining the location of the permanent administrative seat of WHO (Art. 43), and preparing an agreement which will define the privileges and immunities to be accorded to the Organization by its Members (Art. 68). The procedure controlling entry into force of the Constitution, moreover, requires that each instrument of acceptance shall be deposited with the Secretary-General who in turn must register the Constitution in accordance with Art. 102 of the UN Charter and inform the states parties to it of the date it comes into force (Arts. 70, 81, and 82).

On the substantive side the Health Assembly is specifically directed to consider any recommendations bearing on health made to the Organization by the UN General Assembly, the Economic and Social Council, the Security Council, or the Trusteeship Council, and to report to these bodies on the steps taken by WHO to give effect thereto (Art. 18, par. i). The obligation to report is reaffirmed in the next clause relating to the provisions of any agreement entered into by WHO with the Economic and Social Council in accordance with Art. 63 of the UN Charter (par. j), while Art. 69 makes it mandatory upon the Organization to conclude such an agreement.

Clearly it is the intent of all these provisions that WHO shall function as one of the "planets" in the "solar" system of the United Nations. Even so, the founders of the Organization gave emphatic expression to their conviction that it must retain substantial operational autonomy. This point of view was notably reflected in the name they selected for the new institution, in the position they took as to the location of its permanent seat, and in the character of the agreement they had in mind for its affiliation with the UN.

Four different verbal combinations were considered for the name of the new organization. The United Kingdom and Australia, ardent apostles of "centralization," urged that the phrase "United Nations" should appear in the title, either as "UNHO" or as "HOUN." China, taking a contrary position, stressed the idea of universality conveyed by the term "World." The Netherlands, in a move designed to satisfy both camps, suggested a cumbersome combination of wards: "United Nations World Health Organization" (UNWHO). The vote on this proposal showed seventeen for and thirty against. Having thus rejected what amounted to a *reductio ad absurdum,* the Conference then adopted the simplest and shortest name as best symbolizing the new "world age" and expressing the conviction that "health is a fundamental heritage of all peoples."

When the question of permanent headquarters arose in committee, most of the European and Latin-American members went on record in favor of a European city, preferably Geneva or Paris. While it was admitted that certain administrative advantages would result from locating WHO at the seat of the United Nations, special considerations weighed heavily against any decision which might bind the Organization a year or so later to establish its headquarters in the same place as the UN Secretariat. Among such considerations were the difficulties then being experienced by UN in securing adequate office and housing facilities in New York, the uncertainty as to where the eventual location of UN headquarters would be, and, not least, a strong feeling that since the Pan American Sanitary Bureau would presumably serve as WHO's regional base for the Western Hemisphere, its central office should be situated elsewhere. The fact that the epidemiological work of the Organization could be more conveniently handled from a European center also influenced many of the delegates. The upshot was the acceptance of a text which leaves the task of determining the location of the permanent headquarters to the Health Assembly "after consultation with the United Nations" (Art. 43).

Prior to the first session of the Health Assembly, the Interim Commission is instructed to make studies of possible sites and to submit recommendations thereon to the Assembly. During the second session of the Interim Commission in Geneva (November 1946), the conflict of views as to site broke out afresh. Then the point at issue was the location of *interim* headquarters. The problem was temporarily resolved by the adoption of a resolution (1) which took "note of the establishment of a headquarters office in New York capable of assuring indispensable liaison with the United Nations and the fulfilment of other functions of the Interim Commission," but (2) which authorized "the Executive Secretary to set up an office in Geneva to facilitate the activities" of the Commission. Administratively this was not an entirely happy solution: New York is the nominal headquarters but most of the Commission's work is being performed on the other side of the Atlantic.

The final point calling for comment concerns a provision in the Arrangement setting up the Interim Commission. Article 1 (c) of this instrument prescribes that any agreement (or agreements) negotiated with the UN, while providing for "effective coördination between the two organizations in pursuit of their common purposes," shall "at the same time recognize the autonomy of the Health Organization within the field of its competence as defined in its Constitution." Here again may be noted a persistent desire that the functional independence of the new agency should not be jeopardized—a desire likely to be asserted with considerable force when the UN–WHO negotiations actually get under way.[26]

* * *

[26] It should be noted, in passing, that until WHO itself comes into being the preparatory work is being financed from sums advanced by the Secretary-General of UN from his Working Capital Fund. The General Assembly, on 14 December 1946, approved a recommendation from the Economic and Social Council that a sum not exceeding $1,300,000 be lent to the Interim Commission to meet its budgetary needs for 1946–47,

It would be premature to attempt to make here any final appraisal of the accomplishments of the International Health Conference of 1946 —let alone hazard a prediction as to the long-range prospects for WHO. Suffice it to say that, given a world politically at peace, an orderly coördination of coöperative efforts in the international health field now becomes possible. The unfortunate confusion of jurisdiction and responsibility among separate agencies which handicapped inter-governmental health work during the inter-war period will no longer exist. The new "Magna Carta" of health, if it receives sustained and generous support from the major countries of the world, and if it succeeds in escaping the curse of bureaucratic timidity, should afford a powerful impetus for progress in man's unceasing struggle against disease, stunted growth, and social maladjustment.

---

on condition that the amount actually spent will be repaid to the United Nations within two years after WHO comes into being. Preliminary estimates for 1948, approved by the Interim Commission in April 1947 "as the best available index to the possible cost" of financing the permanent Organization during its initial year, call for an expenditure budget of $4,800,000, of which $1,175,000, however, would be earmarked for repayment of a portion of the UN loan and the first instalment of a working capital fund. The World Health Assembly will in no way be legally bound to accept these estimates.

[4]

WORLD HEALTH AND WORLD POLITICS

CHARLES E. ALLEN

The nations of the modern world community have been working together on international health problems for a century and a half. They have collaborated because they have realized that disease does not respect national boundaries. In doing so, these states have learned that their self-interests are best served by world-wide collective action to eradicate communicable disease and to promote positive health conditions everywhere.

International health collaboration became necessary as the result of the increased volume, range and speed of trade and travel. Early in the nineteenth century, many European governments invoked quarantine measures at their home ports as a protection against ship-borne cholera and plague epidemics from the East. However, such unilateral measures soon proved so inefficient and detrimental to commerce that the major European nations were forced to work together to solve their mutual health problems within the framework of expanding trade relations.

These states found it necessary to cooperate in a two-fold manner: by establishing collective sanitary councils at strategic points on the shipping routes from the East, and by periodic general conferences for the formulation of international sanitary regulations. The sanitary councils at Tangier and Alexandria were effective in instigating and supervising port quarantine and health measures, but the work of the Constantinople and Teheran councils was seriously hampered by Anglo-German rivalry in the Near East. These localized arrangements were not adequately supplemented by international sanitary regulations inasmuch as the eleven health conferences held between 1851 and 1903 produced only fragmentary and modest regulations without provision for their continued administration and enforcement.

Even so, it is significant that such rudimentary forms of international health collaboration as the sanitary council and the general conference preceded the creation of public health services within nations and the discovery of the specific causes of disease. These latter developments, which took place during the last third of the nineteenth century, lent new impetus to the growth of international health collaboration. The gradual establishment of national health offices furthered the recognition of health as an

CHARLES E. ALLEN is a research assistant at the Hoover Institute and Library on War, Revolution and Peace, assisting Dr. C. Easton Rothwell in the preparation of a forthcoming book entitled *International Organization and World Politics*. This article, in expanded form, will serve as one of the case studies in this book.

28 INTERNATIONAL ORGANIZATION

important aspect of public welfare, and provided functional channels for the more effective formulation and implementation of international sanitary measures. The discoveries of the precise causes of disease by Pasteur and Koch, followed by rapid progress in bacteriology, provided the knowledge with which to attack disease at its source.

These three main factors — transportation, national health services and medical knowledge — provided both the need and the means for effective international health work. The need for such work became steadily more acute during the latter part of the nineteenth century as faster ships reduced travel time between continents below the incubation period of many communicable diseases, and made it imperative to suppress such disease at its source. Under these conditions, maximum national protection required the development of effective public health services in all countries and the coordination of their activities through international institutions. Thus, the pressure of necessity, reinforced by advances in preventive and curative medicine and in domestic public health organization, finally persuaded nations to move beyond the previous localized and *ad hoc* arrangements to the creation of permanent international health organizations.

The first such organization emerged in the Western Hemisphere where the Pan-American Sanitary Bureau was established in 1902. Seven years later, the first universal health organization, the International Office of Public Health, was brought into existence. Since then, international efforts to improve world health have been carried forward almost entirely through regional and universal organizations. When the League of Nations was established, the promotion of world health was explicitly recognized as essential to universal well-being. This led to the creation of the League Health Organization, which was partially coordinated with both the International Office of Public Health and the Pan American Sanitary Bureau. Notwithstanding the positive accomplishments of these three agencies, their separate operations produced a confusion of jurisdiction and responsibility that made it necessary to bring all international health work under the aegis of a single world-wide organization. Consequently, in 1946 the nations agreed to establish the World Health Organization to supersede or integrate all existing international health agencies.

II

Development of International Health Organizations

In the course of development through forty years, international health organizations have been assigned greatly expanded functional responsibilities by the member states and have been granted moderate increases of authority. This growth of responsibility and authority has been, on the whole, gradual and progressive although sharp advances occurred with the creation of new health organizations after the two world wars.

The International Office of Public Health served initially as a clearing-house through which its member nations could exchange information about the presence and spread of disease. Its functional responsibilities increased rapidly as states employed the IOPH as the medium for formulating recommendations for the revision and expansion of international sanitary conventions, and for the study of many health factors not previously considered to be of international concern. However, the IOPH acquired only modest authority with which to carry out its responsibilities. Through the 1926 Sanitary Convention, 39 states accepted the compulsory reporting of cases of communicable disease to the IOPH. In the 1938 Convention certain nations went further by agreeing to recognize the Permanent Committee of the IOPH as the technical advisory board on all sanitary conventions, and by undertaking to consult the Committee immediately whenever difficulties arose concerning the 1938 Convention. Either because of indifference or fear of interference with national prerogatives, this provision was not accepted by enough states to become generally operative. Thus, the IOPH functioned until 1946 without acquiring any significant authority to facilitate its work.

The general spirit of internationalism in the 1920's, coupled with the pioneer accomplishments of the IOPH, persuaded nations to assign to the League Health Organization broader responsibilities on "matters of international concern for the prevention and control of disease." The Health Organization's activities ranged widely over the fields of medicine, sanitation, scientific coordination and medical education. It furthered the work initiated by the IOPH in many ways, including the development of a permanent and effective epidemiological intelligence system which eventually covered areas with eighty percent of the world's population.

In addition, the Health Organization assumed responsibilities in many new fields, the most significant being, perhaps, its direct assistance to governments whose own health services were incapable of meeting difficult domestic disease problems. As a result of requests from Greece in 1928 and from China in 1929, the Health Organization assisted these governments in reorganizing their public health services. These activities marked the extension of international responsibility from quarantine to the strengthening of undeveloped national health services as the means for attacking disease within its country of origin. During its later years, the Health Organization pioneered the application of preventive health measures to such related matters as nutrition, housing and even health insurance.

The Health Organization assumed these broadened and diversified responsibilities without a commensurate increase of powers. The Health Or-

30   INTERNATIONAL ORGANIZATION

ganization, as one of the League's technical advisory bodies, could not take
direct action without the approval of the League Council. Nevertheless, it
enjoyed considerable freedom of action because both the Council and the
Assembly lacked the time and the specialized knowledge to supervise
health work closely. Even so, states reacted quickly whenever the Health
Organization's work touched on national sensitivities. In 1933 the British
delegate in the Council criticized Health Organization studies on the most
suitable methods for safeguarding public health in particular countries
during the depression because his government considered such matters to
be the exclusive responsibility of the nation concerned. And Japan complained, without effect, that the League's considerable health assistance to
China after 1937 exceeded the proper jurisdiction of that organization.

An extraordinary advance in the evolution of international health institutions was achieved in 1946 with the founding of the World Health Organization, whose responsibilities and powers far exceed those of its predecessors. The WHO Constitution represents the broadest and most liberal
concept of international responsibility for health ever officially promulgated. The progressive spirit of this Constitution finds expression in its
positive definition of health as a "state of complete physical, mental, and
social well-being" in a total world environment, rather than in the traditionally negative sense of the mere absence of disease.

Specifically, WHO is charged with responsibility for promoting: 1) maternal and child health and welfare; 2) mental health; 3) improved nutritional, sanitary, recreational, economic, living and working conditions; and
4) prevention of accidental injuries. WHO is also to study and report on
improved administrative and social techniques affecting public health and
medical care from preventive and curative points of view, including hospital services and social security. Within this broad scope, WHO is concentrating upon three critical diseases — malaria, tuberculosis and venereal
disease — for which new control methods are available, as well as upon
three general problems — maternal and child health, nutrition and environmental sanitation. Part of this program will involve an integrated attack
on the major health problems of selected "demonstration" areas. WHO
also has set up a $10 million supplemental budget for assisting underde-
veloped areas to master their health problems as its part of an over-all
United Nations program of technical assistance for the economic development of such areas. Moreover, WHO will initiate the first international
action in the field of mental health by gathering data from three population groups: rural communities, industrial units and university students.
In addition to all these programs, WHO has reactivated and extended the
many services of its predecessor organizations, and has provided valuable

direct assistance to more than twenty countries, notably Greece, China and Egypt.

Although WHO has no formal authority to bind its member nations, it has been granted considerably greater operational autonomy and quasi-legislative powers than its predecessors possessed. Its general policy-determining body, the World Health Assembly, is empowered to adopt conventions and agreements by two-thirds majority, and to adopt recommendations and technical regulations by a simple majority. The Health Assembly was given such powers because the earlier methods for concluding sanitary conventions, which necessitated action through both the IOPH and *ad hoc* conferences, had proved cumbersome and ineffective. In addition, ratifications of the five principal sanitary conventions concluded during the past 30 years had been so fragmentary that all states faced a bewildering variety of obligations toward others and many nations, including some in key locations on trade routes, remained bound only by obsolete conventions. In order to improve this chaotic situation, procedures for ratification are strengthened under the WHO Constitution to obtain the maximum possible adherence to international health agreements. Each member nation is obligated either to accept or to reject new conventions within eighteen months after the date of their adoption by the Assembly. Technical regulations, which are usually less controversial than conventions, automatically come into force for all members except those which declare their rejection within a stated period. Further, all members are required to report annually to WHO on the progress achieved in improving the health of their peoples, including the action they have taken in respect to international agreements.

Viewed in retrospect, the growth of international health organizations that culminated in WHO is of two-fold significance. On the one hand, it provides tangible evidence that nations have found it mutually advantageous to extend their collaboration on world health in a systematic and regularized manner. This has led them to establish progressively stronger world organizations to deal with health problems and to vest in them increasingly broad responsibilities. On the other hand, this institutional development discloses that the member states have not granted to health organizations increased authority commensurate with their broadened responsibilities. Notwithstanding their recognition that collective action is essential to combat and prevent disease, the nations of the world community have not been willing to yield enough power of decision to make any international health organization more than a purely collaborative agency. Consequently, these organizations have been seriously limited in their capacities to fulfill their assigned responsibilities. Since the nation state has remained the critical center of decision, the effectiveness of international health organizations has depended upon the extent to which the member states have been able to act together to achieve common health objectives which they regard as important to their respective national interests. In order to estimate the significance of international health organizations, therefore, it is essential to examine how individual countries have regarded these organizations and acted within them.

III

National Behavior in Health Organizations

The attitudes of individual nations toward health organizations and their behavior within them are not only a test of the significance and effectiveness of such organizations. They are also a mirror of the forces of world politics which affect the field of health, and of the manner in which these forces influence international health organizations. National attitudes and behavior can be estimated in terms of two major criteria: the extent and meaning of national participation in health organizations, including the willingness of member states to support these bodies financially; and the response of member nations on significant issues that have arisen within such organizations. These issues show what kinds of questions in the health field find common acceptance and what kinds evoke controversy based upon conflicts of national interest. They also provide critical tests of the ability of health organizations to withstand divisive forces and to exert a cohesive influence in the world community.

National Participation. Over the past century there has been a progressive growth in the number of nations that have participated in international conferences and organizations dealing with world health. This long-range trend, steady except for the interruptions of two world wars, can be measured in terms of the growth from the twelve states which attended the first health conference in 1851 to the 66 nations which have joined the World Health Organization. Most of this increase in national participation has taken place during the forty years that have elapsed since the founding of the IOPH.

In 1909, the International Office of Public Health began operations with eighteen members. By 1946 its membership had grown to a total of some forty-seven sovereign states and twenty-five dependencies. No comparable measurement can be made for the League Health Organization because its organs were composed of individual experts serving on behalf of the entire League membership, and of individuals drawn from the IOPH. However, the World Health Organization, with a clearly identifiable membership of its own, has acheived the largest national participation in the history of health institutions.

This growth has brought a corresponding extension of the geographic area represented in health organizations. Even so, a high degree of universality has been attained only recently. Participation in health gatherings from 1851 until the 1930's was predominantly European, and other states contiguous to Europe generally participated earlier and more continuously than those in more distant areas. The most indifferent states have been the Latin American Republics which placed primary reliance upon regional rather than universal health organizations until 1946, and subsequently resisted complete assimilation into the World Health Organization.

The growth of national participation clearly indicates a vastly increased interest in international collaboration on health matters. At the same time, this participation has reflected some of the political and ideological forces at work in the world. These forces have affected national participation most strongly in the case of those states which have repudiated institutionalized health collaboration either by their refusal to join or by their withdrawal from health organizations. Sometimes repudiation has been motivated by comparatively minor elements such as the pique which apparently lay behind German and Austrian refusal to join the IOPH in the beginning because its headquarters were located in Paris rather than in Central Europe. More frequently, repudiation has resulted from major political and ideological cleavages in the world community. Such cleavages led to the withdrawal of the Axis Powers from the League and the consequent termination of their relations with its Health Committee; to the reluctance to bring Spain into WHO, a reflection of the general United Nations ban against granting the Franco Government membership in any of its agencies; and to the recent Soviet withdrawal from WHO.

These examples demonstrate one way in which a broad willingness to work together for world health has been weakened by extraneous political factors, especially during periods of severe international tension. The total picture suggests, nevertheless, that the common will to deal with health on an international scale has been strong enough to resist and survive many of these tensions. It is significant that even those nations which eventually repudiated international health organizations had been willing to collaborate on health questions earlier and with more persistence than on other matters infested with greater political content. For instance, a German national was coopted to serve on the League Health Committee in 1921, five years before Germany became a member of the League. Despite its earlier pique, Germany joined the IOPH in 1928. Similarly, Russia's initial membership in the IOPH, which had terminated with the Bolshevik Revolution, was

34   INTERNATIONAL ORGANIZATION

renewed in 1926, eight years before Soviet participation in the League.
Perhaps of more significance was Japan's continued relationship with the
League's Health Committee until January 1939, six years after that
country had decided to withdraw from the League's political agencies.
Even after terminating relations with the League's central health body,
Japan continued to supply epidemiological information to the Eastern
Bureau of the Health Organization.

More important is the fact that the great majority of the nations of the
world community have maintained uninterrupted membership in international health organizations. Although the political controversies that have
arisen in health organizations have not affected vital interests of these
states, their continued membership also indicates that most nations have
been willing to compose their short-run differences in order to attain the
long-run advantages of regularized collaboration on health matters. Thus,
most of the dissentions arising from world politics have proved to be con-
tainable within international health institutions.

The influence of political forces within health organizations has been
manifested, among other ways, through the prerogatives which various
categories of states have enjoyed in these organizations. The great powers
of every period have received *de facto* permanent representation on important committees, although efforts to formalize this practice have been
thwarted on the ground that all states have an equal interest in world
health. Until recently, non-self-governing territories have had no direct
representation, inasmuch as the administering nations were regarded as
the sole spokesmen for their native subjects. The category of "associate
membership" in WHO was created for such territories, despite opposition
from the colonial powers, as a result of pressure from newly emergent
states and from other nations which believed that native peoples should
be allowed to speak for themselves on their own health problems.

The significance of national participation is further disclosed by the obligations which member states have been willing to assume toward the
financial support of health organizations. Although these nations have
increased the amount of their contributions, particularly in recent years,
financing has not kept pace with the more rapid extension of functional
responsibilities which they have assigned to health bodies. In other words,
the member nations have been unwilling to pay for the effective execution
of more than a portion of the work they have thrust upon the organizations. This deficiency was most serious in the League Health Organization, whose stabilized budget of one million Swiss francs (approximately
$190,000) was so inadequate that an important part of its work could not
have been undertaken without generous grants of nearly $145,000 an-

WORLD HEALTH AND WORLD POLITICS 35

nually by the Rockefeller Foundation. WHO has been much better endowed than its predecessors. Its 1949 budget of $5 million and 1950 budget of $7.5 million make possible a much broader and more effective world health program than in the past. Even these budgets, however, are generally recognized as inadequate to the maximum performance of WHO's essential functions.

This general unwillingness of member states to provide adequate funds to health organizations has assumed damaging proportions in the case of the wealthy nations which bear the major burden of financial support and therefore exert a critical influence on organization budgets. The largest contributors — United Kingdom in the League and the United States in WHO — have not been willing to take the lead in providing either organization with enough money to do the work expected of it. For example, the maximum annual United States contribution to WHO for the indefinite future has been fixed by the Congress at $1,920,000, which just meets the American quota contribution for 1949. The United States objected unsuccessfully to the increased 1950 budget of $7.5 million, which cannot be met unless some way is found for circumventing the restriction imposed by the Congress. Far from recognizing this need, however, the United States sought a 25 per cent reduction in its quota of 39.89 per cent of the total WHO budget. Although other members have opposed such reduction, the 1949 Health Assembly scaled down the United States contribution to 36 per cent with provision for its further reduction to 33 1/3 per cent as world economic conditions permit.

In summary, it may be said that national participation in international health organizations has increased through forty years until it verges upon universality. With this broadened representation from among the states of the world community there has developed a common desire to deal with an ever-wider range of health activities. The common will or consensus to carry out this desire has, on the other hand, been seriously limited in two directions. In the first place, the member states have thus far been unwilling to transfer to the organizations sufficient authority or enough funds to enable them to carry out their growing functions. And in the second place, some states have been willing to put political or ideological considerations above concern for health in deciding the question of their own membership or that of other political units. Despite these limitations, the common will to meet world health problems has become strong enough to withstand and even to modify at times some of the forces of world politics. Further tests of this interaction will be found in a more thorough examination of the response of member nations on critical issues within international health organizations.

36   INTERNATIONAL ORGANIZATION

Issues of World Politics. The international health organizations that
preceded WHO may have been somewhat less affected by issues originating from the general pattern of world politics. The comparatively shel-
tered existence of the IOPH and the League Health Organization was
largely due to the non-political character of their work which seldom extended beyond purely technical health matters. However, the broadened
concept of world health which WHO has adopted, and the increased
range and capacities of that Organization have projected world health
into the arena of world politics at a number of points. The resulting issues
which have arisen within WHO and within previous health organizations
will, for convenience, be treated as issues involving primarily organizational, economic and ideological factors.

Organizational Issues. The most important organizational issues have
arisen in connection with long-standing efforts to bring all international
health work within a single universal institution. Such efforts were
thwarted in the early 1920's by the United States, which refused to permit
the IOPH to become the League of Nations' health agency because such
a move would have brought the United States into formal relationship
with the League. The changed American attitude toward international
organization, coupled with greater need for unified world health work,
brought general agreement at the International Health Conference of
1946 for the integration of all existing organizations with WHO. Provisions for the dissolution of the two previous universal organizations, the
IOPH and the League Health Organization, were quickly formulated.
However, serious difficulties arose over the role of regional organizations
within the WHO system. The most significant issue concerned the future
status of the 44-year old Pan American Sanitary Organization, whose
member nations generally opposed its subordination to WHO. This opposition reflected the same intense regional loyalty of the Latin American
states which previously had complicated the problem of inter-relating the
inter-American system with the United Nations system on political and
security matters.

At the Health Conference, the United States, the Latin American Republics and the Arab states (who had just formed their own regional health
bureau) favored a loose federal relationship in which such regional organizations as the PASO would exercise considerable operational autonomy.
Other states pressed for a degree of centralization that would give WHO
clear authority over regional health agencies, and the Soviet bloc even
urged the complete absorption of such agencies into WHO. These divergent views were finally accommodated within a broadly-worded compromise which provided for the integration of regional agencies, such as the
PASO, with WHO as soon as practicable (Article 54 of the WHO Consti-

WORLD HEALTH AND WORLD POLITICS 37

tution). Integration in this sense was understood to mean that the regional branches of WHO would be subject to the general authority of the central organization while retaining considerable freedom of action on exclusively regional health matters.

Subsequent negotiations between WHO and PASO authorities disclosed that most of the Latin American states were unwilling to effectuate any such integration. The Health Declaration of Havana in October 1946, strongly implied that the Latin American states should withhold their ratifications to the WHO Constitution until assured of a substantial measure of independence for their regional organization. This attitude evoked sharp criticism from many nations, particularly the United States which reaffirmed its full support of Article 54 and emphasized its intention to work vigorously for the unqualified acceptance of that integration formula. Nevertheless, in the 20-month period which elapsed between the signing of the Constitution and its entry into force in April 1948, only two of the 20 Latin American Republics (Haiti and Mexico) had ratified. This extremely low ratio of acceptances suggests that many Latin American states retained their traditional conviction about the superior advantages of regional over universal health organization, and it may indicate that ratifications were withheld in hopes of forcing more favorable terms for the PASO as the price of Latin American participation in WHO.

Nevertheless, most other nations continued to insist strongly upon a meaningful degree of PASO integration with WHO. Such insistence, coupled with patient and skillful negotiation, finally produced an initial working agreement between WHO and PASO in October 1948. This agreement, which became effective in May 1949 after the fourteenth PASO member ratified the WHO Constitution, represents a considerable retreat by the Latin American bloc. It requires that the PASO function as a regional office in conformity with the policies and procedures established by WHO. The progress thus made toward final integration has been most encouraging.

Economic Issues. International health organizations have been affected by very few issues of a clearly economic character, as distinguished from the previously discussed matter of financial support. One of these distinctive economic issues arose during the formulation of the WHO Constitution. The United States had proposed that the Health Assembly be empowered to adopt regulations to prevent member states from importing biologic, pharmaceutical and similar products which did not conform to standards established by the Assembly. However, the Soviet Union and certain Latin American countries argued that this provision would serve to protect the few highly industrialized states to the disadvantage of the many nations with infant drug industries. Because these objections might have increased the simple majority requirement for adoption of technical regulations, the United States proposal was withdrawn.

Ideological Issues. The most numerous and most serious issues of world politics affecting health organizations have been those of an essentially ideological character. These issues have varied greatly in potency, ranging from mild and easily resolvable differences to irreconcilable conflicts between widely divergent ideological beliefs.

The most significant ideological issue of the League period arose in 1932 over a Health Committee report on maternal welfare and infant hygiene. This report was sharply criticized in the League Assembly for its recommendation that contraceptives be used to prevent pregnancy in such cases of ill-health as tuberculosis and diseases of the kidney and heart. A number of nations, particularly those with strong Catholic populations, insisted that the report be revised because it offended religious beliefs and moral and legal principles. The report was subsequently modified.

A somewhat similar issue arose during the Health Conference of 1946 over the question of WHO's responsibilities in the controversial field of health insurance. Although there was general agreement on the desirability of improving medical care for low income groups, some nations and particularly the United States strongly opposed WHO involvement in "socialized" medicine. The American delegation, conscious of the strongly held attitudes at home, urged that the question of health insurance should be left to the exclusive jurisdiction of the International Labor Organization. However, many other states, notably the European and Scandinavian countries with national health insurance programs, argued that health and social security were so interrelated that WHO should promote such matters. A compromise was reached by providing that WHO's role on social security matters would be confined to fact-finding, analysis and reporting in collaboration with other interested agencies. Even this degree of attention to such matters disturbed segments of American opinion and evidently contributed to the two-year delay in United States ratification of the WHO Constitution. Further, the United States, in ratifying, reserved the right to withdraw on a one-year notice, and provided that nothing in the WHO Constitution would in any manner commit this country to enact any specific legislative program. Although Article 81 of the WHO Constitution does not admit of reservations on ratification, the member nations of the first World Health Assembly unanimously approved the admission of the United States to WHO in July 1948. Many states praised American contributions to the advancement of public health, and presumably were aware that the United States would provide nearly forty per cent of the total funds of WHO.

WORLD HEALTH AND WORLD POLITICS 39

More significant than this assertion of primarily American interests have been two recent issues upon which most of the member states lined up in accordance with the prevailing ideological divisions of the world community. One of these was the issue of "associate membership" in WHO for non-self-governing territories. At the Health Conference of 1946, China led the large group of nations which favored granting such territories membership with all rights and privileges except voting and office-holding. This was sharply opposed by a group of states led by the colonial powers (United Kingdom, France, New Zealand, South Africa, etc.) which advocated that participation by such territories be confined to regional branches of WHO. However, the Conference finally approved the principle of associate membership at the central level, and also adopted, over British opposition, a Liberian proposal that associate members be represented by natives instead of foreign officials. The Soviet Union then attempted unsuccessfully to secure for associate members explicit rights of full discussion on health matters within their own territories. This later became implicit as associate members were given rights of participation in the Health Assembly and regional bodies, except that they cannot vote or hold office in major organs or committees dealing with financial and constitutional matters.

Ideological forces were manifested more acutely when the shadow of Franco Spain was cast upon the debate over admission into WHO. At the 1946 Health Conference, the injection of the Spanish matter transformed the relatively innocuous constitutional question of how new members should be admitted to WHO into a serious ideological issue. This issue split the Conference into two highly contentious groups of nations which reflected the basic ideological cleavage existing in the world community on the Spanish question.

The twenty Latin American Republics, with strong sympathies for Spain, led the group advocating that new members be admitted by a simple majority decision of the Health Assembly. It was clear that such a lenient rule would greatly facilitate future Spanish admission to WHO. However, this proposal was opposed by the other group, led by the Soviet bloc, which urged establishment of a two-thirds majority rule. This more stringent requirement would, in effect, provide the anti-Franco states with a collective veto over future Spanish admission. The Latin American bloc picked up some support from states which considered the principle of universality more important that the specific issue of Spain. For example, Canada, despite its dislike for Franco Spain, espoused the simple majority proposal on the grounds that the exclusion from WHO of any country, regardless of its political attitude, would seriously weaken the world-wide defenses against disease. Such appeals for universality, however, made little impression upon nations which considered Franco Spain an undesirable partner in any international enterprise, either for pure ideological reasons or because of reluctance to revise the existing position of the United Nations.

The intensity of feeling on both sides forced the issue to a roll call vote, a necessity which has seldom occurred in international health organizations. By an extremely narrow margin, 25 to 22, the Conference adopted the simple majority provision. The voting alignment graphically depicted the sharp crystallization of opinion on this issue. The majority was composed of 19 of the 20 Latin American Republics (Argentina was absent); four of the six Arab member nations (Lebanon abstained, Iran voted negative); plus Canada and the Philippines. The minority group included all seven European member states; all six Soviet bloc member nations; five of the six British Commonwealth member states; plus the United States, Ethiopia, Liberia and Iran. Four of the five great powers (China abstained) were in the minority group. This victory, however, has not been followed by efforts to secure Spain's admission to WHO, largely because of the General Assembly's subsequent recommendation that the Franco Government be debarred from membership in any United Nations agency.

Far more portentous than any of the previously discussed episodes was the joint withdrawal of the three Soviet Republics from WHO on February 16, 1949. All three states — the USSR, Byelorussian SSR and Ukrainian SSR — said that WHO's work on the control of disease and the dissemination of medical knowledge was unsatisfactory and not worth the expense of continued membership. However, the evidence indicates that the Soviet decision to withdraw was probably not due to health and organizational factors as alleged, but was almost certainly the result of political considerations.

Historically, the Soviet Government began to cooperate with other states on health matters because it needed outside aid to combat the serious epidemics raging in a Russia torn by war and revolution. Consequently, the USSR participated in the Warsaw Health Conference of 1922, and cooperated with the League of Nations' special Epidemic Commission and later with its Health Committee. At the same time, the Soviet Union was proclaiming its hostility to the League as an alliance of capitalist states against the USSR. This apparent inconsistency was justified by the USSR on the grounds that the Health Committee dealt with humanitarian and not political questions.

By joining the IOPH in 1926, the Soviet Union indicated its recognition of the general advantages of collaboration on health matters even through an agency which could not supply material aid to the Soviet health serv-

WORLD HEALTH AND WORLD POLITICS 41

ices. After the USSR was admitted to the League in 1934, a Soviet national served on the Health Committee until Soviet expulsion from the League in December 1939. During its period of membership in both of these health organizations, the Soviet Union behaved in a generally cooperative manner.

Soviet representatives displayed the same cooperative spirit during the first two years of WHO by working side-by-side with other members in a number of cases and even commending the organization's performance. The Russian attitude changed abruptly at the first Health Assembly in June 1948 where the Soviet bloc unleashed a storm of savage criticism at WHO. The catalog of charges and inferences is too long to be reproduced here, but their general nature was strikingly similar to the Russian line in the political organs of the United Nations. In the Health Assembly, the USSR and its supporters simply used the subject of health as a vehicle for political attacks on the west and for propagandizing their own political and ideological beliefs.

In the Soviet view, WHO's work had been deficient in many respects. WHO had failed to give sufficient aid to the war-devastated countries — namely Poland, Yugoslavia, Byelorussia and the Ukraine — which had received only $303,000 out of the total fund of $1,250,000 in 1947. Moreover, WHO had wasted large sums on its subordinate bodies instead of generously providing grants and medical supplies unconditionally to national health services. The Soviet bloc made clear that it wanted more goods and money, and less advice.

The main theme of Soviet criticism was that WHO's work was superficial because it had neglected the root causes of disease. These causes, the Soviets explained, lay in the social and economic structure of various countries. In colonial areas, epidemics were caused by the poverty that resulted from imperialist exploitation. In more industrialized countries, disease problems were the natural outgrowth of capitalism. For example, venereal disease was traceable to basic social ills like prostitution which, in turn, resulted from such factors as unemployment and the unequal status of women. The USSR claimed success in coping with such problems because its health services were organized to provide adequate medical care to the entire population on an equal footing, irrespective of social or financial position. Hence, the USSR considered that WHO could achieve its aims only by promoting the gradual nationalization of health services, on the basis of the nationalization of important industries, after the Soviet model. Throughout this argument, the Soviet bloc implied that all these deficiencies resulted from the domination of WHO by the western nations, particularly the United States.

Despite these assertions, the real reasons for the subsequent Russian

42 INTERNATIONAL ORGANIZATION

withdrawal from WHO remain obscure. The abrupt reversal of Soviet attitude, signalized by its acrimonious attacks of an ideological and partisan nature, strongly suggests that the Russian decision was inspired more by political motives than by dissatisfaction with the work of WHO. Whatever the precise motivation, it is significant that the Russians chose to explain their withdrawal by specifically denying the worth of WHO's collective action against disease. This marked the first time that any state has repudiated world health collaboration by directly renouncing the fundamental concepts upon which such collaboration has been built. By its recent attitude, the Soviet Union has deprecated the value of combatting disease through collective efforts on both the medical and social levels in a world where capitalist institutions continue to prevail. By its withdrawal from WHO, the USSR has, in effect, disavowed the idea of world health in favor of an exclusive concern for health matters within its own sphere — a deliberate and anachronistic attempt to achieve isolationism in health. This behavior by one of the two most powerful states in the present world constitutes the most serious challenge to international collaboration for health since its inception.

The Soviet satellites have threatened periodically to follow the Russians out of WHO unless the organization provides them with considerable quantities of needed medical supplies. They have charged that the United States is deliberately withholding technical information about the manufacture of penicillin and other antibiotics and thereby causing numerous deaths in the "new democracies." Nevertheless, these states are continuing in membership probably because their tangible benefits in aid and supplies from WHO greatly exceed their quota contributions to the organization.

IV

The Significance of International Health Organization

Virtually all nations have come to recognize that health problems must be dealt with on a world scale through a permanent and universal organization. They have demonstrated this by accepting the obligations of membership in WHO and by assigning it global responsibilities for the eradication of major diseases and for the positive promotion of health. WHO and its predecessors have proved their capacity to foster world health in many ways, including epidemiological intelligence and biological standardization. The usefulness of international health organizations in combatting disease has been dramatically illustrated by WHO's recent assistance in the suppression of malaria in Greece and the effective control of a cholera epidemic in Egypt. Beyond these tangible accomplishments, health organizations have rendered invaluable service by raising the standards of public health and preventive medicine throughout the world. The demonstrated value of world health work has, in fact, become so important to most nations that they have been willing to subordinate their particular national, regional or ideological interests in order to carry it forward.

Despite these advances, the World Health Organization has not developed beyond the embryonic stage as a world institution. Like other international bodies, it has not surmounted the barrier of state-centered decision-making (national sovereignty), and its powers and finances remain inadequate to the maximum performance of its tasks. Moreover, the broad consensus of agreement among nations, which must be attained for fully effective world health work, is vulnerable to those deep political and ideological cleavages that affect the whole range of international relations. Cleavages of this character and magnitude have twice impaired world health efforts by precipitating the withdrawal of the Axis powers from the League and of the Soviet Union from WHO. It is to be anticipated that future political rifts among the major centers of world power will likewise hamper collaborative efforts to improve health.

Even though formal cooperation on health continues to be susceptible to the forces of world politics, the practical necessity of world-wide cooperation becomes more imperative with every advance in technology. This compulsion limits the freedom of action of nations which, for political or ideological reasons, refuse to participate in international health organizations. Germany, Japan and the USSR found it necessary to engage in limited and informal cooperation on health matters even when they were non-members of the League of Nations. It is probable that the Soviet Union will be driven to the same course in the more interdependent world of the present day.

The sheer need to cooperate will probably continue to nourish the growth of world health institutions. This growth will be conditioned, perhaps critically, by the climate of world politics. Unless the political climate worsens drastically, however, the World Health Organization will be able to contribute much to human well-being and, by its example, may stimulate effective international cooperation in other fields. In these ways, WHO can contribute, however modestly, to the eventual strengthening of world order.

[5]

The Return of Infectious Disease

Laurie Garrett

SINCE WORLD WAR II, public health strategy has focused on the eradication of microbes. Using powerful medical weaponry developed during the postwar period—antibiotics, antimalarials, and vaccines—political and scientific leaders in the United States and around the world pursued a military-style campaign to obliterate viral, bacterial, and parasitic enemies. The goal was nothing less than pushing humanity through what was termed the "health transition," leaving the age of infectious disease permanently behind. By the turn of the century, it was thought, most of the world's population would live long lives ended only by the "chronics"—cancer, heart disease, and Alzheimer's.

The optimism culminated in 1978 when the member states of the United Nations signed the "Health for All, 2000" accord. The agreement set ambitious goals for the eradication of disease, predicting that even the poorest nations would undergo a health transition before the millennium, with life expectancies rising markedly. It was certainly reasonable in 1978 to take a rosy view of Homo sapiens' ancient struggle with the microbes; antibiotics, pesticides, chloroquine and other powerful antimicrobials, vaccines, and striking improvements in water treatment and food preparation technologies had provided what seemed an imposing armamentarium. The year before, the World

LAURIE GARRETT is the author of *The Coming Plague: Newly Emerging Diseases in a World Out of Balance*. She is a medical and science reporter for *Newsday*.

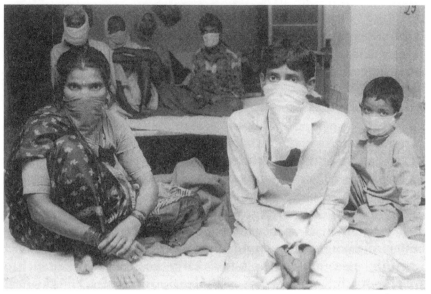

Suspected carriers of plague virus in a New Delhi hospital, October 1994.

Health Organization (WHO) had announced that the last known case of smallpox had been tracked down in Ethiopia and cured.

The grandiose optimism rested on two false assumptions: that microbes were biologically stationary targets and that diseases could be geographically sequestered. Each contributed to the smug sense of immunity from infectious diseases that characterized health professionals in North America and Europe.

Anything but stationary, microbes and the insects, rodents, and other animals that transmit them are in a constant state of biological flux and evolution. Darwin noted that certain genetic mutations allow plants and animals to better adapt to environmental conditions and so produce more offspring; this process of natural selection, he argued, was the mechanism of evolution. Less than a decade after the U.S. military first supplied penicillin to its field physicians in the Pacific theater, geneticist Joshua Lederberg demonstrated that natural selection was operating in the bacterial world. Strains of staphylococcus and streptococcus that happened to carry genes for resistance to the drugs arose and flourished where drug-susceptible strains had been driven out. Use of antibiotics was selecting for ever-more-resistant bugs.

Laurie Garrett

More recently scientists have witnessed an alarming mechanism of microbial adaptation and change—one less dependent on random inherited genetic advantage. The genetic blueprints of some microbes contain DNA and RNA codes that command mutation under stress, offer escapes from antibiotics and other drugs, marshal collective behaviors conducive to group survival, and allow the microbes and their progeny to scour their environments for potentially useful genetic material. Such material is present in stable rings or pieces of DNA and RNA, known as plasmids and transposons, that move freely among microorganisms, even jumping between species of bacteria, fungi, and parasites. Some plasmids carry the genes for resistance to five or more different families of antibiotics, or dozens of individual drugs. Others confer greater powers of infectivity, virulence, resistance to disinfectants or chlorine, even such subtly important characteristics as the ability to tolerate higher temperatures or more acidic conditions. Microbes have appeared that can grow on a bar of soap, swim unabashed in bleach, and ignore doses of penicillin logarithmically larger than those effective in 1950.

> Medicine thought it had beaten infectious disease, until the AIDS epidemic broke out.

In the microbial soup, then, is a vast, constantly changing lending library of genetic material that offers humanity's minute predators myriad ways to outmaneuver the drug arsenal. And the arsenal, large as it might seem, is limited. In 1994 the Food and Drug Administration licensed only three new antimicrobial drugs, two of them for the treatment of AIDS and none an antibacterial. Research and development has ground to a near halt now that the easy approaches to killing viruses, bacteria, fungi, and parasites—those that mimic the ways competing microbes kill one another in their endless tiny battles throughout the human gastrointestinal tract—have been exploited. Researchers have run out of ideas for countering many microbial scourges, and the lack of profitability has stifled the development of drugs to combat organisms that are currently found predominantly in poor countries. "The pipeline is dry. We really have a global crisis," James Hughes, director of the National Center for Infectious Diseases at the Centers for Disease Control and Prevention (CDC) in Atlanta, said recently.

The Return of Infectious Disease

DISEASES WITHOUT BORDERS

DURING THE 1960s, 1970s, and 1980s, the World Bank and the International Monetary Fund devised investment policies based on the assumption that economic modernization should come first and improved health would naturally follow. Today the World Bank recognizes that a nation in which more than ten percent of the working-age population is chronically ill cannot be expected to reach higher levels of development without investment in health infrastructure. Furthermore, the bank acknowledges that few societies spend health care dollars effectively for the poor, among whom the potential for the outbreak of infectious disease is greatest. Most of the achievements in infectious disease control have resulted from grand international efforts such as the expanded program for childhood immunization mounted by the U.N. Children's Emergency Fund and WHO's smallpox eradication drive. At the local level, particularly in politically unstable poor countries, few genuine successes can be cited.

Geographic sequestration was crucial in all postwar health planning, but diseases can no longer be expected to remain in their country or region of origin. Even before commercial air travel, swine flu in 1918-19 managed to circumnavigate the planet five times in 18 months, killing 22 million people, 500,000 in the United States. How many more victims could a similarly lethal strain of influenza claim in 1996, when some half a billion passengers will board airline flights?

Every day one million people cross an international border. One million a week travel between the industrial and developing worlds. And as people move, unwanted microbial hitchhikers tag along. In the nineteenth century most diseases and infections that travelers carried manifested themselves during the long sea voyages that were the primary means of covering great distances. Recognizing the symptoms, the authorities at ports of entry could quarantine contagious individuals or take other action. In the age of jet travel, however, a person incubating a disease such as Ebola can board a plane, travel 12,000 miles, pass unnoticed through customs and immigration, take a domestic carrier to a remote destination, and still not develop symptoms for several days, infecting many other people before his condition is noticeable.

Laurie Garrett

Surveillance at airports has proved grossly inadequate and is often biologically irrational, given that incubation periods for many incurable contagious diseases may exceed 21 days. And when a recent traveler's symptoms become apparent, days or weeks after his journey, the task of identifying fellow passengers, locating them, and bringing them to the authorities for medical examination is costly and sometimes impossible. The British and U.S. governments both spent millions of dollars in 1976 trying to track down 522 people exposed during a flight from Sierra Leone to Washington, D.C., to a Peace Corps volunteer infected with the Lassa virus, an organism that produces gruesome hemorrhagic disease in its victims. The U.S. government eventually tracked down 505 passengers, scattered over 21 states; British Airways and the British government located 95, some of whom were also on the U.S. list. None tested positive for the virus.

In the fall of 1994 the New York City Department of Health and the U.S. Immigration and Naturalization Service took steps to prevent plague-infected passengers from India from disembarking at New York's John F. Kennedy International Airport. All airport and federal personnel who had direct contact with passengers were trained to recognize symptoms of *Yersinia pestis* infection. Potential plague carriers were, if possible, to be identified while still on the tarmac, so fellow passengers could be examined. Of ten putative carriers identified in New York, only two were discovered at the airport; the majority had long since entered the community. Fortunately, none of the ten proved to have plague. Health authorities came away with the lesson that airport-based screening is expensive and does not work.

Humanity is on the move worldwide, fleeing impoverishment, religious and ethnic intolerance, and high-intensity localized warfare that targets civilians. People are abandoning their homes for new destinations on an unprecedented scale, both in terms of absolute numbers and as a percentage of population. In 1994 at least 110 million people immigrated, another 30 million moved from rural to urban areas within their own country, and 23 million more were displaced by war or social unrest, according to the U.N. High Commissioner for Refugees and the Worldwatch Institute. This human mobility affords microbes greatly increased opportunities for movement.

The Return of Infectious Disease

THE CITY AS VECTOR

POPULATION EXPANSION raises the statistical probability that pathogens will be transmitted, whether from person to person or vector—insect, rodent, or other—to person. Human density is rising rapidly worldwide. Seven countries now have overall population densities exceeding 2,000 people per square mile, and 43 have densities greater than 500 people per square mile. (The U.S. average, by contrast, is 74.)

High density need not doom a nation to epidemics and unusual outbreaks of disease if sewage and water systems, housing, and public health provisions are adequate. The Netherlands, for example, with 1,180 people per square mile, ranks among the top 20 countries for good health and life expectancy. But the areas in which density is increasing most are not those capable of providing such infrastructural support. They are, rather, the poorest on earth. Even countries with low overall density may have cities that have become focuses for extraordinary overpopulation, from the point of view of public health. Some of these urban agglomerations have only one toilet for every 750 or more people.

Most people on the move around the world come to burgeoning metropolises like India's Surat (where pneumonic plague struck in 1994) and Zaire's Kikwit (site of the 1995 Ebola epidemic) that offer few fundamental amenities. These new centers of urbanization typically lack sewage systems, paved roads, housing, safe drinking water, medical facilities, and schools adequate to serve even the most affluent residents. They are squalid sites of destitution where hundreds of thousands live much as they would in poor villages, yet so jammed together as to ensure astronomical transmission rates for airborne, waterborne, sexually transmitted, and contact-transmission microbes.

But such centers are often only staging areas for the waves of impoverished people that are drawn there. The next stop is a megacity with a population of ten million or more. In the nineteenth century only two cities on earth—London and New York—even approached that size. Five years from now there will be 24 megacities, most in poor developing countries: São Paulo, Calcutta, Bombay, Istanbul, Bangkok, Tehran, Jakarta, Cairo, Mexico City, Karachi, and the like. There the woes of cities like Surat are magnified many times

Laurie Garrett

over. Yet even the developing world's megacities are way stations for those who most aggressively seek a better life. All paths ultimately lead these people—and the microbes they may carry—to the United States, Canada, and Western Europe.

Urbanization and global migration propel radical changes in human behavior as well as in the ecological relationship between microbes and humans. Almost invariably in large cities, sex industries arise and multiple-partner sex becomes more common, prompting rapid increases in sexually transmitted diseases. Black market access to antimicrobials is greater in urban centers, leading to overuse or outright misuse of the precious drugs and the emergence of resistant bacteria and parasites. Intravenous drug abusers' practice of sharing syringes is a ready vehicle for the transmission of microbes. Underfunded urban health facilities often become unhygienic centers for the dissemination of disease rather than its control.

THE EMBLEMATIC NEW DISEASE

ALL THESE factors played out dramatically during the 1980s, allowing an obscure organism to amplify and spread to the point that WHO estimates it has infected a cumulative total of 30 million people and become endemic to every country in the world. Genetic studies of the human immunodeficiency virus that causes AIDS indicate that it is probably more than a century old, yet HIV infected perhaps less than .001 percent of the world population until the mid-1970s. Then the virus surged because of sweeping social changes: African urbanization; American and European intravenous drug use and homosexual bathhouse activity; the Uganda-Tanzania war of 1977-79, in which rape was used as a tool of ethnic cleansing; and the growth of the American blood products industry and the international marketing of its contaminated goods. Government denial and societal prejudice everywhere in the world led to inappropriate public health interventions or plain inaction, further abetting HIV transmission and slowing research for treatment or a cure.

The estimated direct (medical) and indirect (loss of productive labor force and family-impact) costs of the disease are expected to top $500 billion by the year 2000, according to the Global AIDS Policy

The Return of Infectious Disease

Coalition at Harvard University. The U.S. Agency for International Development predicts that by then some 11 percent of children under 15 in sub-Saharan Africa will be AIDS orphans, and that infant mortality will soar fivefold in some African and Asian nations, due to the loss of parental care among children orphaned by AIDS and its most common opportunistic infection, tuberculosis. Life expectancy in the African and Asian nations hit hardest by AIDS will plummet to an astonishing low of 25 years by 2010, the agency forecasts.

Medical experts now recognize that any microbe, including ones previously unknown to science, can take similar advantage of conditions in human society, going from isolated cases camouflaged by generally high levels of disease to become a global threat. Furthermore, old organisms, aided by mankind's misuse of disinfectants and drugs, can take on new, more lethal forms.

A White House–appointed interagency working group on emerging and reemerging infectious diseases estimates that at least 29 previously unknown diseases have appeared since 1973 and 20 well-known ones have reemerged, often in new drug-resistant or deadlier forms. According to the group, total direct and indirect costs of infectious disease in the United States in 1993 were more than $120 billion; combined federal, state, and municipal government expenditures that year for infectious disease control were only $74.2 million (neither figure includes AIDS, other sexually transmitted diseases, or tuberculosis).

THE REAL THREAT OF BIOWARFARE

THE WORLD was lucky in the September 1994 pneumonic plague epidemic in Surat. Independent studies in the United States, France, and Russia revealed that the bacterial strain that caused the outbreak was unusually weak, and although the precise figures for plague cases and deaths remain a matter of debate, the numbers certainly fall below 200. Yet the epidemic vividly illustrated three crucial national security issues in disease emergence: human mobility, transparency, and tensions between states up to and including the threat of biological warfare.

When word got out that an airborne disease was loose in the city, some 500,000 residents of Surat boarded trains and within 48 hours dispersed to every corner of the subcontinent. Had the microbe that

Laurie Garrett

caused the plague been a virus or drug-resistant bacterium, the world would have witnessed an immediate Asian pandemic. As it was, the epidemic sparked a global panic that cost the Indian economy a minimum of $2 billion in lost sales and losses on the Bombay stock market, predominantly the result of international boycotts of Indian goods and travelers.

As the number of countries banning trade with India mounted that fall, the Hindi-language press insisted that there was no plague, accusing Pakistan of a smear campaign aimed at bringing India's economy to its knees. After international scientific investigations concluded that *Yersinia pestis* had indeed been the culprit in this bona fide epidemic, attention turned to the bacteria's origin. By last June several Indian scientists claimed to have evidence that the bacteria in Surat had been genetically engineered for biowarfare purposes. Though no credible evidence exists to support it, and Indian government authorities vigorously deny such claims, the charge is almost impossible to disprove, particularly in a region rife with military and political tensions of long standing.

Even when allegations of biological warfare are not flying, it is often exceedingly difficult to obtain accurate information about outbreaks of disease, particularly from countries dependent on foreign investment or tourism or both. Transparency is a common problem; though there is usually no suggestion of covert action or malevolent intent, many countries are reluctant to disclose complete information about contagious illness. For example, nearly every country initially denied or covered up the presence of the HIV virus within its borders. Even now, at least ten nations known to be in the midst of HIV epidemics refuse to cooperate with WHO, deliberately obfuscating incidence reports or declining to provide any statistics. Similarly, Egypt denies the existence of cholera bacteria in the Nile's waters; Saudi Arabia has asked WHO not to warn that travelers to Mecca may be bitten by mosquitoes carrying viruses that cause the new, superlethal dengue hemorrhagic fever; few countries report the appearance of antibiotic-resistant strains of deadly bacteria; and central authorities in Serbia recently rescinded an international epidemic alert when they learned that all the scientists WHO planned to send to the tense Kosovo region to halt a large outbreak of Crimean-Congo hemorrhagic fever were from the United States, a nation Serbia viewed with hostility.

The Return of Infectious Disease

The specter of biological warfare having raised its head, Brad Roberts of the Center for Strategic and International Studies is particularly concerned that the New Tier nations—developing states such as China, Iran, and Iraq that possess technological know-how but lack an organized civil society that might put some restraints on its use—might be tempted to employ bioweapons. The Federation of American Scientists has sought, so far in vain, a scientific solution to the acute weaknesses of verification and enforcement provisions in the 1972 Biological Weapons Convention, which most of the world's nations have signed.

That treaty's flaws, and the very real possibility of bioweapons use, stand in sharp focus today. Iraq's threat in 1990-91 to use biological weapons in the Persian Gulf conflict found allied forces in the region virtually powerless to respond: the weapons' existence was not verified in a timely manner, the only available countermeasure was a vaccine against one type of organism, and protective gear and equipment failed to stand up to windblown sand. Last June the U.N. Security Council concluded that Iraqi stocks of bioweaponry might have been replenished after the Gulf War settlement.

More alarming were the actions of the Aum Shinrikyo cult in Japan in early 1995. In addition to releasing toxic sarin gas in the Tokyo subway on March 18, cult members were preparing vast quantities of *Clostridium difficile* bacterial spores for terrorist use. Though rarely fatal, clostridium infections often worsen as a result of improper antibiotic use, and long bouts of bloody diarrhea can lead to dangerous colon inflammations. Clostridium was a good choice for biological terrorism: the spores can survive for months and may be spread with any aerosol device, and even slight exposure can make vulnerable people (particularly children and the elderly) sick enough to cost a crowded society like Japan hundreds of millions of dollars for hospitalizations and lost productivity.

BETTMANN
The Ebola virus

The U.S. Office of Technology Assessment has calculated what it would take to produce a spectacular terrorist bioweapon: 100 kilo-

Laurie Garrett

grams of a lethal sporulating organism such as anthrax spread over Washington, D.C., by a crop duster could cause well over two million deaths. Enough anthrax spores to kill five or six million people could be loaded into a taxi and pumped out its tailpipe as it meandered through Manhattan. Vulnerability to terrorist attacks, as well as to the natural emergence of disease, increase with population density.

A WORLD AT RISK

A 1995 WHO survey of global capacity to identify and respond to threats from emerging disease reached troubling conclusions. Only six laboratories in the world, the study found, met security and safety standards that would make them suitable sites for research on the world's deadliest microbes, including those that cause Ebola, Marburg, and Lassa fever. Local political instability threatens to compromise the security of the two labs in Russia, and budget cuts threaten to do the same to the two in the United States (the army's facility at Fort Detrick and the CDC in Atlanta) and the one in Britain. In another survey, WHO sent samples of hantaviruses (such as Sin Nombre, which caused the 1993 outbreak in New Mexico) and organisms that cause dengue, yellow fever, malaria, and other diseases to the world's 35 leading disease-monitoring facilities. Only one—the CDC—correctly identified all the organisms; most got fewer than half right.

Convinced that newly emerging diseases, whether natural or engineered, could endanger national security, the CDC requested $125 million from Congress in 1994 to bolster what it termed a grossly inadequate system of surveillance and response; it received $7.3 million. After two years of inquiry by a panel of experts, the Institute of Medicine, a division of the National Academy of Sciences, declared the situation a crisis.

Today's reality is best reflected in New York City's battle with tuberculosis. Control of the W-strain of the disease—which first appeared in the city in 1991-92, is resistant to every available drug, and kills half its victims—has already cost more than $1 billion. Despite such spending, there were 3,000 TB cases in the city in 1994, some of which were the W-strain. According to the surgeon general's annual

The Return of Infectious Disease

reports from the 1970s and 1980s, tuberculosis was supposed to be eradicated from the United States by 2000. During the Bush administration the CDC told state authorities they could safely lower their fiscal commitments to TB control because victory was imminent. Now public health officials are fighting to get levels down to where they were in 1985—a far cry from elimination. New York's crisis is a result of both immigration pressure (some cases originated overseas) and the collapse of the local public health infrastructure.

National preparedness has further eroded over the past five years in the face of budgetary constraints. Just as WHO cannot intercede in an epidemic unless it receives an invitation from the afflicted country, the CDC may not enter a U.S. state without a request from the state government. The U.S. system rests on an increasingly shaky network of disease surveillance and response by states and territories. A 1992 survey for the CDC showed that 12 states had no one on staff to monitor microbial contamination of local food and water; 67 percent of the states and territories had less than one employee monitoring the food and water of every one million residents. And only a handful of states were monitoring hospitals for the appearance of unusual or drug-resistant microbes.

> Migration and megacities have made mankind more vulnerable to microbes, in peacetime and in biowarfare.

State capacity rests on county and municipal public health, and there too weaknesses are acute. In October, dengue hemorrhagic fever, which had been creeping steadily northward from Brazil over the past eight years, with devastating results, struck in Texas. Most Texas counties had slashed their mosquito control budgets and were ill prepared to combat the aggressive Tiger mosquitoes from Southeast Asia that carry the virus. In Los Angeles County that month, a $2 billion budget shortfall drove officials to close all but 10 of the 45 public health clinics and to attempt to sell four of the county's six public hospitals. Congress is contemplating enormous cuts in Medicare and Medicaid spending, which the American Public Health Association predicts would result in a widespread increase in infectious disease.

Laurie Garrett

PRESCRIPTIONS FOR NATIONAL HEALTH

BOLSTERING research capacity, enhancing disease surveillance capabilities, revitalizing sagging basic public health systems, rationing powerful drugs to avoid the emergence of drug-resistant organisms, and improving infection control practices at hospitals are only stop-gap measures. National security warrants bolder steps.

One priority is finding scientifically valid ways to use polymerase chain reaction (popularly known as DNA fingerprinting), field investigations, chemical and biological export records, and local legal instruments to track the development of new or reemergent lethal organisms, whether natural or bioweapons. The effort should focus not only on microbes directly dangerous to humans but on those that could pose major threats to crops or livestock.

Most emerging diseases are first detected by health providers working at the primary-care level. Currently there is no system, even in the United States, whereby the providers can notify relevant authorities and be assured that their alarm will be investigated promptly. In much of the world, the notifiers' reward is penalties levied against them, primarily because states want to hush up the problem. But Internet access is improving worldwide, and a small investment would give physicians an electronic highway to international health authorities that bypassed government roadblocks and obfuscation.

Only three diseases—cholera, plague, and yellow fever—are subject to international regulation, permitting U.N. and national authorities to interfere as necessary in the global traffic of goods and persons to stave off cross-border epidemics. The World Health Assembly, the legislative arm of WHO, recommended at its 1995 annual meeting in Geneva that the United Nations consider both expanding the list of regulated diseases and finding new ways to monitor the broad movement of disease. The Ebola outbreak in Kikwit demonstrated that a team of international scientists can be mobilized to swiftly contain a remote, localized epidemic caused by known nonairborne agents.

Were a major epidemic to imperil the United States, the Office of Emergency Preparedness and the National Disaster Medical System (part of the Department of Health and Human Services) would be at the helm. The office has 4,200 private-sector doctors and nurses throughout

The Return of Infectious Disease

the 50 states who are at its disposal and committed to rapid mobilization in case of emergency. The system is sound but should be bolstered. Participants should be supplied with protective suits, respirators, mobile containment laboratories, and adequate local isolation facilities.

As for potential threats from biological weapons, the U.S. Department of Energy has identified serious lapses in Russian and Ukrainian compliance with the Biological Weapons Convention. Large stockpiles of bioweapons are believed to remain, and employees of the Soviet program for biological warfare are still on the state payroll. Arsenals are also thought to exist in other nations, although intelligence on this is weak. The location and destruction of such weapons is a critical priority. Meanwhile, scientists in the United States and

> Few countries are eager to tell the world about contagious outbreaks.

Europe are identifying the genes in bacteria and viruses that code for virulence and modes of transmission. Better understanding of the genetic mechanisms will allow scientists to manipulate existing organisms, endowing them with dangerous capabilities. It would seem prudent for the United States and the international community to examine that potential now and consider options for the control of such research or its fruits.

To guard against the proliferation of blood-associated diseases, the blood and animal exports industries must be closely regulated, plasma donors must be screened for infections, and an internationally acceptable watchdog agency must be designated to monitor reports of the appearance of new forms of such diseases. The export of research animals played a role in a serious incident in Germany in which vaccine workers were infected with the Marburg virus and in an Ebola scare in Virginia in which imported monkeys died from the disease.

Nobel laureate Joshua Lederberg of Rockefeller University has characterized the solutions to the threat of disease emergence as multitudinous, largely straightforward and commonsensical, and international in scope; "the bad news," he says, "is they will cost money."

Budgets, particularly for health care, are being cut at all levels of government. Dustin Hoffman made more money last year playing a disease control scientist in the movie *Outbreak* than the combined annual budgets for the U.S. National Center for Infectious Diseases and the U.N. Programme on AIDS/HIV.🌐

[6]

Ghosts of Kigali

*Infectious disease and global stability at
the turn of the century*

ANDREW T. PRICE-SMITH

> *Beyond the enormous suffering of individuals and families,
> South Africans are beginning to understand the cost [of
> HIV/AIDS] in every sphere of society, observing with growing
> dismay its impact on the efforts of our new democracy to
> achieve the goals of reconstruction and development.*[1]

AS THE SPECTRE OF THE COLD WAR and the traditional security threats associated with it recede into the past, international relations and national security analysts have begun to embrace concepts of human security and preventive defence, arguing that factors such as environmental degradation, resource scarcity, and overpopulation now pose more significant threats to global security. But another threat looms large on the horizon, namely the proliferation of emerging and re-emerging infections on a global scale. Indeed, the HIV pandemic is entrenched in subsaharan Africa and accelerating through eastern Europe and south and east Asia. Other widening pandemics include the

*This article was written when Andrew Price-Smith was Research Director, Program on Health
and Global Affairs, Centre for International Studies, University of Toronto; and Lecturer,
Department of Political Science, University of Waterloo. He is now a Post-Doctoral Research
Fellow at CIESIN, Columbia University. He would like to thank David Welch, Janice Gross
Stein, Louis Pauly, Marc Levy, Mark Zacher, Stephen S. Morse, Nils-Petter Gleditsch, Franklyn
Griffiths, Robert Matthews, Wesley Wark, David Fidler, Peter Gizewski, Laurie Garrett, Jim
Whitman, Jay Keystone, Patrick Kelley, Peter Zoutis, Ann-Marie Kimball, Thomas Homer-
Dixon, and Ron Deibert for their insightful comments and critiques.*

1 Nelson Mandela, 'AIDS: facing up to the global threat,' Address to the World
Economic Forum, Davos, 3 February 1997.
http://www.us.unaids.org/highband/speeches/mandela.html, 2 (20 April 1997).

re-emergence of such old scourges as tuberculosis, malaria, cholera, and dengue. New threats have also appeared in the form of hanta, ebola, legionella, and such antibiotic resistant organisms as vancomycin-resistant enterococci and methycillin-resistant staphylococcus aureas.

A primary purpose of international relations theory is to construct models that will assist in averting the premature loss of human life and productivity as a result of war. Indeed, as Thomas Hobbes claimed, it is the central function of the state to guarantee the physical safety of its citizens from both internal and external forms of predation.[2] However, traditional concepts of security usually ignored the greatest source of human misery and mortality, the microbial penumbra that surrounds our species. It is time to consider the additional form of ecological predation wherein the physical security and prosperity of a state's populace is directly threatened by the global phenomena of emerging and re-emerging infectious disease.[3]

Emerging and re-emerging infectious diseases (ERIDs) are significant obstacles to the political stability and economic development of seriously affected societies. Thus, the global resurgence of infectious disease presents a direct and significant long-term threat to international governance and prosperity.[4] Over the broad span of human history infectious disease has consistently accounted for the greatest proportion of human morbidity and mortality, easily surpassing war as the foremost threat to human life and prosperity. Historians have long argued that infectious disease has had a profound impact on the evolution and, at times, the dissolution of societal structures, governments, and empires.[5] Indeed, Robert Fogel argues that much of England's

2 See Thomas Hobbes, *Leviathan*, ed C.B. Macpherson (Harmondsworth: Penguin 1968).

3 Until very recently the concept of microbial threats to human security had not been explored. Two recent works which begin to do so are Laurie Garret, 'The return of infectious disease,' *Foreign Affairs* 75 (January/February 1996), 66-79; and Dennis Pirages, 'Ecological security: micro-threats to human well-being,' paper presented at the International Studies Association, annual meeting, San Diego CA, April 1996.

4 Andrew T. Price-Smith, *Contagion and Chaos: Infectious Disease and its Effects on Global Security and Development*, CIS Working Paper no 1, 1998 (Toronto: Centre for International Studies, University of Toronto, January 1998).

5 See William H. McNeill, *Plagues and Peoples* (Toronto: Doubleday 1989); Alfred W. Crosby, *Ecological Imperialism: The Biological Expansion of Europe, 900-1900* (New York: Cambridge University Press 1994); Crosby, *The Colombian Exchange: Biological and Cultural Consequences of 1492* (Westport CT: Greenwood 1972); Sheldon Watts, *Epidemics and History: Disease, Power, and Imperialism* (New Haven CT: Yale University Press 1997); and Hans Zinsser, *Rats, Lice, and History* (New York: Little, Brown 1934).

Andrew T. Price-Smith

prosperity, if not the Industrial Revolution itself, resulted from the conquest of high morbidity and mortality in Britain during the late 18th and early 19th century,[6] largely because of significant advances in public health and in the increasingly equitable distribution of food. However, even in the era of modern medicine, states annually suffer much greater mortality and morbidity from infectious disease than from casualties incurred during inter- and intra-state military conflict.

According to the World Bank, of the 49,971,000 deaths recorded in 1990, infectious disease was responsible for 16,690,000 (34.4 per cent), while war accounted for 322,000 (0.64 per cent) or a ratio of 52:1.[7] Thus the relative destruction wrought by disease compared to deaths from military actions is significant. From the standpoint of human security, then, disease is a relatively greater threat to human well-being than war, and yet the subject is poorly understood within the general policy community.

Statistics gathered by the Harvard-based Global AIDS Policy Coalition show that in 1995 approximately 22 million people were infected with HIV/AIDS, and 4.7 million new infections occurred globally. Of the new infections, 2.5 million were in Southeast Asia and 1.9 million in subsaharan Africa; the industrialized world accounted for approximately 170,000 new cases.[8] The pace of the HIV/AIDS pandemic is accelerating: a total of 33.4 million people are now infected; there are 5.8 million new infections annually; and 2.5 million people died from HIV/AIDS related causes in 1998.[9] This translates into an increase

6 See Robert W. Fogel, 'The conquest of high mortality and hunger in Europe and America: timing and mechanisms,' in David Landes, Patrice Higgonet, and Henry Rosovsky, eds, *Favorites of Fortune: Technology, Growth and Economic Development Since the Industrial Revolution* (Cambridge MA: Harvard University Press 1991); Fogel, 'Nutrition and the decline in mortality since 1700: some preliminary findings in long-term factors in American economic growth,' in Stanley L. Engerman and Robert E. Gallman, eds, *Conference on Research in Income and Wealth*, vol 41 (Chicago IL: University of Chicago Press 1986); and Fogel, *Economic Growth, Population Theory, and Physiology: The Bearing of Long-term Processes in the Making of Economic Policy*, working paper no. 4638 (Cambridge MA: National Bureau of Economic Research, April 1994).

7 Statistics on the causes of global deaths in 1990 are derived from World Bank, *World Development Report 1993: Investing in Health* (New York: Oxford University Press 1993), 224-5.

8 Global AIDS Policy Coalition, Johnathan Mann, ed, *Status and Trends of the HIV/AIDS Pandemic as of January, 1996* (Cambridge MA: Harvard School of Public Health, François-Xavier Bagnoud Center for Health and Human Rights, 18 January 1996), 2.

9 See UNAIDS, *AIDS Epidemic Update: December 1998*, 2-3, at http://www.unaids.org/highband/document/epidemio/wadr98e.pdf

in the global pace of infection of 24 per cent since 1995. In terms of the absolute magnitude of mortality, the HIV pandemic now rivals the greatest plagues in history, including the Black Death of Middle Ages Europe and the influenza pandemic of 1918, both of which killed over 20 million people. To date the HIV pandemic has resulted in the infection of 47 million, 14 million of whom died, and the contagion is spreading rapidly throughout south and Southeast Asia, eastern Europe, and Latin America.[10]

The heart of the HIV pandemic beats in subsaharan Africa where many states are now reporting HIV seroprevalence levels in excess of 10 per cent. Indeed, South Africa, Kenya, Uganda, Zambia, Namibia, Swaziland, Botswana, and Zimbabwe all have seroprevalence levels ranging from 10 to 25 per cent of the population.[11] Botswana, for example, has seen rates rise from 10 per cent in 1992 to 25.1 per cent in 1997 - an increase of 250 per cent over five years.[12] In South Africa total HIV infection levels rose from 1.4 million in 1995 to over 3 million in 1998,[13] or an increase of more than 200 per cent in 3 years. Some regions within these states have even higher infection levels. HIV prevalence in KwaZulu-Natal in South Africa has now reached 30 per cent, and Francistown in Botswana reports that 43 per cent of its citizens are infected.[14] Certain towns along the South African-Zimbabwe border claim astonishing rates of approximately 70 per cent.[15]

The pandemic is expanding into eastern Europe at an ever-increasing pace. A former Russian minister of health, Tatyana Dmitriyeva, has predicted that over one million Russians will be infected with HIV by 2000.[16] Ukraine has seen HIV incidence soar from a modest 44 cases in

---

10 *Ibid*, 3.

11 Namibia and Swaziland currently report HIV seroprevalence levels in excess of 20 per cent; Zimbabwe and Botswana have the dubious distinction of having infection levels of over 25 per cent of the total population. Individual country annual seroprevalence statistics are available at http://www.unaids.org/highband.

12 Lawrence K. Altman, 'Parts of Africa showing HIV in 1 in 4 adults,' *New York Times*, 24 June 1998, A1.

13 Suzanne Daly, 'A post-apartheid agony: AIDS on the march,' *New York Times*, 23 July 1998, A1.

14 Donald McNeil, Jr, 'AIDS stalking Africa's struggling economies,' *New York Times*, 15 November 1998, A1.

15 André Picard, 'UN warns of alarming gap in prevention of AIDS,' *Globe and Mail* (Toronto), 24 June 1998, B4.

16 Cited in Murray Feschbach, 'Dead souls,' *Atlantic Monthly*, January 1999, 26.

Andrew T. Price-Smith

1994 to an astonishing 110,000 cases as of mid-1998.[17] The epidemic is also spreading throughout India's vast population at a rapacious pace. Five years ago, HIV was practically unheard of in India; now almost 1 per cent of all pregnant women tested throughout the country are HIV positive.[18] By 1997 the epidemic was already firmly entrenched in some regions such as Nagaland along the Burmese border (7.8 per cent HIV seroprevalence) and nearby Manipur (over 10 per cent).[19] Indeed, with the exception of the developed world and certain states such as Uganda and Thailand which have seen some reduction in the rate of new infections, the HIV pandemic continues to expand at a truly alarming pace.

Other diseases once thought to be under control are reappearing as global scourges. Tuberculosis has been making such a steady comeback that the World Health Organization (WHO) declared it to be a global crisis in 1993. WHO estimates that '8.9 million people developed tuberculosis in 1995, bringing the global total of sufferers to about 22 million, of whom about 3 million will have died in the same space of time.' In the absence of increased effectiveness and availability of tuberculosis control measures, over 30 million tuberculosis deaths and more than 90 million new infections are forecast by the turn of the century. Furthermore, tuberculosis is making inroads into the industrialized nations, particularly Canada and the United States where it infects disadvantaged urban and incarcerated populations and then spreads throughout society. In the United States, reported cases of tuberculosis had declined from 84,300 in 1953 to 22,200 in 1984, a drop of approximately 4 per cent per annum. However, from 1985 to 1993, the number of cases increased by a cumulative 14 per cent, and the pace continues to accelerate.[20] Similarly, Zimbabwe has reported massive increases in incidence, from 5,000 cases in 1986 to 35,000 cases in 1997.[21] Murray Feschbach notes that the incidence in Russia,

17 'HIV rising in CIS countries,' *Globe and Mail*, 22 April 1998, A16.

18 Lawrence K. Altman, 'Dismaying experts, HIV infections soar,' *New York Times*, 24 November 1998, F7.

19 John Stackhouse, 'Nagaland choking in grip of AIDS,' *Globe and Mail*, 1 December 1997, A11.

20 *World Health Report 1996*, 27, 28.

21 Michael Specter, 'Doctors powerless as AIDS rakes Africa,' *New York Times*, 6 August 1998, A1.

too, is increasing rapidly and, based on estimates provided by the Russian Ministry of the Interior, predicts that the result will be 1.75 million Russians deaths per year by 2000.[22]

Malaria also continues its relentless expansion into former regions of endemicity. For example, in 1989 it claimed 100 lives in Zimbabwe and debilitated many thousands; by 1997 the number had risen to 2,800 deaths, an astonishing rate of increase for a disease that was once thought to be under control.[23] Indeed, the best available estimates project that malaria currently claims 5,000 lives every day in Africa or some 1.8 million per year. Global estimates put the total annual death rate at upwards of 2.7 million and indicate that malaria debilitates as many as 500 million people every year.[24] Ellen Ruppel Shell claims that the global incidence of malaria has increased by approximately 400 per cent between 1992 and 1997 and notes that the disease has re-emerged in North America from urban centres in California to Michigan, from New York City to Toronto.[25]

Meanwhile familiar pathogens continue to exact their toll on humanity with relentless vigour. Acute lower respiratory infections are responsible for the death of nearly 4 million children annually, while diarrhoeal diseases such as adnovirus and rotavirus kill nearly 3 million infants every year. Viral hepatitis is another global scourge. A minimum of 350 million people are chronic carriers of the hepatitis B virus and an additional 100 million harbour the hepatitis C virus. According to WHO projections, at least 25 per cent of these carriers will die from related liver disease.[26] To make matters worse, many of the ten million new cases of cancer diagnosed in 1995 were caused by viruses, bacteria, and parasites. WHO calculates that 15 per cent of all new cancer cases (1.5 million) are the result of exposure to infectious agents, and this percentage will no doubt increase as our knowledge of both infectious disease and cancer advances.

22 Feschbach, 'Dead souls,' 27.

23 Specter, 'Doctors powerless as AIDS rakes Africa,' A1.

24 Ellen Ruppel Shell, 'Resurgence of a deadly disease,' *Atlantic Monthly*, August 1997, 47, 48.

25 *Ibid*, 45. Malaria's re-emergence as an endemically transmitted pathogen in Toronto has been verified by Kevin Kain of the Tropical Disease Unit, Toronto General Hospital. Comments made to the author, 30 October 1998.

26 *World Health Report 1996*, 2.

Andrew T. Price-Smith

New evidence is linking many other supposedly chronic or genetic diseases such as heart disease and multiple sclerosis to common infectious agents (chlamydia and herpes, respectively) which promote long-term disease processes within human hosts.[27] If certain conditions such as cancer, heart disease, and multiple sclerosis are indeed pathogen-induced, then the global burden of disease may be far greater than was previously thought.

While it is relatively easy to see that emerging and re-emerging infectious diseases are central agents of misery throughout the developing world, it is not often apparent that infection-induced mortality has been on the rise in the developed world as well. For example, the United States, which has enormous levels of state capacity, has seen a steady increase in mortality from infectious disease over the last two decades, from 15,360 deaths in 1979 to 77,128 ERID-induced deaths in 1995,[28] for a significant increase of 502 per cent.

Interdisciplinary models that combine the natural and social sciences require a fundamental reconceptualization of standard definitions of national interest and security. Constricting definitions that focus exclusively on the relative military capability of states are increasingly sterile in the face of the many global challenges of the post-cold war world. Threats to human welfare such as global environmental degradation, resource scarcity, and infectious disease present policy-makers with difficult dilemmas. Novel global collective action solutions are exceptionally difficult to achieve given the primacy of national sovereignty in an arena of international anarchy. In articulating the complex linkages between increasing disease prevalence and state capacity, some light can be shed on the association between the prevalence of infectious disease and growing poverty and political destabilization in regions such as subsaharan Africa.

To begin with a specific definition: emerging infectious diseases are pathogen-induced human illnesses which have increased in incidence, lethality, transmissibility, and/or have expanded their geographical range since 1973.[29] Re-emerging diseases are those pathogen-induced

27 Note the evidence compiled by Paul Ewald, cited in Judith Hooper, 'A new germ theory,' *Atlantic Monthly*, February 1999, 41-53.

28 See http://cdc.gov/nchswww/fastats for this data.

29 1973 is a significant date. Up until the early 1970s, advances in public health contributed to the dramatic fall in infectious disease-induced morbidity and mortality on a global scale. Thus the prevalence of infectious disease reached its nadir circa

human illnesses that were previously controlled or were declining in range and/or incidence, but are now expanding - not just in range and incidence, but also in drug-resistance and increasing transmissibility and/or lethality. Pathogens are defined as viral, bacterial, parasitic, or proteinic organisms or agents that live in a parasitic and debilitating relationship with their human host.

Pathogenic microbes exist independently throughout the earth's biosphere, the vast majority of them in the zoonotic pool, outside of human ecology. In a very real way these pathogens are independent variables and are exogenous to the state because they are global phenomena (existing at the system level). They may cross over from the zoonotic reservoir into the human ecology at any time according to the principles of chaos. A classic example is falciparum malaria, which seems to have crossed over from various avian species to humans at some time within the last five thousand years. Because of the recent nature of the crossover, falciparum is far deadlier to humans than its cousin vivax, which has had a much longer time to adjust to its human hosts.

After pathogenic agents enter the human ecology (and become endogenized within human societies) their effects are magnified by intervening variables called 'disease amplifiers.' Examples of potent amplifiers are phenomena such as environmental degradation, warfare, climate change, the misuse of antibiotics, changes in the speed of human transportation technologies, famine, natural disasters, and global trade,[30] all of which generate changes in viral traffic that result in ERIDs. Thus ERIDs are a product of the synergy between the independent variable (pathogens) and the intervening variables.

States and societies may at any point use adaptive resources to mitigate the effects of ERIDs on state capacity. But a state's ability to adapt is limited by several factors. First, the initial level of state capacity

1973. In that year a new pathogen 'rotavirus' was recognized, the first of many new pathogenic agents which would emerge in the coming decades. Essentially, 1973 is the turning point in the 'health transition' where the curve of infectious disease incidence stops declining and begins to ascend. See Report of the National Science and Technology Committee, Committee on International Science, Engineering, and Technology (CISET) Working Group on Emerging and Re-Emerging Infectious Diseases, *Global Microbial Threats in the 1990s* (Washington DC: White House), September 1995.

30 Stephen S. Morse, ed, *Emerging Viruses* (New York: Oxford University Press 1993).

Andrew T. Price-Smith

determines the scale of adaptive resources that can be mobilized to deal with the ERID problem. States with higher initial capacity have greater technical, financial, and social resources available to them to cope with crises. State adaptation is also affected by exogenous inputs of capital and social and technical ingenuity, courtesy of international organizations such as the WHO, the United Nations Children's Fund, and non-governmental organizations (NGOs) such as the International Committee of the Red Cross. Adaptation may be compromised by certain outcomes generated by intervening variables, such as war, famine, and ecological destruction.

There is a logically positive association between state capacity and state adaptation because greater initial capacity means that there are more human, economic, and technical resources within the state to mobilize to deal with various crises. The lower the initial value of state capacity, the fewer the resources that can be mobilized to offset the crisis. This relationship operates in a reciprocal spiral: greater initial capacity leads to greater adaptive ability, which should in turn reduce the ERID-induced loss to state capacity. Thus states that have lower state capacity when ERIDs afflict them generally suffer much greater losses than states with high initial capacity. The only means by which states with lower state capacity can ameliorate the effects of ERID is through exogenous inputs which give them greater resources to mobilize and advance tactical knowledge to deal with the crisis.[31]

INTRA-STATE EFFECTS OF ERID
A brief explanation of the effects of ERID on state capacity, in the domains of economics and governance, is in order. The destructive effects of ERIDs reverberate throughout all levels of the economy from households and firms to sectors such as resource extraction, agriculture, insurance, and banking. When infected workers are debilitated or killed, the productivity of the workforce is reduced, particularly in labour-intensive sectors such as agriculture or mining.[32] Infectious dis-

31 This methodology (and the use of surrogate measures of disease prevalence such as infant mortality and life expectancy) can be found in Andrew T. Price-Smith, *Wilson's Bridge: A Consilient Methodology for the Analysis of Complex Biological-Political Relationships*, CIS Working Paper no 8, 1998 (Toronto: Centre for International Studies, University of Toronto, November 1998).

32 See Randall M. Packard, *White Plague, Black Labor: Tuberculosis and the Political Economy of Health and Disease in South Africa* (Berkeley: University of California Press 1989).

ease imposes additional costs on the household in lost savings and in labour substitution, particularly in those units in the lower economic strata of society. Income inequalities between the lower and upper classes are thereby exacerbated. ERIDs also change household expenditure patterns as money earmarked for food, clothing, shelter, and so on is spent on medication instead. Thus ERIDs generate economic shocks to the household, changing savings and consumption patterns, eroding aggregate household wealth, and making significant labour substitution necessary. Rising levels of infectious disease also decrease incentives to invest in child education, as children spend more time working to support debilitated or bereaved family members. Nor is there much incentive to allocate resources to educate a child if that child is likely to die of some infection in the near future.[33] And when whole communities are affected, the problems are compounded.

Thus, the negative effects of an ERID on economic productivity include decreases in worker productivity, labour shortages and increased absenteeism, higher costs imposed on household units (particularly on the poor), reductions in per-capita income, reduced savings, capital flight, reductions in national gross domestic product, and increases in income inequalities within a society which may in turn generate increased governance problems. An ERID also impedes the settlement of marginal regions and the development of natural resources, negatively affects tourism, and results in the embargoing of infected goods. A prime example is the European Union's recent ban on all beef-related products from Britain, from foodstuffs to soaps to cosmetics, for fear of contamination with the bovine spongiform encephalopathy (BSE) prion (infected proteins) that causes Creutzfeld-Jacob disease in humans. All told, increasing disease prevalence poses a serious threat to the economic health of societies across the globe.

In the domain of governance, high levels of ERID incidence undermine the capacity of political leaders and their respective bureaucracies to govern effectively as the infection of government personnel results in the debilitation and death of skilled administrators who oversee the day-to-day operations of governance. For example, AIDS has resulted in a significant winnowing of educated and skilled workers from govern-

33 These hypothetical causal relationships are empirically confirmed via diachronic national and global correlations in Andrew T. Price-Smith, *Statistical Evidence of a Negative Association between Infectious Disease and State Capacity: 1951-1991*, CIS Working Paper no 1, 1999 (Toronto: Centre for International Studies, University of Toronto).

Andrew T. Price-Smith

ment, industry, and education in Tanzania. The destructive impact of ERID-induced mortality in capital-intensive institutions generates institutional fragility that will undermine the stability of nascent democratic societies. As the burden of disease on the population of a state increases, the resulting poverty and physical destruction visited on the populace will over time erode governmental legitimacy. Therefore, ERID-induced poverty, morbidity and mortality, migration, and psychological stresses wear upon the economic and social fabric of society and will contribute to repression and the collapse of democracy as a weakening state seeks to maintain order while the government's legitimacy erodes and as governmental institutions become increasingly fragile. This in turn poses problems for the United States and the administration of President Bill Clinton, whose strategy of 'engagement and enlargement' places a premium on establishing and strengthening democratic regimes on a global level.

The presence of ERIDs in military populations jeopardizes military readiness, international co-operation, national security, and the ability of a state to preserve its territorial integrity. At the intra-state level, ERIDs reduce force strength through the death or debilitation of military personnel, deplete the supply of healthy recruits, and generate costs that limit military budgets, all of which impairs a state's capacity to defend itself against a potential aggressor and limits a state's ability to project power for peacekeeping or coercive measures.

The adaptive capability of states depends on their current and future supply of technical and social ingenuity, on their domestic reservoirs of capacity, and on the contribution that outside actors make in the form of capital, goods, and technical assistance. Thomas Homer-Dixon's concept of ingenuity is a partial factor in the ability of states to adapt to crises. While the ingenuity model that he has constructed deals with the issue of economic development in a climate of resource scarcity and environmental degradation, the concept is useful in determining the capacity of a state to adapt in the face of significant challenges. Homer-Dixon argues that 'resource scarcity can simultaneously increase the requirement and impede the supply [of ingenuity], producing an "ingenuity gap" that may have critical consequences for adaptation and, in turn, social stability.'[34] Similarly, the negative economic and

---

34 Thomas F. Homer-Dixon, 'The ingenuity gap: can poor countries adapt to resource scarcity?' *Population and Development Review 21* (September 1995), 589.

social effects of ERID can also increase the requirement for ingenuity while limiting its supply.[35] The lesson to be drawn from the ingenuity argument is that the longer we wait to address the problem of infectious disease, the greater the costs of generating the levels of ingenuity that will be required to resolve the problem.

Because of low initial levels of state capacity and ingenuity in the developing world, the global proliferation of infectious disease presents the greatest threat to the least developed societies. This has given rise to a disturbing tendency on the part of some Western scholars, policy-makers, and the media to see ERIDs as a threat to the populations only in those societies. But hubris and denial are shortsighted and bound to lead to significant downstream losses for developed societies as well. The natural world is of course infinitely complex and interdependent. As the human species continues to alter the global environment, that environment will produce corresponding responses, such as the continuing emergence of human pathogens. As we have seen from the emergence of AIDS, hepatitis, drug-resistant tuberculosis, and 'flesh eating disease,' the developed world remains vulnerable to the ravages of infection.[36]

The negative effects of ERIDs on state capacity at the unit level produce related pernicious outcomes at the systems level. Within the domain of economics, as an ERID produces a significant drag on the economies of affected countries, we may see chronic underdevelopment, which may in turn exert a net drag on global trade and impair global prosperity. In all likelihood, because of the nature of spiral dynamics inherent in the relationship between an ERID and state capacity, countries with low initial levels will suffer greater losses over time from an increasing prevalence of infectious disease within their populations. Because of the spiral effect, an ERID's negative influence on the economic development of states may exacerbate the economic divide between North and South. Furthermore, the negative effects of infectious disease are not confined to the developing world. At the systems level, trade goods from ERID-affected regions may be subject to inter-

35 The determinants of adaptation are: the change in the requirements for adaptation - that is, how difficult the job is - and whether the necessary knowledge, adaptive strategies, and technologies can be supplied, when and where required and at the optimal time.

36 Note the significant penetration of developed societies by pathogens such as HIV, Hepatitis C and B, and our continuing vigilance against another lethal influenza pandemic.

Andrew T. Price-Smith

national embargo (as was the case with British beef and BSE and with influenza-infected chickens in Hong Kong). As infectious agents continue to emerge and re-emerge, and as agricultural crops and animal stocks become increasingly infested, we should expect that (presumably infected) trade goods from affected states will be embargoed, tourism may decline, and economic damage will likely intensify.

One conclusion which can be drawn from the emergence of prion-induced Creutzfeld-Jacob, ebola, HIV, and plague is that people are extremely risk-averse when it comes to the emergence of new pathogens. The result may be paranoia, hysteria, and xenophobia that may impair rational decision-making in the foreign policy of an affected state. The epidemic of pneumonic plague (yersina pestis) in western India during the autumn of 1994 gives some idea of how the psychological effects of the outbreak of an infectious disease may affect both state capacity and an afflicted state's relations with its neighbours. The very rumour of plague in Surat prompted the frenetic exodus of over 300,000 refugees from the city who then carried the pestilence with them to Bombay, Calcutta, and as far as New Delhi.[37] Out of fear, Pakistan, Bangladesh, Nepal, and China rapidly closed their borders to both trade and travel from India. Some even restricted mail from the affected state: India had become an instant international pariah. As the plague spread, concern mounted, and international travel to and with India became increasingly restricted. On 22 September 1994, the Bombay stock exchange plunged and soon after many countries began to restrict imports from India, placing impounded goods in quarantine or turning them back altogether at the border.[38]

As the crisis deepened, the Indian army was called in to enforce a quarantine in the affected area. Doctors who had fled Surat were forced back to work under threat of legal prosecution by the government. In the aftermath of an epidemic that killed 56 people, the Indian government was notified by the Center for Disease Control in Atlanta that the yersina pestis bacillus was an unknown and presumably new strain. To Indian authorities this information was 'unusual,' and they promptly accused rebel militants (Ultras) of procuring the bacillus from a pathogen-manufacturing facility in Almaty, Kazakhstan, with the object of manufacturing an epidemic in India. As a result of para-

37 'The old enemy,' *Economist*, 1 October 1994, 40.

38 Hamish MacDonald, 'Surat's revenge: India counts the mounting costs of poverty,' *Far Eastern Economic Review*, 13 October 1994, 76.

noia on the part of Indian officials, the inquest into the epidemic was transferred from public health authorities to the Department of Defence.[39] Beyond the acrimony that the plague fostered between India and its Islamic neighbours, the economic toll has been estimated at a minimum of US$1 billion in lost revenue from exports and tourism.[40] While the loss may seem trivial, it dealt a serious blow to a developing economy and had negative repercussions throughout numerous sectors.

As the events in Surat and the current BSE scare in Europe show, infectious disease and the irrational behaviour that it generates may worsen relationships between states and/or cultures.[41] The recent panic in Britain over BSE or 'Mad Cow Disease' has resulted in the embargo of many beef-derived British products and dictated the cull of a significant proportion of Britain's beef stocks. BSE has frightened the British population as scientists talk about the possibility of thousands of Britons infected with a new variant of Creutzfeld-Jacob disease, and Britain's European partners have summarily banned the import of British beef in violation of Europen Community trade law.[42]

Increasing levels of ERID correlate with a decline in the state capacity of affected countries. The decline, coupled with an increase in pathogen-induced deprivation and increasing demands upon the state, is accompanied by an attendant increase in the incidence of chronic substate violence and state failure. State failure frequently produces chaos in affected regions, as neighbouring states seal their borders to prevent the massive influx of ERID-infected refugee populations. Adjacent states may also try to fill the power vacuum and seize valued territory from the collapsing state, prompting other proximate states to do the same, thereby exacerbating regional security dilemmas. As ERID incidence and lethality increase, deprivation will mount and state capacity will decline, which in turn will generate increasing levels of

39 'Were Ultras responsible for Surat plague?' *Hindustan Times*, 9 July 1995.

40 'Was it the plague?' *Economist*, 19 November 1994, 38-40.

41 For an analysis of human reaction and aversion to risk, with the attendant irrational behaviour that results, see Roger E. Kasperson et al, *The Social Amplification of Risk: A Conceptual Framework* (Worcester MA: Center for Technology, Environment, and Development, Clark University, 1989).

42 As of 23 March 1996, France, Italy, Germany, and Belgium, among others, had banned British beef imports. John Darnton, 'France and Belgium ban British beef over cow disease,' *New York Times*, 22 March 1996, A4; David Wallen, 'European partners ban U.K. beef,' *Globe and Mail*, 22 March 1996, A1, A10.

Andrew T. Price-Smith

stress and demands upon government structures and undermine its legitimacy. Thus, ERID-induced stresses may combine with other environmental, demographic, and economic stressors to create riots, rebellions, and insurgencies. As the prevalence of ERID increases and the geographical range of pathogens expands, the number of failing states may rise, necessitating increased humanitarian intervention by United Nations security forces to maintain order in affected regions. As we have seen from its experiences in central and west Africa, the United Nations is unlikely to have a lasting effect in restoring order to areas where ERID incidence and lethality remain high.

CONCLUSIONS

The global resurgence of infectious disease has significant implications for state survival, stability, and prosperity, as well as ramifications for interstate relations. The premature death and debilitation of a significant proportion of a state's population erodes worker productivity and undermines state prosperity, induces high levels of psychological stress in the populace, fosters internal migration and emigration, threatens a state's ability both to defend itself and to project force, generates institutional fragility, and undermines the legitimacy of authority structures, thereby impairing the state's ability to govern effectively. While ERID acts as a stressor on state capacity, it simultaneously generates poverty and misery within the population which may result in deprivation conflicts, widespread insurrection, and governance problems.[43] At the global level, ERID-induced poverty generates a drag on both regional development and global prosperity. Disease-induced poverty and instability may exacerbate migration from the biologically onerous regions of the South to the prosperous and relatively benign regions of the North. Furthermore, as ERID-induced shortcomings in the realms

43 For further literature on deprivation conflicts and state failure, see Jack Goldstone, *Revolution and Rebellion in the Early Modern Era* (Berkeley: University of California Press 1991); Thomas F. Homer-Dixon, 'On the threshold: environmental changes as causes of acute conflict' and 'Environmental scarcities and violent conflict: evidence from cases,' both in Sean M. Lynn-Jones and Steven E. Miller, eds, *Global Dangers: Changing Dimensions of International Security* (Cambridge MA: MIT Press 1995), 43-83, 144-82; Colin Kahl, 'Population growth, environmental degradation, and state-sponsored violence: The case of Kenya, 1991-93,' *International Security* 23(autumn 1998), 80-119; Kalevi J. Holsti, *The State, War, and the State of War* (Cambridge: Cambridge University Press 1996); Ted Gurr, *Why Men Rebel* (Princeton: Princeton University Press 1970); and Edward Rice, *Wars of the Third Kind: Conflict in Underdeveloped Countries* (Berkeley: University of California Press 1988).

of governance and defence impair state survival, the international community may be called on to intervene and restore order in affected states.

It is likely that plagues have contributed to the collapse of governance over the broad span of history: they hampered the Athenian war effort during the Peloponnesian war, contributed to the demise of Byzantine Rome and to the destruction of the feudal order in Europe, and were the primal force in the annihilation of the pre-Colombian societies in the Americas after their first contacts with Europeans.[44] This dynamic is not relegated to the annals of history but continues to affect state capacity in the modern era. Because of the negative association between infectious disease and state capacity, the global proliferation of emerging and re-emerging diseases (particularly HIV, tuberculosis, and malaria) is a threat to international economic development and global governance. The growing destabilization of subsaharan Africa is at least partly due to the exceptionally high ERID levels in the region, particularly HIV/AIDS and malaria. Indeed, extreme governance problems in the Democratic Republic of the Congo, Rwanda, Uganda, and Burundi are likely related to increasing ERID stresses on state capacity.

Based on the experience of subsaharan Africa, we can project that the continuing and rapid spread of HIV and other ERIDs in eastern Europe and south and west Asia will erode state capacity in those regions as well, generating widespread poverty and political instability in seriously affected nations. In particular, the proliferation of infectious diseases such as HIV and tuberculosis threatens the economic well-being and political stability of several key states in the world, notably Russia, Ukraine, India, South Africa, Thailand, perhaps China. To promote global stability and prosperity significant resources will have to be allocated to public health infrastructures within these countries, and public health will have to become a central component of foreign development assistance packages.

Global phenomena such as infectious diseases frequently act in concert with other global collective action problems, such as environmental degradation, resource scarcity, and overpopulation, to strain state capacity. This synergy between stressors of state capacity will increas-

44 This conclusion is based on the negative empirical association between infectious disease and state capacity. The statistical evidence shows that the arguments of historians for linking plagues with the collapse of empires and societies are likely accurate. See, for example, Michael Oldstone, *Viruses, Plagues and History* (New York: Oxford University Press 1998).

Andrew T. Price-Smith

ingly destabilize seriously affected states and in some cases entire regions (such as subsaharan Africa). We will have to foster increased communication and co-operation between the global policy and medical communities and provide increased resources for surveillance, containment, and co-operative policy measures if we ever hope to check the global proliferation of emerging and re-emerging diseases. Above all, the gravity of these issues has to be brought to the attention of the heads of all governments, as the greatest weapon in stemming the global tide of infection is political will.

Tangible actions that governments should take include establishing a global disease surveillance system which incorporates the successful civil-society model of the ProMED network that currently monitors disease outbreaks. Governments should also collect 'health intelligence' so as to monitor the progression of diseases through the populations of states that either cannot provide accurate statistics on disease prevalence or refuse to do so for political reasons. Policy-makers should also take action to reduce the pace of global environmental degradation, curb the abuse of anti-microbial medications within their societies, and provide increased funding for research to develop vaccines and other anti-microbial agents.

Although the World Health Organization has been the principal actor in tracking disease emergence and proliferation, it faces several problems in dealing with these issues. Even though funding is increasingly diverted within the WHO to infectious surveillance, treatment, and control, these programmes are generally underfunded, understaffed, and less than effective in fighting ERIDs on so many fronts. Thus, greater resources should be given to the WHO to increase its capacity, and these funds should be specifically targeted to deal with the greatest current ERID threats (HIV, tuberculosis, and malaria). The United States and Japan are currently developing a policy framework for greater co-operation in checking the spread of ERIDs within and between their own territories. Furthermore, the G-7 states are exploring means by which they might collaborate to reduce the threat of emerging diseases to their populations. While these efforts have not produced any concrete results in the form of multilateral anti-contagion regimes, they are a step in the right direction. Given the will, policy-makers can orchestrate the required redistribution of fiscal resources, ingenuity, and technology to stem the rising tide of disease and thus help to promote global prosperity and stability.

[7]

The Politics of
Global Health Governance:
Whatever Happened to
"Health for All by the Year 2000"?

Caroline Thomas and Martin Weber

The discourse on global health governance (GHG) has received a significant boost in the context of the renewed efforts to tackle the global acquired immunodeficiency syndrome (AIDS) pandemic. Although there is a large body of literature that deals with questions relevant to GHG from the perspectives of various issues and interest groups, the discipline of international relations (IR) has proved slower in providing systematic approaches to interpreting and analyzing GHG. There are various reasons for this, but among the most significant is probably the general paucity of the IR global governance literature to date.[1] A great amount of scholarly effort is still directed primarily at clarifying global governance conceptually, at amending existing theoretical approaches toward its inclusion, and at developing methodologies that reflect these theoretical concerns adequately. The case of GHG offers a number of interesting insights that ought to advance conceptual as well as political debates.

In this article, we approach the problems of GHG by considering the competing political projects that underpin respective GHG conceptions, the actors that represent, defend, and advance them, and the structures that frame debates and policy initiatives. We begin by briefly outlining the scope and nature of the current global health situation, arguing that the main challenge for contemporary GHG is to reestablish within the policy environment the linkage between specific disease-oriented health care interventions and the underlying socioeconomic context. In the next part, we analyze the changing nature and orientation of GHG over the past twenty-five years, using the declarations made at Alma Ata in 1978 and Okinawa in 2000 as signposts indicating two very different trends in GHG. Within this section, we explore the political legacies of two phases of global governance, in broad-brush terms of social democracy and neoliberalism, as a backdrop against which to chart, analyze, and interpret shifts in the GHG discourses. In the final part of the article, we explore recent inputs into the GHG discourse from a wide spectrum of actors, ranging from the World Health Organization (WHO) through to activist nongovernmental organizations (NGOs). We suggest that in their varying hues, these actors have attempted to reintroduce the wider social concerns constitutive of a more integrated approach to health care, which would locate specific interventions within a broader project of socioeconomic transformation.

Setting the Scene: The Challenge for GHG

To an outsider looking in, advances made in responding to health challenges seem inadequate when considered against the exacerbated health risks and problems faced by large populations. As Gro Harlem Brundtland formulated the problem in her address to the World Health Assembly (WHA) in 1998, "Never have so many had such broad and advanced access to healthcare. But never have so many been denied access to health."[2] Crucially, "growing health disparities between the world's wealthy and the world's poor" offset the measurable advances in global health care, such as a general rise in life expectancy from forty-eight years in 1955 to sixty-six in 1998.[3]

Poverty and inequality continue to provide the key context of terminal health problems, with the immediate cause for most deaths among the poor being a disease for which there is a cure. The WHO suggests that 50–90 percent of drugs in the developing and transitional economies are paid for out of pocket, reaffirming that the burden falls heaviest on the poor.[4]

The inequality issue has been highlighted in the context of the recent debate over human immunodeficiency virus (HIV) and poverty—informed significantly by the controversial remarks on the causes of HIV-related deaths by Thabo Mbeki—and the ensuing campaign for broad-based access to antiretroviral (ARV) drugs. Perhaps more than any other disease, HIV/AIDS reflects entrenched and growing global disparities, inequality, and exclusion, together with a salient retrenchment of a North-South divide.[5]

The most challenging problem for GHG, and one that is certainly not composed of but rather exposed more starkly by the AIDS crisis, remains the reestablishment of the linkage in the policy environment between disease-oriented health care intervention and the broader socioeconomic environment. Inequality of access to health mirrors broader socioeconomic inequality. It is in this sense that the GHG agenda must engage with the implications of a health policy environment that has been shaped pervasively by inequalities reproduced through global economic governance.

How are these challenges reflected in current approaches to GHG and to what extent are they likely to be met? In the next section, we reconstruct briefly the different legacies of two phases in global governance, each of which respectively spawned distinctly different academic and policy approaches. We argue that the issues raised between these two clusters are constitutive of the current crisis in GHG.

GHG Discourses: From Alma Ata to Okinawa

The aim of this section is to explore and analyze the changing nature and orientation of GHG from the Alma Ata conference of 1978 to the Okinawa G8 summit of 2000. Each of these occasions resulted in major statements of GHG. However, to do this, it is first necessary to sketch the shifting history of global governance from the 1970s to the present—from the relatively open, multilateral UN-forums to the formalized and narrowly defined policy environments of the neoliberal global governance institutions of the 1980s to the present. This broader historical trajectory of global governance provides the context and important insights for our analysis of GHG from Alma Ata to Okinawa.

Shifting History: Two Legacies of "Global Governance"

We consider two legacies of global governance, representing two phases in its historical trajectory. The first phase broadly covers the 1970s when the prospects for multilateralism were relatively strong and the UN system was the forum for the development of global governance. This phase was marked by the plausibility of global social democracy; it encompassed the call for a New International Economic Order (NIEO) and the Alma Ata declaration, a milestone in health care discourse. The second phase covers the late 1970s onward, when the institutional development of global governance occurred more noticeably through global economic institutions, such as the International Monetary Fund (IMF), the World Bank, and more recently the World Trade Organization (WTO).

During the earlier phase, global governance appeared most clearly focused and unfolding through the UN system. The reasons for this are varied. However, a few trajectories shaped the possibility of a window of opportunity for a social democratic project of global governance during

190   *The Politics of Global Health Governance*

the 1970s and, in its late stages, up until the early 1980s. With the
period of détente in the bipolar world system and the relative decline of
U.S. global hegemony, the UN provided a forum for the emergence
of a coalition of postcolonial states that culminated in the formation of
the G-77 and the proclamation of the need for an NIEO.[6] This coalition
was initially very successful at turning the primary focus in the UN
away from the concerns immediately associated with the remits of the
Security Council and onto the UN's role in shaping the perceptions and
policies on global socioeconomic problems.

The upshot for the shape and form of global governance anticipated
in this context was clearly a conception based on international global
governance, requiring an executive function by UN agencies—for
instance, the UN Conference on Trade and Development (UNCTAD)
and, complementarily, significant increases in funds to these bodies.
The world economic background to these efforts to consolidate multilateral governance in the sense of an NIEO was the capacity crisis of the
late 1960s and early 1970s in advanced capitalist economies[7] and the
gradual transition from an international to a global world economy.[8]

The implications of the NIEO for GHG can be assessed only tenta-
tively, as the NIEO did not include explicit policy framework recommendations on this issue. Yet its general thrust of integrating economic
and social concerns means that the undeniable exacerbation of the
global health crisis through economic inequality would have constituted
a much smaller problem than what is currently experienced.[9]

The 1978 Alma Ata declaration, which enshrined health as a fundamental human right, and its subsequent adoption by the WHO's World
Health Assembly (WHA) in 1981, belong in the context of the politics
of the NIEO. The declaration itself was drafted in the spirit of UN
multilateralism[10] as a declaration of intent in solidarity of the signatories. The adoption by the WHO/WHA of the goals of the declaration to
provide egalitarian health care on a global scale in accordance with a
needs-based approach offers an important insight. It highlights the way
in which UN governance at that historical juncture moved closer than
ever to bridging the gap between declarative/symbolic global politics,
on the one hand, and substantive policy development, on the other. The
UN system was responsive to and transmissive of what was at least a
social-democratic, if not transformative, agenda for global governance.
The combined political might of the tentative OPEC/G-77 coalition
"democratized" the UN more substantially during a time of East-West
stalemate and a lapse in hegemonic leadership in the North. Despite the
more radical challenges continuously posed by the members of, for
instance, the Third World Forum,[11] the expressive social-democratic

compromises can be seen to have commanded both plausibility and practicability in at least a general sense.

The second phase of global governance discussed here is characterized by governance according to neoliberal principles, with the Okinawa summit providing a milestone for the health policy discourse during this period. The phase began during the late 1970s, as the challenges to the political thrust of the NIEO were stepped up. There was a shift in emphasis in the institutional focus of global governance. Whereas the G-77's agenda was advanced mainly through the more parliamentary structures of the UN system, the response to the challenge posed by the call for an NIEO was fashioned through the functionally delimited policy domains of global financial institutions (GFIs) and the evolving multilateral trading system under the General Agreement on Tariffs and Trade (GATT). If the third world challenge to a crisis-ridden and crisis-inducing Northern economic hegemony drew its political force partly from the generality of its reform and transformation demands, the reassertion of Northern dominance proceeded via the piecemeal framing and reconstructing of economic reform proposals and packages along "Reagonomics" lines. Thus, disciplinary neoliberalism[12] in global political economy became extended through institutions in which the political momentum created for the G-77 proved relatively powerless. The constitutive purposes and remits of these institutions circumscribed the modes of engagement. Contemporaneously, a governance agenda was advanced for the structuring of developing states' political institutions. This focused on the administrative and law enforcement–oriented functions of the state/bureaucracy complex that were to be legitimized via democratic minimalism.

GHG: Alma Ata to Okinawa

In this section, the broader changes charted above provide a map for analyzing the changing nature and orientation of GHG. This can be studied by examining in more detail developments from the Alma Ata–inspired "Health for All" strategy in 1981 to the current UN health goals, sanctioned at the G8 summit in Okinawa in July 2000.

The 1978 declaration of Alma Ata cemented the notion of health care as a universal human entitlement and thus as a good, access to which should not be determined by particular economic circumstances. This was to be secured by a participatory process of comprehensive primary health care (PHC) in the context of multisectoral development. The WHO commented that the shape of PHC "is determined by social goals, such as the improvement of the quality of life and maximum health benefits to the greatest number."[13] Thus the declaration was in the spirit of the UN General Assembly, which had already incorporated health as a fundamental human right in the Covenant on Economic, Social and Cultural Rights. The Alma Ata declaration affirmed the responsibility and the crucial role assumed by states and the international community in providing sustainable health care but complemented this affirmation with an explicit recognition of the significant contributions made by households and communities. At least in intent, this was to reflect the experiences of health care improvements induced in the developing world by the establishment of rural health care systems and extension services based on community level access. In 1981, the WHO's WHA endorsed the "health for all by the year 2000" strategy, which was to translate the Alma Ata declaration of 1978 into a reality.

When considering the current global health situation, it is not only obvious that health for all was not achieved by the year 2000, but also that the prospects for significant progress have not improved. At the international level, health goals have been revised and are defined much more narrowly now around specific diseases and specific goals of quantifiable scope,[14] precluding any comprehensive engagement with the issues of universal human rights and socioeconomic transformation, which had previously been identified as crucial to integrated approaches. In May 1998, the WHA, recognizing that the original health for all goals would not be achieved by 2000, passed the new World Health Declaration and endorsed the new policy "Health for All in the 21st Century."[15] While this renewed health for all policy endorses social-democratic principles in terms of a fundamental human right to health, the policy responses supported by the WHO to achieve this goal in the context of globalization, such as public-private partnerships, are the subject of critical evaluation.[16] (See below in relation to policy responses to the challenge of HIV/AIDS.)

These shifts in the scope and general nature of GHG indicate the relocation of the global political project from the more discursively sensitive UN bodies, whose anchoring in parliamentary structures ensure at least some form of a forum of "political will–formation" for global governance, to the functionally defined GFIs and the WTO, ostensibly presented as "nonpolitical" but exhibiting the legitimation problems diagnosed for "new constitutionalism."[17] This means that whereas the achievement of health as a human right as envisaged at Alma Ata required health to be seen as a public good,[18] the neoliberal development orthodoxy of the 1980s and early 1990s interpreted it instead in terms of its privatization potential. The overarching neoliberal development strategy—based on the promotion of economic growth through structural adjustment of national economies and the liberalization of trade, investment, and finance—was to provide the context for the development of global and national health care policies. The new economic orthodoxy that envisaged the comprehensive withdrawal of state influence in markets had the effect of crowding out any political momentum created for cooperative approaches that included redistributive provisions.

This development strategy affected health governance and the actual health of peoples and people both indirectly and directly. The relationship between the neoliberal development project and health inequality has been explored in a number of highly critical recent publications.[19] The role of the market in determining entitlement to health increased, while the role of the state decreased.[20] Importantly, the PHC strategy was modified/derailed almost before it got going. Selective primary health care (SPHC) became the mantra. In terms of policy response, this meant a focus on specific interventions, such as immunization and oral rehydration, rather than an integrated approach to social transformation and community empowerment. The latter had been regarded as crucial to the success of comprehensive health care regimes. Capturing the logic of the SPHC approach quite well, Banerji refers to such interventions as "prefabricated global initiatives" and notes a resemblance between them and the equally prefabricated structural adjustment solutions that pay little regard to local variations (see below).[21]

Expressed in terms of the conception of "society" or societies, underpinning the political shift toward such approaches, the responses to challenges to GHG became framed in terms of functional differentiation. The market-based logic of production and distribution of health "hardware" (drugs and the machinery for health-oriented infrastructure) is set apart operationally from concerns and problems that cannot be expressed in terms of the logic of an economic system.[22]

The piecemeal policy approach to health interventions took place in the direct context of another component of neoliberal global governance: structural adjustment programs (SAPs). The indirect effects of SAPs on health are well documented (for example, the UN Children's Fund, 1987)[23] and have generally lead to criticisms of the dilemmas they have posed for Southern states and societies. Equally, the direct effects have been studied, as seen, for instance, in reports on the exclusion of those who cannot pay through the imposition of user fees and other cost-recovery mechanisms.[24] Confronting the trends toward the comprehensive introduction of payments for what were previously understood to be "public goods," Stephen Browne, director of poverty programs at the UN Development Programme (UNDP), remarks that "user

194   *The Politics of Global Health Governance*

fees are a deterrent to universal education and universal health."[25] World Bank research shows that user fees in health and education result in a lower take-up rate and that the abolition of such fees generally has the desired converse effect. Moreover, user fees beyond the health sector often impact directly on health.[26]

During the 1990s, there was a gradual realization that the process of economic globalization was accompanied by an increasingly pertinent uneven distribution of economic benefits. This resulted in a modification of the overarching global development policy to ameliorate its worst effects. Thus, there was a greater emphasis on targeted poverty reduction through such mechanisms as safety nets and microcredit, public-private partnerships, and debt relief through the Heavily Indebted Poor Countries initiative (HIPC).[27] The notion of good governance became fashionable, and greater efforts were made by multilateral institutions to involve civil society in policy development and implementation. During this period, as already implied in our survey of the greater political trajectories, the WHO lost ground also as a policy provider to the World Bank. In addition to the poor leadership of the WHO's director-general, Hiroshi Nakajima, the enhanced role accorded to the World Bank by the major donors in the context of the restructuring of development policy meant that the World Bank became the main source of funding for the health sector. With its direct links into ministries of finance and ministries of planning, the World Bank became the main multilateral agenda setter in the health field.[28]

This modification in the overarching development strategy and the changing relations between key multilateral institutions were reflected in health policy. On the face of it, there appeared to be an increasing realization in official policy circles that a better balance had to be struck between the goals of economic growth and social and environmental goals, including health. In 1993, the World Bank published its report "Investing in Health," which announced the importance of growth with equity. Some analysts applaud the report for pressing all the right buttons, such as the importance of female education and greater access to health care, but others make a more critical assessment. David Werner and David Sanders, for example, suggest that while the report on first reading sounds "comprehensive, even modestly progressive," in reality this was not the case.[29] For them, the Bank's "new" approach represented 1980s wine in 1990s bottles. Growth, trickle down, and structural adjustment principles underlay the new terminology, which borrows the concepts of social democracy more or less out of political expediency.[30]

In the late 1990s, again reflecting the approach and terminology of global development policy, the emphasis in global health policy was on increasing the involvement of a wide range of stakeholders. Emphasis was placed on public-private partnerships and on the role of benefactors to tackle specific health problems, such as malaria (Rollback Malaria Campaign), vaccines (Global Alliance for Vaccines and Immunization, GAVI), and the problem of access to drugs for the treatment of HIV/ AIDS (UNAIDS-pharmaceutical industry initiative). At Okinawa, the notion of an enhanced role for the private sector and for public-private partnerships was given further legitimacy.

Market-based entitlement thus increasingly meant that those who needed drugs did not have access to them because they could not afford to buy them. As for arguments stressing the failure of states, it is true that most had failed to implement PHC, partly due to a lack of political will and partly due to numerous other constraints, including those imposed by structural adjustment, fluctuating commodity prices, crippling debt repayments, arms purchases, and corruption.

However, where PHC had been seriously attempted (such as in Cuba, India [Kerala], and Costa Rica) there had been great successes.[31] In all these cases, policies toward enhancing socioeconomic equality had been actively pursued by the national or federal state government. Yet in the mid- to late 1990s, the emphasis was still on a narrowly circumscribed role for the state, so the concept of public provision (national or global) was not seen as an appropriate alternative. While rhetorically "stakeholder partnerships" were (and are) the order of the day, typically not all stakeholders are included, as we see below in relation to HIV/AIDS, and not all partnerships function in the spirit of the concept.

This exploration of changing ideas and practice of health governance from Alma Ata to Okinawa would be inadequate without reference to the WTO, the most recent global economic governance body with significant development implications. The WTO impacts on health across a variety of areas, from the general level of "trade creep" over public health concerns to the particular areas, such as the Agreement on the Application of Sanitary and Phytosanitary Measures (SPS).[32] The question of intellectual property rights under the trade-related intellectual property rights (TRIPS) agreement (see below) are important in terms of structuring access to medicines and issues of equity. Also potentially crucial in terms of equity over the next few years will be the General Agreement on Trade in Services (GATS). Although a GATS may not inherently prejudice the development of more inclusive and comprehensive approaches to GHG, the current agenda remains firmly tied to the disembedding logic referred to above and reflects in particular the interests of beneficiaries from trade in financial capital rather than the "localized" goods and services.[33] Critics have warned of the consequences of further entrenchment of the disembedding logic with reference to the provision of health based on public goods.[34] Explored in the context of WTO/GATS implications for the adaptive pressure on domestic health care policies, they make a pertinent point. The neoliberal hegemony, spearheaded in particular by U.S. trade negotiators, produces restrictions on the prospects for public health services in conjunction with enhanced prospects for corporate profit but offers little or no prospect for addressing persistent inequalities.[35]

It is interesting to note that over this period, the emphasis in the presentation of the ill health–poverty relationship has changed. Ill health, of course, contributes to poverty, as it directly affects the often subsistence-oriented economic activities of poor people. Decreasing productivity leads to increasing poverty. The vicious cycle is completed when this in turn leads to further deterioration in health. However, over the last two decades, the presentation of the balance of this relationship has shifted from ill health as a result of poverty, prevailing socioeconomic structures, and the dominant model of development, to conceptions of health in terms of opportunity for poverty reduction and for development. Whereas poverty was portrayed as the primary cause of ill health, now the emphasis has shifted, and ill health is presented more as a key cause of poverty and loss of economic productivity and earnings. The latter is clear in the December 2001 report of the WHO's Commission on Macroeconomics and Health, chaired by Jeffrey Sachs.[36]

These developments may galvanize some dedicated funding for particular problems, and this is both very necessary and urgent.[37] However, ultimately they may not serve well the realization of health as a human right. The consumer-oriented rhetoric of health service provision contained in the new rhetoric places the emphasis on the potential of medicine to remedy health problems, and indirectly poverty, rather than focusing on issues of equity and social transformation as the route to health. To view HIV, malaria, tuberculosis (TB), and other diseases in terms of lost economic productivity conceals that there is a growing body of evidence that suggests that socioeconomic factors influence health and well-being more than medical intervention.[38] While this analysis does not dismiss the importance of such interventions—clearly they are vital—it does suggest that it would be a mistake to take our eyes off the comprehensive need for socioeconomic transformation.

HIV/AIDS and the Legacies of Alma Ata and Okinawa

The HIV/AIDS crisis, having been neglected by key agents of global governance for twenty years, became the focus of attention at the turn of the new century. On 10 January 2000, the UN Security Council met to discuss the challenge of HIV/AIDS, and in July 2001, a UN General Assembly Special Session (UNGASS) was convened to address the problem. The G8 has also considered the problem. Therefore, over the last two years in a relatively short space of time, this disease has been transformed from a health issue into a security issue and most recently into a development issue.

As the symptoms of HIV are treatable and the disease itself can today be controlled to enhance both the patient's life prospects and quality of life, the issue of access to medication assumes an obvious pertinence in this case.[39] When considered in the context of the immensity of the problem, plus the unequal global distribution of the burden of the disease, it is obvious that countries with the greatest constraints on their budgets would be the very ones having to spend the most on HIV-related care. How is this challenge reflected in current approaches of GHG?

The global response to date has focused on piecemeal investments based on loans, discounts, or donations. Policy has been framed in terms of the rights of corporations rather than the human right to health. Corporations are keen to uphold their patent rights, thus safeguarding profits (mostly accrued in the North) into the future. The efforts of a few developing countries to pursue legitimate strategies to secure drugs for their people at more affordable prices have been obstructed by pharmaceutical companies and by some Northern governments, notably the United States.[40] (In theory, the WTO's TRIPS allows for the use of compulsory licensing [Article 31] and parallel importing [Article 6] to increase access to affordable drugs for infected citizens).[41]

The piecemeal approach outlined above is often presented in the language of partnerships. A key problem with these "partnerships" is that they are not based on substantive conceptions of equality that underpin, for instance, the health for all ideal, and that those in whose interests they are avowedly developed are in general excluded from their negotiation. For serious partnerships to develop, developing countries must be fully involved in deliberations with companies and UN organizations.[42]

The global policies currently in vogue for tackling the HIV/AIDS pandemic are likely to bring only limited short-term gains while enhancing significantly risks and vulnerabilities in the future. A cursory glance at the conditions for establishing workable societywide health infrastructures for administering ARVs makes this clear. Unless GHG in conjunction with the national and localized extension agencies get it right, a focus on "providing drugs" is likely to lead to significant adverse effects—for instance, increases in patient risks and the accelerated emergence of drug-resistant strains.[43]

There is growing recognition in several quarters that GHG, in order to be relevant in the context of the massive and deepening global inequality, poverty, and exclusion that characterize the AIDS pandemic, must facilitate the socioeconomic conditions that make health for all realizable. Under current conditions, and given the magnitude of the problem, this seems conditional on comprehensive regulatory and sociopolitical intervention with great emphasis on redistribution. So far this is absent in the GHG response.

The Reform of GHG

The "Okinawa" agenda for GHG has been dominated by a limited set of actors who, albeit to differing degrees, have either encouraged and/or legitimated the continued disembedding of GHG from these wider concerns for social justice from which it is inseparable. There have been a few expressions of concern (such as by UNICEF), directed toward bringing about a reintroduction of wider social concerns within the current formal global governance patchwork. Yet these arguments for a more integrated approach have been without significant effect. In the light of recent clashes over access to HIV-related medication, the WHO has been playing a more confident role under the leadership of Gro Harlem Brundtland and her successor. In particular—and echoing the concerns of the G-77 coalition in the context of the NIEO—the WHO has taken on explicitly the issue of the inequality of access. In May 1999, the fifty-second World Health Assembly gave the WHO the mandate to do more work on trade-related issues, including the impact of global trade governance on access to drugs. The WHO was asked to study the effects of international trade agreements on health. NGOs are working with the WHO to track prices and access to essential drugs.[44] This research is seen as directly linked with enhancing Southern governments' political clout with reference to negotiating and defending affordable access. In the course of the engagement of global economic governance over health concerns, this newly emboldened coalition of interests and outlooks has aided the developing country "victory" at the Doha Round of the WTO.[45] Doha included a formal commitment to the health emergency measures already contained under TRIPS article 31, which had been the subject of the pharma-industry's challenge to Southern governments (most notably Brazil and South Africa).[46] Since Doha, however, continued bilateral pressure by the United States has restricted and delayed the production of cheaper generic drugs, thus revealing the hollow nature of the Doha victory.[47]

Agents of Change

If recent attempts to shape GHG into more egalitarian terms have echoed the agenda set by the Alma Ata declaration, it is important to acknowledge that today the circumstances and the form and thrust of such a political project differ significantly. This can be gauged with reference to the range of actors—and their efficacy—involved in contesting the current consensus and the institutional and organizational environment within which this contest occurs. We have outlined the latter above—a more formalized global arena of political institutions, rules, and modes of interaction that evolved out of the 1980s–1990s efforts to secure and institute international commerce. With regard to the former, the agents of "egalitarian" politics of GHG belong, in general, to a more pluralized context of complex alliances, cooperation, and multiple publics on which the force of the political challenge depends. We consider, in turn, states, organizations, and social movements.

States. Rather than reflecting, as in the case of the NIEO, a relatively coherent challenge to the dominant world order, backed up by a strong coalition, today's state actors involved in contesting the inegalitarian distribution of entitlements to health care involve a few, relatively well positioned representatives of Southern concerns. The relatively higher economic performance of, for instance, Brazil and South Africa renders their status as markets, rather than as recipients of health care aid, more plausible, at least in the midterm future. Hence, the focus of pharmaceutical companies on preventing such states from establishing norms of "good practice," which contravene the corporate agenda of securing profits projected on intellectual property agreements. The states mentioned above have acted individually. However, as documented by the Doha Round, we are beginning to see strength in numbers and more concerted action internationally. This was already clear, for example, at the Geneva World Summit for Social Development in June 2000, when G-77 countries pushed a proposal for the final conference text to protect essential medicines from patentability. Although they did not achieve this, they did succeed in getting an affirmation of countries' rights to freely exercise their legal options.[48]

Organizations. The organizational side can be approached by considering the top-down and bottom-up continuum of organizational actors. On the one hand, there are the institutions of global economic governance (World Bank, IMF, WTO) projecting claims to a new "post–Washington Consensus," with greater emphasis on social and political questions and less focus on the economic orthodoxies of the SAP period. Yet its current programs typically continue to stress market-based responses to the challenges posed by globalization. While this captures some degree of the imbalance that persists in the *international* system, where Northern countries continue to hold on to advantageous subsidies and tariff barriers, the focus on trade liberalization distorts again the way in which the benefits of trade-led growth get distributed. The *international* focus on terms of trade and balance of trade distracts from an analysis of the *global* reproduction of inequality and immiseration.[49]

The bottom-up perspective in the field of organizational actors has seen NGOs, government-related international nongovernmental organizations (GRINGOs), and government-organized nongovernmental organizations (GONGOs) gain greater access to global governance bodies, a development that is often offset by a degree of decoupling from their social movement bases, where such a base existed or was important in propelling the respective organizations onto the international political scene. The move from protest to consultation entails, politically, a narrowing of the informal power base, which often enabled the accession of the NGOs in the first place. This highlights, on the one hand, the problematic representative status of NGOs and, on the other hand, the implications of conceptions of cooperation versus co-optation.[50] More generally, to assume that NGOs and their hybrid siblings are unequivocal agents of progressive change is, of course, hugely misleading. Many NGOs effectively function as lobbying groups, often with narrow agendas and sometimes in ways more conducive to the continuation of existing power relations (see, for example, the role of the International AIDS Economics Network [IAEN], which is, at best, politically ambivalent). The conflictual map of civil society, drawn already by Hegel, serves as a warning against shortcutting assessments of political efficacy and purpose of its agents.[51]

Social movements. Social movements are "by definition fluid phenomena."[52] They differ from organizations and individual "events" (protests), yet their political clout is crucial to both these aspects of "politics from civil society." Insofar as momentum is building for sustained challenges to currently dominant modes in the formation of global governance, social movements can be seen as the sites at which politicization occurs; thus events such as the reiterative protest assertions in the context of global summits begin to take on features of a social movement.

Health activists, scholars, and citizens concerned with the encompassing conception of health policy outlined above are part of this reassertion of "egalitarian" politics, realizing, for instance, the potential significance of the WTO, not only for general issues of inequality but for health issues in particular.[53] Awareness raising and campaigning on health trade issues are gathering momentum as activists see the importance of putting health at the center of trade debates rather than on the periphery. Responses occur both in targeted issue areas, where campaigns focus on expertise-driven intervention in the technical processes of policymaking, and in the broader context of fostering general public debate about the nature of emerging global health governance.

The twin roles of NGOs and (egalitarian) social movements in constructing a governance-relevant "complex multilateralism"[54] in the more general sense is discernible in their persistence to promote more comprehensive conceptions of social justice, which address not only the distribution of health care, but also the conditions of health in general. Ultimately, the challenge of health is viewed by these actors as basically the challenge of socioeconomic equity and development from the local to the national, regional, and global level. As Robert Beaglehole and Ruth Bonita note, "The main variation in health status among countries result from environmental, socio-economic and cultural factors, and medical care is of secondary importance."[55]

Conclusion

Reform of health governance will have to occur at many levels, yet its constraints are now significantly constructed internationally and at the global level. The required changes will have to be profound to make a significant and sustainable difference. There are examples of great achievements on very limited resources where social equity is prioritized. (For instance, TB control programs are cited as successful in this respect.)[56] However in some regions, notably Africa, the challenge symbolized by AIDS, but laden with far-reaching ramifications, is so great that possibly little short of a Marshall Plan is needed to make a big difference.

Is this likely? There are few signs of it at the moment, but there are, at least, signs of limited reform. Poverty reduction is back on the World Bank agenda and equity has returned to the policy discourses of the WHO agenda. Gro Harlem Brundtland stated in 1999 that the problem of "access . . . amounts to a moral problem, a political problem and a problem of credibility for the global market system," an assertion that at least helps to focus the ongoing debates in more inclusive terms.[57] The market-driven agenda for health policy implementation relied crucially on the continued promises of the eventual trickle-down of economic benefits from a generally buoyant global economy. However, the current slowdown and impending recessions may refocus and reinvigorate the politics of "re-embedding," of redistribution, and of the protection of social and political achievements, rather than their erosion through their colonization with market rationalities. Perhaps the pendulum is just beginning to swing back in favor of social justice, and the next step will be a more vigorous promotion of health in terms of public goods at all levels, from the local to the global. ⊕

Notes

Caroline Thomas is professor of global politics at Southampton University. She has a long-standing interest in third world issues in international relations and has published a number of books on aspects of third world security and global development. Martin Weber is a lecturer in politics and international relations at the University of Aberdeen. He has research interests in international political theory, environmental politics, and global political economy and has published articles and book chapters in these fields.

1. Craig Murphy, "Global Governance: Poorly Done and Poorly Understood," *International Affairs* 14, no. 1 (2000): 3–27.

2. Cited by Joyce Millen, Alec Irwin, and Jim Yong Kim, "Introduction: What Is Growing? Who Is Dying?" in Millen, Irwin, Kim, and John Gershman, eds., *Dying for Growth: Global Inequality and the Health of the Poor* (Monroe, Maine: Common Courage Press, 2000), p. 4.

3. Ibid.

4. WHO, "The Rationale of Essential Drugs," available online at www.who.int/medicines/edm-concept.html (accessed January 2001).

5. The disproportionate impact of major health challenges on Southern countries and the roles of poverty and inequality were noted at the fifty-third World Health Assembly, May 2000.

6. Robert Cox, "Ideologies and the New International Economic Order," in Robert Cox and Tim Sinclair, eds., *Approaches to World Order* (Cambridge: Cambridge University Press, 1996), p. 237.

7. Heloise Weber, "Reconstituting the 'Third World'? Poverty Reduction and Territoriality in the Global Politics of Development," *Third World Quarterly* 25, no. 1 (2004).

8. Cox and Sinclair, *Approaches to World Order,* p. 528.

9. Evidence for the positive effects of redistribution on general well-being is provided in UNICEF's annual State of the World's Children reports, which suggest a link between social equity and health. For particular country experiences,

see David Werner and David Sanders, *The Politics of Primary Health Care and Child Survival* (Palo Alto: HealthWrights, 1997), and Aviva Chomsky, "The Threat of a Good Example: Health and Revolution in Cuba," in Millen et al., *Dying for Growth,* pp. 331–358. David Coburn's article "Income Inequality, Social Cohesion and the Health Status of Populations: The Role of Neoliberalism," *Social Science and Medicine* 51 (2000): 139–150, has stimulated a lively debate.

10. Cox and Sinclair, *Approaches to World Order,* pp. 494–519.

11. Ibid., pp. 380–381.

12. Stephen Gill, "Globalisation, Market Civilisation, and Disciplinary Neoliberalism," *Millennium* 24, no. 3 (1995): 399–424.

13. WHO/UNICEF, *Primary Health Care,* Report of the International Conference on Primary Health Care, Alma Ata, 6–12 September 1978 (Geneva: WHO, 1978), p. 38.

14. The G8 summit in Okinawa, July 2000, set numerical targets on major infectious diseases to be achieved by 2010. See http://www.g8kyushu-okinawa.go.jp/ (accessed 1 March 2001).

15. See http://www.who.int/archives/hfa/default.htm (accessed July 2002).

16. Caroline Thomas, "Trade Policy and the Politics of Access to Drugs," *Third World Quarterly* 23, no. 2 (2002): 251–264.

17. Gill, "Globalisation, Market Civilisation, and Disciplinary Neoliberalism."

18. We are aware of the problems created for using "public goods" as a normative standard in the context of the adoption of the public goods discourse by the IFIs and the WTO. The issue requires an in-depth critical reconstruction of shifts in the conception of what is properly such a good. For the purpose of our argument, public goods are conceived ideally as provided equally on a not-for-profit and needs basis.

19. Debabar Banerji, "A Fundamental Shift in the Approach to International Health by WHO, UNICEF, and the World Bank: Instances in the Practice of 'Intellectual Fascism' and Totalitarianism in Some Asian Countries," *International Journal of Health Services* 29, no. 2 (1999): 227–259; Millen et al., *Dying for Growth;* Evelyne Hong, *Globalisation and the Impact on Health: A Third World View* (Penang, Malaysia: Third World Network, 2000), available online at www.twnside.org.sg (accessed 10 December 2000).

20. Werner and Sanders, *The Politics of Primary Health Care and Child Survival;* Daniel Drache and Terry Sullivan, eds., *Market Limits in Health Reform: Public Success, Private Failure* (London: Routledge, 1999).

21. Banerji, "A Fundamental Shift," p. 239.

22. Elmar Altvater and Brigit Mahnkopf, "The World Market Unbound," *Review of International Political Economy* 4, no. 3 (1997): 448–471.

23. Giovanni Cornia, Richard Jolly, and Frances Stewart, eds., *Adjustment with a Human Face,* vol. 1: *Protecting the Vulnerable and Promoting Growth,* A Study by UNICEF (Oxford: Clarendon Press, 1987).

24. Werner and Sanders, *The Politics of Primary Health Care and Child Survival,* pp. 102–104.

25. Lean Ka-Min, "User Fees Blamed for Cholera Outbreak in South Africa," 26 October 2000, available online at http://www.twnside.org.sg/title/cholera.htm (accessed 21 November 2000).

26. Ibid., p. 1.

27. Heloise Weber, "The Imposition of a Global Development Architecture: The Example of Microcredit," *Review of International Studies* 28, no. 3, (July 2002): 537–556.

28. Kent Buse and Catherine Gwin, "World Health: The World Bank and Global Cooperation in Health: 'The Case of Bangladesh,'" *Lancet*, no. 351 (1998), pp. 665–669; Kamran Abbasi, "The World Bank and World Health: Changing Sides," *British Medical Journal*, no. 318 (27 March 1999): 865–869.

29. Werner and Sanders, *The Politics of Primary Health Care and Child Survival*, p. 104.

30. Alex Callinocos, *Against the Third Way* (London: Routledge, 2000).

31. Chomsky, "The Threat of a Good Example."

32. Meri Koivusalo and Michael Rowson, "The WTO: Implications for Health Policy," *Medicine, Conflict and Survival* 16 (2000): 175–191; Meri Koivusalo, *The World Trade Organisation and Trade-Creep in Health and Social Policies*, GASPP Occasional Paper No. 4 (Helsinki: STAKES, 1999).

33. Altvater and Mahnkopf, "The World Market Unbound," p. 459.

34. David Price, Allyson Pollock, and Jean Shaoul, "How the WTO Is Shaping Domestic Policies in Health Care," *Lancet* 354, no. 9193 (27 November 1999).

35. Ibid., p. 1891.

36. Jeffrey Sachs, ed., *Macroeconomics and Health: Investing in Health for Economic Development* (Geneva: WHO, 2001).

37. WHO, *World Health Report* (Geneva: WHO, 2000).

38. Thomas McKeown, *The Origins of Human Disease* (Oxford: Blackwell, 1988); J. Fraser Mustard, "Health, Health Care and Social Cohesion," in Drache and Sullivan, *Market Limits in Health Reform*, pp. 329–350.

39. Panos Institute, *Beyond Our Means? The Cost of Treating HIV/AIDS in the Developing World* (London: Panos, 2000), p. 3; Paul Rogers, "War on Want," available online at www.opendemocracy.net (posted 13 February 2002).

40. Thomas, "Trade Policy and the Politics of Access to Drugs."

41. Ibid.

42. Manto Tshabalala-Msimang, "Cheaper AIDS Drugs for South Africa? Minister Tells of Progress," Health Systems Trust, available online at http://hst.off1:.za/view.oho3?id=20001004 (accessed 24 October 2000).

43. A. D. Harries et al., "Preventing Antiretroviral Anarchy in Sub-Saharan Africa," *Lancet* 358, no. 4 (2001): 410–414.

44. Margaret Duckett, "Compulsory Licensing and Parallel Importing," ICASO Background Paper, July 1999, p. 7, available online at www.icaso.org (accessed 10 October 2000).

45. Sanjoy Bagchi, "What Happened at Doha?" *Economic and Political Weekly*, India (29 December 2001).

46. Patrick Bond, "A Political Economy of South African AIDS," *ZNet Commentary*, 16 July 2000, available online at www.spiraldynamics.com/documents/hotspots/Africa/SA_AIDS_Bond.htm (accessed 22 November 2000); Thomas, "Trade Policy and the Politics of Access to Drugs"; see also www.tac.org.za/archive.htm (accessed December 2000).

47. Oxfam, "US Bullying on Drug Patents: One Year After Doha," Oxfam Policy Paper No. 33, available online at www.oxfam.org.uk/policy/papers/33bullying/33bullying.html (accessed 22 November 2002).

48. Celia Oh, "TRIPS and Pharmaceuticals: A Case of Corporate Profits over Public Health," available online at http:twnslde.org.sg/title/twr120a.htm (accessed 14 November 2000).

49. Julian Saurin, "The Global Organisation of Disaster Triumphant," paper presented at the ISA biannual global convention in Chicago, February 2001.

50. Inge Kaul, Isabelle Grunberg, and Marc Stern, eds., *Global Public Goods: International Cooperation in the Twenty-first Century* (New York: Oxford University Press, 1999); Lincoln Chen, Tim Evans, and Richard Cash, "Health as a Global Public Good," in Kaul, Grunberg, and Stern, *Global Public Goods,* pp. 284–304; Inge Kaul and Michael Faust, "Global Public Goods and Health: Taking the Agenda Forward," *Bulletin of the World Health Organisation* 79, no. 9 (2001).

51. See, for an extensive discussion, Alejandro Colas, *International Civil Society* (Cambridge: Polity Press, 2002).

52. Donatella Della Porta and Mario Diani, *Social Movements: An Introduction* (London: Blackwell, 1999), p. 17.

53. Ronald Labonte, "Healthy Public Policy and the WTO: A Proposal for an International Health Presence in Future Trade/Investment Talks," *Health Promotion International* 13, no. 3 (1998): 245–256; Enis Baris and Kari McLeod, "Globalization and International Trade in the Twenty-first Century: Opportunities for and Threats to the Health Sector in the South," *International Journal of Health Services* 30, no. 1: 187–210.

54. Robert O'Brien, Anne-Marie Goetz, Jan Aart Scholte, and Marc Williams, *Contesting Global Governance* (Cambridge: Cambridge University Press, 2000), p. 206.

55. Robert Beaglehole and Ruth Bonita, "Public Health at the Crossroads: Which Way Forward?" *Lancet* 351, no. 21 (February 1998): 590–592.

56. Harries et al., "Preventing Antiretroviral Anarchy in Sub-Saharan Africa," pp. 410–411.

57. Gro Harlem Brundtland, "Towards a Strategic Agenda for the WHO Secretariat," Statement by the Director General to the Executive Board at Its 105th Session, WHO, EB105/2, 24 January 2000, p. 7.

Part II
Globalization and Global Health

[8]

The globalization of public health: the first 100 years of international health diplomacy

David P. Fidler[1]

Abstract Global threats to public health in the 19th century sparked the development of international health diplomacy. Many international regimes on public health issues were created between the mid-19th and mid-20th centuries. The present article analyses the global risks in this field and the international legal responses to them between 1851 and 1951, and explores the lessons from the first century of international health diplomacy of relevance to contemporary efforts to deal with the globalization of public health.

Keywords Public health administration/history; World health/trends; International cooperation/history; Diplomacy; Communicable disease control/history; Drug and narcotic control/history; Employment/standards; Alcoholic beverages/supply and distribution; Water pollution/prevention and control; International law; Treaties (*source: MeSH*).

Mots clés Administration santé publique/histoire; Santé mondiale/orientations; Coopération internationale/ histoire; Diplomatie; Lutte contre maladie contagieuse/histoire; Contrôle drogues et stupéfiants/histoire; Emploi/ normes; Boissons alcoolisées/ressources et distribution; Pollution eau/prévention et contrôle; Droit international; Traités (*source: INSERM*).

Palabras clave Administración en salud pública/historia; Salud mundial/tendencias; Cooperación internacional/ historia; Diplomacia; Control de enfermedades transmisibles/historia; Control de medicamentos y narcóticos/ historia; Empleo/normas; Bebidas alcohólicas/provisión y distribución; Contaminación del agua/prevención y control; Derecho internacional; Tratados (*fuente BIREME*).

Bulletin of the World Health Organization, 2001, **79**: 842–849.

Voir page 848 le résumé en français. En la página 848 figura un resumen en español.

Introduction

Contemporary analyses of public health make much of its globalization and the national and international impact of this. Commentators argue that globalization creates challenges for the governance of global health, including the need to construct international regimes capable of responding to global threats to public health. These problems are not new: the globalization of public health led to the development of international health diplomacy and international regimes for public health beginning in the mid-19th century. This article analyses the first 100 years of international health diplomacy in order to elucidate what lessons the past holds for the governance of global health today and in the future.

The term "globalization" has been introduced only recently into analyses of world affairs. Most definitions of globalization indicate that it refers to the process of increasing interconnectedness between societies such that events in one part of the world increasingly have effects on peoples and societies far away (*1*). The idea that events in one

part of the world have health effects in countries far away is familiar to historians. Thus McNeill analysed the formation of a Eurasian and then a global infectious disease pool from 500 BC to 1700 AD (*2*). The quarantine practices of European states in the 14th century marked the beginning of modern public health (*3, 4*). The history of public health is, in fact, that of the processes of increasing interconnectedness between societies such that events in one part of the world have health effects on peoples and countries far away.

International cooperation on the control of global risks to human health did not begin until the mid-19th century. Today's commentators argue that the factors accounting for globalization, such as information technology, trade and the flow of capital, undermine the state's control over what happens in its territory (*5*). Globalization forces individual states to cooperate with each other and build partnerships with non-state actors, such as multinational corporations and nongovernmental organizations, in order to develop global governance. Experts distinguish international governance, defined as intergovernmental cooperation, from global governance, which involves the interaction of states, international organizations, and non-state actors to shape values, policies and rules (*6*). In public health, the shift from national to global

[1] Professor, Indiana University School of Law, 211 South Indiana Avenue, Bloomington, IN 47405, USA (email: dfidler@indiana.edu).

Ref. No. **01-1313**

governance began in the mid-19th century, when international health diplomacy emerged because of concern about infectious diseases. During the next 100 years this facet of diplomacy expanded as states, international organizations, and non-state actors tackled global threats to public health through international law and institutions.

The public health risks that acquired global significance during this period were associated with infectious diseases, opium and alcohol, occupational hazards, and transboundary pollution. These matters are discussed below, as are the legal and institutional responses of states and international organizations; the role of non-state actors in global health governance from the mid-19th century until the mid-20th century; the effectiveness of the global health governance regimes constructed in this period; and the lessons of the first century of international health diplomacy for people currently struggling with global risks to public health and the politics they generate.

Global public health risks, 1851–1951

Infectious diseases

International health diplomacy began in 1851, when European states gathered for the first International Sanitary Conference to discuss cooperation on cholera, plague, and yellow fever (7). These states had previously dealt with transboundary disease transmission through national quarantine policies. The development of railways and the construction of faster ships were among the technological advances that increased pressure on national quarantine systems (8). However, disease control became a subject of diplomatic discussion as a result of the cholera epidemics that swept through Europe in the first half of the 19th century. National policies not only failed to prevent the spread of the disease but also created discontent among merchants, who bore the brunt of quarantine measures and urged their governments to take international action. In today's parlance, cholera was an emerging infectious disease that caught Europeans unprepared.

The next 100 years witnessed an evolution in international cooperation on infectious diseases. States convened conferences, adopted treaties, and created several international health organizations to facilitate cooperation on infectious diseases. The work of Koch and Pasteur encouraged international cooperation as germ theory allowed diplomats to shape more informed policies and rules. By the end of 1951 this scientific and diplomatic process had produced the World Health Organization and a single set of international legal rules on infectious disease control, the International Sanitary Regulations (9). Over the course of a century, the global threat of infectious diseases had produced processes, rules, and institutions for global health governance.

International trade in narcotic drugs and alcohol

The international trade in opium was lucrative for the European powers. This was especially true for Great Britain, which forced China to allow the importation of opium from other British colonial territories, particularly India, after the Opium War of 1839–42 (10). Improvements in sailing technology, especially the development of the clipper ship, enabled the opium trade to expand, thus solidifying the economic links between Europe, the Americas, and Asia (10). International concern about the deleterious social and health effects of the opium trade grew during the latter half of the 19th century. The International Opium Commission held its first meeting in 1909 (11, 12). In response to the global health threat presented by narcotic drugs, states negotiated nine treaties on their control between 1912 and 1953.

The second half of the 19th century also saw Western states engaging in diplomacy about the adverse effects of alcohol on indigenous people in colonial areas. In 1884, Great Britain proposed that an international understanding be entered into for the protection of the indigenous peoples of the Pacific Ocean by prohibiting the supply of liquors to them (13, 14). Similar concerns found expression in the 1890 General Act of the Brussels Conference Relating to the African Slave Trade and in the 1899 Convention Respecting Liquor Traffic in Africa (15, 16).

Regulation of the alcohol trade to Africa continued into the 20th century. In 1901 the US Senate proposed that "the principle ... that native races should be protected against the destructive traffic in intoxicants should be extended to all uncivilized peoples by enactment of such laws and the making of such treaties as will effectually prohibit the sale by the signatory powers to aboriginal tribes and uncivilized races of opium and intoxicating beverages" (14). Using this resolution, in 1902 the USA proposed a universal treaty on limiting liquor sales "in the western Pacific, or in any other uncivilized quarter where the salutary principle of liquor restriction could be practically applied" (14). In the 1919 treaty regulating alcohol importation in most of sub-Saharan Africa, the signatories stated that the prohibition of alcohol importation was necessary because alcohol was "especially dangerous to the native populations by the nature of the products ... or by the opportunities which a low price affords for their extended use" (17). In addition, Western states exhibited concern about the illicit trade in alcohol among themselves, as evidenced by numerous regional and bilateral treaties.

Occupational safety and health

The industrial revolution that swept across Europe in the 19th century triggered concerns about health threats posed by dangerous working conditions. The mistreatment of workers by industrial enterprises became a global phenomenon that produced efforts to create international labour standards. Concerns about occupational safety and health continued into the 20th century and led to the creation of the International Labour Organisation (ILO) in 1919. The ILO's constitution emphasized the global nature of the threat to occupational safety and health, in asserting "conditions of labor exist involving such injustice, hardship, and privation to large numbers of people as to produce unrest so great that the peace and harmony of the world are imperiled; and an improvement in those conditions is urgently required" (*18*).

Transboundary water pollution

The industrial revolution created new environmental and health threats that transcended national boundaries and raised the need for international cooperation. Birnie & Boyle, analysing 19th-century and early 20th-century treaties regulating the uses of international rivers and lakes, observed that "early European practice frequently prohibited industrial or agricultural pollution harmful to river fisheries or domestic use" (*19*). Transboundary air pollution was the subject of the 1938 Trail Smelter Arbitration, whereby Canada was held responsible for damage caused in the USA by emissions from a Canadian smelting facility (*20, 21*). While not as geographically widespread as the problems presented by infectious diseases, transboundary pollution emerged in the 1851–1951 period as another public health threat that had to be tackled through international law.

International law, international institutions and global public health risks

Analyses of global public health risks have frequently mentioned international law and international organizations. When a state needs to cooperate with other countries to confront a threat, international law often becomes a central instrument in the crafting of a common approach. Globalization undermines a state's ability to control what happens in its own territory. Consequently, it is necessary to construct procedures, rules, and institutions through international law. Arguments about the importance of international legal regimes to the production of global "public goods" underscore the importance of international law in dealing with global problems (*22*). A great quantity and diversity of international legal regimes on global health risks emerged during the 1851–1951 period.

Infectious diseases

The series of International Sanitary Conferences that began in 1851 and continued for almost a century, together with other diplomatic efforts, produced many treaties on infectious disease control (Table 1). Also important to the development of international legal regimes on infectious diseases was the creation of international health organizations with a mandate to facilitate cooperation on infectious diseases. Four such organizations emerged during the 1851–1951

period: the Pan American Sanitary Bureau in 1902, the Office International de l'Hygiène Publique in 1907, the Health Organisation of the League of Nations in 1923, and WHO in 1948.[a]

International trade in narcotic drugs and alcohol

States also used treaties and international organizations to control international trade in opium and alcohol. The treaties on narcotic drug control that were negotiated between 1912 and 1953 are listed in Table 2. Advice on these treaties was provided by international health organizations, such as the Office International de l'Hygiène Publique and the Health Organisation of the League of Nations (*8*). The League of Nations created an Opium Advisory Committee in 1921, which examined international opium traffic (*11*). The Pan American Sanitary Bureau was involved in combating drug addiction in the Americas during the first half of the 20th century (*23*).

Treaties concerning alcohol sought to control illicit regional or bilateral traffic or to restrict the importation and sale of alcohol in Africa (Table 3 and Table 4). The 1919 treaty regulating alcohol traffic in Africa created a central bureau to oversee implementation under the authority of the League of Nations (*17*). The Health Organisation of the League of Nations began working on alcoholism in 1928 (*24*).

Occupational safety and health

States also turned to international law and international organizations in connection with the improvement of occupational safety and health standards (Table 5). The founding of the ILO in 1919 catalysed the creation of international labour law because this body adopted numerous treaties on the improvement of standards.

Transboundary air pollution

European and North American states used treaties to regulate pollution in international watercourses in the latter half of the 19th century and the first half of the 20th century (Table 6). The rules in the treaties were not uniform in their approach: some strictly prohibited pollution, while others tolerated pollution caused by reasonable uses of international watercourses (*19*). Treaties on transboundary air pollution did not, however, develop in the 1851–1951 period. The best-known international legal dispute on transboundary air pollution in this period, the Trail Smelter Arbitration (1938), involved the application of customary international law rather than a treaty. Nevertheless, it demon-

---

[a] States also created the Organisation International des Epizooties in 1924 to deal with the international transmission of animal diseases, and the International Convention for the Protection of Plants (1929) and the International Plant Protection Convention (1951) to focus on transnational aspects of plant life and health.

strated that international law applied to transbound-ary air pollution. The arbitral panel held that "no state has the right to use or permit the use of its territory in such a manner as to cause injury by fumes in or to the territory or the properties or persons therein, when the case is of serious consequence and the injury is established by clear and convincing evidence" (20).

Non-state actors and the globalization of public health, 1851–1951

A feature of contemporary globalization is the growing importance of multinational corporations and nongovernmental organizations on both global health problems and global governance (25). The involvement of non-state actors in globalization largely distinguishes global governance from inter-national governance. Between 1851 and 1951, merchants involved in moving people and goods around the world contributed to the spread of infectious diseases and to the international trade in opium and alcohol. Commercial enterprises, frus-trated by national quarantine systems, exerted pressure on states to launch and sustain diplomacy on infectious disease control (26). Nongovernmen-tal organizations, such as the Rockefeller Founda-tion and the International Union Against Tuberculosis, cooperated with international health organizations in tackling infectious diseases and other public health problems (8). The International Bureau Against Alcoholism, established in 1907, urged governments to limit alcohol imports, especially in Africa (24).

A major development came with the provision in the ILO constitution that delegations of Member States should all include representatives from industry and labour unions who should have the right to vote alongside but independently of govern-ment representatives (18). ILO is also empowered to receive representations from employers' and work-ers' organizations if they consider that a Member State is not complying with ILO treaties to which it is a party. This gives non-state actors an important role in monitoring international labour standards (18).

The growth in the importance of nongovern-mental organizations in global health between 1851 and 1951 can be demonstrated by comparing the treaties establishing the Office International de l'Hygiène Publique and WHO. The 1907 treaty creating the Office International de l'Hygiène Publique contains no mention of nongovernmental organizations or of the possibility that it could collaborate with them (27). On the other hand, WHO's constitution provides that it can consult and cooperate with nongovernmental organizations (28). While not as robust as the ILO constitution in respect of the use of non-state actors, WHO's constitution recognizes the importance of public–private partner-ships between international health organizations and nongovernmental organizations.

Table 1. **Treaties dealing with infectious diseases, 1892–1951**

Year	Treaty
1892	International Sanitary Convention
1893	International Sanitary Convention
1894	International Sanitary Convention
1897	International Sanitary Convention
1903	International Sanitary Convention replacing the 1892, 1893, 1894 and 1897 International Sanitary Conventions
1905	Inter-American Sanitary Convention
1912	International Sanitary Convention, replacing the 1903 International Sanitary Convention
1924	Pan American Sanitary Code
1924	Agreement Respecting Facilities to be Given to Merchant Seaman for the Treatment of Venereal Disease
1926	International Sanitary Convention, modifying the 1912 International Sanitary Convention
1927	Additional Protocol to the Pan American Sanitary Convention
1928	Pan American Sanitary Convention for Aerial Navigation
1930	Convention Concerning Anti-Diphtheritic Serum
1930	Agreement Regarding Measures to be Taken Against Dengue
1933	International Sanitary Convention for Aerial Navigation
1934	International Convention for Mutual Protection Against Dengue Fever
1938	International Sanitary Convention, amending the 1926 International Sanitary Convention
1944	International Sanitary Convention, modifying the 1926 International Sanitary Convention
1944	International Sanitary Convention for Aerial Navigation, modifying the 1933 International Sanitary Convention for Aerial Navigation
1946	Protocols to Prolong the 1944 International Sanitary Conventions
1951	International Sanitary Regulations

Table 2. **International treaties on the control of narcotic drugs, 1912–1953**

Year	Treaty
1912	International Opium Convention
1925	Agreement Concerning the Manufacture of, Internal Trade in, and Use of Prepared Opium
1925	International Opium Convention
1931	Convention for Limiting the Manufacture and Regulating the Distribution of Narcotic Drugs
1931	Agreement for the Control of Opium Smoking in the Far East
1936	Convention for the Suppression of the Illicit Traffic in Dangerous Drugs
1946	Protocol amending the treaties of 1912, 1925 and 1931
1948	Protocol for Bringing Under International Control Drugs Outside the Scope of the 1931 Convention for Limiting the Manufacture and Regulating the Distribution of Narcotic Drugs
1953	Protocol for Limiting and Regulating the Cultivation of the Poppy Plant, the Production of, and International and Wholesale Trade in, and Use of Opium

Effectiveness of global health governance regimes, 1851–1951

In general, the development of international legal regimes on matters of public health has been impressive. However, the mere enumeration of treaties does not give any indication of their influence on public health. Indeed, the treaties might even be

Table 3. **Treaties on the alcohol trade in Africa, 1890–1919**

Year	Treaty
1890	General Act of the Brussels Conference Relating to the African Slave Trade, Articles XC-XCV
1899	Convention Respecting Liquor Traffic in Africa
1906	Convention Respecting Liquor Traffic in Africa
1919	Convention Respecting Liquor Traffic in Africa

Table 4. **Regional and bilateral treaties regulating illicit trade in alcohol, 1887–1936**

Year	Treaty
1887	Convention Respecting Liquor Traffic in the North Sea
1922	France–Switzerland Convention on the Control of Movement of Intoxicating Liquors
1924	US–UK Convention on Regulation of Liquor Traffic
1924	US–Germany Convention on the Regulation of the Liquor Traffic
1924	US–Sweden Convention on Liquor Traffic
1924	US–Denmark Convention on Liquor Traffic
1924	US–Panama Convention on the Prevention of Smuggling of Intoxicating Liquors
1924	US–France Convention on Preventing Smuggling of Intoxicating Liquors
1924	US–Netherlands Convention on Regulation of the Liquor Traffic
1924	US–Norway Convention on the Regulation of Liquor Traffic
1925	Convention for the Suppression of Contraband Traffic in Alcoholic Liquors in the Baltic Sea
1925	US–Belgium Treaty on Smuggling Alcoholic Liquors into the United States
1928	US–Greece Convention on the Regulation of Liquor Traffic
1932	Finland–Hungary Convention on Prevention of Smuggling Alcoholic Goods
1933	UK–Finland Treaty on the Suppression of the Illicit Importation of Alcoholic Liquors
1933	Sweden–Finland Treaty on Illicit Importation of Alcoholic Beverages
1935	Denmark–Sweden Convention on the Prevention of Smuggling of Alcoholic Beverages
1936	Czechoslovakia–Finland Agreement on the Suppression of the Illicit Importation of Alcoholic Liquors into Finland

seen as rearguard actions against advancing health risks generated by modernizing technologies and the processes of globalization.

Domestic sanitary and public health reforms were more significant than treaties in reducing morbidity and mortality attributable to infectious diseases in many Western countries during the first half of the 20th century (*29*). Doubts about the treaties were raised as early as 1894 by Koch, who criticized those targeting cholera as superfluous because the proper policy was for every country "to seize cholera by the throat and stamp it out" (*7*). In 1947 the US Department of State argued that many states were bound only by obsolete conventions or by no treaties at all (*30*). Experts believed that states were slow to adapt treaty regimes to changes in scientific knowledge and patterns of international trade (*30, 31*). The treaties were also not considered important in connection with public health law generally (*32*). Furthermore, the existence of multiple

international health organizations complicated their efforts on infectious diseases and other issues (*33*).

Questions abound in connection with the international legal regimes established to deal with traffic in narcotic drugs and alcohol. Brewley-Taylor observed that "European nations were unwilling to surrender national sovereignty over domestic drug control or relinquish profitable opium monopolies in their colonies until the League [of Nations] was effectively dead" (*12*). While missionaries claimed that the 1890 treaty regulating alcohol sales in Africa "was to a good degree effective in the Congo region" (*14*), it is not clear whether this regime protected Africans from alcohol and the adverse consequences of its abuse. The USA initiated most of the bilateral treaties on illicit alcohol trade after its own unsuccessful prohibition of alcohol consumption in 1919. International legal analysis of the liquor treaties in the 1920s focused not on public health but on whether their enforcement conformed to the international law of the sea (*34*).

The efforts of ILO to improve standards for occupational safety and health were undermined by friction associated with its treaty-making, by the failure of ILO Member States to ratify or comply with treaties, and by the world economic depression (*35*). Industrial development continued to increase air and river pollution. The later treaties in this period relating to international rivers in Europe clearly showed increased tolerance of pollution as industrial demands on river resources continued to grow (*19*). In connection with transboundary air pollution, the precedent of the Trail Smelter Arbitration remained unique, indicating that such pollution became routine as industrialization spread around the world.

Conclusion: lessons for the contemporary globalization of public health

In the first 100 years of international health diplomacy, global health governance across a range of public health issues was attempted by states, international health organizations, and non-state actors An enormous body of international law on public health, now largely forgotten, was created. The following characteristics marked this period of global health governance: 1) a tendency for health risks to become global because of the growth in international commerce; 2) a need for states to cooperate through international law in order to confront global threats to health; 3) the involvement of nongovernmental organizations and multinational corporations; and 4) mixed results achieved by international legal regimes.

In contemporary discourse about the globalization of public health, experts emphasize the global nature of public health threats, e.g. those associated with pathogenic microbes and the trade in tobacco products. Similarly, calls for international cooperation and legal action against global health risks abound. WHO is revising the International Health

Regulations (*36*) and leading the negotiation of the Framework Convention on Tobacco Control (*37*). Experts have called for international agreements on alcohol control (*38*), the rights of the mentally ill (*39*), the funding of global vaccine supplies (*40*), pandemic influenza vaccine supplies (*41*), and the improvement of access to essential drugs and vaccines (*42*). Increased prominence is being given to international law in the field of public health (*31, 43, 44*). Experts stress the importance of participation by non-state actors in matters of global public health (*45*). In terms of global health governance, history appears to be repeating itself

However, the 1851–1951 period teaches us to be realistic about what states, international health organizations, and non-state actors can accomplish using international law as a means of dealing with global health problems. Earlier experience in the construction and revision of international legal regimes relating to public health serves as a warning in connection with WHO's efforts to revise the International Health Regulations and create the Framework Convention on Tobacco Control. WHO Member States rejected innovative changes to the International Health Regulations proposed in 1998, e.g. those relating to syndromic reporting and the establishment of a committee of arbitration to deal with violations of the rules (*46*). What form the revised International Health Regulations will take remains unclear. The content of the Framework Convention on Tobacco Control has yet to be agreed among states (*47*). The history of efforts to achieve international control of narcotic drugs and alcohol suggests that an effective treaty on tobacco control will be difficult to achieve.

The 1851–1951 period of global health governance exhibits the same paradox as has been identified by the contemporary analysis of the globalization of public health: globalization jeopardizes disease control nationally by eroding sovereignty, while the assertion of national sovereignty can frustrate disease control internationally (*48*). The first 100 years of international health diplomacy proved how vulnerable global health governance was to the machinations of states and the volatile dynamics of international politics. Economic and technological interconnectedness in the period caused public health risks to become global more effectively than they fostered international cooperation to control them. Furthermore, the behaviour of the great powers undermined global health governance. Imperialism, two world wars, and a global economic depression weakened international cooperation on public health. The efforts of Western states to regulate the Asian opium trade and the trafficking of liquor to Africa seem hypocritical when one considers the exploitation of Asians and Africans at the hands of these countries.

Current concerns about global health threats from infectious diseases, narcotic drugs, alcohol, tobacco, labour standards, and environmental pollution suggest that global health governance still lags

Table 5. Treaties on international labour standards related to occupational safety and health, 1906–1937

Year	Treaty
1906	Convention Respecting the Prohibition of Night Work for Women in Industrial Employment
1906	Convention Respecting the Prohibition of the Use of White (Yellow) Phosphorus in the Manufacture of Matches
1919	ILO C1 Hours of Work (Industry) Convention
1919	ILO C3 Maternity Protection Convention
1919	ILO C4 Night Work (Women) Convention
1919	ILO C5 Minimum Age (Industry) Convention
1919	ILO C6 Night Work of Young Persons (Industry) Convention
1920	ILO C7 Minimum Age (Sea) Convention
1921	ILO C10 Minimum Age (Agriculture) Convention
1921	ILO C13 White Lead (Painting) Convention
1921	ILO C14 Weekly Rest (Industry) Convention
1921	ILO C16 Medical Examination of Young Persons (Sea) Convention
1925	ILO C17 Workmen's Compensation (Accidents) Convention
1925	ILO C18 Workmen's Compensation (Occupational Diseases) Convention
1930	ILO C29 Forced Labour Convention
1932	ILO C32 Protection Against Accidents (Dockers) Convention
1935	ILO C45 Underground Work (Women) Convention
1937	ILO C62 Safety Provisions (Building Industry) Convention

Table 6. Treaties dealing with pollution of transboundary international rivers and lakes, 1869–1944

Year	Treaty
1869	Convention Between the Grand Duchy of Baden and Switzerland Concerning Fishing in the Rhine Between Constance and Basel
1882	Convention between Italy and Switzerland Concerning Fishing in Frontier Waters
1887	Convention Establishing Uniform Provisions on Fishing in the Rhine and Its Tributaries
1892	Convention Between Luxembourg and Prussia Regulating Fisheries in Boundary Waters
1893	Convention Decreeing Uniform Regulations for Fishing in Lake Constance
1906	Convention between Switzerland and Italy Establishing Uniform Regulations Concerning Fishing in Border Waterways
1909	United States-Canada Boundary Waters Treaty
1922	Agreement between Denmark and Germany Relating to Frontier Watercourses; Provisions Relating to the German-Belgian Frontier
1923	Agreement between Italy and Austria Concerning Economic Relations in Border Regions
1944	United States-Mexico Colorado River Treaty

behind the ability of human societies to create and spread disease. The revision of the International Health Regulations and the work on the Framework Convention for Tobacco Control mirror the pattern seen in the 1851–1951 period. Efforts in global health governance are belated reactions to developing and established epidemics, reducing the prospects for successful international cooperation. Just as Great Britain forced China to accept the opium trade in the 19th century, the USA and other great powers spread the tobacco pandemic through their efforts to break into the markets of developing countries with cigarette imports. The myopic approach of the great powers has also been evident in the controversies surrounding access to essential drugs and medicines, e.g. HIV/AIDS therapies, in the developing world. Contemporary global health governance is vulnerable to the machinations of the great powers and the resentments of those who remain alienated by international politics.

Global health governance in the 21st century faces problems not seen in the first 100 years of international health diplomacy, e.g. those relating to genetic engineering and access to essential drugs. New technologies, such as the Internet, provide non-state actors with more powerful resources with which to influence the direction of global health governance. For these and other reasons, looking backwards can offer lessons of only limited value. States, international health organizations, and non-state actors confront such 21st-century challenges with tools of global health governance that have remained largely unchanged since the 19th and early 20th cen-

turies. This suggests that, in the final analysis, the tools are unlikely to bring about the differences that are needed. These are more likely to be achieved if states internalize public health effectively as an interest and value. Towards the end of the 1851–1951 period, the WHO constitution envisioned health as a fundamental human right. This is a far cry from the scientifically ignorant, selfish national fears that drove public health on to the diplomatic agenda in the mid-19th century. Contemporary *angst* about global public health reveals that WHO's vision remains unfulfilled after more than 50 years of the organization's existence. Today, it is vital that human societies should move closer to fulfilling this vision instead of remaining trapped in the patterns established between 1851 and 1951. ∎

Conflicts of interest: none declared.

Résumé

La mondialisation de la santé publique : les cent premières années de la diplomatie sanitaire internationale

Ce sont les menaces qui pesaient sur la santé publique dans le monde au XIXe siècle qui ont suscité l'apparition d'une diplomatie sanitaire internationale. De nombreux régimes internationaux applicables à la santé publique ont été instaurés entre le milieu du XIXe et le milieu du XXe siècle. Le présent article analyse les risques mondiaux dans ce domaine et l'ensemble de dispositions légales mises en place pour y faire face au niveau international entre 1851 et 1951, ainsi que les éléments de la diplomatie sanitaire internationale dont pourraient s'inspirer les efforts déployés actuellement face à la mondialisation de la santé publique.

Resumen

Globalización de la salud pública: los primeros 100 años de la diplomacia sanitaria internacional

Las amenazas mundiales que se cernieron sobre la salud pública en el siglo XIX dispararon el desarrollo de la diplomacia sanitaria internacional. Numerosas pautas internacionales sobre cuestiones de salud pública se establecieron entre mediados del siglo XIX y mediados del siglo XX. En el presente artículo se analizan los riesgos mundiales en este campo y las respuestas jurídicas internacionales articuladas contra ellos entre 1851 y 1951, y se examinan las lecciones de la diplomacia sanitaria internacional que más interés revisten para los esfuerzos actualmente desplegados a fin de abordar la globalización de la salud pública.

References

1. **Smith S, Baylis J.** Introduction. In: Smith S, Baylis J, eds. *The globalization of world politics.* Oxford, Oxford University Press, 1997: 1–11.
2. **McNeill WH.** *Plagues and peoples.* New York, Doubleday, 1977.
3. **Rosen G.** *A history of public health.* New York, MD Publications, 1958.
4. **Porter D.** *Health, civilization, and the state: a history of public health from ancient to modern times.* London, Routledge, 1999.
5. **Scholte JA.** The globalization of world politics. In: Smith S, Baylis J, eds. *The globalization of world politics.* Oxford, Oxford University Press, 1997: 13–30.
6. **Lee K, Dodgson R.** Globalization and cholera: implications for global governance. *Global Governance,* 2000, **6**: 213–236.
7. **Howard-Jones N.** *The scientific background of the Sanitary Conferences, 1851–1938.* Geneva, World Health Organization, 1975.
8. **Goodman NM.** *International health organizations and their work,* 2nd ed. London, Churchill Livingstone, 1971.
9. *International Sanitary Regulations. World Health Organization Regulations No. 2.* Geneva, World Health Organization, 1951 (WHO Technical Report Series, No. 41).
10. **Trocki CA.** *Opium, empire and the global political economy: a study of the Asian opium trade 1750–1950.* London, Routledge, 1999.
11. **Jennings JM.** *The opium empire: Japanese imperialism and drug trafficking in Asia, 1895–1945.* Westport, CT, Praeger, 1997.
12. **Brewley-Taylor DR.** *The United States and international drug control, 1909–1997.* London, Pinter, 1999.
13. **Moore JB.** *Digest of international law, volume II.* Washington, DC, Government Printing Office, 1906.

14. *Protection of native races against intoxicants.* Washington, DC , United States Senate, 1902 (Document No. 200, 57th Congress, 1st Session).

15. General Act of the Brussels Conference Relating to the African Slave Trade, 2 July 1890. *Consolidated Treaty Series,* 1890, **173**: 293–324.

16. Convention Respecting Liquor Traffic in Africa, 8 June 1899. *Consolidated Treaty Series,* 1898–1899, **187**: 346–351.

17. Convention Relating to Liquor Traffic in Africa, 10 September 1919. *Consolidated Treaty Series,* 1919, **226**: 1–7.

18. Constitution of the International Labour Organisation, 28 June 1919. In: *American Journal of International Law Supplement,* 1936, **30**: 68–80.

19. **Birnie PW, Boyle AE.** *International law and the environment.* Oxford, Clarendon Press, 1992.

20. Trail Smelter Arbitration. *American Journal of International Law,* 1939, **33**: 182–212.

21. Trail Smelter Arbitration. *American Journal of International Law,* 1941, **35**: 684–734.

22. **Kaul I, Grunberg I, Stern MA.** Defining global public goods. In: *Global public goods: international cooperation in the 21st century.* Oxford, Oxford University Press, 1999: 2–19.

23. *Pro salute novi mundi: a history of the Pan American Health Organization.* Washington, DC, Pan American Health Organization, 1992.

24. **Bélanger M.** *Droit international de la santé [International health law].* Paris, Economica, 1983.

25. **Willetts P.** Transnational actors and international organizations in global politics. In: Smith S, Baylis J, eds. *The globalization of world politics.* Oxford, Oxford University Press, 1997: 287–310.

26. **Howard-Jones N.** Origins of international health work. *British Medical Journal,* 1950, **1**: 1032–1037.

27. Rome Agreement Establishing the Office International d'Hygiène Publique, 9 Dec. 1907 In: Goodman, NM. *International health organizations and their work,* 2nd ed. London, Churchill Livingstone, 1971: 101–104.

28. Constitution of the World Health Organization, 22 July 1946. In: *Basic documents,* 40th ed. World Health Organization, 1994: 1–18.

29. **Winslow CEA.** *The conquest of epidemic disease: a chapter in the history of ideas.* Princeton, NJ, Princeton University Press, 1943.

30. International health security in the modern world: the sanitary conventions and the World Health Organization. *Department of State Bulletin,* 1947, **17**(437): 953–958.

31. **Fluss SS.** International public health law: an overview. In: Detels R et al., eds. *Oxford textbook of public health, volume 1,* 3rd ed. Oxford, Oxford University Press, 1997: 371–390.

32. **Tobey JA.** *Public health law,* 2nd ed. New York, The Commonwealth Fund, 1939.

33. **Howard-Jones N.** *International public health between the two world wars: the organizational problems.* Geneva, World Health Organization, 1978.

34. **Hackworth GH.** *Digest of international law, volume I.* Washington, DC, Government Printing Office, 1940.

35. **Alcock A.** *History of the International Labor Organization.* New York, Octagon Books, 1971.

36. **Fidler DP.** *International law and infectious diseases.* Oxford, Clarendon Press, 1999.

37. **Taylor AL, Bettcher DW.** WHO Framework Convention on Tobacco Control: a global "good" for public health. *Bulletin of the World Health Organization,* 2000, **78**: 920–929.

38. **Jernigan DH et al.** Towards a global alcohol policy: alcohol, public health and the role of WHO. *Bulletin of the World Health Organization,* 2000, **78**: 491–499.

39. *WHO, raising awareness, fighting stigma, improving care: Brundtland unveils new WHO global strategies for mental health, sees poverty as a major obstacle to mental well-being.* Geneva, World Health Organization 1999 (press release WHO/67, 12 November 1999); see also: *World health report 2001 – Mental health: new understanding, new hope.* Geneva, World Health Organization (in press).

40. **Barton J.** Financing of vaccines. *Lancet,* 2000, **355**: 1269–1270.

41. **Fedson D.** *The epidemiology of influenza vaccination: implications for global vaccine supply for an influenza pandemic* (unpublished paper).

42. **Pécoul B.** Priorities for research and development. Paper presented at: *International Conference on Infectious Diseases,* Okinawa, 7–8 December 2000.

43. **Taylor AL et al.** International health instruments. In: Detels R et al., eds. *Oxford textbook of public health,* 4th ed. Oxford, Oxford University Press (in press).

44. **Fidler DP.** *International law and public health.* New York, Transnational Publishers, 2000.

45. **Fidler DP.** The potential role of transnational civil society in health development in the Americas: lessons from the NGO revolution in international law and international relations. In: Bambas A et al., eds. *Health and human development in the new global economy.* Washington, DC, Pan American Health Organization, 2000: 173–194.

46. *Provisional draft of the International Health Regulations.* Geneva, World Health Organization, 1998.

47. *Framework Convention on Tobacco Control.* Geneva, World Health Organization, 2001 (unpublished document WHO/A/FCTC/INB2/2, 9 January 2001).

48. **Fidler DP.** Globalization, international law, and emerging infectious diseases. *Emerging Infectious Diseases,* 1996, **2**: 77–84.

[9]

Global public health: revisiting healthy public policy at the global level

Ilona Kickbusch and Evelyne de Leeuw

We are in a period of significant change for public health. The Ottawa Charter for Health Promotion acknowledged this process through its subtitle: 'the move towards a new public health'. Initially, the new public health debate focused on public health revival, intersectorality and citizen participation. It found its exemplar expression at the local level through the Healthy Cities approach (Ashton and Seymour, 1988). Recently a new discussion has emerged which focuses on public health at a global level. It reflects on the balance between national and international responsibility for public health, revisits the mandate of international organizations, the social responsibility of private companies and the role and legitimacy of non-governmental organizations.

This new global dimension of public health was at the center of the Jakarta Conference on 'New players for a new era'. Tobacco, HIV/AIDS, environmental pollution, food safety, invasive lifestyles, none of these stops at national borders. Yet common action between countries is frequently neglected in favor of anxiously guarded national interests. The Jakarta Conference responded to the tension between globalization and governance with the call for a global alliance for health promotion—giving expression to the need for a new institutional form of global health action (WHO, 1997). How can we take this idea further?

GLOBALIZATION AND PUBLIC HEALTH: LOSS OF INTERNAL SOVEREIGNTY

Globalization was initially understood as a purely economic phenomenon, associated with rapid flows of capital, the growth of global corporations and extreme global inequities. Increasingly though the political, social and cultural dimensions of globalization are being discussed—most recently in the Reith Lectures by Anthony Giddens

(Giddens, 1999). The lectures highlight the temporal, spatial and cognitive dimensions of globalization, and illustrate its pervasiveness both in the developed and developing world. Giddens identifies two schools of thought in relation to globalization: the skeptics who refute that significant change is taking place and the radicals who argue 'that not only is globalization very real, but that its consequences can be felt everywhere'. He comes down firmly, as do the authors of this editorial, on the side of the radicals.

The public health community has only just begun to look at the impact of globalization on health. The contributions by Yach and Bettcher have described globalization as increasing interdependence rather than as a qualitatively new phenomenon (Yach and Bettcher, 1998). Lee has broadened the debate one step further by illustrating the impact of the spatial, temporal and cognitive dimensions of globalization on health concerns and disease patterns, but also defines globalization as increased interdependence (Lee, 1998). Kickbusch and Quick have drawn attention to the many new players in the health arena and identified the need for connecting in new types of partnerships (Kickbusch and Quick, 1998).

A key point this editorial wants to make is that globalization is more than increased interdependence and interconnectedness, be it of nations, people, capital or information. This distinction matters in relation to the policy response of countries. Globalization—contrary to interdependence —challenges the internal sovereignty of nation states. It implies 'a new sphere of action independent of territory', which restricts the policy-making capacity of individual governments within their own territory because the instruments at their disposal cannot reach into the operational sphere of many global players. Reinicke in his excellent book *Global Public Policy* illustrates this development using examples from finance, crime and trade (Reinicke, 1998). It is important that we embark on a similar detailed analysis for the health arena.

Health, which at first instance seems to be the field most destined for joint action independent of territory (how often have we heard and used the phrase that disease knows no borders), remains a policy domain most protectively linked to the nation state. But even as countries defend their internal sovereignty over health care policy they are losing sovereignty over policies related to health determinants: the marketing, distribution and sale of consumer goods and lifestyles (e.g. tobacco and food), the growth of a global health industry (e.g. pharmaceuticals and insurance), the global spread of environmental pollution and infectious disease, the health impact of the global financial system. How then can governments respond other than through new forms of protectionism or extreme competition to attract the global players into their own front yard?

GLOBAL PUBLIC HEALTH

In order to emphasize the interaction between countries and trends in globalization, Frenk and Chacon have suggested the term 'new international health' (Frenk and Chacon, 1992). Having experienced the discussion around the 'old' and 'new' public health following the Ottawa Charter, we believe that this would be an unfortunate choice. It would also not reflect the essentially new dimension of globalization. We suggest to follow the reasoning developed by Reinicke for a global public policy, and propose the term 'global public health'. The challenge before us is to develop a framework that defines its characteristics, and through a series of detailed case studies identifies forms of social organization, mechanisms and instruments for global public health action.

If we look at the present system of international health co-operation we see two key trends: a significant increase in the players in the international health arena; and subtle but systematic erosion of internal sovereignty. Countries maintain their internal sovereignty as a constitutional right within the specialized health agency of the United Nations: the World Health Organization. But 'back home', internal sovereignty in health is being significantly challenged if not eroded in a wide range of countries through a myriad of factors: the actions of transnational corporations, conditionalities set by the IMF, premises of the health

care reform efforts of the World Bank, priorities set by bilateral aid agencies and the agreements reached at the World Trade Organization or the European Union. This erosion is not just directed at developing countries as a form of post-colonial interference but also significantly affects the developed world. It is a global phenomenon.

In response to this development, global public health would 'aim' to fill the governance gap related to those health issues and health development processes that are independent of territory, and to balance the impact of globalization on internal health sovereignty. It would in a novel way bring together the health agendas of the developed and the developing world.

What 'form' should global public health take? There are of course many schools of thought as to the appropriate response to these pressures. Reinicke postulates that the only response which will enable nation states to maintain their policy-making capacity is by voluntarily pooling internal sovereignty, others see a clear need to bring all key players—governmental and non-governmental—together in a process of 'governance without governments', and yet others wish to see a significant strengthening of the UN system. A new system will probably contain elements of all three strategic responses.

NETWORKS AND REGIMES

We are only at the very beginning of understanding the social organization and the new quality of the dynamics between actors that flows from globalization. Therefore, we need to experiment with the institutional response required. Just as the League of Nations was founded as a new mechanism to ensure the external sovereignty of nation states, mechanisms need to be created that allow countries to pool internal sovereignty and work together for a common purpose in a new form of governance while including other social actors beyond the state.

Manuel Castells has described the network as the new organizational form of governance for the 21st century, because it transcends space and time and shares and redistributes power and resources in a new form of social organization (Castells, 1996). This also increasingly means allowing other actors—non-governmental organizations and the private sector—to participate in an organized system of governance. The network approach is only beginning to take shape in the health arena: the fight against HIV/AIDS can be seen as perhaps one of the first truly global public health networks (Gordenker *et al.*, 1995), the Healthy Cities Movement as another (Kickbusch, 1999). A range of UN organizations, the World Bank as well as the new leadership of WHO are experimenting with partnership-oriented approaches, which could provide the nucleus for new forms of governance.

But governance would go beyond intensified co-operation. In the economic and environmental field, many authors argue for new forms of joint decision-making by regime formation involving a broad range of state and non-state actors, a case in point being the ozone regime (Young, 1997). Elements and components of such global regimes for public health exist with the international health regulations, the International Code for the marketing of breast milk substitutes, the Codex Alimentarius and the proposal to develop an International Framework Convention on Tobacco Control. In fact, regimes can be seen as a form to collectively operationalize internal sovereignty at the global level and indeed most regimes at this stage are state organized.

Following such a line of thought we could define global public health as the collective ability to conduct healthy public policy at a global level through a network of public, private, non-governmental, national, regional and international organizations by regime formation.

HEALTH AS A GLOBAL PUBLIC GOOD

We need to address the tension between globalization and global health governance with urgency. The focus of the debate so far has been more concerned with the 'leadership' of specific agencies or the usual call for more co-ordination between the various actors. It must look more systematically at how to strengthen countries in their health policy capacity at the global level and how to increase the accountability for the health impacts of global actors outside of the health arena. The duties and obligations at all levels of governance need to be mapped out with greater clarity, and mechanisms need to be devised that deal with non-compliance, all the more so because non-adherence at any level can have significant global health consequences.

But in order to move ahead, there is need of a common sense of purpose. Two—mutually not exclusive—frameworks can help to move the debate to a new arena. One is to follow in the footsteps of the debate on the environment and reframe health as a 'commons'. International commons (Young, 1997) are 'physical or biological systems that lie wholly or largely outside the jurisdiction of any individual member of international society but that are of interest to two or more of them—or their nationals—as a valued resource'. This relates well to the Ottawa Charter and its definition of health as a resource. The other approach is to define health as a 'global public good' (Kaul *et al.*, 1999) whose benefits 'reach across borders, generations and population groups' and thus calls for a global public policy response.

Understanding healthy public policy at the global level as part of the move towards a global public health must tackle three challenges: the framing of health as a valued global commons/public good; the response to globalization through a new inclusive system of global health governance; and the development of global regimes, codes of conduct and mechanisms of accountability in pursuit of improved global health. This will imply new roles and responsibilities for all concerned: the international organizations, nation states, civil society and the private sector.

THE ROLE OF SCHOOLS OF PUBLIC HEALTH

Schools of public health should be at the forefront of analyzing these developments, mapping the emerging global public health patchworks and networks, and proposing new instruments and mechanisms for the global response. They need to provide public health professionals with the knowledge and skills to respond strategically and effectively. Research agendas and training curricula need to incorporate new global perspectives. We need to complement 'international health' with a global public health perspective, as outlined above. The policies and strategies that flow from this will be significantly different from today and require us to strengthen not only the science but also particularly the art of public health. They will transcend traditional disciplinary boundaries as much as they transcend national sovereignty. And they transcend a simplistic division of the world into global, national and local. Indeed, the term 'glocal' is now being used to express this intense interaction (Kickbusch, 1999). Law, economics, policy sciences, management,

288   *I. Kickbusch and E. de Leeuw*

network sociology and international relations need to be connected systematically with the global public health agenda. Joint degrees and research programs are pathways to enhancing our understanding of the driving forces and the possible avenues for intervention through global public health action.

We urge schools of public health and public health associations to recognize the dimensions of global public health action, and to integrate them into their teaching, research and daily practice.

Ilona Kickbusch
Chair, Editorial Board
Yale University
Evelyne de Leeuw
Maastricht University

REFERENCES

Ashton, J. and Seymour, H. (1988) *The New Public Health.* Open University Press, Milton Keynes.

Castells, M. (1996) *The Rise of the Network Society.* Blackwell, Oxford.

Frenk, J. and Chacon, F. (1992) Bases Conceptuales para la Education e Investigacion en Salud Internacional. In *Organizacion Panamericana de la Salud.* WHO/PAHO, Washington, pp. 209–224.

Giddens, A. (1999) Reith Lectures. Http://news.bbc.uk

Gordenker, L., Coate, R. A., Jönsson, C. and Söderholm, P. (1995) *International Cooperation in Response to AIDS.* Pinter, London.

Kaul, I., Grunberg, I. and Stern, M. A. (eds) (1999) *Global Public Goods.* Oxford University Press, New York.

Kickbusch, I. and Quick, J. (1998) Partnerships for health in the 21st century. *World Statistics Quarterly*, **51**, 68–74.

Kickbusch, I. (1999) Global + local + glocal public health. *J. Epidemiol. Community Health*, **53**, 0–1.

Lee, K. (1998) Globalization and health policy. Discussion paper no. 1. London School of Hygiene and Tropical Medicine, London.

Reinicke, W. H. (1998) *Global Public Policy.* Brookings Institution Press, Washington D.C.

Yach, D. and Bettcher, D. (1998) The globalization of public health I and II. *American Journal of Public Health*, **88**, 735–741.

Young, O. R. (1997) *Global Governance.* MIT Press, Cambridge, MA.

World Health Organization (WHO) (1997) The Jakarta Declaration on leading health promotion into the 21st century. *Health Promotion International*, **12**, 261–264.

[10]

Globalisation and the prevention and control of non-communicable disease: the neglected chronic diseases of adults

R Beaglehole, D Yach

The growing global burden of non-communicable diseases in poor countries and poor populations has been neglected by policy makers, major multilateral and bilateral aid donors, and academics. Despite strong evidence for the magnitude of this burden, the preventability of its causes, and the threat it poses to already strained health care systems, national and global actions have been inadequate. Globalisation is an important determinant of non-communicable disease epidemics since it has direct effects on risks to populations and indirect effects on national economies and health systems. The globalisation of the production and marketing campaigns of the tobacco and alcohol industries exemplify the challenges to policy makers and public health practitioners. A full range of policy responses is required from government and non-governmental agencies; unfortunately the capacity and resources for this response are insufficient, and governments need to respond appropriately. The progress made in controlling the tobacco industry is a modest cause for optimism.

Globalisation—the increasing interconnectedness of countries and the openness of borders to ideas, people, commerce, and financial capital—has beneficial and harmful effects on the health of populations.[1,2] The effect of the current phase of globalisation, or more properly reglobalisation,[3] on health has been debated worldwide.[1,2,4] Most attention has been directed towards control of infectious diseases and national security threats, provision of affordable medicines, and changes required in international trade and finance agreements to improve access to treatment. Broader policy concerns include the relation between globalisation and equity and the changing role of the state and governance for health.[5]

By contrast, the growing burden of non-communicable diseases—mainly heart disease, stroke, cancer, diabetes, and obesity—has been neglected. In this article, we assess the relation between globalisation and non-communicable disease epidemics, summarise the evidence in support of preventing such disease, and outline the required global and national responses.

The global burden of non-communicable disease

This year there will be an estimated 56 million deaths globally, of which 60% will be due to non-communicable diseases:[6] 16 million deaths will result from cardiovascular disease (CVD), especially coronary heart disease (CHD) and stroke; 7 million from cancer; 3·5 million from chronic respiratory disease; and almost 1 million from diabetes. Mental health problems are leading contributors to the burden of disease in many countries and contribute substantially to the incidence and severity of many non-communicable diseases including CVD and cancer.[7]

Table 1 shows that non-communicable diseases are leading causes of death in developing and developed countries. Only in Africa do communicable diseases cause more deaths than non-communicable diseases; this year

Lancet 2003; **362:** 903–08

WHO, Geneva, Switzerland (R Beaglehole DSc, D Yach MBChB)

Correspondence to: Dr R Beaglehole, Evidence and Information for Policy, WHO, 20 Avenue Appia, CH-1211 Geneva 27, Switzerland (e-mail: beagleholer@who.int)

2·8 million CVD deaths will occur in China and 2·6 million in India. Non-communicable diseases contribute substantially to adult mortality with the highest rates being in central and eastern European countries (figure).[7] They add to health inequalities within and between countries, mainly affecting poor populations largely because of inequalities in the distribution of major risk factors.[8–10] The global pattern of death will increasingly be dominated by non-communicable diseases; by 2020, CHD and stroke are expected to be the leading causes of death and loss of disability-adjusted life years.[6]

Causes of non-communicable disease

The burden of non-communicable disease results from past and cumulative risks; the future burden will be determined by current population exposures to risk factors. Although the major risk factors for non-communicable disease epidemics are more complex than those for infectious disease, they are well known and account for almost all such events;[11,12] many are common to the main categories of non-communicable diseases and most are modifiable and operate in the same manner in all regions of the world, with some quantitative differences.[13]

The ageing of populations, mainly due to falling fertility rates and increasing child survival, are an underlying determinant of non-communicable disease epidemics. Additionally, global trade and marketing developments are driving the nutrition transition towards diets with a high proportion of saturated fat and sugars. This diet, in combination with tobacco use and little physical activity, leads to population-wide atherosclerosis and the widespread distribution of non-communicable disease.

Table 2 shows the contribution of the major non-communicable disease risk factors to the burden of disease. In developed countries, seven of the ten leading risk factors contributing to the burden of disease are for non-communicable disease, compared with six and three of ten in developing countries with low and high rates of mortality, respectively. In most developing countries, non-communicable disease risk factor levels have increased during the past decade, portending an increase in the rate of non-communicable diseases in the next two decades.

PUBLIC HEALTH

World			Developed countries			Developing countries		
Rank	Cause	% of total deaths	Rank	Cause	% of total deaths	Rank	Cause	% of total deaths
1	Ischaemic heart disease	12·4%	1	Ischaemic heart disease	22·6%	1	Ischaemic heart disease	9·1%
2	Cerebrovascular disease	9·2%	2	Cerebrovascular disease	13·7%	2	Cerebrovascular disease	8·0%
3	Lower respiratory infections	6·9%	3	Trachea, bronchus, lung cancers	4·5%	3	Lower respiratory infections	7·7%
4	HIV/AIDS	5·3%	4	Lower respiratory infections	3·7%	4	HIV/AIDS	6·9%
5	COPD	4·5%	5	COPD	3·1%	5	Perinatal conditions	5·6%
6	Perinatal conditions	4·4%	6	Colon and rectum cancers	2·6%	6	COPD	5·0%
7	Diarrhoeal diseases	3·8%	7	Stomach cancer	1·9%	7	Diarrhoeal diseases	4·9%
8	Tuberculosis	3·0%	8	Self-inflicted injuries	1·9%	8	Tuberculosis	3·7%
9	Road traffic accidents	2·3%	9	Diabetes	1·7%	9	Malaria	2·6%
10	Trachea, bronchus, lung cancers	2·2%	10	Breast cancer	1·6%	10	Road traffic accidents	2·5%

COPD=chronic obstructive pulmonary disease. Developed countries include European countries, former Soviet countries, Canada, USA, Japan, Australia, and New Zealand.

Table 1: **Estimates of the ten leading causes of death in 2000**[6]

Effects of globalisation

Financial and economic globalisation and the World Trade Organization (WTO) rules that regulate trade, can improve population health status by increasing national incomes. However, the poorest and most excluded countries have not experienced this benefit.[14] Global rules and power imbalances constrain the ability of countries and national health services to respond adequately to health problems. Although national governments can shape international trade rules their influence has been limited by insufficient resources, expertise, and technical support; although advances were made in promoting access to pharmaceuticals at the WTO Ministerial Meeting in Doha in 2001.[15]

Globalisation directly and indirectly affects the development of non-communicable disease epidemics.[1] The indirect effects of globalisation are mediated by national economic performance and act through changes in household income, government expenditure, the exchange rate, and prices. National income is especially important because of its effects on public sector resources available for health and on household health-related behaviours—in particular in low-income households. The direct negative health effects of the modern phase of globalisation are illustrated by the increasingly globalised production and marketing of tobacco, alcohol, and other products with adverse effects on health.[2,16]

Protection of domestic producers by many developed countries and their regional organisations, impacts on non-communicable disease epidemics. For example, US and European Union (EU) agricultural subsidies limit competition from primary producers of fresh produce in developing countries and seriously reduce these countries' national incomes. Subsidisation of tobacco production by

the EU shows the continuing power of tobacco interests and is a major policy anomaly hindering progress on tobacco control; the EU spends about €1 billion on tobacco production subsidies and only €10–20 million on agricultural diversification and tobacco control programmes.[17] The importance and urgency of removing such agricultural subsidies was endorsed in Doha and again during the Johannesburg World Summit on Sustainable Development. Recent pronouncements by the EU suggest that subsidies tied to production might soon be lifted.

Modern information and communication technologies have positive and negative effects on health. Global marketing of tobacco and alcohol, and salty, sugary, and fatty foods now reaches most parts of most countries. A significant proportion of global marketing is targeted at children younger than 14 years. Worldwide, 600 million urban-based 5–14-year-olds spend more than US$200 billion per year on themselves and influence parental spending of more than ten times that amount.[18] A large proportion of this money is spent on fast food, soft drinks, cigarettes, and alcohol. Advertisers increasingly use sophisticated means to ensure that their messages "slip below the radar of critical thinking";[19] take advantage of weak regulatory environments; and have used false, misleading, or deceptive advertising to reach their targets.

Globalisation and the tobacco pandemic

Tobacco is the only consumer product that, when used as recommended by its manufacturers, eventually kills half its regular users. Transnational tobacco companies are aggressively exploiting the potential for growth in tobacco sales in developing countries. The main targets of the industry and associated marketing campaigns are women and young people;[20] in many developing countries, marketing strategies are used that have long been banned in many developed countries. Tobacco companies have consistently denied the adverse effects of tobacco, especially via passive smoking.[21,22] More than 30 years ago, Philip Morris scientists were concerned that "the public have not yet arrived at the consensus that smoking causes heart disease, so cardiovascular developments must be watched extremely carefully".[23] The response was to publicly deny evidence of adverse effects and encourage scientists to carry out spurious research aimed at confusing the public and delaying action. For many years, tobacco companies have deliberately subverted the tobacco control efforts of WHO.[24]

There is a strong link between increased tobacco consumption and free trade and tobacco-related foreign direct investment.[25] In the 1980s, bilateral agreements negotiated between the USA and several Asian countries under threat of sanctions resulted in an overall increase in

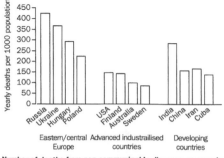

Number of deaths from non-communicable diseases per year in men aged 15–59 years

Developed countries (n=1·4 billion)		Developing countries			
		High mortality (n=2·3 billion)		Low mortality (n=2·4 billion)	
Cause	% of total DALYs	Cause	% of total DALYs	Cause	% of total DALYs
Tobacco	12·4%	Underweight	14·0%	Alcohol	6·3%
Blood pressure	11·0%	Unsafe sex	11·7%	Underweight	5·8%
Alcohol	9·3%	Unsafe water, sanitation, and hygiene	5·6%	Blood pressure	5·0%
Cholesterol	7·6%	Indoor smoke from solid fuels	3·8%	Tobacco	4·2%
Body-mass index	7·5%	Zinc deficiency	3·3%	Body-mass index	2·7%
Low fruit and vegetable intake	3·9%	Iron deficiency	3·2%	Cholesterol	2·1%
Physical inactivity	3·3%	Vitamin A deficiency	2·9%	Iron deficiency	2·0%
Illicit drugs	1·9%	Blood pressure	2·5%	Low fruit and vegetable intake	1·9%
Underweight	1·3%	Tobacco	1·9%	Indoor smoke from solid fuels	1·9%
Iron deficiency	0·8%	Cholesterol	1·9%	Unsafe water, sanitation, and hygiene	1·8%

DALYs=disability-adjusted life years. See *World Health Report 2002* for full list. Developed countries include USA, Japan, and Australia; low-mortality developing countries include China, Brazil, and Thailand; and high-mortality developing countries include India, Mali, and Nigeria.

Table 2: **Contribution of top ten risk factors to global burden of disease[6]**

demand for tobacco, with the highest increase in poor countries.[26] New cross-border challenges such as internet commerce and the illicit trade in tobacco products—often sanctioned by the major tobacco company executives—pose additional challenges. Online marketing by major tobacco manufacturers has increased substantially over the past 3 years, and one company, R J Reynolds, began marketing its new brand, Eclipse, only through the internet. Some websites offer toll-free numbers for offline orders of tobacco products.[22] WTO member governments are allowed to implement the laws and regulations necessary for comprehensive tobacco control policies, provided these are applied equally to all tobacco products irrespective of country of origin; countries vary greatly in their political willingness and capacity to implement these policy measures.[22]

Globalisation, nutrition transitions, and alcohol

Replacement of a traditional diet rich in fruit and vegetables by a diet rich in calories provided by animal fats and low in complex carbohydrates, is happening in all but the poorest countries.[27] Such changes will in general lead to increased rates of many non-communicable diseases, although not necessarily stroke rates, in countries previously protected by balanced and healthy diets. Asia is experiencing a particularly striking shift in consumption patterns, although rates of coronary disease are still low, and stroke rates have fallen substantially in Japan. The rapidity of the transition and the reductions in the energy expended on physical activity in all but the poorest countries, especially in urban areas,[28] are reflected in the rapid rise of urban obesity;[29] in China the prevalence of obesity in urban children aged 2–6 years increased from 1·5% in 1989 to 12·6% in 1997.[30]

During the past 50 years there has been a remarkable and fundamental transformation in farming,[31] food processing,[32] distribution,[33] transportation,[33] shopping practices,[34,35] and the consumption of food outside of the home.[36] Cooking has changed with the development of microwave ovens and other techniques.[37] Changing patterns of production and consumption underlie the emergence of non-communicable disease epidemics and threaten attainment of sustainable development goals.[38]

The alcohol industry is almost as globalised as the tobacco industry.[39] The role of alcohol consumption in non-communicable disease epidemics is complex. There is a direct relation between alcohol consumption and liver cirrhosis, some cancers, and most causes of injuries and violence. Alcohol reduces the risk of CVD, but only very low amounts are needed to achieve this benefit. Binge drinking is an important cause of CVD and is implicated

in the substantial decline in middle-aged life expectancy in Russian men since the collapse of the Soviet Union.[40]

Global policies for non-communicable disease prevention and control

Prevention

Rates of non-communicable disease, notably of lung cancer in men and CVD, have fallen substantially in many wealthy countries. For lung cancer, the reduction in mortality is due to the substantial fall in tobacco consumption by men as a result of active dissemination of scientific research results by politically engaged doctors.[41] However, in many European countries and in Korea, China, and Jordan, lung cancer epidemics are increasing, especially in women. This increase is a result of an increase in smoking by women and the inability of traditional health promotion programmes to counter tobacco marketing campaigns directed towards young women. The reasons for declines in CVD mortality are complex and include improved management of high risk people, in particular in the USA, and in some countries, such as Finland, prevention programmes for reducing population risk levels in combination with other environmental changes.[42]

The application of existing knowledge could make a major, rapid, and cost-effective contribution to the prevention and control non-communicable disease epidemics.[43] However, there are important constraints on the implementation of effective policies. The agenda of most international donors is dominated by the notion that communicable diseases should be prevented and treated before non-communicable diseases receive attention. The report of The Commission on Macroeconomics and Health paid scant attention to the growing burden of non-communicable diseases,[4] with the exception of the cost-effectiveness of tobacco cessation, perhaps because of the misconception that non-communicable diseases are still the preserve of wealthy countries and populations. Although the epidemiological transition is well advanced in all but the poorest countries, the institutional response to disease prevention and control is still based on the infectious disease paradigm. Consequently, the global and national capacity to respond to non-communicable disease epidemics is woefully inadequate and few countries have implemented comprehensive prevention and control policies. Furthermore, some commercial entities involved in producing and promoting unhealthy products exert an adverse influence on health policy. The influence of the tobacco industry has been well documented,[21] and recently the effect of some major food companies on US dietary guidelines and food policy has been described.[44] Appropriate policies are available to

PUBLIC HEALTH

Advocacy	World No Tobacco Day: frequent high-level media coverage
Norms and international legal instruments	Framework Convention on Tobacco Control
Surveillance and surveys	Global Youth Tobacco Survey (now in 110 countries)
Intersectoral action	UN Task Force on Tobacco Control
Research and training	Canadian and USA support for global research and training
Partnerships	Tobacco-Free Sports: Smoking Cessation

Table 3: **Progress in developing formal global responses to tobacco**

promote physical activity in urban environments. However, their implementation is still at an early stage, their effects are not well documented, and they face powerful opposition.[45]

Tobacco control
Table 3 shows progress in developing a global response to the tobacco threat and provides a model for response to non-communicable disease epidemics. An international treaty directed towards the control of tobacco use has been adopted after 3 years of negotiation. The Framework Convention on Tobacco Control (FCTC) is linking the science of tobacco control with the political process of negotiating an international treaty and possible associated protocols on tobacco control priorities, such as advertising restrictions, illicit trade in tobacco products, packaging and labelling, and product regulation.[46] The process of developing the FCTC has led to a coherent UN system-wide approach to tobacco control with demand reduction as the primary goal. This global coherence is being translated into equally important and complementary actions within countries.[47]

Global advocacy
Advocacy is scarce at the global level for non-communicable disease prevention and control, and what there is tends to be fragmented and risk-factor or disease specific. The lack of connection between evidence and action in the USA[48] applies globally. Many potential advocacy groups have their origins in specialist organisations of health professionals, and have not coalesced to become powerful promoters of broad prevention and control policies.[43] This lack of advocacy for health promotion contrasts with the growing dominance of commercial and consumer groups who have placed treatment at the centre of health policy debates and funding priorities. Stronger and broader alliances of major health professional bodies, consumer groups, enlightened industries, and academics are needed to effectively prioritise prevention of major risk factors for non-communicable diseases.

Partnerships and interactions
WHO and governments alone cannot address the challenges of non-communicable disease prevention and control. Unlike tobacco control, partnerships and new forms of interaction are critical. Interaction with international consumer groups and commercial food multinationals is essential if progress is to be made in improving the quality of and access to healthy food and increased physical activity. WHO has started to develop a strategy to address diet and physical activity in relation to chronic diseases. The process has already led to the development of dietary guidelines, and extensive consultations are underway between WHO, governments, consumer groups, multinationals, and UN partners to define complementary roles in tackling

obesity, CVD, and diabetes. Several food multinationals have announced changes in product competition and marketing practices; if widely implemented, these changes could harness the benefits of globalisation and promote public health.[49] WHO is also working with the alcohol industry to assess whether its self-regulatory approaches will reduce marketing to young people and promote safe drinking.

Capacity and resources
National capacity for non-communicable disease prevention and control is weak[50] and the institutional response to capacity development has not kept pace with epidemiological transition. Substantial investment is needed in the capacity of countries to plan and manage health projects for infectious disease[51,52] and even more so for non-communicable disease. Donors and governments have been reluctant to invest in national institutions and infrastructures. Global commitment is needed to assure sustainable progress in policy development and implementation for non-communicable diseases, among other aspects of public health. During the past two decades, WHO's tropical disease research programme, funded by a consortium of donors, has developed an impressive network of communicable disease researchers[53] and provides a useful model for efforts in non-communicable disease. The USA National Institutes for Health, through their Fogarty International Center, and Canada's International Development Research Center have begun to invest modestly in tobacco control research in developing countries; this needs to be expanded to other aspects of non-communicable diseases.

Global norms and standards
There is an increasing need to establish global norms, both legally binding and non-binding, across many spheres to balance otherwise unrestrained influences of powerful actors. Relevant public health professionals need to master technical issues in international trade regulation. They could then influence bodies such as WTO, where health issues are increasingly considered,[5] and develop stronger WHO-led norms that could be used to resolve trade disputes about products with health effects. The proposed FCTC is one example of a legally-binding global norm; non-binding instruments important for non-communicable disease control include the Codex Alimentarius Commission (with its probable increased focus on food labelling and health claims), but more will be needed. Treaties are not the solution to the complex issues related to nutrition transition or physical inactivity. Multistakeholder and intergovernmental mechanisms and other non-binding measures are better options, especially in relation to children and to marketing of alcohol and foods. Such approaches are already being used in improving labour conditions, environmental quality, and human rights.[54]

Reorientation of health services
Untold lives are lost prematurely because of inadequate acute and long-term management of non-communicable disease, many of which have simple and cheap treatments. For example, excellent evidence shows the effectiveness of fairly cheap interventions for CVD.[55] Even in wealthy countries, the potential of these interventions for secondary prevention is far from fully utilised[56] and the situation in poorer countries is even less satisfactory. Effective means of preventing, treating, and providing palliative care for cancer exist[57] but are not implemented in most countries. There are many opportunities for

coordinated non-communicable disease risk reduction, care, and long-term management; for example, smoking cessation is a priority for all patients.[58]

Conclusion

The pace of globalisation of the major risks for non-communicable diseases is increasing. However, the prospects for non-communicable disease prevention and control are only slowly improving. Sustained progress will occur when governments, relevant international agencies, non-governmental agencies, and civil society acknowledge that public health must include non-communicable diseases and their risk factors. The challenges are enormous and the ongoing tobacco wars indicate that progress will remain slow until the response to non-communicable disease epidemics is scaled up in a manner commensurate with their burden.

Conflict of interest statement
Both authors are full-time employees of WHO.

Acknowledgments
We thank Douglas Bettcher for useful comments on an earlier version. There was no funding source for this article.

References

1 Woodward D, Drager N, Beaglehole R, Lipson D. Globalization and health: a framework for analysis and action. *Bull World Health Organ* 2001; **79**: 875–81.

2 Yach D, Bettcher D. The globalization of public health, I: threats and opportunities. *Am J Public Health* 1998; **88**: 735–38.

3 Helliwell JF. Globalization: myths, facts and consequences. Benefactors Lecture, Toronto, 2000. Toronto: CD Howe Institute, 2000. http://www.cdhowe.org/PDF/helliwell.pdf (accessed February, 2003).

4 The Commission on Macroeconomics and Health. Macroeconomics and health: investing in health for development. Geneva: World Health Organization, 2001. http://www3.who.int/whosis/cmh/cmh_report/e/report.cfm?path=cmh,cmh_report&language=english (accessed July, 2003).

5 Zwi AB, Yach D. International health in the 21st century: trends and challenges. *Soc Sci Med* 2002; **54**: 1615–20.

6 WHO. The world health report 2002. Geneva: World Health Organization, 2002.

7 WHO. The world health report 2001. Geneva: World Health Organization, 2001.

8 Kunst AE, Groenhof F, Mackenback JP. Occupational class and cause specific mortality in middle aged men in 11 European countries: comparison of population based studies. *BMJ* 1998; **316**: 1636–42.

9 Mackenbach JP, Cavelaars AEJM, Kunst AE, et al. Socioeconomic inequalities in cardiovascular disease mortality: an international study. *Eur Heart J* 2000; **21**: 1141–51.

10 Leon DA, Watt G. Poverty, inequality and health: an international perspective. Oxford: Oxford University Press, 2000.

11 Stamler J, Stamler R, Neaton JD, et al. Low risk-factor profile and long-term cardiovascular and non-cardiovascular mortality and life expectancy. Findings for 5 large cohorts of young adult and middle-aged men and women. *JAMA* 1999; **282**: 2012–18.

12 Magnus P, Beaglehole R. The real contribution of the major risk factors to the coronary epidemics: time to end the 'only 50%' claim. *Ann Int Med* 2001; **161**: 2657–60.

13 Rodgers A, Lawes C, MacMahon S. Reducing the global burden of blood pressure-related cardiovascular disease. *J Hypertens Suppl* 2000; **18**: S3–6.

14 United Nations. Conference on trade and development. Least developed countries report 2002: escaping the poverty trap. Geneva: United Nations, 2002.

15 World Trade Organization. Doha WTO Ministerial 2001: ministerial declaration. Geneva: World Trade Organization, 2001. http://www.wto.org/english/thewto_e/minist_e/min01_e/mindecl_e.htm (accessed February, 2003).

16 Bettcher DW, Yach D, Guindon GE. Global trade and health: key linkages and future challenges. Bull World Health Organ 2000; **78**: 521–34.

17 DG AGRI. Expenditure FEOGA/EAGGF—communication from DG AGRI—Directorate E (organization of markets in specialised crops). In: European Network for Smoking Prevention, Community Fund for Tobacco Research and Information. ENSP briefing document. Brussels: European Network, 2002.

18 McNeal J. Children as consumers of commercial and social products. Washington: PAHO, 2000.

19 Walsh D. Slipping under the radar: advertising and the mind. Paper presented at WHO symposium: "Marketing to young people". Treviso, Italy, April, 2002.

20 Brands A, Yach D. Women and the rapid rise of noncommunicable diseases. NMH reader no 1. Geneva: World Health Organization, 2002.

21 Ong EK, Glantz SA. Constructing "sound science" and good epidemiology": tobacco lawyers and public relations firms. *Am J Public Health* 2001; **91**: 1749–57.

22 Yach D, Bialous SA. Junking science to promote tobacco. *Am J Public Health* 2001; **91**: 1745–48.

23 Saleeby Jr RN. Review of directory of ongoing research in smoking and health. Bates number 1000211682/1689. Philip Morris USA, Aug 30, 1971.

24 Zeltner T, Kessler DA, Martiny A, Randera F. Tobacco industry strategies to undermine tobacco control activities at the World Health Organization. Report of the Committee of Experts on Tobacco Industry Documents. Geneva: World Health Organization, 2000.

25 Bettcher D, Subramaniam C, Guindon E, et al. Confronting the tobacco epidemic in an era of trade liberalization. WHO/NMH/TFI/01.4. Geneva: World Health Organization, 2001.

26 Taylor AL, Chaloupka F, Guindon GE, Corbett M. Trade policy and tobacco control. In: Jha P, Chaloupka F, eds. Tobacco control in developing countries. Oxford: Oxford University Press, 2000.

27 Popkin BM. The Bellagio Conference on the Nutrition Transition and its Implications for Health in the Developing World. Bellagio, Italy, Aug 20–24, 2001. *Public Health Nutr* 2002; **5**: 93–280.

28 DiGuiseppi C, Roberts I, Li L, Allen D. Determinants of car travel on daily journeys to school: cross sectional survey of primary school children. *BMJ* 1998; **316**: 1426–28.

29 Popkin BM. An overview on the nutrition transition and its health implications: the Bellagio meeting. *Public Health Nutr* 2002; **5**: 93–103.

30 Luo J, Hu FB. Time trends of obesity in pre-school children in China from 1989 to 1997. *Int J Obes Relat Metab Disord* 2002; **26**: 553–56.

31 Goodman D, Watts MJ. Globalising food. London: Routledge, 1997.

32 Brown SA. Revolution at the checkout counter. Cambridge: Harvard University Press, 1997.

33 Paxton A. The food miles report. London: SAFE Alliance, 1994.

34 Raven H, Lang T. Off our trolleys? Retailing and the hypermarket economy. London: Institute of Public Policy Research, 1995.

35 Marsden R, Flynn A, Harrison M. Consuming interests: the social provision of foods. London: University College Press, 2000.

36 Ebbeling CD, Pawlak DB, Ludwig DS. Childhood obesity: public-health crisis, common sense cure. *Lancet* 2002; **360**: 473–82.

37 Mintz SW. Tasting food, tasting freedom: excursions in eating, culture, and the past. Boston: Beacon Press, 1996.

38 von Schirnding YER, Yach D. Unhealthy consumption threatens sustainable development. *Revista de Saudé Pública* 2002; **36**: 379–82.

39 Jernigan DH. Thirsting for markets: the global impact of corporate alcohol. Marin County: Marin Institute for the Prevention of Alcohol and Other Drug Problems, 1997.

40 McKee M, Shkolnikov V, Leon DA. Alcohol is implicated in the fluctuations in cardiovascular disease in Russia since the 1980s. *Ann Epidemiol* 2001; **11**: 1–6.

41 Royal College of Physicians. Smoking and health. London: Pitman Medical Publishing, 1962.

42 Beaglehole R, Dobson A. The contributions to change: risk factors and the potential for prevention. In: Marmot M, Elliott P, eds. Coronary heart disease epidemiology, 2nd edn. Oxford: Oxford University Press, 2003.

43 Beaglehole R. Global cardiovascular disease prevention: time to get serious. *Lancet* 2001; **358**: 661–63.

44 Nestle M. Food politics: how the food industry influences nutrition and health. Berkeley: University of California Press, 2002. ISBN: 0520224 655.

45 Kahn EB, Ramsey L, Brownson RC, et al. The effectiveness of interventions to increase physical activity: a systematic review. *Am J Prev Med* 2002; **22**: 73–107.

46 Taylor A, Bettcher D. A WHO framework convention on tobacco control: a global public good for health. *Bull World Health Organ* 2000; **78**: 920–29.

47 Economic and Social Council Ad Hoc Inter-Agency Task Force on Tobacco Control. Report of the Secretary-General. New York: Economic and Social Council, 2002. http://www.un.org/esa/coordination/ecosoc/SG_UNTF_ECOSOC.pdf (accessed February, 2003).

48 McGinnis JM. Does proof matter? Why strong evidence sometimes yields weak action. *Am J Health Promot* 2001; **15**: 391–96.

PUBLIC HEALTH

49 Barboza D. Food giant puts health initiative on the table. *International Herald Tribune*, July 2, 2003. http://www.iht.com/articles/101495. html (accessed August, 2003).

50 Alwan A, MacLean D, Mandil A. Assessment of national capacity for noncommunicable disease prevention and control. Geneva: World Health Organization, 2001.

51 Morrow RH. Macroeconomics and health. *BMJ* 2002; **352:** 53–54.

52 Berwick DM. A learning world for the Global Fund. *BMJ* 2002; **325:** 55–56.

53 Nchinda T. Research capacity strengthening in the South. *Soc Sci Med* 2002; **54:** 1699–711.

54 UN Nongovernmental Liaison Service (NGLS). Voluntary approaches to corporate responsibility: readings and a resource guide. Geneva: United Nations, 2002.

55 Yusuf S. Two decades of progress in preventing vascular disease. *Lancet* 2002; **360:** 2–3.

56 Campbell CN, Thain J, Deans GH, et al. Secondary prevention in coronary heart disease: baseline survey of provision in general practice. *BMJ* 1998; **316:** 1430–34.

57 WHO. National cancer control programmes: policies and managerial guidelines, 2nd edn. Geneva: World Health Organization, 2002.

58 WHO. Innovative care for chronic conditions: building blocks for action. Geneva: World Health Organization, 2001.

[11]

EPIDEMIC DISEASE AND NATIONAL SECURITY

SUSAN PETERSON

THE UNITED NATIONS Security Council's January 2000 meeting on AIDS marked the first time in the institution's history that it addressed a health issue. In his speech to the Security Council, then-vice president Al Gore called for a "new, more expansive definition" of security that includes emerging and reemerging infectious diseases (IDs) like acquired immune deficiency syndrome (AIDS).[1] That same month, a National Intelligence Estimate on the security implications of global infectious diseases concluded that "these diseases will endanger U.S. citizenry at home and abroad, threaten U.S. armed forces deployed overseas, and exacerbate social and political instability in key

Susan Peterson is associate professor at the College of William & Mary.

The author thanks Dave Brown, Anthony DeVassy, Jason Fabricante, Joe MacAvoy, and Karen Willmer for research assistance, and the College of William and Mary for financial support. She also thanks Ben Frankel, Sean Lynn-Jones, Michael Tierney, several anonymous reviewers and, especially, Andrew Cortell, Jonathan Mercer, and Heather Scully for their careful readings and thoughtful comments.

1. The White House, Office of the Vice President, "Remarks prepared for delivery by Vice President Al Gore, United Nations Security Council Opening Session," 10 January 2000, www.whitehouse.gov/ONAP/pub/vp_sc2.html (8 July 2000). Since 1996, the Clinton administration had argued that "[e]merging infectious diseases present one of the most significant health and security challenges facing the global community." The White House, Office of Science and Technology Policy, "Fact Sheet: Addressing the Threat of Emerging Infectious Diseases," 12 June 1996, www.fas.org/irp/offdocs/pdd_ntsc7.htm (10 September 1999). The policy was announced in response to National Science and Technology Council, Committee on International Science, Engineering, and Technology, Working Group on Emerging and Re-emerging Infectious Diseases, "Global Microbial Threats in the 1990s," www.whitehouse.gov/WH/EOP/OSTP/CISET/html/ciset/html (10 September 1999). Also, see Al Gore, "Emerging Infections Threaten National and Global Security," www.state.gov/www/global/oes/health/task_force/article.htm (6 August 2001), reprinted from *American Society for Microbiology News* 62, no. 9 (1996): 448–49. Clinton's was not the first U.S. administration to explore the link between security and public health. In October 1988, a Department of Defense (DoD) working group had issued a report that, among other things, examined the effects of the Human Immunodeficiency Virus (HIV) that causes AIDS on U.S. security. The document is reprinted as "Economic and Demographic Trends and International Security. A U.S. Analysis," *Population and Development Review* (September 1989): 587–99.

countries and regions in which the United States has significant interests."[2] Thirteen months later, Colin Powell, the Secretary of State for a new administration that initially had dismissed the link between health and security and eliminated the position of Special Advisor for International Health Affairs on the National Security Council, also described Africa's AIDS crisis as a U.S. national security concern.[3]

These pronouncements echo a decade of books and essays that warn of the dangers of IDs and call for "a fundamental reconceptualization of standard definitions of national and international security."[4] Nevertheless, the promise of systematic analysis of the link between IDs and security remains largely unfulfilled.[5] Most scholars and practitioners who explore the link between disease and security do so from within the "human security" tradition, which seeks to expand the concept of security beyond the state to include basic human needs like health. Their arguments remain at the margins of the security literature, however, because their appeal to human security does not resonate with more traditional approaches to national and international security, which focus on physical threats to the state. As Daniel Deudney writes, "Not all threats to life and property are threats to security. Disease, old age, crime and accidents routinely destroy life and property, but we do not think of them as 'national security' threats or even threats to 'security'.... If everything that causes a decline in human well-being is labeled a 'security' threat, the term loses any analytical usefulness and becomes a loose synonym of 'bad'."[6]

2. National Intelligence Council (NIC), "The Global Infectious Disease Threat and Its Implications for the United States," NIE 99-17D, January 2000, www.cia.gov/publications/nie/report/nie99-17d.html (17 November 2000). David F. Gordon is the principal author of this document.

3. Jeffrey Sachs, "The Best Possible Investment in Africa," *New York Times*, 10 February 2001, A15.

4. Andrew T. Price-Smith, "Ghosts of Kigali: Infectious Disease and Global Stability at the Turn of the Century," *International Journal* 54, no. 3 (summer 1999): 432. Popular and academic works on IDs include Laurie Garrett, *Betrayal of Trust: The Collapse of Global Public Health* (New York: Hyperion, 2000); Laurie Garrett, *The Coming Plague: Newly Emerging Diseases in a World Out of Balance* (New York: Farrar, Straus, and Giroux, 1994); David P. Fidler, *International Law and Infectious Diseases* (Oxford: Clarendon Press, 1999); David P. Fidler, "The Return of 'Microbialpolitik'," *Foreign Affairs* (January/February 2001): 80–81; Arno Karlen, *Man and Microbes: Disease and Plagues in History and Modern Times* (New York: G. P. Putnam's Sons, 1995); Andrew T. Price-Smith, *The Health of Nations: Infectious Disease, Environmental Change, and Their Effects on National Security and Development* (Cambridge: MIT Press, 2002); Richard Preston, *The Hot Zone* (New York: Random House, 1994); and Stephen Peter Rosen, "Strategic Implications of AIDS," *The National Interest* , no. 9 (fall 1987): 64–73.

5. A recent exception is P. W. Singer, "AIDS and International Security," *Survival* 44, no. 1 (spring 2002): 145–58.

6. Daniel Deudney, "The Case Against Linking Environmental Degradation and National Security," *Millennium* 19, no. 3 (1990), 463–64. Deudney makes this comment about attempts to link the environment and security. Also, see Marc A. Levy, "Is the Environment a National Security Issue?" *International Security* 20, no. 2 (fall 1995): 35–62.

Historians should find such reasoning puzzling, since epidemic disease has shaped human history, generally, and military conflict, in particular.[7] Thucydides describes how, during the Peloponnesian Wars, disease demoralized the Athenian people, undermined the political leadership, and weakened the army, preventing it from achieving key military objectives.[8] More than 2,300 years later, the 1918 influenza epidemic killed 25 million people, including 500,000 Americans. The Spanish flu struck 294,000 allied troops in the fall of 1918 alone. Nearly 23,000 died, and the disease caused significant, if short-lived problems on both the allied and German sides.[9] It seems clear, in short, that catastrophic IDs like AIDS can and have threatened national security.

This article asks whether, when, and how epidemic disease endangers national security, rather than assuming that anything that undermines the nation's health automatically challenges its security. In what follows, first, I attempt to move beyond efforts to persuade nations and individuals to broaden their concept of security to include basic human needs, including freedom from disease, by investigating the two main causal mechanisms by which IDs can threaten *national* security: (1) IDs may contribute to violent conflict by altering the balance of power among states, fostering foreign policy conflicts, or creating economic and political instability; and (2) IDs can alter the outcome of international conflicts either deliberately, through the use of biological weapons or the targeting of public health, or inadvertently, by eroding military readiness.

Second, I briefly examine whether these processes threaten the national security of the United States and conclude that IDs do not challenge U.S. security as directly or to the extent that many scholars and practitioners currently claim. Certainly, there are important security elements and consequences of AIDS and other catastrophic infectious diseases. At the same time, however, these security implications are often limited relative to the other consequences of epidemic disease. The most direct disease threat to the United States today comes from its vulnerability to biological weapons attack. Because this threat is so apparent, it has been and will be possible, if far from simple, to mobilize public support to meet it. It will be significantly more difficult to rally Americans against two less direct, longer term threats—to the health of armed forces and,

7. See, esp., Frederick F. Cartwright, *Disease and History* (New York: Thomas Y. Crowell, 1972); Jared Diamond, *Guns, Germs, and Steel: The Fates of Human Societies* (New York: Norton, 1997); William H. McNeill, *Plagues and Peoples* (New York: Anchor Books, 1998); and Hans Zinsser, *Rats, Lice and History* (Boston: Little, Brown for the Atlantic Monthly Press, 1935).

8. Thucydides, *History of the Peloponnesian War*, trans. Rex Warner, rev. ed. (London: Penguin Books, 1972), 151–56 (Bk. 2, 47–55). The disease was probably smallpox. Zinsser, *Rats, Lice and History*, 119–27.

9. Alfred W. Crosby, *America's Forgotten Pandemic: The Influenza of 1918* (Cambridge: Cambridge University Press, 1989), 11, 157–66.

most significantly, to the social, economic, and political stability of certain key regions—especially Russia—that also challenge American security. Particularly in the aftermath of 9/11, perhaps the greatest indirect and long run threat that IDs like AIDS pose to U.S. security is their potential to undermine democratic transition and fuel anti-Americanism and terrorism. This connection, however, is a tenuous and distant one, and it will be relatively difficult to seek support for aid to countries ravaged by IDs on the basis of U.S. security concerns alone.

Third, I examine the question of whether it matters that scholars and policy officials make a rhetorical link between epidemic disease and national security if the empirical relationship between the two variables is weak. Numerous students of international health draw this connection to gain attention and resources to fight infectious disease. As P. W. Singer notes, "Conceptualizing AIDS as a security threat, thus is not just another exercise in expounding on the dangers of the disease.... [I]t strengthens the call for serious action against the menace of AIDS. It is not just a matter of altruism, but simple cold self-interest."[10] By overdrawing the link between ID and security, however, public health and human security advocates may sabotage their own attempts to motivate developed nations to fight AIDS in Africa and elsewhere. Students of global health might take a lesson from earlier analyses of the relationship between the environment and national security: Linking an urgent issue to security may raise awareness, but it likely also will hinder much of the cooperation that human security and public health advocates seek and that the disastrous humanitarian and development effects of IDs demand.[11] Appealing to the national interest of advanced industrialized states like the United States to justify a massive commitment to international disease control will likely fail, because the true security implications of IDs for the United States remain limited and indirect. Such a strategy then relieves westerners of any moral obligation to respond to health crises beyond their own national borders, unless or until those crises directly and immediately impact national security.

The article is divided into four sections. The first part examines the severity of the global ID problem today. The second part compares different definitions of security—human and national or international—by which to measure whether and to what extent epidemic disease threatens security. The third part examines the relationship between IDs and national security, defined as protection of the state from physical threats. The fourth part reviews the implications

10. "AIDS and International Security," 158.
11. See Deudney, "Case Against Linking Environmental Degradation and National Security," 466–69. For a related argument about health, see Eoin O'Brien, "The Diplomatic Implications of Emerging Diseases," in *Preventive Diplomacy: Stopping Wars before They Start*, ed. Kevin M. Cahill (New York: Basic Books and the Center for International Health and Cooperation, 1996), 254.

of the argument and revisits the issue of why it matters whether we view AIDS and other IDs as security threats or primarily as health and development challenges.

CATASTROPHIC INFECTIOUS DISEASE IN THE MODERN WORLD

HUMAN HISTORY is replete with stories of epidemic infections. These epidemics tend to follow a cyclical pattern, since they often produce immunity in survivors, and the microbes must await a new generation of hosts to infect. Alternatively, the disease-causing microbes migrate to geographically distant and immunologically vulnerable populations, producing a pandemic, or global outbreak. In this sense, AIDS is just one more disease—albeit a very deadly one—in a long line of devastating IDs. Until the early twentieth century, plague, smallpox, influenza, and other scourges decimated human populations around the globe. Many in the West thought that technological progress had halted the spread of these diseases and that they had been replaced with a second generation of diseases—the so-called diseases of affluence—including heart disease, diabetes, and cancer. Yet IDs remain a significant and growing threat. Their "third wave" includes newly emerging threats like AIDS as well as remerging threats like plague, cholera, and tuberculosis (TB).[12]

Despite unprecedented progress in disease control, IDs remain a major killer. In 1998, 13.3 of the 53.9 million deaths worldwide—or 25 percent of all deaths—resulted from IDs. These illnesses accounted for 45 percent of all deaths in Southeast Asia and Africa. In the hour it takes to read this paper, more than 1,500 people worldwide will die of an ID; at least half will be under the age of five. To put these numbers in perspective, the World Health Organization (WHO) estimates that since 1945 three diseases alone—AIDS, TB, and malaria—have claimed 150 million lives, many times the approximately 23 million deaths from wars.[13]

As this last comparison suggests, a handful of diseases pose the greatest threat to human health. Almost 90 percent of all deaths and half of all premature deaths from IDs result from six diseases—AIDS, pneumonia, TB, diarrhoeal diseases, malaria, and measles.[14] AIDS is spreading the most quickly and with

12. "Can AIDS Be Stopped?" *New York Review of Books*, 14 March 2002, www.nybooks. com/articles/15188 (5 March 2002).

13. The figure is for wars from 1945 to 1993. World Health Organization, "Removing Obstacles to Healthy Development, Report on Infectious Diseases" (Geneva: WHO, 1999), graph 1, chap. 1, graph 22. Available online at www.who.int/infectious-disease-report/ (7 August 2001).

14. WHO, "Removing Obstacles," chap. 2.

the most catastrophic consequences. At the end of 2002, more than 42 million people worldwide were living with AIDS or the human immunodeficiency virus (HIV) that causes it, according to the Joint United Nations Programme on HIV/AIDS (UNAIDS) and the WHO. More than 5 million people were newly infected in 2002 alone. Short of a cure in the very near future, they will join the 26 million who have died since the start of the epidemic. HIV discriminates in its choice of victims: 95 percent of all people living with the virus reside in the developing world, and more than 29 million live in sub-Saharan Africa. Four countries, all in southern Africa, have infection rates above 30 percent; in Botswana 38.8 percent of adults are HIV-positive.[15] In 1998, 200,000 Africans lost their lives to war, but more than 2 million died from AIDS.[16]

As devastating a disease as AIDS is, it is not the only pressing ID threat.[17] Each year, more than 275 million people contract malaria, and 1.5 million die from it. Three thousand people, three out of four of them children, die from the illness each day. Malaria remains largely a disease of the developing world, but a third major scourge more clearly threatens north and south alike: Like many other diseases once thought to be on the verge of eradication, TB now infects eight million people a year, killing one-and-a-half million. It kills even more people who are infected with HIV. Nearly one-third of the earth's total population has latent TB infections, but TB is only the most widespread disease making its deadly comeback. Recent years also have witnessed numerous outbreaks of cholera, anthrax, yellow fever, and plague. In addition to these known killers, new ones continue to emerge. At least 30 new diseases have been identified over the last several decades, including Lassa fever, Ebola hemorrhagic fever, Marburg virus, Legionnaires' disease, hantavirus pulmonary syndrome, Nipah virus, Hepatitis C, new variant Creutzfeldt-Jakob disease (the human disease believed to be linked to bovine spongiform encephalopathy or mad cow disease), and of course HIV/AIDS.[18]

15. UNAIDS and WHO, *AIDS Epidemic Update* (Geneva: UNAIDS, December 2002).

16. UNAIDS, *Report on the Global HIV/AIDS Epidemic* (Geneva: UNAIDS, June 2000), 21, available online at www.unaids.org/ (7 August 2001).

17. The following figures are from WHO, "Removing Obstacles," chap. 2, graph 37, and graph 31; Scott R. Lillibridge, "Emerging Infectious Disease: Threats to Global Security," in *Preventive Diplomacy: Stopping Wars before They Start*, rev. ed., ed. Kevin M. Cahill (New York: Routledge and Center for International Health and Cooperation, 2000), 293; and Hiroshi Nakajima, "Global Disease Threats and Foreign Policy," *The Brown Journal of World Affairs* 4, no. 1 (winter/spring 1997): 319–32.

18. Garrett, *Coming Plague*; WHO, "Removing Obstacles," chap. 10 and graph 32. In 1995, CISET identified twenty-nine new diseases that had emerged and twenty that had reemerged since 1973. For extensive discussions of the emergence and reemergence of ID at this point in human history, see Laurie Garrett, "The Return of Infectious Disease," *Foreign Affairs* 75, no. 1 (January/February 1996): 66–79; NIC, "Global Infectious Disease Threat"; Nakajima, "Global Disease Threats"; and Price-Smith, *Health of Nations*, esp. chap. 5.

DEFINING SECURITY: HUMAN SECURITY VS. NATIONAL SECURITY

DIFFERENT TERMS—"human security" and "national security"—reflect disparate definitions and referents of security, as well as conflicting assessments of the significance of and appropriate response to IDs. Scholars and practitioners within the first tradition view catastrophic IDs as security problems by definition, since they threaten the lives of large numbers of people, while national security analysts and scholars gauge the degree of threat these diseases pose to the territorial integrity and political independence of the state. Members of the two schools talk past each other at nearly every turn, stymieing any serious engagement over whether and how IDs threaten security.

HUMAN SECURITY

Much of the recent surge in concern about IDs comes out of a desire to protect human security. This approach emphasizes the welfare of individuals or people collectively. As Roland Paris notes, "Human security is the latest in a long line of neologisms—including common security, global security, cooperative security, and comprehensive security—that encourage policymakers and scholars to think about international security as something more than the military defense of state interests and territory."[19] Most students of human security date the concept from 1994, when the United Nations Development Programme issued its annual *Human Development Report*, calling for

> ...another profound transition in thinking—from nuclear security to human security.
>
> The concept of security has for too long been interpreted narrowly: as security of territory from external aggression, or as protection of national interests in foreign policy or as global security from the threat of a nuclear holocaust. It has been related more to nation-states than to people.... Forgotten were the legitimate concerns of ordinary people who sought security in their daily lives. For many of them, security symbolized protection from the threat of disease, hunger,

---

19. "Human Security: Paradigm Shift or Hot Air?" *International Security* 26, no. 2 (fall 2001): 87–102. Also, see Edward Newman, "Human Security and Constructivism," *International Studies Perspectives* 2, no. 3 (August 2001): 239–51; Emma Rothschild, "What is Security?" *Daedalus* 124, no. 3 (summer 1995): 53–98; Mejid Tehranian, ed., *Worlds Apart: Human Security and Global Governance* (London: I. B. Tauris, 1999), esp. chap. 2; and Caroline Thomas and Peter Wilkins, eds., *Globalization, Human Security, and the African Experience* (Boulder: Lynne Rienner, 1999), esp. chap. 1.

unemployment, crime, social conflict, political repression and environmental hazards.[20]

Theoretically, the human security approach harkens back at least as far as Barry Buzan's distinction between individual and national security and his view of the state as a threat to individual security.[21] Rothschild traces the understanding of security as an individual good to the late Enlightenment period.[22] From these arguments, flow many contemporary analyses of so-called nontraditional security threats like epidemic disease.

Public health advocates and students of IDs often champion increased mobilization against diseases that threaten security in the broad sense of human well-being. Indeed, these arguments often invoke the concept of "health security."[23] Implicitly or explicitly, health security advocates view IDs as threats to human security because of the enormous loss of life they cause.[24] As Gore argued in his January 2000 UN speech, "the heart of the security agenda is protecting lives—and we now know that the number of people who will die of AIDS in the first decade of the 21st century will rival the number that died in all the wars in all the decades of the 20th century."[25]

Linking disease and security is a means of highlighting a dire problem, capturing scarce resources, and accelerating national, international, and transnational responses.[26] Peter Piot, executive director of UNAIDS, explains public health advocates' tendency to invoke the security term this way: "Whether we conceptualize AIDS as a health issue only or as a development and human security issue is not just an academic exercise. It defines how we respond to the epidemic, how much is allocated to combating it, and what sectors of govern-

20. United Nations Development Programme, *Human Development Report 1994* (New York: Oxford University Press), 22.

21. Barry Buzan, *People, States & Fear: The National Security Problem in International Relations* (Chapel Hill: University of North Carolina Press, 1983), esp. chap. 1.

22. "What is Security?"

23. The first use of this term I find is in "International Health Security in the Modern World: The Sanitary Conventions and the World Health Organization," *Department of State Bulletin*, 16 November 1947, 953–58. For contemporary examples, see Lillibridge, "Emerging Infectious Disease"; and esp. Price-Smith, *Health of Nations*.

24. See Peter Piot, "Global AIDS Epidemic: Time to Turn the Tide," *Science* 288, 23 June 2000, 2176–78; Deniis Pirages, "Microsecurity: Disease Organisms and Human Well-Being," *Washington Quarterly* 18, no. 4 (fall 1995): 5–12; Price-Smith, "Ghosts of Kigali": and Laura Reed and Majid Tehranian, "Evolving Security Regimes," in Tehranian, *Worlds Apart*, 23–53.

25. "Remarks, United Nations Security Council Opening Session."

26. Rothschild outlines the ways different "principles of security" have been used to contest existing policies and influence the distribution of power and wealth. "What is Security?" 58–59.

ment are involved in the response."[27] In short, "sometimes national security says it all."[28]

Sometimes, however, national security may say too much. The literature on environmental security suggests that arguments for linking security and disease have at least three flaws. First, they invite the question of whether *any* serious health, environmental, economic, or other problem automatically constitutes a security threat. They provide no guidance on how to make trade-offs among different security values, such as health and military defense, or between health security and other presumably nonsecurity values, such as conservation, environmental preservation, or economic development.[29] Second, that the study of IDs has remained on the fringes of the international relations field despite countless calls for the two areas to be joined suggests that the security community remains cool to the idea of human security.[30] From their positions on the margins, advocates of human security are unlikely to influence debates about national security. Unless a link is drawn between epidemic disease and national security, not human security, security elites will pay little attention. Third, it is not clear what is gained by linking epidemic disease and human security, rather than relying on public health, development, or humanitarian arguments.

Indeed, public health advocates' appeal to the high politics of security may have unwanted effects. It implies, first, that human health is less important than, and can be justified only in terms of its impact on, security. Moreover, these arguments contain an internal contradiction that may impede health cooperation. To paraphrase Deudney's claims about efforts to link the environment and security, human security advocates usually argue that it is necessary to challenge the utility of thinking in purely national terms if we are to deal effectively with issues like AIDS, but they then turn around and appeal to nationalism to achieve their goals.[31] Finally, equating health with security may imply that a national military response to public health crises is needed, when

---

27. Piot, "Global AIDS Epidemic," 2177. Also, see Peter Piot, "AIDS and human security," Statement by Peter Piot, UNAIDS Executive Director, United Nations University, Tokyo, Japan, 2 October 2001, www.unaids.org/whatsnewpercent5Cspeechespercent5Cengpercent5Cpiot021/00tokyo.htm (14 November 2001).

28. David E. Sanger, "Sometimes National Security Says It All," *New York Times*, Week in Review, 7 May 2000, 3.

29. Marc A. Levy makes this argument about environmental threats to security: "Is the Environment a National Security Issue?", 35–62. Also, see Paris, "Human Security," 94.

30. In fact, Deudney points out, the concept is not widely embraced outside certain progressive circles. "Case Against Linking Environmental Degradation and National Security," 469.

31. Deudney, "Case Against Linking Environmental Degradation and National Security," esp. 468. Also, see Levy, "Is the Environment a National Security Issue?" esp. 44–46.

52   SECURITY STUDIES 12, no. 2

the goal of health for all might be served better by independent international,
or transnational organizations.[32]

NATIONAL SECURITY

If some public health advocates embrace the mantle of human security because they believe it will secure scarce resources for their cause, it stands to
reason that national security would make an even more effective rallying cry.
Indeed, a small group of practitioners and scholars addresses the impact of IDs
on national security, more narrowly and conventionally defined.[33] Security, in
this sense, refers to the preservation of the state—its territorial integrity, political institutions, and national sovereignty—from physical threats. This definition of national security is consistent with another common definition, "the
study of the threat, use, and control of military force,"[34] although it also allows
for nonmilitary or nontraditional threats to the state.[35] Physical threats to the
state may emanate from either or both of two sources. Traditionally, the security field has focused on external threats largely because security studies developed in the United States, which has faced few serious internal threats. Area
specialists and students of comparative politics, who may study military defense issues in nondemocratic or developing states, are more likely to concentrate on internal threats to governments and states.

Since the end of the cold war, numerous students of national and international security have sought to expand the boundaries of the field to include

32. On this point, see O'Brien, "Diplomatic Implications of Emerging Disease," 254.

33. I use the terms "national security" and "international security" interchangeably. The
latter term largely replaced the former by the 1980s, but the content of the field remained
much the same, the study of military threats to the state. See David A. Baldwin, "Security
Studies and the End of the Cold War," *World Politics* 48, no. 1 (October 1995): 125. Some
students of security claim that "[t]raditional conceptions of 'national security' are concerned
with the well-being of the state," whereas "[t]he concept of 'international security' explicitly
acknowledges that the security of one state is connected with the security of others." Jonathan Ban, "Health, Security, and U.S. Global Leadership," Special Report 2, *Health and Security
Series* (Chemical and Biological Arms Control Institute, 2001), 5. Also, see International Crisis Group, "HIV/AIDS as a Security Issue," ICG Report, Washington/ Brussels, 19 June
2001. These definitions are not mutually exclusive, however, since the latter simply emphasizes a long recognized aspect of the former.

34. Stephen M. Walt, "The Renaissance of Security Studies," *International Studies Quarterly*
35, no. 2 (June 1991): 211–39. For other discussions, see Baldwin, "Security Studies"; Joseph
S. Nye Jr. and Sean M. Lynn-Jones, "International Security Studies: A Report of a Conference on the State of the Field," *International Security* 12, no. 4 (spring 1988): 5–27; and Richard
Smoke, "National Security Affairs," in *Handbook of Political Science*, vol. 8, *International Politics*,
ed. Fred I. Greenstein and Nelson W. Polsby (Reading, Mass.: Addison-Wesley, 1975), 247–
362.

35. In this sense, I combine Paris's "national security" and "redefined security" categories.
"Human Security," 98.

nontraditional threats like terrorism, civil war and ethnic conflict, economic threats, crime, drugs, cyberterrorism, and disease. What binds these disparate topics together and allows scholars to examine the security dimensions of each is that they can all threaten territorial integrity, national institutions, or sovereignty. "[T]he referent is still in many ways the state...although the [nature of the] challenge—and the response—may have changed."[36]

Most of the voices raised in support of expanding the concept of security to encompass IDs belong to the human security school, but a number also couch their arguments in more conventional national security rhetoric.[37] On 25 March 1998 U.S. ambassador Wendy R. Sherman told a Department of State Open Forum, "[Infectious diseases] endanger the health of Americans and our national security interests."[38] In a 1996 speech to the National Council for International Health, Gore similarly noted, "Today, guaranteeing national security means more than just defending our borders at home and our values abroad or having the best-trained armed forces in the world. Now it also means defending our nation's health against all enemies, foreign and domestic."[39] A 1998 USAID report on the impact of AIDS on national militaries likewise concluded, "the HIV/AIDS pandemic now represents a direct threat...to national and international security and peace in many parts of the world."[40]

These claims avoid many of the problems of the human security school by considering how IDs threaten the state, but they often suffer from two other problems. First, as many public health advocates note, traditional security language has difficulty capturing the nature of a transnational threat like IDs. Health threats like catastrophic ID, however, need not be threats to national security to warrant decisive action. They only become security threats when

36. Newman, "Human Security and Constructivism," 246. Newman includes this "new security" as a variant of human security. For post–cold war attempts to examine nontraditional threats to national security, see Thomas Homer-Dixon, *Environment, Scarcity and Violence* (Princeton: Princeton University Press, 1999); Ethan Kapstein, *The Political Economy of National Security: A global perspective* (Columbia: University of South Carolina Press, 1992); Jessica Tuchman Mathews, "Redefining Security," *Foreign Affairs* 68, no. 2 (spring 1989): 162–77; Norman Myers, "Environment and Security," *Foreign Policy*, no. 74 (spring 1989): 23–41; and Phil Williams and Stephen Black, "Transnational Threats: Drug Trafficking and Weapons Proliferation," *Contemporary Security Policy* 15, no. 1 (April 1994): 127–51.

37. For a work that does both, see International Crisis Group, "HIV/AIDS as a Security Issue," ICG Report, Washington/ Brussels, 19 June 2001.

38. Wendy R. Sherman, "Emerging Infectious Diseases Are a National Security Challenge to the United States," Remarks Before the Open Forum on Emerging Infectious Diseases, Department of State Open Forum, Washington, D.C., 25 March 1998, www.state.gov/www/policy_remarks/1998/980325_sherman_diseases.htm (6 August 2001).

39. Gore, "Emerging Infections Threaten National and Global Security."

40. USAID, "Military Populations" AIDS Briefs, 22 May 1998, www.usaid.gov/regions/afr/hhraa/aids_briefs/military.htm (14 August 2001). For other examples, see Sir George Alleyne, "Health and National Security", *Bulletin of the Pan-American Health Organization* 30, no. 2 (June 1996): 158–63; and WHO, "Removing Obstacles," graph 22.

they threaten the territory, institutions, or sovereignty of the state. Second, the causal relationships between ID and security remain ill-defined, mostly because proponents of this link, like their colleagues in the human security camp, often make the connection largely for rhetorical purposes.[41] Many link national security to human security without considering whether all threats to individuals necessarily threaten the security of states and whether those that do necessarily threaten all states. For example, the head of the Pan American Sanitary Bureau notes, "Attention to health and well-being, which goes beyond concern about the international spread of disease, will be key for ensuring the global security that is essential to the security of modern states."[42] The referent of security by the end of the sentence is the state, but it is not clear why the threat to the health and well-being of individuals—described at the beginning of the sentence—automatically translates into a threat to the physical security of the state. Section III addresses this issue by examining key causal relationships between epidemic disease and national security, defined as preservation of the state, its institutions, and sovereignty.

CATASTROPHIC INFECTIOUS DISEASE AND NATIONAL SECURITY: THE CAUSAL LINKS

FOR THE FORESEEABLE future, IDs will continue to claim more lives than war and to jeopardize the security of many states. The relevant questions are what states and under what conditions. The heart of the link between IDs and national security concerns the effect of catastrophic disease on violent conflict.[43] IDs may be thought of as "war-starters" and "war-outcome determinants."[44] That is, they may threaten national security in either or both of two ways—by contributing to the outbreak of violent conflict or by deliberately or inadvertently influencing the outcome of conflict. Viewed in this way, IDs present a humanitarian problem of staggering proportions, but they do not always

41. Important, if partial, exceptions include Alleyne, "Health and National Security"; Garrett, "Return of Infectious Disease"; Price-Smith, "Ghosts of Kigali"; and Price-Smith, *Health of Nations*.

42. Alleyne, "Health and National Security," 162. Piot makes a similar point in "Global AIDS Epidemic," 2177.

43. Actually, the relationship between IDs and security is a reciprocal one, since the search for security through war, militarization, or defense spending can also influence the emergence and spread of ID. I discuss this in Susan Peterson, "The Forgotten Horseman of the Apocalypse: Epidemic Disease and National Security" (unpub. ms., 4 September 2001).

44. Donald Burke, Frederic D. Daniell, and John Lowe, "Berlin Seminar," *AIDS and Society: International Research and Policy Bulletin* 4 (July/August 1993), 4; United States, Department of State, "United States International Strategy on HIV/AIDS," July 1995, 40–41.

or automatically pose a security threat. For the United States and most western states, and with the exception of biological weapons, IDs pose only indirect and long-term threats, around which it will be difficult to mobilize public support.

EPIDEMIC DISEASE AND THE OUTBREAK OF MILITARY CONFLICT

Catastrophic ID may contribute to the outbreak of military conflict within or between states, although it is relatively unlikely to be a war-starter on its own. In theory, there are at least three paths by which IDs may provoke war—by influencing the relative balance of power among adversaries, generating disputes between nations over appropriate health and human rights policies, and engendering domestic instability. In practice, the last of these presents the most significant threat, but only to some states. For the United States, ID-induced conflict poses only an indirect and long run security threat.

Balance of power. The first hypothesized relationship between disease and war holds that catastrophic ID may alter the balance of power among competitors. Realist scholars of international politics maintain that shifts in the relative capabilities of states can precipitate war, particularly when national leaders perceive that the balance is shifting against them.[45] Some students of environmental security similarly suggest that severe environmental threats can disturb the international balance of power and increase the risk of military conflict, including preventive war.[46] A preventive war may be particularly likely during or following an ID outbreak if one nation remains relatively immune to the disease. One can imagine, for example, that the diminished size of native North American populations might have led Europeans to anticipate an easy victory in their attempt to conquer and settle the continent. The earliest European "discoverers" introduced epidemic diseases that killed as many as 95 percent of North American Indians between 1492 and the late 1600s, when European settlers arrived in significant numbers.[47] There is little evidence, however, that these ID-induced power shifts played a role in the timing or outbreak of this or any other historical war of conquest. European conquerors did

45. See especially Robert Gilpin, *War & Change in World Politics* (Cambridge: Cambridge University Press, 1981); and Stephen Van Evera, *Causes of War: Power and the Roots of Conflict* (Ithaca: Cornell University Press, 1999), esp. chap. 4.
46. David A. Wirth, "Climate Chaos," *Foreign Policy*, no. 74 (spring 1989): 10.
47. Diamond, *Guns, Germs, and Steel*, 78. Also see Donald Joralemon, "New World Depopulation and the Case of Disease," *Journal of Anthropological Research* 38, no. 1 (spring 1982): 108–27, reprinted in *Biological Consequences of European Expansion, 1450–1800*, ed. Kenneth F. Kiple and Stephen V. Beck (Aldershot, Hampshire: Ashgate, 1997), 71–90.

not know when they set out for the Americas that they carried deadly diseases that would prove more lethal than their swords.

This incentive for war is less likely to emerge in the contemporary international system because of several differences between this and earlier periods. The major epidemics of our time strike entire regions, like sub-Saharan Africa, or strike simultaneously on different continents with little respect for national political boundaries. Partly, this is because high-speed travel and trade have exposed national populations to numerous epidemic diseases and conveyed immunity on diverse populations. Additionally, technological changes mean that the contemporary balance of power depends on numerous factors other than the size of a state's military or general population, factors like weapons of mass destruction, advanced aircraft, and missile technology. Unlike other diseases, moreover, AIDS kills all its victims rather than conferring immunity on survivors. Nearly all individuals, therefore, are equally vulnerable to the disease if they are exposed to it via the dominant routes of transmission—sexual activity, blood or blood product exchange, transmission from mother to child during pregnancy, or intravenous (IV) drug use that involves sharing contaminated needles. These reasons would suggest that ID outbreak is relatively unlikely to prompt a preventive war.

Unlike individuals, however, nations are not equally vulnerable. Differences in resources, state strength, the organization of society, and the relationship between state and society influence the way states respond to epidemics.[48] Weak, resource-poor states are particularly susceptible to AIDS and other IDs, which may undermine political and economic stability and social cohesion. Below, I discuss the likelihood that this process will produce civil conflict. It is unlikely, however, given the reasons already discussed, that it will produce a preventive war between states.

Foreign policy conflict. In theory, ID outbreaks may prompt disputes among states over appropriate policy responses in a number of areas, including freedom of movement for people and goods. Nineteenth-century leaders employed quarantine as their primary instrument of ID control. In the first decade of the AIDS epidemic, despite a half century of human rights advances, some people again viewed quarantine as a reasonable reaction to a frightening new scourge. Cuba instituted mandatory testing and compulsory isolation of its HIV-positive population in sanatoriums, and in 1987 the West German minister of the interior ordered border police to turn back any foreigner suspected of carrying HIV.[49] The United States, which continues to deny entry to HIV-

48. Homer-Dixon *Environment, Scarcity and Violence*; Price-Smith, *Health of Nations.*
49. On nineteenth century quarantine policy, see Neville M. Goodman, *International Health Organizations and Their Work* (Edinburgh: Churchill Livingstone, 1971), chaps. 2–3. On Cuba,

positive immigrants and visitors, bowed to international pressure in the 1990s and allowed waivers for short-term trips to visit family, receive medical treatment, conduct business, or attend scientific or health conferences. Another foreign policy dispute revolves around the issue of intellectual property rights. Major pharmaceutical companies and the U.S. government advocate protection of patents on AIDS drugs and oppose the production in other countries of inexpensive, generic versions of these medications.[50]

Nevertheless, states are unlikely to come into conflict with other states over such health-related foreign policy disputes for at least two reasons. First, and somewhat paradoxically, disease may theoretically reduce the likelihood of such conflicts arising. As disease increases, a society may devote a greater proportion of national budgets and human resources to disease control. Some states already weakened by disease may not want to bear the additional costs of lost trade and military conflict and so may respond to epidemics by turning inward to deal with this and related domestic issues.[51] Second, disease actually may facilitate international cooperation. In the nineteenth century, for instance, disparate national quarantines produced international collaboration, not military conflict. States recognized the trade benefits of standardizing quarantine policies and met regularly to hammer out regulations on disease prevention and control. The current dispute over AIDS therapies suggests a similar lesson: Pharmaceutical corporations negotiate with foreign governments and companies to make their medications available at significantly lower prices in developing than in developed countries, while preserving their patents. David Gordon argues that, in the long run, the ID threat will "further energize the international community and most countries to devote more attention and resources to improved ID surveillance, response, and control capacity."[52]

Social effects. The final hypothesized relationship between IDs and war suggests the greatest threat to national security: By causing severe economic, political, and social effects, epidemic disease can produce domestic instability, civil war, or civil-military conflict, or it may lead a state to lash out against another state. "There is a growing realization that national security depends in great measure on domestic stability, which is in turn heavily influenced by

---

see Marvin Leiner, *Sexual Politics in Cuba: Machismo, Homosexuality, and AIDS* (Boulder: Westview, 1994), chap. 5. The German example is from Rosen, "Strategic Implications," 72.

50. For example, see Carl Mortished, "AIDS Drugs Price War Threatens Big Firms," *Times* (London), 16 July 2001, Business section.

51. Thanks to Andrew Cortell for discussion of this issue. For the argument that multinational disease control efforts may reduce or prevent violent conflict, see Peter J. Hoetz, "Vaccine Diplomacy," *Foreign Policy* no, 124 (May/June 2001): 68–69; and Ban, "Health, Security, and U.S. Global Leadership," 9.

52. NIC, "Global Infectious Disease Threat," 28.

human development—embracing economic, environmental, health, and political concerns."[53]

In many states, particularly in sub-Saharan Africa, IDs like AIDS produce devastating consequences for all economic actors, from the household and firm to the industry and state.[54] At the household level, ID effects are dramatic: Income declines precipitously when bread-winners sicken and die, health care and burial costs mount, savings are depleted, surviving children leave school to work or care for sick relatives, food consumption drops, malnutrition and poverty worsen, and medical expenditures soar. UNDP estimates that AIDS lowers the income of affected households by 80 percent; food consumption drops 15–30 percent; and primary school enrollments decline 20–40 percent.[55] In Thailand, rural families affected by AIDS spend the equivalent of an average annual income on treatment during the last year of an AIDS patient's life, while in Nigeria subsistence farmers spend as much as 13 percent of their total household income on malaria treatment.[56]

Because AIDS is spread largely by sexual behavior, it strikes people in their economically most productive years, with ruinous consequences for numerous sectors of the economy. Agriculture may be hardest hit with the most catastrophic results, given its importance in the economies of most developing countries. A 2001 UN Food and Agriculture Organization study estimates that by year's end AIDS will have claimed 26 percent of the agricultural work force in the ten most affected African nations.[57] In Zimbabwe, for instance, the output of largely subsistence communal agriculture has dropped 50 percent in the last five years, leading some experts to warn of a food crisis in the near fu-

---

53. Alleyne, "Health and National Security," 159.

54. For efforts to examine disease effects on these different actors or levels of the economy, see Desmond Cohen, "The Economic Impact of the HIV Epidemic," Issues Paper No. 2 (UNDP HIV and Development Programme, 1992), www.undp.org/hiv/publications/issues/english/issue02e.htm (5 March 2002); Desmond Cohen, "Socio-Economic Causes and Consequences of the HIV Epidemic in Southern Africa: A Case Study of Namibia," Issues Paper no. 31 (UNDP HIV and Development Programme, 1998), www.undp.org/hiv/publications/issues/english/issue31e.htm (5 March 2002); ICG, "HIV/AIDS As a Security Issue," 9–14; Price-Smith, *Health of Nations*, chap. 3; Andrew T. Price-Smith, "Praetoria's Shadow: The HIV/AIDS Pandemic and National Security in South Africa," Special Report 4, *Health and Security Series* (Chemical and Biological Arms Control Institute; and UNDP, "HIV/AIDS Implications for Poverty Reduction," UNDP Policy Paper (Background Paper prepared for the United Nations Development Programme for the UN General Assembly Special Session on HIV/AIDS, 25–27 June 2001), available online at www.undp.org/hiv (7 August 2001).

55. "HIV/AIDS Implications for Poverty Reduction," 2.

56. UNAIDS, *Report on the Global HIV/AIDS Epidemic*, 27; WHO, "Removing Obstacles," chap. 3. When adults die from any cause in Zimbabwe, small farm output drops by approximately 45 percent, but when AIDS is the cause of death output declines by 61 percent. UNDP, "HIV/AIDS Implications for Poverty Reduction," 10.

57. Cited in ICG, "HIV/AIDS as a Security Issue," 11.

ture.[58] Price-Smith notes that both demand- and supply-side shocks induced by IDs will compromise productivity in agriculture and other economic sectors, including education, mining, tourism, and health.[59]

Sectors dependent on skilled workers and professionals may be particularly hard hit. AIDS disproportionately attacks the middle and professional classes in a society—its teachers, scientists, technicians, and managers—and may prompt surviving elites to flee. Individual businesses bear much of the cost of AIDS in the form of lost work time and benefits. In South Africa, 7.2 percent of total salary costs involve AIDS expenses.[60] One Kenyan company reports a 500 percent increase in funeral expenses and 1,000 percent increase in the cost of health care between 1989 and 1997.[61] With life expectancy plummeting, many companies hire two or more workers for every one job.[62]

AIDS, and IDs more generally, crush national economies, which face labor shortages and diminished productivity. Life expectancy at birth has fallen to about 34 in Sierra Leone, 48 in South Africa, and 42 in Uganda.[63] The U.S. Bureau of the Census estimates that life expectancy in Botswana in 2010 without AIDS would have been nearly 75; with AIDS it will be less than 30.[64] In Zimbabwe and Zambia, as well, life expectancy in 2010 will be half of what it would have been without AIDS—in Zimbabwe, 35 rather than 70, and in Zambia, 30 instead of 60.[65] By 2010, there will be 71 million fewer people in South Africa because of AIDS.[66] This decline is producing alarming demographic trends: Because AIDS most often strikes women in their child-bearing years and HIV may be transferred from a pregnant woman to her child *in utero*, mortality rates among children are soaring. In Kenya, child mortality has risen more than 20 percent since 1986 and now exceeds its level of more than two decades ago. Men and women in their 20s and 30s, a decade or more after they have become sexually active, are dying of AIDS at astonishing rates. Nearly 90 percent of all fifteen-year-old boys in Botswana will become HIV-infected at some point in their lives; the figure is more than 65 percent in South Africa and nearly 70 percent in Zimbabwe. There soon will be more adults in their 60s and 70s than in their 40s or 50s in these societies

58. UNAIDS, *Report on the Global HIV/AIDS Epidemic,* 33.

59. *Health of Nations*, 91–103.

60. UNDP, "HIV/AIDS Implications for Poverty Reduction," 9.

61. UNAIDS, *Report on the Global HIV/AIDS Epidemic*, 33.

62. Robert E. Fritts, ret. ambassador, U.S. Department of State, personal conversation with author, November 2000.

63. World Health Organization, *The World Health Report 2000: Health Systems: Improving Performance* (Geneva: World Health Organization, 2000), 157–63; WHO, "Removing Obstacles," chap. 2.

64. Cited in UNDP, "HIV/AIDS Implications for Poverty Reductions," 8.

65. Cohen, "Socio-economic Causes and Consequences," 10.

66. UNDP, "HIV/AIDS Implications for Poverty Reductions," 7.

60   SECURITY STUDIES 12, no. 2

because of AIDS deaths.[67] The lost generation is the economically most productive segment of society and the one that in most countries supports the oldest,
youngest, and most vulnerable members.

These trends are devastating the national economies of sub-Saharan Africa.
In high prevalence countries, AIDS will cut GDP growth rates by 0.5 to 1.0 percent a year.[68] Channing Arndt and Jeffrey D. Lewis forecast that South African
GDP will be 17 percent lower in 2010 with AIDS than it would have been without the disease, and an alternative measure that they call "non-health, non-
food absorption" will be 22 percent lower. Even after accounting for AIDS-
induced population decline, per capita GDP in South Africa will be 8 percent
lower in 2010 with AIDS than without it.[69] These findings are consistent with
John T. Cuddington's claims that AIDS may reduce Tanzania's GDP in 2010 by
15–25 percent compared to what it would have been without AIDS. Despite a
population size that is 20 percent smaller than in a world without AIDS, per
capita GDP is still projected to decline by as much as 10 percent.[70]

Not surprisingly, IDs promise dire social and political consequences. It has
become commonplace to note that AIDS is producing a generation of orphans:
As many as 11 percent of children in some African states had lost one or both
parents by 1997, compared with about 2 percent before the AIDS era.[71] This
means that millions of children already have been orphaned, and that number
will reach the tens of millions in the next decade. This generation—which is
likely to be homeless, poor, hungry, uneducated, increasingly desperate, and
decreasingly bound by social norms and laws—presents a challenge to political
stability, particularly in societies where criminal opportunities and weapons are
readily available.

> AIDS orphans are a vulnerable group, and may be recruited into military
> activities or into crime with promises of food, alcohol and drugs, as well
> as need for "family". In chilling words, a recent CIA report on the threat
> of HIV/AIDS to national security concluded that AIDS "…will produce a

---

67. UNAIDS, *Report on the Global HIV/AIDS Epidemic*, 21–26.

68. Desmond Cohen, "The HIV Epidemic and Sustainable Human Development," Issues
Paper no. 29 (UNDP HIV and Development Programme, 1998), www.undp.org/hiv/publi-
cations/issues/english/issue29e.htm (5 March 2002).

69. Channing Arndt and Jeffrey D. Lewis, "The Macro Implications of HIV/AIDS in
South Africa," Africa Region Working Paper Series, no. 9 (World Bank, Africa Region Public
Expenditures Effectiveness Project, November 2000). For further discussion of the national
costs of malaria and AIDS, see Price-Smith, *Health of Nations*, 109–16.

70. "Modeling the Macroeconomic Effects of AIDS, with an Application to Tanzania,"
The World Bank Economic Review 7, no. 2 (1993): 173–89.

71. UNAIDS, *Report on the Global HIV/AIDS Epidemic*, 28.

huge and impoverished orphan cohort unable to cope and vulnerable to exploitation and radicalization."[72]

One major foundation of any political system, education, is being devastated. More than one-third of children orphaned by AIDS drop out of school.[73] The disease also depletes the supply of teachers. In South Africa, as many as one-third of teachers are HIV positive. In Zambia, the number is 40 percent, and in Swaziland, 70 percent.[74] A recent World Bank study of Malawi asserts that roughly 40 percent of education personnel in that country will die from AIDS.[75] In the Central African Republic, 107 of 173 schools have closed recently because of a lack of teaching staff. As many teachers in that country died between 1996 and 1998 as retired. They died an average of ten years before the minimum retirement age of 52, and 85 percent of those who died were HIV positive.[76] Over all, Africa will lose ten percent of its educators to AIDS by 2005, setting the continent back a century in education levels.[77] AIDS erodes a state's technical and managerial capacity by incapacitating and killing government personnel at the same high rates at which it strikes other skilled workers and elites. In September 2000, Zimbabwe's president, Robert Mugabe, took the unusual step of announcing that AIDS had claimed three of his cabinet ministers and many traditional tribal chiefs.[78] In South Africa, the spokesman for Presidents Nelson Mandela and Thabo Mbeki died at age 36 of what is generally regarded to be an AIDS-related illness.[79] The human costs of AIDS reach every level of the polity. Eighty-six percent of all employee deaths at the Kenya Revenue authority in 1998 and 75 percent of all police deaths in 1996–98 were AIDS related.[80] More than one-fourth of South African police forces

72. UNDP, "HIV/AIDS Implications for Poverty Reductions," 12. HIV/AIDS has already been blamed for much of the recent violence in Zimbabwe, violence perpetrated by "alienated youths [who] form their own political organizations well beyond the boundaries of constitutional politics or democratic parties." "Another Nail in Zimbabwe's Coffin," *Africa News Service*, 5 December 2000, cited in Lyndy Heinecken, "Strategic Implications of HIV/AIDS in South Africa," *Conflict, Security & Development* 1, no. 1 (April 2001): 113.

73. UNDP, "HIV/AIDS Implications for Poverty Reductions," 9.

74. ICG, "HIV/AIDS as a Security Issue," 16.

75. This is in addition to the regular attrition through retirement, relocation, and death from other causes. Cited in Desmond Cohen, "The HIV Epidemic and the Education Sector in sub-Saharan Africa," Issues Paper no. 32 (UNDP HIV and Development Programme, 1999), www.undp.org/hiv/publications/issues/english/issue32e.htm (5 March 2002).

76. UNAIDS, *Report on the Global HIV/AIDS Epidemic*, 29.

77. ICG, "HIV/AIDS as a Security Issue," 16.

78. "Mugabe Announces that AIDS had Killed Ministers," Panafrican News Agency Wire Service, 7 September 2000.

79. Kurt Shillinger, "Mbeki Aide's Death Renews HIV Debate," *Boston Globe*, 31 October 2000, A8.

80. ICG, "HIV/AIDS as a Security Issue," 10, 14–15.

are probably now infected.[81] In Botswana, a lawyer relays his frustration with a legal system that cannot function properly because of the loss of court officials, and in Uganda political decentralization is hampered because AIDS has decimated local government in some regions.[82]

How might these political and economic effects produce violent conflict? Price-Smith offers two possible answers: Disease "magnif[ies]…both relative and absolute deprivation and…hasten[s] the erosion of state capacity in seriously affected societies. Thus, infectious disease may in fact contribute to societal destabilization and to chronic low-intensity intrastate violence, and in extreme cases it may accelerate the processes that lead to state failure."[83] Disease heightens competition among social groups and elites for scarce resources. When the debilitating and deadly effects of IDs like AIDS are concentrated among a particular socio-economic, ethnic, racial, or geographic group, the potential for conflict escalates. In many parts of Africa today, AIDS strikes rural areas at higher rates than urban areas, or it hits certain provinces harder than others. If these trends persist in states where tribes or ethnic groups are heavily concentrated in particular regions or in rural rather than urban areas, AIDS almost certainly will interact with tribal, ethnic, or national differences and make political and military conflict more likely. Price-Smith argues, moreover, that "the potential for intra-elite violence is also increasingly probable and may carry grave political consequences, such as coups, the collapse of governance, and planned genocides."[84]

The likelihood that IDs will produce violent conflict by generating these social effects depends on at least three factors. Homer-Dixon and Price-Smith offer the first two.[85] First, other stressors like environmental degradation or scarcity may interact with and exacerbate IDs. Second, the strength of the state before the onset of epidemic disease strongly influences the extent to which IDs produce these social, political, and economic effects and thereby provoke military conflict. "There is a logically positive association between state capac-

81. Price-Smith, "Praetoria's Shadow," 24.

82. Desmond Cohen, "Responding to the Socio-Economic Impact of the HIV Epidemic in Sub-Saharan Africa: Why a Systems Approach is Needed" (UNDP HIV and Development Programme, March 1999), www.undp.org/hiv/publications/issues/english/issue34e.htm (5 March 2002).

83. *Health of Nations*, 121. Thomas Homer-Dixon makes a similar argument about environmental degradation. The social and economic effects of environmental stresses weaken the capacity of the state and its relationship to society, reducing its ability to respond creatively to environmental problems and heightening the possibility of violent conflict. Homer-Dixon, *Environment, Scarcity, and Violence*.

84. *Health of Nations*, 124.

85. See Homer-Dixon, *Environment, Scarcity, and Violence*; and Price-Smith, *Health of Nations*, esp. 121.

ity and state adaptation because greater initial capacity means that there are more human, economic, and technical resources within the state to mobilize to deal with various crises.... Thus states that have lower state capacity when IDs afflict them generally suffer much greater losses than states with high initial capacity."[86] The states of sub-Saharan Africa are doubly doomed: Lacking the state capacity to assemble an effective defense against IDs, they are then hit with epidemics that they lack the financial and technical resources to fight.

Third, whether AIDS or other IDs generate severe economic and political effects leading to violent conflict also may depend on prevailing beliefs about religion, society, and medicine. Populations judge their governments' responses to health crises according to their dominant social beliefs. In the nineteenth century, where and when the theory prevailed that disease was contagious, quarantine was the preferred policy response to disease outbreak. Where and when the idea prevailed that disease was acquired through bad air and filth, rather than contagion, people demanded sanitary reform instead.[87] Religious traditions, like Christianity and some forms of Buddhism, that explain human suffering and comfort survivors, may placate individuals and at least temporarily insulate governments against charges that they are not responsive to the health needs of their peoples.[88] In the Middle East and North Africa, social values in predominantly Islamic countries may limit the spread of HIV, but they also inhibit the prevention, reporting, and treating of sexually transmitted diseases, and they likely shield the government.[89] Moral stigma may perform a similar function. Syphilis reached epidemic dimensions in the First World War, for example, because the stigma surrounding it led to poor medical management.[90] A similar shame continues to mark AIDS sufferers, leading many governments to delay and populations to tolerate inaction.

This provides yet another reason that IDs will continue to pose the most serious threat to developing states. With western industrialization came secularization and scientific advancement. In the 1980s, nonetheless, social beliefs posed a significant obstacle to AIDS control and prevention in some developed countries because of bias against the homosexual population, which suffered disproportionately from the disease. These prejudices, as well as prevailing beliefs about sexuality, continue to hinder progress in some segments of western society. The problem is likely to be even more serious in less developed

86. Price-Smith, "Ghosts of Kigali," 434.
87. See Goodman, *International Health Organizations and Their Work*, chap. 2.
88. McNeill argues that such religions developed in countries where disease was prevalent. *Plagues and Peoples*, 149–50.
89. NIC, "Global Infectious Disease Threat," 3–4.
90. McNeill, *Plagues and People*, 289.

states, where traditional customs like wife inheritance and genital mutilation spread AIDS directly and where the role of women and the stigma surrounding AIDS create intolerance and silence that allow the disease to spread unchecked. In a highly publicized case in December 1998, neighbors beat to death a volunteer for a South African AIDS organization for bringing shame on their community by publicly acknowledging that she was HIV-infected.[91] In June 2001, in a three-day special session on AIDS, the UN General Assembly passed a Declaration of Commitment, a global AIDS plan that includes specific goals and time frames. The final document explicitly addressed "harmful traditional and customary practices," but not before agreement was nearly scuttled and language about high risk populations was deleted because Islamic nations opposed wording that would obligate them to help gay men, one of the high risk groups.[92]

Figure 1

EPIDEMIC DISEASE AND MILITARY CONFLICT

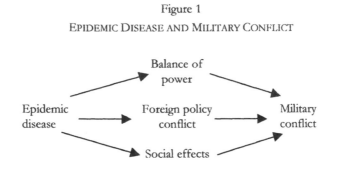

Not all the causal pathways identified in figure 1 threaten national security. There can be little doubt, however, that ID seriously threatens national security, traditionally defined, when large numbers of people die, national economies crumble, and social structures and political institutions weaken and fail, particularly when these factors generate violent conflict. Many sub-Saharan states that are resource-poor and institutionally weak face such threats unless other states, international institutions, or nongovernmental organizations (NGOs) provide significant financial, medical, and administrative assistance. That IDs threaten security in these states, however, does not necessarily or automatically compromise U.S. security.

91. UNICEF, *The Progress of Nations 1999* (New York: UNICEF, 1999), 17.
92. Jennifer Steinhauer, "U.N. Redefines AIDS as Political Issue and Peril to Poor," *New York Times*, 28 June 2001, A4.

U.S. NATIONAL SECURITY

Indeed, none of the mechanisms illustrated in figure 1 immediately or directly threatens U.S. security. Large numbers of Americans die each year from IDs. In fact, the number of deaths from IDs in the United States doubled between 1980 and 1999.[93] These numbers, however, pale in comparison to those in sub-Saharan Africa and other regions, and they do not threaten the state in the way they do in other countries. As Price-Smith points out, "the United States has less to fear from the direct threat of infectious disease (or other environmentally induced health threats) to its population than do developing countries with much lower endogenous capacity."[94] This does not mean, of course, that the United States can afford to bury its head in the sand.

Epidemic disease may exacerbate domestic conflict in key states where vital U.S. interests are at stake. In Russia, for instance, HIV rates have risen dramatically in the past two years and are poised to explode. The 1999 infection rate in Moscow was three times that of all previous years combined.[95] In fact, AIDS is spreading more quickly in Russia than in any other country in the world. According to a 2002 National Intelligence Council (NIC) estimate, between one and two million Russians (or 1.3–2.5 percent of the adult population) is currently infected, and that number is expected to increase to 5–8 million (or 6–11 percent) by 2010.[96] Much of this increase is fueled by IV drug use, commercial sex, and, especially, the prison system, in which inmates may be held for up to two years before being charged and in which more than a million convicts are periodically released through amnesty programs. As Nicholas Eberstadt notes, "Russia's prison system, in other words, functions like a carburetor for HIV—pumping a highly concentrated variant of the infection back through the general population."[97]

In June 2001, Russia's first deputy minister of health, Gennadi Onishchenko, called AIDS "a direct threat to the nation's security."[98] This may be true for several reasons. First, AIDS will exacerbate Russia's projected population decrease. In less than 25 years, it is estimated, Russia's population will decline by 12–13 million, even if the nation faces only a mild HIV/AIDS

93. Erica Barks-Ruggles, "The Globalization of Disease: When Congo Sneezes, Will California Get a Cold?" *Brookings Review* 19, no. 4 (fall 2001): 30–33.

94. Price-Smith, *Health of Nations*, 138.

95. UNAIDS, *Report on the Global HIV/AIDS Epidemic*, 18.

96. "The Next Wave of HIV/AIDS: Nigeria, Ethiopia, Russia, India, and China," ICA 2002-040, September 2002, 8. David F. Gordon is the principal author.

97. "The Future of AIDS," *Foreign Affairs* 81, no. 6 (November/ December 2002): 26. Also see NIC, "Next Wave," 11–12.

98.David E. Powell and Heidi A. Kostin, "Rapid Spread of AIDS in Russia Imperils a Generation," *Boston Globe*, 10 February 2002.

epidemic. In the face of the more severe epidemic now feared, that decline will reach 25 million, with a concurrent drop of 11 million in Russia's working-age population.[99] By 2050, it is estimated, the population of the "superpower" may plummet by as much as one-third to 95–100 million people.[100] The director of the Federal Research Center for AIDS Prevention in Moscow, Vadim Pokrovskii, sums up the problem this way: "In Africa, there are high birth rates, but in Russia the birth rate is low. If we have a rate of only three percent infected, population would fall by six percent.... In Russia, AIDS is scarier than in Africa. There the population is replaced. In Russia it will not be."[101]

Second, and closely related, AIDS is likely to cause severe economic problems. A recent World Bank study predicts that HIV/AIDS will reduce annual economic growth in Russia by one percent by 2020.[102] While Russia's GNP per person of working age could be expected to increase by 50 percent by 2025 without HIV/AIDS, the disease will significantly reduce worker output and decimate the working-age population. The result, Ebertadt projects, is that under even the mildest epidemic-scenario now predicted, Russia's future GNP will remain stagnant through 2025.[103]

Finally, these demographic and economic problems, combined with the disease's effect on military readiness, may undermine political stability in Russia. The chairman of the Defense Ministry's Medical Commission reports that 37 percent of all draft-age men in Russia cannot serve because of serious health problems. Fifty-five percent of those drafted can perform only limited duties because of poor health. In 2001, over 2,000 servicemen were dismissed from the Russian Army for being HIV-positive.[104] In the not too distant future, in short, AIDS could further erode Russia's ability to staff a conventional army and potentially lead Moscow to rely more on a deteriorating nuclear force to maintain its great power status.

99. Eberstadt, "Future of AIDS," 37. Eighty-seven percent of new HIV infections in Russia occur among 15 to 30 year olds. Lisa McAdams, "Looming AIDS Crisis in Russia to Have Profound Impact on Society," Voice of America, 27 November 2002, available from Center for Defense Information, *Russia Weekly*, no. 233, www.cdi.or/russia/233-2-pr.cfm (29 January 2003).

100. Ban, "Health, Security, and U.S. Global Leadership," 35.

101. Peter Graff, "INTERVIEW—AIDS in Russia 'scarier than Africa' yet ignored," Reuters.

102. Cited in NIC, "Next Wave," 24.

103. "Future of AIDS," 40–41.

104. Powell and Kostin, "Rapid Spread of AIDS in Russia Imperils a Generation." Also, see NIC, "Global Infectious Disease Threat," 34; and David L. Heyman, Executive Director for Communicable Diseases World Health Organization, Statement before the Committee on International Relations, U.S. House of Representatives, 29 June 2000, www.who.int/infectious-disease-report/dlh-testimony/testmo.pdf (24 September 2001).

China is in the early stages of a similar HIV/AIDS explosion. Reported infections were 67.4 percent higher in the first six months of 2001 than for the same period in 2000, and the rate of infection among Chinese drug users is ten times as high today as it was in 1995.[105] Seven of China's 22 provinces already are experiencing full-blown epidemics, while nine more face similar fates in the near future.[106] According to a recent United Nations study, current trends indicate that 20 million Chinese will be HIV-positive by 2010.[107] The problem is especially acute, because many Chinese blame their government for the AIDS crisis. Until recently, government officials have refused to acknowledge the epidemic publicly. More importantly, government actions helped spread AIDS throughout central China. There, government-owned or -operated blood collection centers paid poor farmers to donate blood. Blood of the same type was pooled and centrifuged to separate out the plasma. The leftover red blood cells then were pooled and reinjected into the donors, preventing anemia and allowing donors to give blood more frequently. Not surprisingly, there have been a growing number of protests against the government by farmers trying to publicize their plight.[108]

HIV/AIDS will have serious human and economic costs in China, but it is relatively unlikely to cause the kind of widespread disruption that could jeopardize China's regional status. The spreading epidemic could curtail the international investment that has helped fuel China's economic growth. As the recent NIC study notes, however, China has several things going for it that Russia does not. First, although domestic AIDS spending remains low, the Chinese government has recently taken great strides in acknowledging the extent of the epidemic, seeking assistance, and organizing a public health response. Second, the sheer size of China's population will mute the epidemic's impact. Even an infected population of fifteen million would represent just two percent of the adult population of China.[109]

Another nuclear-armed state, India, also faces a looming epidemic. Infection rates remain low—7 of 1,000 adults are HIV-positive. Five to eight million people in India, however, currently live with the disease, and that number is expected to rise to 20–25 million (3–4 percent of the adult population) by 2010.

105. Elisabeth Rosenthal, "China Now Facing an AIDS Epidemic, a Top Aide Admits," *New York Times*, 24 August 2001, A10.

106. Bates Gill, Jennifer Chang, and Sarah Palmer, "China's HIV Crisis," *Foreign Affairs* 81, no. 2(March/April 2002): 96–110; quote from 97.

107. Rosenthal, "China Now Facing an AIDS Epidemic." According to NIC estimates, 10–15 million (1.3–2 percent of Chinese adults) will be infected by 2010. "Next Wave," 8.

108. Rosenthal, "China Now Facing an AIDS Epidemic"; and Elisabeth Rosenthal, "Spread of AIDS in Rural China Ignites Protests," *New York Times*, 11 December 2001.

109. NIC, "Next Wave," 20, 24.

68   SECURITY STUDIES 12, no. 2

In some areas of northeast India, more than 70 percent of the mostly male IV drug-using population is infected, suggesting that infection rates in the general population may soon soar.[110] Public awareness of AIDS remains low, but the Indian government responded relatively early to the epidemic, creating the National AIDS Control Organization in 1986, and India possesses a relatively strong public health infrastructure. As in China, moreover, the NIC estimates that the effects of India's epidemic will be lessened by being diffused among a large population.[111] For the present, significant unrest in Russia, India, or China remains a distant and remote possibility for American policy makers and the public, even though it is becoming increasingly obvious that Russia, in particular, faces a severe ID threat in the near future. If scholars and policy makers are to draw a credible link between ID and U.S. national security, it is here that they should look.

Nevertheless, the more immediate threat is to sub-Saharan Africa, and it is here that scholars and practitioners have focused their attention by arguing that U.S. security is linked to stability in Africa. In February 2001, Secretary of State Powell announced that the AIDS epidemic in Africa is a national security issue.[112] In May of the same year, Powell told South African students, "Africa matters to America," citing $30 billion in U.S.-African trade.[113] In the aftermath of the events of 9/11, the West in general and the United States in particular have a heightened security interest in Africa. Disease can contribute to instability and violence. Indeed, high infant mortality—which exists in sub-Saharan Africa largely because of IDs—is strongly correlated with the likelihood of state failure in partial democracies.[114] Failed states may breed anti-western sentiment and even terrorism.[115] Alternatively, they may influence domestic actors in the United States to pressure their government to intervene on humanitarian grounds. Once U.S. troops are committed, whether alone or as part of a multilateral force, U.S. security is clearly engaged.

These security concerns likely will not seem terribly compelling to Americans for at least three reasons. First, they may appear relatively remote possi-

---

110. UNAIDS, Report on the global HIV/AIDS epidemic, 12–13; NIC, "Next Wave," 8.

111. "Next Wave," 24.

112. Sachs, "Best Possible Investment in Africa," A1.

113. "Powell: U.S. committed to Africa's economic growth," CNN.com, 25 May 2001, www.cnn.com/201/WORLD/africa/05/25/powell.speech/index.htm (4 February 2002). For the text of Powell's speech, see Secretary Colin L. Powell, "Remarks at the University of Witwatersrand," Johannesburg, South Africa, U.S. Department of State, 25 May 2001, www.state.gov/secretary/rm/2001/3090.htm.

114. NIC, "Global Infectious Disease Threat," 32.

115. For a recent statement of this argument, see "Blair urges action on Africa," BBC News, 6 February 2002, news.bbc.co.uk/hi/english/uk_politics/newsid_1803000/1803567.stm. (6 February 2002).

bilities, particularly at a time when the United States is dealing with immediate and direct security threats. Second, even if Americans think about the longer run, there are more obvious candidates for state-sponsored terrorism or state failure than the states of sub-Saharan Africa, particularly the Islamic states of the Middle East and North Africa. Third, regardless of current interest in Africa, that continent has never figured heavily in U.S. security and foreign policy calculations. Americans see few material or strategic interests at stake, particularly in sub-Saharan Africa. As Helen Epstein and Lincoln Chen state, "In 1999, the UN Security Council declared AIDS in Africa an international security issue, because it further destabilizes already politically fragile African nations. How much, however, does this really matter to the West, particularly the United States? The postwar history of the West's relationship with Africa suggests that when millions of Africans die, or when African states collapse, Western leaders often look away."[116] Secretary Powell's own words confirm this. In February 2000, less than a year before assuming office, he said, "While Africa may be important, it doesn't fit into the national strategic interests, as far as I can see them."[117]

It seems obvious, in short, that epidemic disease can contribute to violent conflict, particularly by engendering domestic instability, and in that way can threaten the national security of affected states. At present, however, most ID-induced unrest poses at most an indirect and medium to long term threat to U.S. security, suggesting that a rhetorical linkage to national security may not be the most effective way of inspiring public and political support for AIDS-ravaged Africa. Russia, where IDs may pose the most immediate threat to U.S. interests, is receiving relatively little attention in discussions of disease threats to U.S. national security.

EPIDEMIC DISEASE AS A DETERMINANT OF WAR OUTCOME

Even when disease plays little role in the outbreak of war, it can influence the course and outcome of military conflict. In theory, IDs can be "war-stoppers" or "war-outcome-determinants," contributing to one side's victory and another's defeat, depending on their differential impact on the adversaries. As figure 2 suggests, disease can influence the outcome of contemporary conflict in at least three ways: the deliberate dissemination of biological agents; the targeting by conventional means of public health; and the unintentional impact of epidemic disease on military readiness.

116. "Can AIDS Be Stopped?"
117. Alex Duval Smith, "AIDS, Trade and War Top Powell's African Agenda," *The Independent* (London), 25 May 2001, 20.

Figure 2

DISEASE AND THE OUTCOME OF MILITARY CONFLICT

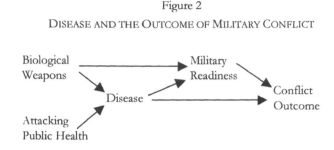

Biological weapons and disease. Biological warfare has been described as "public health in reverse" because of its potential to disperse deadly infectious agents.[118] Because biological weapons potentially pose direct security threats to the United States and other countries, because they are not new threats, and because they fit more easily within traditional definitions of security, attempts to link disease and security in this way should resonate with the American public and policy makers.

Biological weapons are living organisms, most commonly self-replicating micro-organisms—including bacteria, viruses, fungi, and rickettsia—deliberately disseminated to cause disease and death in humans or animals.[119] Since 1972, 144 parties to the Biological Toxins and Weapons Convention have agreed not to develop, produce, stockpile, acquire, or retain biological weapons. At least eleven states nevertheless have some sort of biological weapons program. These efforts produce or are capable of producing numerous IDs. As Americans are all too aware, anti-human biological weapons agents include *bacillus anthracis* (anthrax), which produces fever, severe respiratory problems, shock, pneumonia, and death within days of exposure.[120] Anthrax is not a particularly effective agent, however, since it is not contagious and, in many cases, is susceptible to treatment. Smallpox is extremely contagious, by contrast, and spreads through the inhalation of virus droplets. It can incubate for more than 12 days before sickening its victims for up to several weeks with

118. Jonathan B. Tucker, "The Biological Weapons Threat," *Current History* 96, no. 609 (April 1997): 167.

119. They also may include nonliving, non-self-replicating agents that are either secreted by living organisms or synthetically produced to be similar to agents secreted by living organisms. See Malcolm Dando, *The New Biological Weapons: Threat, Proliferation, and Control* (Boulder: Lynne Rienner, 2001), esp. 18.

120. Information on the effects of anthrax and smallpox is taken from "Biological Weapons Agents," Chemical and Biological Weapons Nonproliferation Project, Henry L. Stimson Center, www.stimson.org/cwc/bwagent.htm (10 November 2000).

vomiting, lesions, fever, and in 35 percent of stricken people, death. In 1980, after the WHO announced that smallpox had been eradicated, stocks of the disease were destroyed and, officially, samples exist only in the Centers for Disease Control (CDC) in Atlanta and the State Centre for Research on Virology and Biotechnology in Siberia. For this reason, until very recently, there was no commercially available supply of smallpox vaccine.[121]

Anti-animal and plant pathogens also make potent biological weapons.[122] Diseases like Newcastle disease, bovine spongiform encephalopathy ("mad cow disease"), avian influenza, swine fevers, anthrax, brucellosis, and—among the most contagious and most costly—foot-and-mouth disease can disrupt cattle, hog, and poultry production. In the process, such agroterrorism can cause significant threats to the agricultural sector, disrupt trade and, in extreme cases, provoke famine. As Dorothy Preslar has noted, terrorism against agricultural targets may pose a greater threat than against human targets because it "[i]s not as repugnant to prevailing sensibilities; [c]annot easily be proved intentional...; [c]an be instigated without violating international arms control agreements; [and w]ill incite neither a crushing military response nor [an] international man-hunt."[123] Crop diseases may be introduced to spread famine and disrupt the economy. Because they are highly sensitive to humidity, temperature, and sunlight and they cannot circulate airborne as far or as fast as many human and animal diseases, however, crop diseases would be more difficult to disseminate.[124]

Unlike nuclear and chemical weapons, biological agents are relatively simple and inexpensive to manufacture and easy to conceal. They can be made in facilities otherwise devoted to legitimate medical and pharmaceutical research at a fraction of the cost of other weapons. One government analyst has calculated that a penny's worth of anthrax is the equivalent in lethality of $1,500 of

121. Fifteen million doses of the vaccine stored at the CDC were scheduled to be destroyed when the last remaining smallpox virus was destroyed. Routine civilian immunization against smallpox halted nearly two decades ago, and human immunity to the disease is thought to fade within 15 years of vaccination. After 9/11, the U.S. government ordered large quantities of smallpox vaccine for the first time in decades. More recently, the government confirmed that existing doses could be diluted safely and that a private company had unexpectedly found 70-90 million doses. Justin Gillis, "Smallpox Vaccine Supply Could Be Stretched," *Washington Post*, 29 March 2002, A10.

122. These diseases may also pose security threats when they occur naturally rather than secondary to a terrorist attack.

123. Dorothy B. Preslar, "The Role of Disease Surveillance in the Watch for Agroterrorism or Economic Sabotage," November 2000, www.fas.org/ahead/bwconcerns/agroterror.htm (16 April 2002).

124. Anne Kohnen, "Responding to the Threat of Agro-terrorism: Specific Recommendations for the United States Department of Agriculture," BCSIA Discussion Paper 2000-29, ESDP Discussion Paper 2004-04, John F. Kennedy School of Government, Harvard University, October 2000, 10.

Global Health

nuclear power.[125] It can be difficult to stabilize biological agents, but relatively easy to deliver them to their targets. They can be sprayed efficiently as respirable aerosols from a truck or small plane. Only ten grams of anthrax spores spread over one square mile would kill as many people as would a metric ton of sarin gas.[126] As Garrett notes, "Enough anthrax spores to kill five or six million people could be loaded into a taxi and pumped out its tailpipe as it meandered through Manhattan."[127]

Despite strong prohibitions against biological weapons and warfare, ID has been used as a weapon of war throughout history. Greek, Roman, and Persian armies tossed dead bodies in enemy wells to poison the water supply. In the fourteenth century, the Black Plague spread to Europe—where it ultimately claimed as much as one-third of the population—from what is now Ukraine, after Tartar soldiers catapulted their own plague victims over the fortress walls as weapons against their Italian foes.[128] The British employed smallpox in their fights against native Americans in the 1754–63 French and Indian War and against U.S. troops in the Revolutionary War.[129] During their southern campaign in the Revolutionary War, the British used infected African slaves, whom they had enticed to fight the Americans with the promise of freedom, as weapons of war.[130] During the Second World War, the Japanese Imperial Army's Unit 731 developed biological weapons to disperse anthrax, typhoid, cholera, plague, and at least a dozen other IDs and tested these weapons on Chinese civilians.[131] More recently, Stefan Elbe argues, African armies have used HIV/AIDS as a psychological, and perhaps even biological, weapon.[132]

Although the risk of biological warfare is modest, it remains one of the most significant and immediate security threats that disease poses for the West, par-

---

125. Michael T. Osterholm and John Schwartz, *Living Terrors: What America Needs to Know to Survive the Coming Bioterrorist Catastrophe* (New York: Delacourt Press, 2000), 8.

126. Tucker, "Biological Weapons Threat," 168.

127. Garrett, "Return," 76.

128. Tucker, "Biological Weapons Threat," 169; J. M. Roberts, *History of the World* (New York: Oxford University Press, 1993), 413.

129. For example, see John Duffy, "Smallpox and the Indians in the American Colonies," *Bulletin of the History of Medicine* 25, no. 4 (1951): 340, reprinted in Kiple and Beck, *Biological Consequences of the European Expansion*, 249.

130. See Elizabeth A. Fenn, *Pox Americana: The Great Smallpox Epidemic of 1775–82* (New York: Hill and Wang, 2001).

131. See Peter Williams and David Wallace, *Unit 731: The Japanese Army's Secret of Secrets* (London: Hodder and Stoughton, 1989); Sheldon H. Harris, *Factories of Death: Japanese Biological Warfare, 1932–45, and the American Cover-Up* (New York: Routledge, 1994); and Nicholas D. Kristof, "Unmasking Horror—A Special Report; Japan Confronting Gruesome War Atrocity," *New York Times*, 17 March 1995, A1.

132. "HIV/AIDS and the Changing Landscape of War in Africa," *International Security* 27, no. 2 (fall 2002): 167–71. Also, see Singer, "AIDS and International Security."

ticularly the United States.[133] These weapons pose two distinct challenges. First, a state's pursuit of biological weapons capabilities could provoke preventive war by other states fearful of that power. Concerns about Iraq's budding biological, chemical, and nuclear capabilities provoked the 1981 Israeli attack on an Iraqi nuclear reactor, helped fuel two wars against Iraq, and prompted the decade of inspections and air strikes between the two Persian Gulf Wars. Second, biological agents could be used as weapons of war or terrorism. State use remains relatively unlikely, however, given normative prohibitions against the use of biological weapons and the deadliness of other available weapons. Despite its extensive biological and chemical weapons program, for example, Iraq did not use these weapons during the 1991 Persian Gulf War and, as of this writing, has not used them in the current conflict. At present, moreover, most states lack the capability to launch a successful biological weapons attack. Non-state actors and some rogue states are more likely to use these weapons of the weak against a domestic population, government, or other target. Certainly, there is no shortage of states or terrorist groups with grievances to air, and these actors will care less, if at all, about international public opinion. That Osama bin Laden actively sought to acquire weapons of mass destruction supports Richard Falkenrath's claim that the rise of religious and anti-American terrorist groups will weaken the bias against causing mass fatalities and using nuclear, chemical, or biological weapons to do so.[134]

Biological weapons pose a substantial and direct threat to U.S. national security. On the one hand, the United States presents the most likely target for such terrorist attacks, even if the overall likelihood of such an attack remains small. On the other hand, key states that the United States considers strategically important might acquire, use, or become a target of biological weapons and indirectly threaten U.S. interests. The U.S. government recognized this potential, for example, when it designated $100 million to defuse the biological weapons threat from the former Soviet Union by converting former weapons

133. There have been 121 incidents involving the use of biological agents in the last four decades. Jeremy Laurance, "U.S. on Alert for Smallpox Terror Attack," *Independent on Sunday* (London), 22 April 2001, 2. In addition to extensive scientific, medical, and public health literatures on biological weapons, see Richard K. Betts, "The New Threat of Weapons of Mass Destruction," *Foreign Affairs* 77, no. 1 (January/February 1998): 26–41; Malcolm R. Dando, *Biological Warfare in the 21st Century: Biotechnology and the Proliferation of Biological Weapons* (London: Brassey's, 1994); Peter R. Lavoy, James J. Wirtz, and Scott D. Sagan, *Planning the Unthinkable: How New Powers Will Use Nuclear, Biological, and Chemical Weapons* (Ithaca: Cornell University Press, 2000); Joshua Lederberg, ed., *Biological Weapons: Limiting the Threat* (Cambridge: MIT Press, 1999); John D. Steinbruner, "Biological Weapons: A Plague Upon All Houses," *Foreign Policy*, no. 109 (Winter 1997–98): 85–113; Tucker, "Biological Weapons Threat."

134. Richard A. Falkenrath, "Confronting Nuclear, Biological and Chemical Terrorism," *Survival* 40, no. 3 (autumn 1998): 43–65.

facilities and employing scientists previously involved in the Soviet biological warfare program.[135]

Given the immediate and direct nature of the threat, and especially following the 2001 anthrax attacks, it should be relatively easy (compared with efforts to link economic instability in Africa to U.S. security) to link biological weapons to American national security in the public mind and therefore to mobilize domestic support for antiterrorist and counterterrorist activities. In 1998, President Clinton announced that he expected a biological or chemical attack within the next five years. The following year, R. James Woolsey, director of Central Intelligence under Clinton, described biological terrorism as the "single most dangerous threat to [U.S.] national security in the foreseeable future."[136] More recently, Secretary of Health and Human Services, Tommy Thompson, responded to the anthrax threats by announcing that "[p]ublic health is a national security issue."[137] Scholars may differ on the perceived likelihood of attack, but few would deny that disease—when used deliberately as a weapon of war—poses a significant threat to national security. Indeed, it has long been recognized as such and included in planning for war and homeland defense.

Targeting public health. Biological agents are not the only way to deliberately disseminate disease during war. Armed forces have often targeted civilians—anand civilian health—as part of a deliberate military strategy, and the use of this tactic seems only to have risen since the end of the cold war. What Jack Chow calls "'humanitarian' warfare—aggression through the control and denial of vital human needs—now complements or even substitutes for direct force."[138] Two tactics of humanitarian warfare, in particular, link ID and national security. What Chow calls "war by starvation" emphasizes the political and strategic value of food. In Sudan, Somalia, and Ethiopia, soldiers and warlords have struggled to control the food supply as a means of increasing their military and political power. This deliberate use of starvation inevitably spreads IDs, given the link between malnutrition and disease. What Chow terms "war by privation" is somewhat broader and includes "deliberate cutoffs of food,

135. See Michael Dobbs, "Soviet-Era Work on Bioweapons Still Worrisome: Stall in U.S. Dismantling Effort Could Pose Proliferation Threat," *Washington Post*, 12 September 2000, A1. For information on the Soviet Union's extensive biological warfare program, see Ken Alibek (with Stephen Handelman), *Biohazard: The Chilling True Story of the Largest Covert Weapons Program in the World* (New York: Delta/Random House, 1999).

136. Quoted in Contagion and Conflict: Health as a Global Security Challenge, A Report of the Chemical and Biological Arms Control Institute and the CSIS International Security Program (Washington, D.C.: Center for Strategic and International Studies, 2000), 37–38.

137. Sheryl Gay Stolberg, "Health Secretary Testifies About Germ Warfare Defenses," *New York Times*, 4 October 2001, B7.

138. "Health and International Security: U.S. Policy on World Health," *Washington Quarterly* 19, no. 2 (spring 1996): 63–77. The authors of the CSIS report, "Contagion and Conflict," call this "community warfare." See chap. 2.

water, medicine and heat."[139] In Sudan, for instance, government troops routinely target hospitals.[140] In Kosovo, Yugoslav president Slobodan Milosovec targeted medical care as far back as 1989–90 when he ordered the firing of thousands of Albanian professionals, closing 75 percent of all state-run medical facilities. This contributed to 170 epidemics between 1990 and 1998. In fighting in 1998, ethnic Albanians were prevented from receiving or forced to pay for medical care that ethnic Serbs received free, and numerous hospitals and out-patient clinics were deliberately destroyed. After the NATO bombing campaign began, government troops and paramilitary units destroyed 90 more country-based health care clinics run by the Mother Teresa Society. Providing medical assistance to members of the Kosovo Liberation Army was labeled terrorism, and doctors were harassed routinely for providing medical aid to people in areas of conflict.[141]

The United States determined that it had strategic interests in Kosovo worth fighting for, so Serbian engagement in war by privation influenced U.S. national security. When the United States becomes militarily involved for humanitarian reasons in areas with little or no strategic value, humanitarian warfare also may threaten its ability to meet its military objectives. In this case, however, the threat is an indirect one and one that is already captured in traditional considerations of military strategy and tactics.

Military readiness. Even when disease is not deliberately used, it can alter the evolution and outcome of military conflict by eroding military readiness and morale. As Jared Diamond notes, "All those military histories glorifying great generals oversimplify the ego-deflating truth: the winners of past wars were not always the armies with the best generals and weapons, but were often merely those bearing the nastiest germs to transmit to their enemies."[142] During the European conquest of the Americas, the conquistadors shared numerous lethal microbes with their native American foes, who had few or no deadly diseases to pass on to their conquerors. When Hernando Cortez and his men first attacked the Aztecs in Mexico in 1520, they left behind smallpox that wiped out half the Aztec population. Surviving Aztecs were further demoralized by their vulnerability to a disease that appeared harmless to the Europeans, and on their next attempt the Spanish succeeded in conquering the Aztec nation.[143] Spanish conquest of the Incan empire in South America followed a similar

---

139. Chow, "Health and International Security."
140. CSIS, "Contagion and Conflict," 29.
141. CSIS, "Contagion and Conflict," 30–31.
142. Diamond, *Guns, Germs, and Steel,* 197.
143. By 1618, Mexico's population had fallen from 20 million to 1.6 million. McNeill, *Plagues and Peoples,* 19–20; Diamond, *Guns, Germs, and Steel,* 210.

pattern: In 1532 Francisco Pizarro and his army of 168 Spaniards defeated the Incan army of 80,000. A devastating smallpox epidemic had killed the Incan emperor and his heir, producing a civil war that split the empire and allowed a handful of Europeans to defeat a large, but divided enemy.[144] In modern times, too, pandemic infections have affected the ability of military forces to prosecute and win a war. The German Army chief of staff in the First World War, General Erick Von Ludendorf, blamed Germany's loss of that war at least partly on the negative effects of the 1918 influenza epidemic on the morale of German troops.[145] In the Second World War, similarly, malaria caused more U.S. casualties in certain areas than did military action.[146] Throughout history, then, IDs have had a significant potential to decimate armies and alter military history.

Still, IDs' impact in the contemporary international system may be somewhat different. Unlike other diseases, AIDS has an incubation period of ten years or more, making it unlikely that it will produce significant casualties on the front lines of a war. It will still, however, deplete force strength in many states. On average, 20–40 percent of armed forces in sub-Saharan countries are HIV-positive, and in a few countries the rate is 60 percent or more. In Zimbabwe, it may be as high as 80 percent.[147] In high incidence countries, AIDS significantly erodes military readiness, directly threatening national security. Lyndy Heinecken chillingly describes the problem in sub-Saharan Africa:

> AIDS-related illnesses are now the leading cause of death in the army and police forces of these countries, accounting for more than 50% of in-service and post-service mortalities. In badly infected countries, AIDS patients occupy 75% of military hospital beds and the disease is responsible for more admissions than battlefield injuries. The high rate of HIV infection has meant that some African armies have been unable to deploy a full contingent, or even half of their troops, at short notice.... [In South Africa, because] participation in peace-support operations outside the country is voluntary, the S[outh] A[frican] N[ational] D[efence] F[orce] is grappling with the problem of how to ensure the availability of sufficiently suitable candidates for deployment at short notice. Even the use of members for internal crime prevention and border control, which subjects them to adverse conditions or stationing in areas where local in-

144. "If it had not been for the epidemic, the Spaniards would have faced a united Empire." Diamond, *Guns, Germs, and Steel,* 67–81, quoted at 77.

145. Crosby, *America's Forgotten Pandemic,* 27.

146. Agency for International Development, *Malaria: Meeting the Global Challenge* (Boston: Oelgeschlager, Gunn & Hain, 1985) 4.

147. Heinecken, "Strategic Implications of HIV/AIDS in South Africa," 109. Also, see Elbe, "HIV/AIDS and the Changing Landscape of War in Africa."

frastructure is limited, presents certain problems. Ordinary ailments, such as diarrhoea and the common cold, can be serious enough to require the hospitalization of an immune-compromised person, and, in some cases, can prove fatal if they are not treated immediately.[148]

Armed forces in severely affected states will be unable to recruit and train soldiers quickly enough to replace their sick and dying colleagues, the potential recruitment pool itself will dwindle, and officers corps will be decimated. Military budgets will be sapped, military blood supplies tainted, and organizational structures strained to accommodate unproductive soldiers.

HIV-infected armed forces also threaten civilians at home and abroad. Increased levels of sexual activity among military forces in wartime means that the military risk of becoming infected with HIV is as much as 100 times that of the civilian risk. It also means that members of the armed forces comprise a key means of transmitting the virus to the general population; with sex and transport workers, the military is considered one of the three core transmission groups in Africa.[149] For this reason, conflict-ridden states may become reluctant to accept peacekeepers from countries with high HIV rates.

Rather than contributing directly to military defeat in many countries, however, AIDS in the military is more likely to have longer term implications for national security. First, IDs theoretically could deter military action and impede access to strategic resources or areas. Tropical diseases erected a formidable, although obviously not insurmountable, obstacle to colonization in Africa, India, and Southeast Asia. French and later American efforts to open the Panama Canal, similarly, were stymied until U.S. mosquito control efforts effectively checked yellow fever and malaria. Second, in many countries AIDS already strains military medical systems and their budgets, and it only promises to divert further spending away from defense toward both military and civilian health. Third, AIDS in the military promises to have its greatest impact by eroding a government's control over its armed forces and further destabilizing the state. Terminally ill soldiers may have little incentive to defend their government, and their government may be in more need of defending as AIDS siphons funds from housing, education, police, and administration. Finally, high military HIV/AIDS rates could alter regional balances of power. Perhaps 40–50 percent of South Africa's soldiers are HIV-infected. Despite the disease's negative impact on South Africa's absolute power, Price-Smith notes, AIDS may increase that nation's power relative to its neighbors, Zimbabwe and

---

148. Heinecken, "Strategic Implications of HIV/AIDS in South Africa," 109–11. Also, see Price-Smith, "Praetoria's Shadow," 18–22.

149. USAID, "Military Populations"; Heinecken, "Strategic Implications of HIV/AIDS in South Africa," 109.

Botswana, with potentially important regional consequences.[150] AIDS poses obvious threats to the military forces of many countries, particularly in sub-Saharan Africa, but it does not present the same immediate security problems for the United States. The authors of a Reagan-era report on the effects of economic and demographic trends on security worried about the effects of the costs of AIDS research, education, and funding on the defense budget,[151] but a decade of relative prosperity generated budget surpluses instead. These surpluses have evaporated, but concerns about AIDS spending have not reappeared and are unlikely to do so for the foreseeable future, given the relatively low levels of HIV-infection in the United States. AIDS presents other challenges, including prevention education and measures to limit infection of U.S. soldiers and peacekeepers stationed abroad, particularly in high risk settings, and HIV transmission by these forces to the general population. These concerns could limit U.S. actions where American interests are at stake.[152]

AIDS' effects on the militaries of key states also could erode vital U.S. interests by undermining allies' military readiness or friends' and foes' political stability. As discussed above, Russia will be among the states hardest hit with potentially serious consequences for the international balance of power. IDs may not prevent the U.S. military from fighting and winning wars, in short, but they still impact U.S. national security. They do not, however, and for the foreseeable future will not, degrade security in the direct ways or to the extent that many health security advocates suggest.

MISSTATING THE THREAT

A T THE START OF the twenty-first century, human beings face what may be the worst plague in history, a disease so devastating that it has already surpassed in absolute terms the most notorious epidemics of earlier generations. In response, politicians, health professionals, and scholars plead with the West to recognize the threat this modern plague presents to human security. They attempt to persuade nations and individuals to broaden their thinking about security to encompass basic needs like health. From there, it is often only one small rhetorical step to the argument that AIDS and other IDs threaten national and international security. Intellectually, however, that step is much

---

150. Price-Smith, "Praetoria's Shadow," 19, 31.
151. "Economic and Demographic Trends," 598.
152. In 2000, the Security Council adopted its first resolution on a health issue, asking member states to initiate AIDS testing and prevention programs among their peacekeeping forces.

steeper. It must include a serious analysis of whether and how epidemic IDs challenge national security, more narrowly construed as the preservation of the state's territory, institutions, and sovereignty.

Using this definition, we see that epidemic disease outbreak can endanger national security. First, it may generate violent conflict by creating significant domestic economic and political instability. Second, epidemic disease historically has altered the outcome of international conflicts, and this remains possible today. Biological agents—including epidemic IDs—can be weapons of war and thereby directly and immediately threaten security. Combatants may deliberately target public health and spread disease to weaken and demoralize an enemy population. Or IDs can reduce military readiness in the hardest hit countries. For many states, particularly in sub-Saharan Africa, ID-induced civil unrest and declining military power directly threaten security, but these pose only long term threats to the United States. ID-induced instability in Russia may pose a less distant challenge to U.S. interests, but that threat has received scant attention to date. For other states, IDs spread by war may add another level to the security threats inherent in violent conflict but, again, this remains a distant threat to the United States. Only biological weapons pose a significant, immediate, and direct threat to the nation's security for the foreseeable future.

The most catastrophic contemporary disease and the first lethal pandemic disease in the lifetimes of most readers of this paper, HIV/AIDS poses the greatest humanitarian crisis of this or perhaps any generation, but it does not now pose a significant security threat to most developed states. A humanitarian and even a security threat to southern Africa does not necessarily threaten other states' security unless southern Africa is of vital interest to them. So far, the United States has been wary of such arguments, choosing instead to rely on humanitarian justifications for its brief and often late incursions into places like Somalia and Rwanda. As the United States relies more on West African states like Nigeria and Angola for oil, the balance between humanitarian and security concerns may shift more toward the latter.[153] This still seems a distant likelihood, however, as the United States continues to focus its efforts on stabilizing its major source of imported oil, the Middle East.

Why should it matter whether policy makers and scholars overdraw the link between IDs and security? Security provides a relatively poor rationale for addressing health threats like AIDS. From a national security perspective, in fact, AIDS poses a far smaller threat to most states than it does from almost any other viewpoint, including health, human rights, economic and political

---

153. On the projected impact of AIDS in Nigeria, see NIC, "Next Wave."

development, and social and economic justice. It is not clear, moreover, that anything is gained by adopting the rhetoric of national security to address IDs.

Ironically, at least two things may be lost. First, the appeal to national security relieves states without major public health threats of any moral obligation to respond to health crises of monumental proportions in the developing world, since it suggests that only national security concerns can justify significant expenditures on disease control. Historically, narrow self-interest has not motivated a sustained commitment to international health cooperation. In the nineteenth century, when epidemic disease in less developed states provoked divergent national quarantine policies within Europe and endangered gains from trade, European states negotiated common quarantine standards and made significant strides in international disease control. By the mid-twentieth century, however, developed states had acquired powerful medical, pharmaceutical, and public health weapons to fight epidemic disease in their own countries and had lost interest in helping the developing world transition to better health. Narrow self-interest is no more likely to promote the sustained commitment that will be necessary to fight AIDS in Africa and elsewhere. Even in the shorter run, in fact, public opinion is more likely to support foreign aid that serves humanitarian than strategic ends. As David H. Lumsdaine notes about twentieth-century foreign aid practices, "The principle of help to those in great need implicit in the very idea of foreign aid led to steady modification of aid practices, which focused then more on the needs of the poor and moved them away from donor interests."[154]

Second, policymakers' and scholars' attempts to whip up support for ID control by making it a national security issue may generate security dilemmas. The more some states accept and attempt to paint epidemic disease as a security threat, the greater the chance that national disease-control and antiproliferation policies aimed at biological weapons will arouse suspicion in other states. Paradoxically, international organizations and NGOs then may be called upon to play a greater role in global health efforts, as the purely national and bilateral efforts of states become increasingly suspect. In this regard, it may be more fruitful to view disease and health issues as concerns for U.S. foreign policy deserving of multilateral responses, rather than as narrow security threats requiring bilateral policy responses that may provoke suspicion.[155]

154. *Moral Vision in International Politics: The Foreign Aid Regime, 1949–1989* (Princeton: Princeton University Press, 1993), 5, 43, quoted at 5.
155. For a work that views disease as a foreign policy, rather than a security, concern, see Jordan S. Kassalow, "Why Health is Important to U.S. Foreign Policy," (New York: Council on Foreign Relations and Milbank Memorial Fund, 2001).

If well-intentioned people seek to rally support among western governments for anti-AIDS efforts in Africa, portraying disease as a security issue may be exactly the wrong strategy to employ. Rather, the world must face AIDS for what it is and will be for the foreseeable future—a health tragedy of unprecedented and staggering proportions that cries out for international and transnational humanitarian assistance, not for the garrisoning of states behind national boundaries and national security rhetoric.

Part III
Communicable Disease

[12]

THE LESSONS OF THE PANDEMIC

George Soper

THE pandemic which has just swept round the earth has been without precedent. There have been more deadly epidemics, but they have been more circumscribed; there have been epidemics almost as widespread, but they have been less deadly. Floods, famines, earthquakes and volcanic eruptions have all written their stories in terms of human destruction almost too terrible for comprehension, yet never before has there been a catastrophe at once so sudden, so devastating and so universal.

The most astonishing thing about the pandemic was the complete mystery which surrounded it. Nobody seemed to know what the disease was, where it came from or how to stop it. Anxious minds are inquiring to-day whether another wave of it will come again.

The fact is that although influenza is one of the oldest known of the epidemic diseases, it is the least understood. Science, which by patient and painstaking labor has done so much to drive other plagues to the point of extinction has thus far stood powerless before it. There is doubt about the causative agent and the predisposing and aggravating factors. There has been a good deal of theorizing about these matters, and some good research, but no common agreement has been reached with respect to them.

The measures which were introduced for the control of the pandemic were based upon the slenderest of theories. It was assumed that the influenza could be stopped by the employment of methods which it was assumed would stop the other respiratory diseases. This double assumption proved to be a weak reed to lean upon. The respiratory diseases as a class are not under control. They constitute the most frequent cause of death, yet it is not known how they can be prevented.

Three main factors stand in the way of prevention: First, public indifference. People do not appreciate the risks they run. The great complexity and range in severity of the respiratory infections confuse and hide the danger. The infections vary from the common cold to pneumonia. They are not all separate entities by any means. An attack which begins as a coryza or rhinitis may develop into a pharyngitis, tonsilitis, laryngitis, bronchitis or pneumonia. The gravity increases with the progress toward the lungs. The infection sometimes seems to begin in the chest, sometimes in the throat, sometimes in the head. It may stop where it started or pass through several phases. This is the story of the common cold. It is generally more discomforting than dangerous. Most people get well without skillful treatment, or indeed any great interference with business. No specific virus is known to produce it.

There is another group of diseases, a more unusual one, which is often at first confused with the foregoing. This includes the specific infections such as diphtheria, measles and scarlet fever. Influenza is in this class. The symptoms at the beginning may be identical with those of the common cold and the true nature of the disease escape notice until the patient shows unmistakable and alarming symptoms. By that time other persons may be infected.

The second factor which stands in the way of prevention is the personal character of the measures which must be employed. The enteric infections can be controlled by procedures of a general sort which impose no great restriction upon the conduct of the individual, but this is not true of the respiratory infections. The waste products of influenza containing the infective virus are not deposited in a vessel or sewerage system where they can be properly dealt with as in typhoid. The excreta of the nose and throat are projected into the air and allowed to pollute the hands, the food, the clothing and, in fact, the entire environment of the infected person. This is done unconsciously, invisibly, unsuspectingly. General methods directed against

this kind of germ distribution must necessarily be of limited value.

It is an epidemiological point of great interest that the kind of preventive measures which must be taken in order to control the respiratory infections devolve upon the persons who are already infected, while those who are liable to contract the disease can do little to protect themselves. The burden is placed where it is not likely to be well carried. It does not lie in human nature for a man who thinks he has only a slight cold to shut himself up in rigid isolation as a means of protecting others on the bare chance that his cold may turn out to be a really dangerous infection.

Third, the highly infectious nature of the respiratory infections adds to the difficulty of their control. The period of incubation varies considerably; in some infections it may be as short as a day or two. And the disease may be transmissible before the patient himself is aware that he is attacked.

This list of the obstacles which stand in the way of controlling the respiratory diseases may fittingly be closed by remarking that healthy persons often carry about in their persons the germs of disease, thereby unconsciously acting as a continuing danger to themselves and a menace to others. It is not to be wondered at, therefore, that of all the things which were done to stop the spread of influenza, nothing seems to have had any material effect upon it.

This may all seem very discouraging but it need not depress anybody. The control of typhoid once seemed an impossible task. To rightly measure a difficulty is often the first step toward overcoming it.

What is said here of the influenza pandemic is put forward only as the writer's view at the present time. Nobody can now speak authoritatively upon this subject. When all the facts are brought together some of the ideas which are held to-day may be found to require modification. We are still too close to the event to fully measure it. Individual researches and the efforts of innumerable workers, must be reported and evaluated. The mass of statistical data which has accumulated in cities, towns, camps and hospitals must be assorted, tabulated and studied before it will be possible to speak with anything like finality as to the efficacy of the measures of control employed.

Until this is done, it will be impossible to give the number of persons attacked, their age, sex, condition and race, the complications and sequelæ of the disease, much less the relations which these facts bear to the preventive measures. This work is now engaging the attention of many experts. Public health officers, skillful workers in bacteriology and pathology and able clinicians who have had opportunity to study the disease intensively are making their reports. It will be months and perhaps years before the records of all the scientific study connected with the pandemic are brought to a conclusion.

A good deal may confidently be expected of the work which has been done from so many angles and in so many places. How far the mysteries which have obscured the true nature of influenza for so many years will be cleared up must be left for time to show.

No disease is more difficult to study than pandemic influenza. It comes, it spreads, it vanishes with unexampled suddenness. It possesses such terrific energy that little time is afforded during its visitations in which to study it in a careful and painstaking manner. Both its total absence and its great prevalence stand in the way of its study.

But, it will be asked, is influenza entirely absent in the intervals between epidemics? Opinion is divided on this point. Some hold that pandemic influenza is a separate infection. Others think it is always with us. It does not ordinarily manifest such a fatal aspect as that recently seen, but many of the symptoms of the usual epidemic and the extraordinary pandemic influenza are the same. Perhaps the recent pandemic is best explained on the assumption that a particularly virulent type of the common infection was to blame.

All attempts at excluding influenza from a community seem to have failed. There is

one and only one way to absolutely prevent it and that is by establishing absolute isolation. It is necessary to shut off those who are capable of giving off the virus from those who are capable of being infected, or vice versa. This is a very difficult procedure. First, it is difficult because it is impossible to discover all the virus producers. Second, it is difficult because it is impossible to know who are and who are not immune. Complete isolation is not feasible for entire cities nor for parts of cities, nor for individuals in cities. It is feasible for some small towns and villages, and some have tried it with success. The fact that in many instances the attack has been merely postponed by no means invalidates the principle.

It is natural to suppose that a phenomenon of such general nature as the influenza pandemic has had an equally general cause and the only cause which most people can think of as general enough to give rise to a world pandemic is one which possesses an atmospheric or terrestrial character. This is a very old conception and one which has survived all others so far as the general public is concerned. In one of its forms it is known as Sydenham's theory of epidemic constitution. In spite of the repeated statement that this theory has been discredited, there are many well-informed persons who believe as Sydenham did that there are general conditions beyond our knowledge which help to cause disease to assume a different aspect and prevalence in some years and at some seasons than at others.

As late as the pandemic of 1889–90 it was thought by many that the cause of the influenza outbreak was in some way connected with world conditions and quite independent of human intercourse. To-day there are some who think that the extraordinarily cold winter of 1917–18 followed by the hot summer was largely responsible for the recent pandemic. Others believe that the great war precipitated the plague. Not a few think that the infection was spontaneously developed in many places at about the same time. The arguments which have been made in support of these suppositions are often ingenuous if not convincing. Unfortunately, they seldom stand the test of scientific analysis.

The weight of evidence now available indicates that the immediate cause of the great pandemic of 1918 was an infective virus which passed from person to person until it had spread all over the world. The method of spread is believed to have been the same as in other respiratory infections. The reasons for the belief that it was transmitted in this manner lies chiefly in the fact that the pandemic spread rapidly, and no more so, than people traveled from point to point.

Nobody so far has positively shown what the virus is, nor how it leaves or enters the body, nor at what period in the disease it may be transmitted to others. Some hold that the Pfeiffer bacillus is the causative agent, others believe that there is a filterable virus which acts independently or in conjunction with the Pfeiffer bacillus. Nearly all agree that the influenza and pneumonia were independent diseases and that the high fatality was due to a very remarkable reduction of resistance to the pneumonia brought about by the influenza. Being of the respiratory type, it is believed that the virus leaves the body by way of the nose and mouth. It is supposed to enter the body by way of the nose, mouth or eyes.

But, it may be asked, if the influenza and the Pfeiffer bacillus are always with us, why should the disease suddenly become so different from its ordinary type in respect to severity, infectivity and complications? Nobody has answered these questions.

There are various ways of replying to them. One is to assume that the infective poison was brought into civilized countries from some distant point where it originated. Another is to suppose that it developed locally. It is not possible to follow these theories through all their details here. The arguments are not convincing by any means. Certainly a complete explanation of the pandemic requires a demonstration of how the disease developed wherever that development took place.

The development of the disease was undoubtedly a complicated biological phenomenon. A virus was produced which was capable of overcoming the resistance of a large proportion of those who were exposed to it. Reductions in virulence are familiar occurrences in connection with infective poisons. Controlled attenuations have been at the foundation of a great deal of the best work in immunology since the time of Pasteur. Increases are less often observed, but it is a well established fact that a virus which has practically lost its pathogenic properties can be exalted to a high state of virulence by inoculating it into susceptible animals. The spontaneous recrudescences of virulent disease in epidemics which sometimes appear to have originated in mild epidemic infections suggest the same process.

Reasoning by analogy it would appear not unlikely that an influenza virus which existed somewhere, perhaps among persons who had become accustomed to it and had consequently gained a toleration to it, was introduced among others to whom it was a stranger and who were consequently particularly susceptible to it. This would naturally result in an outburst which might attain pandemic proportions.

The pandemic has shown among other things how widely and how quickly respiratory infections may travel. It has shown what an enormous interchange of germs takes place in the respiratory apparatus of those who live in cities and towns and villages. It is disquieting to find how readily and frequently the bacterial products of the sick gain entrance into the noses and mouths of other persons, but the facts must not be hidden if to acknowledge them will do any good.

The pandemic calls attention not only to the fact that there is an interchange of mouth germs wherever people meet, but it illustrates how frequently respiratory infections may occur to which little or no attention is given. Some people think that pandemics of colds occur from time to time which are almost as universal as was the recent influenza. Their pandemic character is not suspected because they are so mild. A pandemic of influenza swept over the United States five months before the fatal wave but it attracted notice only in a few places.

The frequent presence of epidemics of colds affords the groundwork upon which other respiratory diseases should be studied. It has been well said by Sir Arthur Newsholme, Medical Officer of Health to the Local Government Board of England, that until the common respiratory infections are studied and controlled, it will be impossible to understand and manage influenza. With this opinion the present writer heartily agrees. The way to study influenza is to study the common cold. The place to study the common cold is a village or other circumscribed environment. The time to study it is now.

The great lesson of the pandemic is to call attention to the prevalence of respiratory diseases in ordinary times, to the indifference with which they are ordinarily regarded and to our present inability to protect ourselves against them. They are not amenable to control through sanitary works as are typhoid, malaria and so many other diseases. They must be controlled by administrative procedures, and by the exercise of appropriate measures of self protection.

Will there be another visitation? Nobody can positively answer this question. Influenza commonly sweeps in more than one wave over a country. America experienced an unmistakable, but mild, wave before the great one of September and October and since then there have been local disturbances corresponding to fresh outbreaks in many places. In England a new and alarming prevalence has been reported. It would not be surprising if there should be another pandemic in the United States.

The steps which should be taken to suppress the disease if it breaks out afresh are such as seem best for the maintenance of general health and protection from respiratory infections as a class. If doubt arises as to the probable efficacy of measures which seem so lacking in specificity it must be remembered that it is better for the public morale to be doing something than nothing and the general health will not suffer for the additional care which is given it.

First as to the things which it is desirable not to do. It is not desirable to close theaters, churches and schools unless public opinion emphatically demands it. It is not desirable to make the general wearing of masks compulsory. Patients should not be masked except when traveling from one point to another —they need air. Suspects should wear masks until their cases are positively diagnosed. Influenza patients should be kept separate from other patients. A case of influenza should be dealt with as though it was as contagious as a case of small-pox: there is danger in the presence of the sick, in his eating utensils, in his clothes and in the air into which he coughs and sneezes, if indeed these respiratory symptoms are present. He is to be regarded as much more seriously ill than his visible symptoms perhaps indicate.

It is worth while to give more attention to the avoidance of unnecessary personal risks and to the promotion of better personal health. Books have been written on the subject. The writer's idea of the most essential things to remember are embodied in the following twelve condensed rules which were prepared in September, recommended by the Surgeon-General of the Army and published by order of the Secretary of War to be given all possible publicity:

1. Avoid needless crowding—influenza is a crowd disease.

2. Smother your coughs and sneezes—others do not want the germs which you would throw away.

3. Your nose, not your mouth was made to breathe through—get the habit.

4. Remember the three C's—a clean mouth, clean skin, and clean clothes.

5. Try to keep cool when you walk and warm when you ride and sleep.

6. Open the windows—always at home at night; at the office when practicable.

7. Food will win the war if you give it a chance—help by choosing and chewing your food well.

506 *SCIENCE* [N. S. Vol. XLIX. No. 1274

8. Your fate may be in your own hands—wash your hands before eating.

9. Don't let the waste products of digestion accumulate—drink a glass or two of water on getting up.

10 Don't use a napkin, towel, spoon, fork, glass or cup which has been used by another person and not washed.

11. Avoid tight clothes, tight shoes, tight gloves—seek to make nature your ally not your prisoner.

12. When the air is pure breathe all of it you can—breathe deeply.

GEORGE A. SOPER
SANITARY CORPS,
    U. S. A.

[13]

Communicable disease control: a 'Global Public Good' perspective

RICHARD SMITH,[1] DAVID WOODWARD,[2] ARNAB ACHARYA,[3] ROBERT BEAGLEHOLE[4] AND NICK DRAGER[2]

[1]Health Economics, Law and Ethics Group, School of Medicine, Health Policy & Practice, University of East Anglia, Norwich, UK, [2]Strategy Unit, Director General's Office, World Health Organization, Geneva, Switzerland, [3]Institute of Development Studies, University of Sussex, Brighton, UK and [4]Department of Health Service Provision, World Health Organization, Geneva, Switzerland

Despite the increasing 'globalization' of health, the responsibility for it remains primarily national, generating a potential mismatch between global health problems and current institutions and mechanisms to deal with them. The 'Global Public Good' (GPG) concept has been suggested as a framework to address this mismatch in different areas of public policy. This paper considers the application of the GPG concept as an organizing principle for communicable disease control (CDC), considering in particular its potential to improve the health and welfare of the developing world.

The paper concludes that there are significant limitations to the GPG concept's effectiveness as an organizing principle for global health priorities, with respect to CDC. More specifically, there are few areas of CDC which qualify as GPG, and even among those that *can* be considered GPGs, it is not *necessarily* appropriate to provide *everything* which can be considered a GPG. It is therefore suggested that it may be more useful to focus instead on the failure of 'collective action', where the GPG concept may then: (1) provide a rationale to raise funds additional to aid from developed countries' domestic budgets; (2) promote investment by developed countries in the health systems of developing countries; (3) promote strategic partnerships between developed and developing countries to tackle major global communicable diseases; and (4) guide the political process of establishing, and mechanisms for providing and financing, global CDC programmes with GPG characteristics, and GPGs which have benefits for CDC.

In short, the GPG concept is not without limitations and weaknesses as an organizing principle, but does provide, at least in some areas, guidance in improving *collective action* at the international level for the improvement of global CDC.

Key words: public goods, globalization, communicable disease control

1. Introduction

It has long been recognized that our health is affected by the health of others, and that the strength of this effect depends on the scope of interactions between people (Szreter 1988). During the 20th Century, globalization (in its broadest sense) has highlighted the *global* interconnectedness of health. In particular, the ability of communicable diseases to travel faster and further than ever before has led to more than 20 diseases re-emerging or spreading since the 1970s, many in drug-resistant form (WHO 2000). It is thus clearer than ever that securing one country's health requires securing the health of others (Folland et al. 1997).

However, despite globalization, the responsibility for health remains primarily national, generating a potential mismatch between global health problems and current institutions and mechanisms to deal with them (Fidler 1998; Jamison et al. 1998). The Global Public Good (GPG) concept has been suggested as a framework to address this mismatch in different areas of public policy (Cornes and Sandler 1996; Sandler 1997; Chen et al. 1999; Arhin-Tenkorang and

Conceição 2003; Smith et al. 2003). This paper considers the specific application of the GPG as an organizing principle for communicable disease control (CDC), considering in particular its potential, through focusing on *mutual* benefits to developing and developed nations, to improve the health and welfare of the developing world.

Following this introduction, section 2 outlines briefly the concept of GPGs and places CDC within the GPG paradigm. Section 3 then considers the production of CDC as a GPG, section 4 the agendas and incentives of the players involved in CDC production, and section 5 implications for financing CDC. Section 6 concludes by assessing the value of the GPG concept as an organizing principle with respect to CDC.

2. The GPG concept and communicable disease control

Public goods yield benefits that are *non-rival* in consumption (they can be enjoyed simultaneously by all in a specified community) and *non-excludable* (from which no-one in that community can be prevented from consuming). For example, no vessel can be excluded from the warning a lighthouse provides, and the warning received by one does not prevent others from also benefiting equally from that warning (Cornes and Sandler 1996).

Public goods also provide a 'consumption externality': a benefit (or harm) is provided to someone due solely to the fact that the good is being consumed by others (Atkinson and Stiglitz 1980; Varian 1992). Communicable diseases have important *externality* effects since preventing one person from contracting a communicable disease (or treating it successfully) clearly benefits the individual concerned, but also benefits others by reducing their risk of infection. For example, while measles vaccination provides complete protection to those children who are vaccinated, others also benefit from a lower risk of catching measles. Similarly, the control of communicable diseases within one country reduces the probability of their transmission to other countries.

The benefits of CDC are thus *non-rival*, in that one person's lower risk of contracting a disease does not limit the benefits of that lower risk to others. However, its production requires *excludable* inputs (private goods), such as vaccination, clean water or condoms, as well as *non-excludable* inputs, such as knowledge of preventive interventions and best practice in treatment. In this sense CDC may be *partially excludable*, where no-one can be excluded from benefiting from a lower risk, but some can benefit more than others, such as the case of measles vaccination above (Sandler and Arce 2002).

However, the non-rival nature of CDC means that even if it is *feasible* to exclude some people from some of these mechanisms, it is not *desirable*. For example, imagine a society where some families vaccinate their children and some do not. This decision is based on the expected costs and benefits to the families themselves and their children, and not to others. The marginal benefit of vaccination to those not vaccinating must therefore be less than the marginal cost in time and/or money. However, the gain to *society* is much larger than it is to the family, as a higher rate of vaccination affords greater protection *to others* by decreasing exposure. Thus, although people *could* be excluded from vaccination, these external benefits make their exclusion socially sub-optimal (Bart et al. 1996). The extent to which mechanisms for CDC are (or could be made) excludable is therefore important, primarily in determining *how* it can be provided and financed.

Global public goods are public goods with significant cross-border benefits on a global level (Woodward and Smith 2003). Since not *all* communicable diseases are *global*, or prone to cross-border transmission, clearly only some elements of CDC will be *global* public goods (as distinct from regional or national public goods). For example, malaria control benefits only endemic areas, and diarrhoeal disease is primarily a disease of poverty, thus their impact is limited to specific geographic or socio-economic populations, and hence is somewhat less than 'global'. It is therefore only for a *sub-set* of communicable diseases that CDC can be considered a *global* public good; for example, HIV/AIDS, tuberculosis and eradicable diseases, such as polio, for which

effective low-cost preventive interventions (e.g. vaccination) are available and there is no non-human reservoir.[1]

Importantly, public good attributes (or non-rivalry in consumption and non-excludability) create a paradox: although there is significant benefit to be gained from them, since many people can benefit without reducing the benefit to others, there is no commercial incentive for their production because 'non-exclusion' means that a price cannot be enforced. With *national* public goods, government therefore intervenes in either finance, such as taxation or licenses, or direct provision. For *global* public goods the situation is exacerbated because no 'global government' exists to regulate or enforce finance or production. The central issue addressed by GPGs is therefore how best to ensure *collective action at the international level*, which is a theme running throughout the remainder of this paper.

3. The production of communicable disease control: a GPG perspective

Like any 'good', CDC requires a wide range of inputs; from public goods to private goods, and from the disease-specific to the generic. Some are essential to produce CDC, others only make its attainment more likely, easier, cheaper or faster, affecting its economic viability or political feasibility. However, all together determine whether or not CDC will be produced. In considering the effectiveness of the GPG concept as an organizing principle for global health priorities with respect to CDC, it is therefore necessary to consider briefly what the GPG concept may reveal of the nature of the production of CDC. This section therefore outlines the GPG concept with respect to four broad categories of inputs.

3.1 Knowledge and technology

CDC relies heavily on the generation and transmission of knowledge about the incidence of disease (surveillance) and the means of its control (e.g. best practice for prevention and treatment). Surveillance information and knowledge of best practice are both national and (potentially) global public goods in their own right, and the consequent lack of commercial incentive for their production necessitates public provision, with appropriate international support and coordination.

Medical knowledge[2] is also a GPG *in principle,* but the embodiment of that knowledge within (e.g. pharmaceutical) products, together with patent regimes, makes knowledge 'artificially' excludable, limited to those who can afford to purchase the products. Nonetheless, the products may be necessary to produce CDC, just as private goods are needed for the production of other public goods (e.g. bricks and labour in the case of the lighthouse), and it will therefore be necessary to ensure access to them in order for CDC to be produced (Ghosh 2003; Smith and Coast 2003; Thorsteinsdóttir et al. 2003).

For knowledge to contribute effectively to CDC, it must also be *applied*, which requires effective health systems. For example, surveillance requires countries both to produce information and to act on it, which in turn requires an effective health infrastructure and appropriate technical expertise at the national level. Similarly, knowledge of best practice and medical technologies depend on effective health services for their application. Thus, as discussed in section 3.3. below, where health systems are inadequate to allow knowledge to be applied effectively, their strengthening will be important to the provision of CDC (Powles and Comim 2003).

There may also be a need for an 'international research network', or 'international research council', to rationalize research priorities, balance developed and developing country interests and avoid duplication. The 'Medicines for Malaria Venture', a public-private partnership, supported by the World Health Organization (WHO) and the World Bank to coordinate research on antimalarial products, provides an example of such international support and cooperation for diseases of international concern (Butler 1997; Gallagher 1997; Mons et al. 1998). Together with similar ventures, such as the Global Alliance for TB Drugs, the International AIDS Vaccine Initiative, the International Partnership for Microbicides and the Paediatric Dengue Vaccine Initiative, such initiatives indicate that a variety of GPG-like entities are emerging that redress important private, and public, market failure in CDC production, and therefore also the problems of failure in international collective action (as indicated below).

3.2 International collective action

CDC requires appropriate policies and regulations, varying according to the disease concerned, which are public goods at the corresponding (national, regional and/or global) level (Fidler 2003). This requires international collective action (highlighted above), as well as intervention by national governments, which could be enhanced if: (1) decision-making processes in those international bodies which develop international policies and regulatory regimes were fully representative of developing countries and their populations; and (2) health considerations were fully and effectively taken into consideration in non-health fora where decisions have potential effects on health (e.g. international agreements concerning pharmaceutical patents).

3.3 National health systems

The absence of functioning health systems in some countries is an important constraint on GPG provision, rendering the production of some GPGs impossible, and increasing the cost and/or reducing the benefits of others, thus increasing the likelihood of under-provision or preventing benefits from being universal. In many developing countries, for example, per capita expenditure on health is a fraction of the US$30–40 per person per year considered necessary for an effective health system (Evans et al. 2001), so that disease surveillance and reporting are non-existent, facilities poorly staffed, and basic public health and health service infrastructure sorely lacking.

To the extent that effective health systems are necessary to universalize the benefits from some potential health-related GPGs (e.g. medical technologies and best practice), they may be considered as *access goods*: private goods necessary for someone to benefit from a public good, as a household's connection is required for it to benefit from a clean water or sanitation system. This suggests that they might appropriately be treated *as if they were GPGs* (Powles and Comim 2003). International collective action in the finance of, and support to, *health systems* would therefore improve the provision of CDC, with the GPG concept suggesting that efficiencies may be gained by taking a more 'horizontal' (system-wide) approach to the provision of inputs.

Donors have traditionally worked in countries through 'vertical' (disease-specific) programmes, partly as a means of limiting the problems of working through under-resourced health systems. However, while such programmes have often been successful, at least in the short term, they have been seen as inappropriate, giving rise to problems of coordination, skewing priorities from national towards donor concerns, diverting scarce human and other resources away from general health services, and generating costly duplication between parallel programmes (LaFond 1995; Koivusalo and Ollila 1997). In developing a more 'horizontal' approach, looking at health systems, the GPG concept highlights the importance of managing relations between national level health programmes, and designing international support for them, in such a way as to ensure that 'vertical' programmes facilitate and promote the effectiveness of overall health systems, and do not create inefficiencies in GPG production or health service provision more generally.

The GPG perspective thus provides an additional rationale for the international support of health systems in countries where they are critically weak. It also highlights the long-term view required of GPG provision, to take account of the potential for health system strengthening to contribute to *future* provision as well as the direct benefits of *immediate* provision.

3.4 Non-health system inputs

A mixture of non-health sector private goods (e.g. nutrition, living conditions and education), and national public goods or club goods (e.g. water and sanitation systems) are critical to health. While their absence is unlikely to *prevent* CDC, they may have a substantial effect on its production. Poverty reduction, food subsidies, supplements and fortification, housing improvement, and water and sanitation provision may play a major role in the control of many communicable diseases. GPG considerations may thus strengthen the case for supporting such programmes.

4. Communicable disease control: ensuring international collective action

At the 'core' of the public goods concept is the existence of a *collective action problem*: the community as a whole is better off if these goods are provided, but their non-rival and non-excludable characteristics require collective action to avoid free-riding (individuals benefiting from the actions of others without reciprocating) and the 'prisoner's dilemma' (lack of communication and information about each participant's actions, and lack of enforcement mechanisms, impeding cooperation).[3] Fundamental to securing the provision of *global* public goods is therefore the political process of ensuring collective action at the international level. This requires consideration of the major players and their agendas, and the dynamics of international cooperation.

Major players for developing and implementing CDC strategies are: (1) national governments, as potential beneficiaries, sources of funding (internally and externally), and providers of many of the mechanisms for control; (2) international agencies, as fora for consensus-building and collective decision-making, coordinators, promoters and channels of government support, and supporters of control mechanisms and regulatory frameworks; and (3) pharmaceutical and other commercial companies, as developers and suppliers of relevant medical technologies, and as political players at the national and international levels.

However, the problem is that these players' agendas (their preferences or priorities) do not necessarily coincide with each other, or with public health priorities. For example, it is unlikely that each *national* agenda will give equal priority to control of the same communicable diseases, or to CDC relative to other priorities; and companies' agendas will inevitably differ from those of governments and international agencies. The more divergent these agendas are, the greater is the potential for free-riding and the prisoner's dilemma to compromise CDC. For example, the interdependence between countries for CDC in particular creates a potential for free-riding. If many nations adopt strategies, one country may avoid involvement (or not contribute financially) and still benefit from the global reduction in incidence. Conversely, however well one country performs within its own borders, it cannot hope to insulate itself from the results of inaction by others. Impediments to international cooperation, and the role of international bodies in facilitating it, are therefore central to consideration of the potential for the GPG concept to assist CDC.

The value of the GPG concept in this respect is in highlighting the importance of assessing where CDC is on different players' agendas, why it is there, and its costs and benefits to them, in order to support means to move forward its provision. Resolving collective action problems requires a clear understanding of the nature, scale and timing of costs and benefits to different countries, and other parties, *and* proactive efforts to reconcile different interests and priorities. Thus, for example, to ensure informed decision-making, it may be preferable to extend the decision-making process, to encompass an initial agreement in principle with full agreement following after a period of intensive technical and economic analysis. This requires international fora that are legitimate, credible and effective in decision-making, and in which national public interests are effectively and proportionally represented. A markedly unequal distribution of power may limit the commitment of some countries to decisions taken, undermining GPG, and hence CDC, provision.

5. Paying for communicable disease control: a GPG perspective

Controlling communicable disease is expensive.[4] For example, in Sub-Saharan Africa alone, increasing the coverage of malaria and HIV/AIDS prevention, and the treatment of malaria and tuberculosis, to 70% of the population by 2015 would cost an *additional* US$10–17bn per year (at 2001 prices). Providing care for 50%, and treatment for 62%, of people with HIV/AIDS would cost a *further* US$24–41bn per year. Even on optimistic assumptions for economic growth, together they would represent around 8–14% of national income in 2015 (Arndt and Lewis 2000; Kumaranayake et al. 2001). Thus, who pays, and how they pay, are crucial elements of a global approach to CDC, and critical under a GPG perspective, for collective action.

5.1 Who should – or could – pay?

In an ideal world, the cost of providing GPGs would be allocated between countries in proportion to their benefits. However, health care expenditure, reflecting income, is very low in many developing countries. This impedes effective global collective action through undermining the political will to cooperate, and limiting effective participation in international CDC. Even the creation of a legal *duty* does not ensure *compliance*, as this depends on having adequate resources to fulfil such obligations (Fidler 1996, 1997).

Further, where countries with inadequate resources do participate in global programmes, financial and human resources may be diverted from other essential activities, with possible adverse effects on health, including other aspects of CDC. The opportunity cost of these resources is far greater in developing than developed countries, creating tensions in securing global cooperation, and reducing the net health benefits. Circumventing this problem requires that financial and other contributions reflect each country's *ability* to contribute, as well as its potential benefits from the GPG. In practice, this means that financing needs to come predominantly from the developed world.

Contributing to the production of a GPG may mean that resources (whether domestic or foreign) are spent on activities that do not accord with national priorities, in at least some countries. This issue is at its most acute, for example, in the latter stages of a disease eradication programme. The Polio Eradication Initiative's estimated external financial needs – excluding volunteer time and governments' contributions to control efforts in their own countries – are estimated at US$370m in 2001–2.[5] If the incidence of polio remains at the 2001 level (537 cases[6]), this implies a cost of around US$0.7m per case. Reallocating this money to more *immediate* health priorities could improve health outcomes in the short term, although these benefits might be outweighed in the long term by the major (and permanent) costs (health and financial) from the resulting failure of the eradication effort, even accounting for the cost of continuing vaccination in the case of non-eradication, variations in discount rates and most plausible future scenarios to achieve eradication (Aylward et al. 2003). Diverting existing development assistance to finance

GPGs could also generate negative effects on health elsewhere, and these opportunity costs would need to be explicitly assessed. Clearly, much of this analysis depends upon the time frame for assessing benefits. In the case of eradication, the benefits are infinite, but even in areas of control they may run to many years in the future, meaning that the willingness to forgo benefits now is a critical issue.

The main GPG contribution here is to show that supporting other countries' CDC strategies is *not* a question of humanitarian aid, but a self-interested *investment* (as alluded to earlier) in domestic health: while recipient countries also benefit, the *primary* objective for the developed countries is to improve *their own* health. This suggests that national health budgets in donor countries are a more appropriate source of funding, leaving existing aid monies unaffected, and thus increasing total funding to developing countries rather than merely reallocating it between uses.

Another possible source of finance is the non-government sector. NGOs play an important role in the provision of CDC, particularly as health-service providers. In this capacity, they are likely to fund their activities largely from their own resources. However, few NGOs have sufficient resources to provide significant financing for CDC-related activities of other actors at a global level. Private foundations and philanthropic trusts may be a more feasible funding source, as in the case of Rotary International's financial support for the Polio Eradication Initiative (PEI). However, the relatively limited resources available overall from such institutions (compared with developed country governments) means that their main role is catalysing larger contributions from public sector institutions, rather than direct funding.

The commercial sector may also be a possible source of financing in some areas of CDC, principally through 'in-kind' contributions, such as donation of vaccines or pharmaceuticals.[7] In other cases, however, they may have little incentive to support GPG provision. The incentives for pharmaceutical company involvement in disease eradication, for example, depend on the additional demand for their eradication-associated products in the short term off-setting the long-term loss of markets for preventive and treatment products. Similarly, although commercial companies may play a critical role in the development of *new* technologies required for CDC, their role is often in the subsequent development and mass production of discoveries initially made in public research facilities, as with antimicrobial and vaccine development. However, in the current political climate, it is likely that the private sector would be looked to, at least for collaboration in the development of new therapies (Buse and Walt 2000a,b). In this case, specific incentives for research and development may be required, including alterations to patents regimes, purchase funds and/or public-private partnership in investment (Buse and Waxman 2001).

5.2 Financing mechanisms

Although numerous possible mechanisms can be envisaged for financing GPGs, there are four main strategies that might be pursued:[8]

(1) *Voluntary contributions.* These are the most straightforward option, but are particularly prone to the free-rider problem – as demonstrated by the meagre contributions thus far to the Global Fund for AIDS, Tuberculosis and Malaria[9] – since each country has an incentive to minimize its contribution.

(2) *Coordinated contributions.* Contributions that are negotiated between countries, or determined by an agreed formula, form the basis for core funding of most international organizations. While this may limit the 'free-rider' problem, each country has an incentive to negotiate the lowest possible contribution for itself (or the formula that will produce this result). Rewarding contributions with influence, to avoid this problem, skews power towards the richest countries (e.g. the IMF and World Bank); but without such incentives (or effective sanctions), countries have little incentive to pay their contributions in full (e.g. US contributions to the United Nations). Basing contributions on an existing formula may be more effective: the starting point for financial contributions to the PEI was contributions to WHO funding. However, as the PEI demonstrates, the free-rider problem remains.

(3) *Global taxes.* Taxes, such as the 'Tobin tax'[10], are theoretically the most efficient means for financing GPGs, comparable to the use of national taxes to provide national public goods. However, substantial opposition remains from some developed countries, limiting the prospects of securing funding from this source for the foreseeable future.

(4) *'Market' based systems.* Some form of market type system could contribute to the provision of some GPGs while being largely self-financing. However, as the USA's withdrawal from the carbon-trading system proposed in the Kyoto Agreement demonstrates, without effective enforcement mechanisms, the free-rider problem remains.

The global nature of CDC, and the vast range of countries involved, make it unlikely that voluntary – or even coordinated – contributions can be relied upon to generate sufficient revenues in many cases. For CDC to be financed as a GPG is therefore likely to require market-based and/or global tax systems, depending on the aspect of CDC concerned and the type of GPG involved.

Disease eradication, for example, is a prime case of a 'weakest-link' GPG; it is provided *only* when the disease has been eliminated in the worst-performing country. Control of non-eradicable diseases, such as HIV/AIDS, is, by contrast, a 'weighted-sum' GPG, with marked variations in the effects of control efforts in different countries. The primary benefits of reducing cross-border transmission, and the greatest ability to pay, are in low-incidence countries, while the need for control is greatest in high-incidence countries, which are least able to pay. In both cases, cross-subsidy between countries is therefore essential (and, for eradication, increasingly so over time). Market mechanisms have been suggested as the most efficient manner with which to tackle this with respect to antimicrobial resistant diseases (Smith and Coast 1998). However, clearly more consideration of the most appropriate (that is, efficient *and* feasible) systems is required on a case-by-case basis, rather than a generic recommendation being given here.

6. Conclusion

This paper has outlined several key aspects of the GPG concept, and applied it to the case of CDC to explore the usefulness of the concept as an organizing principle for health care priorities. Two important implications arise from the discussion presented in this paper.

First, the GPG concept's limited coverage means that it is clearly limited as an organizing principle for global health priorities,[11] as this would mean neglecting most aspects of health. It must not, therefore, be allowed to detract from other motivations for international health programmes, such as social justice, equity, altruism, poverty reduction and economic benefits (Mooney and Dzator 2003).

Second, even among those limited aspects of CDC which *can* be considered GPGs, there are limits to the GPG concept's effectiveness as a means of identifying international objectives, as it is not *necessarily* appropriate to provide *everything* which can be considered a GPG. Eradicating a disease is, by its nature, a GPG; but if the cost outweighs the potential benefits for technical or economic reasons, non-GPGs may be a better use of funds.

The GPG concept is therefore severely limited as an organiz-ing principle for health care priorities. However, it may perhaps be more appropriate to focus on the 'core' feature of the GPG concept, *collective action*, and on the application of this concept to the development of effective and represen-tative mechanisms for international decision-making as the primary means of developing appropriate priorities, policies and programmes for health at the global level (Smith and Woodward 2003). The discussion provided in this paper suggests that the GPG concept may then, when focussed on the failure and resolution of collective action, be a useful framework to:

- raise additional funds for global CDC programmes from developed countries' domestic budgets, to supplement aid funds;
- promote investment by developed countries in the health systems of developing countries, as 'access goods';
- promote strategic partnerships between developed and developing countries, particularly in the generation and dissemination of knowledge, to tackle major global communicable diseases; and to
- guide the political process of establishing, and mechanisms for providing and financing, global CDC programmes with GPG characteristics, and GPGs which have benefits for CDC.

In short, the GPG concept is not without limitations and weaknesses as an organizing principle, but does provide, at least in some areas, guidance for improving *collective action* at the international level for the improvement of global CDC.

Endnotes

[1] Further detail on classifying a variety of communicable diseases as global public goods can be found in Woodward and Smith (2003).

[2] Defined here broadly, comprising 'a wide variety of elements, from the understanding of health risks, through the impact of preventive, diagnostic, curative and palliative procedures, to the effect of different delivery systems for medical technologies' (Gosh 2003, p. 119).

[3] It should be noted that the extent of these two problems varies across different types of public good. For example, the 'weakest link' public good will encounter a less severe prisoner's dilemma than the 'summation' public good. However, this does not affect the general argument advanced in this paper.

[4] Of course, one could see such expenditure as an investment (a healthy population being a productive population, prevention saving treatment etc.) rather than a consumption item. However, the nuances of this debate are beyond the scope of this paper, suffice to say that it is assumed for the discussion here that countries would, *ceterus paribus*, wish to avoid such expenditure if possible.

[5] From: [http://www.polioeradication.org/all/news/_files/pdf/FinalPolioFinancial01_05.pdf].

[6] From: [http://www.who.int/inf/en/pr-2002-25.html].

[7] The experience of PEI suggests that the potential for direct financial contributions is limited. The private commercial sector has contributed less than 2% of the financial costs (i.e. excluding the opportunity cost of volunteer time).

[8] Again, for more information on each of these options see Smith et al. (2003).

[9] The Global Fund for AIDS, Tuberculosis and Malaria is an international fund, financed by donations from governments, private foundations and corporations, to support programmes for health, principally HIV/AIDS, tuberculosis and malaria. It is to be run by governments independently of, but with advice and support from, the UN system.

[10] The Tobin tax refers to a proposal by Nobel Economics Laureate James Tobin (Tobin 1978) to levy a tax at a very low rate on all currency conversion transactions conducted through the inter-national clearing system.

[11] Indeed, as Preker et al. (2000) point out, (global) public goods theory is defined by consumption rather than production characteristics, and as such provides no organizational basis to the provision or financing of such goods.

References

Arhin-Tenkorang D, Conceição P. 2003. Beyond communicable disease control: health in the age of globalisation. In: Kaul I, Conceição P, Le Goulven K, Mendoza RU (eds). *Providing Global Public Goods: managing globalisation*. New York: Oxford University Press, chapter 4.

Arndt C, Lewis JD. 2000. *The macro implications of HIV/AIDS in South Africa: a preliminary assessment*. Africa Region Working Paper No. ARWPS-9. Washington, DC: World Bank.

Atkinson A, Stilitz J. 1980. *Lectures in public economics*. New York: McGraw Hill Publishing Co.

Aylward B, Acharya A, Englands S, Linkins J, Agocs M. 2003. Polio eradication. In: Smith RD, Beaglehole R, Drager N, Woodward D (eds). *Global Public Goods for health: a health economic and public health perspective*. Oxford: Oxford University Press, chapter 2.

Bart KJ, Foulds J, Patriarca P. 1996. Global eradication of poliomyelitis: benefit-cost analysis. *Bulletin of the World Health Organization* **74**: 35–45.

Buse K, Walt G. 2000a. Global public-private partnerships: Part I – A new development in health? *Bulletin of the World Health Organization* **78**: 549–61.

Buse K, Walt G. 2000b. Global public-private partnerships: Part II –

What are the health issues for global governance? *Bulletin of the World Health Organization* **78**: 699–709.

Buse K, Waxman A. 2001. Public-private health partnerships: a strategy for WHO. *Bulletin of the World Health Organization* **79**: 748–54.

Butler D. 1997. Time to put malaria control on the global agenda. *Nature* **386**: 535–6.

Chen L, Evans T, Cash R. 1999. Health as a Global Public Good. In: Kaul I, Grunberg I, Stern M (eds). *Global public goods: international co-operation in the 21st Century*. New York: Oxford University Press.

Cornes R, Sandler T. 1996. *The theory of externalities, public goods, and club goods*. 2nd Edition. Cambridge: Cambridge University Press.

Evans D, Tandon A, Murray CJL, Lauer JA. 2001. Comparative efficiency of national health systems: cross national econometric analysis. *British Medical Journal* **323**: 14–21.

Fidler D. 1996. Globalisation, international law, and emerging infectious diseases. *Emerging Infectious Diseases* **2**: 77–84.

Fidler D. 1997. Return of the fourth horseman: emerging infectious diseases and international law. *Minnesota Law Review* **81**: 771–868.

Fidler D. 1998. Legal issues associated with antimicrobial drug resistance. *Emerging Infectious Diseases* **4**: 169–77.

Fidler DP. 2003. International law. In: Smith RD, Beaglehole R, Drager N, Woodward D (eds). *Global Public Goods for health: a health economic and public health perspective*. Oxford: Oxford University Press, chapter 9.

Folland S, Goodman A, Stano M. 1997. *The economics of health and health care*. New Jersey: Prentice Hall, chapter 22.

Gallagher R. 1997. Global initiative takes shape slowly. *Science* **277**: 309.

Ghosh J. 2003. Medical knowledge. In: Smith RD, Beaglehole R, Drager N, Woodward D (eds). *Global Public Goods for health: a health economic and public health perspective*. Oxford: Oxford University Press, chapter 6.

Jamison D, Frenk J, Knaul F. 1998. International collective action in health: objectives, functions and rationale. *The Lancet* **351**: 514–7.

Koivusalo M, Ollila E. 1997. *Making a healthy world: agencies, actors and policies in international health*. London: Zed Books.

Kumaranayake L, Conteh L, Kurowski C, Watts C. 2001. *Preliminary estimates of the cost of expanding TB, Malaria and HIV/AIDS activities for Sub-Saharan Africa*. Working Paper No. WG5:26. Geneva: Commission on Macroeconomics and Health.

LaFond A. 1995. *Sustaining primary health care*. London: Earthscan.

Mons B, Klasen E, van Kessel R, Nchinda T. 1998. Partnership between south and north crystalises around malaria. *Science* **279**: 498–9.

Mooney G, Dzator J. 2003. Global public goods for health: a flawed paradigm? In: Smith RD, Beaglehole R, Woodward D, Drager N (eds). *Global Public Goods for health: a health economic and public health perspective*. Oxford: Oxford University Press, chapter 12.

Powles J, Comim F. 2003. Public health infrastructure and knowledge. In: Smith RD, Beaglehole R, Woodward D, Drager N (eds). *Global Public Goods for health: a health economic and public health perspective*. Oxford: Oxford University Press, chapter 8.

Preker AS, Harding A, Travis P. 2000. "Make or buy" decisions in the production of health care goods and services: new insights from institutional economics and organizational theory. *Bulletin of the World Health Organization* **78**: 779–90.

Sandler T. 1997. *Global challenges: an approach to environmental, political and economic problems*. Cambridge: Cambridge University Press: chapter 5.

Sandler T, Arce D. 2002. A conceptual framework for understanding global and transnational public goods for health. *Fiscal Studies* **23**: 195–222.

Smith RD, Coast J. 1998. Controlling antimicrobial resistance: a proposed transferable permit market. *Health Policy* **43**: 219–32.

Smith RD, Coast J. 2003. Antimicrobial drug resistance. In: Smith RD, Beaglehole R, Woodward D, Drager N (eds). *Global Public Goods for health: a health economic and public health perspective*. Oxford: Oxford University Press, chapter 4.

Smith RD, Beaglehole R, Woodward D, Drager N (eds). 2003. *Global Public Goods for health: a health economic and public health perspective*. Oxford: Oxford University Press.

Smith RD, Woodward D. 2003. Global public goods for health: use and limitations. In: Smith RD, Beaglehole R, Woodward D, Drager N (eds). *Global Public Goods for health: a health economic and public health perspective*. Oxford: Oxford University Press, chapter 13.

Szreter S. 1988. The importance of social intervention in Britain's mortality decline c.1850–1914: a reinterpretation of the role of public health. *Journal of the Society of Social History and Medicine* **1**: 1–37.

Thorsteinsdóttir H, Daar AS, Smith RD, Singer PA. 2003. Genomics knowledge. In: Smith RD, Beaglehole R, Woodward D, Drager N (eds). *Global Public Goods for Health: a health economic and public health perspective*. Oxford: Oxford University Press, chapter 7.

Tobin J. 1978. A proposal for Monetary Reform. *Eastern Economic Journal* **4**: 153–9.

Varian H. 1992. *Microeconomic analysis*. New York: W.W. Norton and Company.

WHO. 2000. *Global Polio Eradication Initiative: Strategic Plan, 2001–2005*. WHO/Polio/00.05, Department of Vaccines and Biologicals. Geneva: World Health Organization.

Woodward D, Smith RD. 2003. Global Public Goods for health: concepts and issues. In: Smith RD, Beaglehole R, Woodward D, Drager N (eds). *Global Public Goods for health: a health economic and public health perspective*. Oxford: Oxford University Press, chapter 1.

Biographies

Richard Smith trained in economics and health economics at the University of York, and is currently a Reader in Health Economics at the University of East Anglia. His research interests range across many facets of health economics, most recently focusing on the monetary and non-monetary assessment of health benefits, the economics of antimicrobial resistance, primary care reform and the impact of globalization on health and health services.

David Woodward is a development economist working for the Strategy Unit of the World Health Organization. He was previously an economic adviser in the British Foreign and Commonwealth Office, and a technical assistant to the British Executive Director at the IMF and World Bank, and has worked on a wide range of development issues for non-government organizations, UNDP, UNCTAD and the Institute of Child Health (University of London).

Arnab Acharya trained in theoretical economics at the Universtity of Illinois and public health at Harvard University. He is a research fellow at the Institute of Development Studies where he conducts research on public health and poverty. His current fields of research are poverty and health, cost-effectiveness analysis of public health measures, and ethical issues in economic development.

Robert Beaglehole trained in medicine in New Zealand and in epidemiology and public health at the London School of Hygiene and Tropical Medicine and the University of North Carolina at Chapel Hill. He is on leave from his position as Professor of Community Health at the University of Auckland, New Zealand and working as a public health adviser in the Department of Health Service Provision at the World Health Organization, Geneva on strengthening the public health workforce in developing countries.

Nick Drager has an MD from McGill University and a Ph.D in Economics from Hautes Études Internationales, University of Geneva. He is Coordinator in the Strategy Unit in the Office of the Director General of the World Health Organization. His current work focuses on emerging global public health issues related to globalization and trade.

Correspondence: Richard Smith, Health Economics, Law and Ethics Group, School of Medicine, Health Policy & Practice, University of East Anglia, Norwich, NR4 7TJ, UK. Tel: +44 (0)1603 593617, fax: +44 (0)1603 593604, email: Richard.Smith@uea.ac.uk

[14]

The Global Governance of Communicable Diseases: The Case for Vaccine R&D*

DANIELE ARCHIBUGI and KIM BIZZARRI

Fighting communicable diseases such HIV/AIDS, tuberculosis (TB, and malaria has become a global endeavor, with international health authorities urging the development of effective vaccines for the eradication of these global pandemics. Yet, despite the acknowledged urgency, and given the feasibility of effective vaccine development, public and private research efforts have failed to address a response adequate to the magnitude of the crisis. Members of the academic community suggest bridging this gap by devising research pull mechanisms capable of stimulating private investments, confident that competition-based market devices are more effective than public intervention in shaping scientific breakthroughs. With reference to the economics of innovation, the paper argues that, whilst such an approach would lead to a socially suboptimal production of knowledge, direct public intervention in vaccine R&D activities would represent a far more socially desirable policy option. In recognition of the current financial and political fatigue affecting the international community towards communicable disease control, the paper resorts to the theories of global public goods (GPGs) to provide governments, both in the North and in the South, with a powerful rationale for committing to a cooperative approach for vaccine R&D. The paper encourages the creation of a Global Health Research Fund to manage such exercise and proposes enshrining countries' commitments into an International Health Treaty. The paper ends by providing a number of policy recommendations.

I. INTRODUCTION: THE CURRENT MISMATCH BETWEEN GLOBAL HEALTH NEEDS AND GLOBAL HEALTH RESEARCH

A. CURRENT DISTRIBUTION OF COMMUNICABLE DISEASES

At the dawn of the twenty-first century, despite 150 years of international health cooperation and numerous high-profile health summits, communicable disease control is still lacking adequate international political action:

* Address correspondence to Daniele Archibugi, Consiglio Nazionale delle Ricerche, Via dei Taurini, 19 00185 Roma, Italy. Telephone: Tel. +39-0649937838; e-mail: daniele.archibugi@cedrc.cnr.it

forty-two million people are currently living with HIV/AIDS around the world, thirty-nine million in developing countries (the South) alone. Infection rates are also on the increase: five million new HIV/AIDS infections were reported in 2002, with over 70 percent of these occurring just in sub-Saharan Africa (WHO 2003). Similarly, tuberculosis (TB) is responsible for the death of over two million individuals, and the infection of another seventeen million every year (WHO & UNICEF 2002), with an incidence of infection that is thirteen times higher in developing countries than in the industrialized world (the North). Malaria also, despite having been eradicated in the North[1] through an overall improvement in environmental conditions, still claims over one million lives and 400 million new infections each year in the South (Harvard Malaria Initiative 2000). The economic and social repercussions that entire regions experience as a result of these pandemics are tremendous. The United Nations (2001) estimates that AIDS alone will cause South Africa's GDP to fall by 17 percent by 2010, without taking into account falling workers' productivity, declining savings and investment, rising business costs, and decreasing life expectancy. Many other countries are also facing similar prospects, and comparable patterns are envisaged for malaria and TB (WHO & UNICEF 2002). As well as contributing to the economic decay, social fragmentation, and political destabilization of already volatile and strained societies, these global pandemics are also jeopardizing past and present development efforts aimed at bridging the increasing widening socio-economic divide between the North and the South.[2]

B. THE NEED FOR VACCINE R&D

Leading health organizations (International Aids Vaccine Initiative 2001; Médicins sans Frontières 2001a; WHO & UNICEF 2002) have argued with much vigor in favor of preventative immunization as representing the most effective tool in the fight against communicable diseases – the eradication of smallpox in 1977 as a result of WHO's Smallpox Eradication Programme representing the most remarkable example (see Fenner 1988 for a detailed analysis of the program's achievements). Yet, despite the success of preventative immunization and the authoritative opinion of experts, resources devoted to vaccine R&D continue to be minimal. The case of AIDS is exemplary. The annual HIV/AIDS vaccine R&D expenditure still represents just 10 percent – about US$400 million – of the annual global HIV/AIDS anti-retroviral R&D spending (Esparza 2000; International Aids Vaccine Initiative 2002). For malaria and TB, vaccine R&D figures are even more disconcerting. The Malaria Vaccine Initiative[3] estimates that the total R&D for a malaria vaccine has not exceeded US$55 million, whilst for TB, the World Health Organization and United Nations' Children Fund (WHO & UNICEF 2002: 61) estimate that, since the early 1990s, vaccine R&D has not exceeded US$150 million.

C. STRUCTURE AND OBJECTIVES OF THIS STUDY

The paper will explore the possible explanations as to why vaccine R&D for major communicable diseases has been so inadequate in addressing the current health crisis. The following sections will provide an overview of current private and public research efforts in vaccine R&D, and will highlight the importance of incentives in determining R&D investments, arguing that geo-economic factors are responsible for the current lack of incentives. Through a global public goods approach, Section IV provides a rationale for convincing the international community to cooperate in the fight against communicable disease control by focussing on vaccine research and development. Sections V and VI advance estimates concerning the ideal R&D resources required, and propose the creation of an Global Health Research Fund for a coordinated approach to the management of these resources. Section VII supports the creation of an International Health Treaty in an attempt to insure member states' respect of their financial obligations to the proposed fund. The paper concludes by providing a number of policy recommendations.

II. THE CURRENT STATE OF SCIENTIFIC KNOWLEDGE

A. HOW FAR ARE WE FROM HITTING THE TARGET?

The economics of innovation teach that, given the de facto uncertainty of all scientific investigation, no clear linear relationship between input and output can be assumed – the case for a cure for cancer being exemplary. Particularly with reference to the delivery of a vaccine for AIDS, malaria, and TB, experts believe science is still ten to fifteen years away from yielding the desired results (Kaufmann 2000; Malaria Vaccine Initiative 2003; WHO & UNICEF 2002). Despite this technical hurdle, it is the opinion of the very same experts that a knowledge gap alone does not explain the minimal investment geared towards vaccine R&D. To quote the authoritative opinion of the Rockefeller Foundation's deputy director, Scott Halstead, "the major impediment to basic vaccine science is not a gap in knowledge, rather a lack of serious financial commitments that precludes the yielding of tangible results" (Rabinovich, 1994). An opinion that is also shared by many other experts in the field, including Médecins sans Frontières (2001), the International AIDS Vaccine Initiative (2001, 2002), and the WHO and UNICEF (2002).

Though, if indeed a lack of incentives, as opposed to a knowledge gap, were to explain the current undermining of global efforts to fight communicable diseases, two aspects would need to be considered: (a) the type, and amount, of R&D expenditure of both profit-seeking and public non-profit agents; and (b) the influence that the distribution of the disease burden across countries exerts on global research agendas.

36   *LAW & POLICY*   *January 2005*

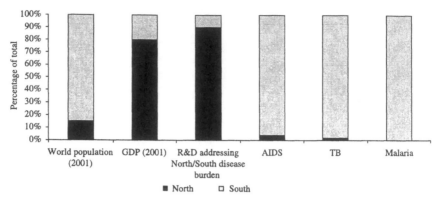

Sources: For World Population, see World Bank (2003: 235, Table 1, col. 1); for GDP, see World Bank (2003: 239, Table 3, col. 1); for R&D addressing North/South disease burden, see Médicins Sans Frontières (2001a); for AIDS, see UNAIDS & WHO (2002: 6); for TB, see UNDP (2002: 173, Table 7, col. 9); for Malaria, see UNDP (2002: 173, Table 7, col. 8).

North: high income countries. South: all others. (See UNDP 2002).

Figure 1. North/South Health and Resource Inequalities.

B. THE PRIVATE FUNDING OF HEALTH-RELATED R&D

The UNDP (2001) reports that of the 1393 new drugs developed between 1975 and 1999, only sixteen (less than 1 percent) of these were relevant to tropical illnesses – including communicable diseases. The World Health Organization Commission on Macroeconomics and Health (2001: 90–91) explains that industry involvement in R&D activities concerning all major disease killers is very limited, and in the majority of cases it is simply non-existent. Similarly, the Harvard School of Public Health revealed in a recent study that, of the world's twenty-four largest drug companies, none maintain an in-house malaria research program (Médicins Sans Frontières 2001b).

This can be interpreted as a reflection of the profit-driven nature of private R&D. As Figure 1 illustrates, the bulk of the disease burden is confined to the South, also home to the highest concentration of the world's poor, where 80 percent of the world's population concentrates just 20 percent of the world's GDP. As a consequence, this low purchasing power of the South has impeded the high "social" demand for vaccine R&D to be matched by an equally high "market" demand necessary to stimulate private investment. This would explain why, of the eleven different HIV clades currently identified, private vaccine research is focussing on clade B, the clade prevalent in Europe and North America – responsible for just 4 percent of the disease burden – whilst clades A and C, prevalent in Africa and responsible for 70 percent of all HIV/AIDS infections, receive minimal research effort (Barnet & Whiteside 2002; Kremer 2001). Moreover, the social pressure exerted over investors to treat their inventions as indivisibilities – as exemplified by the celebrated case between the South African government and the pharmaceutical industry over the AIDS anti-retroviral cocktail drug (May 2002; Seckinelgin 2002) – could cause private investors to be discouraged further from investing in a field already surrounded by much scientific uncertainty, and lacking adequate market demand.

C. STIMULATING PRIVATE R&D: THE ROLE OF "PURCHASING COMMITMENTS"

Many economists have attempted to devise a variety of mechanisms to stimulate privates' investment in neglected areas of medical research. One of the most celebrated proposals, indeed welcome by many IGOs (see the World Health Organization. Commission on Macroeconomics and Health 2001; Kaul et al. 2003: UNDP 2001) has been that of "purchasing commitments" (Kremer 2001). As described by Kremer, purchasing commitments entail a clear financial pledge by international organizations, such as UNICEF or WHO, to purchase a successful vaccine when and if developed. Kremer argues that, by committing to purchase a successful vaccine, the public sector would provide private investors with the market demand necessary to stimulate their interests, whilst it would leave the entire burden of the costs, and the risks associated with R&D activities, on the shoulders of the private sector. Although the private sector clearly necessitates of encouragement for investing in non-profitable markets, this approach presents a fundamental hurdle that deserves mentioning.

Purchasing commitments entail an entirely competitive spirit among research entities. As the economics of scientific and technological innovation teach, optimal knowledge production is reached by maximizing diffusion of all intermediate results, or rather through a highly cooperative approach to scientific inquiry (Nelson 1962). By contrast, the exclusivity of a prize, as suggested by Kremer, would force the various competing agents to maintain secret all intermediate results of their research, with an ultimate detrimental effect to vaccine knowledge production. Thus, despite the utility of encouraging private research in neglected areas of medical research, "purchasing commitments" are far from providing an ideal policy solution.

D. THE ROLE OF THE PUBLIC SECTOR

Back in 1962, Arrow had warned against the dangers of leaving to market forces alone the responsibility for providing the financial incentives necessary to stimulate scientific R&D since, the lack of profitable markets, indivisibilities, and scientific uncertainty, would cause private resources to be suboptimally allocated (Arrow 1962). With reference to activities with strong social implications, many classical economists, including Smith,

Malthus, Ricardo, and indeed Arrow, suggested moreover that – in the event of a market failure – the state should bare the costs of their provision (Desai 2003). Within modern capitalist societies, the state and the market share the provision of a number of activities. With reference to scientific R&D, the public sector performs a variety of research activities through (a) a number of publicly owned infrastructures – such as academic research laboratories – and (b) by outsourcing research projects to private operators – as has been the experience of both space and military R&D programs. Especially within medical science, publicly funded R&D has played a fundamental role in major drug-lead discoveries. Publicly funded R&D has developed a number of antibiotics for many communicable diseases, drugs for treating tuberculosis, various types of chemotherapy to treat cancer, and more recently the development of anti-retrovirals for the treatment of HIV/AIDS (UNDP 2001). It is estimated that 70 percent of all drugs with therapeutic gains have been the direct result of the public sector's involvement (ibid.).

III. THE GEO-POLITICS OF VACCINE R&D

A. THE NORTH-SOUTH PARADOX

If a lack of profitable markets explains the privates' disinterests towards communicable disease control, what could explain the public sector's disengagement? Figure 1 suggests that geo-political factors may be involved.

On one side of the hemisphere, the South concentrates 20 percent of the world's GDP, 90 percent of the total disease burden, and just 10 percent of the total R&D budget. In contrast, on the other side of the hemisphere, the North concentrates 80 percent of the world's GDP, 90 percent of the World's R&D budget, and less than 10 percent of the world's disease burden. These conditions have conferred the North, not only the resources and the competencies necessary to address these diseases, but also the power to set the global health research agenda. Regrettably though, many governments in the North, especially European, have favored financially the R&D of non-targeted academic activities and commercial areas that would increase the international competitiveness of national firms, rather than R&D activities that would benefit humanity as a whole (European Council 2002). The result has been a paradoxical situation, in which countries affected by the diseases lack the resources and expertise necessary to combat them, whilst countries holding both the resources and the expertise to fight them, lack a direct incentive for doing so.

B. THE NORTH/SOUTH HEALTH DIVIDE: A MATTER OF POLITICAL WILL

The case of the Global Fund To Fight AIDS, Tuberculosis and Malaria (GFATM) is exemplary to this political and financial *fatigue* of Northern government towards fighting communicable diseases globally. Established in 2002, under the auspices of the UN Secretary General, the fund has aimed at raising a total of US$8 billion a year through country's voluntary donations to fight major communicable diseases – although the Fund focuses on disease prevention and cure, as opposed to vaccine research and development (Tan, Upshur & Ford 2003). Despite the apparent initial political support from the international community, the fund has suffered severe financial constraints ever since its foundation. Most countries have in fact met only partially their financial obligations to the fund, with the USA in particular having contributed just 10 percent of the US$10 billion it agreed to donate by 2008 (Cunningham 2003). Far from being the exception, the Fund's lack of support follows the general trend that has distinguished Official Development Assistance (ODA) since the fall of the Berlin Wall, or rather a decreasing political and financial support to building bridges between the North/South socio-economic inequalities (World Bank 2003: 13).

Faced with this political indifference, many attempts have been made over the past thirty years to provide convincing arguments for inciting the North to play a proactive role in international cooperation, including global communicable disease control.

A most powerful rationale that has recently emerged, and has captured the interest of governments, and international governmental and non-governmental organizations, is that of global public goods (GPGs). Indeed, by looking at communicable disease control through a global public goods' lens, a persuasive justification can be developed for the North's cooperation in the fight against communicable diseases. The following section explores this rationale.

IV. VACCINE KNOWLEDGE AND COMMUNICABLE DISEASE CONTROL
AS GLOBAL PUBLIC GOODS

A. GLOBAL PUBLIC GOODS (GPGs): A DEFINITION

In her pioneering work, *Providing Global Public Goods: Managing Globalisation*, Kaul (2003) defines GPGs as goods exhibiting the following characteristics:

- non-excludable benefits – entailing the technical impossibility of excluding any one individual from consuming the good (i.e., the atmosphere, judicial systems, national defense);
- and/or non-rival benefits – by which the consumption of the good by one individual does not deprive others from consuming the same good (i.e., knowledge, see below);
- and whose benefits extend to all countries, people, and generations.

To these technical properties, Kaul adds a fourth and normative aspect, namely the dependency on international cooperation for an effective provision of GPGs.

Additionally, Kaul also distinguishes between what she defines *intermediate* global public goods, and *final* global public goods, or rather, global public goods whose provision is dependent upon the production of associate goods (Kaul, 2003). For the purpose of our argument, Kaul's definition will set the frame within which it shall be argued that both the control of communicable diseases, and the knowledge necessary to develop a vaccine for their eradication, can be considered global public goods – the former, final; and the latter, intermediate.

B. VACCINE KNOWLEDGE AS A GPG

In 1962, Arrow postulated that knowledge could be duplicated and diffused at zero or very low costs (Arrow 1962). Although this assumption has proven wrong for the majority of technological applications (see Pavitt 1999), in the case of the chemical and pharmaceutical industries the costs of knowledge duplication and diffusion can be minimal – given adequate supporting infrastructure (Mansfield, Schwartz & Wagner 1981). Moreover, knowledge is unique in its ability to diffuse from one individual to another without depriving the original withholder from continuing to enjoy its consumption and associated benefits. As noted by Thomas Jefferson, "he who receives an idea from me, receives instructions himself without lessing me" (Stiglitz 1999).

These de facto non-excludable and non-rival characteristics have distinguished knowledge as a public good (Correa 2003). However, in order to qualify as a *global* public good, vaccine knowledge would have to benefit more than one group of countries, populations, and generations. At present, the scientific community is concerned that, due to the geographic variation of the HIV virus genetic make-up, country-specific vaccines may fail to prove effective globally (Kremer 2001). International cooperation for the development of a universally effective vaccine might therefore be jeopardized by the self-interest of certain countries to develop a vaccine specific to their own needs only. Also looking at communicable disease control from a global public good perspective provides a convincing argument for pursuing cooperatively the development of a universal vaccine for communicable diseases.

C. COMMUNICABLE DISEASE CONTROL AS A GPG

The GPG character of communicable disease control is best understood by juxtaposing it against the direct and indirect threats that the underprovision of communicable disease control poses globally. The following examples will highlight how, despite the unequal repartition of the disease burden across countries, communicable diseases bring states into a shared fate, consequently calling upon governments to act cooperatively in fighting against communicable diseases:

- *Cross border transmission* – international travel and trade are causing an increase in prevalence within industrial countries of diseases previously endemic to the South. In Switzerland, for example, new HIV infections are exhibiting similar characteristics to those fuelling the AIDS epidemic in Africa (Tenkorang & Conceiçao 2003). Similarly, the recent West Nile virus infections reported in the U.S., illustrate the physical boundless nature of communicable diseases (Kaul & Faust 2001);
- *Costly provision of national public goods* – the cross-border transmission of communicable diseases represents a direct negative externality for the country into which the disease enters – since the disease-importing country will have to bear the costs associated with the imported disease (i.e., prevention, treatment, vaccination, mortality, etc). This was recognized by the United States Congress in 2000, when it acknowledged in its Global AIDS and Tuberculosis Relief Act (2000), that "because of the ease of transmission of tuberculosis, its international persistence and growth pose a direct public health threat to those nations that had previously largely controlled the disease." Indeed, by failing to achieve global eradication, even disease-free countries will still have to incur the costs associated with immunization and treatment. The case of polio is exemplary. The incomplete eradication of polio is estimated to be costing the world US$1.5 billion a year (Aylward 2000). By contrast, it has been estimated that by achieving the eradication of smallpox, the United States recoups its contributions to the smallpox eradication programs once every twenty-six days. That is, every twenty-six days, the benefits accruing from *not* having to deal with smallpox, equal the U.S.'s total eradication costs (Tenkorang & Conceiçao, 2003);
- *Socio-economic repercussions* – as discussed in the introduction, HIV/AIDS is responsible for massive economic and social devastation in sub-Saharan Africa (Bell, Devarjan & Gersbach 2003). The United States assert that HIV/AIDS in Africa constitutes a national security threat not only because of cross-border HIV transmission, but because it has the potential to destabilize the region and harm the economic, political, humanitarian, and strategic interests of other countries (Fidler 2001).

D. THE NECESSITY OF INTERNATIONAL COOPERATION FOR COMMUNICABLE DISEASE CONTROL

The examples reported above illustrate the non-excludable and non-rival characteristics associated with communicable diseases, highlighting the strong intergenerational and social and economic implications for all countries, including those currently disease-free. In particular, they highlight the GPG character of communicable disease control, given the inherent impossibility to exclude any one country from benefiting from the direct and indirect advantages accruing from the eradication of the diseases. Three main conclusions can therefore be drawn with reference to the GPG argument:

1. Vaccine R&D can be considered the *intermediate* GPG necessary for reaching the *final* GPG of communicable disease control.
2. The GPG character of both vaccine R&D and communicable disease control provides a strong case for public intervention in their provision.
3. The effectiveness of their provision will dependent on the international community's capacity to act cooperatively, since individual efforts will not be effective unless supported by a global structure.

Thus, despite the different degrees of threat posed to countries by communicable diseases, the global public good character of communicable disease control brings countries into shared fate. Consequently, countries should also be brought together as partners in reforming appropriately their public policy choices. The following section proposes an ideal framework on which countries should build a cooperative approach to the financing of vaccine R&D.

V. CREATING A GLOBAL HEALTH RESEARCH FUND

A. A CENTRAL FUNDING ORGANIZATION

In its 2001 report, the WHO Commission on Macroeconomics and Health proposed the creation of a Global Health Research Fund (GHRF) to support basic, biomedical, and applied sciences research on health problems of the poor. Although the report provides no details as to how this fund should be structured nor managed, we support amply its creation and we suggest a number of features that should characterise the fund:

- The GHRF should act as a complementary financing mechanisms to the Global Fund to Fight HIV/AIDS, Malaria and TB (GFAMT) by concentrating its mandate exclusively on vaccine research and development (hence knowledge production) – whilst the GFAMT would continue to provide financial support to outreach activities. The complementarity of the two funds would guarantee the global public good character of the vaccines developed;
- The fund would fall under the UN umbrella and, ideally, it would be coordinated by WHO in collaboration with all other UN agencies that might have a direct interest in the activities of the Fund, such as the United Nations Development Programme (UNDP), the United Nations Peoples Fund (UNFPA), and the United Nations Children Fund (UNICEF);
- WHO would be appointed as the primary coordinator of the fund, since WHO is the only global institution to benefit from the mandate to oversee international health cooperation and to guarantee the protection and promotion of global health commons. Moreover, WHO holds the ability

to convene a broad array of actors, develop consensus, and mobilize resources. With respect to legitimacy, the World Health Assembly is currently attended by 191 member states, all of which have equal voting rights irrespective of size of financial contribution (Buse & Walt 2000). No other health-related organization can claim near universal membership of nation states, nor does it benefit from a technical network-support as extensive as that of WHO;

• The fund would be subject to the supervision of a Health Research Council – directly accountable to the World Health Assembly – and would be composed by members representing all stakeholders with an interest in vaccine R&D. Namely, these should include WHO and other UN representatives, scientists, members of academia, NGOs, industry, and southern peoples' groups, in order to account for both scientific and non-scientific matters, keep research activity within its scope, and avoid targeted research being transformed into disciplinary research;

• The fund should also function as a catalyst and cooperate with all international research initiatives geared towards the development of a vaccine for communicable diseases, such as WHO's own vaccine research programs, the WHO/UNAIDS Initiative for Vaccine Research, the Tropical Disease Research program – co-sponsored by WHO, UNDP, and World Bank – the International Aids Vaccine Initiative (IAVI), and the Global Alliance for Vaccine and Immunisation (GAVI);

• The fund should also aim at increasing funding to those groups obtaining more encouraging results. This evaluation would be performed by scientific peer review – a practice now common to many research-funding bodies, such as the U.S. National Institute of Health and the UK Medical Research Council. Members of the scientific community should also be encouraged to exchange information with other research groups on a constant basis. This could be effectively managed by the Global Forum for Health Research established by WHO in 1996, and through customary academic channels – such as scientific journals, conferences, academic courses, Internet, and electronic fora.

B. EFFECTIVELY MANAGING THE PRIVATE OUTSOURCING OF R&D

There is no requirement that public financial commitment must also be performed by public institutions. As discussed earlier, in the case of space and defense, outsourcing R&D activity to private research centres has become a common practice – especially in the United States. Though, as argued also earlier, private contractors tend to disclose the minimum information, especially if they can trade any additional or unexpected result achieved via separate contracts. This can represent a major obstacle for the achievement of optimal knowledge production. The public contracting party would therefore need to master a high degree of competence in contract dealing and a strong leadership in directing research.

C. PRIVATELY FUNDED RESEARCH

Although this paper advocates a greater public commitment towards vaccine research, one cannot, and should not, aim at preventing private and profit-seeking agents from carrying out R&D activities in the field of immunization. Even in a residual position, the outcome of business-funded R&D could prove crucial to medical research. In the instance that the development of a successful vaccine for combating communicable diseases were the result of privately funded R&D, it would be necessary to negotiate the terms and conditions for licensing agreements – such as the type of remuneration (or compensation), and the exclusivity of the patent. Nothing should prevent the GHRF to purchase any successful vaccines through its annual budget. Alternatively, the GFATM could negotiate with patent holders the licensing right to reproduce and diffuse the vaccine via the payment of a royalty fee – issues associated with the duplication and diffusion of knowledge fall however outside the scope of argument (see Pogge (2002) for a radical proposition concerning the diffusion of essential knowledge to the developing world).

VI. FINANCING VACCINE R&D FOR COMMUNICABLE DISEASES

A. THE COSTS OF DEVELOPING A VACCINE FOR AIDS, MALARIA, AND TB

Estimates concerning the costs of drug development are very heterogeneous. Figures vary from US$50 million (WHO & UNICEF 1996) to almost US$900 million (Frank 2003; Tufts Center for the Study of Drug Development 2003) – though this appears to depend on whether the costs of clinical, pre-clinical, and post-approval tests are all accounted for (for a complete overview see DiMasi 1991; Frank 2003; WHO & UNICEF 1996; Miller 1998; TB Alliance 2001; Tufts Center for the Study of Drug Development 2003). The authoritative WHO Commission on Macroeconomics and Health (2001: 81) estimates that the cost of developing a vaccine for HIV/AIDS, malaria, and TB would require an ideal yearly R&D budget of US$1.5 billion. The Commission fails though to indicate how long this commitment would be required for – ideally until successful vaccines are developed. As mentioned earlier on, experts are of the opinion that HIV/AIDS, malaria, and TB vaccines are still ten to fifteen years out of reach (Kaufmann 2000; Malaria Vaccine Initiative 2003; WHO & UNICEF 2002), an opinion that is also supported by the economics of science. Grabowski and Vernon (1994) have shown that research projects in the medical/pharmaceutical field last on average ten years.

According to these estimates therefore, the cost of developing a vaccine for AIDS, malaria, and TB would require US$1.5 billion a year, for a potential fifteen-year period. This would total a comprehensive R&D

budget of US$22.5 billion, a substantial sum, compared to the current patterns of vaccine R&D expenditure – which according to estimates here provided do not exceed US$600 million a year. Nevertheless, US$22.5 billion is an affordable sum for most countries in the North. The fight against communicable diseases would therefore be comparable in size to the Manhattan project, though it would have a far more socially constructive objective.

B. A PROPOSED DISTRIBUTION OF THE FINANCIAL BURDEN

Table 1 illustrates a proposed distribution of the financial burden across countries according to the "Ability to Pay Principle" – or rather based on countries' GDP.[4] The largest overall contribution would come from the North, with the United States responsible for providing the single largest contribution, followed by that of the European Union and Japan. Developing countries would also provide a substantial financial contribution.

A considerable share of the funding should also be geared towards building local knowledge in, and transferring technology to, the South through the strengthening of programmes such as those initiated by IAVI and GAVI (see http://www.iavi.org and http://www.gavi.org), which aim at training local scientists by working in close collaborations with research laboratories in the North. Empowering the South with technical competencies necessary to perform medical R&D will contribute to bridging the current North/South health gap. However, the acquisition of knowledge is a long process that requires learning capacity, absorption of competencies, and the building of local know-how (e.g., Lundvall & Johnson 1994; Pavitt 1999; Polanyi 1962).

Table 1. A Tentative Distribution of Requirements for Vaccine R&D

	2001 GDP US$ billions	Vaccine R&D Requirements (total 15 years)* US$ billions	Vaccine R&D Requirements (per year)* US$ billions
World Total	31400.0	22.5	1.50
High Income Countries *of which*	25372.0	18.2	1.12
USA	9780.8	7.0	0.47
European Union 15	7181.7	5.1	0.34
Japan	4523.3	3.2	0.22
Low and Medium Income Countries	6025.0	4.3	0.29

*Proposals for pledges to an International Vaccine Fund Proportional to GDP.
Source: World Bank and elaborations.

46 *LAW & POLICY* *January 2005*

VII. IMPLEMENTATION AND IMPLICATIONS: THE CASE FOR
AN "INTERNATIONAL HEALTH TREATY"

A. A PROPOSED INTERNATIONAL HEALTH TREATY

How could the idea here advocated of a GHRF be implemented? Vaccine R&D is certainly not the only area where a greater international coopera-tion, and internationally binding legal commitments have been advocated. For many years, it has been suggested to reinforce international health law in order to overcome some of the basic hurdles that constrain the WHO mandate, namely that of voluntary compliance mechanisms (see Fidler 2001). As has been well documented, WHO has historically preferred to use recommendations and persuasion to guide member states through the adoption of appropriate public health policies. Consequently, member states' compliance with WHO recommendations have remained voluntary, leaving public-health sovereignty of states legally unfettered by WHO's actions.

Among many critics, James Love (2003; Love & Hubbard 2004) has sug-gested creating an international health treaty as a mechanism for inciting governments' interest in communicable disease control. In particular, Love identified in an international health treaty the most appropriate legal mechanisms for ensuring countries' commitments towards funding R&D activities, including vaccine R&D for communicable diseases. Although this paper's primary objective is to provide a science policy approach to com-municable disease control, we believe that the general normative framework advocated by Love would benefit greatly the proposal of establishing a global health research fund. In particular, an international health treaty would need to focus on three main points:

Point 1. The Treaty would clearly stipulate that WHO member states have a legal and moral obligation not only to control communicable diseases, but also to promote the right to health both domestically and internationally, given the global public good character of communicable disease control. Member states would carry out this obligation through specific actions defined in Points 2 and 3;

Point 2. Member States would be required to meet the financial obligations to the GHRF – as proposed in Table 1 – and to the GFAMT in order to ensure the GPG character of communicable disease control;

Point 3. Member States would need to develop a coherent approach to health policy implementation by ensuring that domestic policies reflected international commitments (i.e., shift financial priorities from military to health programmes, devise tax incentives for the creation of philanthropic medical research foundations, promote international technology transfer programs, increase number of doctoral positions in the field of immunology).

An international health treaty would have the advantage to enshrine within international law the global public good character of communicable disease control and vaccine R&D, including the necessity for a cooperative approach to their provision. It would moreover provide governments with the necessary legal stimuli to meet their obligations to the GHRF.

VIII. CONCLUSIONS

In this paper we have applied the concept of global public goods as a powerful tool for a robust and rational approach to the cause of communicable disease control and vaccine R&D. More specifically, a GPGs-based approach has supported three main arguments:

1. The fact that both communicable disease control and vaccine knowledge require a form of global governance based on direct public intervention. This is also supported by the view that market forces alone are not the most appropriate device to provide financial investment for R&D devoted to basic human necessities;
2. The North has both direct and indirect incentives to commit its financial and technical resources to communicable disease control, even when affected just marginally by the diseases. Yet, an active involvement of developing countries will also needed to generate appropriate capabilities in the long term and to achieve effective results on the field;
3. The distinction between *final* and *intermediate* GPGs has also allowed to make a strong case for focussing on vaccine R&D as an affective means of reaching the goal of eradicating communicable diseases – a proposition supported by ample evidence within the literature (i.e., WHO & UNAIDS 1999; WHO & UNICEF 1996, 2002).

The paper has also supported the argument in favor of the creation of a Global Health Research Fund to manage and coordinate R&D activity aimed at vaccine development, and has moreover proposed an ideal structure of the fund's mandate and operations. By reference to the economics of innovation and theories of GPGs, we have argued that the fund should be complementary to the GFATM in order to ensure the public good character of a vaccine by having the GHRF charged with the production side of knowledge, whilst the GFATM would insure its reproduction and global diffusion. The complementary role of the two funds could contribute substantially to the bridging of the North/South health divide. Although the development of a vaccine for AIDS, malaria, and TB would require US$22.5 billion – over a third of the current total health R&D spending – this sum is realistic by all means. The financial burden could be split across countries on the basis of the ability-to-pay principle. This would be consistent with the GPG character of fighting communicable diseases, since it would require countries to contribute proportionally to their financial and

48   *LAW & POLICY*   *January 2005*

technical capabilities to produce the good of communicable disease control, as opposed to their share of the global disease burden. In recognition of the historical limitations of international law, we suggested ensuring a strong and continuous political/financial commitment by the international community by including a binding obligation to fund vaccine R&D in the proposal of an international health treaty.

Given the advocacy aspect of our argument, it might be useful to make it explicit which communities are we addressing. First, we address global civil movements, an increasingly important player in international politics. Global civil movements have already played a crucial role in steering government priorities in key areas such as environment, disarmament, and human rights (see, e.g., Glasius, Kaldor & Anheier 2001, 2002, 2003). Concerning the health agenda, global movements have been particularly active in matters of knowledge diffusion, or rather access to drugs (see Shiva 2001). However, despite the present need to challenge the rules governing IPR regimes and realigning social needs with international trade law (see Coriat & Orsi 2002; Heller & Eisenberg 1998; Thurow 1997), we would urge these movements to also include in their priorities the need to increase publicly funded R&D for neglected diseases, since knowledge production is a precondition for its diffusion. As argued extensively in the paper, the current underprovision of communicable disease control is a reflection of lacking research environments, and not of diffusion mechanisms.

Second, we are addressing the academic community. In many cases, scientists hold the ability to direct strategically the priorities of their research. Governments do not have the information to direct scientific investigation unless there are scientists providing them with the technical expertise. Scientists could therefore devote increasing attention to the welfare implications and consequences of their work, and induce governments to devote more resources to global health priorities.

Last but not least, we address science policy analysts and advisors. In the last two decades there has been an increasing focus on science and technology as shapers of economic performance, rather than enhancers of social well-being. The circle of scholars of science and technology policy has been a close advisor to policymakers. If today, so much attention has been placed upon technologies for industrial innovation, and so little towards medical research for developing countries, it is due, in part, to the choices and priority setting of this community.

Whether governments will listen to a request for a change in priority setting will depend on the ability of global movements, scientific communities, and science and technology policy advisors to pursue common objectives.

DANIELE ARCHIBUGI *is a Technological Director at the Italian National Research Council in Rome. He works in the field of technological change and global governance. He is currently spending a semester as Lauro De Bosis Professor at the Department of Government of the Harvard University. Among his recent books, he has edited* Debating

Cosmopolitics *(Verso, London, 2003) and co-edited* The Globalising Learning Economy *(Oxford University Press, 2001).*

KIM BIZZARRI *is currently collaborating with the Italian National Research Council in Rome through the Italian Ministry of Foreign Affairs' research grant schemes.*

NOTES

1. The only high-income country with reported malaria cases is Korea (UNDP 2003: 258, Table 7, column 8).
2. North: OECD countries; South: all other countries.
3. Personal communication with Dr Walter Brandt, Senior Programme Officer, Malaria Vaccine Initiative, 17 June 2003.
4. According to the principle, the financial contribution capacity of countries is proportional to the country's GDP – membership fees to the United Nations for instance are calculated on the basis of the ability-to-pay principle.

REFERENCES

Arrow, Kenneth (1962) "Economic Welfare and the Allocation of Resources For Invention." In *The Rate and Direction of Inventive Activity*, edited by R. Nelson. National Bureau of Economic Research. Princeton, N.J.: Princeton Univ. Press.

Aylward, Bruce (2000) "When is a Disease Eradicable? 100 Years of Lessons Learned," *American Journal of Public Health* 90: 1515–20.

Barnett, Tony, and Alan Whiteside (2002) *AIDS in the 21st Century: Disease and Globalisation.* New York: Palgrave MacMillan.

Bell, Clive, Shantayanan Devarajan, and Hans Gersbach (2003) *The Long-run Economic Costs of AIDS: Theory and Application to South Africa.* Washington, D.C.: World Bank.

Buse, Kent, and Gill Walt (2000) "The United Nations and Global Public-Private Health Partnerships." Paper presented at the Workshop: Public-Private Partnerships in Public Health, Harvard School Of Public Health, Boston, 7–8 April.

Correa, Carlos (2003) *Managing the Provision of Knowledge: The Design of Intellectual Property Laws.* In *Providing Global Public Goods: Managing Globalisation*, edited by I. Kaul, P. Conceição, K. Le Goulven & R. Mendoza. New York: Oxford Univ. Press.

Cunningham, Anne Marie (2003) "The Global Fund – All You Ever Wanted To Know." Available at http://www.geocities.com/jvidalalaball/TheglobalFund.doc.

Coriat, Benjamin, and Fabienne Orsi (2002) "Establishing a New Intellectual Property Rights Regime in the United States: Origins, Content and Problems," *Research Policy* 31: 1491–1507.

Desai, Meghnad (2003) *Public Goods: A Historical Perspective.* In *Providing Global Public Goods: Managing Globalisation*, edited by I. Kaul, P. Conceição, K. Le Goulven & R. Mendoza. New York: Oxford Univ. Press.

DiMasi, Joseph (1991) "Cost Of Innovation In The Pharmaceutical Industry," *Journal of Health Economics* 10(2): 107–42.

Esparza, Jose (2000) "Is an AIDS Vaccine Possible?," *UN Chronicle* 37(3): 22–23.

European Council (2002) *Presidency Conclusions.* Barcelona European Council. Brussels: EC.

Fenner, Frank (1988) *Smallpox and Its Eradication.* Geneva: WHO.

Fidler, David (2001) *International Law and Global Communicable Disease Control.* Geneva: WHO Commission on Macroeconomics and Health.

Frank, Richard (2003) "New Estimates of Drug Development Costs," *Journal of Health Economics* 22: 325–30.

Glasius, Marlies, Mary Kaldor, and Helmut Anheier (eds.) (2001) *Global Civil Society Yearbook.* Oxford: Oxford Univ. Press.

Glasius, Marlies, Mary Kaldor, and Helmut Anheier (Eds) (2002) *Global Civil Society Yearbook.* Oxford: Oxford Univ. Press.

Glasius, Marlies, Mary Kaldor, and Helmut Anheier (Eds) (2003) *Global Civil Society Yearbook.* Oxford: Oxford Univ. Press.

Grabowski, Henry George, and James Vernon (1994) "Returns to R&D on New Drugs Introductions in the 1980s," *Journal of Health Economics* 13: 383–406.

Harvard Malaria Initiative (2000) "The Ancient Scourge of Malaria." Available at http://www.hsph.harvard.edu/Malaria.

Heller, Michael, and Rebecca Eisenberg (1998) "Can Patents Deter Innovation? The Anticommons in Biomedical Research," *Science* 280: 698–701.

International AIDS Vaccine Initiative (2001) *A New Access Paradigm: Public Sector Actions to Assure Swift, Global Access to AIDS Vaccine.* New York: IAVI.

International AIDS Vaccine Initiative (2002) *When Will an AIDS Vaccine be Found? The State of Global Research.* New York: IAVI.

Kaufmann, Stephan. (2000) "Is the Development of a New Tuberculosis Vaccine Possible?," *Nature America* 6: 955–59.

Kaul, Inge, Pedro Conceição, Katell Le Goulven, and Ronald Mendoza (eds.) (2003) *Providing Global Public Goods: Managing Globalisation.* New York: Oxford Univ. Press.

Kaul, Inge, and Michael Faust (2001) "Global public goods and health: taking the agenda forward," *Bulletin of the World Health Organization* 79: 869–74.

Kremer, Michael (2001) *Public Policies to Stimulate Development of Vaccines and Drugs for Neglected Diseases.* Working Paper No. WG2. Geneva: Commission on Macroeconomics and Health.

Love, James (2003) "From TRIPS to RIPS: A Better Trade Framework to Support Innovation in Medical Technologies." Workshop on Economic issues related to access to HIV/AIDS care in developing countries held on 27 May 2003. Marseille: Agence nationale de recherches sur le sida/Institute d' économie publique.

Love, James, and Tim Hubbard (2004) "A New Trade Framework for Global Healthcare R&D," *PLoS Biology* 2(2): 147–50.

Lundvall, Bengt Ake, and Björn Johnson, (1994) "The Learning Economy," *Journal of Industry Studies* 1(2): 23–42.

Mansfield, Edwin, Mark Schwartz, and Samuel Wagner (1981) "Imitation Costs and Patents: An Empirical Study", *Economic Journal* 91: 907–918.

Mazzoleni, Robert, and Nelson, Richard (1998) "The Benefits and Costs of Strong Patent Protection: A Contribution to the Current Debate," *Research Policy* 27: 273–84.

May, Christopher (2002) "Unacceptable Costs: The Consequences of Making Knowledge Property in a Global Society," *Global Society* 16(2): 123–44.

Médicins Sans Frontières (2001a) *Fatal Imbalance: The Crisis in Research and Development for Drugs for Neglected Diseases.* Geneva: MSF.

Médicins Sans Frontières (2001b) *A Survey of Private Sector Drug Research and Development.* Switzerland: the Drugs for Neglected Diseases Working Group.

Miller, Henry (1998) "Rising Costs hold up Drug Discovery," *Nature*: 395: 835.

Nelson, Richard (1962) *The Rate and Direction of Inventive Activity:* National Bureau of Economic Research. Princeton, N.J.: Princeton Univ. Press.

Pavitt, Keath (1999) "On the Nature of Technology." In *Technology, Management, and Systems of Innovation*, edited by K. Pavitt. Cheltenham, UK: Edward Elgar.

Pogge, Thomas (2002) *World Poverty and Human Rights.* Cambridge: Polity Press.

Poku, Nana (2002) "Global Pandemics: AIDS." In *Governing the Global Polity*, edited by D. Held & A. McGrew. Cambridge: Polity Press.

Polanyi, Michael (1962) *Personal Knowledge. Towards a Post-Critical Philosophy.* London: Routledge & Kegan Paul.

Rabinovich, Regina (1994) "Vaccine Technologies: View to the Future," *Science* 265: 1401–4.

Seckinelgin, Hakan (2002) "Time to Stop and Think: HIV/AIDS, Global Civil Society, and People's Politics." In *Global Civil Society*, edited by M. Glasius, M. Kaldor & H. Anheier. Oxford: Oxford Univ. Press.

Shiva, Vandana (2001) *Protect or Plunder?: Understanding Intellectual Property Rights.* London: Zed Books.

Stiglitz, Joseph (1999) "Knowledge as a Global Public Good." In *Global Public Goods: International Cooperation in the 21st Century*, edited by I. Kaul et al. New York: Oxford Univ. Press.

Tan, Darrel (2003) "Global Plagues And The Global Fund: Challenges," *BMC International Health and Human Rights* 3(2): 1–9.

TB Alliance (2001) *The Economics of TB Drug Development.* New York: TB Alliance.

Tenkorang Dyna Arhin, and Pedro Conceiçao (2003) "Beyond Communicable Disease Control: Health in the Age of Globalisation." In *Providing Global Public Goods: Managing Globalisation*, edited by I. Kaul et al. New York: Oxford Univ. Press.

Thurow, Lester (1997) "Needed: A New System of Intellectual Property Rights," *Harvard Business Review* (Fall): 95–103.

Tufts Center for the Study Of Drug Development (2003) *Outlook 2003 Report.* Boston: Tufts CSDD.

United Nations (UN) (2001) *HIV/AIDS: a Call To Action.* Paper presented at the African Summit On HIV/AIDS, Tuberculosis and Other Related Communicable Diseases, 24–27 April, Abuja, Nigeria.

United Nations Development Programme (UNDP) (2001) *Human Development Report 2001. Making New Technologies Work for Human Development.* New York: Oxford Univ. Press.

United Nations Development Programme (UNDP) (2003) *Human Development Report 2003. Millennium Development Goals: A Compact Among Nations to end Human Poverty.* New York: Oxford Univ. Press.

World Bank (2003) *World Development Report, Sustainable Development in a Dynamic World: Transforming Institutions, Growth, and Quality of Life.* New York: Oxford Univ. Press.

World Health Organization (WHO) (2003) *The World Health Report 2003.* Geneva: WHO.

World Health Organization (WHO) and UNAIDS (1999) *Report of the Overview of Vaccine Research in WHO and UNAIDS.* Geneva: WHO.

World Health Organization (WHO). Commission On Macroeconomics and Health (2001) *Investing for Economics Development.* Geneva: WHO.

World Health Organization (WHO) and United Nations Children's Fund (UNICEF) (1996) *The State of the World's Vaccines and Immunization.* Geneva: WHO.

World Health Organization (WHO) and United Nations Children's Fund (UNICEF) (2002) *State Of The World's Vaccine and Immunisation.* Geneva: WHO.

LAWS CITED

United States

Global AIDS and Tuberculosis Relief Act, Pub L No 106–264, HR 3519 (2000)

[15]

Germs, governance, and global public health in the wake of SARS

David P. Fidler

Indiana University School of Law, Bloomington, Indiana, USA, and Centre for International Studies, University of Oxford, Oxford, United Kingdom.

A revolution in the governance of global infectious disease threats is under way, accelerated by events triggered by the outbreak of SARS in 2003. This review article analyzes pre-SARS trends in the governance of infectious diseases, examines the impact of the SARS outbreak on these trends, and posits that germ governance is now a criterion of "good governance" in world affairs.

The study of infectious diseases has traditionally focused on scientific and medical issues, and advances in biotechnology suggest that new, perhaps revolutionary, scientific and medical developments are on the horizon. Important as these developments might become, another revolution is under way in a historically neglected area — governance of global infectious disease threats. Public health has experienced a governance revolution of such significance that infectious disease control now represents an important criterion of "good governance" in world affairs. This development is historically unprecedented and deserves more consideration and critical analysis than it has received to date.

This article is presented in three parts: (i) a description of discernable trends in the governance of infectious disease control prior to the outbreak of severe acute respiratory syndrome (SARS) in 2003; (ii) an analysis of how the global containment of SARS has affected these trends; and (iii) a discussion of how, in the wake of SARS, infectious disease control has emerged onto the "good governance" agenda that developed in other areas of post–Cold War international relations.

Germs and governance

"Governance" refers to how societies structure responses to the challenges they face. Analyses of emerging and re-emerging infectious diseases (EIDs) have made clear that national and international societies are confronting increased microbial threats (1–3). The US Institute of Medicine has argued that the world faces successive "perfect microbial storms" (4). Whether the focus is bioterrorism, HIV/AIDS, SARS, or avian influenza, germs increasingly pose dangers to human societies.

"Germ governance" concerns how societies, both within and beyond national borders, structure their responses to pathogenic challenges. Governance involves government, but the concepts are not synonymous. Making them synonymous would mean governance cannot exist in international relations because no world government exists. The global nature of the microbial threat requires that governance address the borderless challenges presented by infectious diseases.

Horizontal and vertical germ governance

Historically, public health governance has been divided into governance within states and governance between states. In terms of germ governance, two strategies have developed during the course of international efforts on infectious diseases — horizontal and vertical.

Horizontal germ governance. Horizontal strategies concentrated on states as the dominant actors, focused on threats that complicated trade and travel between states, and utilized international law to structure cooperation on public health problems (Figure 1) (5). This approach conceptualized infectious diseases as exogenous threats to a state's national interests that could only be mitigated through international cooperation (6). How a country organized public health internally was not a subject of horizontal germ governance. Horizontal strategies largely served the trade interests of the strongest countries in the international system — the great powers — and dominated international cooperation on public health from the mid-19th century until the end of World War II (7).

The WHO's International Health Regulations (IHR), first adopted as the International Sanitary Regulations in 1951, provide the best contemporary example of the horizontal germ governance approach. The IHR continue the governance approach developed in the international sanitary conventions of the late 19th and first half of the 20th century. The IHR's objective is to ensure the maximum security against the international spread of diseases with minimum interference with world trade and travel (8). The IHR identified specific infectious diseases (e.g., cholera, plague, and yellow fever) and required WHO Member States to report outbreaks of these diseases and to limit trade- and travel-restricting health measures taken in response to outbreaks in other countries to those prescribed in the Regulations (8) (see box, *The WHO's International Health Regulations*).

Vertical germ governance. Vertical strategies conceptualize infectious diseases as threats within states rather than as exogenous threats to a state's interests and power (5). The objective is not to manage germ traffic between states but to reduce disease threats within states (Figure 2). The human right to health strongly influenced the development of the vertical germ governance approach; and this right requires scrutiny of domestic health systems, a feature not present in the horizontal approach (6). Vertical germ governance developed in the post–World War II period, as illustrated by: (i) the turn by the WHO away from horizontal strategies and toward disease eradication and access to primary health care (9); and (ii) the prominence of human rights concepts, such as the right to health, seen in the WHO's "Health for All" campaign (10) and the global strategy for the control of HIV/AIDS (11). The vertical approach highlighted the inadequacy of domestic public health systems in developing countries. Vertical approaches sought to include non-state actors, such as nongovernmental organizations (NGOs), thus challenging the state's monopoly on germ gover-

---

Nonstandard abbreviations used: emerging and re-emerging infectious disease (EID); global public goods for health (GPGH); International Health Regulations (IHR); International Monetary Fund (IMF); nongovernmental organization (NGO); severe acute respiratory syndrome (SARS); Trade-Related Aspects of Intellectual Property Rights (TRIPS); World Trade Organization (WTO).

Conflict of interest: The author has declared that no conflict of interest exists.

Citation for this article: *J. Clin. Invest.* **113**:799–804 (2004). doi:10.1172/JCI200421328.

Regulating microbial traffic between states

Figure 1
Horizontal germ governance focuses on infectious disease threats moving between states through international trade and travel and developed through international sanitary conventions adopted in the late 19th and first half of the 20th centuries; this approach is currently applied in the WHO's IHR.

nance prevalent in the horizontal strategy. During the post–World War II period when both horizontal and vertical approaches operated, no synthesis of these frameworks occurred.

The impact of EIDs

Prior to the 1990s, infectious disease control, of whatever variety, was a neglected aspect of international relations. Although international cooperation on infectious diseases had been occurring since the mid-19th century, germ governance never represented "high politics" between states and was of little interest to scholars of world politics (12). Concern about infectious diseases developed in the 1990s and early 21st century as EIDs, such as HIV/AIDS, tuberculosis, and malaria, increased the global microbial threat. During this period, germ governance received more attention, resulting in a higher political profile for infectious disease control. In this ferment concerning infectious diseases, important trends emerged.

In terms of horizontal governance, the traditional regime for infectious disease control, the WHO's IHR (8), diminished in importance for many reasons, including the IHR's application to only a small number of diseases. International trade law, as found in the agreements of the World Trade Organization (WTO), grew in significance because of the adoption of new agreements that directly affected the relationship between trade and public health (5). Largely because of the HIV/AIDS pandemic, vertical strategies, especially the human rights approach, gained strength, particularly concerning access to antiretroviral drug therapy in developing countries (5). The battle over the impact of the WTO's Agreement on Trade-Related Aspects of Intellectual Property Rights (TRIPS) on access to essential medicines represented a clash between traditional horizontal and vertical approaches (see box, *The WTO's TRIPS Agreement*).

Despite this clash, bifurcation of horizontal and vertical strategies began to break down into a hybrid approach that exhibits characteristics from both strategies. The first aspect of this hybrid strategy involved a move from "international governance" toward "global governance." International governance is defined as governance among sovereign states (including intergovernmental organizations, such as the UN, WHO, and WTO) (13) and is essentially the same concept as horizontal governance. Global governance refers to the involvement of not only states and intergovernmental organizations but also non-state actors, such as NGOs (e.g., Médecins Sans Frontières) and multinational corporations (e.g., pharmaceutical companies) (13). Global governance incorporates non-state actors and radically differs from state-centric horizontal strategies because it posits that governments alone cannot handle global microbial threats.

The vertical process of global governance was, however, harnessed to the traditional horizontal objective of mitigating transboundary microbial traffic. The WHO's decision in 1995 to revise the IHR revealed the growing importance of global governance in interstate disease control. A key change proposed by the WHO was to allow the WHO to use information from nongovernmental sources for epidemiological surveillance of infectious disease outbreaks (14). This proposal would terminate the existing IHR's sole reliance on government-provided surveillance information. In short, states would be better protected from microbial traffic by ending the state's monopoly on disease surveillance.

The second aspect of the hybrid strategy involved the substantive outcomes of germ governance. Horizontal strategies traditionally sought to reduce: (i) the economic burden that public health measures imposed on trade and travel; and (ii) a state's vulnerability to microbial importation. The objective of this approach was to protect mainly developed countries (6). Influenced by the notion of human rights, vertical governance traditionally sought to improve individual health status, particularly in developing countries (6). In the last decade, a hybrid objective — global public goods for health (GPGH) — arose. GPGH have been variously defined, but the basic concept focuses on producing goods (e.g., antimicrobial drugs) and services (e.g., surveillance), the consumption of which is non-rival and non-excludable, across different geographical regions (15). The concept of GPGH is more expansive than the national interest paradigm of horizontal governance but less universal than the human rights approach of vertical governance. Analyses of global infectious disease problems, such as the report by the WHO's Commission on Macroeconomics and Health (16), advocated increasing GPGH production. Mechanisms developed for this purpose included the establishment of public-private partnerships (17) (e.g., the Global Fund to Fight AIDS, Tuberculosis, and Malaria), which proliferated to such an extent that the WHO observed that these partnerships were improving the landscape of infectious disease control (3).

Finally, another significant development in infectious disease policy in the 1990s and early 21st century was bioterrorism. Even before the anthrax attacks in the United States in 2001, bioterrorism fears had risen in the United States and other countries (18). Experts realized that bioterrorism preparedness called for robust public health systems, especially surveillance (19). Countries fearful of bioterrorism, particularly the United States, launched initiatives to improve domestic public health capabilities and international cooperation on bioterrorism preparedness

Public health action to reduce infectious disease prevalence inside states

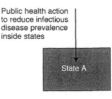

Figure 2
Vertical germ governance focuses on reducing the infectious disease prevalence inside states rather than regulating the transboundary movement of pathogenic microbes and is the approach taken in the promotion of the right to health, disease eradication programs, and programs to increase access to primary health care and essential medicines.

The WHO's International Health Regulations

The WHO's IHR are currently the only set of international legal rules on infectious disease control binding on WHO Member States. In 1951, the WHO decided to consolidate into a universal set of rules a number of sanitary conventions that had been adopted from the late 19th century through World War II; these new rules, called the International Sanitary Regulations, were later renamed (in 1969) the International Health Regulations. The WHO last revised the IHR in 1981, when smallpox was removed from the list of infectious diseases subject to the regulations. Currently, the IHR apply to only three diseases — cholera, plague, and yellow fever. WHO Member States are required to notify the WHO of outbreaks of these diseases and not to punish afflicted countries with trade- or travel-restricting measures that are more restrictive than those prescribed in the IHR. In 1995, the WHO began a process of revising the IHR in order to deal with the challenges of infectious disease control in the era of globalization. The WHO expects to complete this revision process in 2005.

(see box, *Bioterrorism's impact on germ governance*). These developments connected germ governance to national security, an unprecedented circumstance for public health (20).

The ferment concerning infectious disease control suggested that a new governance era was developing. Approaches such as global health governance and GPGH gave momentum to hybrid strategies; but the effectiveness and sustainability of these new ideas remained unclear. Initiatives created to address HIV/AIDS provided a troubling example of the uncertain impact of public-private partnerships on germ governance. For example, as 2003 began, the Global Fund to Fight AIDS, Tuberculosis, and Malaria reported that it was nearly bankrupt because financial contributions from states were inadequate (21). If the emerging strategies of germ governance could not handle the strain of existing microbial problems, what would happen when the next infectious disease crisis broke upon the world?

The impact of the SARS outbreak on germ governance

The SARS outbreak of 2003 had profound impact on approaches to infectious disease control. This author has written at length elsewhere about SARS' impact on governance and the globalization of infectious diseases (22, 23), and has argued that the SARS outbreak represents "the coming-of-age of a governance strategy for infectious diseases more radical than any previous governance innovation in this area of international relations" (23). The following section highlights the governance revolution triggered by the global containment of SARS.

According to the WHO, SARS was the first severe infectious disease to emerge in the globalized society of the 21st century (24). Although SARS had features, such as its cross-border mobility, similar to those of diseases subject to horizontal governance in the past, the mechanisms of such governance were irrelevant to SARS. Because SARS was a new syndrome, it was not a disease subject to the IHR; thus, these rules were not applicable to the global control of SARS. The SARS outbreak put the final nail in the coffin of relying on traditional horizontal strategies for germ governance, for three reasons.

First, the global campaign to control SARS demonstrated the power of global health governance mechanisms. The WHO's ability to access nongovernmental sources of epidemiological informa-

tion (e.g., media reports, e-mails, and the Internet) played a critical role in SARS' containment. In dealing with the Chinese government's unwillingness to report openly the scale of China's SARS problem, the WHO benefited from access to nongovernmental information (e.g., from individual Chinese doctors and media reports) about the extent of the SARS problem in China (23). In an example of historic miscalculation, China attempted to maintain control of epidemiological information in a context saturated by the Internet, e-mail, and mobile phones. China's initial refusal to notify the WHO of suspected and confirmed SARS cases in a timely, transparent, and verifiable manner ran headlong into the global governance mechanism of the WHO's integration of nongovernmental information into global infectious disease surveillance.

Equally important was the effect such integration had on other states. Despite not being under any legal obligation to report SARS cases, every state affected by SARS (except China) reported this information to the WHO early and rapidly. Such behavior by states during a serious outbreak was unprecedented. This astonishing situation reflects the realization that epidemiological information in the global age does not, and will not, respect sovereignty. The incorporation of nongovernmental information into surveillance elevates the importance of non-state actors in germ governance and constricts state sovereignty concerning outbreak management.

Second, the global campaign to control SARS demonstrated the power of GPGH in the context of a dangerous epidemic. The WHO coordinated efforts to produce GPGH as part of the attempt to contain SARS in three areas: the production of (i) surveillance information; (ii) scientific research on the causative agent of SARS; and (iii) guidelines regarding the clinical management of SARS cases (23). Just as with the surveillance achievements, the degree of global cooperation on identifying the causative agent of SARS and developing guidelines for the clinical treatment of infected patients was unprecedented. Production of these GPGH occurred through the participation of states, intergovernmental organizations, and non-state actors, and thus represents further evidence for the need for hybrid germ governance strategies.

Third, the SARS epidemic induced the WHO to exercise unprecedented power against states affected by an infectious disease. Under the terms of traditional horizontal governance, states restrict the authority of intergovernmental organizations in order to maintain maximum flexibility for sovereignty (23). During the SARS outbreak, however, the WHO independently issued global

The WTO's TRIPS Agreement

The WTO's TRIPS Agreement harmonizes intellectual property rights among WTO Member States, including patent rights, by establishing minimum levels of protection that each WTO Member State must give to the intellectual property of other WTO Member States. The TRIPS Agreement contains safeguards, such as the rights to engage in parallel licensing and compulsory licensing that allow WTO Member States to address public health problems. Despite the existence of these safeguards, the TRIPS Agreement became the source of public health controversy in connection with efforts to increase access to essential medicines, such as patented antiretrovirals, in developing countries. This controversy eventually produced the WTO's Doha Declaration on the TRIPS Agreement and Public Health in 2001, which stated that the TRIPS Agreement does not and should not prevent WTO Member States from taking measures to protect public health.

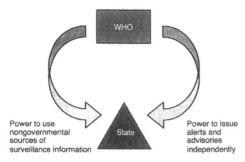

Figure 3
The global health governance "pincer" captures how the WHO's power to use nongovernmental sources of surveillance information on infectious diseases and to issue alerts and advisories independently of its Member States reduces the sovereign state's discretion in how it responds to infectious disease outbreaks.

alerts and geographically specific travel advisories (25) that caused affected states economic damage. The travel advisories were particularly radical, for three reasons.

First, neither the WHO Constitution nor the IHR grant the WHO independent authority to recommend that travelers postpone nonessential travel to WHO Member States affected by an epidemic (26). The WHO itself had not even included such authority in its pre-SARS proposals to revise the IHR (14). Under those proposals, any WHO recommendations concerning an outbreak of international concern would be issued with the advance agreement of the country or countries affected (14). In issuing alerts and advisories regarding SARS, the WHO acted independently, without the consent (or even the consultation) of targeted countries.

Second, through the alerts and advisories, the WHO exercised power against its Member States. These actions resulted in political and economic damage in the states concerned. One would search the annals of international organizations in vain to find examples of such an organization wielding real power against multiple Member States without express authorization. Although the states affected by these advisories complained (e.g., Canada) about the WHO's actions (26), none publicly challenged such radical governance behavior by the WHO during the outbreak. At the World Health Assembly meeting in May 2003, the Member States of the WHO formally empowered it to take such actions in the future when necessary (27).

Third, the WHO issued travel advisories directly to non-state actors − travelers − rather than directing its recommendations to Member States (23). This action revealed that during the SARS outbreak, the WHO governed using principles that resonated with vertical rather than horizontal strategies. Not only did non-state actors play a pivotal role in SARS surveillance but they also were direct subjects of WHO governance actions.

From a governance perspective, the WHO's power to use nongovernmental sources of information and to issue alerts and advisories created a global health governance "pincer" (Figure 3) (23). The pincer squeezes state sovereignty by using nongovernmental sources of surveillance information to minimize a state's discretionary power to report or withhold information about outbreaks, and by increas-

ing political and economic incentives for participation in global cooperation in order to maximize the prospects of domestic containment of a pathogenic threat and thus avoid advisories.

The governance response to SARS also brought into play the notion of human rights (23), which was a prominent factor in the development of vertical strategies. Global HIV/AIDS policy has, since the late 1980s, stressed respect for civil and political rights (e.g., non-discrimination) and the right to health (e.g., access to primary health care and treatment) (28). SARS was a novel pathogen for which no adequate diagnostic, vaccine, or therapeutic technologies existed (25). SARS containment depended on isolation and quarantine in many countries, which raised questions about the precautions required to ensure public health while protecting human rights (23). The concerns expressed about human rights in connection with SARS isolation and quarantine would not arise under traditional horizontal governance. In the SARS outbreak, unlike in the case of HIV/AIDS, infringements of human rights were largely thought justified in order to facilitate domestic containment and mitigation of transboundary spread.

Although this overview only highlights some features of SARS' impact on germ governance, it provides a glimpse into a radical and unprecedented event in the history of governance of infectious diseases. SARS is seminal in another respect: the outbreak put infectious disease control on the agenda of "good governance" in world politics.

Germs and "good governance"
The post–Cold War period saw "good governance" promoted within transition and developing countries by developed states and international development organizations, such as the World Bank (29) and the International Monetary Fund (IMF) (30). Good governance is a complex concept, but it essentially represents a set of procedural and substantive indicators by which to measure the quality of a country's governance. Procedurally, good governance requires, for example, participatory, accountable, and transparent governance. Substantively, good governance involves democracy, the rule of law, market-based economics, and the protection of human rights.

Health's place in the the good governance project evolved over time. Critics assailed early good governance policies, such as IMF demands that developing countries restructure their economic policies in return for financial assistance (i.e., structural adjustment policies), for having adverse health consequences in developing countries because of a myopic focus on economic criteria (31). The prominence of health issues increased as experts connected the achievement of good governance with positive health outcomes. A

Bioterrorism's impact on germ governance

The growing threat of bioterrorism has significantly affected germ governance, especially in the United States. To combat the bioterrorist threat, the US federal government has allocated more money to improve bioterrorism preparedness and response capabilities at federal and state levels, passed new statutes to empower federal agencies to respond more effectively to bioterrorism, and launched new programs, such as the smallpox vaccination campaign, to reduce US vulnerability to bioterrorist attack. The United States has also led efforts to intensify international cooperation against bioterrorism, as illustrated by the establishment of a Global Health Security Initiative among the G-8 countries and Mexico and cooperation with the WHO on bioterrorism preparedness and response.

US interagency task force wrote in 1995 that, because civil instability and strife provide breeding grounds for microbes, "efforts to promote good governance... are not out of place in a discussion of how to deal with new and re-emerging diseases" (32). Such good governance–health linkages asserted that better public health would flow from progress towards good governance but did not maintain that public health was itself a good governance indicator.

Health's rise as a good governance issue also appeared in the context of foreign aid when donor countries and international organizations began to require that aid-recipient countries increase investments in the health sector. The Bush administration's Millennium Challenge Account, from which developmental assistance is provided to those countries that rule justly, invest in their people, and encourage economic freedom, requires, for example, that recipient countries invest in health to be eligible for US aid (33). Such requirements factored increased commitment to health into calculations concerning good governance reforms in developing countries.

The developments traced above concerning infectious disease control deepen the good governance–health relationship by making public health an independent criterion of good governance. In other words, without good germ governance a country does not have good governance. This perspective radically differs from hopes that good governance reforms will produce better public health or from equating increased investments in health as evidence of good governance. The perspective is radical because it posits that public health is itself, like democracy and the rule of law, an indicator of good governance.

The severity of the infectious disease threat supports elevating public health in this way. Experts have argued that infectious diseases pose direct and indirect threats to basic functions of governance, including political institutions (34), economic development (16), the protection of human rights (35), and national security (20, 36). Reflecting on the HIV/AIDS pandemic in developing countries, US Secretary of State Colin Powell has argued, for example, that "HIV/AIDS carries profound implications for prosperity, democracy and security" (37).

When confronting the microbial menace, it is not sufficient to argue that democratic reforms and larger health budgets will produce infectious disease control. South Africa's HIV/AIDS disaster has occurred under a democratically elected government. SARS pushed Canada's expensive system of universal health care to the brink, prompting the government to review the nation's public health policy and infrastructure (26). Upon reflecting on SARS, WHO officials stressed the critical general governance role of infectious disease control in arguing that "[t]he SARS experience... made one lesson clear early in its course: inadequate surveillance and response capacity in a single country can endanger national populations and the public health security of the entire world" (38). A concept of good governance not informed by germ governance is flawed from the perspectives of democracy, human rights, economic development, and national security, all of which experts believe are threatened by resurgent infectious diseases.

Conclusion

Germ governance in the wake of SARS is at a revolutionary moment. The evolution of germ governance before and during SARS, and the elevation of such governance as an element of good governance, place public health in exciting but uncharted waters. In the aftermath of SARS, public health can no longer be considered a secondary priority at any level. In the post-SARS environment, the Canadian National Advisory Committee on SARS and Public Health stressed the importance of public health in governance by quoting Benjamin Disraeli's argument that "public health was the foundation for 'the happiness of the people and the power of the country. The care of the public health is the first duty of the statesman' " (26). Although germ governance has not achieved this level of importance, it has become an increasingly significant benchmark against which the health of national, international, and global governance is measured.

Revolutions do not always end happily, and the revolutionary moment for germ governance may be short-lived because the momentum of the new, radical developments and hybrid strategies may prove to be unsustainable. Countries have begun, for example, to formally question aspects of the WHO's travel advisory power (39). In addition, no one should have any illusions of the Herculean implications, particularly for building public health capacity in developing countries, of maintaining that public health constitutes an independent factor for assessing the quality of governance in an era of a resurgent microbial threat. The recent avian influenza scare in Asia provides further evidence of the dangerous times germ governance faces. Solidifying, sustaining, and advancing the germ governance revolution constitutes a seminal challenge for 21st-century humanity.

Address correspondence to: David P. Fidler, Indiana University School of Law, 211 South Indiana Avenue, Bloomington, Indiana 47405, USA. Phone: (812) 855-6403; Fax: (812) 855-0555; E-mail: dfidler@indiana.edu.

1. 1992. *Emerging infections: microbial threats to health in the United States*. J. Lederberg, R.E. Shope, and S.C. Oaks, editors. National Academy Press. Washington, D.C., USA. 312 pp.

2. 1999. *Removing obstacles to healthy development*. World Health Organization. Geneva, Switzerland. 68 pp.

3. 2003. *Global defence against the infectious disease threat*. M.K. Kindhauser, editor. World Health Organization. Geneva, Switzerland. 242 pp.

4. 2003. *Microbial threats to health: emergence, detection, and response*. M.S. Smolinski, M.A. Hamburg, and J. Lederberg, editors. National Academy Press. Washington, D.C., USA. 367 pp.

5. Fidler, D.P. 2003. Emerging trends in international law concerning global infectious disease control. *Emerging Infect. Dis.* 9:285–290.

6. Fidler, D.P. 2004. Caught between paradise and power: public health, pathogenic threats, and the axis of illness. *McGeorge Law Review*. In press.

7. Howard-Jones, N. 1975. *The scientific background of the International Sanitary Conferences 1851–1938*. World Health Organization. Geneva, Switzerland. 110 pp.

8. 1983. *International Health Regulations (1969)*. 3rd annotated edition. World Health Organization. Geneva, Switzerland. 79 pp.

9. Arhin-Tenkorang, D., and Conceição, P. 2003. Beyond communicable disease control: health in the age of globalization. In *Providing global public goods: managing globalization*. I. Kaul, P. Conceição, K. Le Goulven, and R.U. Mendoza, editors. Oxford University Press. Oxford, United Kingdom. 484–515.

10. 1978. Declaration of Alma Ata. In *Report of the International Conference on Primary Health Care*. World Health Organization. Geneva, Switzerland. 79 pp.

11. Mann, J.M. 1999. Human rights and AIDS: the future of the pandemic. In *Health and human rights: a reader*. J.M. Mann, S. Gruskin, M.A. Grodin, and G.J. Annas, editors. Routledge. London, United Kingdom. 216–226.

12. Lee, K., and Zwi, A. 2003. A global political economy approach to AIDS: ideology, interests, and implications. In *Health impacts of globalization: toward global governance*. Palgrave Macmillan. London, United Kingdom. 13–32.

13. Dodgson, R., Lee, K., and Drager, N. 2002. *Global health governance: a conceptual overview*. Centre on Global Change & Health. London, United Kingdom. World Health Organization. Geneva, Switzerland. 35 pp.

14. 2002. *Global crises, global solutions: managing public health emergencies of international concern through the revised International Health Regulations*. World Health Organization. Geneva, Switzerland. 28 pp.

15. Smith, R., and Woodward, D. 2003. Global public goods for health: use and limitations. In *Global public goods for health: health economic and public health perspectives*. R. Smith, R. Beaglehole, D. Woodward, and N. Drager, editors. Oxford University Press. Oxford, United Kingdom. 246–265.

16. Commission on Macroeconomics and Health. 2001. *Macroeconomics and health: investing in health for eco-*

nomic development. World Health Organization. Geneva, Switzerland. 210 pp.

17. 2002. *Public-private partnerships for health.* M. Reich, editor. Harvard University Press. Cambridge, Massachusetts, USA. 208 pp.

18. Carter, A., Deutch, J., and Zelikow, P. 1998. Catastrophic terrorism: tackling the new danger. *Foreign Affairs.* **77**:80–94.

19. Heymann, D.L. 2003. Emerging and epidemic-prone diseases: threats to public health security. In *Biological security & public health: in search of a global treatment.* K.M. Campbell and P. Zelikow, editors. Aspen Institute. Washington, D.C., USA. 49–55.

20. Fidler, D.P. 2003. Public health and national security in the global age: bioterrorism, pathogenic microbes, and *Realpolitik. George Washington International Law Review.* **35**:787–856.

21. Global Fund to Fight AIDS, Tuberculosis, and Malaria. 2003. Press Release: Global Fund awards $866 million in grants to fight AIDS, TB and malaria; United States takes chair of Global Fund Board; Tommy Thompson is elected. Jan. 31. http://www.globalfundatm.org/journalists/press%20releases/pr_030131b.html.

22. Fidler, D.P. 2003. SARS: political pathology of the first post-Westphalian pathogen. *J. Law Med. Ethics.* **31**:485–505.

23. Fidler, D.P. 2004. *SARS, governance and the globalization of disease.* Palgrave Macmillan. London, United Kingdom. In press.

24. 2003. *Severe Acute Respiratory Syndrome (SARS).* Resolution of the Fifty-Sixth World Health Assembly. World Health Assembly, WHA56.29. May 28. Geneva, Switzerland. 4 pp.

25. 2003. *Severe Acute Respiratory Syndrome (SARS): status of the outbreak and lessons for the immediate future.* World Health Organization. Geneva, Switzerland. 13 pp.

26. National Advisory Committee on SARS and Public Health. 2003. *Learning from SARS: renewal of public health in Canada.* Health Canada. Ottawa, Canada. 234 pp.

27. 2003. *Revision of the International Health Regulations.* Resolution of the Fifty-Sixth World Health Assembly, WHA56.28. May 28. Geneva, Switzerland. 3 pp.

28. UNAIDS. HIV/AIDS, Human Rights & Law. http://www.unaids.org/en/in+focus/hiv_aids_human_rights.asp.

29. World Bank. 1994. *Development in practice: governance – the World Bank's experience.* World Bank. Washington, D.C., USA. 86 pp.

30. International Monetary Fund. 1997. *Good governance: the IMF's role.* International Monetary Fund. Washington, D.C., USA. 14 pp.

31. Fidler, D.P. 1999. Neither science nor shamans: globalization of markets and health in the developing world. *Indiana Journal of Global Legal Studies.* **7**:191–224.

32. National Science and Technology Council Committee on International Science, Engineering, and Technology (CISET) Working Group on Emerging and Re-Emerging Infectious Diseases. 1995. *Infectious diseases – a global health threat.* CISET. Washington, D.C., USA. 55 pp.

33. Millennium Challenge Account. http://www.mca.gov.

34. Price-Smith, A.T. 2002. *The health of nations: infectious disease, environmental change, and their effects on national security and development.* The MIT Press. Cambridge, Massachusetts, USA. 232 pp.

35. Gruskin, S., and Tarantola, D. 2002. Health and human rights. In *Oxford Textbook of Public Health.* 4th edition. R. Detels et al., editors. Oxford University Press. Oxford, United Kingdom. 311–335.

36. Brower, J., and Chalk, P. 2003. *The global threat of new and reemerging infectious diseases: reconciling U.S. national security and public health policy.* RAND. Santa Monica, California, USA. 166 pp.

37. Powell, C. 2003. Remarks at Bill Signing Ceremony for the U.S. Leadership Against HIV/AIDS, Tuberculosis, and Malaria Act of 2003. May 27. http://www.state.gov/secretary/rm/2003/20969.htm.

38. Heymann, D.L., and Rodier, G. 2003. Global surveillance, national surveillance, and SARS. *Emerging Infect. Dis.* Feb. http://www.cdc.gov/ncidod/EID/vol10no2/03-1038.htm.

39. Reuters. 2004. WHO urged to ease up on travel alerts. Jan. 22. http://www.cnn.com/2004/HEALTH/01/22/WHO.warnings.reut/index.html.

[16]

Preparing for the Next Pandemic

Michael T. Osterholm

FEAR ITSELF

DATING BACK to antiquity, influenza pandemics have posed the greatest threat of a worldwide calamity caused by infectious disease. Over the past 300 years, ten influenza pandemics have occurred among humans. The most recent came in 1957–58 and 1968–69, and although several tens of thousands of Americans died in each one, these were considered mild compared to others. The 1918–19 pandemic was not. According to recent analysis, it killed 50 to 100 million people globally. Today, with a world population of 6.5 billion, more than three times that of 1918, even a "mild" pandemic could kill many millions of people.

A number of recent events and factors have significantly heightened concern that a specific near-term pandemic may be imminent. It could be caused by H5N1, the avian influenza strain currently circulating in Asia. At this juncture scientists cannot be certain. Nor can they know exactly when a pandemic will hit, or whether it will rival the experience of 1918–19 or be more muted like 1957–58 and 1968–69. The reality of a coming pandemic, however, cannot be avoided. Only its impact can be lessened. Some important preparatory efforts are under way, but much more needs to be done by institutions at many levels of society.

MICHAEL T. OSTERHOLM is Director of the Center for Infectious Disease Research and Policy, Associate Director of the Department of Homeland Security's National Center for Food Protection and Defense, and Professor at the University of Minnesota's School of Public Health.

Preparing for the Next Pandemic

THE BACKDROP

OF THE THREE types of influenza virus, influenza type A infects and kills the greatest number of people each year and is the only type that causes pandemics. It originates in wild aquatic birds. The virus does not cause illness in these birds, and although it is widely transmitted among them, it does not undergo any significant genetic change.

Direct transmission from the birds to humans has not been demonstrated, but when a virus is transmitted from wild birds to domesticated birds such as chickens, it undergoes changes that allow it to infect humans, pigs, and potentially other mammals. Once in the lung cells of a mammalian host, the virus can "reassort," or mix genes, with human influenza viruses that are also present. This process can lead to an entirely new viral strain, capable of sustained human-to-human transmission. If such a virus has not circulated in humans before, the entire population will be susceptible. If the virus has not circulated in the human population for a number of years, most people will lack residual immunity from previous infection.

Once the novel strain better adapts to humans and is easily transmitted from person to person, it is capable of causing a new pandemic. As the virus passes repeatedly from one human to the next, it eventually becomes less virulent and joins the other influenza viruses that circulate the globe each year. This cycle continues until another new influenza virus emerges from wild birds and the process begins again.

Some pandemics result in much higher rates of infection and death than others. Scientists now understand that this variation is a result of the genetic makeup of each specific virus and the presence of certain virulence factors. That is why the 1918–19 pandemic killed many more people than either the 1957–58 or the 1968–69 pandemic.

A CRITICAL DIFFERENCE

INFECTIOUS DISEASES remain the number one killer of humans worldwide. Currently, more than 39 million people live with HIV, and last year about 2.9 million people died of AIDS, bringing the cumulative total of deaths from AIDS to approximately 25 million. Tuberculosis

Michael T. Osterholm

(TB) and malaria also remain major causes of death. In 2003, about 8.8 million people became infected with TB, and the disease killed more than 2 million. Each year, malaria causes more than 1 million deaths and close to 5 billion episodes of clinical illness. In addition, newly emerging infections, diarrheal and other vector-borne diseases, and agents resistant to antibiotics pose a serious and growing public health concern.

Given so many other significant infectious diseases, why does another influenza pandemic merit unique and urgent attention? First, of the more than 1,500 microbes known to cause disease in humans, influenza continues to be the king in terms of overall mortality. Even in a year when only the garden-variety strains circulate, an estimated 1–1.5 million people worldwide die from influenza infections or related complications. In a pandemic lasting 12 to 36 months, the number of cases and deaths would rise dramatically.

Recent clinical, epidemiological, and laboratory evidence suggests that the impact of a pandemic caused by the current H5N1 strain would be similar to that of the 1918–19 pandemic. More than half of the people killed in that pandemic were 18 to 40 years old and largely healthy. If 1918–19 mortality data are extrapolated to the current U.S. population, 1.7 million people could die, half of them between the ages of 18 and 40. Globally, those same estimates yield 180–360 million deaths, more than five times the cumulative number of documented AIDS deaths. In 1918–19, most deaths were caused by a virus-induced response of the victim's immune system—a cytokine storm—which led to acute respiratory distress syndrome (ARDS). In other words, in the process of fighting the disease, a person's immune system severely damaged the lungs, resulting in death. Victims of H5N1 have also suffered from cytokine storms, and the world is not much better prepared to treat millions of cases of ARDS today than it was 85 years ago. In the 1957–58 and 1968–69 pandemics, the primary cause of death was secondary bacterial pneumonias that infected lungs weakened by influenza. Although such bacterial infections can often be treated by antibiotics, these drugs would be either unavailable or in short supply for much of the global population during a pandemic.

The arrival of a pandemic influenza would trigger a reaction that would change the world overnight. A vaccine would not be available

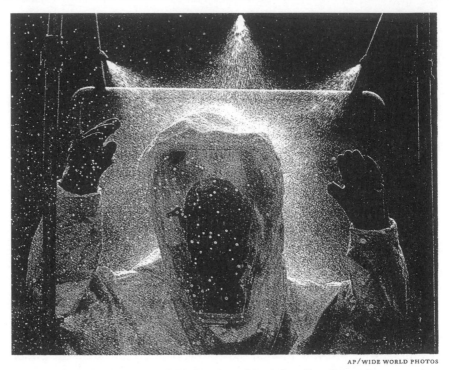

AP/WIDE WORLD PHOTOS

Ready for action? Bioterror drill, Charlotte, North Carolina, September 30, 2002

for a number of months after the pandemic started, and there are very limited stockpiles of antiviral drugs. Plus, only a few privileged areas of the world have access to vaccine-production facilities. Foreign trade and travel would be reduced or even ended in an attempt to stop the virus from entering new countries—even though such efforts would probably fail given the infectiousness of influenza and the volume of illegal crossings that occur at most borders. It is likely that transportation would also be significantly curtailed domestically, as smaller communities sought to keep the disease contained. The world relies on the speedy distribution of products such as food and replacement parts for equipment. Global, regional, and national economies would come to an abrupt halt—something that has never happened due to HIV, malaria, or TB despite their dramatic impact on the developing world.

The closest the world has come to this scenario in modern times was the SARS (severe acute respiratory syndrome) crisis of 2003. Over a period of five months, about 8,000 people were infected by a novel human

Michael T. Osterholm

coronavirus. About ten percent of them died. The virus apparently spread to humans when infected animals were sold and slaughtered in unsanitary and crowded markets in China's Guangdong Province. Although the transmission rate of SARS paled in comparison to that of influenza, it demonstrated how quickly such an infectious agent can circle the globe, given the ease and frequency of international travel. Once SARS emerged in rural China, it spread to five countries within 24 hours and to 30 countries on six continents within several months.

The SARS experience teaches a critical lesson about the potential global response to a pandemic influenza. Even with the relatively low number of deaths it caused compared to other infectious diseases, SARS had a powerful negative psychological impact on the populations of many countries. In a recent analysis of the epidemic, the National Academy of Science's Institute of Medicine concluded: "The relatively high case-fatality rate, the identification of super-spreaders, the newness of the disease, the speed of its global spread, and public uncertainty about the ability to control its spread may have contributed to the public's alarm. This alarm, in turn, may have led to the behavior that exacerbated the economic blows to the travel and tourism industries of the countries with the highest number of cases."

> SARS gave a taste of the devastating impact a killer flu pandemic could have on the global economy.

SARS provided a taste of the impact a killer influenza pandemic would have on the global economy. Jong-Wha Lee, of Korea University, and Warwick McKibbin, of the Australian National University, estimated the economic impact of the six-month SARS epidemic on the Asia-Pacific region at about $40 billion. In Canada, 438 people were infected and 43 died after an infected person traveled from Hong Kong to Toronto, and the Canadian Tourism Commission estimated that the epidemic cost the nation's economy $419 million. The Ontario health minister estimated that SARS cost the province's health-care system about $763 million, money that was spent, in part, on special SARS clinics and supplies to protect health-care workers. The SARS outbreak also had a substantial impact on the global airline industry. After the disease hit in 2003, flights in the Asia-Pacific area decreased

Preparing for the Next Pandemic

by 45 percent from the year before. During the outbreak, the number of flights between Hong Kong and the United States fell 69 percent. And this impact would pale in comparison to that of a 12- to 36-month worldwide influenza pandemic.

The SARS epidemic also raises questions about how prepared governments are to address a prolonged infectious-disease crisis—particularly governments that are already unstable. Seton Hall University's Yanzhong Huang concluded that the SARS epidemic created the most severe social or political crisis encountered by China's leadership since the 1989 Tiananmen crackdown. China's problems probably resulted less from SARS' public health impact than from the government's failed effort to allay panic by withholding information about the disease from the Chinese people. The effort backfired. During the crisis, Chinese Premier Wen Jiabao pointed out in a cabinet meeting on the epidemic that "the health and security of the people, overall state of reform, development, and stability, and China's national interest and image are at stake." But Huang believes that "a fatal period of hesitation regarding information-sharing and action spawned anxiety, panic, and rumor-mongering across the country and undermined the government's efforts to create a milder image of itself in the international arena."

Widespread infection and economic collapse can destabilize a government; blame for failing to deal effectively with a pandemic can cripple a government. This holds even more for an influenza pandemic. In the event of a pandemic influenza, the level of panic witnessed during the SARS crisis could spiral out of control as illnesses and deaths continued to mount over months and months. Unfortunately, the public is often indifferent to initial warnings about impending infectious-disease crises—as with HIV, for example. Indifference becomes fear only after the catastrophe hits, when it is already too late to implement preventive or control measures.

READY FOR THE WORST

WHAT SHOULD the industrialized world be doing to prepare for the next pandemic? The simple answer: far more. So far, the World Health Organization and several countries have finalized or drafted

Michael T. Osterholm

useful but overly general plans. The U.S. Department of Health and Human Services has increased research on influenza-vaccine production and availability. These efforts are commendable, but what is needed is a detailed operational blueprint for how to get a population through one to three years of a pandemic. Such a plan must involve all the key components of society. In the private sector, the plan must coordinate the responses of the medical community, medical suppliers, food providers, and the transportation system. In the government sector, the plan should take into account officials from public health, law enforcement, and emergency management at the international, federal, state, and local levels.

At the same time, it must be acknowledged that such master blueprints may have their drawbacks, too. Berkeley's Aaron Wildavsky persuasively argued that resilience is the real key to crisis management—overly rigid plans can do more harm than good. Still, planning is enormously useful. It gives government officials, private-sector partners, and the community the opportunity to meet, think through potential dilemmas, purchase necessary equipment, and set up organizational structures for a 12- to 36-month response. A blueprint forces leaders to rehearse their response to a crisis, preparing emotionally and intellectually so that when disaster strikes the community can face it.

Influenza-vaccine production deserves special attention. An initiative to provide vaccine for the entire world must be developed, with a well-defined schedule to ensure progress. It is laudable that countries such as the United States and Vietnam are pursuing programs with long-term goals to develop and produce H5N1 vaccine for their respective populations. But if the rest of the world lacks supplies, even the vaccinated will be devastated when the global economy comes to an abrupt halt. Pandemic-influenza preparedness is by nature an international issue. No one can truly be isolated from a pandemic.

The pandemic-related collapse of worldwide trade and its ripple effect throughout industrialized and developing countries would represent the first real test of the resiliency of the modern global delivery system. Given the extent to which modern commerce relies on the precise and readily available international trade of goods and services, a shutdown of the global economic system would dramatically harm the world's ability to meet the surging demand for essential

Preparing for the Next Pandemic

commodities such as food and medicine during a crisis. The business community can no longer afford to play a minor role in planning the response to a pandemic. For the world to have critical goods and services during a pandemic, industry heads must stockpile raw materials for production and preplan distribution and transportation support. Every company's senior managers need to be ready to respond rapidly to changes in the availability, production, distribution, and inventory management of their products. There is no model for how to revive the current global economy were it to be devastated.

To truly be complete, all planning on international, regional, national, and local levels must consider three different scenarios: What if the pandemic begins tonight? What if it starts one year from now? What if the world is so fortunate as to have an entire decade to prepare? All are possible, but none is certain.

STARTING TONIGHT

WHAT WOULD happen today in the office of every nation's leader if several cities in Vietnam suffered from major outbreaks of H5N1 infection, with a five percent mortality rate? First, there would be an immediate effort to try to sort out disparate disease-surveillance data from a variety of government and public health sources to determine which countries might have pandemic-related cases. Then, the decision would likely be made to close most international and even some state or provincial borders—without any predetermined criteria for how or when those borders might be reopened. Border security would be made a priority, especially to protect potential supplies of pandemic-specific vaccines from nearby desperate countries. Military leaders would have to develop strategies to defend the country and also protect against domestic insurgency with armed forces that would likely be compromised by the disease. Even in unaffected countries, fear, panic, and chaos would spread as international media reported the daily advance of the disease around the world.

In short order, the global economy would shut down. The commodities and services countries would need to "survive" the next 12 to 36 months would have to be identified. Currently, most businesses' continuity plans account for only a localized disruption—a single

Michael T. Osterholm

plant closure, for instance—and have not planned for extensive, long-term outages. The private and public sectors would have to develop emergency plans to sustain critical domestic supply chains and manufacturing and agricultural production and distribution. The labor force would be severely affected when it was most needed. Over the course of the year, up to 50 percent of affected populations could become ill; as many as five percent could die. The disease would hit senior management as hard as the rest of the work force. There would be major shortages in all countries of a wide range of commodities, including food, soap, paper, light bulbs, gasoline, parts for repairing military equipment and municipal water pumps, and medicines, including vaccines unrelated to the pandemic. Many industries not critical to survival—electronics, automobile, and clothing, for example—would suffer or even close. Activities that require close human contact—school, seeing movies in theaters, or eating at restaurants—would be avoided, maybe even banned.

Vaccine would have no impact on the course of the virus in the first months and would likely play an extremely limited role worldwide during the following 12 to 18 months of the pandemic. Despite major innovations in the production of most other vaccines, international production of influenza vaccine is based on a fragile and limited system that utilizes technology from the 1950s. Currently, annual production of influenza vaccine is limited to about 300 million trivalent doses—which protect against three different influenza strains in one dose—or less than one billion monovalent doses. To counter a new strain of pandemic influenza that has never circulated throughout the population, each person would likely need two doses for adequate protection. With today's limited production capacity, that means that less than 500 million people—about 14 percent of the world's population—would be vaccinated within a year of the pandemic. In addition, because the structure of the virus changes so rapidly, vaccine development could only start once the pandemic began, as manufacturers would have to obtain the new pandemic strain. It would then be at least another six months before mass production of the vaccine.

Even if the system functions to the best of its ability, influenza vaccine is produced commercially in just nine countries: Australia, Canada, France, Germany, Italy, Japan, the Netherlands, the United King-

Preparing for the Next Pandemic

dom, and the United States. These countries contain only 12 percent of the world's population. In the event of an influenza pandemic, they would probably nationalize their domestic production facilities, as occurred in 1976, when the United States, anticipating a pandemic of swine influenza (H1N1), refused to share its vaccine.

If a pandemic struck the world today, there would be another possible weapon against influenza: antiviral medicine. When taken daily during the time of exposure to influenza, antivirals have prevented individuals from becoming ill. They have also reduced the severity of illness and subsequent complications when taken within 48 hours of onset. Although there is no data for H5N1, it is assumed antivirals would also prevent H5N1 infection if taken before exposure. There is no evidence, however, that current antiviral influenza drugs would help if the patient developed the kind of cytokine storm that has characterized recent H5N1 infections. But barring this complication, H5N1 should be treatable with Tamiflu (oseltamivir phosphate), which is manufactured by the Roche pharmaceuticals company in a single plant in Switzerland.

In responding to a pandemic, Tamiflu could have a measurable impact in the limited number of countries with sizable stockpiles, but for most of the world it would not be available. Although the company plans on opening another facility in the United States this year, annual production would still cover only a small percentage of the world's population. To date, at least 14 countries have ordered Tamiflu, but the amount of these orders is enough to treat only 40 million people. The orders take considerable time to be processed and delivered—manufacturing can take up to a year—and in an emergency the company's ability to produce more would be limited. As with vaccines, countries would probably nationalize their antiviral supplies during a pandemic. Even if the medicine were available, most countries could not afford to buy it. Critical antibiotics, for treatment of secondary bacterial infections, would also be in short supply during a pandemic. Even now, supplies of eight different anti-infective agents are limited in the United States due to manufacturing problems.

Aside from medication, many countries would not have the ability to meet the surge in the demand for health-care supplies and services that are normally taken for granted. In the United States, for example, there are 105,000 mechanical ventilators, 75,000 to 80,000 of which are in use at any given time for everyday medical care. During a routine influenza season, the number of ventilators being used shoots up to 100,000. In an influenza pandemic, the United States may need as many as several hundred thousand additional ventilators.

A similar situation exists in all developed countries. Virtually every piece of medical equipment or protective gear would be in short supply within days of the recognition of a pandemic. Throughout the crisis, many of these necessities would simply be unavailable for most health-care institutions. Currently, two U.S.-based companies supply most of the respiratory protection masks for health-care workers around the world. Neither company would be able to meet the jump in demand, in part because the component parts for the masks come from multiple suppliers in multiple countries. With travel and transportation restricted, masks may not even be produced at all.

Health-care providers and managed-care organizations are also unprepared for an outbreak of pandemic influenza today. There would be a tremendous demand for skilled health professionals. New "hospitals" in high school gymnasiums and community centers would have to be staffed for one to three years. Health-care workers would

Preparing for the Next Pandemic

probably get sick and die at the same rate as the general public—perhaps at an even higher rate, particularly if they lack access to protective equipment. If they lack such fundamental supplies, it is unclear how many professionals would continue to place themselves in high-risk situations by caring for the infected. Volunteers who are naturally immune as a result of having survived influenza infection would thus have to be found and employed. That means that the medical community's strong resistance to using lay volunteers, which is grounded in both liability concerns and professional hubris, would need to be addressed.

Other unpleasant issues would also need to be tackled. Who would have priority access to the extremely limited antiviral supplies? The public would consider any ad hoc prioritization unfair, creating further dissent and disruption during a pandemic. In addition, there would not even be detailed plans for handling the massive number of dead bodies that would soon outstrip the ability to process them. Clearly, an influenza pandemic that struck today would demand an unprecedented medical and nonmedical response. This requires planning well beyond anything devised thus far by any of the world's countries and organizations.

A YEAR FROM NOW

EVEN IF an H5N1 pandemic is a year away, the world must plan for the same problems with the same fervor. Major campaigns must be initiated to prepare the nonmedical and medical sectors. Pandemic planning must be on the agenda of every school board, manufacturing plant, investment firm, mortuary, state legislature, and food distributor in the United States and beyond. There is an urgent need to reassess the vulnerability of the global economy to ensure that surges in demand can be met. Critical heath-care and consumer products and commodities must be stockpiled. Health professionals must learn how to better communicate risk and must be able to both provide the facts and acknowledge the unknowns to a frightened or panicked population.

If there is a year of lead-time before an H5N1 pandemic, vaccine could play a more central role in the global response. Although the world would still have a limited capacity to manufacture influenza vaccine, techniques that could allow scientists to get multiple doses from a current single dose may increase the supply. In addition to

Michael T. Osterholm

further research on this issue, efforts are needed to ensure the availability of syringes and equipment for delivering vaccine. There must also be an international plan for how the vaccine would be allocated. It is far better to struggle with the ethical issues involved in determining such priorities now, in a public forum, rather than to wait until the crisis occurs.

Prevention must also be improved. Priority should be placed on early intervention and risk assessment. And an aggressive and comprehensive research agenda must be launched immediately to study the ecology and biology of the influenza virus and the epidemiologic role of various animal and bird species.

TEN YEARS LATER

IF DEVELOPED countries begin to transform radically the current system of influenza-vaccine production, an influenza pandemic ten years from now could have a much less devastating outcome. The industrialized world must initiate an international project to develop the ability to produce a vaccine for the entire global population within several months of the start of a pandemic. The initiative must be a top priority of the group of seven industrialized nations plus Russia (G-8), because almost nothing could inflict more death and disruption than a pandemic influenza.

The current BioShield law and additional legislation recently submitted to Congress will act to enhance the availability of vaccines in the United States. This aim is laudable, but it does little to address international needs. The ultimate goal must be to develop a new cell-culture vaccine or comparable vaccine technology that works on all influenza subtypes and that can be made available on short notice to all the people of the world.

WHAT COURSE TO TAKE?

THE WORLD must form a better understanding of the potential for the emergence of a pandemic influenza strain. A pandemic is coming. It could be caused by H5N1 or by another novel strain. It could happen tonight, next year, or even ten years from now.

Preparing for the Next Pandemic

The signs are alarming: the number of human and animal H5N1 infections has been increasing; small clusters of cases have been documented, suggesting that the virus may have come close to sustained human-to-human transmission; and H5N1 continues to evolve in the virtual genetic reassortment laboratory provided by the unprecedented number of people, pigs, and poultry in Asia. The population explosion in China and other Asian countries has created an incredible mixing vessel for the virus. Consider this sobering information: the most recent influenza pandemic, of 1968–69, emerged in China, when its population was 790 million; today it is 1.3 billion. In 1968, the number of pigs in China was 5.2 million; today it is 508 million. The number of poultry in China in 1968 was 12.3 million; today it is 13 billion. Changes in other Asian countries are similar. Given these developments, as well as the exponential growth in foreign travel over the past 50 years, an influenza pandemic could be more devastating than ever before.

Can disaster be avoided? The answer is a qualified yes. Although a coming pandemic cannot be avoided, its impact can be considerably lessened. It depends on how the leaders of the world—from the heads of the G-8 to local officials—decide to respond. They must recognize the economic, security, and health threat that the next influenza pandemic poses and invest accordingly. Each leader must realize that even if a country has enough vaccine to protect its citizens, the economic impact of a worldwide pandemic will inflict substantial pain on everyone. The resources required to prepare adequately will be extensive. But they must be considered in light of the cost of failing to invest: a global economy that remains in a shambles for several years.

This is a critical point in history. Time is running out to prepare for the next pandemic. We must act now with decisiveness and purpose. Someday, after the next pandemic has come and gone, a commission much like the 9/11 Commission will be charged with determining how well government, business, and public health leaders prepared the world for the catastrophe when they had clear warning. What will be the verdict?●

[17]

Should HIV/AIDS Be Securitized? The Ethical Dilemmas of Linking HIV/AIDS and Security

STEFAN ELBE

University of Sussex

Should the global AIDS pandemic be framed as an international security issue? Drawing on securitization theory, this article argues that there is a complex normative dilemma at the heart of recent attempts to formulate the global response to HIV/AIDS in the language of international security. Although "securitizing" the AIDS pandemic could bolster international AIDS initiatives by raising awareness and resources, the language of security simultaneously pushes responses to the disease away from civil society toward military and intelligence organizations with the power to override the civil liberties of persons living with HIV/AIDS. The security framework, moreover, brings into play a "threat-defense" logic that could undermine international efforts to address the pandemic because it makes such efforts a function of narrow national interest rather than of altruism, because it allows states to prioritize AIDS funding for their elites and armed forces who play a crucial role in maintaining security, and because portraying the illness as an overwhelming "threat" works against ongoing efforts to normalize social perceptions regarding HIV/AIDS. These overlooked dangers give rise to a profound ethical dilemma as to whether or not the global AIDS pandemic should be portrayed as a security issue. The article concludes that securitization theory cannot resolve this complex dilemma, but that raising awareness of its presence does allow policy makers, activists, and scholars to begin drawing the links between HIV/AIDS and security in ways that at least minimize some of these dangers.

Now in its third decade, HIV/AIDS is well poised to become one of the most devastating pandemics in modern history. Over the next years, many of the 42 million people living with HIV around the world will unfortunately join the 25 million who have already succumbed to AIDS-related illnesses. Every day the pandemic continues to kill three times as many people than died during the terrorist attacks of September 11, 2001, not least because in some southern African countries national HIV prevalence rates presently exceed a third of the adult population. Nor is the growth potential of the AIDS pandemic exhausted, as HIV rapidly

Author's note: This article was first presented at the 44th Annual Convention of the International Studies Association, Portland, Oregon, February 2003. The author would like to thank members of the Africa Research Group at the London School of Economics, members of the Security Research Group at the University of Wales, Aberystwyth, members of the Africa Research Group at King's College, London, participants in the Twenty-First Century Trust Conference on Disease and Security, as well as Andrew Price-Smith, Robert Ostergard Jr., Alex de Waal, Christopher Coker, Louiza Odysseos, and three anonymous reviewers for their valuable feedback on previous versions of this article.

spreads in parts of Asia, Latin America, the Caribbean, Russia, and Eastern Europe (Eberstadt 2002; Grisin and Wallander 2002; National Intelligence Council 2002). Scholars across a plethora of disciplines, ranging from economics and sociology to development studies and social policy, have rightly recognized that the effects of this pandemic will not be confined to individual human tragedies; HIV/AIDS will have a host of wider political, economic, and social ramifications around the globe that will need to be carefully considered and addressed (Garrett 1994; Bloom and Godwin 1997; Linge and Porter 1997; Godwin 1998; Hope 1999; Whiteside and Sunter 2000; Barnett and Whiteside 2002; Holden 2003; Seckinelgin 2003; Kalipeni 2004; Kauffman and Lindauer 2004). Despite the international scope of the AIDS pandemic, and the growing involvement of a number of prominent international organizations in its management, the discipline of international relations still lags notably behind many of these related fields in studying these effects.[1] Only very recently has the AIDS pandemic begun to make inroads into the core of the field through the efforts of a small group of scholars exploring the implications of the pandemic for international security (Ostergard 2005).

This article wishes to expand the discipline's engagement with the global AIDS pandemic by opening up a novel, normative debate on HIV/AIDS and security. It does so through identifying and outlining a complex ethical dilemma at the heart of recent attempts to frame the global AIDS pandemic as a security issue. On the one hand, a successful "securitization"[2] of HIV/AIDS could accrue vital economic, social, and political benefits for millions of affected people by raising awareness of the pandemic's debilitating global consequences and by bolstering resources for international AIDS initiatives. These benefits cannot be easily dismissed and make a strong case in favor of presenting HIV/AIDS as a security issue. Through the novel application of securitization theory, however, this article also shows how such use of security language is simultaneously accompanied by two very serious and hitherto overlooked normative dangers. First, the securitization of HIV/AIDS could push national and international responses to the disease away from civil society toward state institutions such as the military and the intelligence community with the power to override human rights and civil liberties—including those of persons living with HIV/AIDS. Second, the language of security also brings a "threat-defense" logic to bear on HIV/AIDS, which may ultimately prove counterproductive to international efforts to stem the pandemic because (i) this logic makes such efforts not a function of altruism but of more restrictive and narrow national interests, (ii) because it allows states to prioritize AIDS funding for their armed forces and elites who play a crucial role in maintaining security, and (iii) because the portrayal of the illness as an overwhelming security "threat" works against the efforts of many grassroots AIDS activists seeking to normalize social perceptions regarding persons living with HIV/AIDS. These dangers in turn strongly caution against framing HIV/AIDS as a security issue, giving rise to a profound ethical dilemma at the heart of recent efforts to securitize the global AIDS pandemic. The article concludes that securitization theory cannot, in the end, resolve this complex dilemma, but raising awareness of its presence does allow policy makers, activists, and scholars to begin drawing the links between security and HIV/AIDS in ways that at least minimize some of these dangers.

---

[1] For two rare attempts to probe the implications of health for international relations, see Fidler (1998) and Youde (2005).

[2] The term securitization refers to the process whereby HIV/AIDS is presented by officials of national and international institutions not just as a health or development issue, but also as a pressing matter of national and international security requiring the adoption of emergency measures. See also the more detailed discussion of securitization in "Securitization Theory and HIV/AIDS" of this article.

HIV/AIDS and Security: The Need for a Normative Debate

HIV/AIDS is increasingly being portrayed by a range of international organizations, national governments, non-governmental organizations, and scholars of international relations as having important security implications. This was not always so. In the first two decades since the discovery of HIV/AIDS in the mid-1980s, the disease was conceptualized primarily as a public health and development issue. Although the links between HIV/AIDS and security were sporadically explored in the 1990s by a small number of analysts in the U.S. Central Intelligence Agency and in some security think tanks, the major international turning point in terms of conceptualizing HIV/AIDS as a security issue did not occur until 2000. On January 10 of that year, at the behest of U.S. Ambassador Richard Holbrook and Vice-President Al Gore, the United Nations Security Council officially designated HIV/AIDS as a threat to international peace and security in Africa.[3] It was an immensely symbolic occasion because this was the first meeting of the Council in the new millennium and because it was the first time in the Council's history that it had designated a health issue as a threat to international security. In his position as president of the World Bank, James Wolfensohn (2000) argued on this occasion that "[m]any of us used to think of AIDS as a health issue. We were wrong. . . . Nothing we have seen is a greater challenge to the peace and stability of African societies than the epidemic of AIDS. . . . We face a major development crisis, and more than that, a security crisis." The meeting was accompanied by the declassification of a National Intelligence Estimate entitled *The Global Infectious Disease Threat and Its Implications for the United States*. This estimate spelled out the debilitating impact of HIV/AIDS and other infectious diseases on U.S. national security in sufficient detail to merit the Clinton administration's designation of HIV/AIDS as a threat to the national security of the United States in the spring of that same year.[4] The securitization of HIV/AIDS had begun in earnest.

Since that watershed meeting, there have been a plethora of reports and scholarly studies mapping out the implications of HIV/AIDS for security in greater detail. These studies have sought to assess empirically the multiple ways in which HIV/AIDS has ramifications for human security[5] (Kristoffersson 2000; Fourie and Schönteich 2001; Piot 2001; Chen 2003; Leen 2004), national security (Price-Smith 1998, 2001, 2002; Harker 2001; Heinecken 2001a; Yeager and Kingma 2001; CSIS 2002; Ostergard 2002; Sarin 2003), and international security (National Intelligence Council 2000; Singer 2002; Elbe 2003; Prins 2004).[6] They argue that the social, economic, and political stability of communities (and even entire states) can be undermined in the long run by HIV prevalence rates ranging between 10% and 40% of the adult population (ICG 2001; Pharaoh and Schönteich 2003; ICG 2004), that in some African armed forces HIV prevalence rates are estimated to be between 40% and 60%, raising concerns about their combat effectiveness (Heinecken 2001b; Mills 2000; Elbe 2002), and that HIV/AIDS even has important ramifications for international peacekeeping operations, which because they are staffed by members of these same armed forces, can serve as a vector of the illness where and

---

[3] For an account of the genesis of this meeting, see Sternberg (2002).

[4] That same year, the Clinton administration also invoked national security justifications for other non-military purposes, such as granting China "normal" trading status with the United States. Several decades earlier, in 1955, Dwight Eisenhower had similarly tried to promote his administration's National System of Interstate and Defense Highways on the basis of a national security justification, arguing that such a highway network would be essential for evacuation plans and mobilizing defenses. See Sanger (2000).

[5] For competing definitions of "human security," see United Nations Development Program (United Nations Development Program 1994); Commission on Human Security (2003); and the special issue of *Security Dialogue* (Vol. 35, No. 3: September 2004) on human security.

[6] I have explored competing definitions and meanings of human, national, and international security, as well as the ways in which HIV/AIDS bears on them, in greater detail in Elbe (2005). For other accounts of human and national security, see Fidler (2003) and Peterson (2002/2003).

when they are deployed (Bazergan 2001, 2003; U.S. Government Accountability Office 2001; Bratt 2002; Tripodi and Patel 2002). Although a few scholars (David 2001; Mock 2002; Peterson 2002/2003; Elbe 2003; Bazergan 2003) have since begun to raise questions about the unproblematic way in which some of these empirical relationships are increasingly posited, arguments about the security implications of HIV/AIDS have clearly not fallen on deaf ears. "The national security dimension of the virus is plain," the Director of the Central Intelligence Agency (Tenet 2003) could be heard arguing before a Senate intelligence panel in 2003, "[i]t can undermine economic growth, exacerbate social tensions, diminish military preparedness, create huge social welfare costs, and further weaken already beleaguered states." The United Nations Security Council, moreover, has held three further meetings on HIV/AIDS subsequent to its first one in January 2000 and is planning to have further meetings on this issue in the future—rendering the AIDS pandemic the latest in a long line of wider social issues to become framed as an international security concern.

Despite the evident importance of continuing to empirically assess the security implications of HIV/AIDS, the debate about HIV/AIDS and security cannot be conducted on such narrow empirical grounds alone. This debate urgently needs to be widened because recent attempts to bring the language and analytic apparatus of international security to bear on the global AIDS pandemic raise equally important normative questions about the long-term benefits and drawbacks of using such a security framework to respond to the disease. Amidst the pressing efforts to assess the complex impact of HIV/AIDS on international security, scholars and policy makers in this area have yet to engage in a more comprehensive, systematic, and open debate about the ethical tradeoffs inherent in pursuing such a strategy.[7] This is a striking silence, given that normative concerns clearly form an integral part of the debate about HIV/AIDS and security, never lurking far from its surface. Many of those drawing the links between HIV/AIDS and security do so instrumentally in the hope that this will accrue important humanitarian benefits by bolstering international efforts to combat the spread of the disease. Peter W. Singer (2002:158) argues that presenting HIV/AIDS as a security threat "strengthens the call for serious action against the menace of AIDS. It is not just a matter of altruism, but simple cold self-interest." Many policy makers agree, including the director of the Joint United Nations Program on HIV/AIDS (UNAIDS), who has similarly argued (Piot 2000) that framing HIV/AIDS as a security issue is not merely an academic exercise but "defines how we respond to the epidemic, how much is allocated to combating it, and what sectors of government are involved in the response." In the debate on HIV/AIDS and security, scholarly interest in understanding the wider social dynamics of the AIDS pandemic frequently goes hand-in-hand with an underlying normative commitment to scaling up international efforts to respond to the disease.

This progressive belief in the humanitarian benefits of framing HIV/AIDS as a security issue has not gone entirely unchallenged, however. Taking her cue from earlier debates seeking to link environmental concerns with national security, Susan Peterson (2002/2003:81) has warned that "[i]f well-intentioned people seek to rally support among western governments for anti-AIDS efforts in Africa, portraying disease as a security issue may be exactly the wrong strategy to employ." In her view, such a strategy is unlikely to achieve its objectives because the empirical security implications of HIV/AIDS for the United States are insufficiently strong to motivate a sustained commitment to the issue, and because such a strategy may even begin to trigger novel security dilemmas, fueling further suspicion and rivalry between states, rather than encouraging the more open and multilateral policy approaches needed to address the illness on a global scale. Moreover, even in

---

[7] For two notable exceptions, see the brief discussion in Altman (2000) and Peterson (2002/2003).

heavily affected countries, she finds that these security implications pale in comparison with the much more pressing impact of HIV/AIDS on health, human rights, and development, as well as social and economic justice—making these alternative, non-security framings much more fruitful to pursue in the long run.[8] Crucially, however, Peterson does not only challenge the political efficacy of using security language; in the conclusion to her article she also begins to raise important *normative* reservations about the long-term effects of pursuing such language in relation to HIV/AIDS. Rather than bolstering international efforts to reduce the spread of the disease, she is concerned that such moves may paradoxically end up absolving states from any moral responsibility to react to diseases in the developing world that do not engage their essential national interests. Instead of going through the complicated and ambiguous route of securitizing AIDS, the world should instead "face AIDS for what it is and will be for the foreseeable future—a health tragedy of unprecedented and staggering proportions that cries out for international and transnational humanitarian assistance, not for the garrisoning of states behind national boundaries and national security rhetoric (Peterson 2002/2003:81)." Peterson thus raises for the first time the possibility that the normative aspects involved in framing HIV/AIDS as a security issue may be much more complex and complicated than has hitherto been assumed by participants in the debate, and hence require further analysis.

A more detailed exploration on the ethical implications of securitizing HIV/AIDS becomes unavoidable, then, for at least two reasons. First, as is the case with so many discussions revolving around this highly politicized illness, the debate on the security implications of HIV/AIDS is already deeply invested and infused with a host of subtle normative commitments that need to be brought to the fore and debated more openly.[9] Second, as Peterson's intervention shows, strongly divergent views about the ethical consequences of framing HIV/AIDS as a security issue are beginning to emerge, necessitating more systematic attention to the possible benefits and drawbacks of framing the disease in this manner. Over the past decade, such normative debates have proved similarly unavoidable in relation to a wide variety of other non-military issues framed by the international community as security concerns—ranging from the environment (Deudney 1990; Kakonen 1994; Litfin 1999; Ney 1999; Ostrauskaite 2001) and migration (Weiner 1992/1993; Wæver et al. 1993; Huysmans 1995, 2000; Bigo 1998; Doty 1998; Ceyhan and Tsoukala 2002), to the "war on drugs" (Husak 1992; Aradau 2001), transnational crime (Emmers 2003), and even development more generally (Duffield 2001). Given the growing policy resonance of arguments about the security implications of HIV/AIDS, the time has come to reflect more thoroughly on how such a framing of the pandemic could facilitate international efforts to reduce its spread and how this framing might also be counterproductive to these efforts. This is undoubtedly an enormous task encompassing a multiplicity of actors, issues, and arguments, and one that easily exceeds the limits of a single article; yet it is a task that must be begun if the discipline of international relations is not to restrict itself to merely tracing the impact of HIV/AIDS on international security, but to also actively contribute to finding the most appropriate ways for international political actors to respond to the pandemic.

Securitization Theory and HIV/AIDS

How, then, does one begin such a normative debate? Even though there has been an immense resurgence in normative theorizing in international relations over the

---

[8] These arguments closely parallel those in Deudney (1990).

[9] For more general reflections on the normative questions the AIDS pandemic gives rise to, see Harris and Siplon (2001), and the special section on "Health and Global Justice" in *Ethics and International Affairs* 16 (2), Fall 2002. For pieces on the ethics of conducting research into HIV/AIDS see Kesby (2004) and Craddock (2004).

past decade (Brown 1992, 2002; Nardin and Mapel 1993; Bonanate, Puchala, and Kegley 1995; Frost 1996; Keim 2000; Seckinelgin and Shinoda 2001; Odysseos 2002, 2003), there has been markedly less engagement with the particular ethical tradeoffs involved in bringing the language of international security to bear on wider social issues. For those interested in such questions, the *locus classicus* has quickly become the influential study by Barry Buzan, Ole Wæver, and Jaap de Wilde (1998) entitled *Security: A New Framework for Analysis*.[10] Not only is the "securitization" theory presented in this framework widely considered to be among the most important, original, and controversial contributions to the field of security studies in recent years (Huysmans 1998:480), it also remains the only systematic scholarly study of the ethical implications of widening the security agenda to include an array of non-military issues—making it a natural starting point for a more sustained normative debate about the securitization of HIV/AIDS. Although securitization theory is not exclusively concerned with normative questions, and also has important analytical interests in tracing the detailed social processes through which security threats become constructed by political actors, it is predominantly this normative dimension of the framework that remains indispensable for opening up a wider ethical debate about framing HIV/AIDS as an international security issue.[11]

Indeed, securitization theory can address these normative questions more readily than many longer standing neorealist or neoliberal approaches to international security, because its constructivist account of security remains highly sensitive to the intersubjective and performative nature of portraying social issues as security concerns, that is, of "speaking" security.[12] Securitization theory forms part of a growing body of literature bringing the insights of speech act theory—as pioneered by J. L. Austin (1962) at Harvard University in the 1950s and subsequently developed by several other prominent philosophers and linguists (Searle 1969)—to bear on social and political analysis. Austin (1962:1) famously argued that the point of speech act theory was to challenge the assumption that "the business of a 'statement' can only be to 'describe' some state of affairs, or to 'state some fact,' which it must do either truly or falsely." Even though language certainly encodes information, speech act theory illustrates that language can also do much more than just convey information, and that even when it is used primarily to convey information, language often conveys more than just the literal meaning of the words. Austin became particularly interested in phrases that in themselves constitute a form of action or social activity, that is phrases such as saying "thank you," "you are fired," "I promise," "I bet," "I nominate," etc. These are instances in which a speaker is using language not just for the purposes of description, but also for actually *doing* something with considerable social significance—hence the term speech *acts*. In saying "thank you," for example, one is not making a statement that is either true or false, but is undertaking the act of thanking somebody.

By way of extension, for Buzan, Wæver, and de Wilde, labeling an issue a security issue also constitutes such a performative speech act. For them (1998:26) security "is not interesting as a sign referring to something more real; it is the utterance itself that is the act. By saying the words, something is done (like betting, giving a promise, naming a ship)." Security is thus not viewed by these three scholars as something that exists independently of its discursive articulation,[13] but rather as a particular

---

[10] See also Wæver (1995) and Williams (2003).

[11] A more comprehensive analysis of the securitizing actors, agendas, and strategies has already been undertaken by Sheehan (2002).

[12] In this way, their study forms part of a larger research effort to view security issues as being socially constructed. See, for example, Wendt (1992, 1999), Finnemore (1996), Katzenstein (1996), Adler (1997), Hopf (1998), Barnett and Finnemore (1999).

[13] On this point see also Hansen (2000:288).

form of performative speech act; security is a social quality political actors, such as intelligence agencies, government officials, and international organizations, inject into issues by publicly portraying them as existential threats (Buzan, Wæver, and de Wilde 1998:204). Whereas more traditional approaches to security operate within a specific definition of security, revolving for example around the deployment of armed force in world politics, and then seek to ascertain empirically whether an issue *genuinely* represents a security threat, for securitization theory the designation of an issue as a security threat is primarily an intersubjective practice undertaken by security policy makers. "It is a choice to phrase things in security . . . terms, not an objective feature of the issue . . . ." (Buzan, Wæver, and de Wilde 1998:211); or, as Wæver (1995:65) put it elsewhere, the "[u]se of the security label does not merely reflect whether a problem *is* a security problem, it is also a political choice, that is, a decision for conceptualization in a special way." The leader of a political party, for example, can choose whether to portray immigration as a security issue or as a human rights issue. Similarly, leaders of international organizations can choose whether they portray HIV/AIDS as a health issue, as a development issue, or, as they have done more recently, as an international security issue.

According to the framework of Buzan, Wæver, and de Wilde, the determination of which issues end up on the international security agenda cannot consequently be made solely on the basis of empirical criteria. Much security analysis entails making speculative predictions about future developments, necessitates prioritizing between competing claims with imperfect information, and, especially when it comes to wider social issues, requires deciding about whether an issue is best addressed under the heading of security rather than another competing framework. Inevitably, there is a considerable element of politics involved in determining how a social issue is presented in public debate. An issue can either remain non-politicized if it is not made an issue of public debate or decision, or it can become politicized if it is successfully made part of public policy and subject to a public decision. Finally, in the extreme case, an issue can become "securitized," by which Buzan, Wæver, and de Wilde (1998:23–24) mean very specifically that it is "presented as an existential threat requiring emergency measures and justifying actions outside the normal bounds of political procedure." The security quality of an issue thus does not reside for them in the nature of the issue itself or in the anticipated empirical effects of a particular phenomenon, but it derives from the specific way in which an issue or phenomenon is presented in public debate.

Buzan, Wæver, and de Wilde provide their framework with a high degree of analytical focus by further specifying the precise conditions that collectively make up this "security" speech act. Rather than addressing all instances in which the word "security" is used, or all wider calls for the adoption of emergency measures, securitization theory applies only to those issues that are presented according to the particular logic or grammar of the security speech act (Buzan, Wæver, and de Wilde 1998:25). The four constituent components of this security speech act (Buzan, Wæver, and de Wilde 1998:24, 36) are presence of the following: (i) *securitizing actors* (such as political leaders, intelligence experts, etc.), declaring (ii) a *referent object* (such as a state)[14] to be (iii) *existentially threatened* (e.g., by an immanent invasion),

---

[14] Referent objects of security do not necessarily have to be states or militaries, but more generally "things that are seen to be existentially threatened and that have a legitimate claim to survival" (Buzan, Wæver, and de Wilde 1998:36). Examples of this security grammar can thus be found operating both in regard to military issues and throughout the wider security agenda. For example, it is just as possible for non-governmental organizations (securitizing actors) to declare humanity or the biosphere (referent objects) existentially threatened by greenhouse gases, requiring drastic social changes. Of course, Buzan, Wæver, and de Wilde are aware that, in practice, there are important constraints on which actors can successfully securitize issues. Although it remains a theoretical possibility, they find that individuals and small groups of people are rarely able to establish a wider security legitimacy in their own right. Nevertheless, this flexibility in their framework in principle allows it to be applied to the wider security agenda, including HIV/AIDS, without losing analytic focus as a result.

and who make a persuasive call for the adoption of (iv) *emergency measures* to counter this threat (e.g., declare war or impose a curfew). The framework advanced by Buzan, Wæver, and de Wilde confines itself to analyzing only those issues—be they of a military or non-military nature—that are presented in a manner conforming to all four of these criteria. The term *securitization*, in turn, formally refers to the process whereby an issue is taken out of its non-politicized or politicized status and is elevated to the security sphere by portraying it in a way that meets these four criteria. This is precisely what has happened to the issue of HIV/AIDS in recent years, where arguments have shifted from humanitarian and public health ones to officials in international organizations, governments, and non-governmental organizations (*securitizing actors*) increasingly arguing that beyond these humanitarian considerations, the survival of communities, states, and militaries (*referent objects*) is now being undermined (*existentially threatened*), unless drastic measures (*emergency measures*) are undertaken by national and international actors to better address the global pandemic.[15] HIV/AIDS has become securitized.

This radically constructivist view of security also generates important new tasks for security analysts, who must now begin to reflect in greater depth on the normative consequences of securitizing a particular issue. "Our approach," Buzan, Wæver, and de Wilde (1998:212) insist, "has the basic merit of conceptualizing security as a labeling for which actors can be held responsible rather than an objective feature of threats"; securitization theory "serves to underline the responsibility of talking security, the responsibility of actors as well as of analysts who choose to frame an issue as a security issue. They cannot hide behind the claim that anything in itself constitutes a security issue (Buzan, Wæver, and de Wilde 1998:34)." Because security analysts have a choice about whether or not to present a given issue in the language of security, they need to reflect on the wider consequences of doing so. This also means that the debate about HIV/AIDS and security cannot be waged solely on empirical grounds; for if there is an inevitable choice to "speaking" security in relation to HIV/AIDS, then the debate about the security implications of the disease will remain incomplete, unless the wider normative implications of using such language are assessed as well. Securitization theory was designed with a view to this very task; with its help "it is possible to ask with some force whether it is a good idea to make this issue a security issue—to transfer it to the agenda of panic politics—or whether it is better handled within normal politics" (Buzan, Wæver, and de Wilde 1998:34). Yet because the global AIDS pandemic was securitized only after the publication of their study, this line of inquiry has not yet been pursued specifically in relation to HIV/AIDS.

Raising this normative dimension is all the more important because Buzan, Wæver, and de Wilde think scholars would be mistaken in simply assuming that bringing the language of security to bear on the growing number of social issues is always a favorable political development. After the end of the Cold War, some security scholars quickly faulted such an expansion of the international security agenda on the grounds of the inability of security studies to accommodate such a wide variety of issues without losing analytical focus as a result. Stephen Walt (1991:213) famously argued that expanding the field of security studies to include issues such as pollution, diseases, and economic recessions "would destroy its

---

[15] These specific and narrow criteria also set the securitization of HIV/AIDS distinctly apart from other emergency responses to HIV/AIDS that have occurred within the contexts of public health, development, or even disaster relief, such as the Ryan White Comprehensive AIDS Resource Emergency Act in the United States. The latter clearly calls for emergency measures that provide health care and support for those persons living with HIV/AIDS, whose health needs would otherwise remain unmet. This act, however, is not intended to protect the United States from an existential threat, but instead to "reduce the use of more costly inpatient care, increase access to care for underserved populations, and improve the quality of life for those affected by the epidemic" (U.S. Department of Health and Human Services 2005) In this case, there are no securitizing actors arguing that a referent object is existentially threatened.

intellectual coherence and make it more difficult to devise solutions to any of these important problems." From a different theoretical perspective, Daniel Deudney (1990:464) echoed that "[i]f everything that causes a decline in human well-being is labeled a 'security' threat, the term loses any analytical usefulness and becomes a loose synonym of 'bad'". Buzan, Wæver, and de Wilde, by contrast, have criticized such an expansion on different, normative grounds. Already on the first page of their study, they warn readers of serious intellectual and political dangers involved in securitizing social issues, and hence in widening the security agenda. "Basically, security should be seen as negative, as a failure to deal with issues as normal politics. Ideally, politics should be able to unfold according to routine procedures without this extraordinary elevation of specific 'threats' to prepolitical immediacy" (Buzan, Wæver, and de Wilde 1998:29; Williams 2003:523). In the conclusion to their study (1998:208), they again point to the dangers of securitization, insisting that "[a]voiding excessive and irrational securitization is thus a legitimate social, political, and economic objective of considerable importance." By highlighting the normative choices that are always involved in framing issues as security issues and by warning of potential dangers inherent in doing so, their framework marks an ideal starting point for a deeper debate on the ethical implications of using the language of international security to respond to the global AIDS pandemic.

The Dangers of Securitizing AIDS

What, then, are the specific normative dangers Buzan, Wæver, and de Wilde identify, and how do they pertain to the ongoing securitization of HIV/AIDS? Based on their selection of case studies, such as the securitization of migration in Europe in the 1990s, two general dangers emerge. Both of these dangers result from the unique connotations of the word "security," about which Wæver (1995:47) has observed elsewhere that it "carries with it a history and a set of connotations that it cannot escape. At the heart of the concept we still find something to do with defense and the state. As a result, addressing an issue in security terms still evokes an image of threat-defense, allocating to the state an important role in addressing it. This is not always an improvement." This passage expresses in summary form both the major normative concerns that securitization theorists have about securitization processes, namely that (i) these processes usually lead to a greater level of state mobilization, enabling the state to encroach on an increasing proportion of social life where it might not be desirable (Buzan, Wæver, and de Wilde 1998:4), and (ii) that the language of security attaches to issues a particular "threat-defense" logic that may not always be appropriate or beneficial for addressing these issues. It is worth exploring these two concerns in greater detail.

In many ways, this first concern about excessive state mobilization is deeply liberal, in that it assumes an a priori preference for a minimalist state that maximizes individual liberty, rather than for a state that is heavily involved in the management of social life. Although this is not explicitly mentioned in their framework, Buzan and Wæver have pointed to the liberal nature of such an objection elsewhere when they observe that classical liberalism can itself be understood as a project that seeks to narrow the range of things seen as security threats, so as to enlarge the realm of "normal politics" and to reduce as far as possible the areas of social life within which force could be used (Buzan and Wæver 1998:4; Buzan, Wæver, and de Wilde 1998:210). More specifically, Buzan, Wæver, and de Wilde wish to highlight two concrete threats to democratic politics inherent in using security language in order to incite state mobilization. First, states can use the language of security in order to remove an issue from routine democratic considerations and push it into the higher echelons of the state's inner circles of power, where there is less political transparency and hence also less democratic scrutiny of issues. Second, state representatives often also invoke the term "security" to justify the use of any necessary means to confront the threatening condition or to silence opposition to the state (Buzan, Wæver, and de Wilde 1998:21). Any emergency measures taken by the state can thus be used to override the rule of law and infringe upon valued civil liberties. Hence, Buzan, Wæver, and de Wilde (1998:29) are generally concerned about how the language of security has historically served to silence opposition to the state, how it has given state representatives special powers that could be exploited for domestic purposes, and how it can lead to the suspension of important democratic control mechanisms.

Even though this danger of excessive state involvement has not been hitherto acknowledged in the debate on AIDS and security, advocates of the securitization of HIV/AIDS will need to devote greater attention to this outcome of past securitization processes. In the case of HIV/AIDS, too, framing the issue as a security issue pushes responses to the disease away from civil society toward the much less transparent workings of military and intelligence organizations, which also possess the power to override human rights and civil liberties—including those of persons living with HIV/AIDS. One analyst (Chowka 2000) has pointed out that the designation of HIV/AIDS as a security issue is "a bit frightening and a bit scary ... [b]ecause that means you're going to begin to call in the FBI, you can call in the CIA. If people are talking about things which are decided to be a national security issue, they in fact can be spied upon and civil rights protections can be suspended." Not everyone would go this far, but it is certainly true that in the United States the armed forces and the CIA are becoming increasingly involved in assessing the security implications of HIV/AIDS. It is also true that historically state responses to the disease have frequently been undemocratic and have been characterized by periods of great insensitivity toward persons living with the virus. Calls for quarantining such people, subjecting them to various forms of violence, attempting to bar them from serving in state institutions, and refusing to issue visas to HIV-positive foreigners are only a few of the examples in which persons living with HIV/AIDS have been ostracized and even persecuted by some states for their illness. In the early stages of HIV/AIDS in the United States, Haitians were variously denied housing, required to undergo tests before entering the country, dismissed from jobs, and so forth. In Europe and Russia, moreover, many Africans were similarly targeted because of the perception that they were disease carriers (Schoepf 2004). Portraying HIV/AIDS as a national and international security threat risks fueling such exclusionary and dehumanizing responses and could serve as an implicit legitimization of any harsh or unjust "emergency" policies that states may adopt in relation to persons living with the virus. After all, examples of such measures are not confined to the dustbin of history. In the United States, the Institute of Medicine not long ago proposed a policy of introducing mandatory screening for tuberculosis—a common condition for people living with HIV—for immigrants from countries with high prevalence rates, and it even made the case in favor of linking the permanent residence card (green card) to taking preventative treatment (Coker 2003:2). As recently as February 2003, the British government similarly considered implementing compulsory HIV screening for prospective immigrants amid alleged worries that HIV-positive foreigners are traveling to the United Kingdom to seek treatment (Hinsliff 2003:2). Such moves undoubtedly justify the first normative concern of Buzan, Wæver, and de Wilde that the involvement of the state in the management of wider social issues can also have detrimental effects in terms of placing the management of such an issue behind closed doors, and by paving the way for civil liberties to be overridden if this is deemed necessary by the state.[16]

---

[16] Indeed, this danger is not only inherent in relations between the state and the civilian population, but also *within* state institutions, such as the armed forces. In many of the world's armed forces, security arguments have already been cited for no longer accepting HIV-positive applicants for service.

Participants in this debate will also need to reflect more deeply on the second danger inherent in their efforts to portray the pandemic as an international security issue, namely that such efforts bring the unique "threat-defense" logic of security to bear on an ever-growing range of social issues. Buzan, Wæver, and de Wilde observe on a deeper level how the immense increase in the number of securitization processes occurring over the past decade collectively construes the notion of "security" as a universally good thing—as a desirable condition toward which to push all social relations. The cumulative social effect of this proliferation of securitization processes, of which HIV/AIDS is only the latest manifestation, is thus to convey the impression that working toward a condition of security is always socially beneficial—that "more security" is always better. Buzan, Wæver, and de Wilde (1998:29) find this to be a dangerously narrow view, because the connotations of security also attach a specific "threat-defense" logic to issues that may not always be appropriate or beneficial for their resolution.

This too is a valid normative concern in the case of HIV/AIDS, where the "threat-defense" logic entailed in the language of security can have three detrimental consequences. First, the securitization of the disease removes the issue from the more cosmopolitan and altruistic frameworks of health and development, locating it instead within a state-centric framework, where states are primarily concerned with maximizing power and security, rather than with addressing wider humanitarian concerns. In such a context, national and international action taken on HIV/AIDS is likely to be confined to those instances where it touches upon the selfish security interests of states. States may take action to defend their core security interests, but they are unlikely to undertake measures extending much beyond these narrow concerns. As Susan Peterson points out, responding to HIV/AIDS as a security issue transforms the logic of international action on HIV/AIDS into one based on narrow self-interest, which historically has not proved very effective in terms of addressing global health issues. Indeed it creates the impression that global health issues are not worth addressing in their own right, but only to the extent that they touch upon the core security interests of states, which may mean that in the long run, states will cease to be concerned about global health in areas where it does not concern their core national security interests (Peterson 2002/2003:46, 80). This is an important side effect of the language of security that needs to be borne in mind by those drawing the links between HIV/AIDS and security.

A second and closely related effect of the "threat-defense" logic in the case of HIV/AIDS is that it may adversely shift the identification of national and international funding priorities. Within a security framework, concern about HIV/AIDS will not revolve primarily around how HIV/AIDS affects civilian populations, but around how it affects the core institutions of the state, including the armed forces. In low-income countries in particular, this may mean that scarce resources for medicines are provided on a priority basis to the armed forces and state elites rather than to civilian populations as a whole, or, in the worst case, are diverted from civilian programs to military programs as a result of the portrayal of HIV/AIDS as a security issue. Examples of the latter have not yet been officially documented by NGOs or civil-society organizations, but there is certainly evidence that in many countries members of the armed forces routinely enjoy preferential access to medicines vis-à-vis the civilian population, or have at least moved to the front of the line in terms of receiving access to expensive antiretroviral medicines (ARVs). In Zambia, for example, members of the military have begun to argue that the armed forces should have priority access to more government funding for ARVs, because the military and their families are more at risk because of the nature of their job and because this would contribute to world peace (Allocate More ARVs to Military Personnel, 2003). Similarly, in Rwanda, high-ranking officers increasingly have access to ARVs, but the general population does not (Amnesty International 2004). This is part of a wider development in Africa, whereby the soldiers of many countries now have greater or better access to health care and AIDS medicines than the civilian population.[17] As Radhika Sarin (in Conklin 2003) argues, "quite a few African militaries are committed to providing treatment for their soldiers, such as the Ugandan People's Defense Forces and Nigeria's Armed Forces. These militaries do try and work with military spouses and civilian communities to provide HIV prevention education. However, access to antiretrovirals is very low in many African nations." The portrayal of HIV/AIDS as a security issue thus plays into the hands of those who already have the greatest chances of access to medicines, rather than into the hands of those who are currently least likely to receive such access. Indeed, it may inadvertently help to ensure that soldiers and elites who play a crucial role in the maintenance of national and international security receive access to treatment, without being able to ensure that such treatment is also provided democratically and universally to all who need it. This too is an important normative drawback that needs to be reflected upon in a more sustained manner.

Finally, the "threat-defense" logic inherent in the securitization of HIV/AIDS also works against the grassroots efforts undertaken by many non-governmental organizations and AIDS charities over the past decade in terms of normalizing societal attitudes regarding people living with HIV/AIDS. The goal of many of these groups has been to move away from the perception that people living with HIV/AIDS are dangerous "outsiders" and a threat to society. Rather than avoiding contact with such persons in the quest to be completely safe and secure from the virus, what is needed instead is more tolerance and a better understanding of the illness. Already in the 1980s the writer Susan Sontag described how the view of disease as "invader" is a perennial feature of many public pronouncements about the "war on AIDS," and she famously made the case for abandoning the military metaphor—both in terms of portraying the illness as something that invades the person and that invades entire societies. She (1998:94) felt that the military metaphor "overmobilizes" and "powerfully contributes to the excommunicating and stigmatizing of the ill." In such a context, a strategy of normalization can, from an ethical standpoint grounded in the lived experiences of those living with HIV/AIDS, easily be seen as highly advantageous in terms of cultivating a more inclusive and supportive public posture toward those persons. Ongoing efforts to securitize HIV/AIDS, by contrast, once again work against this goal by portraying the illness as a destructive and debilitating threat, and risk reversing important advances made to date regarding societal attitudes about the illness. In this way, the language of security deployed in international organizations also has important implications at the grassroots level.

The contribution, then, that securitization theory can make toward an ethical debate about whether the global AIDS pandemic should be framed as a security issue is not just methodological but also substantive. While its unique methodological standpoint highlights particularly clearly the choice that analysts have in terms of whether they frame issues such as HIV/AIDS in security terms, its wider normative concerns about excessive state mobilization and its questioning of the usefulness of using the "threat-defense" logic of security to respond to a growing range of social issues help to highlight important and previously overlooked normative dangers inherent in the ongoing securitization of HIV/AIDS—and this despite the fact that securitization theory was formulated well in advance of these more recent efforts. It is also precisely because of such dangers that Buzan, Wæver, and de Wilde (1998:4) generally do not believe that scholars should eagerly rush to publicly present an ever-growing range of issues as security issues; they should aim instead for "desecuritization," that is for shifting issues out of the emergency mode and returning them to routine political processes. Securitization theory thus compels those linking HIV/AIDS and security to think more deeply about whether,

---

[17] For a more comprehensive list of medical provision for HIV/AIDS in the civilian and military populations of African countries, see www.uniformservices.unaids.org/

upon reflection, such efforts should best be abandoned, resisted, and reversed because of these adverse effects. At this stage, the answer to the question of whether HIV/AIDS should be securitized might well be "no." As the next section illustrates, however, such a conclusion would be premature, because in the case of HIV/AIDS, uncovering these ethical dangers does not mark the end of the normative debate about its securitization, but only the beginning of a much more complex and complicated ethical terrain that begins to unfold.

The Benefits of Securitizing AIDS

Taking securitization theory's ethical imperative seriously also necessitates reflecting on the possible benefits a successful securitization of HIV/AIDS could have for persons living with the illness. Buzan, Wæver, and de Wilde (1998:29) insist that although desecuritization remains the abstract ideal of their framework, "one has to weigh the always problematic side effects of applying a mind-set of security against the possible advantages of focus, attention, and mobilization." Pursuing this line of thought shows that the ethical concerns identified above in fact only apply in a qualified manner in the case of HIV/AIDS and that they also have to be balanced with a plethora of competing political, economic, and legal advantages that a successful securitization of the AIDS pandemic could accrue for persons living with HIV/AIDS. For example, although the concern raised by Buzan, Wæver, and de Wilde about excessive state mobilization certainly resonates within the context of a liberal democracy where the state should, *ceteris paribus*, not seek to forcefully interfere with democratic deliberation processes, outside the context of Western democracies, the relationship between state, society, and security is often more complex, so their findings in this regard may consequently be less readily applicable.

In some of the countries most seriously affected by the AIDS pandemic, it is not excessive state mobilization that poses the main problem, but, on the contrary, the utter absence of a meaningful state response to the disease. In several southern African countries there is a widespread desire among persons living with HIV/AIDS for more action to be taken to ensure the provision of medicines—a prominent example of which is the Treatment Action Campaign in South Africa.[18] In many other African countries there are millions of people who do not even have the privilege of being informed about this illness, let alone knowing whether they have contracted the virus or not; yet, their governments remain unable or unwilling to demonstrate leadership on the issue, or to make such medical provisions, or even to prioritize their illness politically. Over the past years, Thabo Mbeki's refusal to instruct the South African government to prioritize efforts to address the AIDS pandemic has been a case in point and continues to receive widespread media attention. It is, unfortunately, only one case among many. Because of the stigmatized nature of the illness, and the long illness cycle, the strategy of denial has been particularly convenient for many governments to pursue in the past, albeit with catastrophic social consequences. What is more, many scholars and AIDS activists view the minimalist (neoliberal) state promoted in Africa through the structural adjustment programs favored by several international political and financial institutions over the past decade as part of the underlying structural conditions facilitating the emergence of the AIDS pandemic, and as contributing to the limited health care infrastructure currently available in many of the countries seriously affected by HIV/AIDS (Lurie 2004). In such a context, where a devastating illness remains largely ignored by states and where a minimalist conception of the state promoted by the international community is not helping the situation, the concern of many political AIDS activists understandably does not revolve around fears of

---

[18] For a good overview, see Sell and Prakash (2004).

excessive state mobilization, but, on the contrary, around the utter absence of adequate state involvement. What is needed is an urgent attempt by the international community and by governments to respond to the disease, which is what those framing HIV/AIDS as a security issue are actively trying to provoke.

The securitization of HIV/AIDS through the United Nations Security Council, because of its high public profile and unique status in international law, is one way of working toward this goal; it tries to increase the political pressure on governments to begin addressing the issue in a way that would help to ensure the survival of millions of persons living with HIV/AIDS, and it tries to encourage them to do so through early and prompt responses to the pandemic. Thus, where Buzan, Wæver, and de Wilde see dangers to democracy emanating from securitization processes because of the potentially oppressive role they accord to the security institutions of states, for some AIDS activists, compelling states hitherto unresponsive to the needs of their people into greater action is an equally important political goal with a strong democratic dimension. However imperfect, it is a way of representing the ignored political voice of those with HIV/AIDS at the highest levels of government.[19] Speaking at the UN Security Council in January 2001, Dr. Peter Piot, Executive Director of UNAIDS (2001), argued that "[t]he simple fact that the Security Council regards AIDS as a significant problem sends a powerful message: AIDS is a serious matter for the global community." In the case of HIV/AIDS, then, the key normative question does not revolve around the quantity or intensity of state involvement, because some state involvement is undoubtedly needed, but around the mode and nature of such state responses.[20] Securitization, in this instance, is not intended to remove the issue of HIV/AIDS from the political sphere and to shift it into the security sphere, but instead to shift it out of its non-politicized status in many countries and to begin a proper politicization of the issue.

By way of extension, where Buzan, Wæver, and de Wilde generally see dangers with pushing issues higher up the echelons of state bureaucracies—and thus away from civilian control—many AIDS activists see this as precisely what is needed for getting many African governments to undertake more sustained efforts and to commit more resources to addressing a pandemic that is already affecting more than 40 million people. To date, the securitization of AIDS at the international level has encouraged political actors to break the silence surrounding HIV/AIDS. For example, the Abuja Declaration on HIV/AIDS, Tuberculosis and other Related Infectious Diseases adopted by several African heads of state and by the Organisation of African Unity in 2001 reasoned that it was necessary to break the silence around HIV/AIDS because HIV/AIDS is not just a health issue, but also a threat to Africa's political stability, and that fighting illnesses such as HIV/AIDS must consequently form a part of Africa's strategy for ensuring durable peace and political security on the continent (OAU 2001). In some instances, moreover, the securitization of HIV/AIDS has also allowed states to shift responsibility for addressing the issue from ministries with only very little political clout to political bodies with greater influence on the political process. Denis Altman (2000) has observed that in countries such as Nigeria, Cote d'Ivoire, and South Africa, where health ministries only enjoy a modest degree of political influence and are perennially short of financial resources, the securitization of the pandemic has helped to move the issue higher up the political agenda, and HIV/AIDS has subsequently become the responsibility of ministries or committees with a greater degree of political clout

---

[19] This is part of deeper tension inherent in securitization theory. By grounding their normative framework in speech act theory, the framework encounters difficulties when dealing with social groups that are not able to voice their views due, for example, to political marginalization. On this point see Hansen (2000:287).

[20] Even among theorists of democracy, there is considerable disagreement regarding the role the state should perform in social life, with some models arguing in favor of a role restricted to the provision of security and with others suggesting that the state must make important social provisions and perform redistributive functions.

and with more resources at their disposal. By illustrating that HIV/AIDS is not only a humanitarian concern but also a security concern affecting the core institutions of states, the securitization of HIV/AIDS can increase the political priority accorded to the issue by governments, which in turn could benefit those living with HIV/AIDS if this is translated into the scaling up of treatment programs.

Finally, where Buzan, Wæver, and de Wilde point to the danger of security arguments being used to override the rule of law, and hence also to threaten civil liberties, from an economic perspective this ability of security concerns to override certain legal provisions is deemed to be a potential advantage. The patents on many AIDS medicines are presently protected by the World Trade Organization's Agreement on Trade-Related Aspects of Intellectual Property (TRIPS)—barring poorer countries from producing generic antiretroviral therapies and other medicines at lower prices, or even importing them from other countries who can procure them at lower costs. Those countries who try to circumvent these restrictions can subsequently be threatened with a variety of political, economic, and legal sanctions. In 1997, some 39 different pharmaceutical companies attempted to legally challenge the South African Medicines and Related Substances Control Amendment Act, which would have enabled South Africa to "parallel" import much cheaper generic HIV/AIDS medicines. The securitization of HIV/AIDS assists groups wishing to weaken the grip of patents on life-saving medicines because these patents could potentially be overridden in light of national security considerations. The TRIPS agreement contains an important set of "security exceptions," including Article 73(b), which notes that nothing contained in the agreement should be construed to "prevent a Member from taking any action which it considers necessary for the protection of its essential security interests" (World Trade Organization 1994). Although no dispute has yet occurred under Article 73 since the establishment of the World Trade Organization, the devastating social and economic impact of HIV/AIDS is raising the possibility of invoking these security provisions. A recent report by the United Nations (Roffe and Melendez-Ortiz 2005:10) has noted that it might be possible to invoke the security exceptions of TRIPS because "it could be argued that pandemics such as HIV affect a nation far beyond purely economic interests and might therefore justify action otherwise inconsistent with the TRIPS Agreement." If states do wish to override these patents on expensive life-saving medicines in the future, or at least maintain pressure on the pharmaceutical companies when negotiating prices, it will be essential for them to demonstrate that the AIDS pandemic constitutes an emergency affecting the security of states, especially as attempts to protect such access to medicines through widening the public health provisions of TRIPS agreed at Doha in 2001 are proving increasingly ineffective and are being actively side-stepped through bilateral free trade agreements (Oxfam 2004; Medecins Sans Frontieres 2005). Some participants in the United Nations Security Council debates on AIDS and international security have already been able to use that forum in order to make precisely this point. The Indian representative (Sharma 2001) has urged the Security Council, in line with its responsibility of maintaining international peace and security, "to rule that Article 73 of the TRIPS Agreement must be invoked to urgently provide affordable medicines that help in the treatment of the epidemic."

This legal dimension to the securitization of HIV/AIDS is becoming even more important because of the strong role that Indian pharmaceuticals have recently been playing in providing generic and affordable AIDS medicines to many developing countries. Because India's Patent Act of 1970 did not apply to medicines, Indian pharmaceuticals have been able to produce generic versions of AIDS drugs for some time. The pressure of their generic products has meant that prices for ARVs have dropped from over U.S.$10,000 annually to, in some instances, U.S.$140 annually, but this has only been possible because some of the provisions of the TRIPS agreement have hitherto not applied to India. What is more, Indian pharmaceuticals have also been at the forefront of developing the three-in-one cocktail pill, which means that patients only need to take two pills instead of six pills a day, making their administration considerably easier. However, as members of the Affordable Medicines and Treatment Campaign point out, India is in the process of changing its Patent Act in a way that would comply with TRIPS, which requires all governments to grant developed countries a 20-year monopoly patent on all essential medicines, including HIV/AIDS drugs. There are several proposed amendments to the Act that would potentially impede generic competition. If the supply of cheap Indian medicines dries up in the near future, this will make the ability to invoke the security exceptions of TRIPS all the more pressing (Grover 2004). In this way, the securitization of AIDS continues to play into the hands of those countries that might wish to invoke legal provisions necessary for procuring life-saving medicines at lower costs, maintaining background pressure on pharmaceutical companies. This illustrates how securitization processes can have normative benefits beyond merely raising attention and resources. Furthermore, it means that where Buzan, Wæver, and de Wilde—coming from a political perspective concerned with civil liberties—point to the dangers of security arguments being used to override the rule of law, from an economic perspective grounded in the attempts of poorer states to access cheap generic medicines, this same ability of security concerns to override legal provisions is deemed to be a crucial potential advantage, and something that the language of security can uniquely bring to the debate in a way that health or development language cannot. In either case, the point here is not that the concern of Buzan, Wæver, and de Wilde is not justified, but rather that in the context of HIV/AIDS, the advantages and disadvantages for those persons living with HIV/AIDS are much more evenly balanced than their normative criticism about excessive state involvement would initially seem to suggest.

The same is true regarding their other warning about the appropriateness of applying security's unique "threat-defense" logic to an ever-growing range of issues, such as HIV/AIDS. Although concern is clearly justified here as well, upon reflection, all three of the adverse side affects that this logic can have in the case of HIV/AIDS emerge in a much more complex form. The state-centric and self-interested nature of security, for example, is not seen by many of those advocating the links between HIV/AIDS and security as a drawback, but on the contrary, as an important asset that can mobilize global responses to HIV/AIDS. "It is a simple truth," Alex de Waal (2003) notes in reflecting on his experience with many African governments over the past decades, "that governments act when they perceive real threats to their power. This is a lesson from government famine prevention strategies: the political impulse is primary ... To date, few African governments have recognized the political threat posed by the HIV/AIDS pandemic." Where humanitarian development or other more altruistically inclined international initiatives have failed to generate sufficient political will and resources, for those advocating the HIV/AIDS-security nexus, the appeal to the naked self-interest of states is the only strategy left in light of the pressing daily humanitarian implications of the pandemic.

Indeed, appealing to the self-interest of states through the language of security can be economically useful in terms of increasing the amount of international attention the AIDS pandemic receives. Securitizing the illness could assist in freeing up more scarce resources for preventing the transmission of HIV in the future, as well as for purchasing medicines to treat those persons already suffering from AIDS. In the United States, arguments about the long-term security implications of AIDS reportedly already informed President Bush's decision to launch his five-year U.S.$ 15 billion Emergency Plan for AIDS Relief (Stolberg 2003).[21] There has been

---

[21] Another important factor was the push for action by evangelical Christian religious groups in the United States. See Burkhalter (2004).

much controversy about the strings attached to this money, about its emphasis on bilateral rather than multilateral programs, as well as the considerable delay in its appropriation, indicating that this was a shrewdly calculated political move, but such resources will undoubtedly be necessary for international efforts to respond to the global pandemic. This shows the ability of leaders to use security arguments in order to justify appropriating such considerable sums and the general expansion in AIDS funding that has taken place in recent years.[22] The logic of security can thus help to maintain such funding in the years ahead as will be necessary for treatment and prevention programs.

The securitization of HIV/AIDS is not only useful in terms of increasing international aid for HIV/AIDS, but it is also an important tool in terms of provoking African governments themselves into taking the issue more seriously within their domestic politics, that is to prioritize HIV/AIDS efforts on their own political agendas and budgets. Highlighting the security implications of HIV on the armed forces, for example, can even serve as an important initial trigger for placing HIV/AIDS on the political agenda (UNAIDS 1998; Elbe 2002). There is evidence from countries such as Uganda, Ethiopia, and Malawi that highlighting this military relationship was crucial in securing wider political leadership on the issue of HIV/AIDS. In Uganda, President Museveni began to take the issue seriously when, in 1986, Fidel Castro took him aside at a meeting of the Non-Aligned Movement in Harare and informed him that 18 out of the 60 military staff that Museveni had sent to Cuba for military training were HIV positive. This spurned Museveni into commencing a wider social program on HIV/AIDS in Uganda (Museveni 1995). Commenting on the response to HIV/AIDS by the Ethiopian army in 1996, de Waal (2003:22) similarly observes how "within the military such as the quasi-democratic 'council of commanders,' a legacy of the army's roots as a revolutionary guerrilla army, allowed the institution to develop and implement its own distinctive AIDS program." There is also some evidence from Malawi indicating that the impact of HIV/AIDS on the army and members of parliament was crucial in prompting political leadership on this issue (Lwanda 2004:40). In this way, highlighting the impact of HIV/AIDS on the armed forces undermines the ability of political leaders to deny the importance of the problem and can present a very obvious way of putting HIV/AIDS on the political agenda, as well as marking an entry point for wider HIV/AIDS programs and efforts. Thus, although in an ideal world HIV/AIDS would be addressed as a humanitarian and altruistic issue, outlining how HIV/AIDS programs would also benefit the national interests of states can help to increase international funding and can spur heavily affected states into action in a way that more altruistic health and development frameworks have not been able to do over the past decade.

This still leaves unresolved, however, the second problem: that the "threat-defense" logic could lead to the redirection of funding priorities toward the core institutions of the state. Will such a security framing not simply shift funding to the elites and the armed forces at the expense of more universal programs? Here, too, there are factors complicating the picture; for even when money is allocated to the military, this money can have a wider beneficial impact. The securitization of HIV/AIDS spurred Congress to allocate $10 million to begin setting up a program to address the spread of HIV/AIDS in selected African militaries. In 2001, this culminated in the Department of Defense HIV/AIDS Prevention Program, which has secured funding in excess of U.S.$35 million through fiscal year 2004 (U.S. Department of Defense 2005). Through this program, the Department of Defense has assisted 35 countries in developing HIV/AIDS prevention programs in the armed

---

[22] It also seems to parallel an insight expounded by William H. Foege, the former director of the Center for Disease Control in Atlanta, Georgia: one must "[t]ie the needs of the poor with the fears of the rich. When the rich lose their fear, they are not willing to invest in the problems of the poor." Quoted in Gellman (2002).

forces. Although these programs primarily focus on military personnel, and their levels of funding are small compared with other expenditures undertaken by the Department of Defense, they can have a broader impact. In Kenya, for example, the U.S. military HIV/AIDS program also extends to soldiers' dependents, with the result that 1,500 Kenyans, half of whom are not soldiers, are now receiving treatment through the program—a program which has also helped train many HIV counselors (Fisher-Thompson 2005). A similar program is currently underway in Tanzania, and a further one is planned for Nigeria. As long as such funding does not come at the expense of funding for civilian programs, the securitization of HIV/AIDS could generate new resources that are crucial for building the health care infrastructure in poor countries and thus for international efforts to mitigate the spread of HIV/AIDS. What is more, as an organization, the armed forces also have a duty to protect the health of their soldiers when deployed abroad. This means that unlike many commercial pharmaceutical companies that lack economic incentives to develop medicines for illnesses affecting the developing world, the U.S. military continues to be engaged in vaccine research for strands of HIV that predominate in Asia and Africa in order to protect troops that might contract HIV while deployed abroad. Historically, many of the medical advances that people still benefit from today originally emerged from military research.

What is more, drawing attention to the role of HIV/AIDS in the armed forces will invariably have to form an important part of international efforts to respond to HIV/AIDS. Although many would clearly oppose privileged access to treatment for the armed forces of developing countries, when the issue of HIV/AIDS is approached from the angle of prevention, a slightly different picture emerges. In a recent overview of new security issues, James Wirtz (2002:311) notes that "it is not clear how military action can help stop the [AIDS] epidemic that is sweeping Africa and other parts of the world." Yet around the world members of the security sector are not only profoundly affected by, but are also important actors in, the AIDS pandemic. Although Wirtz is thus correct in the sense that the security sector cannot (and indeed should not) co-ordinate national or international responses to HIV/AIDS, it is similarly true that such efforts to mitigate the spread of the virus are unlikely to succeed unless they incorporate strategies for targeting members of the security sector. In many countries members of the armed forces mark a high-risk group, and prevalence rates in several militaries around the world are thought to range between two and five times that of comparable civilian populations. A study carried out regarding gonorrhea and chlamydia infections at the Fort Bragg U.S. Army installation in North Carolina, for example, found that even after standardization of rates by age, race, and sex, the adjusted rates for Fort Bragg were higher than state or national averages (Sena et al. 2000). Around the world it is suspected that this is true in many militaries regarding levels of HIV as well, given that one of the transmission routes is through unprotected sexual intercourse. In some African militaries, average HIV prevalence rates are even thought to have reached between forty and sixty percent of the armed forces (National Intelligence Council 2000). Soldiers that are of a sexually active age, and that are very mobile and stationed away from home for long periods of time often valorize violent and risky behavior, can have frequent opportunities for casual sexual relations, and often seek to relieve themselves from the stress of combat. Members of the armed forces can thus be an important vector for transmitting the virus, and will have to play a vital role—not in leading or orchestrating national and international AIDS policy—but rather in terms of taking seriously their role in the pandemic and undertaking responsible steps to reduce the transmission of HIV both within and outside of the ranks. Again, this is not to insist that the armed forces should enjoy privileged access to medicines, but rather to suggest that, given the prominent role of the military sector in the pandemic, international efforts to prevent the spread of the pandemic are unlikely to succeed in the absence of a strategy for also addressing

HIV/AIDS in the military. It makes a big difference, therefore, whether the issue of HIV/AIDS in the military is approached from the perspective of treatment or prevention. Although highlighting HIV/AIDS in the military could thus be seen as detrimental if it leads to privileged access to treatment, from the perspective of global prevention efforts, drawing attention to the role of HIV/AIDS in the armed forces seems inevitable—mitigating against this second problem inherent in bringing the "threat-defense" logic of security to bear on HIV/AIDS.

What, then, of the third concern about the impact of the "threat-defense" logic on grassroots attempts to normalize social responses to the illness? Does the portrayal of HIV/AIDS as a debilitating security threat not just further stigmatize those living with the illness? Here, too, the normative picture becomes much more complicated when the threat is not seen to emanate from a group of persons, but rather from the *virus*. Although many would find the portrayal of persons living with HIV as a security threat to be ethically abhorrent and as something to be avoided at all costs, the question of whether such an assessment is also appropriate regarding the virus itself is much less certain. There is a crucial difference between arguing that "people with HIV/AIDS are a security threat" and arguing that "AIDS is a security threat": while the former aims to be politically exclusionary, and would bring into play a host of normative concerns already outlined by other scholars (Huysmans 1995, 2000) in relation to the securitization of migrants in many countries, the latter can be understood as a more inclusive gesture arguing that those living with HIV/AIDS should receive assistance if they so desire. It is also the latter claim that predominates among those linking HIV/AIDS and security.

What is more, one may well be skeptical about whether, in order to avoid the "threat-defense" logic of security, the optimal long-term relationship between people and the HIV virus really is one of complete normalization and "desecuritization." A certain normalization regarding the perception of people living with the illness would, of course, serve to reduce stigma and discrimination, but it might also culminate in an increased "threat" to life if, as a result, people begin to underestimate the lethal nature of the virus and cease to the take precautions against its transmission. In Western countries, where public reactions to people living with HIV/AIDS have become slightly more normalized compared with much of the 1980s, transmission rates are again increasing—even though there is no cure for HIV/AIDS and the virus may well become drug resistant in the long run (UNAIDS 2002:25). In this way, aiming for normalization regarding the HIV virus might have more adverse side effects. Again, the point here is not that the normative concern of securitization theory is not justified—especially as many political actors may not be able to differentiate at this level of detail and might perceive people living with HIV/AIDS as a threat rather than the key to reversing the global pandemic; the point is that in the case of HIV/AIDS, there are, depending on where precisely the threat is seen to emanate from, also strong arguments complicating any hasty rejection of the securitization of HIV/AIDS. In the case of HIV/AIDS, the ethical picture rapidly becomes much more complex.

In all of these aforementioned instances, then, linking HIV/AIDS and security can also have important benefits for those living with HIV/AIDS, especially in terms of reinforcing national and international efforts to stem the spread of HIV and treating those already suffering from AIDS-related illnesses. Many of these advantages are also unique to the language and apparatus of security, that is benefits that a securitization of HIV/AIDS could bring to the international debate on HIV/AIDS in a way that, as the first two decades of the pandemic's history have shown, portraying HIV/AIDS primarily as a health issue or as a development issue has not been able to achieve. In terms of securing high-level political leadership and increased funding, the framing of HIV/AIDS as a security issue is clearly useful; it is essential in terms of potentially overriding the TRIPS provisions and politicizing the role of the security sector in the pandemic. Given these competing normative benefits and drawbacks of framing the international response to the global AIDS pandemic in the language of security, participants in the debate are left confronting a profound and complex ethical dilemma about whether they should continue to frame HIV/AIDS as a security issue.[23] Indeed, just as there are clear normative dangers inherent in presenting HIV/AIDS as a security issue, there appear to be equally important normative costs involved in not doing so. All of this generates a much more complex and unyielding normative terrain surrounding the securitization of AIDS. At this stage, the answer to the question of whether HIV/AIDS should be securitized could justifiably be both "yes" and "no."

Conclusion

Can this ethical dilemma be resolved? It is not actually the intention of securitization theory to solve this dilemma on behalf of individual policy makers, activists, and scholars. Rather, its purpose is to cultivate among all of these audiences a deeper ethical sensibility about "speaking" security and to encourage them to reflect more thoroughly on whether the language of security is the most appropriate avenue for addressing any particular social issue. Securitization theory, Wæver (1999:334) notes, "puts an ethical question at the feet of analysts, decision makers and political activists alike: why do you call this a security issue? What are the implications of doing this—or of not doing it?" This article has sought to take this challenge seriously and to outline both the possible benefits and dangers of framing HIV/AIDS as a security issue. Yet securitization theory is also very cautious not to prejudge the complexity of issues such as HIV/AIDS. While Buzan, Wæver, and de Wilde (1998:29) have a general preference for resisting securitization processes, they also grant that "although in the abstract desecuritization is the ideal, in specific situations one can choose securitization, only one should not believe this is an innocent reflection of the issue *being* a security threat; it is always a political choice to securitize or to accept a securitization." In the end this choice about whether to endorse or reject securitization processes cannot be made *for* analysts and scholars; it must be made *by* them—independently and with respect to each particular securitization they encounter, as well as with the particular audiences they engage.

What an awareness of this dilemma can do in the case of HIV/AIDS, however, is spur those advocating the links between HIV/AIDS and security to at least do so in ways that seek to minimize some of these aforementioned dangers. There are three ways in which this could be achieved. First, those presenting HIV/AIDS as a security issue could be sure to insist that it is not *exclusively* a security issue, but rather a security issue *in addition* to also being a health issue, a development issue, an economic issue, a social issue, a political issue, a gender issue, etc. In this way, insisting on the security implications of HIV/AIDS does not unreflectively reify the traditional hierarchy between achieving security and the attainment of other social values, such as health. Nor does it simply replace an altruistic logic with a self-interested one. The security dimension of HIV/AIDS could then complement, rather than supersede, existing frameworks, and it would not undermine alternative rationales for global health initiatives, or unduly prioritize the needs of the security community over those of civil society. Second, the ethical dangers of securitizing AIDS could be further minimized by framing the illness as a security *issue*, or as an issue with an important security *dimension*, rather than as a dangerous and overwhelming security *threat*. This would still add considerable political *gravitas* to

---

[23] Nor are there clear historical precedents that one could turn to. There are certainly historical precedents for diseases shaping the unfolding of human history, and indeed influencing battle outcomes. See, for example, Cartwright (1972), Diamond (1997), McNeill (1998), Oldstone (2000), Watts (1997), and Zinsser (1953). There are, however, no diseases in recent history that match the experience of HIV/AIDS in terms of transmission methods, geographic extent, demographic impact, and disease pattern.

international efforts to respond to HIV/AIDS. It would probably also suffice in terms of invoking the security exceptions within TRIPS should this become necessary in the years ahead, and would similarly allow for the role of the security sector in the pandemic to be politicized, without doing so at the cost of playing on excessive fears and further stigmatizing persons living with HIV/AIDS. Finally, those framing HIV/AIDS as a security issue could also take great care to indicate that their primary concern lies with those people living with HIV/AIDS—that the problem lies not with the people living with the virus, but with the virus itself.

Here, then, the uniqueness of the case of HIV/AIDS in relation to previous securitization processes also begins to emerge particularly clearly. For it is a "danger" residing within the human body. If, as a result of the securitization of HIV/AIDS, *persons* living with the virus come to be seen as the threat, then many of the dangers already highlighted by scholars in relation to the securitization of migration and its detrimental effects on migrants come into play. If, however, it is the *virus* that is seen to be the threat, then these concerns are much less applicable, and the parallels reside much closer to environmental security, where nature is part of that which is being securitized. In this case, people living with HIV/AIDS would not be the enemy of global efforts to reduce the pandemic's debilitating consequences, but in fact would be the only hope for achieving viable improvements in the future. Consequently, they would have to be included in these efforts in a way that does not infringe upon their human rights or civil liberties. Precisely because the virus resides inside the human body, however, the case of HIV/AIDS in the end neatly parallels neither the securitization of the environment nor that of migration; it reaffirms instead the need for security analysts to continually assess the effects of linking security and wider social issues with due consideration of the specificities of each particular issue. All of this requires participants in the debate on HIV/AIDS and security to at least follow securitization theory's ethical imperative of thinking much more carefully about the intended audience, about the way in which the term security is used, and about the general language deployed in relation to HIV/AIDS. In the end, however, the securitization of HIV/AIDS undoubtedly remains a gamble on the ability of those presenting HIV/AIDS as a security issue to maintain control over the uses to which this language will be put—albeit a gamble that has perhaps become necessary because of the particular vicissitudes of contemporary world politics.

References

ADLER, EMMANUEL. (1997) Seizing the Middle Ground: Constructivism in World Politics. *European Journal of International Relations* 3(3):319–365.

ALLOCATE MORE, ARVS TO MILITARY PERSONNEL. (2003) Times of Zambia, November 17. ⟨http://www.times.co.zm⟩ (June 28, 2005).

ALTMAN, DENNIS. (2000) Understanding HIV/AIDS as a Global Security Issue. In *Health Impacts of Globalization: Towards Global Governance*, edited by Lee Kelley. London: Palgrave.

AMNESTY INTERNATIONAL. (2004) Marked for Death: Rape Survivors Living with HIV/AIDS in Rwanda. Report AFR 47/007/2004. Available at ⟨http://web.amnesty.org/library/index/en gafr470072004⟩ (Accessed June 28, 2005).

ARADAU, CLAUDIA. (2001) Beyond Good and Evil: Ethics and Securitization/Desecuritization Techniques. *Rubikon*. Available at ⟨http://venus.ci.uw.edu.pl/~rubikon/forum/claudia2.htm⟩ (Accessed June 28, 2005).

AUSTIN, JOHN. (1962) *How to Do Things with Words*. Cambridge: Harvard University Press.

BARNETT, MICHAEL, AND MARTHA FINNEMORE. (1999) The Politics, Power and Pathologies of International Organizations. *International Organization* 53(4):699–732.

BARNETT, TONY, AND ALAN WHITESIDE. (2002) *AIDS in the Twenty-First Century: Disease and Globalization*. Basingstoke: Palgrave.

BAZERGAN, ROXANNE. (2001) UN Peacekeepers and HIV/AIDS. *World Today* 57(5):6–8.

140   *Should HIV/AIDS Be Securitized?*

BAZERGAN, ROXANNE. (2003) Intervention and Intercourse: HIV/AIDS and Peacekeepers. *Conflict, Security and Development* 3(1):27–51.

BIGO, DIDIER. (1998) Sécurité et immigration: vers une gouvernementalité par l'inquiétude. *Cultures et Conflits* 31–32:13–38.

BLOOM, DAVID E., AND PETER GODWIN, EDS. (1997) *The Economics of HIV and AIDS: The Case of South and South East Asia.* New York: Oxford University Press.

BONANATE, LUIGI, DONALD PUCHALA, AND CHARLES W. KEGLEY JR., EDS. (1995) *Ethics and International Politics.* Columbia: University of South Carolina Press.

BRATT, DUANE. (2002) Blue Condoms: The Use of International Peacekeepers in the Fight Against AIDS. *International Peacekeeping* 9(3):67–86.

BROWN, CHRIS. (1992) *International Relations Theory: New Normative Approaches.* New York: Columbia University Press.

BROWN, CHRIS. (2002) *Sovereignty, Rights and Justice: International Political Theory Today.* Cambridge: Polity.

BURKHALTER, HOLLY. (2004) The Politics of AIDS: Engaging Conservative Activists. *Foreign Affairs* 83:8–14.

BUZAN, BARRY, AND OLE WÆVER. (1998) Liberalism and Security: The Contradictions of the Liberal Leviathan. Working papers no. 23, Copenhagen Peace Research Institute, Copenhagen. Available at ⟨http://www.ciaonet.org/wps/bub02/⟩ (Accessed June 28, 2005).

BUZAN, BARRY, OLE WÆVER, AND JAAP DE WILDE. (1998) *Security: A New Framework for Analysis.* Boulder: Lynne Rienner.

CARTWRIGHT, FREDERICK. (1972) *Disease and History.* New York: Barnes & Noble.

CEYHAN, AYSE, AND ANASTASSIA TSOUKALA. (2002) The Securitization of Migration in Western Societies: Ambivalent Discourses and Policies. *Alternatives* 27(1):21–39.

CHEN, LINCOLN, *et al.*, EDS. (2003) *Global Health Challenges for Human Security.* Cambridge: Harvard University Press.

CHOWKA, PETER. (2000) AIDS Deemed a "National Security" Threat by U.S. as South African President Challenges Medical Orthodoxy. Natural Healthline, May 1. Available at ⟨http://www.nat uralhealthvillage.com/newsletter/01may00/aids.htm⟩ (Accessed June 28, 2005).

COKER, RICHARD. (2003) Migration, Public Health and Compulsory Screening for TB and HIV. Asylum and migration working paper 1, Institute for Public Policy Research, London.

COMMISSION ON HUMAN SECURITY. (2003) Human Security Now. Available at ⟨http://www.humanse curity-chs.org/finalreport/FinalReport.pdf⟩ (Accessed June 28, 2005).

CONKLIN, STEVE. (2003) Interview with Radhika Sarin, Author of the Enemy Within: AIDS in the Military. World Watch Institute, Washington, March 28. Available at ⟨http://www.worldwatch.org/ live/discussion/70/⟩ (Accessed June 28, 2005).

CRADDOCK, SUSAN. (2004) AIDS and Ethics: Clinical Trials, Pharmaceuticals, and Global Scientific Practice. In *HIV and AIDS in Africa: Beyond Epidemiology,* edited by Ezekiel Kalipeni, *et al.* Oxford: Blackwell.

CSIS. (2002) *The Destabilizing Impacts of HIV/AIDS.* Washington: Center for Strategic and International Studies. Available at ⟨http://www.csis.org/africa/destabilizing_aids.pdf⟩.

DAVID, MARCELLA. (2001) Rubber Helmets: The Certain Pitfalls of Marshalling Security Council Resources to Combat AIDS in Africa. *Human Rights Quarterly* 23(3):560–582.

DEUDNEY, DANIEL. (1990) The Case Against Linking Environmental Degradation and National Security. *Millennium* 19(3):461–476.

DE WAAL, ALEX. (2003) How Will HIV/AIDS Transform African Governance? *African Affairs* 102: 1–23.

DIAMOND, JARED. (1997) *Guns, Germs and Steel: The Fates of Human Societies.* New York: Norton.

DOTY, ROXANNE. (1998) Immigration and the Politics of Security. *Security Studies* 8(2–3):71–93.

DUFFIELD, MARK. (2001) *Global Governance and the New Wars: The Merging of Development and Security.* London: Zed Books.

EBERSTADT, NICHOLAS. (2002) The Future of AIDS. *Foreign Affairs* 81(6):22–45.

ELBE, STEFAN. (2002) HIV/AIDS and the Changing Landscape of War in Africa. *International Security* 27(2):159–177.

ELBE, STEFAN. (2003) *The Strategic Dimensions of HIV/AIDS. International Institute for Strategic Studies.* Oxford: Oxford University Press.

ELBE, STEFAN. (2005) HIV/AIDS: The International Security Dimensions. In *New Threats and New Actors in International Security,* edited by Elke Krahmann. New York: Palgrave.

EMMERS, RALF. (2003) ASEAN and the Securitization of Transnational Crime in Southeast Asia. *Pacific Review* 16(3):419–438.

FIDLER, DAVID. (1998) Microbialpolitik: Infectious Diseases and International Relations. *American University International Law Review* 14(1):1–11.

FIDLER, DAVID. (2003) Public Health and National Security in the Global Age: Infectious Diseases, Bioterrorism, and Realpolitik. *George Washington International Law Review* 35:787–856.

FINNEMORE, MARTHA. (1996) *National Interests in International Society.* Ithaca: Cornell University Press.

FISHER-THOMPSON, JIM. (2005) Kenya Provides Firm Ground for U.S. Military AIDS Partnership. U.S. Department of State Information Service (USINFO), Washington, February 18. Available at ⟨http://usinfo.state.gov/gi/Archive/2005/Feb/22-541177.html⟩ (Accessed June 28, 2005).

FOURIE, PIETER, AND MARTIN SCHÖNTEICH. (2001) Africa's New Security Threat: HIV/AIDS and Human Security in Southern Africa. *African Security Review* 10(4). Available at ⟨http://www.iss.co.za⟩ (Accessed June 28, 2005).

FROST, MERVYN. (1996) *Ethics in International Relations: A Constitutive Theory.* Cambridge: Cambridge University Press.

GARRETT, LAURIE. (1994) *The Coming Plague: Newly Emerging Diseases in a World out of Balance.* New York: Penguin Books.

GELLMAN, BARTON. (2000) World Shunned Signs of the Coming Plague. *Washington Post*, July 5.

GRISIN, SARAH, AND CELESTE WALLANDER. (2002) *Russia's HIV/AIDS Crisis: Confronting the Present and Facing the Future.* Washington: Center for Strategic and International Studies.

GODWIN, PETER, ED. (1998) *The Looming Epidemic: The Impact of HIV and AIDS in India.* London: Hurst & Company.

GROVER, ANAND. (2004) Letter from the Affordable Medicines Treatment Campaign to India's National Human Rights Commission. Human Rights News, Human Rights Watch, October 11. Available at ⟨http://www.hrw.org/english/docs/2004/10/22/india9556.htm⟩ (Accessed June 28, 2005).

HANSEN, LENE. (2000) The Little Mermaid's Silent Security Dilemma and the Absence of Gender in the Copenhagen School. *Millennium* 29(2):285–306.

HARKER, JOHN. (2001) HIV/AIDS and the Security Sector in Africa: A Threat to Canada. Canadian Security Intelligence Service, Ottawa. Available at ⟨http://www.csis-scrs.gc.ca/eng/comment/com80_e.html⟩ (Accessed June 28, 2005).

HARRIS, PAUL, AND PATRICIA SIPLON. (2001) International Obligation and Human Health: Evolving Policy Responses to HIV/AIDS. *Ethics and International Affairs* 15(2):29–52.

HEINECKEN, LINDY. (2001a) Strategic implications of HIV/AIDS in South Africa. *Conflict, Security and Development* 1(1):109–113.

HEINECKEN, LINDY. (2001b) Living in Terror: The Looming Security Threat to Southern Africa. *African Security Review* 10(4):7–17.

HOLDEN, SUE. (2003) *AIDS on the Agenda: Adapting Development and Humanitarian Programmes to Meet the Challenge of HIV/AIDS.* Oxford: Oxfam.

HINSLIFF, GABY. (2003) Britain Slams the Door on Foreign NHS Cheats. *The Observer*, February 9.

HOPE, KEMPE RONALD, ED. (1999) *AIDS and Development in Africa: A Social Science Perspective.* New York: The Haworth Press.

HOPF, TED. (1998) The Promise of Constructivism in International Relations Theory. *International Security* 23(1):171–200.

HUSAK, DOUGLAS. (1992) *Drugs and Rights.* Cambridge: Cambridge University Press.

HUYSMANS, JEFF. (1995) Migrants as a Security Problem: Dangers of "Securitizing" Societal Issues. In *Migration and European Integration*, edited by Robert Miles and Dietrich Thranhardt. London: Pinter.

HUYSMANS, JEFF. (1998) Revisiting Copenhagen: Or, on the Creative Development of a Security Studies Agenda in Europe. *European Journal of International Relations* 4(4):479–505.

HUYSMANS, JEFF. (2000) The European Union and the Securitization of Migration. *Journal of Common Market Studies* 38(5):751–777.

ICG. (2001) *HIV/AIDS as a Security Issue.* Washington: International Crisis Group.

ICG. (2004) *HIV/AIDS as a Security Issue in Africa: Lessons From Uganda.* Kampala, Uganda: International Crisis Group.

KAKONEN, JYRKI, ED. (1994) *Green Security or Militarized Environment.* Aldershot: Dartmouth Publishing Company.

KALIPENI, EZEKIEL, et al., EDS. (2004) *HIV and AIDS in Africa: Beyond Epidemiology.* Oxford: Blackwell.

KATZENSTEIN, PETER, ED. (1996) *The Culture of National Security: Norms and Identity in World Politics.* New York: Columbia University Press.

KAUFFMAN, KYLE, AND DAVID LINDAUER, EDS. (2004) *AIDS and South Africa: The Social Expression of a Pandemic.* Basingstoke: Palgrave.

KEIM, WILLARD. (2000) *Ethics, Morality and International Affairs*. Lanham: University Press of America.
KESBY, MIKE. (2004) Participatory Diagramming and the Ethical and Practical Challenges of Helping Themselves to Move HIV Work "Beyond Epidemiology." In *HIV and AIDS in Africa: Beyond Epidemiology*, edited by Ezekiel Kalipeni, *et al*. Oxford: Blackwell.
KRISTOFFERSSON, ULF. (2000) HIV/AIDS as a Human Security Issue: A Gender Perspective. Paper presented at the expert group meeting on "The HIV/AIDS Pandemic and Its Gender Implications," 13–17 November, Windhoek, Namibia.
LEEN, MAURA. (2004) *The European Union, HIV/AIDS and Human Security*. Dublin: Dochas.
LINGE, GODFREY, AND DOUG PORTER, EDS. (1997) *No Place for Borders: The HIV/AIDS Epidemic and Development in Asia and the Pacific*. New York: St. Martin's Press.
LITFIN, KAREN. (1999) Constructing Environmental Security and Ecological Interdependence. *Global Governance* 5(3):359–378.
LURIE, PETER, PERCY C. HINTZEN, AND ROBERT A. LOWE. (2004) Socioeconomic Obstacles to HIV Prevention in Developing Countries: The Roles of the International Monetary Fund and the World Bank. In *HIV and AIDS in Africa: Beyond Epidemiology*, edited by Ezekiel Kalipeni, Susan Craddock, Joseph R. Oppong, and Jayati Ghosh. Oxford: Blackwell.
LWANDA, JOHN LLOYD. (2004) Politics, Culture, and Medicine: An Unholy Trinity. In *HIV and AIDS in Africa: Beyond Epidemiology*, edited by Ezekiel Kalipeni, *et al*. Oxford: Blackwell.
MCNEILL, WILLIAM. (1998) *Plagues and People*. New York: Anchor Books.
MEDECINS SANS FRONTIERS. (2005) A Guide to the Post-2005 World: TRIPS, R&D and Access to Medicines. Available at ⟨http://www.msf.org/msfinternational/content/advocacy/accesstoessential medicinescampaign/index.cfm⟩ (Accessed June 28, 2005).
MILLS, GREG. (2000) AIDS and the South African Military: Timeworn Cliché or Timebomb? In *HIV/AIDS: A Threat to the African Renaissance?*, edited by Michael Lange. Johannesburg: Konrad Adenauer Foundation.
MOCK, NANCY. (2002) HIV/AIDS in our Ranks. Presentation to the Woodrow Wilson Center, Washington, June 4. Available at ⟨http://www.certi.org/strategy/military/role_of_the_military.htm⟩ (Accessed June 28, 2005).
MUSEVENI, YOWERI. (1995) Opening Speech at the Ninth International Conference on AIDS and STDs in Africa. Kampala, Uganda, December 10. Available at ⟨http://www.museveni.co.ug⟩ (Accessed March 15, 2005).
NARDIN, TERRY, AND DAVID MAPEL, EDS. (1993) *Traditions of International Ethics*. Cambridge: Cambridge University Press.
NATIONAL INTELLIGENCE COUNCIL. (2000) The Global Infectious Disease Threat and Its Implications for the U.S. Washington DC. Available at ⟨http://www.cia.gov/cia/reports/nie/report/nie99-17d.html⟩.
NATIONAL INTELLIGENCE COUNCIL. (2002) The Next Wave of HIV/AIDS: Nigeria, Ethiopia, Russia, India, and China. Washington, DC. Available at ⟨http://www.cia.gov/nic/special_nextwaveHIV.html⟩.
NEY, STEVEN. (1999) Environmental Security: A Critical Overview. *Innovation: The European Journal of Social Sciences* 12(1):7–30.
OAU. (2001) *Abuja Declaration on HIV/AIDS, Tuberculosis and other Related Infectious Diseases*. Abuja, Nigeria: Organisation of African Unity. Available at ⟨www.un.org/ga/aids/pdf/abuja_declara tion.pdf⟩ (Accessed June 28, 2005).
ODYSSEOS, LOUIZA. (2002) Dangerous Ontologies: The Ethos of Survival and Ethical Theorising in International Relations. *Review of International Studies* 28(2):403–418.
ODYSSEOS, LOUIZA. (2003) On the Way to Global Ethics? Cosmopolitanism, Ethical Selfhood and Otherness. *European Journal of Political Theory* 2(2):187–207.
OLDSTONE, MICHAEL. (2000) *Viruses, Plagues, and History*. Oxford: Oxford University Press.
OSTERGARD, ROBERT L. JR. (2002) Politics in the Hot Zone: AIDS and National Security in Africa. *Third World Quarterly* 23(2):333–350.
OSTERGARD, ROBERT L. JR., ED. (2005) *HIV, AIDS and the Threat to National and International Security*. London: Palgrave.
OSTRAUSKAITE, RASA. (2001) Environmental Security as an Ambiguous Symbol: Can We Securitize the Environment? *Rubikon*. Available at ⟨http://venus.ci.uw.edu.pl/~rubikon/forum/rasa2.htm⟩ (Accessed June 28, 2005).
OXFAM. (2004) Undermining Access to Medicines: Comparison of Five US FTAs. A Technical Note. Available at ⟨http://www.oxfam.org.uk/what_we_do/issues/health/downloads/undermining_access_ftas.pdf⟩ (Accessed June 28, 2005).
PETERSON, SUSAN. (2002/2003) Epidemic Disease and National Security. *Security Studies* 12(2):43–81.
PHARAOH, ROBYN, AND MARTIN SCHÖNTEICH. (2003) *AIDS, Security and Governance in Southern Africa: Exploring the Impact*. Pretoria: Institute for Security Studies.

PIOT, PETER. (2000) Global AIDS Pandemic: Time to Turn the Tide. *Science* 288:2176–2178.

PIOT, PETER. (2001) AIDS and Human Security. Speech delivered at the United Nations University. Tokyo, October 2. Available at ⟨http://www.unaids.org/html/pub/media/speeches01/piot_tokyo_02oct01_en_doc.htm⟩ (Accessed June 28, 2005).

PRICE-SMITH, ANDREW. (1998) Ghosts of Kigali: Infectious Disease and Global Stability at the Turn of the Century. *International Journal* 54:426–442.

PRICE-SMITH, ANDREW. (2001) *The Health of Nations: Infectious Disease, Environmental Change, and Their Effects on National Security and Development.* Cambridge: MIT Press.

PRICE-SMITH, ANDREW. (2002) *Pretoria's Shadow: The HIV/AIDS Pandemic and National Security in South Africa.* Washington: Chemical and Biological Arms Control Institute.

PRINS, GWYN. (2004) AIDS and Global Security. *International Affairs* 80(5):931–952.

ROFFE, PEDRO, AND RICARDO MELENDEZ-ORTIZ. (2005) *Resource Book on TRIPS and Development: An Authoritative and Practical Guide to the TRIPS Agreement.* Geneva: The United Nations Conference on Trade and Development and The International Centre for Trade and Sustainable Development. Available at ⟨http://www.iprsonline.org/unctadictsd/ResourceBookIndex.htm⟩ (Accessed June 28, 2005).

SANGER, DAVID. (2000) Sometimes, National Security Says It All. *New York Times*, May 7.

SARIN, RADHIKA. (2003) A New Security Threat: HIV/AIDS in the Military. *World Watch* (March/April), 17–22.

SCHOEPF, BROOKE GRUNDFEST. (2004) AIDS, History, and Struggles over Meaning. In *HIV and AIDS in Africa: Beyond Epidemiology*, edited by Ezekiel Kalipeni, *et al.* Oxford: Blackwell.

SEARLE, JOHN. (1969) *Speech Acts: An Essay in the Philosophy of Language.* Cambridge: Cambridge University Press.

SECKINELGIN, HAKAN. (2003) HIV/AIDS, Global Civil Society and People's Politics: An Update. In *Global Civil Society Yearbook*, edited by Mary Kaldor, *et al.* Oxford: Oxford University Press.

SECKINELGIN, HAKAN, AND HIDEAKI SHINODA, EDS. (2001) *Ethics and International Relations.* London: Palgrave.

SELL, S., AND A. PRAKASH. (2004) Using Ideas Strategically: The Contest Between Business and NGO Networks in Intellectual Property Rights. *International Studies Quarterly* 48(1):143–175.

SENA, A., W. MILLER, I. HOFFMAN, M. COHEN, P. JENKINS, AND J. McKEE. (2000) Trends of Gonorrhoea and Chlamydial Infections During 1985–1996 Among Active Duty Soldiers at a US Army Installation. *Clinical Infectious Diseases* 30:742–748.

SHARMA, KAMALESH. (2001) Statement by Mr. Kamalesh Sharma, Permanent Representative at the Open Meeting of the Security Council on the Responsibility of the Security Council in the Maintenance of International Peace and Security: HIV/AIDS and International Peacekeeping Operations, January 19. Available at ⟨http://www.un.int/india/ind499.htm⟩ (Accessed June 28, 2005).

SHEEHAN, CARRIE. (2002) Securitizing Global Health Issues: HIV/AIDS in Africa as a U.S. National Security Threat. Paper presented at the International Studies Association, New Orleans, LA, 26 March.

SINGER, PETER. (2002) AIDS and International Security. *Survival* 44(1):145–158.

SONTAG, SUSAN. (1988) *AIDS and Its Metaphors.* New York: Farrar, Straus and Giroux.

STERNBERG, STEVE. (2002) Former Diplomat Holbrooke Takes on Global AIDS. *USA Today*, June 10.

STOLBERG, SHERYL. (2003) Bush Proposal on AIDS Funds Shows Concern about Security. *New York Times*, January 29.

TENET, GEORGE J. (2003) Testimony of Director of Central Intelligence George J. Tenet before the Senate Select Committee on Intelligence. Washington, February 11.

TRIPODI, PAOLO, AND PREETI PATEL. (2002) The Global Impact of HIV/AIDS on Peace Support Operations. *International Peacekeeping* 9(3):51–66.

UNAIDS. (1998) *AIDS and the Military.* Geneva: UNAIDS.

UNAIDS. (2001) AIDS Now Core Issue at UN Security Council. Press Release, New York, January 19.

UNAIDS. (2002) AIDS Epidemic Update: December 2002, Geneva.

UNITED NATIONS DEVELOPMENT PROGRAM. (1994) *Human Development Report, 1994: New Dimensions of Human Security.* New York: Oxford University Press.

U.S. DEPARTMENT OF DEFENSE. (2005) Background Information on HIV/AIDS Prevention Program. Available at ⟨http://www.nhrc.navy.mil/programs/dhapp/background/background.html⟩ (Accessed June 28, 2005).

U.S. DEPARTMENT OF HEALTH AND HUMAN SERVICES. (2005) Ryan White Comprehensive AIDS Resources Emergency (CARE) Act. Available at ⟨http://hab.hrsa.gov/history.htm⟩ (Accessed June 28, 2005).

U.S. GOVERNMENT ACCOUNTABILITY OFFICE. (2001) *U. N. Peacekeeping: United Nations Faces Challenges in Responding to the Impact of HIV/AIDS on Peacekeeping Operations*. Washington: U.S. Government Accountability Office.

WÆVER, OLE. (1995) Securitization and Desecuritization. In *On Security*, edited by Ronnie Lipschutz. New York: Columbia University Press.

WÆVER, OLE. (1999) Securitizing Sectors? Reply to Eriksson. *Cooperation and Conflict* 34(3):334–340.

WÆVER, OLE, BARRY, BUZAN, MORTEN, KELSTRUP AND PIERRE, LEMAITRE. (1993) *Identity, Migration and the New Security Agenda in Europe*. New York: St. Martin's Press.

WALT, STEPHEN. (1991) The Renaissance of Security Studies. *International Studies Quarterly* 35(2): 211–239.

WATTS, SHELDON. (1997) *Epidemics and History: Disease, Power, and Imperialism*. New Haven: Yale University Press.

WEINER, MYRON. (1992/1993) Security, Stability and International Migration. *International Security* 17(3):91–126.

WENDT, ALEXANDER. (1992) Anarchy Is What States Make of It: The Social Construction of Power Politics. *International Organization* 46(2):335–370.

WENDT, ALEXANDER. (1999) *A Social Theory of International Politics*. Cambridge: Cambridge University Press.

WHITESIDE, ALAN, AND CLEM SUNTER. (2000) *AIDS: The Challenge for South Africa*. Cape Town: Human & Rousseau.

WILLIAMS, MICHAEL. (2003) Words, Images, Enemies: Securitization and International Politics. *International Studies Quarterly* 47(4):511–531.

WIRTZ, JAMES J. (2002) A New Agenda for Security and Strategy? In *Strategy in the Contemporary World*, edited by John Baylis, *et al*. Oxford: Oxford University Press.

WOLFENSOHN, JAMES. (2000) Speech delivered to the UN Security Council. New York, January 10.

WORLD TRADE ORGANISATION. (1994) The Agreement on Trade-Related Aspects of Intellectual Property Rights. Available at ⟨http://www.wto.org/english/docs_e/legal_e/27-trips_01_e.htm⟩.

YEAGER, RODGER, AND STUART KINGMA. (2001) HIVAIDS: Destabilizing National Security and the Multi-National Response. *International Review of the Armed Forces Medical Services* 74(1–3):3–12.

YOUDE, JEREMY. (2005) Enter the Fourth Horseman: Health Security and International Relations Theory. *Whitehead Journal of Diplomacy and International Relations* 6(1):193–208.

ZINSSER, HANS. (1953) *Rats, Lice, and History*. Boston: Little, Brown and Company.

Part IV
Health and Trade

[18]

Drug development for neglected diseases: a deficient market and a public-health policy failure

Patrice Trouiller, Piero Olliaro, Els Torreele, James Orbinski, Richard Laing, Nathan Ford

There is a lack of effective, safe, and affordable pharmaceuticals to control infectious diseases that cause high mortality and morbidity among poor people in the developing world. We analysed outcomes of pharmaceutical research and development over the past 25 years, and reviewed current public and private initiatives aimed at correcting the imbalance in research and development that leaves diseases that occur predominantly in the developing world largely unaddressed. We compiled data by searches of Medline and databases of the US Food and Drug Administration and the European Agency for the Evaluation of Medicinal Products, and reviewed current public and private initiatives through an analysis of recently published studies. We found that, of 1393 new chemical entities marketed between 1975 and 1999, only 16 were for tropical diseases and tuberculosis. There is a 13-fold greater chance of a drug being brought to market for central-nervous-system disorders or cancer than for a neglected disease. The pharmaceutical industry argues that research and development is too costly and risky to invest in low-return neglected diseases, and public and private initiatives have tried to overcome this market limitation through incentive packages and public-private partnerships. The lack of drug research and development for "non-profitable" infectious diseases will require new strategies. No sustainable solution will result for diseases that predominantly affect poor people in the South without the establishment of an international pharmaceutical policy for all neglected diseases. Private-sector research obligations should be explored, and a public-sector not-for-profit research and development capacity promoted.

Despite progress made in both the basic knowledge of many infectious diseases and the process of drug discovery and development, tropical infectious diseases such as malaria, leishmaniasis, lymphatic filariasis, Chagas' disease, and schistosomiasis continue to cause significant morbidity and mortality, mainly in the developing world. The burden of infectious diseases has been compounded by the re-emergence of diseases such as tuberculosis, dengue, and African trypanosomiasis. These diseases all predominantly affect poor populations in the less-developed world.[1]

WHO has identified three key factors that can collectively contribute to the burden of illness associated with infectious diseases: failure to use existing tools effectively, inadequate or non-existent tools, and insufficient knowledge of the disease.[2] The discovery and development of most of the current tropical pharmacopoeia was driven by colonial requirements during the first part of the 20th century.[3] As Western interests drifted away from these regions, tropical diseases have become progressively neglected, mainly because they do not offer sufficient financial returns for the pharmaceutical industry to engage in research and development. Tuberculosis—another major poverty-related disease—is also neglected in terms of drug research and development.

Despite an ever-increasing need for safe, effective, and affordable medicines for the treatment of these diseases, drug development has virtually stopped.[4,5] We present an analysis of the trends in drug development over the past 25 years, focusing particularly on neglected diseases, and review future prospects for stimulating research and development through analysis of current public and private sector initiatives aimed at correcting this imbalance in research and development.

Drug development over the past 25 years

We did a quantitative and qualitative analysis of global drug development output over the past 25 years, focusing specifically on neglected diseases. Data on the new chemical entities marketed in this period were compiled by searches of Medline and databases of the US Food and Drug Administration and the European Agency for the Evaluation of Medicinal Products. The data are presented over time and by therapeutic class, indicating innovation level and market share in both absolute terms and relative to the burden of disease expressed as millions of disability-adjusted life-years (DALYs). Although rare, examples of registrations exclusively within developing countries do exist—eg, artemisinin derivatives for malaria developed and manufactured in China.

We found that 1393 new chemical entities were granted a market authorisation between 1975 and 1999 (table 1). Their quantitative distribution in different therapeutic areas shows a bias towards high-income countries. This imbalance was especially pronounced for infectious and parasitic diseases, which account for a third of the worldwide disease burden but only 5% of the disease burden in high-income countries. To quantify the level of

Lancet 2002; **359:** 2188–94

Centre Hospitalier Universitaire, BP 217, 38043 Grenoble cedex 9, France (P Trouiller PharmD); UNDP/World Bank/WHO Special Programme for Research and Training in Tropical Diseases (TDR), WHO, Geneva, Switzerland (P Olliaro PhD); **Department of Immunology, Parasitology and Ultrastructure, VIB-Free University Brussels, St-Genesius Rode, Belgium** (E Torreele PhD); **Munk Centre For International Studies, University of Toronto, Toronto, Canada** (J Orbinski MD); **Boston University School of Public Health, Boston, MA, USA** (R Laing MD); **Médecins Sans Frontières, London, UK** (N Ford MSc); **Drugs for Neglected Diseases (DND) Working Group, Médecins Sans Frontières, Geneva** (P Trouiller, P Olliaro, E Torreele, J Orbinski, R Laing, N Ford)

Correspondence to: Dr Patrice Trouiller
(e-mail: PTrouiller@chu-grenoble.fr)

Therapeutic areas	Approved NCEs 1975–99*	Disability-adjusted life-years (DALYs)†				Proportion of worldwide sales, 1999‡	NCEs by DALY	Drug sales (millions of US$) by DALY
		Number (×10⁶)	World- wide (%)	High-income countries (%)	Low- and middle- income countries (%)			
Central nervous system	211 (15·1%)	159·46	11·5	23·5	10·5	15·1%	1·32	193
Cardiovascular	179 (12·8%)	143·02	10·3	18·0	9·7	19·8%	1·25	283
Cytostatics (neoplasms)	111 (8·0%)	84·87	6·1	15·8	5·2	3·7%	1·31	90
Respiratory (non-infectious)	89 (6·4%)	61·60	4·5	7·4	4·2	9·3%	1·44	307
Anti-infectives and antiparasitics§	224 (16·1%)	409·08	29·6	4·2	31·8	10·3%	0·55	52
HIV/AIDS¶	26 (1·9%)	70·93	5·1	0·9	5·5	1·5%	0·37	44
Tuberculosis‖	3 (0·2%)	28·19	2·0	0·1	2·2	0·2%	0·11	11
Tropical diseases (total)**	13 (0·9%)	130·35	9·4	0·3	10·2	0·2%	0·10	3
Malaria	4 (0·3%)	39·27	2·8	0·0	3·1	0·1%	0·10	5
Other therapeutic categories	579 (41·6%)	524·54	37·94	31·08	38·59	41·9%	1·10	163
Total	1393 (100%)	1382·56	100	100	100	100%	1·01	148

*Sources: IMS Health drug monitor 1999 (http://www.imshealth.com); EMEA and FDA data; reference 5. †Data from WHO World Health Report, 1999. ‡Total pharmaceutical sales for 1999 was US$204 700 million (IMS health). Includes private pharmacy sales for all drug classes except anti-infectives and parasitics, which also include public pharmacy sales. §Includes antibiotics, antituberculosis drugs, antivirals, vaccines, and immunoglobulins. ¶Including 20 AIDS antiviral drugs and six drugs for opportunistic infections; atovaquone is also quoted under malaria. ‖Pyrazinamide, rifabutin, rifapentine. **Benznidazole, nifurtimox (Chagas' disease); albendazole (helminthic infection); eflornithine (human African trypanosomiasis); artemether, atovaquone+proguanil, halofantrine, mefloquine (malaria); ivermectin (onchocerciasis); oxamniquine, praziquantel (schistosomiasis) and two reformulations of already approved drugs: liposomal amphotericin B (leishmaniasis) and pentamidine (African trypanosomiasis). After 1999, two new drugs were registered for malaria: artemether and artemether/lumefantrine.

Table 1: **New chemical entities (NCEs) approved between 1975 and 1999 by drug class and relative to disease burden and drug sales**

neglect, we calculated the ratio of the number of new drugs marketed and the disease burden for major disease categories. For the period considered, the number of new chemical entities per million DALYs was 0·55 for infectious and parasitic diseases, compared with values two to three times higher (ranging between 1·25 and 1·44) for the main diseases of the high-income countries. The ratio for all infectious diseases combined was mostly accounted for by 20 antiretroviral drugs developed in the past 5–15 years, the development of which benefited from a serious political commitment from wealthy countries, as well as major investment from the pharmaceutical industry that was motivated by the high potential return on investment in high-income countries.[6] For tuberculosis and malaria, the numbers of new chemical entities per million DALYs are as low as 0·1.

We examined specifically registration of new chemical entities for tropical diseases (defined here as parasitic diseases [malaria, African trypanosomiasis, Chagas' disease, schistosomiasis, leishmaniasis, lymphatic filariasis, onchocerciasis, intestinal nematode infections], leprosy, dengue, Japanese encephalitis, trachoma, and infectious diarrhoeal diseases) and tuberculosis. These infectious diseases represent a substantial burden among developing countries, and together account for 11·4% of the global disease burden. We found that only 1% of the 1393 new chemical entities marketed between 1975 and 1999 were registered for these diseases: 13 for a tropical disease indication, and three for tuberculosis (table 1).

Not unexpectedly, drug development outcomes closely follow the existence of viable markets. US$307 million per million DALYs is spent worldwide on non-infectious respiratory diseases, compared with $3 million per million DALYs for tropical diseases. Drugs for cardiovascular and central-nervous-system diseases account for 35% of worldwide pharmaceutical sales, and represent 28% of the 1393 new chemical entities. This imbalance is also shown in the overall level of pharmaceutical industry investments for research and development: of the $35·3 billion[7] invested in 1999, 10·1% was spent on infectious diseases. By contrast, estimates suggest that the total investment (public and private sector) in drug research and development for malaria, tuberculosis, leishmaniasis, and African trypanosomiasis was less than $70 million.[8]

An average of 55·7 new chemical entities were developed each year, with an innovation index averaging

0·313 throughout the whole period (table 2). The innovation index is defined as the number of group 1 new chemical entities per total number of new chemical entities, where group 1 drugs have a substantial and important gain over existing therapies (eg, breakthrough drugs), and group 2 drugs offer little or no therapeutic gain (eg, "me-too" drugs). In other words, 68·7% (959 new chemical entities) of the 1393 registered products present little or no therapeutic gain compared with what was already available. Conversely, the innovation index for neglected diseases is 1, indicating that when the development attention is limited, only innovative drugs are developed. Moreover, all of the 16 newly developed drugs for neglected diseases have been included in the latest WHO Essential Drugs List, whereas less than 2% (21) of all other drugs were included in this list. Overall, despite vast scientific and technological advances in the processes and organisation of drug research and development, no significant increase in the number of drugs delivered or improvement in the degree of innovation has been seen.

Table 3 lists drugs currently under clinical investigation. We found some activity for malaria, leishmaniasis, onchocerciasis, lymphatic filariasis, tuberculosis, schistosomiasis, and leprosy, but no clinical development activity for other neglected diseases (eg, African trypanosomiasis, Chagas' disease, and dengue). Of all drugs in develop-

Period	Number of approved NCEs	Innovation Index	NCEs listed in 1999 WHO EDL	NCEs listed in WHO EDL indicated for a neglected disease
1975–79	248	0·339	2*	0
1980–84	256	0·308	16†	6
1985–89	277	0·278	8‡	4
1990–94	280	0·314	4§	1
1995–99	332	0·324	7¶	5
Total	1393	..	37	16
5-year average	279	0·313	7	3

NCEs=new chemical entities. *Cisplatin, levothyroxine. †Aciclovir, benznidazole, captopril, cimetidine, cetriaxone, clavulinic acid, factor VIII concentrate, factor IX complex, iohexol, nifedipine, nifurtimox, oxamniquine, pentamidine, praziquantel, pyrazinamide, testosterone enantate. ‡Albendazole, ceftazidine, ciprofloxacine, fluconazole, ivermectin, halofantrine, mefloquine, zidovudine. §Atenolol, ciclosporin, eflornithine, imipenem-cilastatin. ¶Liposomal amphotericin B, artemether, atovaquone, etoposide, nevirapine, rifabutine, rifapentine. Italics indicate approval for a neglected-disease indication.
Sources: EMEA and FDA data;
IMS statistics; WHO essential drug list (EDL, available at www.who.int/medicines/edl/edl11-alpha.html); reference 5.

Table 2: **Innovation during 1975–99**

PUBLIC HEALTH

ment for all neglected diseases, six research and development projects can be classified as mid-late development projects, and an additional 12 early development projects are ongoing. This number compares with an estimated 2100 compounds in clinical development for all other diseases during 1999–2000.[7]

There is no indication that drug development for neglected diseases will significantly improve in the near future. A recent study by the Drugs for Neglected Diseases working group (an independent group established by Médecins Sans Frontières to examine drug development for neglected disease) and the Harvard School of Public Health questioned the world's top 20 pharmaceutical companies on their research and development activities for malaria, tuberculosis, African trypanosomiasis, Chagas' disease, and leishmaniasis. 11 companies responded, representing 29% of the worldwide pharmaceutical market for 2002. Of these companies, seven reported spending less than 1% of their research and development budget over the previous fiscal year on any of the five diseases, and eight spent nothing on the three most neglected diseases (African trypanosomiasis, Chagas' disease, and leishmaniasis).[8]

Overall, the biggest advance in drug research and development and new chemical entity outputs for neglected diseases has been in malaria, for which four new chemical entities have been approved between 1975 and 1999, and 18 projects were in clinical development in 2001. The new approaches to antimalarial therapies rely mainly on artemisinin derivatives discovered in China in the 1970s, which are particularly effective in combination with other drugs in slowing the development and spread of drug resistance. Malaria represents the largest proportion of public and private research expenditures for tropical diseases (includes research on drugs, vaccines, environmental interventions, and vector-control programmes) and accounted for 56% of the 1988–99 Tropical Disease Research (TDR) budget, 2% of the total US National Institutes of Health budget, and 4% of the UK Wellcome Trust's budget.[9] The other neglected diseases are poor relatives when compared with malaria (table 3).

Moreover, the mean time for clinical development is longer for neglected diseases than for other indications. In the USA, the mean time for clinical development during the 1990s was 8·8 years for neglected diseases, compared with 5·4 years for other indications.[10] The comparatively poor performance is attributable to the low market viability of these compounds, and hence suboptimum funding compared with potentially more profitable projects. Whereas the development of all 16 new chemical entities for neglected diseases received at least some level of public-sector support, this sector is also failing: thus far there is no example of the public sector as applicant for a drug registered for a neglected indication (although a submission to the US, UK, and Swiss authorities made in 2001 by TDR for rectal formulation of artesunate is awaiting assessment).

The data presented here quantify the degree of neglect and poor outcome in terms of drugs to control the infectious diseases that disproportionately affect impoverished populations. Although substantial advances in molecular biology and pathophysiology have been made—including the ongoing genome sequencing of the parasites that cause malaria, leishmaniasis, and African trypanosomiasis—these advances are not translating into new products directed at the needs of patients.[11,12] More is known and published on the biology of leishmania and trypanosomes than any other parasite, yet virtually no products result from this wealth of knowledge.[13] This absence is mainly a consequence of inadequate investment in drug research and development for neglected

Disease	Early development*	Mid–late development	Studies with registered entities
Malaria	Chlorproguanil/dapsone/artesunate (Liverpool University [UK], GSK, TDR, MMV)	Chlorproguanil/dapsone (TDR, GSK, DFID, WHO)	Artemether/lumefantrine (Novartis)
	Pyronaridine/artesunate (TDR, Shin Poong, MMV)	Artesunate rectal (TDR, Knoll Sherer, Scanpharm, Novartis)	Artesunate/mefloquine (WT, TDR, MSF)
	Modified side-chain chloroquine (Tulane University [TX, USA])	Tafenaquine (etaquine: WRAIR, GSK, NIH)	Artesunate/sulfadoxine/pyrimethamine (TDR, MSF, IDA, WT)
	Dihydroartemisinin (Artecef BV)	..	Artesunate/amodiaquine (TDR, MSF)
	Fosmidomycin (Jomaa Pharmaka GmbH, TDR)	..	Dihydroartemisinin/piperaquine (Guangzhou University [China], WT, WHO)
	Desbutyl halofantrine (GSK)	..	Dihydroartemisinin/mefloquine (Thai Government, TDR)
	..	..	Artesunate/atovaquone/proguanil (WT)
	..	..	Azythromycin combinations (WRAIR, NIH, Pfizer)
Leishmaniasis (visceral)	Sitamaquine (WR6026: WRAIR, GSK)	Paromomycin (TDR, IOWH, MSF, IDA)	Amphotericin B liposomal (Cornell & Banaras Hindu University [India])
	..	Miltefosine oral (TDR, AstaMedica)	..
Onchocerciasis	Moxidectin (TDR)	..	Ivermectin/albendazole (TDR)
	Oral eflornithine (Aventis, TDR)	..	Ivermectin/levamisole (TDR)
	..	..	Albendazole/levamisole (TDR)
	..	..	Ivermectin/doxycycline (TDR, Nocht Institute [Germany])
Lymphatic filariasis	..	..	Ivermectin/albendazole (TDR)
	..	..	Ivermectin/doxycycline (TDR, Nocht Institute)
	..	..	Albendazole/diethylcarbamazine (TDR)
Schistosomiasis	Artemether (TDR)		Praziquantel/albendazole (TDR)
Chagas' disease	..		..
Leprosy	..	Oxofloxacin/rifampicin (TDR)	..
Tuberculosis	Moxifloxacin	..	..
	Gatifloxacin	..	..

Sources: WHO, Special Programme for Research and Training in Tropical Diseases (TDR). GSK=GlaxoSmithKline; MMV=Medicines for Malaria Venture, Switzerland; WT=Wellcome Trust, UK; MSF=Médecins Sans Frontières; WRAIR=Walter Reed Army Institute of Research, USA; IDA=International Dispensary Association, Netherlands; IOWH=International One World Health; DFID=Department for International Development, UK; NIH=National Institutes of Health, USA. *No absolute distinction can be made between early and mid–late development.

Table 3: **Drugs under clinical development for a neglected-disease indication in 2001**

diseases. For example, investment in research for malaria, at $42 per fatal case, is at least 80 times lower than for HIV/AIDS and 20 times lower than for asthma.[14] The other neglected diseases lag even further behind.

Current incentives and technology transfer

The pharmaceutical industry argues that research and development is a "costly and risky activity".[15] This argument is put forward to explain the lack of research and development into diseases of the poor, and to justify the high price of new chemical entities. Developed countries offer viable market incentives for research and development through individual purchasing power and purchasing through government-run health insurance programmes. In Europe, for instance, these mechanisms cover two-thirds of drug costs for 80–100% of the population[16] as opposed to 35% in Latin America and less than 8% in Africa.[17] With public spending on drugs at around $239 per head per annum in countries belonging to the Organisation for Economic Cooperation and Development (OECD), the pharmaceutical industry has a strong incentive to develop drugs for this market. By contrast, most developing countries spend less than $20 per year and per head on all health programmes (less than $6 in sub-Saharan Africa, including drug expenditures[18]). This situation results from a market too small to attract private-sector investment in research and development for the diseases that mainly affect developing countries.

Measures envisaged to overcome this limitation in both public and private markets are either incentives devised to encourage private investment towards the development of new cost-effective drugs (often referred to as push and pull mechanisms), or public-private partnerships.

Push mechanisms are incentives that operate upstream during the research and development process, and involve costs to the public sector without a guarantee that a viable drug will be delivered (such as tax credits for and public investment in research and development, which lower the cost). Pull mechanisms operate downstream, and offer public incentives for development of a product (examples include patent extensions and advance purchase commitments). In exchange for this increased market attractiveness or market subsidy, private pharmaceutical companies are expected to increase their research and development efforts.[19] There are examples of push and pull mechanisms, or a blend of the two, being applied to areas of the pharmaceutical sector with variable effects.

Orphan drug legislation is an example of push and pull elements combined, which uses a blend of tax credits, market exclusivity, and intellectual property protection. The US Orphan Drug Act, which grants market exclusivity for rare diseases of national public-health priority in the USA, is generally regarded as a domestic success story.[20] Drawing a parallel between rare and neglected diseases drugs is tempting. However, orphan legislation operates within a market logic: reasons for success in the USA, are inapplicable in the countries mainly affected by neglected diseases, and so far no drug candidates for a neglected disease indication have been developed and marketed through US and European orphan legislations.[21] Moreover, market prices for orphan drugs are extremely high (the annual cost of life-long treatment with alglucerase for Gaucher's disease is about $150 000 per patient[22]), whereas the average annual per-head health-care expenditure in sub-Saharan Africa is currently $6.[23] Push mechanisms might contribute to fast-track research and development or give a wealth of new lead compounds through public investment. But if there is no viable market for these candidate drugs (patient or

government purchasing power), there will be no incentive to develop them further. In the USA, 39% of new chemical entities in clinical development are abandoned because profit prospects are poor.[24]

Orphan-type legislation is therefore unlikely to provide the solution to drug development for tropical diseases. In any case, whether the pharmaceutical industry—one of the most profitable industrial sectors today[25] thanks to extended market monopolies—should be given further market incentives is to be questioned. The ongoing debate surrounding industry's claim that drug research and development is extremely costly,[26] and the uncovering of the pharmaceutical industry's innovation deficit,[27] lend further weight to such concerns.

Another mechanism that has been mainly applied to vaccines is differential pricing between industrialised and developing countries, allowing research and development investments to be recouped in wealthier countries so that lower prices can be charged in developing countries (eg, pricing at production costs plus a small margin).[28] Whether differential pricing can be applied to drugs is currently being explored, but it would be unlikely to offer much for the most neglected diseases that exist exclusively in poor countries.

In 1998, more than 90% of the worldwide pharmaceutical production by value, and 97% of research and development activities, occurred in developed countries.[29] With few exceptions, the countries concerned with neglected diseases lack adequate capacity to undertake research and development activities for neglected diseases. To counter this polarity, building of local research and development and production capacity through technology transfer is being examined as a tool to generate long-term solutions as well as economical development. The transfer of capacities requires an enabling environment at both the provider and the receiver end—in most cases, the private sectors of developed and developing countries. Capacity building and technology transfer has been promoted for many years by such groups as the United Nations Development Programme,[30] TDR, and the Drugs for Neglected Diseases Working Group. It can be promoted via bilateral and multilateral development cooperation, but priority-setting must be well adapted to the specific needs and capabilities of the concerned countries, who themselves must place neglected diseases higher up the political agenda. Emerging economies could be the first target of action, and solutions for the poorest countries could be grafted on successful drug production facilities in those countries.

This issue of technology transfer inevitably leads to the consequences of the implementation of provisions of the World Trade Organisation TRIPS (Trade-Related Intellectual Property Rights) agreement. Whether intellectual property rights can significantly affect technology transfer (which is included as an objective in Article 7 of the TRIPS agreement) and foreign direct investment towards developing countries is unclear.[31]

A broader question with respect to intellectual property rights protection is how viable it is as a system for stimulating research and development and delivering the most needed medicines. The costs to national governments of extended intellectual property protection and subsidies need to be considered. Intellectual property regimes are in essence a pull mechanism intended to promote research and development. There is no conclusive evidence that further strengthening of intellectual property rights (through for example roaming patent extensions—a proposal favoured by the pharmaceutical industry) results in benefits to public health. In the OECD countries, between the 1980s and 1990s, the effective patent life of drugs was extended by 6 years as a result of several "patent term restoration" measures that conferred a total average patent life of 14 years from marketing (such as the Hatch-Waxman Act of 1984 in the USA and the Supplementary Protection Certificate of 1993 in Europe). But while the total number of products registered increased slightly in the same period, the mean innovation index remained unchanged (table 2). Judging from the lack of research and development for tropical diseases in the past 25 years, market incentives provided by intellectual property rights do not work when market prospects are poor or non-existent.

Regulations are an important element in the research and development process, and have been adapted by Western regulatory authorities to respond better to specific priority health needs. For example, fast-track registration was successful in speeding up the delivery of medicines for HIV/AIDS. Such measures result, in particular, in shorter review times for drugs considered as responding to health priorities: the mean approval time in the USA is 11·8 months (ranging from 26·4 months for respiratory agents to 4·6 months for AIDS antiretrovirals).[32]

In the West, drug regulation follows strict guidelines defined by the International Conference on Harmonisation of regulatory requirements for registration of pharmaceuticals (ICH). But neglected diseases are not a priority in the West, and region and context-specific expertise and regulatory capacity is therefore needed in countries where these diseases are endemic so that review and registration of novel compounds or new chemical entities can occur in a way that is relevant to the priorities of disease-endemic countries.

For example, malaria control has improved significantly in some Asiatic countries because of the availability of new and effective drugs, notably artemisinin derivatives, registered in several disease-endemic countries. Yet corresponding drug dossiers may not strictly conform to ICH guidelines. Initiatives to harmonise drug regulation at a regional level currently underway in southeast Asia (ASEAN technical cooperation in pharmaceuticals) and South America (MERCOSUL treaty) are examples of initiatives that should be strengthened.

Double standards of drug quality, safety, and efficacy are not acceptable, and standards set by WHO must be adhered to as the minimum normative criteria. But guidance on regulatory procedures based more on technological advances than on nationally determined health priorities are increasingly being applied, with the net effect of inhibiting drug development capacity in the developing world. Specific procedures should be designed to allow for a better assessment of the risk-benefit ratio of drugs for neglected diseases, allowing for speedier and more effective drug development.

Public-private partnerships

Public-private partnerships (PPPs) attempt to fill gaps in the health needs of developing countries through the establishment of public-private collaboration, networks, and partnerships.[33,34] The private sector includes for-profit (pharmaceutical companies) and not-for-profit (charities, foundations, and philanthropic institutions) groups, whereas the public sector includes international organisations, development and aid agencies, governments, and academia.

Recently, PPPs have altered the international health landscape, particularly in the pharmaceuticals sector, as a new paradigm for drug development activities. They have resulted from a gradual convergence of the private-for-profit and public sectors (under pressure of international organisations such as the World Bank), concerned engagement by the not-for-profit sector, and the pharmaceutical industry's need to improve its image.

Traditional examples of public institutions working in partnership with the private sector on individual drug development projects include TDR and the US Walter Reed Army Institute of Research (WRAIR). The antimalarial drug mefloquine, for example, was discovered by the WRAIR and later developed jointly with industry and TDR. The PPP concept has more recently evolved into more structured and product-based collaborations, mainly for products that have already reached advanced phases of development.

There were various examples of ad-hoc agreements during the 1990s to develop drugs between TDR and WRAIR and drug companies, sometimes with government-donor support. However, the progressive withdrawal of the pharmaceutical industry from the tropical-disease sector widens the gaps in the drug development process, especially at the point of transition between discovery and early development. To address this problem, recent agreements between the public and private sector also focus on the discovery process, for example to access industry's chemical libraries (such as the agreement between the Japanese pharmaceutical industry association, the Japanese government, and TDR). Most of these types of partnerships have depended on a coincidence of priorities among partners who each contribute assets or funds to develop specific products.

The most recent trend favours disease-based initiatives, as exemplified by the Medicines for Malaria Venture (which accounts for most of today's antimalarial drug development projects) and the Global Alliance for Tuberculosis. Both initiatives focus mainly on converting drug candidates into registered entities using a social venture capital model funded by the public and philanthropic sectors. They are managed as not-for-profit ventures, operate in collaboration with several partners ranging from the traditional pharmaceutical industry to corporations, academia, and development agencies,[35] and rely on business drug development models and a medium-term secured budget including newer sources of funding (such as the Gates Foundation).

Industry has played a part in the establishment of these new ventures, is represented through their boards, and is a development partner, contributing both facilities and assets and receiving funds. However, company engagement is limited: of the 14 active or planned projects of the Medicines for Malaria Venture, five still have no industrial partner, and six companies are involved in the remaining nine projects (GlaxoSmithKline alone accounts for three).

Much hope is placed in public-private partnerships, but it is too early to say how successful these initiatives will be.[34] Moreover, developing a drug is one thing, but consideration must also be given to ensuring equitable access. Engagement with an industry whose strategy has so far largely been to maximise profit in the West, rather than establish an equitable pricing policy worldwide,[7] requires careful management of intellectual property. Donor agencies, for their part, must do more to assist in drug procurement: current financial pledges to the Global Fund for AIDS, TB and Malaria, at less that one fifth of the estimated requirement, indicate that much greater political will is required.

PPPs clearly do not provide the solution for all tropical diseases. They exist for tuberculosis and malaria because these diseases rank higher in the public-health priorities of developed countries than other, more neglected diseases and represent a potential market for industry. For other neglected diseases that do not represent a health threat to the developed world, public and private sector engagement for neglected diseases is likely to be more difficult to motivate.

Conclusions

Despite impressive advances in science, technology, and medicine, society has failed to allocate sufficient resources to fight the diseases that particularly affect the poor. There is a dearth of research and development into neglected diseases to control the re-emergence of human African trypanosomiasis, to replace the ineffective and toxic drugs for Chagas' disease, to overcome resistance to antileishmanial and antimalarial drugs, and to develop more effective drugs for tuberculosis to shorten treatment and address multidrug-resistant disease.

Market prospects and return on investment dictate the pharmaceutical industry's investments, leaving many medical needs unmet. Only 16 new chemical entities marketed in the past 25 years were for tropical diseases and tuberculosis, and all were developed with public-sector involvement. Whereas on average two in three new drugs developed in this period offer little or no therapeutic advance over existing treatments, all new drugs for neglected diseases represent a clear therapeutic benefit, and all are included in the WHO Essential Drug List, which indicates the importance of new drugs for neglected diseases.

National governments and international organisations have recently increased efforts to correct the imbalance between a decreasing supply and a growing demand for drugs that meet the needs of poor countries. A range of market push and pull measures are being proposed to attract the pharmaceutical industry to invest or reinvest in the neglected diseases area. In parallel, various PPPs have been established, combining respective capacities and resources. Although all such efforts are certainly necessary, their possible effect is likely to be insufficient to meet the vast and increasing health needs of poor people in the developing world.

Patent life has increased in the past 20 years, but the rate of innovation has not. Moreover, only one in three new drugs developed in the past 25 years represent a clear therapeutic advance. This finding raises the question of whether continuously increasing patent protection is an effective stimulus for innovation. The existing global patent system will clearly not answer global population health needs, and certainly will not provide the answer for neglected diseases: a market monopoly incentive is irrelevant when market prospects are absent.

The chronic neglected disease crisis calls for a substantial and long-term response, and will probably require a paradigm shift in health and research and development policy. Governments in the North and South must lead in restarting research and development for diseases that are currently ignored. A well defined, needs-driven research and development agenda is needed to assist policy makers, funding agencies, and the research community in setting priorities. These can be implemented through competent and durable research and development networks in the South, to be built or strengthened via focused capacity and technology sharing.

The private sector must also do more. There is currently an imbalance between private-sector rights and obligations under international agreements. The public sector—ie, the main buyer of pharmaceuticals—provides the private sector with patent incentives for innovation, but has little say over the research agenda. Governments can and do oblige industry to do necessary research in other sectors. A neglected-disease research obligation could be framed that would require industry to reinvest a percentage of pharmaceutical sales into neglected disease research and development, either directly or through public programmes.

For the most neglected diseases such as African trypanosomiasis or leishmaniasis, which might not account for much of the global disease burden, but which represent a significant disease burden in affected countries, a new approach is needed. The Drugs for Neglected Diseases working group is currently exploring the feasibility of an international not-for-profit initiative that would focus on drug development projects for the most neglected diseases. Such an initiative would remove the process of researching and developing life-saving drugs from a market-driven logic. Without a shift to needs-driven research and development, the needs of millions in the developing world will continue to be ignored.

Conflict of interest statement
None declared.

Acknowledgments
We thank all other members of the Drugs for Neglected Diseases working group for their contributions.

References

1   Murray HW, Pépin J, Nutman TB, Hoffman SL, Mahmoud AF. Recent advances, tropical medicine. London: BMJ Publishing, 2001: 490–94.
2   WHO. Adhoc Committee (of the WHO) on health research relating to future intervention options. Investing in health research and development. Geneva: WHO, 1996.
3   Janssens PG, Kivits M, Vuylsteke J. Médecine et hygiène en Afrique centrale de 1885 à nos jours. Brussels: Fondation Roi Baudoin, 1992: 590.
4   Pecoul B, Chirac P, Trouiller P, Pinel J. Access to essential drugs in poor countries: a lost battle? *JAMA* 1999; **281:** 361–67.
5   Trouiller P, Olliaro P. Drug development output from 1975 to 1996: what proportion for tropical diseases? *Int J Infect Dis* 1999; **3:** 61–63.
6   Folkers GK, Fauci AS. The AIDS research model: implications for other infectious diseases of global health importance. *JAMA* 2001; **286:** 458.
7   Health IMS. Market Report, 1999. http://www.ims-global.com//insight/report/market_growth/report0600.htm (accessed March 11, 2002).
8   Pécoul B, Orbinski J, Torreele E, eds. Fatal imbalance: the crisis in research and development for drugs for neglected diseases. Geneva: Médecins Sans Frontières/Drugs for Neglected Diseases Working Group, 2001.
9   Anderson J, MacLean M, Davies C. Malaria research, an audit of international activity. Prims Report number 7. London: Wellcome Trust, 1996.
10 DiMasi J. New drug development in the United States from 1963 to 1999. *Clin Pharm Ther* 2001; **69:** 286–96.
11 Stephenson I, Wiselka M. Drug treatment for tropical parasitic infections: recent achievements and developments. *Drugs* 2000; **60:** 985–95.
12 Vial H, Traore M, Fairlamb A, Ridley R. Renewed strategies for drug development against parasitic diseases. *Parasitol Today* 1999; **10:** 393–94.
13 Wirth D. A harvest not-yet reaped: genomics to new drugs in leishmania and trypanosomes. Geneva: DND Working Group, 2001.
14 Unit for Policy Research in Science and Medicine (PRISM). Malaria research: an audit of international activity. London: Wellcome Trust, 1996.
15 DiMasi JA, Grabowski HG, Vernon J. R&D costs innovative output, and firm size in the pharmaceutical industry. *Int J Econ Bus* 1995; **2:** 201–19.

PUBLIC HEALTH

16 Kanavos P. Pharmaceutical pricing and reimbursement in Europe. Richmond: PJB Publications, 1999.

17 WHO. Health reform and drug financing: overview of experiences, options and priorities for action. Geneva: WHO, 1997: 9.

18 World Health Organization. WHO Medicines Strategy: framework for action in essential drugs and medicines policy 2000–2003. Geneva: WHO/HTP/EDM, 2000. http://www.who.int/medicines/strategy/strategy.pdf (accessed March 2, 2002)

19 Webber D, Kremer M. Perspectives on stimulating industrial research and development for neglected infectious diseases. *Bull World Health Organ* 2001; 79: 735–41.

20 Haffner M. Orphan drug development: international program and study design issues. *Drug Inf J* 1998; 32: 93–99.

21 Trouiller P, Battistella C, Pinel J. Is orphan drug status beneficial to tropical diseases control? Comparison of the American and future European orphan drug acts. *Trop Med Int Health* 1999; 4: 412–20.

22 Goldman DP, Clarke AE, Garber AM. Creating the costliest orphan: the Orphan Drug Act in the development of Ceredase. *Int J Tech Assess Health Care* 1992; 8: 583–97.

23 Makinen M, Waters H, Rauch M, et al. Inequalities in healthcare use and expenditures: empirical data from eight developing countries and countries in transition. *Bull World Health Organ* 2000; 78: 55–65.

24 DiMasi J. Risks in new drug development: approval successes rates for investigational drugs. *Clin Pharm Ther* 2001; 69: 297–307.

25 Fortune500. Top performing industries, 2000. http://www.fortune500.com (accessed March 11, 2002).

26 Young B, Surrusco M. Rx R&D myths: the case against the drug industry's R&D "scare card". Washington DC: Public Citizen Publication, 2001 http://www.citizen.org/publications/release.cfm?ID=7065 (accessed June 11, 2002).

27 Drews J. Innovation deficit revisited: reflection on the productivity of pharmaceutical R&D. *Drug Discov Today* 1998; 3: 491–94.

28 Kadar M. La Mutation du Marché Mondial des Vaccins. *Rev Préscrire* 1995; 15: 844–47.

29 European Federation of Pharmaceutical Industries and Associations. The pharmaceutical industry in figures. Brussels: EFPIA, 2000. http://www.efpia.org (accessed March 11, 2002).

30 United Nations Development Programme. Human Development Report, 2001: making new technologies work for human development. New York: Oxford University Press, 2001.

31 Correa C. The case of pharmaceuticals. In: Correa C, ed. Intellectual property rights, the WTO and developing countries: the TRIPS agreement and policy options. London: Zed Books, 2000: 42–45.

32 Kaitin K, Healy E. The new drug approvals of 1996, 1997, and 1998: drug development trends in the user fee era. *Drug Inf J* 2000; 34: 1–14.

33 Buse K, Walt G. Global public-private partnerships, part II: what are the health issues for global governance? *Bull World Health Organ* 2000; 78: 699–709.

34 Buse K, Walt G. Global public-private partnerships, part I: a new development in health? *Bull World Health Organ* 2000; 78: 549–61.

35 Wheeler C, Berkley S. Initial lessons from public-private partnerships in drug and vaccine development. *Bull World Health Organ* 2001; 79: 728–34.

[19]

Trade policy and the politics of access to drugs

CAROLINE THOMAS

ABSTRACT   *This article explores the relationship between trade policy and access to drugs, using the ARV drugs as an example. It begins by noting the moral problem of inequality in access to drugs. It goes on to explore the political problem in terms of the discrepancy between what is legal/permissible under WTO rules, and what is permissible/desirable under the terms of US trade policy. Finally, it explores the problem of credibility for global health governance and the global market system in terms of access to drugs.*

> Never have so many had such broad and advanced access to healthcare. But never have so many been denied access to health. (Gro Harlem Brundtland, the Director-General of WHO, December 1998)

> Access ... amounts to a moral problem, a political problem and a problem of credibility for the global market system. (Brundtland, 2000)

Significant advances have been made in global health over the past 50 years; for example, life expectancy has increased from 48 in 1955, to 66 in 1998. However, we cannot overlook the fact that these advances are 'marred by growing health disparities between the world's wealthy and the world's poor' (Millen *et al*, 1999: 4). Nowhere are these disparities seen more clearly than in the experience of access to drugs. In spring 2001 the issue of access to drugs was catapulted onto the global political agenda as a transnational alliance of NGOs stepped up their campaign to widen access to anti-retroviral (ARV) drugs for HIV/AIDS sufferers worldwide (see below). These NGOs have argued that the efforts of a few developing countries to pursue legitimate strategies to secure drugs for their people at affordable prices have been obstructed by the combined might of the pharmaceutical industry, and the US government.

This article explores the relationship between trade policy and access to drugs, using the ARV drugs as an example. It begins by noting the moral problem of inequality in access to drugs. It goes on to explore the political problem in terms of the discrepancy between what is legal/permissible under WTO rules, and what is permissible/desirable under the terms of US trade policy. Finally, it explores the problem of credibility for global health governance and the global market system in terms of access to drugs.

Caroline Thomas is in the Department of Politics, University of Southampton, Highfield, Southampton, Hants, SO17 1BJ.

CAROLINE THOMAS

The moral problem: inequality in access to drugs

Perhaps more than any other disease, HIV/AIDS reflects entrenched and growing global inequality and exclusion, and the continuation of the North–South divide. The problem is overwhelmingly (95%) a problem of the South; in particular, it reflects the continuing marginalisation of Africa (Booker, 1999). About 40 million people worldwide are HIV positive; 28 million of these are African. HIV/AIDS remains incurable, although with appropriate combinations of drugs quality of life can be improved and life expectancy considerably enhanced.

The results of the disease are very different, depending on whether one's fate is to be born in the developed or developing countries:

> The inequalities are striking. In developed countries, there may be one pharmacist for every 2000 to 3000 people. A course of antibiotics to cure pneumonia can be bought for the equivalent of two or three hours wages. One year's treatment for HIV infection costs the equivalent of four to six months' salary. And the majority of drugs costs are reimbursed.

> In developing countries, there may be only one pharmacist for one million people. A full course of antibiotics to cure common pneumonia may cost one month's wages. In many countries, one year's HIV treatment—if it were purchased—would consume the equivalent of 30 years' income. And the majority of households must buy their medicines from their own pockets. (Scholtz, 1999)

'Today, hundreds of thousands of people with the disease in the industrialized world lead full, healthy lives, thanks to antiretroviral (ARV) drugs. In the developing world, perhaps only one in a hundred of those needing treatment have full access to ARVs. The vast majority of people living with AIDS in the developing world receive either no medical treatment or only palliative care to reduce pain and suffering' (Panos, 2000: 3). Of those HIV infected, Panos estimates that 12 million in the developing world need ARV drugs now. The overwhelming majority won't get them. Moreover, even if the drugs were available, an appropriate infrastructure would need to be developed for their delivery. In a global environment where aid commitments have fallen over the past decade, and where debt reduction has been slow in coming, the costs of such infrastructural development are prohibitive.

In 2000 the Panos Institute, London, undertook a thorough study of the costs of treating HIV/AIDS (Panos, 2000). It estimated that, worldwide, $60 billion a year was needed at 2000 prices to pay for ARVs, and that this would rise (p 1). To put this figure in context, this was less than 25% of the US annual military budget, and it is $8 billion more than the amount annually spent on obesity in the USA (Piot, quoted in UNAIDS/WHO press release, 28 November 2000). In the case of a country like Zambia, to buy the necessary drugs at current prices for those who need them would cost US$2 billion; that is 57% of Zambian GDP. Panos has estimated that in the developing world it costs roughly $ 4000–6000 per person per year for a course of ARV drugs, and the associated tests and consultations (Panos, 2000: 3).

Despite the denials of pharmaceutical companies, the fact is that *differential access to ARV drugs because of cost contributes to the uneven global experience*

TRADE POLICY AND THE POLITICS OF ACCESS TO DRUGS

of HIV/AIDS. These drugs are produced largely, but not wholly, in the North, and many of them are under patent. Some of them are not on the WHO list of Essential Drugs, because they are too expensive. A few developing countries, such as India and Brazil, have the ability to produce generic versions of some of these patented drugs. These are much cheaper than their patented cousins. The price of patented drugs puts them out of reach of the overwhelming majority of sufferers. Mindful of this, the African Development Forum in Addis Ababa argued in its December 2000 final declaration that: 'A substantial reduction in the prices of antiretroviral drugs and treatments for opportunistic infections is required. African governments, donors and international financial institutions must work in partnership to reduce the price of drugs to a level commensurate with production costs' (African Development Forum, 2000).

For a concrete example of price differentials between patented drugs and generic cousins, let us consider the example of fluconazole, which is used to treat cryptococcal meningitis, among other things. Ten per cent of people with AIDS suffer from this, in some areas, 25%. Without treatment, life expectancy is one month. The drug is under patent to Pfizer until 2004 in the USA. However, since not all countries recognise patents on medicines, it is also being produced generically elsewhere. Médecins sans Frontières (MSF) reported in the *Lancet* on 16 December 2000 that the company has refused to grant voluntary licenses for poor countries to enable them to import an affordable generic supply. As Table 1 shows, if South Africa imported generic fluconazole to treat this problem, this 'would have a striking effect on access and adherence to treatment' (Perez-Casas *et al* for MSF).

TABLE 1

MSF comparative study of generic and patented flucanozole: wholesale prices of 200mg capsules, June 2000

Manufacturer	Country of production	Country of distribution	Price per unit (US$)
Biolab	Thailand	Thailand	0.29
Cipla	India	India	0.64
Bussie	Colombia	Guatemala (negotiated)	3.00
Pfizer		Thailand	6.20
Vita	Spain	Spain	6.29
Pfizer		South Africa	8.25
Pfizer		Kenya	10.50
Pfizer		Spain	10.57
Pfizer		Guatemala (negotiated)	11.84
Pfizer		USA	12.20
Pfizer		Guatemala (not negotiated)	27.60

CAROLINE THOMAS

The political problem: the politics of access to ARV and other drugs

Since the late 1990s a small number of developing countries, with the support of a transnational alliance of NGOs, has been battling for affordable access to essential ARV drugs. It has been estimated that the cost of ARVs will have to be reduced by 95% before they can be affordable to all who need them (Panos, 2000: 2). The efforts of a few developing countries to pursue legitimate strategies to secure drugs for their people at affordable prices have been obstructed by the combined might of the pharmaceutical industry, and the US government. Interestingly, these developing countries have been fighting only for what they are legally entitled to under the WTO Trade Related Intellectual Property (TRIPS) agreement: that is, the use of compulsory licensing and parallel importing to increase access to affordable drugs for their infected citizens. Richard Laing (1999) argues that manufacturers of proprietary drugs would not be affected in any significant way by changes in pricing such as compulsory licensing, as the proportional contribution of Asia, Africa, and the CIS is so small to both turnover and profit of these pharmaceutical giants. However, the manufacturers of the ARV drugs do not agree.

WTO/TRIPS and access to drugs

The issue of patent protection has been high on the international trade agenda since the establishment of the WTO in 1995. The TRIPS agreement sets a minimum standard for intellectual property protection in all member countries' national legislation. In the case of pharmaceuticals, patent protection is extended for a minimum of 20 years. Developing countries had until 2000 (or 2006 for the least developed) to bring their national policies into line with this. In theory at least the TRIPS does allow countries to protect public health. Under Article 8.1, it says that: 'members may ... adopt measures necessary to protect public health and nutrition, and to promote the public interest in sectors of vital importance to their socio-economic and technological development'. Under certain circumstances, TRIPS allows countries to pursue parallel importing (Article 6, Exhaustion of Rights) and compulsory licensing (Article 31).

- Parallel imports refer to importing a patented drug from a third party in another country where it is sold for less. Under Article 28 of the TRIPS, patent owners have the right to prevent third parties from 'making, using, offering for sale, selling or importing' a product, but it is states who determine when these rights are 'exhausted'. Under Article 6, states can take whatever action they deem necessary at the point of exhaustion. This allows for parallel imports as national policy, which is permitted under EU, US and Japanese patent laws (Love, 1999).
- Compulsory licensing permits the manufacture (anywhere) and use of generic drugs without the agreement of the patent holder. Under Article 31 of WTO/TRIPS rules, states can issue such licenses for a number of reasons, not only national emergencies, so long as they adopt adequate safeguards such as compensation. In such emergencies, however, as in the case of non-

TRADE POLICY AND THE POLITICS OF ACCESS TO DRUGS

commercial public use, or to correct anti-competitive practices, they do not need to make prior efforts to negotiate a licence on reasonable commercial terms with the patent holder (Love, 1999).

Under WTO rules, decisions regarding the appropriate amount of compensation paid to patent holders are decided under the national law of the country issuing the licence. These national laws determine the ability of the country to import drugs via compulsory licences. Love points out that 'the TRIPs does have some limits on the ability of a country to export under a compulsory license, but drugs can be acquired from non-WTO member countries, and from WTO member countries where the drug is off patent, or where exports are not the predominant activity, or in countries that provide patent exceptions for imports into countries that have TRIPs compliant compulsory licenses' (Love, 1999). Only a small number of developing countries have the medical and industrial infrastructure to produce these drugs themselves, and also a stratum of the population able to purchase them. As Wright points out, these are the very countries in which pharmaceutical companies would like to expand their market (Wright, 1999: 4). These countries have found that going down this road elicits a heavy-handed response from the USA. Indeed, one author has commented that: 'compulsory licensing ... is a dangerous weapon, in terms of generating a very dramatic response' (Laing, 1999: 3).

US power and the issue of access

The USA argues that the TRIPs is the minimum standard acceptable for patent rights, and in its bilateral dealings it encourages other countries to go for more than the minimum required under international law. This position was clarified by Lois Boland of the US Patent and Trademarks Office in the Geneva conference on compulsory licensing in March 1999: 'In our bilateral discussions, we continue to regard the TRIPs agreement as an agreement that establishes minimum standards for protection and, in certain situations, we may, and often do, ask for commitments that go beyond those found in the TRIPs agreement' (Boland, 1999).

The US government has successfully put Thailand under pressure to change its patent and trade laws so that they are more restrictive than what is allowed under TRIPs. James Love, of the Consumer Project on Technology (CPT) in Washington, DC, comments:

> The problem for developing countries is not whether compulsory licensing of pharmaceuticals is legal, because it clearly is legal. It's the political problem of whether they will face sanctions from the United States government, for doing things that they have a legal right to do, but which the United States government does not like. In the case of Thailand, that country clearly could have done compulsory licensing on these drugs for meningitis and AIDS. They had a statute in place that gave them the authority to do it, and it was consistent with international law. But the US government threatened trade sanctions, and used a carrot and stick approach to persuade the Thai government not to do something which would have been legal under international law. (Cited by James, 1999)

The USA has been less successful in the case of South Africa. South Africa

CAROLINE THOMAS

became the focus of a bipartisan US campaign to get it to amend or repeal the Medicines and Related Substances Control Amendment Act ('Medicines Act') of 1997. Ralph Nader and James Love of CPT have referred to the 'weight of US power, short of military warfare, on South Africa to prevent that country from implementing policies to obtain cheaper sources of essential medicine' (cited by James, 1999: 4). The Medicines Act was passed by the South African Parliament in 1997. However, it was challenged in the local High Court by over 40 pharmaceutical companies, who claimed it was unconstitutional. The dispute was stuck there until April 2001 (see below). A key aim of the act was to enable the government to purchase generic drugs at affordable prices. The health system was undergoing major reform, with the right to health care for all being constitutionally embedded in 1996. This made the issue of drug prices all the more important (Bond, 1999: 767).

The Medicines Act included a raft of provisions for increasing access to affordable drugs. However, the one which most offended the USA was Clause 15(c):

> The Minister may prescribe conditions for the supply of more affordable medicines in certain circumstances so as to protect the health of the public, and in particular may ... prescribe the conditions on which any medicine which is identical in composition, meets the same equality of standard and is intended to have the same proprietary name as that of another medicine already registered in the Republic ... may be imported. (Cited in Bond, 1999: 768)

The USA objected to the legitimisation of parallel importing and compulsory licensing. Leon Brittan of the EU wrote to South African Vice-President, Thabo Mbeki, in support of the US position, claiming that South African laws were at variance with WTO obligations and that EU companies would be hurt by this action (Taylor, 14 March 2000).

South Africa was punished for not coming into line by being put on the US trade Special 301 Watch List in April 1998. In June 1998 it was denied Generalized System of Preferences (GSP) treatment for four items, pending progress on intellectual property protection. In 1999 the pressure intensified when US Trade Representative (USTR) Charlene Barshefsky, citing South Africa's advocacy role in the World Health Assembly, called for an 'out of cycle' review of South Africa to be held in September 1999 (Bond, 1999: 776). The 30 April USTR 301 report on South Africa claimed that South African representatives 'have led a faction of nations in the WHO in calling for a reduction in the level of protection provided for pharmaceuticals in TRIPS' (USTR, 11999). As leader of the Non-Aligned grouping at that time, South Africa was well placed to give the issue of access to medicines greater importance on the world health agenda, and to increase support globally for this. At no time, however, did it call for a change in the TRIPS. At the 52nd World Health Assembly, January 1999, a unanimous resolution was passed which gave health a place in trade negotiations.

The USA eventually backed down *vis à vis* South Africa and ended trade pressures (Love, 1999). In May 2000 South Africa was removed from the trade watch list. Why does the USA take this stand against various methods for making drugs more affordable? One reason of course is that pharmaceutical lobbies in the USA are incredibly powerful. Consider that promotional spending by US

TRADE POLICY AND THE POLITICS OF ACCESS TO DRUGS

companies in 1997 was $4.2 billion, equivalent to the total drug sales in Africa. (Laing, 1999: 3). Consider that Pfizer has more staff in its marketing department than work at the whole of the WHO (Koivusalo, 1999: 38). These companies exert pressure on the US government to promote and defend their interests abroad. This is not new.

The case of Bangladesh in the early 1980s is an infamous example of US foreign policy serving the interests of pharmaceutical companies, rather than public interest in broad access to health. The efforts of the Bangladeshi government to streamline spending on drugs by use of a list of essential drugs met with a very hostile reaction from the companies, who urged the US government to encourage the government of Bangladesh to change its mind. This it did. The US government even includes representatives of the industry in its official visits to other countries. In 2000, for example, the president of Merck joined US State Department officials on a visit to Brazil, the purpose of which was to encourage the Brazilian government to abandon legislation that would increase access to affordable AIDS medications.

US policy seemed to be changing in May 2000, following NGO campaigning on the issue in the election year. President Clinton signed an Executive Order which 'prohibits the US Government [from bringing trade sanctions] with respect to any law or policy in beneficiary sub-Saharan countries that promotes access to HIV/AIDS pharmaceuticals or medical technologies and provides effective and adequate intellectual property protection consistent with the TRIPs agreement' (James, 2000). In other words, the USA would accept the WTO standard on patents, rather than requiring more stringent US trade law standards. While this represented a significant change, critics asked why the step was limited to Africa and to AIDS drugs (Africa Trade Bill, 2000). The AIDS problem extends to other continents, and within Africa there are many other important health challenges such as TB and malaria.

The industry response was hostile. Alan Holmer, the president of the Pharmaceutical Research and Manufacturers of America, commented that the Executive Order sets 'an undesirable and inappropriate precedent, by adopting a discriminatory approach to intellectual property, and focusing exclusively on pharmaceuticals' (reported in Africa Trade Bill, 2000).

The situation has been evolving rapidly. In January 2001 President Bush considered reversing Clinton's Executive Order, so the WTO/TRIPS standard may not satisfy US trade representatives in future (Kaiser Daily, 2001). In terms of equal access to drugs, this would be bad news. Also worrying was that the USA has raised the issue of Brazilian patent laws at the WTO, and asked for an arbitration panel to investigate their conformity with WTO rules. Despite all the US protestations against Thailand and South Africa, it did not take a dispute to the WTO for adjudication. One possible reason was the calculation that it probably would not win. However, with a new government and new relationships with pharmaceutical companies, policy has been shifting and muscles have been flexed. Given the Brazilian success in producing ARV drugs since 1996 and treating patients free of charge, this is potentially a huge blow not only to AIDS sufferers in Brazil, but to those worldwide. Brazil has offered its drugs to other countries. NGOs such as Oxfam and MSF have immediately gone into top gear,

CAROLINE THOMAS

campaigning against the US reversal. The implications of the case go far beyond HIV/AIDS (Act Up Paris, 2001). The findings will set a precedent.

The role of the pharmaceutical giants in issues of access to drugs

The powerful pharmaceutical companies in the North vehemently oppose attempts by developing countries to produce or acquire cheap drugs, especially via methods that would be most likely to result in a sustainable solution. They are opposed to generic production in the South, even though many of them are involved in it themselves in the North (Nogues, 1990). As we have seen above, they are supported in this stance by the US government, which has pursued an aggressive trade policy to ensure a strict definition of international patent protection (Wright, 1999). Companies can and do pressure states and generic drug producers directly to persuade them to change their policies, even if they are acting in accordance with international law. One recent example involves Glaxo Smithkline (GSK) and Ghana. GSK has put Ghana, the 5% of its population HIV infected, and the Indian company Cipla under enormous direct pressure. Indirectly this pressure, in the form of a clear signal, extends to other exporters and potential importers and users of generics.

Cipla has been exporting low-cost generic Duovir (AZT and 3TC) to a Ghanaian drugs distributor, Healthcare Ltd. Glaxo has accused Cipla of patent infringement by violating Glaxo's Combivir (brand name for 3TC and AZT combined in one pill) patent rights. In August 2000 GSK threatened to take Cipla to court. However, it seems that Glaxo's patent rights are not valid in Ghana (Schoofs, 2000; Sharma, 2000). The patent system is not retroactive, and Ghana did not allow patent protection for pharmaceuticals until 1 July 1993. The Global Treatment Access campaign argues that: 'because GSK filed for several patents relevant to Combivir before Ghanaian patent law recognized patents on medication, it is likely that GSK's claim to patent rights to Combivir are completely invalid' (www.globaltreatmentaccess.org/content/camp/...ghana.htm, 30 November 2000). In other words, GSK has no exclusive rights to market the medication in Ghana. At least three out of four of Glaxo's patents on Combivir are from before July 1993. Cipla's and Ghana's actions were lawful.

Yet Glaxo's tactics have been successful; Cipla ceased exports to Ghana, and Healthcare Ltd is afraid to distribute the drugs that have already reached the country. In the meantime Ghana's HIV sufferers continue to die, while Glaxo continues to negotiate price reductions for Combivir through the UNAIDS initiative. Here we have the largest pharmaceutical company in the world (7.3% of the global market, with control of over a third of the ARV market (GSK profiting from barriers to essential medicine, 2000) bullying a poor country as well as a small company, neither of whom were breaking international law.

Why are companies so opposed to generic production, parallel importing, compulsory licensing, etc? The most frequently cited reason is that financial incentives are necessary for Research and Development (R&D). Companies claim that R&D costs involved in developing new drugs are so high that developing countries are ill advised to turn to generics, as this will discourage the transnationals from further R&D to deal with Southern diseases. On the surface, this argument is compelling. If companies do not have lengthy patent protection, they do not have an incentive to pour resources into the development of new drugs. But, for a number of reasons, this argument is highly questionable.

First, if it were really the case, many of the developments of the past five decades would not have occurred through lack of patent incentive. For it is only in recent decades that many developed countries have themselves developed patent laws on drugs (the older US patent laws are an exception). Their pharmaceutical industries for the most part developed without this kind of protection (Nogues, 1990: 82-3; Challu, 1991: 74-77). Challu argues that: 'most industrailized countries adopted product patent protection systems once they had already reached a high degree of economic development' (pp 74-75). Challu (1991: 86) argues that 'the hypothesis that increased patent coverage encourages more invention may be regarded as false, based on empirical evidence from the US, as well as on a world-wide level'.

Second, R&D priorities are set by companies not according to public health needs, but rather according to calculations about maximising the return to shareholders. Developing countries do not represent a lucrative market. The global pharmaceutical market is huge—over $400 billion per annum. Yet Africa accounts for only 1.3% of the global health market. About 90% of the $70 billion invested annually in health R&D by pharmaceutical companies and Western governments is not focused on tropical problems, but increasingly on the problems faced by the 10% of the global population living in developed, industrialised countries. Examples include baldness and obesity. This explains why, of the 1233 new drugs that entered the market between 1975 and 1997, only 13 were targeted specifically at tropical, infectious diseases (Pecoul in HAI, 2000).

In their advertising, companies can be somewhat misleading on this point, as demonstrated by the advert below announcing the union of two large companies.

> Today is the day. Today is the day 139 000 people will die prematurely from disease. Over 25 000 of them will be children under five. But today is also the day that Glaxo Wellcome and SmithKline Beecham become one. This means that for the first time, over 100 000 people will pool their unique talents to seek causes and find remedies for diseases all over the world. They will do so not just with a sense of hope. But with a sense of urgency. Diseases do not wait. Neither will we. (GlaxoSmithKline advert in The Economist, January 2001).

But they haven't poured resources into finding cures for diseases of the poor. Indeed, the Global Forum for Health Research reported in 2000 that less than 10% of global health research funding was allocated to 90% of the world's health problems, mostly concentrated in developing countries (World Bank, 2000).

Third, much R&D is initially paid for by Northern taxpayers. The US government funded much research into tropical diseases such as malaria when it had troops in active service abroad. In the case of ARV and related drugs, the US government, through the National Institutes of Health, has funded primary research. While it is true that pharmaceutical companies spend a significant amount on R&D, one should not forget the high profits they make. An alternative explanation of the companies' dislike of generic production in the South is

CAROLINE THOMAS

that they are acting to ensure that they can continue to protect market share in developed countries and continue charging high prices there. This is especially so in the face of increased competition from generics and tighter drug safety and efficacy regulations *in the North* (Nogues, 1990: 81). Ultimately they are protecting their profits.

Companies claim that the price of drugs reflects, among other things, the costs of R&D. Critics, however, claim the prices of proprietary drugs often reflect what the market will bear rather than the costs of R&D. Duckett illustrates this with the case of Pentamidine, a cheap treatment developed for sleeping sickness. She points out that when this drug was found to be effective in treating AIDS-related pneumocystis cariniii pneumonia, the price increased 500% and the drug evaporated from the market in poor African and Southeast Asian countries (Duckett, 1999: 5).

Public–private partnerships and the challenge of widening access to drugs

During 2000 the success of activists in politicising the issue of access, coupled with bad publicity for pharmaceutical companies and the electoral process in the USA, prompted some new initiatives. Importantly, however, patents continued to be supported over cheaper forms of drugs. In July 2000 President Clinton announced $1 billion Export–Import Bank loans for the import of drugs at patented prices. This met sharp criticism from campaigning groups and Southern countries, which saw it as adding to the already unbearable burden of debt of the poorest countries.

Potentially more significant was the joint UNAIDS/five-company initiative announced in May 2000, and it is to that public–private partnership that we now turn. The partnership between five pharmaceutical companies and UNAIDS aims to bring ARV and related drugs to people in the South who cannot afford to buy them in the market place. Let us look at this partnership to help us establish the efficacy of such arrangements to deal with the challenge of access to drugs. The initiative built on the far more limited version of 1997 that aimed at bringing reduced-priced drugs in limited quantities to four countries (Vietnam, Senegal, Uganda and Cote d'Ivoire). On paper the 2000 version represented a significant scaling up of the attempt to bring more drugs more cheaply to more countries and people. Amidst great fanfare, the companies announced their intentions to the *Washington Post*. However, they omitted any details of how much, for how long, and for whom.

Details published in the *Washington Post* about how the initiative was agreed are quite shocking, revealing a startling lack of partnership between the UN agencies and the companies in negotiating the deal, and a lack of clear vision regarding policy and sustainability. (Gellman, 2000) There was no involvement of Southern governments or concerned civil society groups. Many NGOs were sceptical of the initiative at the beginning, and their concerns have been validated. Seven months after the scheme was launched, MSF published a report card (see Figure 1). The findings were staggering.

Instead of enjoying across-the-board price reductions, poor countries have to negotiate individually with each company for each drug. This both weakens

TRADE POLICY AND THE POLITICS OF ACCESS TO DRUGS

UNAIDS/5 COMPANIES ACCELERATED ACCESS PROGRAMME

- Number of countries that have negotiated price reductions to date (December 2000): One (Senegal)
- Number of people with HIV in sub-Saharan Africa: 26 million
- Number of patients that will benefit in Senegal once this programme is implemented (according to UNAIDS): approximately 900 (out of 79 000 with HIV)
- Number of patients that Brazil has put on antiretroviral therapy by using affordable generic medicines: more than 90 000
- Amount of money Brazil has saved on hospitalizations and treatments for opportunistic infections avoided by successful use of antiretroviral therapy (1997–99): $472 million
- Annual cost of triple combination therapy in USA: $10 000–15 000
- Annual cost of triple combination offered by a generic Indian manufacturer (quality meeting international standards): $800–1000

FIGURE 1
MSF six-month report card on a public–private initiative.

their negotiating position and consumes huge human resources. After a year few benefits had ensued.

The May 2000 initiative represents one of the clearest examples of the pharmaceutical companies' role in influencing the health governance agenda. It has deflected attention from the development of more sustainable solutions, regionally, nationally or locally. Even within its own limited vision, this initiative has failed to deliver. What is more, this initiative was ongoing while 42 companies, including some of those involved in the initiative, were still fighting the Medicines Act in the High Court in South Africa. The case was tied up there until April 2001, and throughout this time people were dying because of a lack of availability of affordable drugs. As mentioned earlier, even if the price of the drugs were to plummet, big investments would be needed to develop the necessary infrastructure for their appropriate delivery. This lack of infrastructure, however, in no way legitimates the continuation of drug prices beyond the means of governments and people.

Looking forward

The focus on the case of access to ARV drugs highlights the problematic role of pricing and patent right protection in devising responses both at the global and the national levels to the AIDS epidemic. In practice the legal provisions under the WTO for compulsory licensing and parallel imports, rather than providing a guarantee for genuine public policy responses in the case of emergencies, instead seem to be providing transnational corporations with an opportunity to contest such policy responses. The prime objective of US trade policy—largely supported by the EU trade Commission—and transnational pharmaceutical companies has been to assert, in principle, the primacy of TRIPs, and thus secure

CAROLINE THOMAS

projected profits: the case of ARVs as elucidated in this article illustrates this.

This stance is sustained by arguing that it is not patents, nor the price of ARVs which are the problem; that many drugs needed in the South are not subject to patent; and that in any case many of the poorest Southern states don't have to comply with the TRIPs until 2006. Access problems are presented from this perspective as mainly the result of infrastructural failings, security issues (military conflicts) and lack of expertise in the concerned Southern states (Ensuring access in developing countries, 2000).

At the broadest level, the issue of access to ARVs underscores the struggle at the global level between two competing political projects. On the one hand, there is the neoliberal project, concerned first with disembedding the market from political influence and second with expanding its reach across social institutions. On the other hand, there is a social-democratic project concerned with the delivery of welfare provisions on a more egalitarian basis rooted in conceptions of social justice. As global protests and increased campaigning in the light of the heavy-handed approach by transnational pharmaceutical companies and the US government began to make the neoliberal stance less acceptable, attempts at a diffusion of that stance came under way. It is in this context that the latest proposals for public–private partnerships have to be understood and evaluated.

As we have seen, the particular public–private initiative outlined in this article is essentially flawed, and reveals some major shortcomings which may turn out to be endemic to the new public–private approach to public health. It raises, for instance, the question of whether it is possible for a true partnership to develop in a situation of structural inequality. What are the prospects for an effective partnership between transnational companies and under-resourced UN agencies, or between multilateral organisations and developing countries?

It is clear that next to the issue of pricing, co-ordinated efforts for managing outreach, distribution and effective administration of drugs have to be in place, efforts which involve a much enhanced role for both the institutions of the UN co-ordinating globally and local agencies, groups and institutions. Yet the current situation reflects the stance, voiced by one African spokesperson, that '... there are discussions about us, excluding us' (Cheaper aids drugs for South Africa?, 2000). Robin Stott points out that for partnerships to be effective, health partners need to make policy and hold budgets together (Stott, 1999: 822). In addition, necessary ingredients for success include drugs access that is broad (in terms of range of therapeutic remedies), inclusive (reaching all who need them) and sustainable (encouraging regional or national self-sufficiency).

What role is there for global governance to make a positive impact on behalf of AIDS sufferers and the states concerned with their welfare, and where could such input originate? The WHO, relatively sidelined as a multilateral agency in the 1990s, is now taking a more active interest in trade policy and may make an important contribution to the current policy debate. In May 1999 the 52nd World Health Assembly gave WHO the mandate to do more work on trade-related issues, including access to drugs. In particular, WHO was asked to study the effects of international trade agreements on health. NGOs are working with the WHO to track prices and access to essential drugs (Duckett, 1999: 7). Governments need these data if they are to comprehensively increase their chances to provide access to

TRADE POLICY AND THE POLITICS OF ACCESS TO DRUGS

AIDS-related medication.

Furthermore, the WHO has a role in helping developing countries understand the health implications of the WTO and the TRIPs. 'Globalization and access to Drugs: Perspectives on the WHO/TRIPs agreement', to help with interpretation and guidance. Southern African Development Co-ordinating Conference (SADDC) countries have called on WHO to participate in WTO negotiations and help draft national laws safeguarding compulsory licensing and parallel importing (Kaiser Daily, 2000). Potentially, UNAIDS could help here as well. Clearly, it would be helpful if model legislation could be drawn up for developing countries to assist them in the development of national intellectual property laws.

Support for a strengthening of the public policy role of UN institutions *vis à vis* the imbalances created through the privileging of investors' interests through the WTO is beginning to build. While states like South Africa, Thailand, Brazil and India have acted individually, we are beginning to see strength in numbers and more concerted action not only in the domestic arena, but internationally. This was clear, for example, at the Geneva World Summit for Social Development, June 2000, when G77 countries pushed a proposal for the final conference text to protect essential medicines from patentability. While they did not achieve this, at least they did succeed in getting an affirmation of countries' rights to freely exercise their legal options (Oh, 2000). The WTO's Doha meeting, November 2001, gives grounds for cautious optimism regarding the primacy of public health over patents.

Furthermore, health activists and scholars are also beginning to realise and challenge the potential significance of the WTO, not only on general issues of inequality, but for health issues in particular (Labonte, 1998; Baris & McLeod, 2000). Awareness raising and campaigning on health-trade issues is gaining momentum, as activists see the importance of putting health at the centre of trade debates, rather than on the periphery. The example of the USA, Brazil and the WTO cited earlier illustrates how rapidly NGOs can organise a response.

Access to drugs is affected deeply by a number of factors, one of which is clearly price. The question is whether the governance framework for public health policy will continue to favour an individual's ability to purchase expensive patented drugs over broad-based access and the expanded use of cheaper generic products. Global health issues cannot be abstracted out of *public* policy. If this is so, then a response to health insecurities framed in terms of the former option can only be an *inappropriate* political response. If the global social policy makers are sincere in their commitment to seeking solutions to the global health crisis, *there is no alternative* but to radically re-write the regulations of the global health governance agenda so as to situate access to health care within the parameters of a true public good: the politically guaranteed provision of health care to all, based primarily on *need* rather than on ability to pay.

References

Act-up Paris (2001) The WTO menaces the survival of 100 000 people with AIDS, press release, 2 February.

African Development Forum (2000) Aids consensus and plan, on the Economic Commission for Africa website at http://www.uneca.org/adf2000, December.

CAROLINE THOMAS

Africa Trade Bill: Clinton issues Executive Order relaxing intellectual property rights (2000) *Kaiser Daily HIV/AIDS Report*, 11 May, at www.http://report.kff.org/archive/aid/2000/05/kh000511.1.htm.

Baris, E & McLeod, K (2000) Globalization and international trade in the twenty-first century: opportunities for and threats to the health sector in the South, *International Journal of Health Services*, 30(1), pp 187–210.

Boland, L (1999) USG position on compulsory licensing of patents, 26 March, available at http://www.haiweb.org/campiagn/cl/boland.html.

Bond, P (1999) Globalization, pharmaceutical pricing, and South African health policy: managing confrontation with US firms and politicians, *International Journal of Health Services*, 29(4), pp 765–792.

Booker, S (1999) Letter to APIC members, 13 June.

Brundtland, G (1998) WHO boss sets out stance on health and human rights, WHO press release, 8 December.

Brundtland, G (2000) 'Towards a strategic agenda for the WHO secretariat: Statement by the Director General to the Executive Board at its 105th session' (WHO, EB105/2), 24 January, p 7.

Challu, P (1991) The consequences of pharmaceutical product patenting, *World Competition*, 15, pp 65–126.

Cheaper AIDS drugs for South Africa? Minister tells of progress (2000) Health Systems Trust, at http://hst.org.za/view.php3?id=20001004, 24 October.

Duckett, M (1999) *Compulsory Licensing and Parallel Importing*, ICASO Background Paper, July.

Ensuring access in developing countries (2000), *Health Horizons*, 39, p 12.

Gellman (2000) An unequal calculus of life and death, *Washington Post*, 27 December.

GSK profiting from barriers to essential medicine (2000) http://www.globaltreatmentacccess.org/120100_HG-GSK_GHANA.html, 1 December.

James, J (2000) Africa treatment access in the news, *AIDS Treatment News*, 343, 19 May.

James, J (1999) Compulsory licensing for bridging the gap—treatment access in developing countries: interview with James Love, Consumer Project on Technology, *AIDS Treatment News Archive*, 5 March, at http://www.aids.org/Immunet/atn.nsf/page/a-314-01.

Kaiser Daily HIV/AIDS Report (2000) Africa: Southern countries lack infrastructure to accept offer of price cuts for AIDS drugs, 21 June.

Kaiser Daily HIV/AIDS Report (2001) 23 January, http://report.kff.org/hivaids).

Koivusalo, M (1999) *The WTO and Trade Creep in Health and Social Policies*, GASPP Occasional Paper, Finland.

Labonte, R (1998) Healthy public policy and the WTO: a proposal for an international health presence in future trade/investment talks, *Health Promotion International*, 13(3), pp 245–256.

Laing, R (1999) Global issues of access to pharmaceuticals and effects of patents, presentation to the AIDS and Essential Medicines and Compulsory Licensing Meeting, Geneva, 26 March, http://www.haiweb.org/campaign/cl/laing.html.

Love, J (1999) Five common mistakes by reporters covering US/South Africa disputes over compulsory licensing and parallel imports, 23 September, http://www.cptech.org/ip/health/sa/mistakes.html.

Millen, J, Irwin, A, Kim J & Gershman, J (2000) Dying for Growth: Global Inequality and the Health of the Poor (Main, MS: Common Courage Press).

Nogues, J (1990) Patents and pharmaceutical drugs: understanding the pressures on developing countries, *Journal of World Trade Law*, 24, pp 81–104.

Oh, C (2000) TRIPS and pharmaceuticals: a case of corporate profits over public health, <http:twnside.org.sg/title/twr120a.htm>.

Panos (2000) Beyond our Means: the cost of treating HIV/AIDS in the developing world (London: Panos).

Pecoul, (2000) cited by HAI, May, at http://www.haiweb.org/news/WHA53en.html.

Perez-Casas, C, Chirac, P, Berman, D & Ford, N for MSF (2000) Access to fluconazole in less-developed countries, *Lancet*, 356, 16 December.

Schoofs, M (2000) Glaxo attempts to block access to generic AIDS drugs in Ghana, *Wall Street Journal*, 1 December.

Sharma, S (2000) Drug majors battle for Ghana's AIDS market, *Indian Express* (New Delhi), 17 November.

Scholtz, Executive Director, Health Technology and Pharmaceuticals, WHO (1999) Views and perspectives on compulsory licensing of essential medicines, 26 March, at http://www.haiweb.org/campaign/cl/scholtz.html.

Stott, R (1999) The World Bank: friend or foe?, *British Medical Journal*, 318, pp 822–823.

Taylor, S (2000) 'Drug Firms Fight Lamy', in *European Voice*, 14 March, at http://www.europeanvoice.com/thisweek/index.html.

USTR (1999) www.ustr.gov/releases/1999/04/99-4.1html.

Wright (1999) Does US trade policy keep AIDS drugs out of reach?, 26 July, at http://hivinsite.ucsf.edu/social/spotlight/2098.4374full.html.

World Bank (2000) WHO calls for Third World medical research, *World Bank Development News*, 11 October.

[20]

THE DILEMMA OF INTELLECTUAL PROPERTY RIGHTS FOR PHARMACEUTICALS: THE TENSION BETWEEN ENSURING ACCESS OF THE POOR TO MEDICINES AND COMMITTING TO INTERNATIONAL AGREEMENTS[1]

JILLIAN CLARE COHEN AND PATRICIA ILLINGWORTH

ABSTRACT

In this paper, we provide an overview of how the outcomes of the Uruguay Round affected the application of pharmaceutical intellectual property rights globally. Second, we explain how specific pharmaceutical policy tools can help developing states mitigate the worst effects of the TRIPS Agreement. Third, we put forward solutions that could be implemented by the World Bank to help overcome the divide between creating private incentives for research and development of innovative medicines and ensuring access of the poor to medicine. Fourth, we evaluate these solutions on the basis of utilitarian considerations and urge that equitable pricing is morally preferable to the other solutions.

'At the beginning of the 21st century, one-third of the world's population still lacks access to the essential drugs it needs for good health. In the poorest parts of Africa and Asia, over 50% of the population do not have access to the most vital drugs.'[2]

[1] The authors wish to acknowledge the very helpful comments of anonymous reviewers and the outstanding research and editing suggestions of Jessica Wolland.
[2] G. H. Brundland. May 1, 2000. Speech to the WHO/Public Interest NGO Pharmaceuticals Roundtable, Third Meeting. Geneva, Switzerland.

28   JILLIAN CLARE COHEN AND PATRICIA ILLINGWORTH

I INTRODUCTION

In this paper, we put forward some possible resolutions to the issue of improving access of the poor to essential medicines. This paper responds in part to arguments put forward in an earlier volume of *Developing World Bioethics* (Volume 1, Number 1, 2001). In that volume, Resnik argued that pharmaceutical firms have social responsibilities and moral obligations to meet the health needs of the populations in developing countries. He argued further that if pharmaceutical firms provide reduced pricing or donations to developing countries, then developing countries in turn should foster an adequate business environment for these firms. That is to say, they should honour intellectual property laws for pharmaceuticals. In response Brock, in the same volume, took issue with Resnik on the grounds that increased social responsibility may be inconsistent with a corporation's duties to its shareholders but was not convinced that developing countries should respect intellectual property protection for pharmaceuticals in return for reduced pricing on pharmaceuticals. We acknowledge the murkiness that is inherent to the discussion of pharmaceutical intellectual property protection and access to medicines for the poor; and the risk that pharmaceutical firms and governments of developing countries may not be able to resolve the thorny issue of intellectual property protection to essential medicines bilaterally. We thus call for the intervention of a third party – perhaps through the financing of drugs by an international organisation, like the World Bank, to help improve access of the poor to essential medicines. While intellectual property protection for pharmaceuticals is not the single cause of the lack of access of medicines to the poor, for the purpose of this article we focus on this issue exclusively and on the World Bank's potential role in it.[3] We use the World Bank simply as a model of an international organisation that could become more central to the provision of medicines for the poorest.

The paper is organised as follows. First, we provide an overview of the Trade Related Aspects of Intellectual Property Rights (TRIPS) Agreement, and its provisions which are relevant for pharmaceutical products and processes. Second, we explain how specific pharmaceutical policy tools can help developing states mitigate the worst effects of the TRIPS Agreement. Third, we provide an overview of the ethical dilemmas that intellectual

---

[3] For example, poor infrastructure, mismanagement, and sometimes corruption, are all variables that can potentially limit the access of the poor to essential medicines.

THE DILEMMA OF IP RIGHTS FOR PHARMACEUTICALS   29

property protection for pharmaceuticals presents. And fourth, we put forward solutions that could be implemented by an international organisation, like the Bank, to help overcome the divide between creating private incentives for research and development of innovative medicines, and ensuring access of the poor to critical medicines.

II BACKGROUND ON THE TRIPS AGREEMENT

The TRIPS Agreement was one of the many trade agreements that were agreed upon during the Uruguay Round and included in the new international trading system, governed by the World Trade Organisation (WTO). The Agreement covers a range of intellectual property issues beyond patents, such as trademarks, industrial designs, and copyright, applicable to any sector.[4] It provides minimum standards for intellectual property law, procedures, and remedies so rights' holders can enforce their rights effectively. The main rule of TRIPS for patents is that they should be available for any invention, whether product or process, in all fields of technology with discrimination. Inventions covered under the patent law have to meet the criteria of novelty, inventive step, and industrial applicability. The minimum obligations for pharmaceuticals are: pharmaceutical products and micro-organisms are patentable for up to twenty years from the date the inventor files for the patent application. Second, there is no discrimination permitted against patent rights for imported products. Third, exclusive marketing rights are granted until patent expiry; and, there are transitional periods for developing countries without pharmaceutical product patents.[5] The Agreement does provide a degree of freedom to member states. For example, states can deny patent protection for specific inventions (Articles 27.2 and 27.3), such as 'diagnostic, therapeutic and surgical methods for the treatment of humans or animals'; and plants and animals (other than micro-organisms) and biological processes (other than microbiological) for their production.[6]

The Agreement also provides governments with the authority to issue a compulsory license for a pharmaceutical license without

---

[4] Patent protection for pharmaceuticals is exclusively examined in this paper.

[5] H. Redwood. 1995. *Brazil: The Future Impact of Pharmaceutical Patents.* Felixstowe, Suffolk. Oldwicks Press.

[6] Jeffrey J. Schott, ed. 2000. *The WTO after Seattle.* Washington, D.C. Institute for International Economics.

30 JILLIAN CLARE COHEN AND PATRICIA ILLINGWORTH

the permission of the patent owner when it can be justified in the public interest. The latter was strengthened further in the Doha Agreement on TRIPS and Public Health (November 2001). Compulsory license refers to when a judicial or government official is allowed by law to grant a license without permission from the holder on the grounds of general interest (such as public health considerations).[7] Proponents of the compulsory licensing system stress that consumer price benefits arise from effectively abrogating the market exclusivity of the patent. The TRIPS Agreement also does not prohibit the parallel importing of drug products. Parallel trade refers to the act of purchasing a drug product that is priced lower in another country and importing it to a country for resale where the same product is priced higher.

III THE COSTS AND BENEFITS OF INTELLECTUAL PROPERTY PROTECTION

The potential costs and benefits of intellectual property protection are well known and have been discussed at length elsewhere. Thus, in this section, we highlight a selection of the arguments on both sides of the debate to serve only as requisite background for our ensuing discussion. The application of intellectual property rights is viewed by some as a beneficial government intervention insofar as it can possibly prevent free-riding behaviour and the attendant 'congestion problem' that is particularly acute when intellectual assets are easy to copy. (This applies to the pharmaceutical sector, as the reverse engineering of patented drugs is not technically demanding.) New knowledge may potentially suffer from overuse in the absence of intellectual property because access to it would not be costly. The overuse of knowledge could minimise the economic value of an innovation and limit incentives for others to pursue advances in knowledge.[8] Intellectual property rights thus mitigate the tendency toward free-riding behaviour by limiting who has the rights to an intellectual asset.

Furthermore, they provide an inventor with some degree of certainty that he can capture a sufficient amount of rent for his innovation effort by preventing congestion behaviour, and thus encourage the pursuit of new knowledge. This argument assumes that pharmaceutical patents provide incentives for firms to invest

[7] Schott, *op. cit.* note 6, p. 41.
[8] K.E. Maskus. September 12–14, 1997. *The International Regulation of Intellectual Property.* Paper prepared for the IESG Conference on International Trade and Investment. Nottingham. p. 3.

THE DILEMMA OF IP RIGHTS FOR PHARMACEUTICALS   31

resources in the research and development of new drug therapies. New drug therapies are desirable if we assume that they can help cure or prevent diseases and improve the health of the population, which in turn, can lead to economic growth.[9] Thus, pharmaceutical patent protection should encourage firms to invest in the research and development of new drug therapies specific to the disease burden of developing states that had previously not protected pharmaceutical patents. We deem this highly unlikely, given existing trends in the research and development of pharmaceuticals. Of the 1393 new drugs approved between 1975 and 1999, only 16 (or just over 1%) were specifically developed for tropical diseases and tuberculosis; diseases which account for 11.47% of the global disease burden.[10]

The TRIPS Agreement imposes minimum standards for pharmaceutical patents for member states of the WTO. Compliance for most developed states, including those with relatively mature production and innovation systems, did not demand significant changes in existing standards and institutions.[11] For developing states, the pharmaceutical patent regime, for the most part, was considerably below the minimum criteria of the TRIPS Agreement. From the standpoint of innovating drug firms in the advanced economies, the TRIPS Agreement corrects deficiencies in the latter regimes that lead to copying of products and ultimately loss of rent for innovating firms. These include the absence of patents for pharmaceutical products, the issuing of compulsory licenses for products without adequately compensating the firm of an innovating product, and a weak or poorly defined system of rules to protect trade secrets, therefore facilitating the imitation and copying of products.[12]

From a public health perspective, intellectual property protection for pharmaceuticals may maintain the uneven direction of product research and development, by limiting the type of drug therapies available to treat disease among the poor.

---

[9] The Bank health sector strategy paper notes, 'no country can secure sustainable economic growth or poverty reduction without a healthy, well nourished, and educated population.' Bank. 1997. *Health, Nutrition, and Population Sector Strategy Paper.* Washington, D.C. Bank Group: 10.

[10] Doctors Without Borders. 2001. *Fat Imbalance: The Crisis in Research and Development for Drugs for Neglected Diseases.* Geneva

[11] C. R. Frischtak. 1993. Harmonization Versus Differentiation in Intellectual Property Rights Regimes. In *The Global Dimensions of Intellectual Property Rights in Science and Technology: A Conference.* M.B. Wallerstein, M.E. Mogee, & R.A. Schoen, eds. Washington, D.C. National Academy Press: 99.

[12] Maskus, *op. cit.* note 8.

32   JILLIAN CLARE COHEN AND PATRICIA ILLINGWORTH

Here is the reason why. Patents impede progress in technology by precluding other firms from cross-learning and building on the original innovation. Patents produce a loss or 'dead-weight burden' insofar as the benefits of the new knowledge to society would have been greater in the absence of a patent regime, and thus reduce the capacity for other firms to exploit the knowledge on a competitive basis.[13] Additionally, the application of pharmaceutical patents could result in the further concentration of production of pharmaceuticals in advanced economies. International drug firms will be free to export finished or semi-finished products, instead of transferring technology. Consequently, foreign direct investment may be lessened.[14]

A much anticipated cost of the TRIPS Agreement is that it gives pharmaceutical firms greater scope for price discrimination, a rational move for profit-maximising firms, but exploitative to persons in developing countries.[15] If drug prices increase, in addition to the obvious implications for public health, this could be potentially politically disastrous for many politicians in developing states who are already under pressure from their constituents to improve access to medicines and lower pharmaceutical prices.

Although the innovating pharmaceutical industry emphasises the importance of patents as an incentive for research and development, there are also powerful economic arguments that counter them. Arrow argued that the entrenched patent monopolist has weaker incentives than a 'would-be' entry firm to initiate an R&D programme that would produce substitutes, even superior quality ones, than for goods, which were already profit-generating.[16] This, in turn, results in sub-optimal outcomes for social welfare.

---

[13] Maskus, *op. cit.* note 8, p. 34.

[14] WHO. March 2001. Globalization, TRIPS and Access to Pharmaceuticals. In *WHO Policy Perspectives on Medicines*. Geneva. WHO.

[15] J. Stiglitz. *Two Principles for the Next Round: Or How to Bring Developing Countries in From the Cold.* Paper prepared for the WTO/Bank Conference on Developing Countries in a Millennium Round, WTO Secretariat, Geneva, 20–21 September 1999. p. 34. (Stiglitz argues further that in the next round of trade negotiations, efforts should be made to explore ways to ensure that developing countries achieve 'most favoured pricing' status.)

[16] K. J. Arrow. 1962. Economic Welfare and the Allocation of Resources for Invention. In *The Rate and Direction of Inventive Activity: Economic and Social Factors*. Princeton, N.J. National Bureau of Economic Research: 609–25. As quoted in: Paul A. David. 1993. Intellectual Property Institutions. In *The Global Dimensions of Intellectual Property Rights in Science and Technology: A Conference*. M.B. Wallerstein, M.E. Mogee & R.A. Schoen, eds. Washington, D.C. National Academy Press: 4.

THE DILEMMA OF IP RIGHTS FOR PHARMACEUTICALS 33

Prior to the TRIPS Agreement, many governments in developing countries had adopted an explicit policy preference not to honour intellectual property protection for pharmaceuticals in an effort to promote self-sufficiency in the production of basic medicines, and as in the case of India, develop a competitive local industry. Domestic producers, both private and public, could, then, supply their populations with basic medicines, at prices often considerably lower than those of the research-based pharmaceutical industry and learn by doing so.

In short, the TRIPS Agreement requires developing states to reform drug policy and thereby limit the drug portfolios of local firms. The potential impacts of this are more costly pharmaceuticals and/or limited access of the population to essential medicines. Developed states, by comparison, have tended to support pharmaceutical patent protection in order to protect revenue streams from their established innovative pharmaceutical industry and to promote investment in technological innovation.[17]

IV RECOMMENDED SOLUTIONS TO LESSEN THE TENSION BETWEEN LOCAL AND INTERNATIONAL IMPERATIVES

Specific pharmaceutical policy tools, such as parallel importing, compulsory licensing and price controls, could potentially mitigate the worst effects of the TRIPS Agreement on drug supplies in developing states. We do not claim that these mechanisms solve the issue of improving access of the poor to essential medicines. However, they are policy tools for governments to use in order to adjust the terms of the treaty to local economic and public health realities.

At the international level, however, possible policy options exist that could help ease the tension between ensuring access of the poorest to essential medicines and intellectual property rights. Our following suggestions do not purport to be original, but we offer new thoughts by assigning responsibility for the realisation of these suggestions to an international global policy maker, and we make use of the World Bank as an example. Each one of the ensuing recommendations is imperfect, entailing trade-offs, either for the local and international pharmaceutical industry or for developing states. However, they present possible resolutions to the increasingly complex problem of providing

---

[17] C. Correa. 2000. *Integrating Public Health Concerns into Patent Legislation in Developing Countries.* Geneva: South Centre.

34 JILLIAN CLARE COHEN AND PATRICIA ILLINGWORTH

incentives for the development of new drug therapies and ensuring equal access of the population to these new therapies.

These are: (1) intensified loans or grants to client states for the purchase of patented medicines; (2) the cancellation of debt and the use of these 'extra' financial resources for pharmaceuticals currently under patent; (3) the purchase of patents from the research-based pharmaceutical industry and the licensing of production of the patented drugs to generic drug firms in client states (a split-TRIPS model); (4) the promotion of a tiered pharmaceutical pricing (equity-pricing) system.

Resolution One: intensified pharmaceutical loans for patented drugs

An international organisation, such as the World Bank, could assume an important role in resolving the conflict surrounding the TRIPS Agreement by providing specific loans and grants to developing countries that could enable them to have the financing they need for the purchase of essential medicines that are protected under the patent treaty. To achieve this, the Bank would need to allocate more financing for pharmaceutical procurement and for the monitoring of the types of drugs that client states purchase through these special loans, to ensure that they are in compliance with intellectual property laws and that the drugs are distributed effectively to those in need.

Alternatively, the Bank could provide its client states with loans to purchase drug patents from pharmaceutical firms and license the production of specific drugs to local firms. This solution would enable public financing to reduce the prices of medicines to their marginal costs of production, and permit the research and development firms to recoup their sunk costs of research and development by ensuring that they receive payment for their products. This Resolution presents potential disadvantages to developing states as well as to the international research-based pharmaceutical industry. Unfortunately, some countries, as noted earlier, may not even have the capacity to manufacture these products. For the international research-based pharma-ceutical industry, the disadvantage is clearly the reduction of rents in developing markets.

Resolution Two: debt cancellation to purchase critical pharmaceuticals

Another possible mechanism that could contribute to abating the conflict surrounding the TRIPS Agreement is for international institutions, like the Bank, to forgive the debt of the poorest

THE DILEMMA OF IP RIGHTS FOR PHARMACEUTICALS 35

countries, and demand as conditions attached to the forgiveness of debt that the 'surplus' money is spent on priority medicines under patent for those in need.[18] This Resolution builds on the Highly-Indebted Poor Countries Initiative (HIPC I) in 1996 and HIPC II in 1999, which the Bank initiated along with the International Monetary Fund (IMF). The HIPC Trust Fund has obtained $2.5 billion in bilateral contributions and pledges from about 20 countries. To date, the Bank has transferred more than $1.3 billion to the Bank component of the Trust Fund.[19]

To ensure that the countries honour their commitment to purchase patented medicines, the debt relief assigned to drug purchases could be transferred directly to the Bank. The Bank would then be responsible for managing the procurement of essential drugs under patent and monitoring their delivery in the targeted client state. This Resolution could benefit both developing states and the pharmaceutical industry. Developing states make gains by having their debts cancelled and probably improving the access of their population to pharmaceuticals. It does not guarantee that increases in drug spending will result in measurable gains in health outcomes. Nor does this Resolution offer a long-term solution to the dilemma of ensuring rents to the research-based pharmaceutical industry and access to patented drugs to the most vulnerable. Finally, it assumes that the Bank will have sufficient human resources to take on these expanded responsibilities.

Resolution Three: purchase of patents by the Bank and licensing of patented drugs to generic drug manufacturers

The Bank could purchase patents from the research-based pharmaceutical industry and make licensing agreements with generic drug firms that may or may not be located in developing states. Using financing provided by donors, the Bank could purchase patents from the research-based pharmaceutical industry and then provide licenses to generic drug manufactures in developing states to produce the requisite medicines and distribute them widely.[20]

---

[18] J. Sachs. February 24, 2000. Submission to the Senate Subcommittee on African Affairs. Washington.

[19] For more information see: http://www.worldbank.org.hipc

[20] R. Weissman. AIDS and Developing Countries: Facilitating Access to Essential Medicines. *Foreign Policy in Focus* 2001; 6.

36 JILLIAN CLARE COHEN AND PATRICIA ILLINGWORTH

This Resolution is a modification of compulsory licensing, which the TRIPS Agreement permits, whereby a government can compel a patent holder to grant licenses to domestic firms. These firms then pay the patent holder a royalty for the license. The benefit of having the Bank purchase the patent from the pharmaceutical firm is that the firm may have more trust that the Bank will deliver a sufficient level of rent. Furthermore, the Bank could exercise some measure of quality control by only agreeing to license out the patented drug to generic drug firms that meet international standards, such as Good Manufacturing Practices (GMPs).

Resolution Four: equity pricing

The pharmaceutical industry currently prices its pharmaceuticals by using a tiered pricing system. This type of pricing refers to market segmentation based on the economic profile of a state. We propose, like others before us, that the research-based pharmaceutical industry offer countries an equity-pricing scheme, based on the economic profile of the poorest consumer in a country. This is based on the concept of price discrimination, whereby a pharmaceutical firm sells the same product to different consumers at different prices. Prices are not based on the costs of production but on what the consumer will and can pay. The Bank, ideally, could assist the pharmaceutical industry and developing states in this type of initiative by acting as a broker between them.

Pharmaceuticals under patent could be subject to different pricing schemes depending on the purchasing power of the poorest consumer and health needs. Consumers in developed states would then find themselves subsidising the pharmaceutical needs of consumers in developing states. For developing states, equity pricing is potentially beneficial because it takes into account social and economic conditions but does not guarantee universal access. For the research-based pharmaceutical industry, equity pricing poses the risk of more intensified parallel imports between states. Parallel importing occurs when drugs are imported from a state where a pharmaceutical product is placed on the market with patent holder consent to another state, without the patent holder's consent. The use of parallel importing is permissible under the TRIPS Agreement and employed by many countries, such as those of the European Union.

THE DILEMMA OF IP RIGHTS FOR PHARMACEUTICALS 37

V SOME MORAL CONSIDERATIONS

Whether to implement one or more of these Resolutions should be made in light of ethical considerations. Although each of the Resolutions is beneficial insofar as it aims to facilitate access to needed medicines for people living in developing countries, we argue that an equity-pricing system is morally preferable. This is not to say that we do not support each Resolution, for the problems that face developing countries are of such a magnitude that all of the Resolutions may need to be implemented. Before developing our argument in favour of Resolution Four, equity pricing, we will look at some of the moral problems raised by Resolutions One, Two, and Three.

Our argument is made against the background of two assumptions about the World Bank: that (1) its resources are limited in light of its mission to fight poverty in the developing world and to '... establish economic growth that is stable, sustainable and equitable'; and (2) that this mission is morally important.[21] This is only to say that the demand for World Bank resources far exceeds the available resources, and that some priority setting is necessary. Although we also assume that pharmaceutical organisations have limited resources, we do not *assume* that their mission is *necessarily* morally important. Nonetheless, our argument will show that once pharmaceutical organisations are acknowledged to have a de facto socially and morally important mission, then arguably they ought to shoulder greater moral responsibility for ensuring access to essential drugs.

We are concerned that Resolution One's proposal to offer additional loans to already heavily indebted countries for the purpose of purchasing essential drugs, will not significantly improve access to drugs and, in turn, reduce the suffering in developing countries. Resolution One ensures that pharmaceutical firms will receive rent on their products and, arguably, this will encourage the innovation of medicines that may help people, including those living in developing countries; although for the latter, current trends do not suggest this will be the case.

However, the prospect of such debt, often in addition to longstanding debt, may have a chilling effect on the willingness and ability of developing countries, especially the least developed, to secure loans for essential drugs for their communities. Our fear then is that Resolution One will do little in the end to relieve the suffering in developing countries.

---

[21] http://www.worldbank.org/about/whatwedo

38   JILLIAN CLARE COHEN AND PATRICIA ILLINGWORTH

From the perspective of justice, it is also worth asking whether, given the health and welfare crisis in developing countries and the economic robustness of the pharmaceutical industry, is it just for developing countries to be further burdened with additional debt when pharmaceutical companies might well assume greater economic responsibility? This is a concern about who ought to shoulder the burden. World Bank funds that are not directed at paying for patented drugs could be directed toward meeting other urgent social needs in the developing world. The pharmaceutical industry argues that they need to charge high prices on their patented property in order ultimately to effectively undertake R&D. However, a recent article in the *Economist* reports that the cost of R&D in the pharmaceutical industry is on the decline.[22] Moreover, as Resnik and later Schüklenk and Ashcroft point out, the developing world is not the primary source of pharmaceutical profits.[23] From a justice-based perspective, increasing the burden on developing countries, even indirectly through the World Bank, when there is another alternative, is morally problematic.

Naturally, we are also concerned that measures, such as loans, will place developing countries in the morally undesirable position of depending on others for additional loans that they may never be able to pay back and will not contribute to the development of sustainable pharmaceutical systems. We assume that this will encourage a cycle in which loan repayment figures importantly, and sound economic development becomes impossible. In the end, Resolution One may do little to alter the burden of disease in developing countries.

Resolution Two, which proposes to forgive debt contingent upon using the forgiven amount for the purchase of needed medicines, also raises moral concerns. First, although the World Bank could offer to forgive the debt contingent on the beneficiary using the forgiven amount to purchase critical drugs, many developing countries cannot now afford to repay their debts because they simply do not have the economic wherewithal to do so. If funds are unavailable to repay loans, they may likewise be unavailable to pay the high cost of patented drugs for the

[22] G. Carr. Survey: The Pharmaceutical Industry: Beyond the Behemoths. *The Economist* February 21, 1998: 16–18.

[23] D. Resnik. Developing Drugs for the Developing World: An Economic, Legal, Moral, and Political Dilemma. *Developing World Bioethics* 2001; 1: 11–22; U. Schuklenk & R. Ashcroft. Affordable Access to Essential Medication in Developing Countries: Conflicts Between Ethical and Economic Imperatives. *Journal of Medicine and Philosophy* 2002; 27: 179–195.

THE DILEMMA OF IP RIGHTS FOR PHARMACEUTICALS 39

millions of people who need them. If so, then developing countries would ultimately be unable to make use of the opportunity afforded by Resolution Two. Thus, as with Resolution One, we assume that Resolution Two will not result in benefits for developing countries.

Second, given the wide-ranging economic and social problems that many developing countries face, it is far from clear that they ought to devote the 'surplus' to pay the high prices of patented pharmaceuticals, and in this way ultimately subsidise the pharmaceutical preferences of the developed world.[24] Using loan forgiveness as an incentive to fashion a developing countries' health policy may be paternalistic.

Third, Resolution Two may also be coercive insofar as the original agreement was not made between free and equal parties. Consider the following. The fairness of a given agreement is determined in part by whether the parties to the agreement are free and equal at the time of the agreement.[25] It is not clear that any agreement between developed and developing countries or NGOs for the purpose of providing necessities to developing countries, is fully voluntary.[26] The pull of poverty, sickness, and death place the bargainers under duress. Even if, strictly speaking, the agreements are valid, they can certainly be challenged under the moral principles that ground the notion of an agreement made freely and without duress. When necessities, such as food, shelter, and medicine are at issue, it is not clear that repayment ought to be demanded in any case. If the initial loan agreement was morally compromised because one of the parties was under great duress, neither equal nor free at the time of the agreement, then the original wrong would only be compounded were the forgiveness of the loan made contingent upon purchasing drugs. In other words, the loan should be forgiven outright.

It might be argued that Resolution Two has the merit of benefiting both the research-based pharmaceutical industry and developing countries by increasing demand for pharmaceuticals, creating incentives and ensuring that developing countries get the drugs they need. Again, as with Resolution

[24] D.J. Ncayiyana. Antiretroviral Therapy Cannot Be South Africa's First Priority. *CMAJ JAMC* 2001; 164: 1857–1858.

[25] This is implicit in the kinds of considerations that are used to negate contracts (e.g. infancy, insanity, undue influence, and duress). See: A.L. Corbin. 1950. *Corbin on Contracts*. St. Paul. West Publishing Company.

[26] See: *Henningsen v. Bloomfield Motors*. Supreme Court of New Jersey, 32 N.J. 358; 161 A.2d 69 (a good case on necessities).

40 JILLIAN CLARE COHEN AND PATRICIA ILLINGWORTH

One, we are not convinced that the resources of the World Bank
(and indirectly the developing countries) should pay for
patented drugs.

Although Resolution Three, like One and Two, has the
potential to make critical medicines more accessible to those in
need in developing countries, it does so at a high cost, since it
also requires the payment of 'market' price for these patents.
Thus, it shares some of the same moral weakness as Resolutions
One and Two.

Resolution Four proposes that an international broker, like the
World Bank, negotiate an equity-pricing system with pharmaceutical firms and that the pharmaceutical industry implement
such a policy. Because this Resolution prices medicine according
to morally relevant factors, such as what countries are able to pay,
it has distinct moral advantage. It ensures that the principle of
charging what the market will bear will not impede access of the
poor to needed medicines. It promises to reduce suffering in a way
that Resolution One, Two, and Three do not. Presumably, most
people would share the view that ability to pay for medicine should
not determine whether someone enhances the quality of his or
her life, or even lives or dies, recalling the extraordinary properties
of medicines. Moreover, it shifts the burden of helping improve
the access of the poor to medicines, to the pharmaceutical
industry. We propose this with the understanding that pharmaceutical corporations have obligations to their shareholders. We
argue, however, that this obligation should not be viewed as an
obstacle to implementing Resolution Four – an equity-pricing
system.

To this end, it will be helpful to evaluate the theoretical model
that has been used to justify the corporate practice of charging
what the market will bear. Although we shall call this the 'primacy
of the shareholder' view, it has been referred to in a number of
ways.[27] According to this principle, the primary duty of organisations is to maximise shareholder profits. Managers who sacrifice
profit may be interpreted to be in breach of their legal Duty of
Care to shareholders.[28]

---

[27] It has been referred to by a number of terms, including fiduciary duty and
classical view. We choose this term because it is most perspicuous for an
interdisciplinary audience.

[28] M. Friedman. 1997. The Social Responsibility of Business is to Increase
Profits. In *Ethical Theory and Business*. T. L. Beauchamp & N.E. Bowie, eds.
Upper Saddle River, NJ. Prentice Hall: 30, 56; Revised Model Business Code 8:
30 (a), 1992.

THE DILEMMA OF IP RIGHTS FOR PHARMACEUTICALS 41

Our discussion of shareholder primacy will be framed around the dialogue that took place between David Resnik and Dan Brock in which they discussed the concept of corporate social responsibility as it applied to pharmaceutical companies.[29] Although a number of related matters were discussed in that dialogue, we will focus only on their discussion of corporate responsibility. Resnik argued that pharmaceutical companies have social responsibilities to the developing world because they, like other moral agents, '. . . have obligations to avoid causing harm and to promote social welfare.'[30] Brock argued that corporations are unlike moral agents insofar as their responsibilities are to their shareholders.[31] Brock seems to be invoking an argument in support of role differentiation. That is, he appears to be arguing that corporations do not have the same moral obligations as individuals because they serve a different social role – one that requires shareholder primacy.

Debunking the myth of shareholder primacy

Indeed, corporations do have legal responsibilities to shareholders. However, it is far from clear that these are as primary as Brock and others appear to assume. We agree with some of the objections that Brock presents against Resnik's arguments. We argue, however, that corporations have considerable social obligations to facilitate access to essential drugs in developing countries. Although these obligations may not rise to the level of legal obligations, they potentially have greater force than mere supererogatory obligations. The view articulated by Schüklenk and Ashcroft, that a social responsibility approach relies too heavily on philanthropic inclinations, may be less problematic than they suppose.[32]

The classical theory of shareholder primacy, and the one that Brock invokes, holds that there is a fiduciary relationship between directors and shareholders that puts the interests of shareholders first. Because Brock does not reference his statement about shareholder primacy, it is difficult to know what argument he has in mind. In any case, many of the most

---

[29] D. Resnik, *op. cit.* note 22; D.W. Brock. Some Questions about the Moral Responsibilities of Drug Companies in Developing Countries. *Developing World Bioethics* 2001; 1: 33–37.

[30] D. Resnik, *op. cit.* note 22.

[31] D.W. Brock, *op. cit.* note 28, p. 34.

[32] Schuklenk & Ashcroft, *op. cit.* note 22, pp. 179–195.

42 JILLIAN CLARE COHEN AND PATRICIA ILLINGWORTH

persuasive statements of this position have come from legal cases, scholars, and the economist Milton Friedman.[33] One of the main legal arguments is based on agency law, according to which shareholders are viewed as the owners (the principals) of the corporation and managers, their agents.[34] This indeed has even deeper roots in master-servant law. Both of these maintain that the agent must act only for the principal, leaving aside other constituencies, including the manager himself. When applied to the modern corporation, however, this argument seems only remotely relevant. The modern corporation is a great departure from the principal-agent model since it is based on the separation of ownership and control of the corporation, with managers assuming a very active role and shareholders a relatively passive one.

The shareholder primacy view has also been justified on the grounds that the shareholders own the corporation, that they are the principals, and that the directors are bound to maximise their wealth. This conception of the modern corporation, called the 'property conception', was articulated by A.A. Berle in the now famous Harvard debate and re-articulated in the popular press by Friedman.[35] In this conception, maximisation of the stockholders' wealth is thought to follow from the fact that they *own* the corporation. However, even if we accept the view that stockholders *own* the corporation, there is nothing about ownership *per se* that necessarily means that the corporation must aim at shareholder profit, especially when shareholders contribute little other than money. Moreover, the common practice of extending stock options certainly weakens any claim of shareholder ownership.[36]

A relatively recent but significant modification to the reasoning in support of shareholder primacy can be found in the 'agency costs' view. According to this view, in the best of all possible worlds, it would be preferable if managers could consider the interests of all of a corporation's constituencies (all

[33] A.A. Berle, Jr. Corporate Powers as Powers in Trust. *Harvard Law Review* 1932; 45: 1049–1074.

[34] One reason to think that this view is wrong when applied to managers is that they are not agents in the classic sense. Modern corporations separate ownership and control of the corporation because owners frequently know little about the corporation while managers know a great deal.

[35] Berle, *op. cit.* note 32; M. Dodd. For Whom Are Corporate Managers Trustees? *Harvard Law Review* 1932; XLV: 1162; Friedman, *op. cit.* note 27, p. 30.

[36] Ibid. p. 1192. See also: F. Black & M. Scholes. The Pricing of Options and Corporate Liabilities. *J. Pol. Econ.* 1973; 81: 637.

THE DILEMMA OF IP RIGHTS FOR PHARMACEUTICALS   43

those who affect the organisation and are affected by it), including among others employees, clients, and the community. Unfortunately it cannot, because any departure from shareholder primacy would entail giving too much discretion to managers, who after all are human and therefore too opportunistic to be given such discretion.[37] Were managers to be given such discretion they would not necessarily act in the interests of society but instead act in their own interest (the classic principal-agent problem). Mark Roe states: '... a stakeholder measure of managerial accountability could leave managers so much discretion that managers could easily pursue their own agenda, one that might maximize neither shareholder, employer, consumer, nor national wealth, but only their own.'[38]

In yet another view, identified as the social entity conception, the corporation is seen as a social construction, with social purposes. According to Merrick Dodd, 'Business – which is the economic organization of society – is private property only in a qualified sense, and society may properly demand that it be carried on in such a way as to safeguard the interests of those who deal with it either as employees or consumers even if the proprietary rights of its owners are thereby curtailed.'[39] Dodd believes the case for social responsibility is even stronger with respect to companies that have strong public dimensions, such as railways and public utilities. Arguably, pharmaceutical companies would fall into this category. In the social entity conception, corporations have much broader social purposes and duties than simply the maximisation of shareholder wealth.[40] From this brief overview of the three main theories of the firm, it can be seen that the theory we adopt will influence what we take to be the duties of pharmaceutical organisations.

Many people take the property conception, coupled with shareholder primacy, as a given. Nonetheless, according to William Allen, the courts and legislatures have endorsed the entity view and the social obligations it supports.[41] Interestingly, one of the ways that the legal system has accomplished this is with the enactment of corporate constituency statutes. These statues

---

[37] Ibid.

[38] M.J. Roe. Symposium Norms and Corporate Law: The Shareholder Wealth Maximization Norm and Industrial Organization. *U. Pa. L. Rev.* 2001; 149: 2063, 2065.

[39] Dodd, *op. cit.* note 34, p. 1162.

[40] Ibid. pp. 1149–150.

[41] W.T. Allen. Our Schizophrenic Conception of the Business Corporation. *Cardozo Law Review* 1992; 14: 276.

44   JILLIAN CLARE COHEN AND PATRICIA ILLINGWORTH

have undermined the primacy of shareholders, in support of
other constituencies, such as employees and the community. In
the United States, at least 29 states have adopted corporate
constituency statues.[42]

Provisions 4 and 5 of the New York statute, for example, permit
directors to consider other constituencies when they act, and to
act on behalf of these other constituencies.[43] Ultimately, corporate constituency statutes realign the focus of a corporation's
duty of care to include others in addition to shareholders. Thus,
managers may well have a (legal) right to consider other
constituencies in addition to shareholders without being in
violation of their obligations to shareholders. Scholarly work on
the theory of the firm – and the corporate constituency statues
that follow from it – show that shareholder primacy can no
longer be taken for granted and that corporations cannot be
shielded from assuming greater social responsibilities on the
basis of it. In this respect, the moral intuitions of many ethicists
seem to have informed and guided the law.

The American firm seems to be responding to imperatives
other than shareholder primacy. If this is so, it is a mistake to
shield pharmaceutical companies from increased moral
responsibility for ensuring access to essential drugs for those in
developing countries on the basis of shareholder primacy.
Moreover, pharmaceutical companies may, in theory at least,
embrace the social entity view. Merck, for example, says in its first
statement of values: 'Our business is preserving and improving
human life.' Second, Merck claims, 'we are committed to the
highest standards of ethics and integrity.'[44]

If we move away from the belief that corporations are obligated
only to shareholders, we can better evaluate Resolution Four. In

----

[42] E.W. Orts. Beyond Shareholders: Interpreting Corporate Constituency
Statues. *George Washington Law Review* 1992; 61: 14–135. See also: R. Roman.
What is the Value of Other Constituency Statutes to Shareholders? [Comment].
University of Toronto Law Journal 1993; XLIII: 533–542.

[43] New York's Corporate Constituency Statute:

> 'In taking action a director shall be entitled to consider without limitations
> ... the effects that the corporation's actions may have ...for any of the
> following: ...

> 4. the corporation's customers and creditors
> 5. the ability of the corporation to provide as a going concern, goods,
> services, employment opportunities and employment benefits and other-
> wise to contribute to the communities in which it does business.'

[44] Merck & Co., Inc. 'Mission Statement: Our Values' at www.merck.com.
overview/philosophy

THE DILEMMA OF IP RIGHTS FOR PHARMACEUTICALS 45

effect, our strategy has been to show that the *role* that was invoked to exempt pharmaceutical companies from assuming greater social responsibility to render aid, namely their duty to shareholders, is a fiction.

Pharmaceuticals for social justice: equity pricing

It is arguable that the pharmaceutical industry could assume a greater role in providing medicines to the neediest. Such action can be justified based on a number of principles, including consequentialism, the principle of beneficence and its social and legal correlate, Good Samaritan laws.[45] In what follows, we will focus on the principle that Peter Singer articulates in his paper, 'Famine, Affluence and Morality.' The principle is as follows: 'if it is in our power to prevent something bad from happening, without thereby sacrificing anything of comparable moral importance, we ought morally to do it.'[46] The application of this principle to the issue at hand is obvious, but it will be helpful to go through the analysis. Relieving pain, suffering, loss and unnecessary death are moral goods by many moral barometers – including consequentialism and the principle of beneficence. Equity pricing can relieve the suffering of many of those in developing countries who need essential drugs, by making those drugs affordable. So clearly, pharmaceuticals can satisfy the first part of Singer's principle – that is, they can prevent something bad from happening, such as suffering and death.

We examine briefly if an equity-pricing scheme could be accomplished without losing something of comparable moral value. The only loss of comparable value would be the loss of other lives. Would the lives saved through equity pricing cause the loss of other lives? We can speculate confidently that the answer is 'no.' It is worth noting that the pharmaceutical industry is the most profitable industry in the US.[47] Moreover, many of the drugs it manufactures are 'me too' drugs, requiring little

---

[45] See for example: The Bill Emerson Food Donation Act. Public Law 104–210 (October 1, 1996), which protects donors (typically grocery stores) who donate food to non-profit organisations from liability for harm caused by the product. Although not typical of Good Samaritan laws, this Act shows that as a community we encourage organisations to render aid that they are uniquely suited to render, especially with respect to necessities.

[46] P. Singer. 2001. Famine, Affluence and Morality. In *Writings on an Ethical Life*. New York. Harper Collins: 107.

[47] Marcia Angell. The Pharmaceutical Industry: To Whom is It Accountable? *NEJM* 2000; 342: 1902–1904.

46   JILLIAN CLARE COHEN AND PATRICIA ILLINGWORTH

innovation while rendering high profits. And the industry spends much more on marketing than on R&D.[48] Many of the drugs that the industry spends money on have little to do with saving lives and much more to do with improving quality of life (e.g. Viagra, Paxil, Ritalin). When we apply Singer's principle, we find that pharmaceutical companies ought to respond more appropriately to the health needs of the poor in developing countries, such as through an equity-pricing system.

VI PENULTIMATE THOUGHTS

A study conducted by MIT in 1995 found that of the 14 drugs the pharmaceutical company had identified as the most medically important in the last 25 years, 11 were partially supported by government funds. Publicly funded science is, thus, an important component of the pharmaceutical industry's R&D.[49] Thus, the view that profits belong solely to the pharmaceutical industry because it has only invested in R&D is not always the case. The industry does invest large amounts in R&D for innovative medicines, but public entities, such as the National Institute for Health, also contribute. This is a large issue that cannot be sufficiently addressed here, but we raise it for consideration.

   Public funds are directed to research that will, ideally, result in helpful medicines that contribute to the public good. This is so for many reasons, including the moral qualities of medicine. Medicines play a foundational role in supporting other community values, such as liberty, equal opportunity, and human flourishing and are critical for the good functioning of health systems. In view of this, they cannot be considered as equivalent to other consumer goods. A similar intuition underlies Dodd's view that public utilities have unique social obligations.[50] In short, we believe that of the four Resolutions, Resolution Four, which advocates equity pricing, has a distinct moral advantage and is likely to be the most practical Resolution to apply.

---

[48] Angell, *op. cit.* note 46.
[49] J. Gerth and S.G. Stolberg. Medicine Merchants: Birth of a Blockbuster; Drug Makers Reap Profits On Tax-Backed Research. *New York Times* April 23, 2000.
[50] Dodd, *op. cit.* note 34, p. 1162.

THE DILEMMA OF IP RIGHTS FOR PHARMACEUTICALS   47

VII CONCLUSIONS

The TRIPS Agreement and pharmaceutical pricing policies present complex ethical dilemmas about ensuring access of the poor to critical medicines. The Treaty may impede efforts to improve access of the poor to medicines under patent, unless creative public policies are put forward. We have argued that there is space for a global policy maker – such as the World Bank – to assume a central and active role. We put forward four potential Resolutions: (1) intensified pharmaceutical loans and grants for patented drugs; (2) debt cancellation to purchase critical pharmaceuticals; (3) purchase of patents by the bank and the licensing of patented drugs to generic drug manufacturers; and (4) equity pricing. These Resolutions are not novel. Some are even well in progress. Indeed, there is a trend toward equity pricing. Because of considerable pressure from public health activists, pharmaceutical companies, such as Merck & Co. and GlaxoSmithKline PLC, are beginning to provide drugs at marginal production costs or less in developing countries.[51] While prices are still out of reach for the poor, they at least demonstrate that equity pricing can be put in practice. We believe we have contributed to the debate about pharmaceutical intellectual property rights by integrating ethical issues and practical solutions and proposing that the pharmaceutical industry can make profits and act in a socially responsible manner.

Patricia Illingworth
Associate Professor
Department of Philosophy and Religion
361 Holmes Hall
Northeastern University
Boston, MA 02155-5000
USA
p.illingworth@neu.edu

Jillian Clare Cohen
Assistant Professor
Leslie Dan Faculty of Pharmacy
University of Toronto

[51] M. Ganslandt, K.E. Maskus and E.V. Wong. Developing and Distributing Essential Medicines to Poor Countries: the DEFEND Proposal, IUI Working Paper Series 552. The Research Institute of Industrial Economics.

48   JILLIAN CLARE COHEN AND PATRICIA ILLINGWORTH

19 Russell Street
Toronto
Ontario
Canada
M5S 2S2
Jillianclare.cohen@utoronto.ca

[21]

TRIPS, Pharmaceutical Patents, and Access to Essential Medicines: A Long Way From Seattle to Doha

Ellen 't Hoen*

I. INTRODUCTION

Infectious diseases kill over 10 million people each year, more than 90 percent of whom are in the developing world.[1] The leading causes of illness and death in Africa, Asia, and South America—regions that account for four-fifths of the world's population—are HIV/AIDS, respiratory infections, malaria, and tuberculosis.

In particular, the magnitude of the AIDS crisis has drawn attention to the fact that millions of people in the developing world do not have access to the medicines that are needed to treat disease or alleviate suffering. Each day, close to eight thousand people die of AIDS in the developing world.[2] The reasons for the lack of access to essential medicines are manifold, but in many cases the high prices of drugs are a barrier to needed treatments. Prohibitive drug prices are often the result of strong intellectual property protection. Governments in developing countries that attempt to bring the price of medicines down have come under pressure from industrialized countries and the multinational pharmaceutical industry.

The World Trade Organization ("WTO") Trade-Related Aspects of Intellectual Property Rights Agreement ("TRIPS" or "Agreement"), which sets out the minimum standards for the protection of intellectual property, including patents for pharmaceuticals, has come under fierce criticism because of the effects that increased levels of patent protection will have on drug prices. While TRIPS does

---

*   Ellen 't Hoen is Coordinator of the Globalisation Project of Médecins sans Frontières ("MSF") Access to Essential Medicines Campaign. She holds a master's degree in law from the University of Amsterdam. The author wishes to thank Ms. Que Mai Do for her assistance in preparing the manuscript.

1.   World Health Organization, *The World Health Report 2001*, 144 (WHO 2000).

2.   See UNAIDS, *Report on the Global HIV/AIDS Epidemic* 125, 129, 133 (UNAIDS 2000), available online at <http://www.unaids.org/epidemic_update/report/Epi_report.pdf> (visited Mar 24, 2002) (outlining the statistics utilized to reach the generally recognized figure of eight thousand deaths per day due to AIDS in the developing world).

offer safeguards to remedy negative effects of patent protection or patent abuse, in practice it is unclear whether and how countries can make use of these safeguards when patents increasingly present barriers to medicine access.

The Fourth WTO Ministerial Conference, held in 2001 in Doha, Qatar, adopted a Declaration on TRIPS and Public Health ("Doha Declaration" or "Declaration") which affirmed the sovereign right of governments to take measures to protect public health. Public health advocates welcomed the Doha Declaration as an important achievement because it gave primacy to public health over private intellectual property, and clarified WTO Members' rights to use TRIPS safeguards. Although the Doha Declaration broke new ground in guaranteeing Members' access to medical products, it did not solve all of the problems associated with intellectual property protection and public health.

II. THE ACCESS PROBLEM AND INTELLECTUAL PROPERTY

A number of new medicines that are vital for the survival of millions are already too costly for the vast majority of people in poor countries. In addition, investment in research and development ("R&D") towards the health needs of people in developing countries has almost come to a standstill. Developing countries, where three-quarters of the world population lives, account for less than 10 percent of the global pharmaceutical market. The implementation of TRIPS is expected to have a further upward effect on drug prices, while increased R&D investment, despite higher levels of intellectual property protection, is not expected.[3]

One-third of the world population lacks access to the most basic essential drugs and, in the poorest parts of Africa and Asia, this figure climbs to one-half. Access to treatment for diseases in developing countries is problematic either because the medicines are unaffordable, have become ineffective due to resistance, or are not sufficiently adapted to specific local conditions and constraints.

Many factors contribute to the problem of limited access to essential medicines. Unavailability can be caused by logistical supply and storage problems, substandard drug quality, inappropriate selection of drugs, wasteful prescription and inappropriate use, inadequate production, and prohibitive prices. Despite the enormous burden of disease, drug discovery and development targeted at infectious and parasitic diseases in poor countries has virtually ground to a standstill because drug companies in developed and developing nations simply cannot recoup the cost of R&D for products

---

3.   See MSF Access to Essential Medicines Campaign and The Drugs for Neglected Diseases Working
      Group, *Fatal Imbalance; The Crisis in Research and Development for Drugs for Neglected Diseases* 10–18
      (Sept 2001), available online at
      <http://www.msf.org/source/access/2001/fatal/fatal.pdf> (visited Mar 24, 2002).

to treat diseases that abound in developing countries.[4] Of the 1,223 new drugs approved between 1975 and 1997, approximately 1 percent (13 drugs) specifically treat tropical diseases.[5]

TRIPS sets out minimum standards and requirements for the protection of intellectual property rights, including trademarks, copyrights, and patents. The implementation of TRIPS, initially scheduled for 2006 by all WTO Members, is expected to impact the possibility of obtaining new essential medicines at affordable prices.

Médecins sans Frontières ("MSF"), together with other non-governmental organizations ("NGOs"), formulated the following concerns related to TRIPS:

- Increased patent protection leads to higher drug prices.[6] The number of new essential drugs under patent protection will increase, but the drugs will remain out of reach to people in developing countries because of high prices. As a result, the access gap between developed and developing countries will widen.

- Enforcement of WTO rules will have a negative effect on local manufacturing capacity and will remove a source of generic, innovative, quality drugs on which developing countries depend.

- It is unlikely that TRIPS will encourage adequate R&D in developing countries for diseases such as malaria and tuberculosis, because poor countries often do not provide sufficient profit potential to motivate R&D investment by the pharmaceutical industry.

- Developing countries are under pressure from industrialized countries and the pharmaceutical industry to implement patent legislation that goes beyond the obligations of TRIPS. This is often referred to as "TRIPS plus." TRIPS plus is a non-technical term which refers to efforts to extend patent life beyond the twenty-year TRIPS minimum, to tighten patent protection, to limit compulsory licensing in ways not required by TRIPS, or to limit exceptions which facilitate prompt introduction of generics.[7]

---

4. See Bernard Pécoul, et al, *Access to Essential Drugs in Poor Countries. A Lost Battle?*, 281 JAMA 361 (1999).

5. See Patrice Trouiller and Piero Olliaro, *Drug Development Output from 1975 to 1996: What Proportion for Tropical Diseases?*, 3 Intl J Infect Diseases 61 (1999).

6. See F. Michael Scherer and Jayashree Watal, *Post Trips Options for Access to Patented Medicines in Developing Countries* 11 (WHO Jan 2001), available online at <http://www.cmhealth.org/docs/wg4_paper1.pdf> (visited Mar 24, 2002) (reporting on three independent studies that found a mean price increase of well over 200 percent with the introduction of product patents).

7. See World Health Organization, *Globalization, TRIPS and Access to Pharmaceuticals* 4 (March 2001), available online at <http://www.who.int/medicines/library/edm_general/6pagers/PPM03%20ENG.pdf> (visited Mar 24, 2002).

Industrialized countries and World Intellectual Property Organization ("WIPO") offer expert assistance to help countries become TRIPS-compliant. This technical assistance, however, does not take into account the health needs of the populations of developing countries. Both of these institutions are under strong pressure to advance the interests of large companies that own patents and other intellectual property rights.

III. IMPORTANT DEVELOPMENTS IN THE DEBATE ON ACCESS TO DRUGS AND INTELLECTUAL PROPERTY

A number of factors have shaped the debate on TRIPS and access to medicines, directly or indirectly impacting the content of the Doha Declaration.

A. BIG PHARMA VS. NELSON MANDELA: TRADE DISPUTE IN SOUTH AFRICA

In February 1998, the South African Pharmaceutical Manufacturers Association and forty (later thirty-nine, as a result of a merger) mostly multinational pharmaceutical manufacturers brought suit against the government of South Africa, alleging that the Medicines and Related Substances Control Amendment Act, No. 90 of 1997 ("Amendment Act") violated TRIPS and the South African constitution.[8]

The Amendment Act introduces a legal framework to increase the availability of affordable medicines in South Africa. Provisions included in the Amendment Act are generic substitution of off-patent medicines, transparent pricing for all medicines, and the parallel importation of patented medicines.[9]

At the start of the litigation, the drug companies could rely on the support of their home governments. For its part, the US had put pressure on South Africa by withholding trade benefits and threatening further trade sanctions, aiming to force the South African government to repeal the Amendment Act.[10] In 1998, the European

---

8.   See *Pharmaceutical Manufacturers' Association of South Africa v President of the Republic of South Africa,* Case No 4183/98 (filed Feb 18, 1998).

9.   Parallel imports are cross-border trade in a patented product, without the permission of the manufacturer or publisher. Parallel imports take place when there are significant price differences for the same good in different markets. For more information, see *Health Care and Intellectual Property: Parallel Imports,* available online at <http://www.cptech.org/ip/health/pi/> (visited Mar 24, 2002).

10.   See Omnibus Consolidated and Emergency Supplemental Appropriations Act, Pub L No 105-277, 112 Stat 2681 (1999):

> [N]one of the funds appropriated under this heading may be available for assistance for the central Government of the Republic of South Africa, until the Secretary of State reports in writing to the appropriate committees of the Congress on the steps being taken by the United States Government to work with the Government of the Republic of South Africa to negotiate the repeal, suspension, or termination of section 15(c) of South Africa's Medicines and Related Substances Control Amendment Act No. 90 of 1997.

Simon Barber, *US Withholds Benefits over Zuma's Bill,* Bus Day 13 (S Africa) (Jul 15, 1998).

Commission joined the US in pressuring South Africa to repeal the legislation.[11] AIDS activists effectively highlighted these policies, profoundly embarrassing then-presidential candidate Al Gore. Confronted at election campaign rallies about his personal involvement in the dispute, demonstrators accused him of killing babies in Africa.[12] As a result of increasing public pressure, the US changed its policies at the end of 1999. By the time the case finally reached the courtroom in May 2000, the drug companies could no longer count on the support of their home governments.

Demonstrators in major cities asked the companies to drop the case; several governments and parliaments around the world, including the European Parliament, demanded that the companies withdraw from the case. The legal action turned into a public relations disaster for the drug companies.[13]

During the course of the trial it became clear that the most contentious section of the Amendment Act was based on a draft legal text produced by the WIPO Committee of Experts,[14] a fact that made it difficult for the drug companies to maintain the position that the Amendment Act violated South Africa's obligations under international law. Eventually, the strong international public outrage over the companies' legal challenge of a developing country's medicines law and the companies' weak legal position caused the companies to unconditionally drop the case in April 2001.

The widely publicized South African court case brought two key issues out into the international arena. First, the interpretation of the flexibilities of TRIPS and their use for public health purposes needed clarification to ensure that developing countries could use its provisions without the threat of legal or political challenge. Second, it became clear that industrialized countries that exercised trade pressures to defend the interest of their multinational industries could no longer exert pressure without repercussions at home.

---

11. See Letter from Sir Leon Brittan, Vice-President of the European Commission, to Thabo Mbeki, Vice-President of South Africa (Mar 23, 1998) ("Section 15c of the [medicines] law in question would appear to be at variance with South Africa's obligations under the TRIPS and its implementation would negatively affect the interest of the European pharmaceutical industry.") [Letter on file with CJIL].

12. See Simon Barber, *Activists Accuse the US of Blocking Access to Drugs,* Bus Day 6 (S Africa) (Apr 19, 1999).

13. See Helene Cooper, Rachel Zimmerman, and Laurie McGinley, *Patents Pending: AIDS Epidemic Traps Drug Firms In a Vise: Treatments vs. Profits,* Wall St J A1 (Mar 2, 2001) ("Can the pharmaceuticals industry inflict any more damage upon its ailing public image? Well, how about suing Nelson Mandela?").

14. See Pat Sidley, *Silent Trump Card Gives State Winning Hand,* Bus Day 2 (S Africa) (Apr 20, 2001).

Chicago Journal of International Law

B. US vs. Brazil: The Brazilian AIDS Program

Since the mid-1990s, Brazil has offered comprehensive AIDS care, including universal access to antiretroviral ("ARV") treatment. An estimated 536,000 people are infected with HIV in Brazil, with 203,353 cases of AIDS reported to the Ministry of Health from 1980 through December 2000. In 2001, 105,000 people with HIV/AIDS received ARV treatment. The Brazilian AIDS program has reduced AIDS-related mortality by more than 50 percent between 1996 and 1999.[15] In two years, Brazil saved $472 million in hospital costs and treatment costs for AIDS-related infections.

At the core of the success of Brazil's AIDS program is the ability to produce medicines locally. In Brazil, the price of AIDS drugs fell by 82 percent over five years as a result of generic competition.[16] The price of drugs that had no generic competitor remained relatively stable, falling only 9 percent over the same period. Brazil has also been able to negotiate lower prices for patented drugs by using the threat of production under a compulsory license.[17] Article 68 of the Brazilian patent law allows for compulsory licensing, which allows a patent to be used without the consent of the patent holder.[18] The Brazil AIDS program serves as a model for some developing countries that are able to produce medicines locally, and Brazil has offered a cooperation agreement, including technology transfer, to developing countries for the production of generic ARV drugs.[19]

In February 2001, the US took action against Brazil at the WTO Dispute Settlement Body ("DSB") over Article 68 of the Brazilian intellectual property law. Under that provision, Brazil requires holders of Brazilian patents to manufacture the product in question within Brazil—a so-called "local working" requirement. If the company does not fulfill this requirement, the patent shall be subject to compulsory licensing after three years, unless the patent holder can show that it is not economically feasible to produce in Brazil or can otherwise show that the requirement to produce locally is not reasonable. If the company is allowed to work its patent by

---

15.   See Tina Rosenberg, *Look at Brazil*, NY Times § 6 at 26, 28 (Jan 28, 2001) ("The treatment program has cut the AIDS death rate nationally by about 50 percent so far.").

16.   See Ellen 't Hoen and Suerie Moon, *Pills and Pocketbooks: Equity Pricing of Essential Medicines in Developing Countries* (MSF Jul 11, 2001), available online at <http://www.accessmed-msf.org/prod/publications.asp?scntid=318200146197&contenttype=PARA> (visited Mar 24, 2002).

17.   See Brazil Ministry of Health, Official Note, *Ministry of Health Announces Compulsory Licensing of Nelfinavir Patent* (Aug 22, 2001) [on file with author]; Jennifer L. Rich, *Roche Reaches Accord on Drug with Brazil*, NY Times C1 (Sept 1, 2001).

18.   Law No 9,279 of May 14, 1996.

19.   See Brazil Ministry of Health, *National AIDS Drug Policy* (May 2001), available online at <http://www.aids.gov.br/assistencia/aids_drugs_policy.htm> (visited Mar 24, 2002) (discussing the Horizontal Technical Co-operation Program in Latin America).

importation instead of manufacturing in Brazil, parallel import by others will be permitted.

The US argued that the Brazilian law discriminated against US owners of Brazilian patents and that it curtailed patent holders' rights. The US claimed that the Brazilian law violated Article 27.1 and Article 28.1 of TRIPS.[20] Brazil argued that Article 68 was in line with the text and the spirit of TRIPS, including Article 5.4 of the Paris Convention, which allows for compulsory licensing if there is a failure to work a patent. Article 2.1 of TRIPS incorporates relevant articles of the Paris Convention.

The US action came under fierce pressure from the international NGO community, which feared it would have a detrimental effect on Brazil's successful AIDS program.[21] Brazil has been vocal internationally in the debates on access to medicines, and on several occasions, including the G-8, the Roundtable of the European Commission, and WHO meetings, Brazil has offered support to developing countries to help them increase manufacturing capacity by transferring technology and know-how. NGOs feared that the US action could have a negative effect on other countries' ability to accept Brazil's offer of assistance. On June 25, 2001, in a joint statement with Brazil, the US announced that it would withdraw the WTO panel against Brazil.[22]

C. THE ROLE OF NGOS

NGOs have played a key role in drawing attention to provisions of TRIPS that can be used to increase access to medicines. One such provision pertains to compulsory licensing, which enables a competent government authority to license the use of an invention to a third-party or government agency without the consent of the patent holder. The patent holder, however, according to Article 31 of TRIPS, retains intellectual property rights and "shall be paid adequate remuneration" according to the circumstances of the case. The first international meeting specifically on the use of compulsory licensing to increase access to AIDS medicines took place in March 1999 at the Palais de Nations in Geneva and was organized by Consumer Project on Technology, Health Action International, and MSF. Later that year, the same group of NGOs organized the Amsterdam Conference on Increasing Access to Essential

---

20. See World Trade Organization, Request for the Establishment of a Panel by the United States, *Brazil Measures Affecting Patent Protection*, WTO Doc No WT/DS199/3 (Jan 9, 2001).

21. See, for example, MSF, *US Action at WTO Threatens Brazil's Successful AIDS Programme*, Press Release (Feb 1, 2001), available online at <http://www.accessmed-msf.org/prod/publications.asp?scntid=2182001228232&contenttype=PARA> (visited Mar 24, 2002).

22. See Helene Cooper, *U.S. Drops WTO Complaint Against Brazilian Patent Law*, Wall St J Eur A2 (June 26, 2001).

Drugs in a Globalized Economy, which brought together 350 participants from 50 countries on the eve of the Seattle WTO ministerial conference. The statement drawn up at this conference ("Amsterdam Statement") focused on establishing a working group in the WTO on TRIPS and access to medicines, considering the impact of trade policies on people in developing and least-developed countries, and providing a public health framework for the interpretation of key features of WTO agreements. The working group was to address questions related to the use of compulsory licensing to increase access to medicines, mechanisms to allow production of medicines for export markets to a country with no or insufficient production capacity, patent barriers to research, and overly restrictive and anti-competitive interpretations of TRIPS rules regarding protections of health registration data. In addition, the working group was to examine "burden sharing" approaches for R&D that permit countries to consider a wider range of policy instruments to promote R&D and to consider the practical burdens on poor countries of administrating patent systems. The Amsterdam Statement also urged national governments to develop new and innovative mechanisms to ensure funding for R&D for neglected diseases.

The Amsterdam Statement has served as a guide for the work of NGOs and other advocates on TRIPS and public health. Many international and national NGOs, such as the OXFAM campaign, "Cut the Cost," the South African Treatment Action Campaign, and Act Up, are now involved in campaigning for access to medicines.

D. THE WTO MINISTERIAL 1999 IN SEATTLE

Though public health and access to medicines did not form part of the official agenda in Seattle in the way it would two years later in Doha, the issue did receive attention for a number of reasons. First, in Seattle a Common Working Paper section on TRIPS contained the following proposal: "to issue . . . compulsory licenses for drugs appearing on the list of essential drugs of the World Health Organization."[23] Since only about 11 of the 306 products on the WHO Model List of Essential Drugs are patented drugs in certain countries,[24] this proposal could have limited the use of compulsory licensing, rather than making sure it became a useful tool to overcome access barriers, such as prohibitive pricing, caused by patent abuse.

Then-US President Clinton chose Seattle as the venue to declare a change in US policy with regard to intellectual property rights and access to medicines. The US government had come under fierce attack from AIDS activists because of its policies

---

23.   Common Working Paper of the EC, Hungary, Japan, Korea, Switzerland, and Turkey to the Seattle Ministerial Declaration 3 (Nov 29, 1999), available online at <http://europa.eu.int/comm/trade/2000_round/friends.pdf> (visited Mar 24, 2002).

24.   High cost or price of a drug in general excludes a drug from the WHO Essential Drug List.

in South Africa. Under the new policy, the US Trade Representative and the Department of Health and Human Services would together establish a process to analyze health issues that arise in the application of US trade-related intellectual property law and policy. In his speech, President Clinton referred specifically to the situation in South Africa and the HIV/AIDS crisis, saying that "the United States will henceforward implement its health care and trade policies in a manner that ensures that people in the poorest countries won't have to go without medicine they so desperately need."[25]

In May 2000, President Clinton confirmed the change in US policy by issuing an Executive Order on Access to HIV/AIDS Pharmaceuticals and Medical Technologies, supporting the use of compulsory licenses to increase access to HIV/AIDS medication in sub-Saharan Africa.[26] Although this policy change contributed to breaking the taboo on the use of compulsory licensing in the health field, attention to TRIPS and medicines at the WTO was diverted by the collapse of the WTO conference in Seattle.[27] However, outside the WTO, the debate on access to medicines, TRIPS, and compulsory licensing became more intense.

E. CHANGING ATTITUDES AMONG GLOBAL PLAYERS

A number of international institutions and UN agencies contributed to the debate on access to medicines and looked into the consequences of stronger intellectual property protection for developing countries as a result of TRIPS.

1. The World Health Organization

The public health community first raised concerns about the consequences of globalization and international trade agreements with respect to drug access during the 1996 World Health Assembly. A resolution on the Revised Drug Strategy ("RDS") set out the WHO's medicines policy.[28] The WHO resolution on the RDS requested the WHO in paragraph 2(10) "to report on the impact of the work of the World Trade Organization (WTO) with respect to national drug policies and essential drugs and make recommendations for collaboration between WTO and

---

25. William J. Clinton, *Remarks at a World Trade Organization Luncheon in Seattle*, 35 Weekly Comp Pres Doc 2494, 2497 (Dec 1, 1999).

26. Exec Order No 13,155, 65 Fed Reg 30,521 (2000).

27. See Kevin Gopal, *With Chaos, A Reprieve. The Collapse of the WTO Talks in Seattle Has, for the Time Being Diverted Attention from the Issue of Compulsory Licensing*, Pharmaceutical Executive 32 (Jan 2000) ("Unlikely as it seems the pharmaceutical industry may have reason to thank the demonstrators who brought Seattle and the ministerial meeting of the World Trade Organization (WTO) to a standstill. Had the demonstrators not disrupted the gathering, the forecast for global pharma might be much cloudier.").

28. See World Health Organization, *Revised Drug Strategy Resolution*, World Health Assembly Resolution WHA 49.14 (1996).

WHO, as appropriate." This resolution gave the WHO the mandate to publish, in 1998, the first guide with recommendations to Member States for implementing TRIPS while limiting the negative effects of higher levels of patent protection on drug availability.[29] The US and a number of European countries unsuccessfully pressured the WHO in an attempt to prevent publication of the guide.[30]

At that time, the WHO's involvement in trade issues was highly controversial. The emphasis on public health needs versus trade interest was seen as a threat to the commercial sector of the industrialized world. For example, in 1998, in response to the draft World Health Assembly's resolution on the RDS and in reference to "considerable concern among the pharmaceutical industry," the European Directorate General for Trade ("DG Trade") of the European Commission concluded: "No priority should be given to health over intellectual property considerations."[31]

However, subsequent resolutions of the World Health Assembly have strengthened the WHO's mandate in the trade arena. In 2001, the World Health Assembly adopted two resolutions in particular that had a bearing on the debate over TRIPS.[32] The resolutions addressed 1) the need to strengthen policies to increase the availability of generic drugs, and 2) the need to evaluate the impact of TRIPS on access to drugs, local manufacturing capacity, and the development of new drugs. As a result, the WHO's work program on pharmaceuticals and trade now includes the provision of policy guidance and information on intellectual property and health to countries for monitoring and analyzing the effects of TRIPS on access to medicines.[33]

2. The UN Sub-Commission for the Protection and Promotion of Human Rights

The UN Sub-Commission for the Protection and Promotion of Human Rights passed a resolution, pointing out the negative consequences for human rights to food, health, and self-determination if TRIPS is implemented in its current form. The resolution was an initial effort to monitor the implications of TRIPS on human rights concerns. Reminding governments of the primacy of human rights obligations over

---

29.   See Germán Velasquez and Pascale Boulet, *Globalization and Access to Drugs: Perspectives on the WTO/TRIPS Agreement* (WHO 2d ed 1999).

30.   See Paul Benkimoun, *Agressions et Menaces contre un Responsable de l'OMS Défenseur de l'Accès du Tiers-monde aux Médicaments*, Le Monde (Aug 23, 2001).

31.   European Commission (DG1), *Note on the WHO's Revised Drug Strategy*, Doc No 1/D/3/BW D (98) (Oct 5, 1998), available online at <http://www.cptech.org/ip/health/who/eurds98.html> (visited Mar 24, 2002).

32.   See World Health Organization, *Scaling up the Response to HIV/AIDS*, World Health Assembly Resolution WHA 54.10 (2001); World Health Organization, *WHO Medicines Strategy*, World Health Assembly Resolution WHA 54.11 (2001).

33.   See World Health Organization, *Technical Cooperation Activities: Information from Other Intergovernmental Organizations*, WHO Doc No IP/C/W/305/Add.3 (Sept 25, 2001).

economic policies and programs, the resolution states that there are "apparent conflicts between the intellectual property rights regime embodied in TRIPS, on the one hand, and international human rights law, on the other."[34] Referring specifically to pharmaceutical patents, the resolution stresses the need for intellectual property rights to serve social welfare needs.

3. The United Nations Development Program

In 1999, the United Nations Development Program's ("UNDP's") Human Development Report made a plea for re-writing the rules of globalization to make them work "for people—not just profits."[35] The report, in particular, draws attention to the high cost of the patent system for developing countries compared to the unequal distribution of the system's benefits. 97 percent of the patents held worldwide are held by individuals and companies of industrialized countries, and 80 percent of the patents granted in developing countries belong to residents of industrial countries. UNDP called for a full and broad review of TRIPS and called upon countries not to create an unsustainable burden by adding new conditions to the intellectual property system. The report suggested that countries present frameworks for alternatives to the provisions of TRIPS and that the room for manoeuvring granted in TRIPS be respected in practice.

4. The European Union

In February 2001, the EU adopted the Program for Action, a program which accelerates action on HIV/AIDS, malaria, and tuberculosis in the context of poverty reduction. The EU program recognized the potential problems of TRIPS and the need to rebalance its priorities. In addition, several European Parliament resolutions reflected a shift in support of a pro-public health approach to TRIPS.[36] As part of this approach, DG Trade changed its policy to acknowledge the concerns of developing countries. Reflecting this change, DG Trade dropped its objections to the use of compulsory licensing to overcome patent barriers to medicine access and became an advocate for a global tiered pricing system for pharmaceuticals.[37] These

---

34. United Nations Economic and Social Council Commission on Human Rights Sub-Commission on the Promotion and Protection of Human Rights Resolution 2000/7, para 2, UN Doc No E/CN.4/SUB.2/RES/2000/7 (2000).

35. United Nations Development Program, *Human Development Report 1999*, 2 (Oxford 1999).

36. See, for example, European Parliament Resolution on Access to Drugs for HIV/AIDS Victims in the Third World, 2001 OJ (C 343) 300.

37. See *World AIDS Day: Lamy Calls for More Action on Access to Medicines After Progress in Doha*, Press Release of Pascal Lamy's speech marking World AIDS Day, European Union Trade Commissioner (Nov 30, 2001), available online at <http://europa.eu.int/comm/trade/speeches_articles/spla87_en.htm> (visited Mar 24, 2002).

policy changes are in stark contrast to previous European Commission policies, which closely track the pharmaceutical industry's agenda.

5. Other Organizations

Other organizations, such as UNAIDS, the World Bank, the Group of 77, and regional organizations such as the Organization of African Unity, added their voice to the debate on TRIPS and access to medicines.

Unable to turn a deaf ear to the growing chorus of critics of TRIPS and its effects on access to medicines, the WTO changed course. In April 2001, when proposing a special TRIPS Council session on access to medicines, Zimbabwe—chair of TRIPS Council—said that the WTO could no longer ignore the access to medicines issue, an issue that was being actively debated outside the WTO but not within it.[38] The voices had been heard; public health would be featured as a key subject at the Doha Conference.

IV. A BRIEF HISTORY OF THE DOHA DECLARATION ON TRIPS AND PUBLIC HEALTH

The Fourth Ministerial Conference of the WTO took place in Doha in 2001 and was a breakthrough in international discussions on TRIPS and access to medicines. The WTO Ministerial adopted a Declaration on TRIPS and Public Health, which put public health before commercial interests and offered much needed clarification in the field of TRIPS and public health.

A. THE AFRICAN PROPOSAL FOR A SPECIAL TRIPS COUNCIL MEETING IN JUNE

Zimbabwe's statement on behalf of the "African Group" about the need to confront the access to medicines issue initiated preparations for the Declaration. Just two months later, in June 2001, the TRIPS Council held its first session devoted to TRIPS and access to medicines. It was the first time that the TRIPS Council discussed intellectual property issues in the context of public health. At that meeting, the African Group proposed issuing separate declarations on access to medicines.[39] Referring to the devastating AIDS crisis in Africa and mounting public concern, Zimbabwe stated: "We propose that Members issue a special declaration on the

38.   See Statement by Zimbabwe to the WTO TRIPS Council (Apr 5, 2001) ("Our intention is to bring into this Council an issue that has aroused public interest and is being actively debated outside this organisation, but one which we cannot afford to ignore.") [on file with CJIL].

39.   Compare *TRIPS and Public Health*, WTO Doc No IP/C/W/296 (June 29, 2001) (working paper submitted by the African group, joined by seventeen developing countries) with *The Relationship Between the Provisions of the TRIPS Agreement and Access to Medicines*, WTO Doc No IP/C/W/280 (June 12, 2001) (working paper submitted by the European Communities).

TRIPS Agreement and access to medicines at the Ministerial Conference in Qatar, affirming that nothing in the TRIPS Agreement should prevent Members from taking measures to protect public health."[40]

In September 2001, the TRIPS Council devoted another full day of discussion to the topic of access to medicines. At this meeting, the African Group, joined by nineteen other countries, presented a draft text for a ministerial declaration on TRIPS and Public Health. A comprehensive text, this proposal addressed political principles to ensure that TRIPS did not undermine the legitimate right of WTO Members to formulate their own public health policies. The text also provided practical clarifications for provisions related to compulsory licensing, parallel import, data protection, and production for export to a country with insufficient production capacity. In addition, the draft included a proposal for evaluating the effects of TRIPS on public health, with particular emphasis on access to medicines and R&D for the prevention and treatment of diseases predominantly affecting people in developing and least-developed countries.

At the meeting, the US, Japan, Switzerland, Australia, and Canada circulated an alternate draft, stressing the importance of intellectual property protection for R&D, arguing that intellectual property contributes to public health objectives globally. The text was aimed at limiting the flexibilities of TRIPS during crisis and emergency situations. The EU circulated its own draft, which proposed a solution to the problem of production for exports to fulfill a compulsory license in a country with insufficient or no production capacity by allowing production under the TRIPS Article 30 exception.

From the onset of the pre-Doha negotiations, the main point of contention was the text proposed by the developing countries: "Nothing in the TRIPS Agreement shall prevent Members from taking measures to protect public health."[41] Some developed countries saw this wording as a new rule that would override the present rules of TRIPS, which do not allow for health exceptions that are inconsistent with TRIPS.[42]

The text drafted by the chair of the WTO General Council, Mr. Stuart Harbinson, that was the basis for the negotiations in Doha left the issue unresolved and instead offered two options for Paragraph 4. The first option read:

> Nothing in the TRIPS Agreement shall prevent Members from taking measures to protect public health. Accordingly, while reiterating our commitment to the

---

40. See WTO Council for Trade-Related Aspects of Intellectual Property Rights, *Special Discussion on Intellectual Property and Access to Medicines* 4, WTO Doc No IP/C/M/31 (Restricted) (July 10, 2001) [on file with CJIL].

41. *TRIPS and Public Health* at summary (cited in note 39).

42. See Agreement on Trade Related Aspects of Intellectual Property Rights, art 8(1), Marrakesh Agreement Establishing the World Trade Organization, Annex 1C, 33 ILM 81 (1994) ("TRIPS Agreement").

TRIPS Agreement, we affirm that the Agreement shall be interpreted and implemented in a manner supportive of WTO Members' right to protect public health and, in particular, to ensure access to medicines for all. In this connection, we reaffirm the right of WTO Members to use, to the full, the provisions in the TRIPS Agreement which provide flexibility for this purpose.

Whereas the second option offered was:

We affirm a Member's ability to use, to the full, the provisions in the TRIPS Agreement which provide flexibility to address public health crises such as HIV/AIDS and other pandemics, and to that end, that a Member is able to take measures necessary to address these public health crises, in particular to secure affordable access to medicines. Further, we agree that this Declaration does not add to or diminish the rights and obligations of Members provided in the TRIPS Agreement. With a view to facilitating the use of this flexibility by providing greater certainty, we agree on the following clarifications.

In Doha, for three days the discussions on TRIPS and public health dominated the trade talks. Early on in the meeting it became clear that a majority of Members preferred the first option of the Harbinson draft, making it the basis for further negotiation. The core supporters of the second option included the US, Japan, Australia, Switzerland, Canada, and Korea. The EU, at this stage, did not take a clear position and claimed it was playing the role of "honest broker." After three days of negotiation among the participating Members, a compromise was reached. The compromise text, which resulted from negotiations primarily between Brazil and the US, read:

We agree that the TRIPS Agreement does not and should not prevent Members from taking measures to protect public health. Accordingly, while reiterating our commitments to the TRIPS Agreement, we affirm that the Agreement can and should be interpreted and implemented in a manner supportive of WTO Members' right to protect public health and, in particular, to promote access to medicines for all.[43]

This text acknowledges the unmitigated right of countries to take measures to protect public health. Thus, if intellectual property rules should stand in the way of doing so (for example, in the case of high prices associated with patented medicines), countries are allowed to override the patent.

In Paragraph 5, the Declaration lays out the key measures and flexibilities within TRIPS that can be used to overcome intellectual property barriers to access to medicines. The discussions at Doha and the Doha Declaration itself make it unambiguously clear that the use of compulsory licenses is in no way confined to cases of emergency or urgency; in fact, the grounds for issuing a compulsory license are unlimited. Members who proposed language that would have limited measures like compulsory licensing to emergency situations, pandemics, or specified diseases such as

---

43.   World Trade Organization, Doha Ministerial Declaration on the TRIPS Agreement and Public Health, para 4, WTO Doc No WT/MIN(01)/DEC/2 (2001) ("Doha Declaration" or "Declaration").

HIV/AIDS were unsuccessful. In addition, the Declaration leaves Members free to determine for themselves what constitutes a national emergency or urgency, in which cases the procedure for issuing a compulsory license becomes easier and faster. The Declaration also resolves the question of whether TRIPS authorizes parallel trade once and for all by noting: "The effect of the provisions in the TRIPS Agreement that are relevant to the exhaustion of intellectual property rights is to leave each Member free to establish its own regime for such exhaustion without challenge."[44]

In addition, the Declaration grants least-developed country ("LDCs") Members an extra ten-year extension—until 2016, instead of 2006—to the implementation deadline for pharmaceutical product patent protection. The negotiating history illustrates that this outcome was not predetermined. Pre-Doha, the US proposed two operative paragraphs, which included this extension of transition periods until 2016 for patents on pharmaceutical products, as well as offering a moratorium on dispute settlement action to sub-Saharan African countries, which do not fall within the LDC grouping. The moratorium covered laws, regulations and other measures that improve access to patented medicines for HIV/AIDS and other pandemics. These proposals were viewed as a "divide and conquer" strategy employed by the US to break the cohesion of the developing countries[45] and the proposal for a moratorium on dispute settlement actions was rejected at Doha. The proposals to extend the deadlines for LDCs were accepted. The extended deadlines are important because they extend the timeframe (until 2016) in which countries may rethink the kind of pharmaceutical intellectual property law they want while still being able to import and produce generic medicines.

The Declaration also refers to the as-yet unfulfilled commitment of developed-country Members to provide incentives to their enterprises and institutions to promote technology transfer to LDCs pursuant to Article 66.2. The ten-year extension might be of limited value because only LDCs will be able to benefit from this provision. Of the 143 WTO members, only 30 are LDCs, representing 10 percent of the world's population. The ten-year extension is also limited to Sections 5 (patents) and 7 (undisclosed information) of TRIPS; the extension does not apply to other provisions of the Agreement relevant to pharmaceuticals, notably Article 70 ("exclusive marketing rights"). Though there seemed to be an understanding among the negotiators in Doha that Paragraph 7 implied that LDCs are not required to provide "mail box" protection or "exclusive marketing rights," this is not clear from the text of the declaration. Paragraph 7 of the declaration refers to pharmaceutical

---

44. Id at para 5(d).
45. See Third World Network Info Service on WTO Issues, *Update on Ministerial Declaration on TRIPS and Public Health*, available online at <http://www.twnside.org.sg/title/info3.htm> (visited Mar 24, 2002) (discussing this and other points of contention between the developed and developing WTO states).

products, which means that LDCs still are under the obligation to provide process patents.

C. OTHER AREAS OF DEBATE

1. *Public Health*: Most of the language aimed at narrowing the scope of the Declaration to health crises and pandemics[46] was replaced with language that referred generally to public health. Indeed, the title itself—Doha Declaration on Public Health— reflects this shift.

2. *Access for All*: Some countries objected to the text that countries have the right "to ensure access to medicines *for all*."[47] In particular, Switzerland objected to the wording, but had difficulty defending a position that advocated access to medicines for some but not for others.

3. *Scope*: A point of strong contention was how far-reaching the Declaration would be. Some WTO Members feared that the negotiations could lead to changes in TRIPS and wanted to include a confirmation that the Declaration was purely a clarifying exercise. They borrowed language from the WTO Dispute Settlement Process Rules to indicate that the Ministerial Declaration would have no formal legal effect to change the rights and obligations TRIPS established.

The text did not, however, make it into the final version of the Declaration. As a result, one could argue that the Declaration actually does go beyond clarifying the already existing rules. A Member can appeal to the Declaration and its negotiating history in the event that a Member's legislation, particularly relating to patents in the health field, is challenged on the grounds that it is incompatible with TRIPS.

D. WHY DOHA CAME TO PASS

Why was it possible to achieve a declaration on such a contentious issue considering that public health hardly played a part in the trade talks two years ago? Mike Moore, WTO Director-General, made it clear on the opening day of the conference that the TRIPS and health issue could be the deal-breaker for a new trade round. Observers point to a number of factors that contributed to the success of the negotiations.[48] First, the developing country Members were extremely well prepared and operated as one bloc. Second, the uncompromising positions of western countries such as the US and Canada were hard to maintain in light of the anthrax crisis and the threat that a shortage of Ciprofloxacine ("Cipro") might occur. Both the US and Canada rapidly expressed their willingness to set aside the patent held by the

---

46. Pandemics refer to diseases, mostly of infectious nature, that travel across borders.
47. Doha Declaration at para 4 (cited in note 43) (emphasis added).
48. See David Banta, *Public Health Triumphs at WTO Conference*, 286 JAMA 2655, 2655–65 (2001).

German company Bayer if other solutions could not be found.[49] The anthrax scare and the threatened shortage of Cipro forced all WTO Members to ask how much of a prisoner they want to be of their own patent systems. Third, a growing and active international NGO movement ensured the issue would be high profile, and that NGOs would monitor different countries' positions.

V. DRUG INDUSTRY RESPONSE TO THE WTO DECLARATION ON TRIPS AND PUBLIC HEALTH

The multinational pharmaceutical industry argued from the beginning that a declaration was not necessary because: a) patents are not a problem,[50] and b) weakening patent protection would have devastating effects on the R&D capabilities of the research-based industry.   Although the International Federation of Pharmaceutical Manufacturers ("IFPMA") officially welcomed the Declaration on TRIPS and Public Health, individuals in the industry expressed their concerns. Indeed, the US pharmaceutical companies asked the USTR to re-open the negotiations even after an agreement on the text of the Declaration was reached.

For more than two years, IFPMA has warned against the dangers of compulsory licensing—ever since NGOs started to propose compulsory licensing systems to overcome patent barriers.   IFPMA's position has not changed. "[C]ompulsory licensing is a threat to good public health by denying patients around the world the future benefits of R&D capabilities of the research-based industry from which new therapies come."[51]

The generic drug industry welcomed the Declaration, in particular the freedom of countries to decide the grounds for compulsory licensing.   The generic drug industry did express concern about possible unilateral pressure to influence countries not to make full use of the Declaration. The industry suggested that the advanced WTO Members should commit to the Declaration in practice by refraining from exerting unilateral pressure. The generic drug contingent expressed disappointment that there was no resolution of the issue that arises when a country with limited production capacity that issues a compulsory license for a medicine cannot find an efficient, affordable, and reliable source of medicines, due to TRIPS restrictions on production and export of medicines. After 2005, production of affordable medicine will increasingly become dependent on compulsory licensing. However, production

---

49.   See Amy Harmon and Robert Pear, *A Nation Challenged: The Treatment; Canada Overrides Patent for Cipro to Threat Anthrax*, NY Times A1 (Oct 19, 2001).

50.   At Doha, the International Federation of Pharmaceutical Manufacturers ("IFPMA") distributed Amir Attaran and Lee Gillespie-White, *Do Patents for Antiretroviral Drugs Constrain Access to AIDS Treatment in Africa?*, 286 JAMA 1886 (2001).

51.   IFPMA, *Access to Medicines: The Right Policy Prescription* (distributed at the WTO 2001) [on file with CJIL].

under a compulsory license is restricted to production "predominantly for the supply of the domestic market."[52] The problem is not the compulsory license itself, but the need to allow exports from a country where the drug is under patent to a country that has issued the compulsory license.

The generic drug industry expressed further disappointment that the Declaration did not offer an interpretation of the data protection issue addressed in Article 39.3 of TRIPS.[53] The concern here is that an overly restrictive interpretation of Article 39.3 will lead to delays in introduction of generic medicines, may provide exclusive marketing rights beyond the patent protection term and increase barriers to the registration of generic medicines including those produced under a compulsory license.

V. The Post-Doha Agenda

A key issue that remained unresolved in Doha is how to ensure that production for export to a country that has issued a compulsory license, but does not have manufacturing capacity, can take place within a country that provides pharmaceutical patents. Since Article 31(f) of TRIPS limits compulsory licensing to uses which are predominantly for the supply of the domestic market, further clarification is necessary to ensure that countries without production capacity can make use of compulsory licensing provisions to the same extent that countries with manufacturing capacity can use these provisions. The Doha Declaration acknowledges the problem in Paragraph 6:

> We recognize that WTO Members with insufficient or no manufacturing capacities in the pharmaceutical sector could face difficulties in making effective use of compulsory licensing under the TRIPS Agreement. We instruct the Council for TRIPS to find an expeditious solution to this problem and to report to the General Council before the end of 2002.

It is increasingly urgent that the production for export issue be resolved. Implementation deadlines for some important producing countries are quickly approaching, thus further limiting the possibilities of producing generic versions of medicines that are protected by patent elsewhere.

Another flaw of the Doha Declaration is that it does not resolve the problem of production for export from markets that provide patents to countries that do not grant pharmaceutical patents (and subsequently do not grant compulsory licenses). This is of particular importance now that the least-developed WTO Members can delay the granting of pharmaceutical product patents until 2016. These countries need to have access to sources of affordable medicines, which threaten to dry up as the 2005 deadline for TRIPS implementation is nearing for producing countries.

---

52. TRIPS Agreement at art 31(f) (cited in note 42).

53. See Jayanta Ghosh, *No Gains from Doha, Say Pharma Firms*, Times (India) (Nov 27, 2001).

Another challenge will be to find ways to make the Doha Declaration on TRIPS and Public Health operational at the regional and national levels. A classic example is the Bangui Agreement, the regional intellectual property agreement for francophone Africa, which was adopted in 1977 and revised in 1999 to ensure TRIPS compatibility, but includes typical TRIPS plus provisions that are not in line with the Doha Declaration.

At the national level, countries should be encouraged to make full use of the Doha Declaration in the process of adjusting national intellectual property laws to become compliant with TRIPS. This will require substantial advice and technical assistance from institutions like WIPO and WTO. While the spirit of the Doha Declaration is to go slowly and to tailor intellectual property laws to national needs, the practice has been to encourage developing countries to go beyond the minimum requirements and speed up the process to become TRIPS-compliant. It will require a "culture change" at WIPO and WTO to adjust the type of technical assistance to developing countries' needs. In addition to increasing their interaction with countries, WIPO and WTO will have to increase their level of collaboration with the public health community, including the WHO, which has become heavily involved in trade discussions as a result of the process that led to the Doha Declaration.

VI. CONCLUSION

The very fact that public health and access to medicines have been singled out as major issues needing special attention in TRIPS implementation indicates that health care and health care products need to be treated differently from other products. By giving countries broad discretion in deciding how to counter the negative effects of TRIPS, the Doha Declaration may stand for the proposition that public health concerns outweigh full protection of intellectual property.

In fact, the Doha Declaration takes a large step toward ensuring that intellectual property protection actually serves the public interest, an interest broader than that of the commercial sector. In the years to come, it will be important to scrutinize closely whether the results of intellectual property protection serve the poor as well as the rich. The Doha Declaration lays out the options countries have available when prices of existing patented drugs are too high for their populations. But Doha did not solve every problem: the lack of R&D investment in new drugs for the particular health needs of the poor remains to be addressed.[54]

---

54. See World Trade Organization, Doha General Ministerial Declaration, para 17, WTO Doc No WT/MIN(01)/DEC/1 (Nov 14, 2001) ("We stress the importance we attach to implementation and interpretation of the Agreement on Trade-Related Aspects of Intellectual Property Rights (TRIPS Agreement) in a manner supportive of public health, by promoting both access to existing medicines and research and development into new medicines and, in this connection, are adopting a separate declaration.").

In the Doha process, developing countries and NGOs pointed to commercial and public sector neglect of the R&D needs of developing countries. Recent studies claim that the R&D cost of a commercial drug company per new pharmaceutical product is $802 million.[55] The Global Alliance for Tuberculosis Drug Development, a non-profit entity for R&D of tuberculosis drugs, estimated that the total R&D cost for a new tuberculosis drug, including the cost of failure, is between $115 million and $240 million.[56] These high R&D costs claimed by the commercial pharmaceutical sector pose some key questions that need to be resolved. Is the present system for funding R&D the most efficient, and is it sufficient to rely on the present intellectual property systems to fuel innovation? Clearly, in the area of neglected diseases, the answer is no.

In an increasingly globalized economy, additional international mechanisms need to be developed to address health needs in developing countries. MSF and others have proposed a radical shift in the way health R&D is financed in particular for drugs for neglected diseases. For example, health R&D could be financed based on burden sharing between countries, or obligating companies to complete essential medical research. Such a proposal might be incorporated into an international treaty on essential health R&D. In the end, the challenge for the coming years will be to encourage essential health R&D not only for the benefit of some, but for the benefit of all.

---

55.   See Tufts Center for the Study of Drug Development, *Tufts Center for the Study of Drug Development Pegs Cost of a New Prescription Medicine at $802 Million*, Press Release (Nov 30, 2001), available online at <http://www.tufts.edu/med/csdd/images/NewsRelease113001pm.pdf> (visited Mar 24, 2002). See also James Love, *How Much Does it Cost to Develop a New Drug*, available online at <http://www.cptech.org/ip/health/econ/howmuch.html> (visited Mar 24, 2002).

56.   For details see The Global Alliance for TB Drug Development, *Drug Development Costs*, available online at <http://www.tballiance.org/3_costs.cfm?rm=economics&sub=costs> (visited Mar 24, 2002).

[22]

THE QUEST FOR GLOBAL GOVERNANCE IN INTELLECTUAL PROPERTY AND PUBLIC HEALTH: STRUCTURAL, DISCURSIVE, AND INSTITUTIONAL DIMENSIONS[*]

Susan K. Sell[**]

ABSTRACT

The contest between competing knowledge networks is raging in the World Trade Organization ("WTO") over diverse interpretations of the Agreement on Trade-Related Aspects of Intellectual Property Rights ("TRIPS"). The sharpest conflict is between trade and public health. To what extent can persuasion and principled argument be a potent asset for the weak to bring about desired change? How can the legal debate over the boundaries of the WTO, and the extent to which declarations, laws, and regulations promulgated in other venues are relevant to WTO deliberations, help developing countries devise strategies to press their concerns more effectively? Given sharply asymmetrical power relationships, what are the prospects for achieving outcomes that better balance public health and commercial concerns? This article argues that principled argument has the potential to alter actors' interests and outcomes. While coercion is a viable weapon of the strong, principled argument can be a potent asset for the weak to bring about desired change. This is especially the case when such discursive strategies are coupled with the strategic use of a variety of institutions.

I. INTRODUCTION

Increasingly, public health policy has had to interact with environmental, trade, economic, and intellectual property policy. Just considering the intersection between public health, trade, and intellectual property, governance in public health is complicated by the diverse institutions involved, including the World Health Organization ("WHO"), the International Monetary Fund ("IMF"), the World Bank, the World Trade Organization ("WTO"), and the World Intellectual Property Organization ("WIPO"). Global governance means devising, implementing, and enforcing policies in a way that accommodates a

---

[*] Prepared for "SARS, Public Health, and Global Governance," Institute for International Law and Public Policy, Temple University Beasley School of Law, Philadelphia, Pa., March 24-25, 2004. I would like to thank Jeff Dunoff, Peter Gourevitch, Jay Smith, and Greg Shaffer for helpful comments on an earlier draft. The usual caveats apply.

[**] Associate Professor of Political Science & International Affairs, The George Washington University.

broad range of stakeholders and publics. Challenges to effective global governance of public health issues include trade pressures, multi-layered governance (i.e., local, national, bilateral, regional, international), the complexity of health policy jurisdiction across multilateral organizations, the simultaneous development of hard and soft law in diverse venues with conflicting mandates, and values, economic coercion, and unequal access to resources and institutions. Among the central features of the quest for global governance in intellectual property and public health are the blurring lines between public and private, the increasing role of the private sector in public policymaking, growing global inequality, constricted autonomy for the weak, and the inappropriateness of "one-size-fits-all" policies for diverse contexts.

The development of global public health policy is shaped by developments in three dimensions: structural, discursive, and institutional. The structural dimension is characterized by glaring economic and political power asymmetries between developed and developing countries. The structural dimension has also fostered the ascendance of the global life sciences industries in public health policymaking. Battles between commercial and social agendas in public health are hardly waged on a level playing field. Given these asymmetries, what are the possibilities available to the weak through discursive and institutional strategies? The current environment presents dangers and opportunities. The "weak" must become adept at playing the multi-level, multi-forum governance game. As Laurence Helfer has pointed out, governments, non-governmental organizations ("NGO"s), and commercial actors are engaging in "regime shifting" that reveals "an acute awareness by government officials, international secretariats, and non-state actors of the fluidity of lawmaking processes, and reveals such actors' keen ability to assess the comparative institutional advantages offered by different negotiating fora for achieving particular goals."[1] Deftly advancing different types of arguments and mobilizing different players in a variety of international institutions, these actors have begun to alter rules and procedures that affect public health. What are the relationships among various international organizations? What perspectives do they promote? Who is defining and shaping these perspectives? When these perspectives conflict, what perspective prevails and why? Are international organizations roughly equal or do they exist in strictly hierarchical relation to each other? How malleable are these relationships? Can discursive and institutional strategies alter these relationships?

Global intellectual property rules in the WTO emerged from a vigorous corporate campaign to link intellectual property and trade. This campaign employed economic expertise, effective discursive strategies, and forum shifting to persuade the United States government to redefine its interests in intellectual property protection. The result was a dramatic global expansion of protections for rights holders and penalties for violators of intellectual property rights. In the wake of TRIPS, a vigorous civil society campaign has mobilized to protest

---

1. Laurence R. Helfer, *Regime Shifting: The TRIPs Agreement and New Dynamics of International Intellectual Property Lawmaking*, 29 YALE J. INT'L L. 1, 71 (2004).

this expansion of rights, particularly in the face of the HIV/AIDS pandemic. Arguing that intellectual property rights should be construed as a public health issue, rather than a trade issue, this civil society campaign has scored some victories in challenging the corporate perspective. This group seeks to limit the expansion of intellectual property rights and reduce such rights for essential medicines in an effort to contain costs and increase access. TRIPS opponents, consisting of consumer groups, NGOs, and a number of developing country governments, have used "counter-experts" to challenge the trade-based conception of intellectual property rights in favor of a public health perspective. The corporate TRIPS architects have been forced to respond to this challenge and engage the debates of the civil society groups.

The contest among these competing knowledge networks is raging in the WTO over diverse interpretations of TRIPS. Moreover, it is animating related deliberations in the WHO and WIPO. Governance in this area is complicated by the fact that different groups are scoring "victories" in some venues, while opposing groups are scoring "victories" in other venues. For instance, while the access to medicines agenda has moved forward in both the WHO and the WTO, WIPO is moving forward with the Substantive Patent Law Treaty deliberations which threaten to reverse any gains achieved in other forums. The United States, at the behest of nongeneric pharmaceutical firms, is pursuing an aggressive course of bilateral and regional intellectual property and investment agreements that further undermine any broader gains for developing countries in the throes of the HIV/AIDS crisis.

This article examines the structural, discursive, and institutional dimensions of the quest to balance public health, trade, and intellectual property. These dimensions help to highlight both the obstacles to, and the opportunities for, advancing public health concerns over competing values when necessary. The international organizations dealing with public health and intellectual property are embedded in a broad structural context of unevenly distributed political and economic power. "[P]olicy content has been closely aligned with global shifts in power and influence among key policy actors."[2] The structure of the organizations varies in reflecting these inequalities. For example, an organization like the IMF mirrors unequal power relationships with weighted voting according to contribution, whereas the United Nations General Assembly's one-nation one-vote system formally obscures these inequalities. Furthermore, one of the major developments in the health sector has been "the rapid growth of public-private partnerships in recent years [that] has given the private sector unprecedented entrée into policy-making circles in national governments and key organizations such as WHO, UNICEF, and the World Bank."[3] Access to and participation in various organizations is uneven, and the costs of participating in venues such as the WTO can be prohibitive for those without substantial resources.

---

2. Kent Buse et al., *Globalisation and health policy: trends and opportunities*, in HEALTH POLICY IN A GLOBALISING WORLD 256 (Kelley Lee et al. eds., 2002).

3. *Id.* at 262.

Discursive dimensions are also important. Information plays an important role in the policy process. However, information is not knowledge.[4] Given bounded rationality, actors employ filters to identify useful and interesting information.[5] People transform information into knowledge by employing different normative frames. Frames are "specific metaphors, symbolic representations, and cognitive cues used to render or cast behavior and events in an evaluative mode and to suggest alternative modes of action."[6] Because agenda setting and advocacy involve both the provision of information and normative frames, they crucially influence policy debates and outcomes.[7] According to John Braithwaite and Peter Drahos, "webs of dialogue" can be an important source of change in international politics. "Webs of dialogue" or "webs of persuasion" describe efforts in which actors seek to alter others' interests. As they suggest, "[i]ssue definition is the first form of persuasion delivered by dialogic webs that is a prerequisite for a global regime."[8] Indeed, in their survey of global business regulation, they conclude that webs of dialogue are much more frequent catalysts of change than webs of coercion.

Global governance in intellectual property protection, as exemplified by TRIPS in the WTO, has come about by the mechanism of coercion.[9] However, in the aftermath of TRIPS, and the contest between those who frame intellectual property as a trade issue and those who frame it as a health issue, webs of dialogue are becoming increasingly important. As Braithwaite and Drahos point out, "[d]ialogic webs offer individuals the possibility of micro action to secure macro change."[10] Competing knowledge networks participate in dialogic webs in their efforts to define issues, persuade others to redefine their interests, and inject normative commitments that shape prescriptions and seek to persuade others that "compliance is morally right."[11] Authors working in the rational choice tradition focus on processes given preferences. As Patrick Jackson has pointed out, rationalist accounts are silent on the issue of legitimacy; "[w]hat

---

4. *See* Edward Comor, *The Role of Communications in Global Civil Society: Forces, Processes, Prospects*, 45 INT'L STUD. Q. 389, 393 (2001) (noting that "people are not intellectual sponges").

5. *See* BRYAN D. JONES, POLITICS AND THE ARCHITECTURE OF CHOICE: BOUNDED RATIONALITY AND GOVERNANCE 26 (2001) (concluding that individual course of action is often dictated by cost/gain analysis); Amos Tversky & Daniel Kahneman, *The Framing of Decisions and the Psychology of Choice*, 211 SCIENCE 453, 453-58 (1981) (noting that a rational decisionmaker, when faced with a choice, will prefer those prospects that offer highest expected utility).

6. Mayer N. Zald, *Culture, Ideology and Strategic Framing, in* COMPARATIVE PERSPECTIVES ON SOCIAL MOVEMENTS: POLITICAL OPPORTUNITIES, MOBILIZING STRUCTURES, AND CULTURAL FRAMINGS 261, 262 (Doug McAdam et al. eds., 1996).

7. Susan K. Sell & Aseem Prakash, *Using Ideas Strategically: The Contest Between Business and NGO Networks in Intellectual Property Rights*, 48 INT'L STUDIES Q. 143, 145 (2004).

8. JOHN BRAITHWAITE & PETER DRAHOS, GLOBAL BUSINESS REGULATION 553 (2000).

9. *See generally* Frederick Abbott, *The Doha Declaration on the TRIPS Agreement and Public Health: Lighting a Dark Corner at the WTO*, 5 J. INT'L ECON. L. 469 (2002) (arguing that Doha Declaration sent clear signal that developing countries intended to protect their interests against political maneuvering by the United States and European Union).

10. BRAITHWAITE & DRAHOS, *supra* note 8, at 7.

11. *Id.* at 553.

vanishes from sight ... are any notions of persuasion, learning, reflective reconsideration, or any of the other activities that go on when a leader tries to render a policy acceptable to an audience."[12] Authors concerned with questions of legitimacy and negotiation processes focus on the *content* of actors' beliefs and principled argument.[13] I will argue that principled argument used in dialogic webs has the potential to alter actors' interests and outcomes. While coercion is a viable weapon of the strong, principled argument can be a potent asset for the weak to bring about desired change—especially when coupled with the strategic use of institutions.

The institutional dimension concerns the broad range of different multilateral institutions that are promulgating laws, declarations, resolutions, and soft law related to global public health. These institutions reflect competing conceptions of which values should be promoted. Since WTO law is binding and enforceable, it is imperative to examine its role and its relationship to other institutions to assess the prospects for and obstacles to global governance in public health. The institutional dimension is also addressed in a lively debate among scholars of international law about the boundaries of the WTO and the extent to which declarations, laws, and regulations promulgated in other venues are relevant to WTO deliberations. It also addresses the question of what role the WTO should play in resolving politically-charged value conflicts. This issue is central to conflicts over intellectual property because a variety of different international organizations have weighed in on the matter, and these organizations reflect competing and conflicting conceptions of intellectual property. Competing values are at stake both outside of and within the WTO. For example, WTO judicial panels hearing cases involving pharmaceutical patent protection face "a major dilemma. [They] cannot simply recognize *a* public good in interpreting the TRIPS Agreement. [They] must rather take account of concerns over competing public goods as reflected in the agreement's provisions."[14] "The ultimate issue in choosing among the production of public goods becomes institutional because different institutions offer different

---

12. Patrick Thaddeus Jackson, *Jeremy Bentham, Foreign Secretary; or, the Opportunity Costs of Neo-Utilitarian Analyses of Foreign Policy*, 9 REV. INT'L POL. ECON. 735, 744 (2002).

13. *See* CECILIA ALBIN, JUSTICE AND FAIRNESS IN INTERNATIONAL NEGOTIATION 1-3 (2001) (outlining considerations that affect international negotiations); NETA C. CRAWFORD, ARGUMENT AND CHANGE IN WORLD POLITICS: ETHICS, DECOLONIZATION, AND HUMANITARIAN INTERVENTION 11-14 (2002) (analyzing process of foreign policy decision making); MARGARET E. KECK & KATHRYN SIKKINK, ACTIVISTS BEYOND BORDERS: ADVOCACY NETWORKS IN INTERNATIONAL POLITICS 1-8 (1998) (examining the ideas and processes through which transnational advocacy networks "multiply channels of access to the international system"); William D. Coleman & Melissa Gabler, *Agricultural Biotechnology and Regime Formation: A Constructivist Assessment of the Prospects*, 46 INT'L STUD. Q. 481, 481-506 (2002) (noting effect that evolving and diverging practices of actors' express principled reasoning and shared understandings have on international governance); Harald Müller, *International Relations as Communicative Action*, in CONSTRUCTING INTERNATIONAL RELATIONS: THE NEXT GENERATION 160, 160-63 (Karin M. Fierke & Knud Erik Jørgensen eds., 2001) (discussing the role of language and argument and the social relations between actors in international negotiations).

14. Gregory Shaffer, *Recognizing Public Goods in WTO Dispute Settlement: Who Participates? Who Decides?*, 7 J. INT'L ECON. L. 459, 464 (2004).

opportunities for actors to participate, affecting which perspectives on the appropriate balancing are advanced."[15] This raises an urgent problem of which perspectives should have pride of place in interpretations of states' rights and obligations.

This article begins by sketching out the broadest structural framework.[16] It goes on to describe the issues at stake.[17] The next section identifies the varieties of discourse and their purveyors.[18] Then it maps out several of the key institutions relevant to trade, intellectual property, and public health.[19] It then offers conclusions and speculates on the possibilities for a way forward.[20]

II. STRUCTURAL DIMENSIONS

A deep structural impetus for economic globalization and liberalization emerged from the increasing mobility of capital. Capital mobility and the ideological shift toward a radical free market agenda served to enhance the power of global corporations and particularly those engaged in knowledge-intensive processes and production. In effect, these structural and ideational factors delivered these corporations to the forefront of global business regulation. The growth of offshore capital markets, the removal of capital controls, financial deregulation, and the cross-border integration of capital markets has created "an explosion in the availability of private liquidity which governments are hard pressed to control."[21] As a consequence, transnational corporations in knowledge-intensive sectors such as computers, software, and pharmaceuticals "have the resources, motivations and capabilities to roam the world searching for the kind of opportunities which promise lucrative rewards."[22] These corporations have become increasingly influential in policymaking in the United States because of their positive trade balances and their contribution to the state's competitiveness goals. Now, "[t]he private interests of the market are integrated into the state, asymmetrically in accordance with their structural power and organizational capacity, through their close relationship to state institutions in the policy decision-making process. . . . "[23] These trends are central to the current discussion because these firms and their governments have rewritten the rules of international trade. Further, they have been pushing high

---

15. *Id.*

16. See *infra* Part II for a discussion of the structural framework of economic globalization and liberalization.

17. See *infra* Part II.A for a discussion of the moral and economic issues related to TRIPS.

18. See *infra* Part III for an analysis of the debate over TRIPS.

19. See *infra* Part IV, V for a discussion of the institutional dimensions related to TRIPS.

20. See *infra* Part VI for a discussion of the possible future implications of TRIPS.

21. RANDALL D. GERMAIN, THE INTERNATIONAL ORGANIZATION OF CREDIT: STATES AND GLOBAL FINANCE IN THE WORLD-ECONOMY 105 (1997).

22. Randall D. Germain, *Globalization in Historical Perspective, in* GLOBALIZATION AND ITS CRITICS: PERSPECTIVES FROM POLITICAL ECONOMY 81 (Randall D. Germain ed., 2000).

23. Geoffrey R. D. Underhill, *Global Money and the Decline of State Power, in* STRANGE POWER: SHAPING THE PARAMETERS OF INTERNATIONAL RELATIONS AND INTERNATIONAL POLITICAL ECONOMY 129 (Thomas C. Lawton et al. eds., 2000).

protectionist norms in intellectual property protection at every conceivable level.

In the name of "competitiveness" the United States relaxed its formerly stringent antitrust (competition) laws. Throughout the 1980s, anti-trust law increasingly recognized that intellectual property rights do not *necessarily* "confer monopolies or even market power in any relevant market."[24] The Reagan administration's concern over its industries' abilities to compete effectively in world markets resulted in a more permissive approach to merger control that reflected the Chicago school of economics.[25] The United States Justice Department argued that "antitrust laws should not be applied in a way that hinders the renewed emphasis on increasing U.S. competitiveness."[26] With regard to intellectual property, both the administrators and the courts have adopted the view that an intellectual property owner has no relevant market power (in terms of antitrust) if close substitutes exist for the product or process. This more flexible approach, when coupled with newly broad definitions of what constitutes a relevant market, redounds to the benefit of the intellectual property owner in comparison to the pre-Chicago approach. The consequence of this new thinking was to remove most intellectual property licensing from antitrust scrutiny. Under the Reagan administration:

> [T]he executive agencies viewed the economic incentives provided by intellectual property rights as legitimate means of extracting the full economic benefit from innovation. Intellectual property rights acted as a "magic trump card" allowing many previously suspect arrangements to proceed without challenge from the [Federal Trade Commission] or [Department of Justice].[27]

The 1980s have been referred to as an "anything goes era" for intellectual property licensing arrangements.[28]

Furthermore, intellectual property rights have been dramatically expanded in recent years to cover things such as computer programs, compilations of data, genes, entire plant species, software algorithms, pharmaceutical products and processes, and "practices in local agriculture, medicine and education which were outside of market relations."[29] This combination of relaxed antitrust

---

24. Jere M. Webb & Lawrence A. Locke, *Intellectual Property Misuse: Developments in the Misuse Doctrine*, 4 HARV. J.L. & TECH. 257, 263 (1991).

25. MARC ALLEN EISNER, ANTITRUST AND THE TRIUMPH OF ECONOMICS: INSTITUTIONS, EXPERTISE, AND POLICY CHANGE 2-3 (1991).

26. PAUL S. HOFF, INVENTIONS IN THE MARKETPLACE: PATENT LICENSING AND THE U.S. ANTITRUST LAWS 19 (1986).

27. Thomas L. Hayslett III, *1995 Antitrust Guidelines for the Licensing of Intellectual Property: Harmonizing the Commercial Use of Legal Monopolies with the Prohibitions of Antitrust Law*, 3 J. INTELL. PROP. L. 375, 382 (1996).

28. *Id.* at 382 n.33 (quoting Richard J. Yurko, *Intellectual Property Guidelines: New, Improved, and . . . Irrelevant?*, MASS. L. WKLY., July 17, 1995, at B9).

29. Christopher Arup, *Competition Over Competition Policy for International Trade and Intellectual Property*, 16 PROMETHEUS 367, 367-81 (1998). *See also* Carlos M. Correa, *TRIPS and Access to Medicines: Internationalization of the Patent System and New Technologies*, 20 WIS. INT'L L.J. 523, 550 (2002) (concluding that developing countries should define patentable subject matter in a manner compatible with their level of development).

policies and expanded intellectual property rights has promoted economic concentration in high technology sectors, and particularly in the life sciences industries. This trend has been well documented by scholars and NGOs.[30] The consequences include enhanced political power of these industries, a reduction in the number of suppliers of certain kinds of technology, a reduction in competition, and higher costs of technology. As Assad Omer suggests:

> Developing countries are confronted with the following dilemma: on the one side, in order to attract more investment and technology they have to press to open up their markets, and on the other side, the reduction of regulatory barriers gives rise to the emergence of anti-competitive behaviour of firms.[31]

Even more ominously, Drahos (with Braithwaite) argues that:

> The globalization of intellectual property rights will rob much knowledge of its public good qualities. When knowledge becomes a private good to be traded in markets the demands of many, paradoxically, go unmet. Patent-based R&D is not responsive to demand, but to ability to pay.... Much of what happens in the agriculture and health sectors of developed and developing countries will end up depending on the bidding or charity of biogopolists as they make strategic commercial decisions on how to use their intellectual property rights.[32]

So what does all this mean for public health? Structural features at the macro level shape the micro level, as manifest in the underprovision of drugs for tropical diseases, public health budgets reduced under IMF conditions, and the constrained ability of governments to meet public health needs. Furthermore, "[t]he weakness of regulatory frameworks in [low and middle income countries] in the face of emerging global health markets leaves their populations especially vulnerable. . . ."[33]

The rise of private power in the context of globalization has also led to the "marked ascendance of private (for profit) sector actors in health policy in recent decades within the context of a 'global shift' in the world economy."[34] Economic concentration in the life sciences industries, coupled with the expanded property rights afforded by TRIPS, has translated "economic power into greater influence over policy-making that has hitherto been seen as the realm of the public sphere."[35] Recent years have witnessed the proliferation of

---

30. *See generally* GRAHAM DUTFIELD, INTELLECTUAL PROPERTY RIGHTS AND THE LIFE SCIENCES INDUSTRIES: A TWENTIETH CENTURY HISTORY (2003) (providing historical perspective on current debates on intellectual property rights in life sciences industries).

31. Assad Omer, *An Overview of Legislative Changes, in* INTERNATIONAL TECHNOLOGY TRANSFER: THE ORIGINS AND AFTERMATH OF THE UNITED NATIONS NEGOTIATIONS ON DRAFT CODE OF CONDUCT 295, 312 (Surendra J. Patel et al. eds., 2001).

32. PETER DRAHOS & JOHN BRAITHWAITE, INFORMATION FEUDALISM: WHO OWNS THE KNOWLEDGE ECONOMY? 167-68 (2003).

33. Buse et al., *supra* note 2, at 260.

34. *Id.* at 261.

35. *Id.*

global private-public partnerships ("GPPPs"). "Health GPPPs are those collaborative relationships which transcend national boundaries and bring together at least three parties, among them a corporation (and/or industry association) and an intergovernmental organisation so as to achieve a shared health-creating goal on the basis of a mutually agreed and explicitly defined division of labour."[36] Among the concerns raised by GPPPs include that of representative legitimacy: "it would appear that GPPPs provide the commercial sector with improved access to decision-making within the U.N., which is not balanced by special access to recipient countries and marginalised groups."[37] An example of a GPPP is the Global Alliance for Vaccines and Immunizations ("GAVI") "launched by Bill Gates together with the executive heads of WHO, UNICEF, the World Bank and Merck & Co."[38] In connection with the HIV/AIDS pandemic, industry has suggested "'long-term donation programs instituted by pharmaceutical companies....'"[39] GPPPs have been initiated to discourage the use of compulsory licensing to facilitate access to medicines. For example, "the Bristol-Myers Squib's partnership with the Joint United Nations Programme on HIV/AIDS ("UNAIDS") and a variety of actors in southern Africa, 'Bridging the Gap,' has been cited as the way forward in lieu of compulsory licensing."[40] In response to these changes, developing countries and NGOs increasingly have mobilized to check this expansion of commercial power.

A. TRIPS AND THE ISSUES

The most important public international law covering intellectual property is TRIPS, administered by the WTO. Unlike most international law, TRIPS is binding and enforceable. The WTO may authorize states to sanction those found to be in violation of the agreement. TRIPS reflects the interests of the owners of intellectual property. Indeed, its very existence and much of its substance owe much to just a handful of global firms based in the United States.[41] TRIPS extends patent rights for twenty years, requires developing countries to offer patent protection for pharmaceuticals, sharply circumscribes the conditions under which states may issue compulsory licenses, and reduces states' autonomy in crafting domestic intellectual property policies that suit their diverse levels of innovation and economic development. From the standpoint of economic development and technology transfer, TRIPS represents the most

---

36. *Id.* at 41, 44.

37. *Id.* at 60.

38. *Id.* at 51.

39. Buse et al., *supra* note 2, at 54 (citation omitted).

40. *Id.* at 55 (citation omitted).

41. *See* DRAHOS & BRAITHWAITE, *supra* note 32, at 12 (noting that small number of U.S. companies heavily influenced blueprint for TRIPS and used their trade power to force developing countries to comply); DUNCAN MATTHEWS, GLOBALISING INTELLECTUAL PROPERTY RIGHTS: THE TRIPs AGREEMENT 7 (2002) (noting that U.S. based multinationals used bilateral trade law as first step towards TRIPS); SUSAN K. SELL, PRIVATE POWER, PUBLIC LAW: THE GLOBALIZATION OF INTELLECTUAL PROPERTY RIGHTS 75 (2003) (concluding that U.S. sector "has been remarkably successful in politicizing IP protection").

challenging public international law. In a sharply worded and bold critique, a United Nations Development Program ("UNDP") report stated that "'[c]ountries at low levels of human technological capability cannot benefit significantly from TRIPS .... Developing countries are not likely to be even at least as well off under TRIPS as they would be outside it.'"[42] While some critics, such as the UNDP, call for TRIPS's abolition, others argue that it is workable for developing countries if interpreted appropriately.[43] Everyone agrees that the short-term consequences will be massive resource transfers from developing countries to owners of intellectual property. The World Bank has estimated that TRIPS should yield an annual nineteen billion dollars for the United States, whereas South Korea would sustain the largest loss – fifteen billion dollars.[44]

Countries that consume and import intellectual property will pay a higher premium to those who produce and export it. Under TRIPS, countries have agreed that importation of a product constitutes "working" the patent. However, importation represents only a passive mode of technology transfer and once again raises concerns that firms will use patents to maintain import monopolies. Those concerns had animated the earlier New International Economic Order ("NIEO") approach to patents.[45] Another consequence of TRIPS is that it offers "hardly any incentive for the patentee to license his technology. The technology holder can serve the large and small markets with his enhanced rights without licensing the technology."[46]

Overall, TRIPS reflects and promotes the interests of global corporations that seek to extend their control over their intellectual property. These firms, acting through the United States government (and with the support of Europe and Japan), largely captured the WTO process and succeeded in making public international law to suit their particular needs. The battle over access to essential medicines revolves around the rights to issue compulsory licenses and to manufacture and export generic versions of brand name drugs. Global brand name pharmaceutical corporations seek to restrict the ability of generic manufacturers to produce and distribute essential medicines. African countries in the grip of the HIV/AIDS pandemic, Brazil, India, and their NGO advocates seek to clarify interpretations of TRIPS that permit compulsory licensing,

---

42. Natasha McDowell, *WTO Patent Rules "Should Be Scrapped,"* Science and Development Network, *at* http://www.scidev.net/NEWS/index.cfm?fuseaction=readnews&itemid=429&language=1 (Feb 26, 2003) (quoting United Nations Development Program).

43. *See* Jerome H. Reichman & David Lange, *Bargaining Around the TRIPS Agreement: The Case for Ongoing Public-Private Initiatives to Facilitate Worldwide Intellectual Property Transactions,* 9 DUKE J. COMP. & INT'L L. 11, 49-68 (1998) (advocating establishment of operational framework outside of TRIPS that would facilitate "cooperative strategies" among WTO member states).

44. Richard Newfarmer et al., *Global Economic Prospects and the Developing Countries* 137 (2001), *at* http://www.worldbank.org/prospects/gep2002/gep2002complete.pdf (last visited Sept. 13, 2004).

45. SUSAN K. SELL, POWER AND IDEAS: NORTH-SOUTH POLITICS OF INTELLECTUAL PROPERTY AND ANTITRUST 28-29 (1998).

46. S.K. Verma, *The TRIPS Agreement and Development, in* INTERNATIONAL TECHNOLOGY TRANSFER, *supra* note 31, at 344.

parallel importing, and generic manufacture and export.

III. DISCURSIVE DIMENSIONS

The debate over TRIPS and access to medicines has galvanized a broad range of stakeholders. Brand name pharmaceutical companies (a.k.a. global pharma), developed and developing country governments, the Office of the United States Trade Representative ("USTR"), NGOs representing public health and consumer interests, and generic drug manufacturers are all participating in this vigorous debate. Among the competing values embedded in TRIPS are the generation of knowledge, the facilitation of "undistorted" trade, and the protection of public health.[47]

On one side of the TRIPS and access to medicines debate are those who support strong intellectual property protection for pharmaceuticals and argue that, if anything, TRIPS is too weak. These advocates highlight the high costs of developing new drugs, the importance of strong property rights as incentives for innovation, and the need for substantial compensation for providing life saving drugs.[48] This view is most prominently associated with the brand name global pharmaceutical industry, the United States, and the USTR. It has also been influential in the WTO. The industry fears that any expansion of cut-rate drugs will undermine their markets, particularly if they find their way into high income industrialized country markets. Global pharma highlights the potential health dangers of widespread generic production, "piracy," and the use of drugs without the supervision, dosing instructions, and regulatory controls covering global pharma's products.[49]

Perhaps the most frequently offered argument from supporters of global pharma is that the big problem is not patents but poverty.[50] This view has been promulgated in industry-supported American think tanks such as the American Enterprise Institute and the International Intellectual Property Institute ("IIPI"). Roger Bate and Richard Tren presented their remarks at an American Enterprise Institute forum on "unelected" NGOs. The United States-based Pharmaceutical Research and Manufacturing Association ("PhRMA"), an industry-lobbying group, is hardly subtle about its efforts to enlist academics to promote its cause. The *Washington Post* has referred to these as "hall-of-mirrors techniques by which special interests amplify their arguments through seemingly

---

47. Shaffer, *supra* note 14, at 460.

48. *See* Henry Grabowski, *Patents, Innovation and Access to New Pharmaceuticals*, 5 J. INT'L ECON. L. 849, 850-53 (2002) (characterizing importance of patents for pharmaceutical innovation).

49. *See* Symposium, *Global Intellectual Property Rights: Boundaries of Access and Enforcement*, 12 FORDHAM INTELL. PROP. MEDIA & ENT. L.J. 675, 729 (2002) (noting "dangers from ineffective sub- or super-potent medicines").

50. *Id.* at 692 (attributing lack of access to drugs to "prevalence of poverty"); John E. Calfee, *Patently Wrong; Free Drugs are No Panacea for Poor Nations*, WASH. TIMES, Jan. 28, 2003, at A21 (concluding that lack of rudimentary health care market renders effect of drug prices irrelevant in poor countries); Roger Bate & Richard Tren, *Do NGOs Improve Wealth and Health in Africa?*, at http://www.aei.org/docLib/20030612_batepub.pdf (June 12, 2003) (attributing high cost of policy mistakes in Africa to above-average poverty rates).

unconnected third parties."[51] For example, in the coming fiscal year, PhRMA has budgeted $1 million for an:

> "[I]ntellectual echo chamber of economists – a standing network of economists and thought leaders to speak against federal price control regulations through articles and testimony." It has set aside $550,000 "for placement of op-eds and articles by third parties" and at least $2 million for outside research and policy groups "to build intellectual capital and generate a higher volume of messages from credible sources" backing industry positions. Overall, the group will devote $12.3 million to "alliance development," . . . with . . . economists, doctors, patients, and minority groups.[52]

PhRMA frequently cites a "Harvard study" that "proves" that patents are no obstacle to access to antiretroviral medicines in Africa.[53] Amir Attaran was an adjunct lecturer in public policy at Harvard, and his coauthor, Lee Gillespie-White, worked for a PhRMA-supported think tank IIPI.[54] The oft-cited paper originated as a study that PhRMA commissioned with its think tank (IIPI) headed by Bruce Lehman, former United States Commissioner of Patents.[55] The United States trade delegation relied on this then unpublished study in its Talking Points in late September 2001 in the run up to the WTO Doha Ministerial meeting.[56]

Substantively, advocates of PhRMA's position object to any weakening of intellectual property protection through public health exceptions. They reject compulsory licensing as a policy tool to bring the costs of essential medicines down. They reject parallel importing,[57] whereby states can take advantage of differential pricing policies and import the cheapest version of the brand name pharmaceutical. Overall, they ardently oppose any efforts to weaken the international system of intellectual property protection. Instead, they advocate increased foreign aid, drug donations from firms, and "protection for international price discrimination against the threat of 'grey market' arbitrage."[58]

On the other side of the debate is an alliance of developing country governments and NGOs campaigning for access to essential medicines. They argue that patent protection *is* a barrier to access and that public health exceptions to patent rules are necessary to prevent needless deaths. They advocate compulsory licensing, generic competition, and fixed rates of compensation for pharmaceutical companies.

Among the most outspoken advocates of this position are James Love of

---

51. *Behind the Lobbying Curtain*, WASH. POST, June 9, 2003, at A20.

52. *Id.*

53. Amir Attaran & Lee Gillespie-White, *Do Patents for Antiretroviral Drugs Constrain Access to AIDS Treatment in Africa?*, 286 JAMA 1886, 1888-91 (2001).

54. *Id.* at 1892.

55. Abbott, *supra* note 9, at 485 n.62.

56. *Id.* at 485.

57. *See* Symposium, *supra* note 49, at 727 (characterizing parallel importing as dangerous).

58. M. Gregg Bloche, *WTO Deference to National Health Policy: Toward an Interpretive Principle*, 5 J. INT'L ECON. L. 825, 838 (2002).

American consumer activist Ralph Nader's Consumer Project on Technology ("CPT"), and Ellen 't Hoen of Médecins Sans Frontières ("MSF"). They consistently have attacked PhRMA's positions on these issues. Ellen 't Hoen points to strong intellectual property protection as one important barrier to access; she argues that patent protection leads to high prices and limited access.[59] MSF and other NGOs have expressed a number of concerns about TRIPS, including high drug prices, reduced availability of quality generic alternatives, inadequate research and development into tropical diseases, and bilateral pressures on developing countries to adopt patent protection that exceeds the requirements of TRIPS.[60] For example, only 13 of 1,233 new drugs marketed between 1975 and 1997 were approved for tropical diseases. As Peter Hammer suggests, "[t]here is a substantial wedge between the public health needs of developing countries and what private drug markets are likely to deliver. As a result, the rhetoric of strong intellectual property rights leading to innovation that meets social needs rings particularly hollow in this setting."[61] Furthermore, Love has challenged PhRMA's claims that its companies spend $500-800 million developing each new drug. Love has argued that the majority of important HIV/AIDS drugs were actually developed by the public National Institutes of Health, and funded by taxpayers' dollars.[62] Love and others have also criticized the Attaran and Gillespie-White 2001 argument.[63]

Brazil, India, and the African group of countries have been leaders in the intergovernmental efforts to address their public health emergencies. As José Viana, a Brazilian trade delegate, remarked, "[t]he Brazilian government has consistently supported the idea that public health should not be subordinate to abuses of economic power."[64] Activists have praised Brazil's policies of providing universal access to HIV/AIDS drugs.[65] Brazil has used the threat of compulsory licensing to negotiate steep drug discounts with global pharma. It also has committed resources to producing generic drugs. Its policies have helped to create a market for high quality generic drugs.[66] Creating a market has

---

59. Ellen 't Hoen, *TRIPS, Pharmaceutical Patents, and Access to Essential Medicines: A Long Way from Seattle to Doha*, 3 CHI. J. INT'L L. 27, 29 (2002).

60. *Id.* at 29-30.

61. Peter J. Hammer, *Differential Pricing of Essential AIDS Drugs: Markets, Politics and Public Health*, 5 J. INT'L ECON. L. 883, 888 (2002).

62. *See* CONSUMER PROJECT ON TECH., BACKGROUND INFORMATION ON FOURTEEN FDA APPROVED HIV/AIDS DRUGS (June 8, 2000) (tabulating number of government versus non-government sponsored clinical trials), *at* http://www.cptech.org/ip/health/aids/druginfo.html.

63. *See* Symposium, *supra* note 49, at 732-35 (labeling Attaran/Gillespie-White argument as biased); CONSUMER PROJECT ON TECH. ET AL., COMMENT ON THE ATTARAN/GILLESPIE-WHITE AND PhRMA SURVEYS OF PATENTS ON ANTIRETROVIRAL DRUGS IN AFRICA, *at* http://www.cptech.org/ip/health/africa/ dopatentsmatterinafrica.html (Oct. 16, 2001) (characterizing omission of data on drug cocktails as a critical flaw).

64. José Marcos Nogueira Viana, *Intellectual Property Rights, the World Trade Organization and Public Health: The Brazilian Perspective*, 17 CONN. J. INT'L L. 311, 311 (2002).

65. *See* Tina Rosenberg, *Look at Brazil*, N.Y. TIMES, Jan. 28, 2001, § 6 (Magazine), at 26, (noting that "Brazil has shredded all the excuses why poor countries cannot treat AIDS").

66. *See* Symposium, *supra* note 49, at 702 (discussing impact of competitive pricing of

encouraged competition. As a recent WHO report concludes, "[c]ompetition is perhaps the most powerful policy instrument to bring down drug prices for off-patent drugs."[67] Above all, the access to medicines campaign endorses the right of developing countries to compulsory license drugs, to produce and export generic drugs, and to take advantage of parallel importing to seek out the lowest cost medicines.

IV. INSTITUTIONAL DIMENSTIONS, THE WTO: SOCIAL ISSUES AND LEGAL DEBATES

Since the WTO administers TRIPS, the "hard law" that public health advocates have sought to clarify and interpret in flexible ways, it is important to examine the role of the WTO in greater detail. Clearly, public health and trade have both social and economic dimensions. NGOs and developing countries have criticized the WTO as being insufficiently responsive to social needs. The question arises, to what extent should social policy be incorporated into the WTO? If so, how should it be incorporated? "While many accept the WTO essentially as currently constituted, others find it increasingly difficult to conceive of a multilateral trade regime confined exclusively to promoting economic efficiency through trade liberalization, in isolation from other values."[68] José Alvarez argues that one's analysis of the WTO is dependent upon one's perspectives on the relevant stakeholders and the WTO's mandate. While some maintain that the WTO strictly exists to serve the "producers of goods," others see the WTO as charged with serving "marginalized developing countries, NGOs and individuals."[69] Indeed, the question is how to balance the interests of these stakeholders within a trade framework. Ultimately, the questions of linking public health, intellectual property, and trade are both normative and political.

We can approach these issues more systematically by considering two analytic dimensions: the reasons behind linking trade and social policy and the mechanisms for doing so. Reasons for linking trade and public health could be:

(1) normative (because linkage is demanded by justice and fairness); (2) coherence (because a free trade regime would simply not make sense if [public health is] ignored); (3) consequentialist (because free trade will adversely affect [public health]); (4) strategic (because linking these issues in creative package deals leads to more effective negotiations as to both); or (5) effectiveness (because the more effective WTO approach to dispute settlement can be usefully

---

pharmaceuticals internationally).

67. *See* Abbott, *supra* note 9, at 472 n.14 (quoting Creese and Quick discussing impact of generic drugs on price competition).

68. *See* Eric Stein, *International Integration and Democracy: No Love at First Sight*, 95 AM. J. INT'L L. 489, 508 n.106 (2001) (discussing debate over integrating public policy issues into WTO).

69. *See* José E. Alvarez, *The WTO as Linkage Machine*, 96 AM. J. INT'L L. 146, 154 (2002) (discussing importance of adopting culturally-competent assessment of social conditions and associated remedies).

"borrowed" to the benefit of [public health]).[70]

A second dimension is the mechanisms for linking these issues. At least three institutional alternatives exist within the WTO for balancing competing policy goals. The first would be to interpret TRIPS flexibly in order to facilitate national solutions to balance conflicting goals; the second would be to apply TRIPS stringently to establish a common floor that all nations would have to meet so as to limit national interpretive discretion; and the third would be for the judicial panel to engage in judicial activism on a case-by-case basis, taking into account the broader policy landscape (e.g., WHO, UNAIDS, The United Nations Conference on Trade and Development ("UNCTAD")).[71] The first route would give developing countries more scope to tailor the TRIPS provisions to their specific needs. The second would rest ultimate authority in the intergovernmental political bargain struck in achieving TRIPS. This approach would leave it up to states to negotiate trade-offs between public health and trade. The third route, frequently advocated by legal scholars pushing non-market agendas, would empower WTO judicial panels to resolve value conflicts. Public health and trade could be linked interpretatively in a top-down manner whereby the WTO's Appellate Body interprets the meaning of the relevant laws (interpretive linkage).

Advocates of a broader stakeholder approach for the WTO, such as Robert Howse, argue that "[r]ather than attempt once again to decide what is 'in' or 'out' of' the WTO, we should try to mold the rules and their interpretation to structure the *interaction* of the trading regime with other powers and authorities, both domestic and international, in a legitimate manner."[72] With this perspective, legitimacy would be the yardstick by which to measure the process and outcomes. As Gregory Shaffer suggests, "scholars of different ideological orientations tend to identify their ideological goals with particular institutions and thus tend to idealize those institutions. Power tends to disappear within their preferred institutions."[73] However, one must examine these institutions in their political context, and that invariably implicates power.

For example while the WTO judicial "interpretive" approach may seem appealing on its face, both Shaffer and Jeffrey Dunoff have made compelling arguments against it. First, as Shaffer points out, structural asymmetries militate against extensive developing country participation in WTO litigation.[74] For example, in many cases the costs of litigating a WTO claim ($300 to 400

---

70. Jose E. Alvarez, *Trade and the Environment: Implications for Global Governance: How Not to Link: Institutional Conundrums of an Expanded Trade Regime*, 7 WIDENER L. SYMP. J. 1, 12 (2001).

71. *See* Shaffer, *supra* note 14, at 468 (describing difficulties in applying TRIPS Agreement in multi-national context).

72. Robert Howse, *The Boundaries of the WTO: From Politics to Technocracy – and Back Again: The Fate of the Multilateral Trading Regime*, 96 AM. J. INT'L L. 94, 112 (2002).

73. Gregory C. Shaffer, *Power, Global Governance and the WTO: The Need for a Comparative Institutional Approach*, in POWER IN GLOBAL GOVERNANCE 3 (Michael Barnett & Raymond Duvall eds., 2004).

74. *See* Shaffer, *supra* note 14, at 472-74 (describing challenges of developing nations' participation in WTO).

thousand in attorneys' fees) are prohibitive. "The 'haves' come out ahead in litigation at the international level where legal expertise is highly specialized and expensive."[75] Dunoff has argued that based on the General Agreement on Trade and Tariffs ("GATT")/WTO record, panels are more likely to decide cases in ways that militate against a non-market outcome.[76] These arguments powerfully question the assumption that judicial activism would tend in a "progressive" direction. Furthermore, "WTO judicial bodies decide ... cases in a highly-charged political context. They are not free from political pressure, even if they do not expressly take it into account. They have their own institutional interests at stake."[77] "The WTO Appellate Body operates not as an ideal neutral judge, but one that takes into account its own institutional interests and shapes decisions to encourage compliance and consensus."[78]

Analysis of the Shrimp/Turtle case pertains to the prospects of the WTO's representation of a broader range of stakeholders. While parallels between access to medicines and the Shrimp/Turtle case are inexact,[79] the Shrimp/Turtle case seems to serve as a Rorschach inkblot test in legal scholarship. Scholarly interpretations of the significance of the case are hardly unambiguous. Some scholars advocating a broader stakeholder approach to trade find hope in the case, whereas others are far more wary. The first group of analysts argues that Shrimp/Turtle provides an important precedent for enlarging the WTO's scope beyond trade. The second group bemoans the Shrimp/Turtle case for stretching the WTO too far. The third group draws more pessimistic conclusions about the significance of the case for WTO judicial activism. I will discuss each group in turn.

Advocates for change and for expanding the WTO's mandate conclude that the Appellate Body report in the Shrimp/Turtle Case "abandoned the WTO's isolationism, that the WTO is a self-contained system . . . . by examining whether an endangered species was an exhaustible resource, by referring to international environmental law."[80] The Appellate Body referred to "a baseline in actual international environmental law that was contained in the Rio Declaration on Environment and Development."[81] Howse cites the recent Beef Hormones and

---

75. Shaffer, *Power, Global Governance and the WTO, supra* note 73, at 11.

76. *See* Jeffrey L. Dunoff, *The WTO in Transition: Of Constituents, Competence and Coherence*, 33 GEO. WASH. INT'L L. REV. 979, 1007-11 (2001) (raising issues regarding scope and effectiveness of WTO's transition).

77. Shaffer, *Power, Global Governance and the WTO, supra* note 73, at 26.

78. *Id.* at 29. *See also* James McCall Smith, *WTO and Dispute Settlement: The Politics of Procedure in Appellate Body Rulings*, 2 WORLD TRADE REV. 65, 74-80 (2003) (arguing that Appellate Body rulings are informed by political expediency and desire to build consensus rather than by notions of fairness or morality).

79. E-mail from Gregory C. Shaffer, Professor of Law, University of Wisconsin Law School, to Susan K. Sell (Nov. 23, 2003) (on file with author).

80. James Thuo Gathii, *Institutional Concerns of an Expanded Trade Regime: Where Should Global Social and Regulatory Policy Be Made?: Re-Characterizing the Social in the Constitutionalization of the WTO: A Preliminary Analysis*, 7 WIDENER L. SYMP. J. 137, 155 (2001).

81. Howse, *supra* note 72, at 110.

Asbestos cases as additional examples of the Appellate Body's use of "a variety of jurisprudential techniques" to address the balance of economic and social values.[82] James Thuo Gathii also notes that the Appellate Body endorsed Article 31 of the Vienna Convention on the Law of Treaties as an interpretive reference for the WTO in the Standards for Gasoline case. In his judgment, "such instructions come down to a 'recognition that the *General Agreement* is not to be read in clinical isolation from public international law.'"[83] Joost Pauwelyn argues that "WTO rules are not the alpha and omega of all possible trade relations between states. Other more detailed or special rules of international law . . . continue to be highly relevant."[84]

These analysts advocate the fuller explicit incorporation of social issues into the WTO and tend to highlight normative and consequentialist arguments to support their position. Further, they advocate interpretive linkage by invoking WTO Appellate Body decisions in defense of their arguments and the possibilities for expanded linkage.[85] Some authors argue that social policy is already deeply embedded in the WTO.[86] For example, M. Gregg Bloche argues that in the WTO system the protection of health has become "a *de facto* interpretive principle when disputes arise over members' treaty obligations."[87] According to Bloche, the Doha Declaration on TRIPS and Public Health "has interpretative weight under the Vienna Convention on the Law of Treaties, as either a 'subsequent agreement between the parties regarding the interpretation' of TRIPS or 'subsequent practice in the application of the treaty which

---

82. *Id.* at 109.

83. Gathii, *supra* note 80, at 156 (quoting WTO Appellate Body Reports on United States - Standards for Reformulated and Conventional Gasoline, May 20, 1996, 35 I.L.M. 603 (1996)).

84. Joost Pauwelyn, *The Role of Public International Law in the WTO: How Far Can We Go?*, 95 AM. J. INT'L L. 535, 540 (2001).

85. *See* Frederick Abbott, *Distributed Governance at the WTO-WIPO: An Evolving Model for Open-Architecture Integrated Governance*, 3 J. INT'L ECON. L. 63, 64 (2000) (discussing policymaking and governance structure of WTO); Bloche, *supra* note 58, at 833-34 (describing Appellate Body decisions); Steve Charnovitz, *The Legal Status of the Doha Declarations*, 5 J. INT'L ECON. L. 207, 211 (2002) (questioning authority of Doha Declarations); Gathii, *supra* note 80, at 155-57 (highlighting Appellate Body decisions supporting integration of public international law); James Thuo Gathii, *The Legal Status of the Doha Declaration on TRIPS and Public Health Under the Vienna Convention on the Law of Treaties*, 15 HARV. J.L. & TECH. 291, 316 (2002) (discussing implications of Doha Declaration); Howse, *supra* note 72, at 109-11 (discussing different approaches for inclusion of Appellate Body in deciding cases); Pauwelyn, *supra* note 84, at 556-61 (describing WTO's conflict resolution process); Robert Howse & Makau Mutua, *Protecting Human Rights in a Global Economy: Challenges for the World Trade Organization*, International Centre for Human Rights and Democratic Development (2000) (discussing the promising implications for transparency and linkage in WTO Appellate Body's use of amicus or intervener briefs in the Turtles case and the need to develop procedures for further outside involvement in dispute resolution for human rights advocates), *available at* http://www.ichrdd.ca/english/commdoc/publications/globalization/wtoRightsGlob.html.

86. *See* Gathii, *supra* note 80, at 138-39 (arguing that social policy issues belong within international trade regime).

87. *See* Bloche, *supra* note 58, at 825 (arguing that WTO has adopted a self-determination health policy for member nations).

establishes the agreement of the parties regarding its interpretation.'"[88] Gathii agrees, arguing that "[w]hat the Doha Declaration . . . does as a matter of law is not insignificant. It mandates reading the TRIPS Agreement in light of its objectives and principles, thereby giving countries a legal basis in the Agreement itself to argue in favor of public policies."[89]

Others argue that the WTO should be restricted to trade, *period*,[90] and advocate an incrementalist, bottom-up approach. These analysts tend to highlight strategic reasons and advocate "negotiation linkage." This group also presents a narrower conception of the WTO's mandate.[91] At the end of the day, these analysts warn about the dangers of expanding the WTO's mandate in the absence of a prior *political* consensus among the member states.[92] They raise concerns about the WTO's resource constraints[93] and the dangers of a damaging backlash if the WTO gets too far ahead of its membership.[94] Both Jagdish Bhagwati and Debra Steger are careful to define their sense of the WTO's ultimate purpose. For Bhagwati, it is to promote "non-coercive trade" as a "mutually beneficial phenomenon."[95] By this yardstick he believes that TRIPS has no place in the WTO. Steger defines the WTO as an institution dedicated to promoting freer trade via the norm of nondiscrimination (and *not* fairness).[96] Bhagwati, unlike the first group of commentators, sharply criticizes the Shrimp/Turtle decision for precisely the reasons that the other commentators praised it. As he states:

> [I]t would be more prudent for it not to let earlier findings be replaced

---

88. *See id.* at 842 & nn.96-97 (explaining practical application of Doha Declaration).

89. *See* Gathii, *Legal Status, supra* note 85, at 305 (describing effects of allowing policy to impact trade regime).

90. *See generally* Jagdish Bhagwati, Afterword, *The Boundaries of the WTO: The Question of Linkage*, 96 AM. J. INT'L L. 126, 133-34 (2002) (advocating altering WTO's comprehensive policy goals via political negotiation between member nations rather than through adjudication by Appellate Body, which can be influenced by non-trade considerations); Debra P. Steger, Afterword, *The Boundaries of the WTO: The "Trade and. . ." Conundrum - A Commentary*, 96 AM. J. INT'L L. 135, 145 (2002) (stating that human rights concerns could be addressed by other international organizations without expanding scope of WTO's mandate).

91. *See* Steger, *supra* note 90, at 137-40 (examining competing positions on public policies and WTO).

92. *See* José E. Alvarez, Foreword, *The Boundaries of the WTO*, 96 AM. J. INT'L L. 1, 4 (2002) (analogizing limits of WTO to political constraints on development of globalization); Alvarez, *supra* note 69, at 157 (urging a culturally competent understanding of public policy and trade regime); Alvarez, *supra* note 70, at 13-14 (arguing member states have different visions of human rights to be considered); Bhagwati, *supra* note 90, at 134 (arguing for global understanding of policy considerations and trade regimes); Steger, *supra* note 90, at 144-45 (suggesting shared norms and values inform policy).

93. *See* Bhagwati, *supra* note 90, at 132 (highlighting limitations of WTO in public policy arena).

94. *See* Alvarez, *Trade and the Environment, supra* note 70, at 15-17 (discussing danger of lack of political consensus).

95. *See* Bhagwati, *supra* note 90, at 127 (recognizing potential impact of free trade on poor nations).

96. *See* Steger, *supra* note 90, at 139 (arguing nondiscrimination – not fairness – is the norm for GATT's free trade mandate).

so drastically as in the shift from the Tuna/Dolphin to the Shrimp/Turtle decisions, which was doubtless influenced to some degree by the environmental lobbies of the North. Instead, such dramatic reversals or changes are better made in negotiations than in courts.[97]

Bhagwati fears the explicit introduction of non-market criteria as opening a "Pandora's box"[98] and favors a stricter compartmentalization of functions between various international organizations. He believes, for example, that labor standards should be addressed in the International Labor Organization ("ILO") and not the WTO. Some see this as a potentially cynical position – to shunt sensitive issues off to venues in which "words don't matter," using less authoritative institutions as a safety valve to defuse controversy.[99] Steger also favors compartmentalization out of acute resource constraints as much as principles. For example, Douglas Irwin has pointed out that the WTO has a staff of only 500 (300 of whom are translators), and an annual budget of just $77 million. By contrast the World Bank employs 6,000 people and has an annual budget of about $8 billion, and even many NGOs have much bigger budgets than the WTO. The World Wildlife Fund's annual budget is $360 million, and Greenpeace has a budget of about $120 million.[100] According to Eric Stein, one must question:

> [W]hether the global commitment to free trade is strong enough to sustain a significant expansion of WTO competence to the full scope of trade-related environmental, social, and sustainable development issues.... For both the 'nationalists' concerned about state sovereignty, and the liberals concerned about democracy, the answer may be to 'stop the integration' and allow other (less integrated) international agencies (e.g., the ILO and mechanisms established by environmental treaties) to deal with the other values.[101]

These analysts trace the development of the GATT/WTO system as a "bottom-up" process.[102] As such, they recommend that its continued evolution rest on a political process of negotiation among member states. Ultimately, these authors see the problems as essentially political and therefore advocate political solutions. Insofar as the WTO is "a system of rules," the "normative problems of interpreting and applying those rules . . . cannot be avoided."[103]

---

97. Bhagwati, *supra* note 90, at 133-34.

98. *Id.* at 133.

99. *See* Helfer, *supra* note 1, at 56-57 (describing safety valves in regime shifting); Gregory C. Shaffer, *The World Trade Organization Under Challenge: Democracy and the Law and Politics of the WTO's Treatment of Trade and Environment Matters*, 25 HARV. ENVTL. L. REV. 1, 38 (2001) (describing consequences of words in binding dispute resolution context).

100. DOUGLAS A. IRWIN, FREE TRADE UNDER FIRE 186 (2002) (noting that WTO has a much smaller budget and relatively greater mission than other comparable international organizations).

101. *See* Stein, *supra* note 68, at 507 (discussing inclusion of public policy issues in WTO).

102. *See* Alvarez, *Trade and the Environment*, *supra* note 70, at 19 (suggesting use of specific problem to discover solution to linkage issue); John H. Jackson, Afterword, *The Linkage Problem – Comments on Five Texts*, 96 AM. J. INT'L L. 118, 125 (2002) (discussing linkage positions).

103. *See* Steger, *supra* note 90, at 138 (critiquing view that GATT is simply a contract).

Steger takes direct aim at the analysts who champion the Appellate Body's potential to expand WTO's purview. As Steger states, "this challenge - of redefining and clarifying the values and policy objectives that the international community believes should trump the value of freer trade - is too big and too important to be left to the judicial branch of the WTO, even at its highest level, the Appellate Body."[104]

A third group of scholars endorses a broader mandate for the WTO, that it conform to a stakeholder model,[105] but disagrees on mechanisms. As Dunoff states:

> Debates within and about the WTO tend to be consequentialist. That is, they tend to argue over what results will follow from adopting this or that rule, and whether such outcomes are desirable. In this context, the 'desirable' outcome is typically understood to be the outcome that maximizes economic welfare. But it is surely a mistake to understand the new trade issues exclusively in consequentialist terms.[106]

Indeed, the new trade issues (such as intellectual property) are distributional and are not about "expanding the pie."[107] While Dunoff and Shaffer subscribe to the broad stakeholder view, they part company with Howse and Gathii insofar as they are leery about a "top-down" Appellate Body incorporation mechanism.

Scholars' emphasizing the deeply political universe of the WTO draw different conclusions from the Shrimp/Turtle case.[108] For instance, Dunoff argues that the Shrimp/Turtle case presents an ambiguous picture for champions of incorporation of "trade and" in the WTO.[109] While heralded as a major step forward insofar as the Appellate Body held that "dispute resolution Panels and the [Appellate Body] itself have legal authority to receive amicus briefs and other materials from NGOs,"[110] in fact the Appellate Body "proceeded to largely ignore the NGO arguments and instead 'focus' solely on the arguments the United States presented in its 'main submission.'"[111] Surveying additional cases, Dunoff concludes that WTO trends are a step backwards for advocates of greater NGO involvement in WTO deliberations. Rather than representing the infusion of independent ideas into the deliberative process, NGO submissions are routinely ignored unless adopted by one of the parties to the dispute. In

---

104. *Id.* at 144.

105. MICHAEL J. TREBILCOCK & ROBERT HOWSE, THE REGULATION OF INTERNATIONAL TRADE 54-56 (2d ed. 1999) (discussing G. Richard Shell's Trade Stakeholder's Model for WTO dispute resolution as "'part of a wide-ranging deliberative process by which an emerging global social system can set its priorities'").

106. *See* Dunoff, *supra* note 76, at 1008 (arguing for a broader, non-consequentialist interpretation of WTO issues).

107. *Id.*

108. *See* Dunoff, *supra* note 76, at 984 (describing process of Shrimp/Turtle case); Smith, *supra* note 78, at 88-89 (discussing differences of opinion following Shrimp/Turtle case and two subsequent rulings).

109. *See* Dunoff, *supra* note 76, at 984-85 (highlighting conflict in brief acceptance policy).

110. *Id.*

111. *Id.* at 985.

essence, this has had the effect of diluting the possibilities of NGO input. "While doctrinal developments deprive NGOs of a powerful rhetorical argument about the closed nature of WTO dispute resolution, the actual procedure used effectively excludes NGOs from WTO dispute resolution."[112]

V. INSTITUTIONAL DIMENSIONS: PUBLIC INTERNATIONAL LEGAL REGIMES, INSTITUTIONS, HARD AND SOFT LAW: WIPO, CBD, UNHCHR, & WHO

The WTO is arguably the most important institution governing global intellectual property policy. However, TRIPS is not the only important public international legal regime covering global intellectual property, and the WTO is not the only significant venue. WIPO, the Convention on Biological Diversity ("CBD"), the United Nations High Commissioner for Human Rights ("UNHCHR"), and the WHO are all actively engaged in making public international law in intellectual property. The following section seeks to map out the broader institutional terrain, focusing on WIPO, the CBD, the UNHCHR, and the WHO. I will devote most of the discussion to the WHO, due to its centrality to the medicines debate. As Stein points out, "any effort to rank [International Intergovernmental Organizations ("IGOs")] in a hierarchical way is fraught with difficulties."[113] However, it is important to highlight each organization's perspective on the issue before discussing the relationships among them.

This discussion of the institutional dimensions of global public policymaking requires exploring the reasons for shifting from one forum to another, the available options, the choice of institutions, and the role of the WTO. According to Helfer, there are four main reasons why actors strategically choose to shift forums: "to help achieve desired policy outcomes[;] to relieve political pressure for lawmaking in other international venues[;] to generate counter[-]regime norms[;] and to integrate those norms into the WTO and WIPO."[114] These reasons are not mutually exclusive. Of these four reasons, only the second, the "safety valve" strategy, is pursued in order to preserve the status quo. "[S]tates and interest groups can use regime shifting as a safety valve, consigning an issue area to a venue where consequential outcomes and meaningful rule development are unlikely to occur."[115] The other three are pursued in order to effect change.

Governments, private actors, and NGOs all engage in forum shifting. Forum shifting can be done horizontally, across institutions, as in the case in which the United States pushed to move intellectual property policymaking from WIPO to GATT for the Uruguay Round.[116] Forum shifting can also involve vertical moves across levels of governance, such as the United States' use of Super 301 of U.S. trade laws to coerce developing countries into adopting higher

---

112. *Id.* at 987.
113. Stein, *supra* note 68, at 495.
114. *See* Helfer, *supra* note 1, at 53 (discussing regime shifting in international law context).
115. *Id.* at 56.
116. SELL, *supra* note 45, at 108.

standards of intellectual property protection, or its more recent efforts to use bilateral and regional intellectual property and investment treaties to secure "TRIPS-Plus" protection in developing countries.[117] Actors may also choose among different institutions favoring those that afford them better access or those whose philosophies resonate more closely with their own goals. For example, actors can select a forum in which previously marginalized issues get a better reception. This can provide them with opportunities to propose and experiment with policy approaches to the issues.[118] Forum shifting can provide governments that are critical of TRIPS a "safe space" in which to exchange information, develop soft law, and craft viable policy alternatives that address their concerns.[119] Such soft law forums as the WHO and the CBD have proven to be significant incubators of alternative approaches, or "counter-regime norms," to TRIPS. As Helfer suggests:

> [E]mbedded in the very idea of counterregime norms is a more strategic understanding of legal inconsistencies, one in which states consciously create conflicts as a way to subvert the prevailing legal landscape and provide fuel for renegotiating principles, norms, and rules to reflect their interests more accurately. . . . [D]eveloping countries and NGOs used precisely this strategic approach in seeking to integrate the new rules developed in biodiversity . . . public health, and human rights regimes into the WTO and WIPO.

> [Such forum shifting] can also function as an intermediate strategy that allows developing countries to generate the political groundwork necessary for new rounds of intellectual property lawmaking in the WTO and WIPO. When adopting this 'integrationist' strategy, developing countries use regime shifting to shore up support from hesitant allies, vet competing reform proposals, and generate common negotiating positions which they then introduce into the two organizations.[120]

This strategy can also support the development of competing discourses that can change the way parties read TRIPS and are willing to apply it.[121] Furthermore, these competing discourses can challenge various domestic political bargains and integrate a broader range of viewpoints and parties into the issues. They can raise the political costs of defending the status quo.[122] With this in mind, the following discussion surveys TRIPS-related activity in diverse forums.

The NIEO negotiations on the revision of the Paris Convention for the

---

117. *See* Peter Drahos, *BITs and BIPs: Bilateralism in Intellectual Property*, 4 J. WORLD INTELL. PROP. 791, 792-93 (2001) (describing how the United States' use, or threatened use, of § 301 investigations on developing countries has created enhanced intellectual property protection).

118. *See* Helfer, *supra* note 1, at 55 (offering rationales behind forum shifting).

119. *See id.* at 58 (suggesting alternative rationales behind regime shifting).

120. *Id.* at 59-60.

121. E-mail from Gregory C. Shaffer, Professor of Law, University of Wisconsin Law School, to Susan K. Sell (Nov. 12, 2003) (on file with author).

122. *See generally* Sell & Prakash, *supra* note 7, at 143-75 (examining role of ideas in influencing policy agendas and outcomes in contemporary intellectual property rights regime).

Protection of Industrial Property took place in WIPO, which administered the Paris Convention. In the mid-1980s, in the waning days of those stalled negotiations, dissatisfied American negotiators shifted intellectual property deliberations out of WIPO and into GATT. Americans, seeking high protectionist norms for intellectual property, favored GATT because it would permit them to link intellectual property protection to trade. The U.S. negotiators anticipated better results owing to the large and attractive U.S. market that could be used as negotiating leverage.[123] The forum shifting of the mid-1980s was a major blow to WIPO's morale and prestige. However, it has bounced back with renewed energy. Since then, WIPO has substantially transformed itself from a relatively sleepy, albeit highly competent, organization into a more entrepreneurial agency with a mission to prove its continued relevance to intellectual property owners.

Unlike many international organizations, WIPO is almost self-sufficient. Rather than relying upon government handouts and grants, WIPO earns nearly ninety percent of its operating budget from its administration of the Patent Cooperation Treaty ("PCT").[124] The biggest users of the PCT are the global corporations engaged in producing knowledge-intensive products and processes, such as the global life sciences industries and the financial services industries. These corporations also are the most ardent champions of high protectionist norms for intellectual property. These budgetary facts behind WIPO undoubtedly compromise its image as a technocratic, objective civil servant.

WIPO actively provides technical assistance to developing countries as they seek to comply with TRIPS. Those who pay WIPO's freight undoubtedly shape its advocacy, and it has urged a number of developing countries to adopt "TRIPS-Plus" provisions in their national legislation. For example, WIPO assisted in formulating the revised Bangui Agreement for the Organisation Africaine de la Propriete Intellectuelle ("OAPI") countries. This agreement goes further than TRIPS by placing greater restrictions on the issuance of compulsory licenses and prohibiting parallel imports.[125] Indeed, in the wake of TRIPS, "[t]he United States regularly sent lawyers for the U.S. pharmaceutical and copyright industries to Geneva as 'faculty' of the World Intellectual Property Organization . . . to teach developing country representatives about intellectual property matters and to draft 'model' laws for their consideration.

---

123. SELL, *supra* note 45, at 137.

124. *See generally* BRUCE G. DOERN, GLOBAL CHANGE AND INTELLECTUAL PROPERTY AGENCIES (1999) (examining nature and relationship among national and international intellectual property agencies); DRAHOS & BRAITHWAITE, *supra* note 32, at 111 (examining global redefinition of intellectual property standards); WIPO, *Revised Draft Program and Budget 2002-2003*, at 2 (June 30, 2001) (estimating that 85% of WIPO's income will continue to come from fees paid by users of WIPO's services, which include its administration of PCT and the Madrid, Hague, and Lisbon systems), *available at* http://www.wipo.int/documents/en/document/govbody/budget/2002_03/rev/pdf/pbc4_2.pdf.

125. *See* COMM'N ON INTELL. PROP. RIGHTS, INTEGRATING INTELLECTUAL PROPERTY RIGHTS AND DEVELOPMENT POLICY (Sept. 2002) (describing usage of compulsory licenses), *available at* http://www.iprcommission.org/papers/text/final_report/reportwebfinal.htm.

Industry successfully lobbied Congress to allocate funds for these 'educational' efforts."[126]

WIPO is also conducting negotiations on a Substantive Patent Law Treaty ("SPLT") that aims for harmonization of patent law globally. After a failed effort that ended in 1991, new talks began in 2001, and many suspect that the momentum behind the renewed effort is animated by a quest to increase property rights protection beyond that embodied in TRIPS. The 1991 effort produced a draft that largely was a hybrid of U.S. and European laws. This prompted one developing country delegate to point out that· "there was a paradox that through a harmonisation process, the majority of countries were being asked to align their law with the provisions of a minority."[127] The current deliberations pose a danger to developing countries insofar as they could universalize TRIPS-Plus standards. Furthermore, it is important to avoid "one-size-fits-all" approaches to intellectual property protection.

But developing countries have also seized opportunities to press their agendas, which are more fully developed in other venues, within WIPO. They sought to link biodiversity issues to the 1999 WIPO Patent Law Treaty negotiations by proposing the incorporation of the CBD recommendation that intellectual property applicants, when using genetic resources, prove that they had obtained informed prior consent to access those resources.[128] In response, WIPO agreed to establish a separate body within WIPO to address intellectual property aspects of resources and traditional knowledge. Subsequently, the Intergovernmental Committee on Intellectual Property, Genetic Resources, Traditional Knowledge and Folklore ("IGC") has conducted a number of studies that reflect the developing countries' concerns as expressed in the CBD's Conference of the Parties ("COP"). While to this point the IGC's activities have "emphasized soft law studies and reports," governments are debating public health, biodiversity, plant genetic resources, and traditional knowledge issues "in hard law negotiations over the SPLT."[129] Developing countries have also requested that the WIPO Secretariat examine the implications of the SPLT for the IGC's work, that "illustrates their increasing recognition of the need to coordinate lawmaking not only across different regimes or across venues ... but also in different fora within the same intergovernmental organization."[130]

The CBD is yet another international law that includes intellectual property elements. Unlike TRIPS and WIPO efforts, it more explicitly and squarely incorporates provisions that developing countries favor. The CBD recognizes the rights of indigenous cultures to preserve their knowledge resources; Article 8(j) recognizes communal knowledge. The CBD conception challenges the TRIPS view that endorses the western, individualistic conception of knowledge

---

126. *See* Shaffer, *supra* note 14, at 476 (describing tactics of United States and European Communities in knowledge game).

127. COMM'N ON INTELL. PROP. RIGHTS, *supra* note 125.

128. Helfer, *supra* note 1, at 62.

129. *Id.* at 71.

130. *Id.*

ownership; this western perspective draws a sharp line between "folklore" and "science." CBD stresses that biological resources are sovereign resources of states, whereas TRIPS enforces private property rights over them. Many developing countries and NGOs endorse CBD as a way of combating "biopiracy" in which global life sciences' corporations expropriate genetic resources and traditional knowledge without authorization or compensation. W.R. Grace's patenting of Indian neem tree seed extracts became a lightning rod for this controversy. Furthermore, the CBD also offers more opportunities for upholding farmers' rights against "biogopolists." Article 8(j) calls for respect and preservation for "innovations and practices of indigenous and local communities embodying traditional lifestyles relevant for the conservation and sustainable use of biological diversity."[131] India has called for the primacy of the CBD over TRIPS 27.3(b) (the provision requiring members to provide protection for plant varieties either by patents or an effective *sui generis* system).

The CBD's COP, the CBD member states that decide how to apply and implement the CBD, has addressed the degree of the CBD's compatibility with TRIPS. "After the entry into force of TRIPs, developing states led by China and the Group of 77 ("G77") and sympathetic NGOs such as the World Wildlife Fund began to express concern over the relationship between intellectual property rights and the CBD's access and benefit sharing rules."[132] The COP convened a panel of experts that led to the adoption of the Bonn Guidelines in 2002, which stipulated that applicants for intellectual property rights should disclose the origin of any genetic resources or related knowledge relevant to the subject matter. Such disclosures are meant to facilitate monitoring whether applicants have received prior informed consent of the country of origin and complied with the country's conditions of access.[133] While the CBD's COP states have urged cooperation with the WTO and WIPO, they have:

> [P]ointedly refrained from ceding jurisdiction over biodiversity-related intellectual property issues to these organizations and instead are attempting to influence the terms of the debate by setting agendas, convening meetings, suggesting topics for further study, proposing a memorandum of understanding with WIPO, and directing the CBD's Executive Secretary to seek observer status with the TRIPS Council.[134]

The WTO Ministerial Declaration of November 2001 instructed the TRIPS Council to examine the relationship between the TRIPS Agreement and the CBD.[135] This is an important development insofar as it constitutes a frank recognition of conflicts that will need to be addressed. It also demonstrates the migration of an issue developed in the CBD into the WTO; the developing countries' proposals were derived from the Bonn Guidelines.[136]

---

131. Convention on Biological Diversity ("CBD"), June 5, 1992, art. 8(j), 31 I.L.M. 818, 825.

132. *Id.* at 33.

133. *See id.* at 29 (discussing importance of COP and need to harness intellectual property rules to promote compliance with convention).

134. Helfer, *supra* note 1, at 34.

135. Abbott, *supra* note 9, at 489.

136. Helfer, *supra* note 1, at 59-62.

Human rights organizations increasingly have devoted their attention to intellectual property issues. Under a human rights rubric, intellectual property is recast as "a social product with a social function and not primarily as an economic relationship."[137] The organizations adopt resolutions, declarations, and reports that are not legally binding. "In July 2000, an NGO consortium composed of the Lutheran World Federation, Habitat International Coalition, and the International NGO Committee on Human Rights in Trade and Investment submitted a statement to the Chair of the Sub-Commission" on the Promotion and Protection of Human Rights.[138] The statement underscored fundamental conflicts between TRIPS and human rights. In November 2000, the UN Committee on Economic, Social, and Cultural Rights held a day-long session on intellectual property rights, which led to the adoption of a statement in November 2001 endorsing a normative framework for intellectual property rights. The UN High Commissioner's report on the impact of TRIPS on human rights addressed the medicines issue.[139] This report endorsed the public health and developing country activists' position on TRIPS and highlighted the high cost of patented drugs as a barrier to health. It also discussed Brazil's program as a positive model for expanding access to medicines. In this venue, NGOs, independent experts, and developing countries have framed the TRIPS rules as "a threat to economic, social, and cultural rights" and have displayed an antagonistic approach to TRIPS.[140] The Sub-Commission on the Promotion and Protection of Human Rights has criticized the WTO quite sharply, stating in one draft report that "the WTO is a 'veritable nightmare' for certain sectors of humanity and criticize[d] WTO rules as 'grossly unfair.'"[141] The WTO Secretariat responded by criticizing the report's methodology, language, and conclusions, claiming that they were unsubstantiated by the evidence. The Secretariat suggested "a meeting with WTO officials to correct the 'significant misunderstandings' included in the report."[142] The Sub-Commission has requested that the High Commissioner for Human Rights seek observer status with the WTO for the ongoing review of TRIPS.[143]

Patrick Wojahn points out that the right to health is guaranteed under numerous conventions including Article 12 of the International Covenant on Economic, Social and Cultural Rights ("ICESCR"), Article 25 of the Universal Declaration of Human Rights, and Article 11 of the Convention on the

---

137. Audrey Chapman, *The Human Rights Implications of Intellectual Property Protection*, 5 J. INT'L ECON. L. 861, 867 (2002).

138. Helfer, *supra* note 1, at 49.

139. UNITED NATIONS HIGH COMM'R FOR HUMAN RIGHTS, THE IMPACT OF THE AGREEMENT ON TRADE-RELATED ASPECTS OF INTELLECTUAL PROPERTY RIGHTS ON HUMAN RIGHTS: REPORT OF THE HIGH COMMISSIONER (2001), *available at* http://www.eldis.org/static/DOC5597.htm (last visited Aug. 19, 2004).

140. Helfer, *supra* note 1, at 46.

141. Dunoff, *supra* note 76, at 998.

142. *Id.* at 999.

143. Chapman, *supra* note 137, at 880.

Elimination of All Forms of Discrimination Against Women.[144] Even though the United States has not ratified the ICESCR, Wojahn argues that the right to health should be considered to be "customary international law" because 143 states are parties to the Covenant and the right to health is included in numerous other treaties.[145] The UN human rights bodies have focused considerable attention on intellectual property issues, spanning public health, technology transfer, agriculture, indigenous peoples, and cultural dimensions of human rights. These bodies would like to see human rights concerns prevail over intellectual property rights. Many of the human rights approaches to health have been developed from the WHO.[146]

The WHO is a specialized agency of the UN system. Its mandate is to direct and coordinate authority for health work.[147] The WHO has the largest budget of all the specialized agencies, with an annual budget of "$1.8 billion dollars contributed by its 193 member states."[148] Since TRIPS, the WHO increasingly has been drawn into trade issues, and NGOs have had considerable access to the institution. In 1999, "the WHO ... granted official status to nearly two hundred NGOs."[149] Even though global pharma has an important voice in the WTO through its powerful OECD member states that contribute significant funding, the WHO has been criticized for its "failure to cooperate with the private sector."[150] The director-general, secretariat, and health expert staff significantly shape agendas and outcomes.

The WHO has been active in the access to essential medicines campaign.[151] Governments and NGOs first deliberated in the WHO over the very issues that led to the Doha Declaration on TRIPS and Public Health. In 1996, public health activists and developing country member states, including Brazil, South Africa, and Zimbabwe, expressed concerns about access to medicines in connection with globalization and TRIPS. The World Health Assembly adopted a resolution on a Revised Drug Strategy that asked the WHO to examine the impact of the WTO on national drug policies and essential drugs and to make recommendations for collaboration between the WTO and the WHO. "This resolution gave the WHO the mandate to publish, in 1998, the first guide with recommendations to Member States for implementing TRIPS while limiting the

---

144. Patrick Wojahn, Comment, *A Conflict of Rights: Intellectual Property Under TRIPS, The Right to Health, and AIDS Drugs*, 6 UCLA J. INT'L L. & FOREIGN AFF. 463, 466 (2001/2002) (explaining that absolute protection of intellectual property rights would conflict with right to health guaranteed by many international agreements).

145. *Id.* at 496.

146. *Id.* at 469.

147. Stein, *supra* note 68, at 497.

148. Mark J. Volansky, Comment, *Achieving Global Health: A Review of the World Health Organization's Response*, 10 TULSA J. COMP. & INT'L L. 223, 229 (2002) (discussing purpose and importance of WHO).

149. Stein, *supra* note 68, at 498.

150. *Id.*

151. Susan K. Sell, *TRIPS and the Access to Medicines Campaign*, 20 WIS. INT'L L.J. 481, 504-06 (2002) (describing WHO's role in campaign to provide access to medicines and practice public health).

negative effects of higher levels of patent protection on drug availability."[152] The WHO Essential Drugs Policy concentrates on the supply and use of about 250 drugs that are considered to be the most essential and important for public sector provision.

In 1998, Zimbabwe's Minister of Health asked Bas van der Heide of the NGO Health Action International ("HAI") to produce a draft resolution for a "Revised Drug Strategy." The Revised Drug Strategy is a document designed to assist developing countries in their health planning and policy implementation. The proposed document drew from work that HAI had been doing with consumer activist Ralph Nader's group CPT headed by James Love. Van der Heide and Love had crafted language for the Free Trade of the Americas negotiations advocating compulsory licensing and parallel importing, as well as stressing the priority of health concerns over commercial interests. "A small technical group within the WHO began to prepare and distribute concrete recommendations for coping with TRIPS by using the built-in flexibility to ameliorate the effects of introducing its requirements. These recommendations included . . . authorizing parallel importation and granting compulsory licenses where appropriate."[153] This incensed the brand name global pharmaceutical industry because the document endorsed the very practices that this sector was fighting through the United States Trade Representative. "The U.S. and a number of European countries unsuccessfully pressured the WHO in an attempt to prevent publication of the guide."[154] Commercial pharmaceutical interests felt that the WHO's involvement in this issue presented a threat to a trade-based approach. The United States has resisted the WHO's efforts to help developing countries gain access to medicines, but the European Community has shifted its views in recent years and has become more supportive of the WHO's role in this area.[155]

In May 1999, the WHO's World Health Assembly unanimously enacted resolution WHA 52.19 calling upon member states to ensure equitable access to essential drugs and review options under international agreements to safeguard access to these medicines.[156] The WHO continues to pursue strategies designed to increase developing countries' access to essential drugs. As Abbott points out:

> A number of training seminars regarding TRIPS implementation have been conducted with public health, patent office, and trade officials. These activities of WHO remain relatively unpublicized because increased attention would risk drawing a stronger reaction from Pharma. However, it is becoming substantially more difficult to find developing country officials who are unaware of compulsory licensing,

---

152. 't Hoen, *supra* note 59, at 36.

153. Abbott, *supra* note 9, at 474-75.

154. 't Hoen, *supra* note 59, at 36.

155. Helfer, *supra* note 1, at 42.

156. WHO, *Revised Drug Strategy* (Mar. 13, 2000), *available at* http://www.who.int/gb/ebwha/pdf_files/WHA53/ea10.pdf.

parallel importation, and the importance of patent application reviews.[157]

In 2001, the WHO adopted two resolutions that addressed the need to strengthen policies to increase access to medicines and the need to evaluate the impact of TRIPS.[158] It also published a bulletin highlighting the WHO's policy guidelines and urging developing countries to refrain from implementing TRIPS-Plus intellectual property provisions.[159]

In the spring of 2001, the Zimbabwean Ambassador Boniface Chidyausiku requested a special TRIPS Council session on access to medicines. The session was held in June. The Quaker United Nations Office in Geneva provided support for developing country delegates, and a number of legal scholars, economists, and activists provided technical support.[160] As expressed by the Brazilian delegate, the meetings were intended to "eliminate the imprecision in international agreements concerning public health. In matters involving public health, developing countries wish WTO judges to interpret the TRIPS Agreement in a manner that benefits public health."[161] The TRIPS Council resolved to continue analyzing the degree of flexibility afforded by TRIPS and planned future meetings on the issue. Momentum to address the issue accelerated throughout the summer and fall. The United States withdrew a WTO intellectual property case against Brazil, the UN General Assembly held a special session devoted to the HIV/AIDS pandemic, and Secretary-General Kofi Annan announced the establishment of a Global Fund to Fight AIDS, Tuberculosis, and Malaria.[162] In September 2001, the TRIPS Council met again to discuss the access to medicines issue. The African group presented a draft text for a ministerial declaration on TRIPS and public health, which emphasized that "[n]othing in the TRIPS Agreement shall prevent Members from taking measures to protect public health."[163]

In the September preparations for the upcoming WTO Doha Ministerial meeting, some participants discussed the possibility of WHO/WTO collaboration in preparing a guide to assist developing countries in implementing TRIPS while protecting public health. An accidentally-leaked memo provided a WTO critique of WHO's role.[164] Australia mistakenly included an e-mail message from the Director of Intellectual Property for the WTO, Adrian Otten, in a

---

157. Abbott, *supra* note 9, at 475.

158. *See* 't Hoen, *supra* note 59, at 36 (arguing that WHA resolutions have strengthened WHO's mandate in trade arena).

159. Helfer, *supra* note 1, at 44 (outlining WHO's approach as detailed in bulletin); WHO, POLICY PERSPECTIVES ON MEDICINES: GLOBALIZATION, TRIPs AND ACCESS TO PHARMACEUTICALS (Mar. 2001) (discussing effect of TRIPS on pharmaceutical access), *available at* http://www.who.int/medicines/ library/edm_general/6pagers/PPM03ENG.pdf.

160. Sell, *TRIPS and the Access to Medicines Campaign*, *supra* note 151, at 512.

161. Viana, *supra* note 64, at 314.

162. *See* Sell, *TRIPS and the Access to Medicines Campaign*, *supra* note 151, at 513 (discussing developments during TRIPS Council sessions in 2001).

163. 't Hoen, *supra* note 59, at 39.

164. Abbott, *supra* note 9, at 475 n.26.

submission to the TRIPS Council and then recalled it. The message states:

> [T]o be frank, I have my doubts about the wisdom and feasibility of attempting a joint guide with WHO and this still remains to be seen ; . . . I do feel very strongly, for reasons indicated below, that we should not send it to WHO prior to Doha.
>
>   . . . .
>
> I have two major concerns on the TRIPS side.
>
> The first and most important is that I think it unnecessarily risky for the WTO Secretariat to share texts on the TRIPS Agreement's provisions on pharmaceuticals with the WHO at this stage . . . . It is important to recognize that there is a network which includes the leading non-governmental people, certain people in the WHO Secretariat, . . . and many developing country delegates and nothing that is given to WHO can be relied upon to remain confidential.
>
> My second concern about TRIPS is that it does not, as yet, contain a section which discusses the positive impact of the TRIPS Agreement on public health, namely through promoting research and development into new drugs.
>
>   . . . .
>
> The main messages that we would want to give are: (a) that open trade and a movement towards more open trade brings with it higher standards of health; and (b) concerns that the WTO rules will stand in the way of legitimate health measures are unfounded.[165]

Not only does the message reveal a somewhat tense relationship between the two organizations, but it also clearly incorporates the PhRMA perspective as revealed in Otten's "second concern." Indeed, PhRMA executives have boasted about their close relationship with and extensive access to the WTO Secretariat.[166]

In the run up to Doha, human rights activists supported the WHO's approach to the medicines issue[167] and participated in the access to medicines lobbying process. More dramatically, in the wake of anthrax attacks in the United States in September 2001, the United States and Canada announced plans to compulsory license ciprofloxacin ("Cipro"). Ultimately, these governments negotiated steep price reductions with Bayer, just as Brazil has done with Roche and others. The irony that the United States was suddenly prepared to do precisely what it had complained about to WTO was lost on no

---

165. Posting of Mike Palmedo, mpalmedo@cptech.org, to IP-Health Listserv, *Adrian Otten Missive on WTO/WHO Cooperation*, at http://lists.essential.org/pipermail/ip-health/2001-September/001900.html (Sept. 21, 2001).

166. *See* Sanjay Basu, *Patents and Pharmaceutical Access*, at http://www.zmag.org/content/showarticle.cfm?ItemID=3694 (May 29, 2003) (explaining pharmaceutical industry's role in debate over access to medicines); Posting of James Love, james.love@cptech.org, to IP-Health Listserv, *Pfizer's McKinnell Says Drug Patent Talks Progress*, REUTERS, Jan. 28, 2003, (noting role played by chairman of world's largest pharmaceutical company in trade negotiations), *at* http://lists.essential.org/pipermail/ip-health/2003-January/004184.html.

167. Chapman, *supra* note 137, at 879.

one. Numerous commentators have noted the political importance of this event in the successful conclusion of the Doha meeting.[168]

In November 2001, WTO members unanimously endorsed the Doha Declaration on TRIPS and Public Health. While not, by its terms, legally binding, it largely embraced the WHO and NGO view that TRIPS should not be a barrier to developing countries seeking access to medicines. This opens the possibility that the norms expressed in the Doha Declaration could become legally binding either through a dispute resolution report that so holds or otherwise.[169] Reactions to the Declaration predictably have been mixed, with PhRMA interpreting it as an endorsement of intellectual property rights, many NGOs and developing countries seeing it as an important victory, and scholars debating what it really means.[170] The Declaration postponed the politically contentious issue of the ability of generic manufacturers to export drugs to countries without manufacturing capacity. This was deferred to the so-called Paragraph 6 negotiations at the TRIPS Council. The WTO deadline for resolving that issue came and went in December 2002. The United States, reflecting the wishes of its brand name pharmaceutical corporations, stood alone and used its veto to block the interpretation that 140 other countries had supported.[171] Meanwhile, the WHO busily tried to craft constructive approaches to this issue.

A May 2003 WHO report endorsed the NGO/developing country approaches to the medicines issue.[172] The report emphasized the neglect of

---

168. *E.g.*, Abbott, *supra* note 9, at 486-88 (discussing how the U.S. and Canadian need for Cipro impacted Doha's outcome); Sell, *TRIPS and the Access to Medicines Campaign, supra* note 151, at 515-16 (describing how U.S. and Canadian thoughts of compulsory licensing of Cipro during Anthrax attacks affected their positions during Doha meeting); 't Hoen, *supra* note 59, at 42-43 (listing U.S. and Canadian reactions to Anthrax scare as one reason for Doha's passage); César Vieira, *Changing Roles of State and Non-State Actors in the Wake of Drugs Access Decisions in South Africa and Brazil*, 17 CONN. J. INT'L L. 319, 320 (2002) (noting how the "U.S. and Canadian approach to obtaining affordable supplies of Cipro to combat Anthrax" factored into the compromise reached at the Doha meeting).

169. Email from Professor Jeffrey Dunoff, Professor of Law, Temple University, Beasley School of Law, to Susan K. Sell, (Nov. 13, 2003) (on file with author).

170. *E.g.*, Charnovitz, *supra* note 85, at 207-08 (struggling to define meaning of Doha Declaration); Carmen Otero Garcia-Castrillión, *An Approach to the WTO Ministerial Declaration on the TRIPS Agreement and Public Health*, 5 J. INT'L ECON. L. 212, 212-19 (2002) (explaining Doha Declaration's contribution to interpretation of TRIPS Agreement); Gary N. Horlick, *Over the Bump in Doha?*, 5 J. INT'L ECON. L. 195, 199-200 (2002) (concluding that effect of Doha Declaration on TRIPS members is unclear); Jeffrey J. Schott, *Comment on the Doha Ministerial*, 5 J. INT'L ECON. L. 191, 195 (2002) (arguing that Doha Declaration created substantial political obstacles); 't Hoen, *supra* note 59, at 43-44 (noting concerns of pharmaceutical manufacturers following Doha Declaration); Alan Wm. Wolff, *What Did Doha Do? An Initial Assessment*, 5 J. INT'L ECON. L. 202, 206 & n.1 (2002) (warning that lack of established mechanisms to meet concerns of developing nations could lead to trade confrontations).

171. Larry Elliott & Charlotte Denny, *U.S. Wrecks Cheap Drugs Deal*, THE GUARDIAN, Dec. 21, 2002 (characterizing pharmaceutical companies' intense lobbying efforts and Vice President Cheney's intervention in talks as instrumental in U.S. refusal to relax global patent laws), *available at* http://www.guardian.co.uk/ international/story/0,3604,864071,00.html.

172. WHO, INTELLECTUAL PROPERTY RIGHTS, INNOVATION AND PUBLIC HEALTH (May 12,

394   *TEMPLE LAW REVIEW*   [Vol. 77

tropical diseases, the Doha Declaration's recognition that pharmaceutical products require special treatment, and the negative effects of patent protection on drug pricing. Further, the report recommended expanded competition as the most effective way to reduce drug prices. The report also took a critical view of "TRIPS-plus" provisions as being detrimental to health care. The director-elect of the WHO, Lee Jong-wook, announced measures that will make Brazil's AIDS policy the foundation for the WHO efforts in this area. He asked the Brazilian Health Minister to release Paulo Teixeira, head of the administration's AIDS program, "to formulate the new policy for combating AIDS throughout the world, based on Brazil's experience."[173] This represents important recognition of Brazil's leadership role, and support for the developing countries' and NGO positions.

The May 2003 World Health Assembly meeting on improving access to essential medicines was particularly volatile. The United States presented a resolution that neglected even to mention the Doha Declaration and did little more than assert the value of strong intellectual property protection as a stimulus for innovation.[174] The U.S. proposal further requested the WHO to refer member states to the WTO and WIPO for assistance in implementing TRIPS obligations.[175] Brazil proposed a resolution, supported by Bolivia, Ecuador, Indonesia, Peru, Venezuela, and South Africa on behalf of the members of the WHO African Region. The Brazilian proposal reflected developing countries' concerns about access to medicines and called for an independent commission to examine the relationship between intellectual property rights, innovation, public goods, and public health. The developing countries sought an international committee much like the UK Commission on Intellectual Property Rights,[176] which was critical of overly strong patent rights as a barrier to access.[177] When it was clear that no one supported the U.S. resolution, the Brazilian, American, and several African delegations worked out a compromise that a WHO committee adopted by consensus. The resolution called for the establishment of a time-limited independent commission, whose terms of reference have yet to be drafted, and it omitted any reference to "TRIPS-Plus" obligations in bilateral and regional trade agreements. NGOs bemoaned the fact that the developing countries' proposals had been watered

---

2003), *available at* http://www.who.int/gb/ebwha/pdf_files/WHA56/ea5617.pdf.

173. Posting of Mike Palmedo, mpalmedo@cptech.org, to IP-Health Listserv, *WHO to Adopt Brazilian Model to Fight AIDS/HIV*, FIN. TIMES LTD., May 21, 2003, *available at* http://lists.essential.org/pipermail/ip-health/2003-May/004779.html.

174. Posting of Nathan Ford, Nathan.FORD@london.msf.org, to IP-Health Listserv, *Sparks Fly Over Patents and Vital Drugs at World Health Assembly*, LANCET, May 31, 2003, *available at* http://lists.essential.org/pipermail/ip-health/2003-May/004816.html.

175. Posting of Cecilia Oh, ceciliaoh@yahoo.com, to IP-Health Listserv, Third World Network Info. Service, *WHO Adopts Resolution on IPRs and Public Health After Wrangling Over Text*, THIRD WORLD NETWORK, May 29, 2003, *available at* http://lists.essential.org/pipermail/ip-health/2003-May/004815.html.

176. *Id.*

177. COMM'N ON INTELL. PROP. RIGHTS, *supra* note 125, at 22.

down in the compromise. However, the Doha Declaration is prominently featured in the resolution, and Member States were urged to arrive at a solution to the Paragraph 6 Doha Declaration impasse prior to the Cancun WTO Ministerial in September 2003.[178]

A TRIPS Council meeting held June 4th through 6th, 2003 ended in a deadlock over the Paragraph 6 issue. Harvey Bale, President of the Geneva-based International Federation of Pharmaceutical Manufacturers Associations, stated that there had been no progress since the talks collapsed in December 2002. He referred to the December sixteenth draft text as "a license to steal" and claimed that "all research-based companies have problems with December 16."[179] However, just before the Cancun Ministerial in September 2003, the United States finally relented in its adamant opposition to developing countries' proposals for a Paragraph 6 solution. Developing countries threatened to hold the Round hostage in the absence of a Paragraph 6 agreement. The WTO members adopted an interpretive decision that "allows developing countries that lack sufficient domestic manufacturing capacity to meet their public health needs by importing generic drugs from other WTO members without restriction as to type of disease or type of emergency."[180] The WTO General Council issued a decision implementing Paragraph 6 of the Doha Declaration that "waived obligations set forth in paragraphs (f) and (h) of Article 31 of the TRIPS Agreement so as to facilitate the grant of 'compulsory licenses' for the supply of medicines from any third country to countries with insufficient manufacturing capacities in the pharmaceutical sector."[181]

Clearly, international organizations involved in intellectual property issues are divided over the merits of diverse multilateral approaches to intellectual property protection. The WTO and WIPO seem to champion the interests of property holders over property users (or producers over consumers), whereas the CBD, the human rights organizations, and the WHO promote approaches that at the very least seek to balance the rights of producers and consumers. These divisions provide opportunities for developing countries and NGOs to change the agenda by reframing issues in ways that enlarge their scope of action. For example, linking intellectual property to environmental protection as in the CBD or to public health as in the WHO can build effective challenges to the more narrow trade-based conception enshrined in the WTO or the economic efficiency notions reflected in WIPO. Redefining intellectual property from being a trade issue to a public health issue resulted in the Doha Declaration.

---

178. WHO, Fourth Report of Committee A (Draft) (May 28, 2003), *available at* http://www.who.int/gb/ebwha/pdf_files/WHA56/ea5666.pdf.

179. Posting of Mike Palmedo, mpalmedo@cptech.org, to IP-Health Listserv, Richard Waddington, *No Shift on Drugs at Trade Talks – Industry Chief*, Reuters, May 22, 2002, *available at* http://lists.essential.org/pipermail/ip-health/2003-May/004773.html.

180. Helfer, *supra* note 1, at 67. *See also* World Trade Organization Council, *Implementation of Paragraph 6 of the Doha Declaration on the TRIPS Agreement and Public Health* (Aug. 30, 2003) (containing WTO General Council's decision to implement relieving measures for developing countries), *available at* http://www.wto.org/english/tratop_e/trips_e/implem_para6_e.htm.

181. Shaffer, *supra* note 14, at 467.

This has opened up an important space for debate on the costs and benefits of intellectual property protection as enshrined in TRIPS.

VI. CONCLUSION AND THE WAY FORWARD

The foregoing has important implications for the access to medicines campaign and the quest for global governance of public health more generally. The access to medicines campaign, in particular, has provided several important lessons. Reframing issues can be an effective way of creating space for debate and reconsideration of the conventional wisdom. By recasting intellectual property as a public health issue, policy makers are increasingly forced to confront the unconscionable trade off between economic gain and unnecessary death. This has raised the political costs for those seeking to defend the status quo. "In a world of asymmetric power, developing countries enhance the prospects of their success if other U.S. and European constituencies offset the pharmaceutical industry's pressure on U.S. and European trade authorities to aggressively advance industry interests."[182] When brought to light through public action and media attention, the use of economic coercion to reduce access to medicines can become "politically unpalatable for U.S. and EC government and corporate elites."[183] By mobilizing to reduce domestic political support for the status quo in the most economically powerful and influential countries, "developing countries retain greater leeway to formulate intellectual property policies to fit their own needs."[184] They will need considerable support to enable them to resist pressures to adopt pernicious TRIPS-Plus provisions in bilateral and regional agreements. Highlighting the unintended and devastating consequences of particular policies can be a powerful rhetorical strategy. The HIV/AIDS pandemic underscored just how costly overly-strong patent protection can be. The anthrax/bio-terror threat in the United States led American policy makers to threaten compulsory licensing of Bayer's cipro to ensure adequate supplies. The access to medicines campaign capitalized on this hypocrisy and it softened the American stance at Doha. Additionally, the SARS epidemic of spring 2003 led to an expansion of the WHO's mandate and a further empowerment of NGOs within the public health context. In May 2003, the WHO assembly approved changes to international health regulations to strengthen the WHO's ability "to respond to global public health threats based on information from non-government sources."[185]

Even without obvious economic power, the African block, Brazil, India, and their NGO advocates have begun to make inroads on global intellectual property policy by strategically shifting forums and advancing new arguments. For

---

182. Shaffer, *supra* note 14, at 480.

183. *Id.* at 476. *See also* Sell & Prakash, *supra* note 7, at 163-65 (noting that NGOs characterize pharmaceutical companies as greedy and responsible for millions of needless deaths).

184. Shaffer, *supra* note 14, at 481.

185. Posting of Mike Palmedo, mpalmedo@cptech.org, to IP-Health Listserv, Frances Williams, *WHO to Gain Advisory Role on Pharmaceutical Patents*, FIN. TIMES, May 28, 2003, *available at* http://lists.essential.org/pipermail/ip-health/2003-May/004803.html.

instance, the CBD recasts intellectual property as both an environmental issue and a potential obstacle to sustainable agriculture. Environmental preservation and the ability of states to feed their own people are powerful values that can lead people to question the primacy of economic efficiency as the sole yardstick by which to measure policy effectiveness. While the WTO and WIPO seem to represent both the economically and politically most powerful, the work of the WHO and the CBD can have an impact on the work of these other agencies. The Doha Declaration on TRIPS and Public Health is a good example of that. Recasting intellectual property as a human rights issue could be an effective strategy to the extent that intellectual property rights are implicated in battles over the rights to food and medicines. No single "reframing" will open up the dialogue and change global policies, but cumulative concerted efforts from a variety of angles could serve to weaken the consensus that backed TRIPS and lead to a more balanced approach to intellectual property rights.

Soft and hard law developed in non-WTO venues via developing countries' strategic forum shifting has enhanced their bargaining power within the WTO and WIPO. Developing countries and their NGO supporters deliberately promoted issue migration, on health from the WHO to the WTO, and on human rights and indigenous people to WIPO:

> [Strategic forum shifting] facilitates a proactive negotiating strategy, enabling governments and NGOs to coordinate their efforts around hard and soft law proposals first vetted and refined in other international venues. This integrationist approach also allows states to justify their demands for reform by invoking rules and principles endorsed by officials of intergovernmental organizations and by legal and technical experts. Support from these seemingly neutral actors gives the demands the imprimatur of legitimacy. And it allows proponents to frame their arguments as rational efforts to harmonize potentially inconsistent treaty obligations and soft law standards that many states have agreed to, rather than as self-interested attempts to distort trade rules or to free ride on foreign creators or inventors. Seen from this perspective, even the soft law intellectual property standards generated in the biodiversity ... public health, and human rights regimes have hard-edged consequences. They act as progenitors of proposals to revise legally binding rules within the WTO and WIPO."[186]

Returning to issues raised at the outset, it is important to bear in mind the relationships among international institutions. Given the fact that the WTO embodies hard law, it exists in somewhat of a hierarchical relationship compared to its soft law counterparts. Beyond the hard/soft law distinction, the WTO has cooperated more extensively with those international institutions (IMF and World Bank) that share its basic pro-market philosophy.[187] Indeed, the WTO also has expressed some overt antagonism toward both the WHO and the

---

186. Helfer, *supra* note 1, at 61.

187. *See* Dunoff, *supra* note 76, at 999 (arguing that the pattern of these relationships could have troubling implications).

UNHCHR. Nonetheless, since much of the debate over TRIPS interpretations will be discursive,[188] "soft law will be an important tool for WTO panels to use in resolving . . . arguments [over competing objectives]."[189] While the deliberate generation of counter-regime norms in alternative forums has many benefits, it also risks the injection of further uncertainty and incoherence into efforts at global governance of public health.[190] Without authoritative guidelines for resolving such issues, it may facilitate outcomes that favor the structurally powerful at the expense of others.

In order to reduce some of the power asymmetries, it would be helpful to institutionalize expertise and technical support for developing country delegations in Geneva. Drahos has suggested the establishment of a "counter Quad" for developing countries that would function somewhat like the Cairns Group of agricultural exporters.[191] The idea is to provide continuity and technical support on diverse issues to help balance information and expertise asymmetries between the resource abundant delegations and most of those from developing countries. This expertise would need to be provided by developing countries' representatives and experts eager to protect developing countries' interests. Support provided by the Quaker United Nations Offices in Geneva during the negotiations over the Doha Declaration on TRIPS and Public Health is a good example of this latter type of assistance. UNCTAD, in conjunction with ICSTD, also has assembled a panel of intellectual property experts that have helped craft reports and documents to assist developing countries' negotiators negotiate intellectual property issues.

At the national level, developing countries should pursue vigorous competition legislation. Competition law can provide an important check on abuses of intellectual property rights. Even though the Reagan administration gutted American antitrust practice with respect to intellectual property rights in the name of competitiveness, consumer groups and developing countries can lobby for competition policies that check the abuses of the new "global knowledge cartels."[192] Indeed, for most of the twentieth century American antitrust laws kept patent power in check.[193] Competition policies can facilitate healthy markets and keep costs down. Technical assistance directed to this end would be invaluable.

While the structural picture poses daunting obstacles to the access

---

188. *See* Shaffer, *supra* note 14, at 476 (presenting ways in which developing countries might advance their interests).

189. *See* Helfer, *supra* note 1, at 77 (discussing prior use of soft law in interpreting international agreements).

190. *See id.* at 75 (noting claims that TRIPS is inconsistent with other international treaty commitments and norms).

191. Peter Drahos, *When the Weak Bargain with the Strong: Negotiations in the World Trade Organization*, 8 INT'L NEGOTIATION 79, 96 (2003) (suggesting regional leaders could form a group to represent developing countries' interests in the most difficult stages of negotiations).

192. DRAHOS & BRAITHWAITE, *supra* note 32, at 206.

193. SELL, *supra* note 41, at 5-6 (noting that, historically, patents have been disfavored as monopolistic in the United States).

campaign, the personal, emotional, and subjective nature of health may give the subject added punch. As Bloche argues, the infiltration of health issues into the WTO through the Agreement on the Application of Sanitary and Phytosanitary Measures ("SPS Agreement") and the Doha Declaration:

> [R]ests on the intensely subjective, highly variable nature of people's beliefs about health danger. We appreciate and respond to health risks in ways shaped much less by statistical magnitudes than by the feelings that these risks evoke and our sense of control over these risks. . . . And public decision-making mechanisms that fail to offer opportunities for community control, or at least engagement, tend to raise people's anxieties about the risk-benefit judgments reached. . . . National, let alone transnational, efforts to systematize and rationalize health policies encounter skepticism and resistance. Pushed too far, these efforts undermine the credibility, indeed the perceived legitimacy, of governments, and public, multinational institutions.[194]

This article has just begun to chart out the relationships among competing knowledge networks, international institutions, and normative concerns in the quest for global governance in public health. An important issue for further research is specifying the conditions under which principled arguments and persuasion help the weak achieve important goals. Neta Crawford, William Coleman, and Melissa Gabler have done important work in this vein and offer excellent ways to begin to address this vital question. Combining this set of concerns with negotiation analysis could be a fruitful way to proceed.[195] Additionally, further examination of relationships among intergovernmental institutions is imperative. It matters a great deal whether they see themselves as in horizontal or hierarchical relation to one another. Analysts should continue to explore the intersection of knowledge networks, governments, multilateral institutions, international law, global business regulation, and social policy.

---

194. Bloche, *supra* note 58, at 845.

195. *See* ALBIN, *supra* note 13, at 1-2 (explaining ability of negotiation to create new solutions to shared problems); Müller, *supra* note 13, at 160-63 (analyzing the social understanding, equitable positions, and argumentation involved in effective international negotiations).

[23]

The framework convention on tobacco control: the politics of global health governance

JEFF COLLIN, KELLEY LEE & KAREN BISSELL

ABSTRACT   *This paper analyses the particular challenges that tobacco control poses for health governance in an era of accelerating globalisation. Traditionally, health systems have been structured at the national level, and health regulation has focused on the needs of populations within individual countries. However, the increasingly global nature of the tobacco industry, and the risks it poses to public health, require a transnational approach to regulation. This has been the rationale behind negotiations for a Framework Convention on Tobacco Control (FCTC) by the Tobacco Free Initiative of the World Health Organisation (TFI/WHO). In recognition of the need to go beyond national governments, and to create a governance mechanism that can effectively address the transnational nature of the tobacco epidemic, WHO has sought to involve a broad range of interests in negotiations. The contributions of civil society groups in particular in the negotiation process have been unusual. This paper explores the nature and effectiveness of these contributions. It concludes with an assessment of whether the FCTC constitutes a significant shift towards a new form of global health governance, exploring the institutional tensions inherent in attempting to extend participation within a state-centric organisation.*

It is estimated that some four million deaths per year can currently be attributed to tobacco, a figure representing around one in 10 adult deaths. By 2030 both the total and the proportion of tobacco-related deaths are expected to have risen dramatically, to some 10 million or one in 6 adult deaths. Such figures suggest that around 500 million people alive today will eventually be killed by tobacco. Nor will this burden be equitably shared. Smoking related deaths were once largely confined to men in high-income countries, but the marked shift in smoking patterns among high- to middle- and low-income countries will be evident in due course by rapidly rising trends in tobacco-related diseases. By 2030 70% of deaths from tobacco will occur in the developing world, up from around 50% currently (WHO, 1999a; Jha & Chaloupka, 1999).

   These sobering statistics reflect a continuing struggle by the public health community to effectively address an issue that has long been understood scien-

Jeff Collin, Kelley Lee and Karen Bissell all work at the Centre on Global Change and Health, London School of Hygiene and Tropical Medicine, Keppel Street, London WC1E 7HT. Karen Bissell also works in the Health Policy Unit of the International Union Against Tuberculosis and Lung Disease.

tifically. Since the first wave of publications linking smoking with lung cancer around 1950 (Levin *et al*, 1950; Wynder & Graham, 1950; Doll & Hill, 1950), much has been learned about the diverse health impacts of tobacco consumption. Despite the clear messages emerging from medical research, however, the establishment of effective regulatory frameworks of tobacco control has been sporadic, and they remain far from adopted in most countries.

The additional challenge in recent decades has been the globalisation of the tobacco industry. Globalisation is a set of processes leading to the intensification of human interaction across three types of boundaries—spatial, temporal and cognitive. The changes wrought by processes of global change are evident in many spheres of social activity, including the economic, political, cultural and technological (Lee, 2001). In terms of tobacco control, the specific challenges of globalisation are:

- facilitated access to markets worldwide by the tobacco industry through trade liberalisation and specific provisions under multilateral trade agreements;
- enhanced marketing, advertising and sponsorship opportunities via global communication systems;
- greater economies of scale ranging from the purchase of local cigarette manufacturers, improved access to ever larger markets and the development and production of global brands; and
- the ability of transnational corporations (TNCs) to undermine the regulatory authority of national governments.

It is therefore unsurprising that transnational tobacco companies (TTCs) have enjoyed record sales and profits since the early 1990s, with the main source of growth being the developing world. While demand has gradually declined in many high-income countries thanks to changing public attitudes towards tobacco use and stronger regulation, changes in the developing world are more than compensating for contraction of traditional markets. Indeed, by expanding their presence in middle and low-income countries, TTCs will continue to remain viable and lucrative businesses in all countries

This paper analyses the particular challenges that tobacco control poses for health governance in an era of accelerating globalisation. Traditionally health systems have been structured at the national level, and health regulation has focused on the needs of populations within individual countries. However, the increasingly global nature of the tobacco industry, and the risks it poses to public health, require a transnational approach to regulation. This has been the rationale behind negotiations for a Framework Convention on Tobacco Control (FCTC) by the Tobacco Free Initiative of the World Health Organisation (TFI/WHO). In recognition of the need to go beyond national governments, and to create a governance mechanism that can effectively address the transnational nature of tobacco issues, WHO has sought to involve a broad range of interests in negotiations. The contributions of civil society groups in particular in the negotiation process have been unusual. The paper explores the nature and effectiveness of these contributions. It concludes with an assessment of whether the FCTC constitutes a significant shift towards a new form of global health governance, exploring the institutional tensions inherent in attempting to extend participation within a state-centric organisation.

Thwarting health governance: the tobacco industry and the limits of tobacco control

> Tobacco use is unlike other threats to global health. Infectious diseases do not employ multinational public relations firms. There are no front groups to promote the spread of cholera. Mosquitoes have no lobbyists. (WHO Committee of Experts, 2000)

The progress of the global epidemic of tobacco-related deaths and disease reflects the extent to which the tobacco industry has been able to thwart the development and implementation of effective tobacco control policies at national, regional and international levels. There are countries such as Canada, Australia, Thailand, Singapore and South Africa that have been able to adopt relatively comprehensive programmes of control measures, programmes that have been successful in checking or reversing increases in smoking prevalence and consumption. It is also clear that there has been a gradual spread of certain basic restrictions on issues such as advertising and youth access.

The existence of a handful of beacon states and the broader profusion of limited regulation should not, however, detract attention from the inadequacies of governance in relation to tobacco. Since the release of internal industry documents following litigation in Minnesota (Ciresi *et al*, 1999), it has become increasingly clear that, in addition to being the primary vectors of the pandemic, TTCs have actively sought to manipulate the policy process to maintain commercial advantage.

At the national level, tobacco companies have largely been able to manage the policy process so as to ensure that they are able to continue trading on advantageous terms and subject to limited hindrance. This is not, of course, to deny the significant variation that exists in the extent to which to health professionals, ministers and NGOs have been able to advance tobacco control objectives, with a concomitant variation in the domestic influence of the tobacco industry. A continuum of industry capacity to thwart effective tobacco control can be identified:

* precluding serious consideration of tobacco control strategies;
* defusing calls for legislation by the voluntary adoption of token self-regulation;
* vetoing proposed legislation, or compromising its effectiveness by amendment;
* undermining effective control measures upon implementation.

At one extreme are those countries within which tobacco interests are sufficiently pervasive to have kept all but the most minimal and ineffective control measures off the policy agenda. The paucity of regulation may reflect the importance of domestic interests, particularly in the small number of national economies that are heavily dependent on tobacco production (Jha & Chaloupka, 1999). In

JEFF COLLIN ET AL

Zimbabwe, for example, tobacco typically accounts for up to one-third of foreign currency earnings, contributes substantially to GDP and employs around 6% of the population, a context in which the close identification of government with industry and the minimal nature of existing tobacco control measures are scarcely surprising (Woelk *et al*, 2000). In other countries the scale of much needed investment by the major tobacco companies may be seen to carry with it an accompanying influence over policy, a phenomenon that has become evident across much of central and eastern Europe and the countries of the former Soviet Union. In Uzbekistan there have been suggestions of a contract between British American Tobacco (BAT) and the government that delimits the anti-smoking measures open to the government (Simpson, 2000). In Kazakhstan the reputation of the government among some journalists as 'the public relations department of Philip Morris' is partially explained by the decision to commemorate victims of mass hunger on 31 May, an apparent spoiling tactic to detract attention from World No Tobacco Day (Krasovsky, 2000). In Hungary BAT's apparent largesse as a major sponsor within the health, education and welfare sectors is not without strings, with its funding of a media centre at the University of Pecs being followed by a request that the university abandon its no-smoking policy (Chapman, 2000).

Where control issues do threaten to appear on the policy agenda, TTCs have long sought to defuse them through the pre-emptive adoption of self-imposed industry codes or voluntary regulation. Such a strategy typically enjoys the twin benefits of projecting an image of corporate responsibility while avoiding meaningful constraint or effective enforcement. As the Health Select Committee of the House of Commons in the UK recently noted, 'voluntary agreements have served the industry well and the public badly' (Health Select Committee, 2000). In the UK tobacco advertising is nominally subject to the Committee on Advertising Practice (CAP) of the Advertising Standards Association. However, documents disclosed during the course of the Health Select Committee's investigations revealed blatant transgressions of CAP rules in a desire to expand the market and in the use of sexual imagery to target the young (Hastings & MacFadyen, 2000). In the USA tobacco companies agreed to the Cigarette Advertising Code in 1964. While the code has been employed to demonstrate that the industry promotes tobacco responsibly, as well as to avoid more rigorous government oversight, the code's key provisions have been persistently violated (Richards *et al*, 1996). Similarly, tobacco firms voluntarily stopped the practice of brand placement in movies in order to avoid the prospect of federal government regulation. The adoption of a revised code of practice in 1989 merely led to a shift from background placements to potentially more powerful actor brand endorsements within films (Sargent *et al*, 2001).

The most striking examples of tobacco company influence in the conduct of the national policy process are provided by those cases where industry intervention via lobbying has apparently shaped the outcome of proposed legislation, resulting in its abandonment or significant amendment. Internal industry documents released as a result of litigation in the USA are illustrative of the scale of such efforts, the resources afforded to them and their frequency of success. A review of activities by Philip Morris International Corporate Affairs in 1986

FRAMEWORK CONVENTION ON TOBACCO CONTROL

proclaims, among other achievements, their success in blocking, diluting and reversing measures to control advertising:

> A law prohibiting tobacco advertising was passed in Ecuador but, after a mobiliza-
> tion of journalists from throughout Latin America and numerous organizations, it
> was vetoed by the President. A similar bill was proposed in Peru, but was sent back
> for reconsideration ... In Venezuela, we were successful in stopping a detrimental,
> self-regulating advertising code, and are now negotiating a new one. Our work in
> Senegal resulted in a new advertising decree which reversed a total advertising ban.
> (Whist, 1986)

A review of Philip Morris' corporate affairs activities across Asia–Pacific similarly notes that 'the region has been successful at fighting off anti-tobacco proposals', exemplified by events in the Philippines where 'we have successfully delayed the passage of national legislation and more recently local legislation' (Dollisson, 1989). Such lobbying success is not, of course, confined to low- and middle-income countries. In what was reportedly the most expensive sustained issue-advocacy campaign in the USA, the tobacco companies spent $43 million in the first half of 1998 in defeating federal legislation sponsored by Senator John McCain (Saloojee & Dagli, 2000).

The efforts of the tobacco companies to minimise the impact of regulation on their trading operations extends throughout the policy process, from agenda setting through to implementation and evaluation. In those situations where industry lobbying has seemingly failed, with the successful passage of legislation, the actual impact of such regulation can subsequently be undermined. This may take the form of a refusal to comply with certain provisions of legislation, as in the case of ingredient disclosure in Thailand. The TTCs appealed directly to cabinet ministers to have this regulation dropped and, when met with government obduracy, BAT and Philip Morris then refused to release requisite information regarding product composition. It wasn't until they received a public commitment from Thailand's health ministry that the information would remain confidential that compliance was secured. This was a proviso without basis in the regulation and reduced its utility to public health activists and consumers (Vateesatokit *et al*, 2000). More subtle expressions of recalcitrance are evident in various efforts to evade or circumvent regulation. 'Brand stretching' or 'trade-mark diversification' is one widely used such strategy. In Malaysia a television advertising ban was easily side-stepped by 'Salem High Country Holidays', via which fruitless attempts to book a vacation indicated that the operation existed solely to promote the Salem brand (Cunningham, 1996). Sports sponsorship offers another means by which advertising restrictions can be overcome in a cost-effective manner. Despite the longstanding ban on cigarette advertising on US television, exposure generated by motor sports sponsorships allows the tobacco companies to achieve an annual equivalent of over $150 million in television advertising (Siegel, 2001).

Recent investigations into the complicity of tobacco companies in the smuggling of cigarettes starkly illustrate the manner in which pressure can be exerted upon governments to enforce a policy change (International Consortium of Investigative Journalists, 2001). Industry arguments that smuggling is a

JEFF COLLIN ET AL

product of high levels of taxation, and particularly of tax differentials between neighbouring states, have been widely employed as a means of exercising political leverage (Japan Tobacco International, 2001; Gallaher, 2001; Brown & Williamson, 2001). In Canada, successive increases in cigarette taxes from 1979 to 1994 brought both a dramatic fall in per capita cigarette consumption and significant increases in tax revenues. These public policy gains were reversed when an industry-orchestrated campaign to induce and highlight awareness of a rise in contraband from the USA led to a rollback in taxation (Cunningham, 1996). The imposition of higher taxes in Sweden in 1996–97 again brought the dual benefit of generating further revenues and falling consumption, but limited evidence of a marginal rise in smuggled cigarettes brought reversal in both tax policy and the associated gains (Joossens *et al*, 2000). The recent decision of the UK government to abandon its previous policy of year-on-year tax increases on cigarettes suggests that growing evidence of the role of tobacco companies in overseeing and facilitating contraband has not diminished the utility of such arguments. This policy reversal is all the more remarkable in that it occurred in the context of an ongoing investigation by the Department of Trade and Industry into the involvement of BAT in smuggling.

In keeping with the primarily national basis of tobacco control to date, the efforts of the industry to minimise its impact have historically focused on policy processes within nation-states. Tobacco companies have, however, been quick to identify both the potential regulatory challenges and the enormous business opportunities inherent in regional and international organisations. Research into industry documents recently undertaken on behalf of the Eastern Mediterranean Regional Office of WHO has disclosed the scale of industry activity designed to prevent meaningful progress towards tobacco control by the countries of the Gulf Cooperation Council (GCC), and particularly within the regular meetings of the Arab Gulf Health Ministers' Conference. Operating under the aegis of the Middle East Tobacco Association (META), the tobacco companies developed a sub-stantial, well resourced and well connected lobby. Among those enlisted to provide information and perform lobbying functions were an Egyptian member of Parliament, a former Assistant Secretary General of the Arab League, and the Kuwaiti Under-Secretary of Health who served as the Secretary General of the GCC Health Ministers (Hammond & White, 2001). Among the issues successfully targeted by the industry were government attempts to restrict smoking in public places, efforts to regulate standards in the manufacture of tobacco products, and proposals for a unified approach to increasing taxation across the region (EMRO, 2001).

Within the EU the gradual transfer of policy competence to the regional level has been accompanied by increasing concern among the major tobacco companies to monitor and intervene in policy making. The diversity of key issues handled by EU institutions, including food regulation, advertising practices, excise tax harmonisation, abolition of duty free and environmental tobacco smoke have encouraged major lobbying efforts by the industry. Analysis of industry documents reveals the astute exploitation of the complex decision-making procedures of EU institutions, as well as the high levels of access to and support within them that tobacco companies have secured. Industry attempts to

FRAMEWORK CONVENTION ON TOBACCO CONTROL

defeat the emergence of a European Directive prohibiting advertising in the early 1990s, for example, combined a clear reading of the requirements of the qualified majority voting system with the active support of key actors and countries. A Philip Morris document assessing the blocking minority within the Council of Ministers, by which the defeat of such a Directive could be attained, urged the use of 'all possible German influence to prevent a weakening of the blocking minority. Work with Chancellor Kohl to put ad ban on Commission subsidiary list' and of the 'successful revision of Dutch code [sic] and contacts with the economics ministry to keep the Health Minister from undermining the Dutch position' (Philip Morris, nda).

At the same time, the industry has appreciated the commercial opportunities provided by greater economic integration within Europe. BAT's assessment of the 1992 single European market programme was that:

> 1992 will give greater impetus to the growth of the international brand segment whilst giving BAT the opportunity to transform its cigarette position within the Community ... BATCo. market strategy is to defend and develop its position in existing Operating Company markets, whilst aggressively taking up the opportunities created in the markets of Southern Europe. (Bingham, 1989).

Tobacco companies have been able to exploit the privileged status accorded to free trade within the emergent European legal system in the event of failure to successfully exert political influence. This was starkly illustrated by the industry response to the eventual passage in 1998 of the Tobacco Advertising Directive, when the blocking minority within the Council of Ministers had been critically undermined following the election of a Labour government in the UK. The European Court of Justice annulled the Directive in October 2000 following litigation brought to it by Germany and by tobacco companies in the English courts (Fennelly, 2001). A subsequent product regulation directive that includes within its provisions a reduction in the tar content of cigarettes and a tightening of rules on product labelling, including a prohibition on misleading descriptors such as 'light' and 'mild', is now to be subject to a legal challenge by BAT and Imperial Tobacco (Clark, 2001).

The tobacco industry has also sought to minimise the impact of potential control measures within international organisations, particularly WHO, while simultaneously exploiting the opportunities presented by trade liberalisation under GATT and WTO. Analysis of tobacco industry documents has revealed the scale of collaborative activities undertaken by transnational tobacco companies to undermine WHO efforts to reduce tobacco consumption. A committee of experts assembled by WHO Director-General Gro Harlem Brundtland identified diverse strategies to defuse the potential impact of WHO initiatives. Tobacco companies sought to influence policy by building relationships with WHO staff, including gaining contacts through hiring or offering future employment to officials, and placing industry consultants in positions within WHO. The industry exerted pressure on relevant WHO budgets in an attempt to further constrain its tobacco control activities, and targeted other UN agencies to detract attention from the scale of the health impact of tobacco. WHO's competence and priorities were attacked in orchestrated campaigns of media and political pressure, the

JEFF COLLIN ET AL

International Tobacco Growers Association was established as a front for lobbying, and large events were staged to distract media attention from the World Conference on Tobacco or Health (WHO Committee of Experts, 2000).

A key element in the attempt to inhibit the development of effective international tobacco control has been the distortion of the conduct and dissemination of scientific research. A clear example is provided by the campaign to manipulate the largest European study into the relationship between environmental tobacco smoke and lung cancer, a study undertaken by the International Agency for Research on Cancer (IARC). Instigated by Philip Morris and involving BAT, RJ Reynolds, Imperial, Rothmans and Reemtsma, a major collaborative effort was launched in an attempt to deflect and constrain the impact of IARC's work. An indication of the significance attached to these efforts is provided by the resources devoted by the industry. Whereas the IARC study itself is estimated to have cost between $1.5–3 million over its 10-year period, Philip Morris alone budgeted $2 million for its IARC plans in 1994 alone and also proposed $4 million to fund studies to discredit IARC's work. BAT took the lead in instigating an international programme of press briefings that served to defuse the impact of the study before its publication, ensuring that the study was widely and incorrectly reported as demonstrating no increase in risk of lung cancer for non-smokers (Ong & Glantz, 2000).

The industry has also dedicated itself to shaping the activities of regulatory bodies that can have some impact on the cigarette production process. The International Standards Organisation (ISO) establishes product standards for tobacco and tobacco products via ISO technical committee 126, the composition and output of which has been demonstrated to be subject to the influence of the tobacco industry (Bialous & Yach, 2001). Documents indicate that its chair is both a former employee of Imperial Tobacco and a consultant to the Tobacco Manufacturers Association, while the work of the committee is reliant upon development work carried out by the industry's Cooperation Centre for Scientific Research Relative to Tobacco (CORESTA):

> The relationship with ISO/TC 126 is such that CORESTA does the science and the collaborative testing and produces recommended methods which are subsequently submitted for conversion into International Standards. If a work proposal is accepted by ISO/TC 126 and study is required, it is almost always referred to the appropriate study group in CORESTA. This procedure has worked extraordinarily well in the revision of ISO 3308, 3402, 4387, 8243 and the issue of 10315 and 10362. (Philip Morris, ndb)

The expansion and entrenchment of a liberal trading regime under the auspices of GATT and WTO represent an opportunity that TTCs have been quick to exploit. The operational context of the industry was transformed by the rapid political and economic changes coincident with the end of the Cold War. In 1993 the then BAT chairman Sir Patrick Sheehy noted that 'the tobacco markets open to our products have actually tripled in size in recent years, under the twin impact of sweeping market liberalisations across the northern hemisphere and the crumbling monolithic communism east of the river Elbe' (Sheehy, 1993). The relationship between trade liberalisation and tobacco consumption has since become increas-

FRAMEWORK CONVENTION ON TOBACCO CONTROL

ingly apparent, a relationship that varies in accordance with national economic circumstances. The Uruguay Round concluded in 1994 brought an expansion of the GATT trading regime to cover agricultural products, including tobacco, an inclusion that is emblematic of a broad dismantling of barriers to tobacco trade through numerous international, regional and bilateral trade agreements (Chaloupka & Corbett, 1998). Such negotiated change has been influential in revitalising the tobacco industry, with a 12.5% increase in unmanufactured tobacco exports between 1994 and 1997, following a decade of minimal growth, and global cigarette exports rising by 42% in the period 1994–96. Trade liberalisation has led to increased consumption of tobacco, but while it has no substantive effect on higher income countries, it has a large and significant impact on smoking in low-income countries and a significant, if smaller, impact on middle-income countries (Taylor *et al*, 2000).

Part of this expansion can be attributed to the willingness and ability of the tobacco transnationals to pursue their interests within the institutional architecture of the international trading regime. The most famous example here is the case of Thailand, where access to a previously closed cigarette market was enforced by a GATT arbitration panel in 1990 following a referral by the US Trade Representative that was prompted by US tobacco companies (Chantornvong & McCargo, 2000; Vateesatokit *et al*, 2000). The Thai case was part of a broader wave of threatened retaliatory sanctions by the USA between 1986 and 1990 that also involved Taiwan, South Korea and Japan. It has been estimated that the subsequent opening of these markets had by 1991 increased per capita cigarette consumption by an average of 10% (Chaloupka & Laixuthai, 1996). A similar international litigiousness on behalf of the tobacco industry is evident in Japan's complaint against the recent product regulation directive of the European Community. Japan, with a large stake in Japan Tobacco, whose 'Mild 7' brand is jeopardised by the directive's product labelling provisions, brought its complaint to the WTO Technical Barriers to Trade Committee even before the formal adoption of the directive (Ryan, 2001).

Revitalising health governance: the Framework Convention on Tobacco Control

The Framework Convention process will activate all those areas of governance that have a direct impact on public health. Science and economics will mesh with legislation and litigation. Health ministers will work with their counterparts in finance, trade, labour, agriculture and social affairs ministries to give public health the place it deserves. The challenge for us comes in seeking global and national solutions in tandem for a problem that cuts across national boundaries, cultures, societies and socio-economic strata. (Brundtland, 2000a)

In a world where many health risks and opportunities are becoming increasingly globalised, influencing health determinants, status and outcomes cannot be achieved through actions taken at the national level alone. The intensification of transborder flows of people, ideas, goods and services necessitates a reassessment of the rules and institutions that govern health policy and practice. This is especially so as the determinants of health are being affected by factors outside

JEFF COLLIN ET AL

the traditional parameters of the health sector—trade and investment flows, collective violence and conflict, illicit and criminal activity, global environmental change, and global communication technologies. Importantly, there is a widespread belief that the current system of international health governance (IHG), focused on the national governments of states, has a number of limitations and gaps. In the light of these challenges, the concept of global health governance (GHG) has become a subject of interest and debate in the field of international health (Dodgson *et al*, 2001).

The distinction between IHG and GHG arises from the challenges of globalisation, as defined above, to health governance. First, the spatial dimension of global change means that health determinants and outcomes are less defined by, and in some cases, disengaged from, territorial space. Traditionally, national health systems are by definition structured along national boundaries and deal with cross-border flows (eg infectious disease control) through international co-operation. Globalisation creates transborder flows that, in many cases, are 'deterritorialised' (unrelated to physical or territorial space) and may thus circumvent territorially based rules and institutions. In the case of tobacco control, trade in tobacco products remains largely within the regulatory control of national governments. However, the trend towards targeting selected populations within and across countries through marketing, advertising and sponsorship conveyed through global communications (eg satellites), for example, has the potential to circumvent national regulatory authority.

A recognition of the limitations of health governance, primarily structured around states, for controlling the global dimensions of the tobacco epidemic is the impetus behind the FCTC. While the convention formally remains an intergovernmental treaty, the involvement of non-state actors in the negotiation process reflects the need to go beyond the state. Civil society organisations have been especially active in tobacco control, and will represent a key resource for implementing and monitoring the provisions of FCTC. Hence, WHO has sought to broaden participation in the FCTC as a means of strengthening the effectiveness of the treaty to deal with a global issue.

A second limitation of IHG illuminated by the tobacco control issue has been the traditional focus of existing agreements on infectious disease. International health co-operation has historically focused on infectious diseases, of which only a small number (eg cholera, plague, yellow fever) have been listed in the International Health Regulations as serious threats to public health. The selection of the diseases covered has been largely predicated by the speed at which they spread across populations, rates of morbidity and mortality and, not least, the capacity of control measures to disrupt international trade interests (Fidler, 2001). Tobacco-related diseases are non-communicable and the timeframe of the epidemic is many decades. As such, tobacco control has not been perceived traditionally as a high priority in public health policy requiring strong international governance mechanisms. The FCTC aims to demonstrate that, despite a slower timeframe for the health impacts to be realised, tobacco is an 'emergency' public health issue requiring firmer action. Moreover, the global aspects of the epidemic give the issue far greater urgency in terms of the ultimate burden of disease on populations around the world.

FRAMEWORK CONVENTION ON TOBACCO CONTROL

Third, and related to the above, the global nature of tobacco control has required a shift in how we think about IHG. The public health community has traditionally perceived its role, in terms of tobacco control, as one of health education and promotion. In large part, as described in this paper, the tobacco industry has played an influential role in downgrading more assertive forms of tobacco control as a legitimate and worthy public health issue. Various arguments have been put forth by the industry to this end, including portraying tobacco control as a preoccupation of high-income countries, describing the risks of tobacco use as relatively low, elevating more immediate health needs such as infectious disease as of greater importance, and questioning the 'politicisation' of WHO's mandate. In response, the FCTC process has sought to broaden the debates around tobacco control beyond public health medicine to include issues of economics, law, environment and good governance. This has again required a broadening of the constituency supporting the FCTC to involve state and non-state actors, health and other policy sectors (eg trade, education, environment), and a wider range of disciplinary expertise.

The FCTC process has thus been employed as a catalyst to encourage broader participation in and engagement with tobacco control issues. An obvious target for this inclusive approach has been WHO member states themselves, clearly the core constituency if a convention is to be adopted and implemented. The 1999 World Health Assembly unanimously adopted resolution 52.18 (World Health Assembly, 1999) to instigate a two-step process leading to negotiation of the FCTC, with working groups to establish its technical foundation, to be followed by the establishment of an Intergovernmental Negotiating Body (INB). A record 50 states took the floor to commit political and economic support (WHO, 2000a). The scale of subsequent member state involvement in the process has been generally impressive, with 148 countries attending the first session of the INB in October 2000 (WHO, 2000b). The demands of such attendance and participation have meant an expanded role for multi-sectoral collaboration on tobacco issues at the national level. Formal and informal committees have been established and regular inter-ministerial consultations in countries as diverse as Zimbabwe, China, Brazil, Thailand and the USA (Woelk *et al*, 2000; Wipfli *et al*, 2001). A notable development has been the negotiation of co-ordinated positions among regional groupings prior to the INB meetings. The Johannesburg Declaration on the FCTC (African Region Meeting 2001) was adopted by 21 countries of the African Region in WHO in March 2001. This common front was widely perceived as having added weight to their contributions to the INB session, emphasising a commitment to progressive control measures in combination with calls for assistance in agricultural diversification (Bates, 2001).

An additional objective of the WHO team handling the FCTC process has been to improve co-ordination and co-operation across UN agencies. A key step here was the 1999 decision to establish an Ad Hoc Inter-Agency Task Force on Tobacco Control under the leadership of WHO. This replaced the UN focal point, previously located within the UN Conference on Trade and Development (UNCTAD), the creation of which had 'opened the door to tobacco industry influence throughout the UN' (WHO Committee of Experts, 2000). Fifteen UN organisations as well as the World Bank, the International Monetary Fund and the

JEFF COLLIN ET AL

WTO are participating in the work of the Task Force (Wipfli *et al*, 2001). Its technical work in support of the negotiation process has included projects on environmental tobacco smoke, deforestation, employment and the rights of the child (Taylor & Bettcher, 2001; WHO & UNICEF, 2001). Success in engaging the World Bank in tobacco control issues has been of particular importance in adding credibility and momentum to the FCTC process. A landmark in this regard was the publication by the World Bank of the 1999 report *Curbing the Epidemic* (Jha & Chaloupka, 1999), the dissemination of which has contributed greatly to recognition of the national economic benefits associated with effective tobacco control. This politically critical message has been reinforced by the more detailed exploration of economic issues surrounding tobacco use in developing countries (Jha & Chaloupka, 2000).

The FCTC process has aimed to encourage the participation of actors traditionally excluded from the state-centric politics of UN governance. Some indication of the breadth of engagement that has been facilitated is provided by the Public Hearings held in October 2000. This exercise, the first such ever hosted by WHO, provided an opportunity for interested groups to register their views before the start of intergovernmental negotiations. Over 500 written submissions were received, while 144 organisations provided testimony during the two-day hearings, encompassing TTCs, state tobacco companies and producer organisations as well as diverse public health agencies, womens' groups and academic institutions (WHO, 2001a).

This unique exercise has done little to pacify industry proclamations of their exclusion from the FCTC process. BAT, for example, has complained that 'the tobacco industry has been denied appropriate access to the international debate on the proposed Convention, compared with other parties, particularly anti-tobacco activists' (BAT, 2001). Such protestations have been accompanied by attempts to undermine the legitimacy of WHO efforts at tobacco control, with the FCTC presented as a threat to national sovereignty for low-income countries. BAT has sought to commandeer the language of subsidiarity in proposing an alternative approach of leaving 'national governments free to develop the most appropriate policies for the specific circumstances of their country' (BAT, 2000b). One means by which tobacco companies have secured greater participation in the FCTC process is by serving on member state delegations during the negotiations, the composition of which is beyond WHO jurisdiction. One example is provided by Turkey, whose delegation to the negotiations has included Oktay Önderer, the Deputy Director General of TEKEL, the state tobacco monopoly (WHO, 1999b; 2000c). BAT is reported successively to have pressed representatives of China's state tobacco company to ensure their inclusion in the Chinese delegation, while a spokesman for Japan Tobacco/RJ Reynolds asserted that the company had successfully made its case against the FCTC in Russia, Romania and Turkey (Loewenberg, 2000).

Given both past experience and ongoing practices, WHO has understandable reservations about the participation of the major tobacco companies in regulatory efforts, and has cautioned governments to be wary of industry proclamations of offering a middle ground or realistic solutions (Brundtland, 2000b). In other spheres, however, WHO has not been reluctant to engage with the corporate sector.

FRAMEWORK CONVENTION ON TOBACCO CONTROL

WHO is committed to exploring the role of nicotine replacement therapy in smoking cessation programmes and has co-operated with pharmaceutical companies. Such collaboration is epitomised by World No Tobacco Day in 2000, the theme of which was smoking cessation with the slogan 'leave the pack behind'. Marketing expertise and financial assistance were accepted by WHO both at headquarters and regional levels for this purpose. There are two pharmaceutical consortia in particular that are interested in working on tobacco control issues: the World Self-Medication Industry (WSMI) and the International Federation of Pharmaceutical Manufacturers Association (IFPMA). A representative of WSMI sat on the Policy and Strategy Advisory Committee (PSAC), an advisory committee that reported to WHO Director General Gro Harlem Brundtland on tobacco control between 1999 and May 2001.

A key element in the opening of participation sought by the FCTC process has been the attempt to find new ways of engaging with international NGOs that are active in tobacco control efforts. WHO has standard practices that govern the terms by which certain NGOs can participate in its proceedings. 'Official Relations' is a status achieved through a multi-year process by international health-related NGOs, usually international federations of national and regional professional NGOs. There are currently 193 NGOs in Official Relations with WHO, entitling them to observe proceedings and to 'make a statement of an expository nature' at the invitation of the chair (WHO, 2000d), generally restricted to a short period at the end of a session. NGOs that are not in Official Relations must find a sponsoring organisation to enter and observe a formal meeting, and are unable to make statements in the name of their organisation.

In order to contribute more fully to the FCTC process, NGOs have sought to ease the narrow parameters of participation enabled by Official Relations status, and to accelerate the protracted process by which this status has traditionally been conferred. Some member states have supported these aspirations to greater involvement, with Canada prominent in requesting greatly expanded NGO participation and the accreditation of expert national NGOs (WHO, 2001b). Following an open consultation held by Canada and Thailand, member states approved recommendations that the process of accreditation should be accelerated and that NGOs in Official Relations should have access to working groups. At the Second Session of the Intergovernmental Negotiating Body, it was reported that the Executive Board of the WHO had agreed to admit NGOs into provisional official relations with the WHO, a status that would be revised yearly throughout the FCTC process (WHO, 2001c). It should be noted that some public health NGOs have been cautious about seeking any radical change in the terms of access and participation, fearing that such expansion could serve to facilitate the entry of tobacco industry front groups into the negotiating process.

Perhaps more important than the formal terms of participation in the negotiating chamber is the scope facilitated by such access for NGOs to play a number of key supporting roles. Prominent among these has been an educative function, with NGOs organising seminars and preparing briefings for delegates on diverse technical aspects of the proposed convention. Lobbying activities have been extensive thanks to policy discussions with governments, letter-writing to delegates and heads of state, advocacy campaigns, press conferences before,

JEFF COLLIN ET AL

during and after the meetings, and the publication of reports into tobacco industry practices and collusion in smuggling (Campaign for Tobacco Free Kids and ASH-UK, 2001; Campaign for Tobacco Free Kids, 2001). The NGOs have also been able to use such access to strengthen the effectiveness of their advocacy role, acting as the public health conscience during proceedings. Particularly important has been exposing the dangerous and obstructivist positions adopted by certain member states, with the negative role of the Bush administration leading to calls from some NGOs for the USA to withdraw from negotiations (ASH-UK, 2001; Bates, 2001). Additionally, prominent tobacco control advocates have occasionally participated in FCTC negotiations from within national delegations, examples including Jon Kapito, Margaretha Haglund and Luc Joossens for Malawi, Sweden and Belgium, respectively (WHO, 2000a). In each of these respects the public health NGOs can be seen as constituting a counterweight to the pressures exerted on national delegations by the tobacco industry (INFACT, 1999).

This pattern of NGO involvement does not preclude questions relating to legitimacy and barriers to entry. At the two working group meetings, in particular, participation was almost exclusively from high-income country NGOs and international health-based NGOs (WHO, 1999b; 2000c). For the subsequent INB meetings, high-income country NGOs and international NGOs have given some financial assistance to enable the participation of NGO representatives from developing countries, while there are hopes that some United Nations Fund money may reach low-income country NGOs for this purpose. The coherence of NGO activities and the scope for impact of developing country activists have, however, been significantly increased as a result of the formation of the Framework Convention Alliance. This grouping of over 60 NGOs was created to improve communication between those groups already engaged in the FCTC process and to address the need for a systematic outreach to smaller NGOs in developing countries (Wipfli *et al*, 2001).

Conclusion

The TTCs have long recognised that tobacco control issues are of supranational significance, transcending the national borders within which policies have primarily focused and disputes have largely been articulated. Such companies have recognised the scope for policy learning, and national regulation has frequently been resisted more through fears of a domino effect on other countries than for fear of direct impacts within the territorial limits of is application (Collin, forthcoming). As far back as 1986 Philip Morris International Corporate Affairs highlighted the essentially global nature of their contest with advocates of tobacco control, noting that 'the issues we face—taxation, marketing restrictions, environmental tobacco smoke (ETS)—are now literally world-wide problems, and the anti-smoking groups use sophisticated tactics to attack us on these issues throughout the world' (Whist, 1986).

The FCTC process constitutes an explicit attempt to counter the globalisation of the tobacco epidemic through a reconfiguration of health governance. It represents a necessary response to the extent to which the spread of a 'global bad for public health' has outstripped the capacity of existing modes of regulation

FRAMEWORK CONVENTION ON TOBACCO CONTROL

(Taylor & Bettcher, 2001). As such, the tobacco epidemic demonstrates poignantly the limitations of national level health governance in a globalising world.

This ambitious undertaking to exercise for the first time WHO's capacity to develop a binding public health treaty clearly constitutes a major innovation in health governance. A more sceptical reading could emphasise the limitations inherent in such a state-centric institution as WHO, and indeed the eventual outcome of the negotiations will inevitably be essentially a more-or-less traditional intergovernmental agreement among member states. Such a narrow focus on the form of the convention itself, however, detracts from the innovative and dynamic features of the FCTC process. The power of the FCTC lies not merely in the product itself but in the process by which it is being negotiated (Taylor, 2000). The breadth of multi-sectoral collaboration at the national level; the co-operation among comparatively marginalised states to heighten their impact on negotiations; the greater involvement of UN agencies and other international organisations in tobacco control; the opening towards civil society—all indicate the innovation of the FCTC as a move closer to global health governance.

There are limitations to the changes that have been introduced. The role of NGOs remains tightly circumscribed, recent procedural amendments notwith-standing. While the strength of the outcome of FCTC negotiations will depend on commitment by WHO member states to meaningful tobacco control measures, the effective implementation of the FCTC at the national and local levels will ultimately rely on important contributions by non-state actors, notably civil society groups. With this need in mind, negotiations for an FCTC must be as open to these groups as possible.

The one exception to this prescription for participation is the need to circum-scribe the involvement of TTCs. Their historic and ongoing practices in consistently undermining tobacco control overtly and covertly, combined with the fundamental incompatibility of public health and industry objectives, mitigates against their being viewed as legitimate stakeholders. Regardless of the validity of ongoing debates concerning the value of public–private partnerships for health, the politics of tobacco remain an important exception.

References

African Region Meeting on the FCTC (2001) Johannesburg Declaration on the Framework Convention on Tobacco Control, 14 March, at http://tobacco.who.int/en/fctc/Regional/AFRO/SA/Jo-declaration-en.pdf, accessed 28 October 2001.

ASH-UK (2001) United States should pull out of tobacco treaty—EU needs new approach, 4 May, at http://www.fctc.org/press13.shtml, accessed 29 October 2001.

BAT (2000b) News release: British American Tobacco proposes 'quantum leap' for sensible tobacco regulation, 29 August, at www.bat.com, 11 September 2001.

BAT (2001) Regulation: Framework Convention on Tobacco Control, at http://www.bat.com/oneweb/sites/uk__3mnfen.nsf/vwPagesWebLive/DO52WQJV?opendocument&TMP=1, accessed 28 October 2001.

Bates, C (2001) Developing countries take the lead on who convention, *Tobacco Control*, 10(3), p 209.

Bialous, S & Yach, D (2001) 'Whose standard is it, anyway?' How the tobacco industry determines the International Organization for Standardization (ISO) standards for tobacco and tobacco products, *Tobacco Control*, 10(2), pp 96–104.

Bingham, P (1989) *The European Community: The Single Market 1992*, Guildford Depository, 3 February, Bates No: 301527819-7858.

JEFF COLLIN ET AL

Brown & Williamson (2001) Corporate social responsibility, at ww.brownandwilliamson.com, accessed 11 August 2001.

Bruntland, GH (2000a) Speech to WHO's International Conference on Global Tobacco Control Law: Towards a WHO Framework Convention on Tobacco Control, New Delhi, 7 January, at http://www.who.int/director-general/ speeches/2000/20000107_new_delhi.html, accessed 29 October 2001.

Brundtland, GH (2000b) WHO Director-General's response to the tobacco hearings statement WHO /6, 13 October, at http://www.who.int/genevahearings/ hearingsdocs/ dghearingsen.rtf, accessed 28 October 2001).

Campaign for Tobacco Free Kids (2001) Illegal pathways to illegal profits: the big cigarette companies and international smuggling, April, at http://tobaccofree kids.org/ campaign/ global/ framework/ docs/Smuggling.pdf, accessed 28 October 2001.

Campaign for Tobacco Free Kids and ASH-UK (2001) Trust us—we're the tobacco industry, April, at www.ash.org.uk/ html/conduct/ html/trustus.html, accessed 28 October 2001.

Chaloupka, F Corbett, M (1998) Trade policy and tobacco: towards an optimal policy mix, in: I Abedian, R van der Merwe, N Wilkins & P Jha (eds), *The Economics of Tobacco Control: Towards an Optimal Policy Mix* (Cape Town: Applied Fiscal Research Centre, University of Cape Town).

Chaloupka, F & Laixuthai, A (1996) *US Trade Policy and Cigarette Smoking in Asia*, Working Paper No 5543 (Cambridge, MA: National Bureau of Economic Research).

Chantornvong, S & McCargo, D (2000) Political economy of tobacco control in Thailand, in: JP Vaughan, J Collin & K Lee (eds) *Case Study Report: Global Analysis Project on the Political Economy of Tobacco Control in Low- and Middle-Income Countries* (London: London School of Hygiene & Tropical Medicine).

Chapman, M (2000) Where there's smoke, *Guardian*, 18 September.

Ciresi, M, Walburn, R & Sutton, T (1999) Decades of deceit: document discovery in the Minnesota Tobacco Litigation, *William Mitchell Law Review*, 25, pp 477–566.

Clark, A (2001) Big tobacco challenges Brussels, *Guardian*, 25 August.

Collin, J (forthcoming) 'Think global, smoke local': transnational tobacco companies and cognitive globalisation, in K Lee (ed), *Globalization and Health: Case Studies* (London: Macmillan/St Martin's Press).

Cunningham, R (1996) *Smoke and Mirrors: The Canadian Tobacco War* (Ottawa: International Development Research Centre).

Dodgson, R., K Lee & N Drager (2001) Global health governance: a conceptual review, *Key Issues in Global Governance*, Discussion Paper No 1 (Geneva: WHO).

Doll, R & Hill, A (1950) Smoking and carcinoma of the lung: preliminary report, *British Medical Journal*, 143, pp 329–336.

Dollisson, J (1989) 2nd Revised Forecast Presentation—Corporate Affairs, 15 June, Bates Number: 2500101311-1323, at www.tobacco.org/ Documents/dd/ddpmbattleasia.html, accessed 28 August 2001.

EMRO (2001) *Voice of Truth Vol 2*, WHO Regional Office for the Eastern Mediterranean, at http://www.emro.who.int/TFI/VoiceOfTruthVol2.pdf, accessed 29 October 2001.

Fennelly, Hon. Mr Justice N (2001) The Tobacco Judgement ERA Conference on Tobacco Regulation in the European Community, Luxembourge, 18–19 May.

Fidler, D (2001) The globalization of public health: the first 100 years of international health diplomacy, *Bulletin of the World Health Organisation*, 79(9), pp 842–849.

Gallaher (2001) http://www.gallaher-group.com, accessed 11 August 2001.

Hammond, R & White, C (2001) *Voice of Truth, Vol 1: Multinational Tobacco Industry Activity in the Middle East: A Review of Internal Industry Documents*, WHO Regional Office for the Eastern Mediterranean, at http://www.emro.who.int/TFI/VOICE%20OF%20TRUTH.pdf, accessed 29 October 2001.

Hastings, G & MacFadyen, L (2000) *Keep Smiling, No One's Going to Die: An Analysis of Internal Documents from the Tobacco Industry's Main UK Advertising Agencies* (London: Tobacco Control Resource Centre and the Centre for Tobacco Control Research).

Health Select Committee (2000) *The Tobacco Industry and the Health Risks of Smoking* (London: HMSO).

INFACT (1999) *Mobilizing NGOs and the Media Behind the International Framework Convention on Tobacco Control*, FCTC Technical Briefing Series No 3, WHO/NCD/TFI/99.3, at http://tobacco.who.int/en/fctc/papers/paper3.pdf, accessed 29 October 2001.

International Consortium of Investigative Journalists (2001) Tobacco companies linked to criminal organizations in cigarette smuggling, 3 March, at http://www.public-i.org/ story_01_030301.htm, accessed 9 August 2001.

Japan Tobacco International (2001) What we stand for, at http://www.jti.com/e/what_we_stand_for/ addiction/what_addiction_e.html, accessed 11 August 2001.

Jha, P & Chaloupka, F (eds) (2000) *Tobacco Control in Developing Countries* (Oxford: Oxford

FRAMEWORK CONVENTION ON TOBACCO CONTROL

University Press).

Jha, P & Chaloupka, F (1999) *Curbing the Epidemic: Governments and the Economics of Tobacco Control* (Washington, DC: World Bank).

Joossens, L, Chaloupka, F, Merriman, D Yurekli, A (2000) Issues in the smuggling of tobacco products, in: P Jha & F Chaloupka (eds), *Tobacco Control in Developing Countries*, pp 393–406 (Oxford: Oxford University Press).

Krasovsky, K (2000) Kazakhstan: PM's 'PR department' ignores tobacco, *Tobacco Control*, 9 (2), p 133.

Lee, K. (2001) 'Globalisation—a new agenda for health?, in: M McKee, P Garner & R Stott (eds), *International Co-operation and Health* (Oxford: Oxford University Press).

Levin, M, Golsdstein, H & Gerhardt, P (1950) Cancer and tobacco smoking: a preliminary report, *Journal of the American Medical Association*, 143, pp 336–338.

Loewenberg, S (2000) Tobacco lights into WHO, industry pushes to influence October treaty debate over global curbs on cigarettes, *Legal Times*, 11 September, at http://lists.essential.org/ pipermail/intl-tobacco/ 2000q3/000276.html, accessed 28 October 2001.

Ong, E & Glantz, S (2000) Tobacco industry efforts subverting International Agency for Research on Cancer's second-hand smoke study, *Lancet*, 355, pp 1253–1259.

Philip Morris (nda) Corporate Affairs/EU Archive—marketing freedoms, Bates No: 2501021740-1746, at www.pmdocs.com, accessed 28 October 2001.

Philip Morris (ndb) Technical Committee TC 126, Philip Morris, Bates No: 2028652539 -2540, www.pmdocs.com.

Richards, J, Tye, J & Fischer, P (1996) The tobacco industry's code of advertising in the United States: myth and reality, *Tobacco Control*, 5(4), pp 295-311.

Ryan, J (2001) Regulatory control of tobacco: EU position, paper presented to the ERA conference on Tobacco Regulation in the European Community, Luxembourg, 18–19 May.

Saloojee, Y & Dagli, E (2000) Tobacco industry tactics for resisting public policy on health, *Bulletin of the World Health Organisation*, 78(7), pp 902–910.

Sargent, J, Tickle, J, Beach, M, Dalton, M, Ahrens, M & Heatherton, T (2001) Brand appearances in contemporary cinema films and contribution to global marketing of cigarettes, *Lancet*, 357, pp 29–32.

Sheehy, P (1993) Speech to the Farmers President's Council Meeting, Guildford Depository, 8 June, Bates No: 601023526-3540.

Siegel, M (2001) Counteracting tobacco motor sports sponsorship as a promotional tool: is the Tobacco Settlement enough?, *American Journal of Public Health*, 9(7), pp 1100–1106.

Simpson, D (2000) Uzbekistan: who's in charge now?, *Tobacco Control*, 9(4), pp 359–361.

Taylor, A (2000) The Framework Convention on Tobacco Control: the power of the Process, paper presented to the 11th World Conference on Tobacco or Health, Chicago.

Taylor, A & Bettcher, D (2001) Sustainable health development: negotiation of the WHO Framework Convention on Tobacco Control, *Development Bulletin*, 54, pp 6–10.

Taylor, A, Chaloupka, F, Gundon, E & Corbett, M (2000) The impact of trade liberalization on tobacco consumption, in: P Jha & F Chaloupka (eds), *Tobacco Control in Developing Countries*, pp 343–364 (Oxford: Oxford University Press).

Vateesatokit, P, Hughes, B & Rittiphakdee, B (2000) Thailand: winning battles, but the war's far from over, *Tobacco Control*, 9, pp 122–127.

Whist, A (1986) Memo to Board of Directors: Subject—Philip Morris International Corporate Affairs, 17 December, Bates Number: 2025431401-1406, at www.pmdocs.com, accessed 12 October 2001.

WHO (1999a) *World Health Report 1999* (Geneva: WHO).

WHO (1999b) Provisional list of participants, first meeting of the Working Group on the Framework Convention on Tobacco Control, A/FCTC/WG1/DIV/1.

WHO (2000a) Framework Convention on Tobacco Control: Introduction, at http://tobacco.who.int/ en/fctc/index.html, accessed 28 October 2001.

WHO (2000b) WHO Framework Convention on Tobacco Control: report by the Secretariat, Geneva, EB/107/30, 6 December.

WHO (2000c) List of participants, Intergovernmental Negotiating Body on the Framework Convention on Tobacco Control, Second session, A/FCTC/INB2/DIV/2 Rev.1.

WHO (2000d) Participation of nongovernmental organizations in the Intergovernmental Negotiating Body, Intergovernmental Negotiating Body on the Framework Convention on Tobacco Control, First session. A/FCTC/INB1/5 Paras 4, 6.

WHO (2001a) FCTC public hearings, at http://tobacco.who.int/ en/fctc/publichearings.html, accessed 28 October 2001.

WHO (2001b) Intergovernmental Negotiating Body on the Framework Convention on Tobacco Control, First Session Part 1–2. Intergovernmental Negotiating Body on the Framework Convention on Tobacco Control, Second session, A/FCTC/INB2/3 Part 2, second session, Para 3.

WHO (2001c) Participation of nongovernmental organizations, Intergovernmental Negotiating Body on

JEFF COLLIN ET AL

the Framework Convention on Tobacco Control, Second session, A/FCTC/INB2/6.

WHO & UNICEF (2001) Tobacco and the rights of the child, WHO/NMH/TFI/01.3.

WHO Committee of Experts (2000) Tobacco company strategies to undermine tobacco control activities at the World Health Organisation, July, at http://filestore.who.int/ ~who/home/tobacco/tobacco.pdf, accessed 29 October 2001.

Wipfli, H, Bettcher, D, Subramaniam, C & Taylor, A (2001) Confronting the global tobacco epidemic: emerging mechanisms of global governance, in M McKee, P Garner & R Stott (eds), *International Co-operation and Health* (Oxford: Oxford University Press).

Woelk, G, Mtisi, S & Vaughan, JP (2000) Political economy of tobacco control in Zimbabwe, in: JP Vaughan, J Collin & K Lee (eds) *Case Study Report: Global Analysis Project on the Political Economy of Tobacco Control in Low- and Middle-Income Countries* (London: London School of Hygiene & Tropical Medicine).

World Health Assembly (1999) WHA Resolution 52.18—Towards a WHO framework convention on tobacco control, at http://tobacco.who.int/ en/fctc/WHA52-18.html, accessed 28 October 2001.

Wynder, E & Graham, E (1950) Tobacco smoking as a possible etiologic factor in bronchogenic carcinoma, *Journal of the American Medical Association*, 143, pp 329–336.

Part V
Global Health Governance

[24]

The World Health Organisation

WHO in crisis

Fiona Godlee

Media attention has been focused on the leadership of the World Health Organisation, rather than on the real factors that limit WHO's effectiveness. These factors relate to the organisation's structure and also to its current priorities, methods, and management. This article examines the objectives and strategy of WHO in view of financial constraints and donor countries' demands; WHO's stated goal of integrated primary health care; staff morale; and the growing dislocation between the regions and headquarters.

The World Health Organisation has an image problem. People know that it exists, and most people know that it eradicated smallpox, but few have a clear idea what it does. Of those I have spoken to, some think it is a sort of world medical association, others see it only as a source of standard technical medical reports, yet others as just another faceless United Nations body where overpaid bureaucrats carve out their careers. Some politicians and doctors in Britain see it as meddling in public health matters that need not concern it when it should be concentrating its efforts on the developing world. Doctors in the developing world respect the WHO for its technical advice and support but criticise the waste of money on salaries and bureaucracy. Its slogan "Health for All by the Year 2000" has entered the international vocabulary, but few people, apart from diehard enthusiasts in the organisation, believe the target can be realised or understand how WHO intends to achieve it.

The media woke up to WHO last year when political and financial scandal seemed set to erupt over the re-election of its director general, Dr Hiroshi Nakajima. The outcome of an external audit fell short of media hopes; it found financial mismanagement and misuse of the organisation's funds but they cleared the director general of any involvement.[1] Amid the reportage of seedy dealings and the repetition of mainly unsubstantiated stories, the real factors that limit WHO's effectiveness received little attention.

It is these factors that I will be exploring in the next few weeks. They relate mainly to the structure of the organisation but also to its current priorities, methods, and management. In order to understand its problems, I have spoken to staff at WHO, former staff, diplomats, civil servants, politicians, and doctors. I have interviewed the director general and attended the annual meeting in Geneva of WHO's governing body, the World Health Assembly. I have also visited two of the regional offices, in Delhi and Copenhagen, and interviewed five of the six regional directors. In this article I will summarise the main criticisms of WHO, first describing its objective and strategy.

Objective and strategy

WHO's objective, as laid down when the organisation was founded in 1948, is "the attainment by all people of the highest possible level of health," where health is defined as complete physical, mental, and social wellbeing and not just the absence of disease and infirmity.[2] WHO's strategy is to act through member states, advising their governments on technical matters, financing the training of local health professionals, and trying to influence health policy decisions.

WHO does not, except with rare exceptions, intervene directly in health care provision or disease prevention—a strategy designed to avoid charges of imperialism and ensure that developments are sustainable in the long term. But this strategy presents the organisation with important problems. Not only is it a major source of misunderstanding (WHO is frequently criticised for its lack of activity "in the field," to which staff reply wearily that "that is not the WHO's role") but it means that WHO has no direct powers to improve people's health. Its success relies entirely on the receptiveness and effectiveness of national governments and the fidelity with which other agencies like Unicef translate its principles into action.

Financial constraints and donors' demands

WHO's activities are seen by many as disparate and uncoordinated. They range over the whole gamut of health issues, from major threats to life such as AIDS and tuberculosis to lesser threats like oral disease. WHO remains committed to what it calls the "full menu" approach and aims to encompass all aspects of health care. Critics say, however, that there is little logic to how resources are allocated and that diseases of the developed world take up a disproportionate amount of WHO's time and money.[3] Donors would like to see WHO focus its attention on a smaller number of essential programmes mainly in the developing world, and they are calling for WHO to set itself clearer priorities in keeping with its limited resources.[4]

WHO is suffering the same financial straits as the rest of the United Nations. Unpaid contributions, largely from the former Soviet Union but also from the

---

Views of WHO: misconceptions but with some truth

WHO should be more visible in the field, handing out vaccines and helping with emergency relief

WRONG—WHO's role is to advocate and advise countries on health care and disease prevention, not to implement interventions. Its aim is to influence long term policy decisions. Its constitution specifies that it should work through national governments, to assist them "upon request, in strengthening health services."

BUT—Some of WHO's most visible and effective programmes, including the smallpox eradication programme, have involved direct intervention. The onchocerciasis control programme, which has already achieved its 1995 target of eliminating the disease as a public health problem, provides drug treatment and case finding facilities and has its own helicopters for spraying blackfly breeding grounds. Many critics believe that WHO should stick to this approach.

WHO is a centralised bureaucracy based in Geneva

WRONG—WHO is one of the most decentralised of the United Nations agencies. It divides the world into six regions, each with its own regional office, which have a high degree of autonomy from Geneva.

BUT—The decentralisation is largely illusory since

WHO's efforts do not easily penetrate beyond the regional offices. WHO's effectiveness in individual countries is variable but often poor. It depends on the energy of country representatives, who are generally undertrained and underresourced.

WHO wastes vast amounts of money

WRONG—Of the four biggest United Nations agencies (in terms of the number of staff), WHO spends the least. Its biennial budget for 1994-5 is $1·8bn, compared with annual NHS spending of $60bn.

BUT—The most recent external audit found that, despite financial constraints, money is wasted on bureaucratic inefficiency and petty corruption.[5]

WHO spends too much on staff

WRONG—WHO is its staff. Its technical advisory and advocacy roles rely entirely on staff activities.

BUT—It does not always attract the best people for the job. The director general believes this is because the United Nations does not pay well enough. Most people think it pays too well and that political appointments and quota systems conspire against achieving meritocracy or excellence. Recent attempts to slim down the payroll have proved largely ineffective.

United States, have left it with a biennial income deficit of $51m.[3] Meanwhile, donor countries (those countries that give funds in addition to their membership fees) are demanding more value for money and a greater say in how their money is spent. They have achieved both objectives in a way that has left WHO increasingly dispersed and uncoordinated. Instead of putting the additional money into WHO's central pot, they are using so called extrabudgetary contributions to support freestanding programmes within WHO. These programmes have their own management committees, which include representatives from donor countries, and they are out of the World Health Assembly's control. Donors can choose which programmes to support and can withdraw money if they don't like what is being done. The situation pleases recipient countries as much as donors. This is because WHO's budget is made up of countries' membership fees, which are based on their population and income. The budget has been frozen by the World Health Assembly for the past 13 years and is losing ground against inflation (figure). As a result, each country's contribution to the budget is falling in real terms, but the extrabudgetary contributions from donors ensure that money is still available for recipient countries.

It is WHO that loses out. These freestanding or

vertical programmes are generally disease specific, dealing, for example, with malaria, AIDS, and diarrhoeal diseases. Their increasing share of the money and the limelight detracts from WHO's routine activities within member countries, especially its efforts to establish integrated networks for primary health care. WHO says that such networks are developing but that their success depends on economic and social development and the existence of an adequate infrastructure, factors over which WHO has little control. Critics maintain, however, that WHO has failed to promote primary health care effectively and that the organisation's efforts in individual countries are hampered by the lack of a clear strategy. A report from the Danish overseas development organisation, Danida, concludes that WHO's budget in individual countries is used for "ad hoc financing of fellowships, study tours, workshops, local cost subsidies and miscellaneous supplies and equipment" rather than being allocated according to a strategic plan.[4]

Some critics also fear that WHO's priorities now reflect donors' preferences rather than rational allocation of resources. In the absence of central priorities, much depends on the energy with which individual programmes lobby for support. Behind the single face of WHO are warring factions arguing over territory and funds, to the confusion of donors and recipients.

Changes in definition of health

WHO's position has been further weakened by its failure to adapt to changes in the definition of health itself. For years male and medical, health has become increasingly multisectorial—encompassing disciplines such as education, development, sociology, and anthropology—and oriented towards women's health and women practitioners. WHO has been slow to respond. Few of its professional staff are women and most of them are medical. Staff are increasingly frustrated by the realisation that the major determinants of health—poverty, education, development, and the environment—are beyond the scope of WHO.

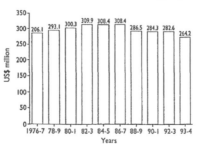

WHO's working budget has been frozen for the past 13 years and is losing ground against inflation

Figure axis labels: US$ million (y-axis); Years (x-axis)

Bar values: 206.1, 293.1, 300.3, 309.9, 308.4, 308.4, 286.5, 284.3, 282.6, 264.2

Year labels: 1976-7, 78-9, 80-1, 82-3, 84-5, 86-7, 88-9, 90-1, 92-3, 93-4

WHO's representatives in recipient countries are stationed inside ministries of health, which limits their influence, especially since health is traditionally one of the government departments with the lowest status. Observers say that the WHO's country representatives are the weak link in an already weak chain of influence, from the organisation's headquarters in Geneva through its six regional offices into national ministries of health. Seen as political appointees, they are given no structured training and few resources and they are often poorly motivated.

Under new management

WHO's structural flaws have become increasingly evident since the change of leadership in 1988. After 15 years under the charismatic visionary Dr Halfden Mahler, WHO staff and donors were unimpressed by Dr Hiroshi Nakajima, who they saw as reserved and a poor communicator. Today people outside the organisation fear that under his direction WHO is losing ground to other international agencies. They see WHO retreating from Dr Mahler's high profile approach, which has made the organisation an influential advocate of international equity and rational use of resources, back into its traditional role of setting standards and providing advice on technical medical matters. Dr Nakajima has the support of developing countries, but Western donors worry about WHO's loss of influence under his direction. Last year they took the unprecedented step of asking Japan to withdraw his candidature for re-election. His re-nomination by the executive board led to allegations that Japan had exerted undue pressure on developing countries, including threats to withdraw trade and aid agreements if they did not vote for Dr Nakajima. Opponents also alleged that WHO's funds had been misused to influence the election.

An external audit to examine the allegations found no corruption but criticised WHO for shortcomings in management and found that the number of contracts let to members of the executive board had doubled in the six months leading up to the election. In his report the external auditor, Sir John Bourne, recommended changes in the regulations governing the letting of contracts to board members. A further report, from a working party of the executive board, chaired by Britain's chief medical officer Dr Kenneth Calman, called for wide ranging changes to WHO's internal organisation.[8] This year's routine external audit found that little had been done in response to either report.

Supporters of Dr Nakajima say that the international climate has changed since Dr Mahler's time and that the worldwide recession has forced donors to demand greater accountability. They argue that under such scrutiny the old leadership would also have been found wanting. Some international observers comment that Dr Nakajima's technical emphasis and conciliatory style—brokering compromises between conflicting vested interests—is perhaps the best approach for WHO in the current climate. As one commentator said, "Countries in the developing world have had enough of the strong man style. They don't take kindly anymore to outspoken, objective oriented approaches to health care." Others note the strong tide in the West towards deregulation and growing calls to dispense with international nannies. They feel that WHO may have to stand back for a while until people again see the need for international bodies to act as advocates for equity and social justice. In the meantime, they say, WHO could do a lot worse than Dr Nakajima.

But even Dr Nakajima's most dedicated staff acknowledge that his severe difficulties in communicating are a major handicap for a United Nations leader. His spoken English and French are poor, and

even Japanese delegates and staff find him difficult to understand. When he speaks privately his passion for the work of WHO is evident, as well as his grasp of the problems it faces; but under stress—at press conferences, for example—he becomes defensive and incoherent. His attempts to establish what he has called "a new paradigm for health" have floundered in a maze of incomprehension.

In the absence of coherent policy and strategy direction, conflicts within the organisation are rife. Departments fight over territory rather than cooperating, and communication between them is poor. "All communications have to go through heads of divisions and up through the hierarchy," said one programme director. "The result is that the right hand never knows what the left hand is doing." WHO's internal structure reflects these personal infightings, with units being allocated to divisions not on a logical basis but according to who has what.

A dive in staff morale

Staff complain that Dr Nakajima's management style is autocratic. The director general has absolute power to hire and fire within headquarters and can post members of staff to any region. Directorial appointments are made at his discretion, bypassing the senior staff selection committee. Under previous director generals such discretionary posts were rarely appointed. Under Dr Nakajima their number has gone up from 66 in 1988 to 114 in 1994 (see table). The

Discretionary appointments in WHO

	1988	1994
Deputy director general	1	0
Special representatives*	0	1
Assistant director general	5	6
Executive directors	0	2
Special rate advisers	1	4
Director D2	24	39
Director D1	1	5
Professional P6	34	57
Total senior staff	66	114
% Of all WHO staff	1·7	2·6

*To United Nations Relief and Works Agency for Palestine Refugees in the Near East.

number of top ranking employees (above director level, all earning around $80000 a year) has nearly doubled since Dr Nakajima took office, from seven in 1988 to 13 today. "We used to have only directors. Now there are executive directors, acting directors, associate directors, and assistant directors," said a senior staff member. "These promotions might be acceptable in a private firm, but they are paid for out of public funds. We feel embarrassed."

No overall policy informs these decisions at present, according to staff representatives in Geneva. When experienced technical staff retire their posts are frozen to save money, causing some programmes to collapse and making it difficult for others to make long term plans. Meanwhile, at senior administrative level promotions have been made beyond the top grade of salary scale recommended by the UN secretary general.

Since Dr Nakajima took office the International Labour Organisation, to which WHO answers on personnel issues, has received an increasing number of appeals from aggrieved staff. Several of the subsequent tribunals have found disregard of the rules and arbitrary decisions by the director general. Soon after taking office he demoted the then director of personnel, Mr Herbert Crockett, over a dispute about Dr Nakajima's housing allowance. A tribunal found that Mr Crockett's demotion was illegal and ordered WHO to reinstate him. He is now employed elsewhere in

Dr Hiroshi Nakajima, WHO's director general

Almost a third of WHO's staff is based in Geneva, one of the world's most expensive cities

the Geneva headquarters. In his place Dr Nakajima appointed a retired member of staff, Mr Mustafa Latif, on repeated short term contracts that enabled him to continue to draw his pension for four years while also receiving a salary. The current director of personnel, Mr Dario Sanvincenti, is a former supply officer with almost no previous experience in personnel management.

The staff association's lawyer in Geneva, Mr Klaus Samson, believes that there is now a serious problem with the way WHO handles its staff. "WHO used to have a good reputation as an employer," he said, "but there has been a striking increase in the number of cases going to tribunal in the past few years and a striking increase in the number that have found against the organisation; six in the past half year." The most recent successful appeal was lodged by a German medical technician, Mrs Gabriele Mussnig, who claimed unfair dismissal and sexual harassment by WHO's representative in Angola, Dr Emmmannuel Ben-Moussi. The ILO found she had been unfairly dismissed and ordered WHO to reinstate her. The tribunal found that WHO had wrongly denied Mrs Mussnig access to her files and tried to prevent her from exercising her right to appeal. The report also said that WHO made no attempt to deny the accusations of sexual harrassment and, despite being a signatory to the United Nations declaration against sexual harassment, has failed to take action against its representative in Angola. He remains in post having received, according to the tribunal report, only a "putative reprimand."[7] "The case is more than just sexual harassment," said the chairman of WHO's staff committee, Dr Jan Stjernsward. "What the judgment brought out is the arbitrariness of the administration and a denial of due process."

Staff morale in Geneva is low and standards are reported to be slipping. Staff talk about growing inertia and an atmosphere of distrust. Skilled technical staff who are able to find jobs outside the organisation are leaving, while those with less chance of finding the same salary elsewhere and those with mainly administrative skills are staying on. Recruiting good replacements is proving difficult. Despite being insulated to a large extent from the discontent in Geneva, some of the regional offices report similar difficulties in recruitment. Lack of motivation is reflected in an increasing fixation among staff about pay, promotion, perks, and allowances.

Staff are WHO's main commodity. Salaries take up a large proportion of the budget, and almost a third of the organisation's employees are based in Geneva, one

of the world's most expensive cities. Staff numbers have increased by nearly a fifth over the past six years, from about 3800 in 1988 to 4500 today, and recent attempts to slim down the payroll have been only partially successful. A voluntary redundancy scheme, intended to save the organisation $4·4m, ended up costing $4·9m in severance payments, and some of the 47 vacated posts have subsequently been refilled.[5] In the face of deepening financial crisis, failure to reduce staff numbers means less and less money for implementing WHO policy.

The regions

Staff in the six regional offices are insulated from the discontent and internal politics in Geneva, but they are embroiled instead in regional politics. For regional directors, getting reelected means maintaining the support of the regional committees, made up of delegates from the ministries of health of member states. Recent reports have questioned the amount of time and energy that regional directors devote to regional politics,[6] and there are growing calls for an overhaul of the way in which regional directors are selected.[4]

Many are also concerned about the growing dislocation between the regions and headquarters. The regional directors have never been directly answerable to the director general or to WHO's governing body, the World Health Assembly, and they enjoy wide-ranging discretionary powers over setting policy, awarding jobs and fellowships, and allocating resources. Their independence was, however, tempered in the past by Dr Mahler's strong personality. Observers say that Dr Nakajima does not command such respect from the regional directors, a fact that has further distanced the regional offices from Geneva's control.

WHO is concerned

WHO is clearly concerned about the criticisms levelled against it. Its apparent openness to scrutiny and readiness to provide information and access to staff are in striking contrast to the generality of international bureaucracies. The staff I spoke to were painfully aware of the organisation's problems and talked openly about them, though few would speak on the record. They seemed deeply committed to WHO's objectives and strategy.

My overall impression is of an organisation whose system conspires against the best efforts of its staff; where staff appear overworked but often have little to show for their efforts; where despite all the institutional barriers a few exceptional people achieve impressive results. As one insider said, "WHO is like an enormous beehive. Some cells work extremely effectively, with dedicated workers doing excellent work against the odds. But there are whole chunks of it that are rotten and where nothing happens."

Conclusion

The World Health Organisation has unique resources in terms of people, knowledge, and experience, but it is suffering a crisis of confidence, both internally and internationally. Sensing the organisation's lack of direction, donors are finding other agencies to invest in. The resulting financial crisis is now preventing the organisation from functioning effectively. In the absence of strong leadership, three long-hidden fault lines in WHO's structure are opening up: the dislocation between management and staff; the dissociation between headquarters and the regional offices; and the contradiction between WHO's high profile, vertical intervention programmes and its stated goal of integrated primary health care.

WHO is entering a period of intense soul searching and internal upheaval. Some insiders fear that it is tearing itself apart. With growing pressure on limited resources, donors are demanding more value for money and greater accountability. Reports from the United Nations, from donors, and from within the WHO itself are demanding radical reform.[1-8] The articles that follow will explore the problems faced by WHO and some possible solutions.

Even WHO's most vociferous critics agree that some form of international health organisation is necessary. The world needs a strong body to take the lead in health matters, to act as an advocate for equity in economic and social development, to set priorities for the use of limited resources, to provide neutral territory for debating sensitive issues, and to give technical advice and support. Such a role can be successfully taken only by an organisation that commands respect and is seen to be above national politics and free from divisive internal wranglings. It remains to be seen whether the World Health Organisation is capable of reform or whether, as some critics feel, it is doomed, like the rest of the United Nations, to flounder in a morass of petty corruption and ineffective bureaucracy. These articles will, I hope, stimulate a much needed debate on WHO's future.

1 World Health Organisation. *Report of the external auditor to the World Health Assembly: allegations of possible financial irregularities during 1992. 46th World Health Assembly.* Geneva: WHO, 1993.

2 World Health Organisation. *Basic documents.* 39th edition. Geneva: WHO, 1992.

3 Tollison RD, Wagner RE. *Who benefits from WHO? The decline of the World Health Organization.* London: Social Affairs Unit, 1993. (Publication No 53.)

4 Daes EIA, Daoudy A. Decentralisation of organisations within the United Nations system. Part three: the World Health Organisation. Report of the Joint Inspection Unit. *General Assembly official records. 48th session.* New York: United Nations, 1994. (Supplement No 34 (A/48/34).)

5 World Health Organisation. *Financial report and audited financial statements for the financial period 1 January 1992-31 December 1993 and report of the external auditor to the World Health Assembly. 47th World Health Assembly.* Geneva: WHO, 1994.

6 Danida. *Effectiveness of multilateral agencies at country level: WHO in Kenya, Nepal, Sudan and Thailand.* Copenhagen: Ministry of Foreign Affairs, 1991.

7 United Nations. *Prevention of sexual harassment.* Geneva: United Nations, 1994.

8 World Health Organisation. *Report of the Executive Board Working Group on the WHO response to global change. Executive Board, 92nd session.* Geneva: WHO, 1993.

[25]

The development of international health policies — accountability intact?

Ilona Kickbusch

Yale School of Medicine, New Haven, CT 06520-8034, USA

Abstract

International health governance as it exists today is facing major structural challenges in view of globalization, the increased transfer of international health risks and the mounting challenge of health inequalities worldwide. As a consequence the capacity of nation states to ensure population health and to address major health determinants has been weakened. This paper explores health as an exemplary field to illustrate that we have entered a new era of public policy which is defined by increasing overlaps between domestic and foreign policy, multilateral and bilateral strategies and national and international interest. Cross border spill overs and externalities of national actions need to move into the core of public policy at the national and global level within a new rules based system. A new perspective on global health governance is further necessitated through the increased number of players in the global health arena. The organizational form that is emerging is based on networks and is characterized by shifting alliances and blurred lines of responsibility. The paper explores the emerging paradox of state sovereignty and makes a set of proposals to pool state sovereignty on health and structure the myriad of networks. Particular attention is given to the role of the World Health Organization within this process of change and adjustment. In using a framework from international relations analysis the paper explores how nation states are socialized into accepting new norms, values and perceptions of interest with regard to national and international health and what challenges emerge for the WHO in "inventing" global health policy.

Keywords: Globalization; Health governance; World Health Organization; Health for All; Global health policy

The challenge

It seems that a new intellectual dynamism has entered the field of international health that has not been there since the late 1970s and early 1980s when the World Health Organization (WHO) launched the Health for All Strategy. Of course such a shift does not take place in a vacuum: the whole field of inter-

E-mail address: ilona.kickbusch@yale.edu (I. Kickbusch).

national relations is in flux since the fall of the Berlin Wall. With the disappearance of the cold war power blocks many questions have been raised as to which interests and issues will drive the international system. This has included a critical look at the UN and its affiliated institutions and agencies with regard to their mandates, their achievements, their interrelationships and — of course — their future. The field of international health has also been subject to scrutiny, not only because issues of leadership and competition have plagued the WHO since the early 1990s, but also because a series of trans-national health threats has alarmed politicians and the general public. After the election of a new Director General of WHO in 1998 expectations are high that the new global health challenges will be tackled with creativity and determination.

At the same time though it has become increasingly clear that the issues at stake are much more profound and reach far beyond one leader, one agency and one specific area of action. While a consensus on the "how" is far from emerging, most authors agree that the international system needs to be "reinvented" to respond to a new global environment. It should be doing something different, in a different way and not be restricted to nation states. The practice of the international community already reflects this as we witness an increasing number of international agreements and "cross national policy patchworks" (Reinicke, 1998). This is illustrated by regime formation on global environmental matters, the involvement of NGOs in the major UN Conferences, the arrival of new philanthropists and the wide array of partnership based initiatives throughout the UN System and beyond. The organizational form that is emerging is network based rather than agency based and is defined by shifting alliances and unclear lines of responsibility and accountability (Castells, 1996). It is this question of "*governance*" that is challenging nation states and international organizations alike.

The shift from international to global health policy

This paper takes its starting point from the view put forward by Kaul, Grunberg and Stern (1999) that we have entered *a new era of public policy*. This era is defined by increasing overlaps between domestic and foreign policy and national and international interest as well as by a widening range of new actors at the local, national, regional and international level. The private sector and civil society are part of a realignment of power. The classic question of international relations analysis: "What do states want?" is being replaced by a quest to understand the shift from a clearly circumscribed international arena to a "dense network of trans-national and international social relations" in terms of *agency* and *accountability*. As the role of the nation state changes so does the role of international organizations within which states have come together to pursue their interests (Finnemore, 1996).

The forces that drive this new environment are usually circumscribed with the term *globalization*. Within the health field there have been a number of recent attempts to map the impact of globalization on health (Lee, 1998; Yach & Bettcher, 1998; Walt, 1994).

Two views emerge that in turn determine the strategic response. If one views globalization as increased interdependence then one might argue for an increased willingness of countries to work together at the international level since it would serve their rational interest without threatening their policy making capacity. If — on the other hand — one views globalization as an essentially new phenomenon which implies an increasing loss of internal sovereignty of nation states then the willingness to pool resources and policies might be less forthcoming and the reaction might rather be one of protectionism, increased competition and insistence in maintaining those spheres of influence that still seem intact. In health both processes are underway. There are indeed areas of quantitative intensification as in the area of infectious disease control and countries seem more willing to agree on a revision of the traffic rules (international health regulations) that structure this interdependence. But the real challenge of globalization lies in the "fundamental qualitative transformation of the international system" (Reinicke, 1998, p. 6).

Globalization is not a phenomenon that has been thrust upon the world by an invisible hand. As Vincente Navarro (1998) rightly contends — power and politics are as much at the center of globalization as of any other sphere of social and political action and nation states have played their part in shaping it, for example by establishing the World Trade Organization. But what has been lacking is a more organized global policy response to ensure the influence of nation states on the new global environment. For the health arena this means we need to move towards developing a *global health policy* which would provide the framework within which new networks of health governance are created and new forms of accountability are developed.

The invention of international health policy

But let us start from the beginning. We have come to speak of international health policy in a rather matter of fact way, as if we knew what it was. "*One of the great paradoxes in the history of health policy is that, despite all the evidence and understanding that has accrued about determinants of health and the means available to tackle them, the national and international policy arenas are filled with something quite different*" (Leppo, 1997). By using the term international health policy lightly we have come to obscure its origins, its rather recent history and its future.

International health policy was invented by WHO in the late 1970. What existed before was a set of "international traffic rules" on disease control and a range of norms and standards without a framework that

I. Kickbusch / Social Science & Medicine 51 (2000) 979–989 981

bound the elements together and gave a common purpose and direction. When set up after the Second World War WHO was to be a technical advisor and information broker with a universalistic goal and a focus on controlling and eradicating disease.

All that changed in the mid-1970s and for a variety of reasons, both contextual and from within the WHO. I would contend — based on the work of Finnemore (1996, p. 5) — that *"states were socialized to accept new norms, values and perceptions of interest"* with regard to both international and national health policy by an international organization. The Alma Ata Declaration (Koivusalo & Ollila, 1997) made it abundantly clear that governments have the responsibility for the health of their people. This was no less than a redefinition of the norms and expectations of the state role with regard to health. States were "taught" by the WHO that a national health policy was part and parcel of modernization and that the organization would advise countries on how to go about establishing such a policy. This was particularly important for the newly created states which were challenged to provide health care for their populations after the collapse of the colonial system. In this new policy environment WHO both defined the problem and provided the solution — and in the process of doing so reinvented itself from being a specialized agency that implemented a set of technical programs to being a leader in health policy development.

The HFA agenda was clearly an initiative by the secretariat and the then director general of the WHO Halfdan Mahler and his closest advisor Joshua Cohen — it was a supply driven initiative, making use of a supportive intellectual and political environment to launch a new comprehensive framework. Looking back it laid the ground for much of the health debate that was to follow to this day by framing health within a triangle of economics, politics and human rights:

- *Economics*: it placed health firmly within the development agenda of the day (Myrdal, 1970; McNamara, 1981) at a time when multi lateral and bilateral agencies were expanding following the increasing number of newly independent countries in the developing world and it set an outcome oriented goal for health policy in linking population health and economic development: citizens should gain access to "a socially and economically productive life",
- *Politics*: it expanded WHOs remit from disease to health (Illich, 1976; Dubos, 1959) and with the eight elements of primary health care set out the core health determinants in the early public health tradition, health policy was a responsibility of the nation state and how health was distributed in society became a political issue: the challenge was "to put health on the political agenda",
- *Human rights*: it linked the health and the equity agenda in its key slogan "Health for all" and defined access to health and health care as a universal right and a global challenge: "health is indivisible".

Just as the World Bank institutionalized and internationalized the concern for global poverty and made it an inextricable part of what development was (Finnemore, 1996), so did WHO with health. The late seventies were a period of immense global economic growth and it seemed reasonable to assume that within 20 years (by the year 2000) the developing countries would have made major strides towards achieving the major HFA goals: improved water and sanitation, maternal and child health, nutrition, education and housing. The framers of the HFA policy institutionalized and "internationalized" the responsibility for the world's health by adding yet another crucial dimension. As the first UN agency the WHO introduced *accountability* and developed a set of indicators to measure health outcomes at the global and the national level. Countries were to report back regularly to the WHO on their progress towards Health For All and the organization would present a "World Health Report" as part of this accountability mechanism. Donor agencies and other international organizations were approached to contribute to the attainment of the HFA goals.

The accountability gap

Accountability refers to holding actors responsible for their actions (Brown & Fox, 1998). But despite best intentions health accountability at the international level did not really work: not for countries, not for donors and not for the many players in the international health system as a whole.

At first instance it seems like a paradox that HFA had its greatest impact in the European region of the WHO. But it is only logical if one assumes that in order to introduce a national Health For All policy a well-established infrastructure needs to be in place which most of the developing countries did not have. HFA placed the nation state in the center and took very seriously the definition of WHO as an intergovernmental agency. Despite the HFA rhetoric it did not really open up to the wider populist movements in health. This was surely unavoidable in a nationalistic period of history when many countries had finally achieved independence from colonialist rule. But for a complex number of reasons most of the developing nations were either too weak and vulnerable, too inexperienced or too corrupt to implement sound and

982   *I. Kickbusch / Social Science & Medicine 51 (2000) 979–989*

democratic health policies. Frequently the investment in external sovereignty — the military — overrode all investment in living standards (Sen, 1999). The cold war competition preferred an arms race to a health race and many donor countries heavily supported this. Developing countries also were restricted in their internal health sovereignty. The preference of donors and agencies lay in vertical programs and medical/technical solutions rather than in infrastructure and human capital investments such as sanitation and community development. Agencies competed over approaches and influence (selective primary health care, Bamako, HIV/ AIDS) as did donors and the increasing numbers of NGOs, particularly at country level. Once the cold war was over pressures increased in the donor countries to show that foreign aid was efficient, made a difference on the spot and fulfilled a national interest "back home" — preference mounted for short term high impact programs following the donors, not the recipients agenda. Notable exceptions — such as Cuba — were not able to maintain the health investment and political commitment due to outside pressures.

Developing countries did not have incentives or capacity to provide reliable data for the HFA evaluation, not only because they had not been able to build the health information infrastructure and competence but also because international aid followed problems not solutions. The increasing dependence on international trade and tourism also led to conscious non or under-reporting of epidemics. The export of health threats to the developing countries was increasing as was the international illicit drug market. And many developing countries acted irresponsibly in terms of both national and international health by refusing to respond to the growing HIV/AIDS epidemic, just as many donor countries followed a non-health agenda when establishing UNAIDS. No established forum systematically addressed these mounting problems. It was left to the NGO community to raise them where ever possible. A notable exception in strengthening accountability and fully involving the NGOs and engaging world public opinion was the International Code for the Marketing of Breast Milk Substitutes which introduced the accountability of the private sector for their marketing and sales practices in the developing world (Keck & Sikkink, 1998; Courtney, 1999).

While WHO was able to significantly shift the normative context in which nation states developed health policies it was not able to establish reliable health accountability at the international level. WHO did not exploit its constitutional mandate to initiate and negotiate international health agreements and it stayed on the sidelines while new agencies such as the World Trade Organization were established and the health industry expanded exponentially. Weak leadership left it totally unprepared for the major political, economic,

ideological and epidemiological shift that occurred in the 1990.

In the late 1980s the world was beginning to change rapidly, national health systems around the world were in crisis and new health problems were looming. It was becoming clear that world health had not progressed to the extent expected. Not only were readily available public health interventions not being implemented — resource problems that reached far beyond the health sector were beginning to result in severe cut backs in the health and social arena around the globe. Poverty and inequality continued to grow both within and between countries. Governments had lost legitimacy and solutions were now expected from private rather than public investment.

Countries were looking to find solutions to their problems and guidance on new rules of the game in a new global environment and the WHO was not able to provide it. It was only pragmatic to look elsewhere, particularly for a new generation of national health leaders that had no special allegiance to the WHO and were frequently not part of the health community. It was at this point that the World Bank entered the scene as an arbiter of health development norms — with a combination of money, prestige and power that WHO could not muster. Paradoxically the World Banks interest in health went back to WHOs approach to the World Bank and the 1993 Investment in Health Report was the long term outcome of a meeting between WHO Director General Halfdahn Mahler and the President of the World Bank MacNamara (Cohen, 1999). In the early 1990s the World Bank stepped into the international health policy void and took on the leadership and socialization function previously held by WHO. The role the developing countries had played in the acceptance of Health for All as part of a social development agenda (expansion) fell to the countries of CCEE and NIS in restructuring their health care systems as part of a privatization agenda (contraction).

Setting the scene for a new agenda

Koivusalo and Ollila (1997) give an excellent and comprehensive overview of agencies, actors and policies in international health as they can be mapped in the late 1990s. They express a deep concern over the loss of a clear value base and accepted policy framework within international health at the end of the 1990s and outline the dangers of both the market and donor driven approaches to health policy which neglect addressing the health determinants central to the HFA Strategy and have become disconnected from the larger context. *"There seems to be an increasing tendency to adjust the capacities of governments to fit these*

I. Kickbusch / Social Science & Medicine 51 (2000) 979–989 983

models, instead of trying to enable those governments committed to improving the health of their citizens to implement policies which would fit their capacities" (Koivusalo & Ollila, 1997).

It is interesting to note that this analysis — like many others on the changing nature of international health — was initially driven by "internal" organizational politics. In 1993 a group of about 20 Member States took the unprecedented step of opposing the re-election of the Director General of WHO. As he began his second term the critics pressed ahead with a "reform agenda" for the organization. Important for the argument of this paper is that the deep frustration of some member states and other actors with the weak WHO (and their response that followed) must also be seen as an expression of the acceptance (and need) of countries of the leadership role of international organizations. They had been successfully socialized into expecting such a role and set about to reestablish it rather than just leaving the organization or letting it decline.

From 1993 onwards a vigorous debate on how to reform the World Health Organization took place: foundations convened meetings, member states commissioned studies, medical journals attempted analysis (Godlee, 1994). Sometimes it seemed as if the WHO was being held accountable for all that had not been achieved in international health. The consensus of all these attempts was that the WHO had failed to respond adequately to both old and new challenges in world health (Lee, Collinson, Walt & Gilson, 1996). Most significantly though it had lost its edge in setting the agenda for international health policy.

The reform discussion was initially motivated politically and focused on WHO as an organization with weak leadership and lack of efficiency. Frequently it was not possible for those involved in debate and analysis to disentangle the agendas. Indeed it seemed at times that WHO had to be more severely criticized than it perhaps deserved in order to create and maintain a strong momentum for change. But as the debate developed it turned its interest to the more significant question: what place for health in the new international (dis)order that was emerging after the cold war, what were the health priorities that needed to be addressed in a rapidly changing environment and what kind of international health policy response was needed in order to act responsibly and adequately. The external and contextual factors have been listed frequently in a variety of ways (see for example Yach & Bettcher, 1998; Lee et al., 1996) and with different weightings as to their relative importance. Let me just summarize them as follows:

- the increasing number of actors in the international health arena;
- the increasing privatization of medical care and the growing global health care market;
- increased importance of health intelligence, data and surveillance for economic development and trade;
- increased feeling of threat through new and reemerging diseases;
- increased awareness of health as a human rights.

Inventing global health policy

Establishing a global agenda

At present we are witnessing a very systematic attempt to return WHO to its leadership role. Just as WHO "invented" international health policy in the 1970s it is now faced with the task of shaping "global health policy" for the 21st century. This of course is at least as complex a balancing act as the introduction of HFA, made more difficult by the fact that compared with the late 1970s WHO is no longer the only and major player in the health arena. HFA established health as a national policy responsibility and at the same time gave the health ministries the message that much of health was created outside of their remit. It proposed that they embark on intersectoral action at the national level to remedy their lack of power in shaping peoples living conditions.

Now WHO must convince member states that it is in their own best interest *to cooperate in a new manner in the global arena* with other global players and to pool significant elements of their internal sovereignty on health in order to shape a "global health policy". This is complicated by the additional fact that many of the policy agreements necessary will need to be reached in organizations other than WHO such as the WTO, the WIPO or the big financial organizations. The agenda is also driven by the necessity for WHO to survive as an organization by binding a very diverse membership through a common purpose. WHO must engage in *identifying global policy challenges and agendas that are relevant to rich and poor countries alike* and provide new legitimacy for health action at a time when inequity is increasing on a global scale and international donor commitment to health is spiraling downward.

A major step in this process has been the promotion of new way of mapping and measuring the worlds health problems and express them (note the language) as the *"global burden of disease"*. No matter what the weaknesses inherent in this approach to measurement we must not underestimate the significant symbolic difference it represents. It provides arguments and evidence for the need to act jointly in view of increased

984 *I. Kickbusch / Social Science & Medicine 51 (2000) 979–989*

common threats and the need for common solutions. As such it establishes a new imperative for action and new dimensions of accountability: if one state neglects to act or is incapable of action all others can be endangered. It also defines what constitutes a legitimate health issue for intervention at the global level as well as providing a measure for accountability.

Establishing a rationale for nation states that developing a global health policy serves their purpose

In order to gain the support of member states to embark on global policy formulation, a process of "learning" (Finnemore, 1996) must be organized at various levels, using a range of illustrative issues and with enlisting the support of actors at the national level. The first set of arguments for a global health approach have come from the infectious disease and the immunization area and have been driven by a parallel agenda of economics and fear. The 1994 World Health Day made the point of the significant saving the world had made through the eradication of small pox and how much the world stands to save in immunization costs if we were able to achieve a similar success in polio eradication. While at first instance this is of interest mainly to the developed world it lays the ground for a more complex economic argument that shows the contribution of better health to overall economic growth and development. Meaning: if we were to invest in healthier populations in the developing world they will be able to contribute significantly to the economic growth in their own societies and in the long run reduce the need for development aid and support global economic growth. This argument was presented by Nobel Prize winner for economics A. Sen to the 1999 World Health Assembly (Sen, 1999).

The Ebola crisis in 1995 was a watershed in international health and — supported by Hollywood and a number of high profile publications (Garrett, 1994) led to a high awareness by politicians and the general public of the potential dangers incurred by new and reemerging diseases. Organizations in the USA have been particularly active in using the mix of economics and threat to lobby for increased commitment to international health in an adverse national political environment. The report by the Board on International Health of the Institute of Medicine which appropriately is called "*Americas vital interest in global (sic!) health*" states categorically: "The direct interests of the American people are best served when the United States acts decisively to promote health around the world." The report gives four reasons for increased involvement and investment:

- protecting our people;
- enhancing our economy;
- advancing our international interests;
- leading from strength.

This type of advocacy at the national level — which presently comes mainly from the academic and the NGO world — is crucial for establishing the new WHO agenda. For example the US advocacy organization for international health, the National Council for International Health (NCIH), reshaped itself recently into the Global Health Council following a similar rational and the interest in global health is growing in prestigious American national institutions and agencies such as the CDC and the National Institutes of Health. The common agenda is to educate American politicians that "*The failure to engage in the fight to anticipate, prevent, and ameliorate global health problems would diminish America's stature in the realm of health and jeopardize our own health, economy, and national security*" (Berkowitz, 1998). It is essential to underline that global public policy aims at strengthening not replacing national policy capacity but by placing it in the global context *accountability* develops two new dimensions: by not investing in health abroad national politicians are endangering their electorate at home (infectious disease) or, by not acting at home national politicians are endangering the health of others (Tobacco export). A key premise of global health policy is that it is not a zero sum game but an investment that generates a return which is shared by the global community as a whole. Even so there are critical voices which question the relevance of the "global agenda" for the priorities of the developing countries (Das, 1999).

Widening the support base for global health and acting as a broker of interests on behalf of the global community

The many analyses produced to define WHOs new role in a changed environment show consistently that a global health policy cannot not hope to be successful if it does not provide a role for the many new players in the international and global arena. Again a difficult balancing act is required: WHO as an intergovernmental agency is forced through a new set of circumstances and driving forces to build new types of alliances with non/state actors and yet maintain its constitutional links with the member states. Reinicke provides a helpful analytical tool to structure this changed environment: the implementation of global public policy depends on two forms of subsidiarity, vertical subsidiarity (think globally act locally) and horizontal subsidiarity, which implies a mix of public private actors doing what each does best in given circumstances.

This means that WHO must create *platforms that allow for consensus building* on global health in relation

I. Kickbusch / Social Science & Medicine 51 (2000) 979–989 985

to both vertical and horizontal subsidiarity. The accountability challenge lies in drawing the divergent actors into a web of joint responsibility that reflects vertical and horizontal power relationships without compromising the integrity of the WHO. In terms of vertical subsidiarity WHO has gained important experiences through the Healthy Cities Program. In terms of horizontal subsidiarity mechanisms for working in partnership with the private sector are increasingly being explored. Most importantly WHO is for the first time exploring the domain of "soft" international law through the development of a global convention on tobacco control. The convention approach could provide a starting point for other instruments of global health policy, fully exploiting the provision of WHO's constitution. Probably what one will see here over time are various complex strategic approaches similar to the triangulation strategies applied in third way politics.

But other issues loom that move WHO more forcefully into the arena of other global policy arenas, organizations and agencies: issues of trade and health, intellectual property rights, food safety, structural adjustment programs, poverty alleviation, women's rights to name but some. A global health policy needs intersectorality at the global level, it needs to get global health responsibility on the agenda of central actors in the global arena: the G8, the Davos summit, the Bretton Wood Institutions, global companies and new global donors. And it must provide the evidence that argues the case for a global health policy. WHO is reshaping itself in this new global arena and is proactively using the profile of its present Director General as a former prime-minister and global player to move beyond ministries of health. In order to reach its constitutional goals it can no longer be reduced to being the technical advisor on health matters to other agencies. It needs a seat at the table when decisions are being made in fora that will significantly effect global health and it needs to show much more effectively that in supporting a health agenda world leaders will also be contributing to the solution of other global problems. From being the worlds "health conscience" WHO should move to become a pro-active "department of consequence" that monitors the health impact of other actors in the global arena on behalf of the global community. Note as an example the "Health Impact Assessment of the EU Common Agricultural Policy" produced by the Swedish National Institute of Health (Dahlgren, Nordgren & Whitehead, 1996).

Framing the rationale and shifting the moral argument for accountability

One subtle but significant shift between an international and global health agenda is the issue on whose behalf WHO acts. To whom is it accountable? As an international/intergovernmental organization it acts on behalf of its member states and their interest. But not only do the member states themselves frequently not act in the best health interest of their populations but increasingly the main reference group of the WHO — the national ministries of health — does not have the power to effect change for health. This is due to a range of developments: decentralization to regional and local health authorities, decisions set by donors or by lending institutions, rules set by regional bodies such as the European Union or other international agreements and regimes and of course the wider forces of globalization.

The global — as I have outlined elsewhere — is not just more interdependence it is another place, a field of action that cannot easily be reached by national policy action as it transcends borders (Kickbusch, 1999). Global health policy — following the rationale of the global disease burden — transcends geographical boundaries. It refers to populations and affinity groups (i.e. the elderly, youth, women) rather than to nation states. But it needs to frame its agenda in a form that appeals to nation states for common action. Ever since the definition of the environment as a global commons there have been proposals to see health in a similar manner. Recently this has been taken up more systematically by Chen, Evans and Cash (1999) in framing health as a global public good. This takes us back to the challenge of a new era of public policy, where "international cooperation and the internalization of cross border spillovers of national actions have to be at the core of public policy" (Kaul et al., 1999, p. 452).

Chen et al. (1999) argue that "globalization may be shifting the balance of health to a global public good". Two forces have contributed to this: the international transfer of risks and the increasing threat to common resources. Indeed, if we take the argument put forward by Leppo early in this paper it is the *determinants of health* that are becoming increasingly global, outside of the remit of national health ministries and even nation states — requiring a qualitatively new response. Global public goods are defined by Kaul et al. (1999) as having *non-excludable, non-rival benefits that cut across borders, generations and populations*. They include natural global commons (such as the ozone layer), human-made global commons (such as information and knowledge) and global policy outcomes such as peace, health and financial stability. Each category of global public goods is faced with a specific policy challenge: the natural commons are faced with over-use, the man made commons with under-use and lack of access, and health and other global policy outcomes with under-supply. WHO's task must be to establish health firmly as a global public good and ensure that it is supplied with fairness globally.

986   *I. Kickbusch / Social Science & Medicine 51 (2000) 979–989*

Ensuring health as a global public good through global governance

Health as a global public good should constitute the core of a global health policy: both as a value and as a resource

Global public goods are produced by a wide array of actors and coalitions, both public and private and at many different levels. The recent explosion of actors in international health underlines the point made by Chen et al. (1999, p. 301) that the future of global health lies in horizontally linked coalitions. They see WHO's role as a center *that"exerts health leadership by becoming the central promoter and facilitator in the production of health as a global public good"*. Health programs are and will be increasingly implemented through partnerships, networks, alliances and coalitions (Kickbusch & Quick, 1998). WHO's role must be to ensure that these networks and patchworks (to paraphrase Reinicke, 1998, p. 228) evolve into networks of governance. What follows are some suggestions grouped along six overlapping areas of action for how WHO could support the development of such a network for health governance and lay the groundwork for global health policy development:

Ensure a reliable information base on global health

Health leadership in the 21st century is inextricably linked to information and knowledge. This includes the regular gathering and analysis of a wide range of health information, global surveillance (Zacher, 1999), development of quality control systems, policy analysis. WHO must become a modern knowledge organization and ensure the rapid, easy and reliable access to the world's expanding information resources on health — and take on the challenge to counteract the inequality of access to information on a global basis. Providing an overview of the global health system, its actors and resource flows will be as important as the epidemiological information on world health. Indeed this mapping constitutes a major first task in the move towards a global health policy. A mechanism could be for the World Health Assembly (WHA) to commission *a global health governance audit*, which would be submitted to the WHA and global health community at regular intervals.

Ensure global health security

Increasingly disease outbreaks are seen as threats to international security, they disrupt development, economies and trade, as witnessed by a series of events in the last few years such as the Plague in India, Ebola in Zaire, the Rift Valley fever in Kenya and outbreaks in Hongkong, Britain and Belgium. Zacher (1999) has underlined the need for protocols on how the global community should respond at all levels to these outbreaks. Following recent discussion of the UN Security Council on HIV/AIDS in Africa it would put the links between security and health on a more permanent base if WHO were formally requested by the UN security council to take on the task of ensuring both a *rapid disease/medical events response* network (including such concerns as bio terrorism) and acting as *the public spokesperson to the global media networks* in the event of major outbreaks. A *special global outbreak fund* would be created for this purpose and be administered by the WHO. Similar protocols and mechanisms need to be developed for the increasingly un-coordinated involvement of many actors in humanitarian relief.

Support countries in developing global health competence and responsibility

Within a global public goods framework countries will need to develop willingness and competence to include across border spillovers and externalities, (the costs of which are carried by others) into their policy considerations. WHO would help develop capacities at country level ranging from reporting capacity to partnership building, helping countries clarify what they give and what they receive within the global community. This also means the recasting of international development assistance as "globalized internal policy". Kaul et al. (1999, p. 451) proposal for "externalities profiles" at national level should be developed for health. An interesting such model has been pioneered by Clyde Hertzman (1996) which measures "the ecological footprint" and relates countries attempts to maximize their health status with overall resource use. In this model for example Costa Rica emerges as the world's healthiest country.

Act as the global health broker

The increasing number of international networks and agreements with impact on health open up a new set of roles for the WHO. It includes:

- the development of mixed regulation with the participation of all interested parties;
- both the initiation and brokering of international agreements on health;
- the negotiating role in conflicts over health effects (such as the TRIPS negotiations); and
- the role to enable partnerships and enhance commitment to mutual goals to address major global health problems including major health inequities (for example the vaccine initiative for tropical diseases).

A range of round tables, platforms and regimes can be

I. Kickbusch / Social Science & Medicine 51 (2000) 979–989 987

established and developed that build trust and establish bridges between the representatives of nation states and the many other actors involved in global health action. Binding a wide range of actors into these processes would also increase the potential for implementation through horizontal subsidiarity as well as for self-regulation. This also must include a new type of exchange between UN agencies active in and relevant to global health. Over time this would lead in an incremental fashion to the development of the parameters and key instruments for a global health policy.

Act as a health oversight body

The functioning of such a system of networks and alliances will depend on a high level of transparency, quality control, outcome analysis and accountability infrastructures. A special sector of WHO could be established (following the ISO model) that monitors the major health networks, partnerships and alliances as part of an accreditation process to the world health community. The results of these oversight studies — based on voluntary disclosure — would be audited by an independent "auditor" or tripartite accreditation body and be reported to the WHO governing bodies. Partnerships, networks and alliances that pass the "global health ISO" would gain special access to the global health policy process. A similar oversight function for the *health consequences of other parts of the UN system* (and maybe the larger international system) could be delegated to the WHO by the ECOSOC, in particular in relation to the interface of economic development and health. Major global players — from UN agencies, Bretton Wood institutions as well as the business and the NGO community — could commit to the global health ISO for voluntary audit and establish themselves as responsible members of the global health community. Such audits could also be considered for member states, as is being practiced by the European office of WHO in the field of health promotion and investment for health (Ziglio, 1997). Care of course must be taken that such a function provides incentives to voluntarily join the audit process and not become a restrictive control measure that excludes rather than includes.

Establish a UN spokesperson on human rights and health

Finally the WHO must be seen by the global community as the organization that ensures accountability on health and human rights. The Director General should — on request of the UN high commissioner on human rights — designate an independent spokesperson on health and human rights that gives a health and human rights report to each World Health Assembly. She must have the right to draw the attention of the international community to health and human rights abuses of any actor in the global health system.

The way forward

Kaul et al. have identified three gaps that stand in the way of moving forward in the area of global public goods: a Jurisdictional gap, a Participation gap and an Incentive gap (Kaul et al., 1999, pp. 450–451). Obviously WHO and the global health community will have to analyze with great care how these gaps can be overcome. Another gap that needs to be addressed and cuts across many of the issues raised is the gap between the local and the global. In many ways governments are now accountable to both domestic and international constituencies in different ways. A very interesting example of this interaction are World Bank Loans where the international NGO community has pushed for more accountability of the World Bank, the donors and the national governments (Brown & Fox, 1998) on behalf of local communities. The challenge will be to explain the new world of international agreements to local constituencies and to convince policy makers at national level of the need for a "globalized internal policy".

Much will depend on the ability to *finance the tasks* outlined above as well as the interventions needed to reduce the untenable global health inequality. Nation States will and should not be willing to continue to cover the costs of international health development as the private health sector expands to become one of the largest and fastest growing industries world wide, including speculation on the capital market. Cleveland, Henderson and Kaul (1996) have put forward a number of interesting proposals of financing alternatives for global public goods: "As a matter of common sense, fund raising for international functions should bear most heavily on those activities which benefit most from a peaceful and predictable world environment. Travel, transport, communications and international transactions are the obvious candidates". New philanthropists — such as Gates, Soros and Turner who come from these sectors — have entered the global health development arena with a high profile and major sums to address key issues such as immunization and maternal mortality. A major next step would be to see them take the initiative to move from philanthropy to support the formation of a financing system that reflects the global responsibility of a wide array of global actors — public and private. A new network based *global health fund* administered by a board of international trustees from the public and the private sector and linked to the WHO for final disbursement could well be envisaged.

In the past the increase of actors has led to a re-duction in consensus, a shift of priorities away from integrated programs to vertical interventions and a competition for resources. The conflict between WHO and UNDP in relation to the responsibility for HIV/AIDS is a case in point, the story of the Children's Vaccine initiative is another (Muraskin, 1998). The loss of orientation after the cold war must now make place for a systematic attempt at a global health policy that deserves the name. It can only be achieved through new mechanisms of governance, some of which I have outlined above. Proposals of this nature could also be further developed and pooled with the support of an alliance of foundations (old and new), supposing they would be willing to invest not just in vertical programs but a new infrastructure for global health governance. There is in my mind no need for new agencies but we do need to adapt the orientation, working structure and composition of those that exist to a global agenda and a networked based infrastruc-ture. Indeed one could envisage *a seminal global health summit* which would gather the global health commu-nity to commit itself to a global health policy for the first decades of the 21st century.

Accountability intact?

Significant health improvement for the world's population is so close within our reach but in order to achieve it we need to be willing to go down new ave-nues — as academics our historical accountability lies in thinking outside the box, as public health pro-fessionals it lies in the courage and capacity to act. Accountability refers to the process of holding actors responsible for their actions. Most of the world's population cannot raise its voice and demand their health rights. They die too young, too soon, without being heard. A global health system worthy of its name must first and foremost address this daunting task of social justice.

Acknowledgements

I would like to thank Joshua Cohen and Lowell Levin for their thoughtful comments.

References

Berkowitz, E. (1998). *To improve human health: a history of the Institute of Medicine.* Washington, DC: National Academy Press.

Brown, L. D., & Fox, J. A. (1998). *The struggle for account-ability: the World Bank, NGOs, and grassroots movement.* Cambridge, MA: MIT Press.

Castells, M. (1996). *The rise of the network society.* Malden, MA: Blackwell.

Chen, L., Evans, T., & Cash, R. (1999). Health as a Global Public Good. In *Global public goods: international co-operation in the 21st century.* New York: Oxford University Press.

Cleveland, H., Henderson, H., & Kaul, I. (1996). The United Nations: policy and financing alternatives. In *The first report of the Global Commission to fund the United Nations.* New York: Apex Press.

Cohen, J. (1999). *Interview for "Oral History of WHO" pro-ject.* New Haven: Yale University.

Courtney, B. (1999). *Global tobacco control: lessons from the infant formula situation.* Yale University, New Haven, CT (unpublished MPH dissertation).

Dahlgren, G., Nordgren, P., & Whitehead, M. (1996). *Health impact assessment of the EU Common Agricultural Policy.* Sweden: Folkhälsoinstitutet.

Das, V. (1999). Public Good, Ethics, and Everyday Life: Beyond the Boundaries of Bioethics. *Daedalus Fall, 128*(4), 99–133.

Dubos, R. (1959). *Mirage of health.* New Brunswick: Rutgers University Press.

Finnemore, Martha (1996). *National Interests in International Society.* Ithaca, NY: Cornell University Press.

Garrett, L. (1994). *The Coming Plague: Newly Emerging Diseases in a World Out of Balance.* New York: Farrar, Straus & Giroux.

Godlee, F. (1994). WHO in crisis. *British Medical Journal, 309.*

Hertzman, C. (1996). What's been said and what's been hid: population health, global consumption and the role of national health data systems. In D. Blane, E. Brunner, & R. Wilkinson, *Health and social organization: towards a health policy for the twenty-first century.* New York: Routledge.

Illich, I. (1976). *Limits to medicine: medical nemesis: the expropriation of health.* London: Boyars.

Kaul, I., Grunberg, I., & Stern, M. (1999). *Global public goods: international cooperation in the 21st century.* New York: Oxford University Press.

Keck, M., & Sikkink, K. (1998). *Activists beyond borders: advocacy networks in international politics.* Ithaca, NY: Cornell University Press.

Kickbusch, I. (1999). Global + local: global public health. *Journal of Epidemiology and Community Health, 53,* 451–452.

Kickbusch, I., & Quick, J. (1998). Partnerships for health in the 21st century. *World Statistics Quarterly, 51,* 68–74.

Koivusalo, M., & Ollila, E. (1997). *Making a healthy world: agencies, actors, and policies in international health.* London: St. Martin's Press.

Lee, K. (1998). Globalization and Health Policy. Discussion paper no. 1, London. London School of Hygiene and Tropical Medicine.

Lee, K., Collinson, S., Walt, G., & Gilson, L. (1996). Who should be doing what in international health: a confusion of mandates in the UN. *British Medical Journal, 312,* 302–306.

Leppo, K. (1997). Introduction. In Meri Koivusalo, & E.

I. Kickbusch / Social Science & Medicine 51 (2000) 979–989 989

Ollila, *Making a healthy world: Agencies, actors, and policies in international health*. London: St. Martin's Press.

McNamara, R. (1981). *The McNamara Years at the World Bank: Major Policy Addresses of Robert S. McNamara, 1968–1981*. Baltimore, MD: John Hopkins University Press for the World Bank.

Muraskin, W. (1998). *The politics of international health: the Children's Vaccine Initiative and the struggle to develop vaccines for the third world*. Albany, NY: State University of New York Press.

Myrdal, G. (1970). *The Challenge of World Poverty: A World Anti-Poverty Program in Outline*. New York: Pantheon Books.

Navarro, V. (1998). Comment: Whose globalization? *American Journal of Public Health, 88*, 742–743.

Reinicke, W. (1998). *Global public policy: Governing without government?* Washington, DC: Brookings Institution Press.

Sen, A. (1999). *Development as freedom*. New York: Oxford University Press.

Walt, G. (1994). *Health policy: an introduction to process and power*. Johannesburg: Witwatersrand University Press.

Yach, D., & Bettcher, D. (1998). The globalization of public health I and II. *American Journal of Public Health, 88*, 735–741.

Zacher, M. (1999). Global epidemiological surveillance: international cooperation to monitor infectious diseases. In I. Kaul, I. Grunberg, & Marc A. Stern, *Global public goods: international cooperation in the 21st century*. New York: Oxford University Press.

Ziglio, E. (1997). *WHO: Investment for health in Hungary*. Report of an Expert Group.

[26]

Globalization and Cholera: Implications for Global Governance

Kelley Lee and Richard Dodgson

Plague and pestilence have become an increasingly popular theme since the end of the Cold War among policymakers, journalists, fiction writers, and film directors searching for new threats to personal and national security. Ill health and, in particular, infectious diseases have generated a spate of popular, and often alarmist, literature.[1] This has been accompanied by growing high-level concern within governments and the medical community with global health issues that threaten national interests.[2] The emphasis in many of these discussions has been on emerging health threats that are perceived to pose potentially sudden and serious dangers to public health.

We begin this essay with the premise that the process of globalization has particular impacts on health and that there is a clear need to better understand and more effectively respond to these impacts. However, without underplaying the dangers posed by health emergencies caused, for example, by the genetic mutation of viral agents or epidemics of emerging infectious diseases, we seek to develop a broader understanding of the historical and structural factors behind the health challenges posed by globalization. As we discuss later, globalization can be defined as a process that is changing the nature of human interaction within a range of social spheres. Globalization's impact on health can be seen as part of a longer historical process firmly located in social change over decades, and perhaps centuries, rather than recent years.

From this perspective, an understanding of global health issues at the turn of the twenty-first century could benefit substantially from the voluminous literature on globalization from international relations, including the subfields of social and political theory and international political economy. This is a rich and highly relevant literature. It documents what structural changes are occurring toward a global political economy, how power relationships are embedded within this process of change, what varying impacts this may have on individuals and groups, and to what extent global governance could effectively mediate this process. These issues counterbalance the strong focus in the health literature on biomedical research, information systems, and other technical solutions. Although

214   *Globalization and Cholera*

health is a classic transborder issue, it continues to receive limited attention in international relations.

We seek to bring together the international relations and health fields for two purposes. First, knowledge of the globalization process can be used to better understand the nature of health issues and the development of effective responses to them. To explore this link, we analyze cholera from the nineteenth century to the present, with particular attention to the seventh pandemic (1961–present). We argue that the particular form that globalization takes has created social conditions that have influenced the transmission, incidence, and vulnerability of different individuals and groups to the disease. Thus, we compare epidemiological patterns of the disease alongside changing patterns of human migration, transportation, and trade.

Second, knowledge of health and disease can be used to better understand the nature of globalization, because globalization is a highly contested concept, infused with embedded interests and having both positive and negative consequences.[3] Cholera has mirrored this process, highlighting the contradictions of globalization in its present form. A significant and often overlooked threat to human health, therefore, is the particular form globalization took in the late twentieth century. Thriving in the midst of increased poverty, widening inequalities within and across countries, pressures to shrink the public sector, and global environmental change, cholera can be seen as a reflection of the ills of globalization itself.

From analysis of this dual relationship between globalization and cholera, we conclude by considering the implications for existing mechanisms of international health cooperation. Following a brief review of measures for the transborder prevention, control, and treatment of infectious diseases, we explore the need for a system of global governance. We propose a definition of global governance for health and discuss key functions and characteristics that may be needed to protect human health on a global scale.

Globalization and Health: A Conceptual Framework

An understanding of the linkages between globalization and health depends foremost on one's definition of globalization and precise dating of the process. In this essay, we define globalization as a process that is changing the nature of human interaction across a range of social spheres, including the economic, political, social, technological, and environmental. This process is globalizing in the sense that many boundaries hitherto separating human interaction are being increasingly eroded. These boundaries—spatial, temporal, and cognitive—can be described as the dimensions of globalization.[4]

The *spatial dimension* concerns change to how we experience and perceive physical space. Roland Robertson writes of "a sense of the world as a single place" because of increased travel, communication, and other shared experiences.[5] Conversely, this "death of distance"[6] has also led to more localized, nationalized, or regionalized feelings of spatial identity. As such, globalization can be seen as a reterritorializing rather than deterritorializing process. Second, the *temporal dimension* concerns change to the actual and perceived time in which human activity occurs, generally toward accelerated time frames. A good example is currency trading of U.S.$1.7 trillion worldwide each day, two-thirds of this amount retraded after less than seven days. The speed of communication (e.g., facsimile, e-mail) and transportation (e.g., high-speed train, Concorde jet) has also accelerated social interaction. Third, globalization has a *cognitive dimension* that affects the creation and exchange of knowledge, ideas, beliefs, values, cultural identities, and other thought processes. Change has been facilitated by communication and transportation technologies that have enabled people to interact more intensely with others around the world. The production of knowledge has also become more globalized through research and development, mass media, education, and management practices. Contrasting forces are at play that, on the one hand, homogenize cognitive processes for better or worse (e.g., global teenager) and, on the other hand, encourage greater heterogeneity (e.g., religious fundamentalism).

In addition to the precise nature of globalization, the timing of the process has been subject to dispute. Some believe that it is a relatively recent phenomenon defined foremost by the activities of multinational corporations and their striving for global economies of scale.[7] While others agree that social relations have become more intense during the past ten to twenty years, they argue that such relations are not fundamentally new. Anthony Giddens and Robertson, for example, argue that globalization has historical roots from the fifteenth century.[8] Giddens asserts that, since the fifteenth century, globalization has developed with modernity. Robertson, however, disputes the view that globalization has followed a single *telos* or that its emergence can be linked to a single force such as modernity. Instead, he argues that there are a number of historical stages to globalization (Table 1), each characterized by what are currently regarded as features of a modern society and global system. These include, for instance, human migration, a system of global trade, urbanization, and the growth of international governance.

It is this conceptualization of globalization occurring across multiple spheres and dimensions and a time frame of centuries that we adopt in this essay as a useful framework for understanding its complex impacts on health. Briefly, the geographical spread of disease can be closely correlated with the migration of the human species across the globe. Robert Clark writes, "In becoming global, humans, plants, animals, and diseases

216   *Globalization and Cholera*

Table 1   Robertson's Historical Stages of Globalization

Stage	Time Scale	Spatial Center	Characteristics
Germinal	Circa 1500–1850s	Europe	Growth of national community, accentuation of the concept of the individual, spread of Gregorian calendar
Incipient	Circa 1850–1870s	Mainly Europe	Shift toward homogeneous unity of the state, formalized international relations
Takeoff	Circa 1870–1920s	Increasingly global	Inclusion of non-European states into international society, World War I, League of Nations
Struggle for hegemony	Circa 1920–1965	Global	Wars or disputes about the shape of the globalization process, atomic bomb, UN
Uncertainty	Circa 1965–present	Global	Inclusion of Third World, moon landing, end of Cold War, environment, HIV/AIDS

Source: Roland Robertson, *Globalization: Social Theory and Global Culture* (London: Sage, 1992).

have coevolved; i.e., evolved together as a package of interdependent life systems."[9] With the spread of human populations came changes to social organization into larger communities with different lifestyles, notably from hunting and gathering to agricultural and animal husbandry, to sustain such communities. Changes to disease patterns followed—increased zoonosis (e.g., tuberculosis, rabies, salmonella, helminths), nutritional ills, and dental decay. The establishment of permanent communities, accompanied by systems of irrigation and often ineffective sanitation and water supplies, led to increased diseases such as malaria and schistosomiasis.[10]

As J. N. Hays points out, human settlements on different continents remained relatively isolated until the late fifteenth century when the age of exploration brought Europe into contact with the Americas. Coinciding with a greater concentration of human populations into larger communities, the impact of the spatial dimension of globalization on health became increasingly evident. Periodically, epidemics could now become pandemics through intercontinental trade, migration, and imperialism. During this period, diseases such as plague and influenza traveled the silk route from Asia into Europe, or by ship to ports throughout the old and new worlds. Similarly, typhus from Asia and syphilis from the Americas were brought to Europe, while Europeans introduced measles, smallpox, typhus, plague, and other diseases to the new world, thus precipitating "the greatest demographic disaster in history."[11]

The greater frequency and intensity of human interaction across continents eventually made the temporal dimension of globalization more prominent. From the seventeenth century, industrialization, rapid urbanization, military conflict, and imperialism brought increased vulnerability to many populations. Coupled with inequalities in living standards and a lack of basic medical knowledge, many communicable diseases (e.g., syphilis, typhus, tuberculosis, and influenza) spread more rapidly than ever before. Another disease, the infamous "potato blight," was also able to travel quickly from the northeast of North America in 1840 to Europe by ship in 1845, eventually causing widespread starvation, notably in Ireland.[12]

By the late eighteenth century, these changes to the spatial and temporal dimensions of health risks and determinants led to greater efforts to develop public health knowledge and practice to respond to them. The nineteenth century brought the initiation of bilateral and regional health agreements, giving way from 1851 to periodic International Sanitary Conferences to promote intergovernmental cooperation on infectious disease control. This was accompanied by major advances in medical knowledge, including vaccination and microbiology, which were increasingly shared at international scientific meetings. This process of knowledge creation and application across countries signaled the cognitive dimension of globalization in health, which gained further momentum with the professionalization of the health field, creation of research and training institutions worldwide, and growth of scientific publications. Yet, as we show later, how health and ill health within and across societies were understood cannot be separated from prevailing beliefs and values characterizing these later stages of globalization. The creation of the World Health Organization (WHO) in 1948 was fueled by the postwar faith in scientific and technical solutions to defeat ill health, a belief that would be seriously shaken by the uncertainty of this phase of globalization in the late twentieth century.

Cholera in the Time of Globalization:
The First Six Pandemics

We argue that an analysis of cholera from the nineteenth century can offer important insights into the nature of globalization and the specific challenges it poses for human health. Cholera is caused by the ingestion of an infectious dose of a particular serogroup of the *Vibrio cholerae* bacterium.[13] The bacterium is usually taken into the body through contaminated water or food, then attaches itself to the lining of the human bowel and produces a poison (enterotoxin). The infection is often mild or without symptoms, but approximately one in twenty cases is severe. In severe cases, cholera is an acute illness characterized by repeated vomiting and profuse watery diarrhea, resulting in rapid loss of body fluids and salts.

218 *Globalization and Cholera*

During this stage, the disease is highly infectious through further contamination of local water, soil, and food. Without treatment, this can lead to severe dehydration, circulatory collapse, and death within hours.[14]

Medical historians have long recognized that the epidemiology of cholera has been intimately linked to social, economic, and political change. Cholera had been confined for centuries to the riverine areas of the Indian subcontinent with occasional appearances along China's coast introduced by trading ships and in the Middle East transported by pilgrims traveling to Mecca. The pattern of the disease changed dramatically, however, in the early nineteenth century with the first of six pandemics over the next hundred years (Table 2). The intensification of human interaction during this period through imperialism, trade, military conflict, and migration (e.g., slave trade) was a significant factor. The first pandemic occurred between 1817 and 1823, with cholera suddenly moving far beyond its historical boundaries. A number of changes contributed to its spread in that period: the movement of British troops and camp followers throughout the region, construction of irrigation canals without sufficient drainage ditches to raise cash crops, building of a national railway system, impoverishment of rural people by land reforms and taxation, and mass migration as a result of economic hardship. For the first time, cholera became endemic throughout South Asia, from which it was then transported to the Far and Middle East via burgeoning trade links (e.g., tea, opium), religious pilgrimage, and notably military expansionism.

The geographical pattern of cholera during the next five pandemics continued to mirror human activity, spreading from country to neighboring country. Corresponding with the intensification of links between Asia, Europe, and the Americas, cholera became a worldwide disease in 1826. From India, the disease moved beyond Asia to Europe, the Americas, and to a lesser extent Africa; it traveled via immigration, troop movements during times of war and peace (e.g., Crimean War), and the slave trade. A particularly important factor was immigration from Europe to North America. Cholera first arrived in New York in June 1832 via immigrants from Dublin who, in turn, traveled inland via wagon train. This extended the second pandemic across North America and then south to the Caribbean and South America. Immigrants then became a repeated source of reinfection, facilitated by the building of the intercontinental railway.[15]

This close link between epidemiology and mode of transport can be observed throughout the history of the first six cholera pandemics. As well as extending the geographical incidence of the disease, the speed at which it spread also corresponded with prevailing technology. Until the twentieth century, cholera was limited to travel by land and sea. Compared to the seventh pandemic, which we discuss later, the rate of spread was relatively slow. For example, it took the disease three months to cross the sea via trade routes from Hamburg (where it arrived in August 1831) to Sunderland in the

Table 2 First Six Cholera Pandemics, 1817–1923

Date	Geographical Pattern of Spread
1817–1823 (6 years)	India (1817) Ceylon, Burma, Siam, Malacca, Singapore (1818–1820) Java, Batavia, China, Persia (1821) Egypt, Astrakhan, Caspian Sea, Syria (1823)
1826–1838 (12 years)	India (1826) Persia, Southern Russia (1829) Northern Russia, Bulgaria (1830) Poland, Germany, Austria, England, Mecca, Turkey, Egypt (1831) Sweden, France, Scotland, Ireland, Canada, United States (1832) Spain, Portugal, Mexico, Cuba, Caribbean, Latin America (1833) Italy (1835)
1839–1855 (16 years)	India, Afghanistan (1839) China (1840) Persia, Central Asia (1844–1845) Arabian Coast, Caspian and Black Seas, Turkey, Greece (1846–1847) Arabia, Poland, Sweden, Germany, Holland, England, Scotland, United States, Canada, Mexico, Caribbean, Latin America (1848) France, Spain, Portugal, Italy, North Africa (1850)
1863–1874 (11 years)	India (1863) Mecca, Turkey, Mediterranean (1865) Northern Europe, North America, South America (1866–1867) West Africa (1868)—limited
1881–1896 (15 years)	India (1881) Egypt (1883) North Africa, Southern Mediterranean, Russia China, Japan United States, Latin America (1887)—limited Germany (1892)
1899–1923 (24 years)	India (1899) Near and Far East Egypt, Russia, Balkan Peninsula Southern Europe, Hungary China, Japan, Korea, Philippines

Sources: Compiled from K. Kiple, ed., *The Cambridge World History of Human Disease* (Cambridge: Cambridge University Press, 1993), pp. 642–649; D. Barua, "The Global Epidemiology of Cholera in Recent Years," *Proceedings of the Royal Society of Medicine* 65 (1972): 423–432.

Note: Accurate historical data on the epidemiology of specific infectious diseases is notoriously incomplete, given the absence of standard reporting systems (e.g., lists of notifiable diseases), incompleteness of demographic data, and differences in disease nomenclature. This table draws on the limited data available to illustrate the general geographic pattern of early cholera pandemics. The spread of the disease by year and country cannot always be provided comprehensively.

northeast of England (where it arrived in October 1831). During later pandemics, the introduction of the steamship led to cholera spreading more quickly across major bodies of water. Hence, in 1848 cholera advanced from Poland to New Orleans in just over seven months. This more rapid

220   *Globalization and Cholera*

move also coincided with the approximate doubling of railway lines and tonnage of steamships in operation,[16] correlating with the rapid spread of the disease throughout the Americas. By the time of the third and fourth pandemics, the spread of cholera into South America was hastened by the opening of the Panama Canal. A similar pattern can be observed in the Middle East with the opening of the Suez Canal.

Another feature during this period was cholera's close association with prevailing social conditions that enabled the disease to spread so widely and repeatedly, in the process becoming endemic in many parts of the world. In India, the cumulative effect of profound changes to local societies and ecology was, as Sheldon Watts writes, the transformation of a merely local disease, endemic in Bengal, into a chronic India-wide problem by 1817 and soon afterward an epidemic disease of worldwide proportions.[17] As cholera spread, it found fertile conditions for epidemic transmission in nineteenth-century industrialization. Poor sanitation, poverty, malnutrition, overcrowding, ignorance, and a lack of basic health services allowed cholera to flourish in the new urban centers of Europe and North America. Such was the link between cholera and social inequality during this period that the disease added impetus to fermenting unrest. In Russia, an uprising by revolutionaries known as the "cholerics" in the 1830s was because of the belief that the disease was actually a plot to kill off the poor. Although Czar Nicholas I quelled the movement, cholera continued to inflame class conflict across Europe.

By the middle of the nineteenth century, health policies to control epidemic diseases began to be adopted. But the link between disease and the squalid conditions of the poor had not yet been made officially. The experiences of Florence Nightingale with cholera during the Crimean War led the British Army to establish sanitary engineering as a new branch.[18] The first U.K. Public Health Act was adopted in 1848, followed by the creation of a General Board of Health, although cholera continued to be blamed on immorality and a lack of "proper habits."[19] Despite John Snow's historic gesture in 1854,[20] it was not until the discovery by Robert Koch in 1883 of the bacillus *Vibrio cholerae* as the causative agent of cholera that the relative inertia of government bodies toward the lack of safe drinking water and sanitation for poor people finally ended. This was gradually followed by the establishment of a public health infrastructure, eventually supported by a system of regulation and social welfare.

Internationally, governments complemented national efforts with meetings to promote cooperation and improve public sanitation. Between 1851 and 1911, twelve International Sanitary Conferences were held, which led to the formation of international public unions, such as the International Association of Public Baths and Cleanliness. In 1907, the Office International d'Hygiène Publique (OIHP) was created to standardize surveillance and reporting of selected communicable diseases, including cholera. Following establishment of the League of Nations, the work of these international public unions continued under the auspices of the League's Health Commission. In particular, the commission "established new procedures for combating epidemics and initiated studies in child welfare, public health training and many other subjects."[21] All of these efforts proved to be the forerunners of increasingly organized international health cooperation, leading to the eventual creation of the World Health Organization in 1948.

In summary, the first six pandemics of cholera can be understood in close relation to the prevailing socioeconomic and political structures of the period. From a local disease, cholera became one of the most widespread and deadly diseases of the nineteenth century, killing estimated tens of millions of people.[22] Not coincidentally, cholera traveled the same routes around the globe as European imperialism. The disease, in this sense, was an integral part of this stage of the globalization process, affected by changing spatial, temporal, and cognitive dimensions of human interaction but, in turn, also influencing the articulation or particular form that globalization has taken. It is within this historical context that the seventh pandemic can be understood.

Globalization and the Seventh Pandemic: Mirror, Mirror on the Wall

The seventh cholera pandemic began in 1961 in Sulawesi, Indonesia, after a gap of thirty-eight years. The disease remained endemic in a number of regions, including South and Southeast Asia, and cases were reported regularly until the 1960s. Nonetheless, there was a declining incidence overall, and worldwide transmission did not occur. The primary reasons were improvements in basic sanitation and water supplies in many countries, backed by international health cooperation. Until 1961, it was thought that cholera was disappearing.

But in 1961, cholera presented a new and unexpected challenge (Table 3). Unlike previous pandemics, which are believed to have been the result of the classical biotype, the cause of this new pandemic was discovered to be a different biotype of *Vibrio cholerae,* known as El Tor.[23] Although less virulent, this new strain has proven more difficult to eradicate. El Tor cholera causes a higher proportion of asymptomatic infections, allowing carriers to spread the disease through contamination of food or water. It survives longer in the environment and shows greater resistance to antibiotics and chlorine. It can also live in association with certain aquatic plants and animals, making water an important reservoir for infection.[24]

From Indonesia, El Tor cholera moved west to reach India and the Middle East by 1966. In 1970, it reached southern Europe (Russia) and

222   *Globalization and Cholera*

Table 3   Seventh and Eighth Cholera Pandemics, 1961–Present

Pandemic, Date, Type[a]	Countries
Seventh pandemic, 1961–present, El Tor biotype	Indonesia (1961)
	Indo-Pakistan Subcontinent (1963–1964)
	West Pakistan (Bangladesh), Afghanistan, Iran, Uzbekistan, Thailand (1965)
	Iraq (1966)
	Laos, South Korea, Hong Kong, Macao, Nepal, Malaysia, Burma, East Pakistan (1969)
	Russia (Astrakhan, Odessa/Kersh), Turkey, Czechoslovakia, France, U.K.,[b] Lebanon, Israel, Syria, Jordan, Libya, Tunisia, Dubai, Kuwait,[b] Saudi Arabia, Somalia, Ethiopia, Guinea, Sierra Leone, Liberia, Ghana, Côte d'Ivoire, Mali, Togo, Dahomey, Upper Volta, Nigeria, Niger, Japan[b] (1970)
	Muscat, Oman, Yemen, Morocco, Algeria, Cameroon, Chad, Mauritania, Senegal, Kenya, Uganda, Madagascar,[b] Spain, Portugal, France,[b] Sweden,[b] West Germany[b] (1971)
	United States (1973)
	Peru, Colombia, Chile, Bolivia, Brazil, Ecuador, Guatemala, Honduras, Mexico, Nicaragua, Panama, Venezuela (1991)
	Argentina, Belize, Costa Rica, El Salvador, French Guyana, Guyana, Surinam (1992)
	Paraguay (1993)
	Zaire, Ukraine (1994)
Eighth pandemic, 1993–present, 0139 Bengal serogroup	India, Bangladesh (1993)
	Pakistan, Thailand (1994)
	10 Southeast Asian countries, United States[b] (1995)

Sources: D. Barua, "The Global Epidemiology of Cholera in Recent Years," *Proceedings of the Royal Society of Medicine* 65 (1972): 423–432; Paul Epstein, "Emerging Diseases and Ecosystem Instability: New Threats to Public Health," *American Journal of Public Health* 85, no. 2 (February 1995): 168–172.

Notes: a. Many serogroups of *Vibrio cholerae* have been identified. During the first to seventh pandemics, only the 01 serogroup (of which two biotypes exist) caused cholera. Its classic biotype caused the first six pandemics and its El Tor biotype caused the seventh pandemic. A different serogroup—0139 Bengal—caused the eighth pandemic, and it is the first non 01 serogroup to have caused cholera.

b. Shows imported cases.

north, east, and west Africa. By 1971, outbreaks had been reported in thirty-one countries, one-third of them experiencing the disease for the first time. In that year, 150,000 cases were reported, including some 50,000 cases in West Bengal refugee camps. In most newly affected countries, the disease caused severe outbreaks with mortality rates of 40 percent or higher.[25] A year later, it reached the southeastern Mediterranean and eastern Europe. M. Narkevich and others describe the pandemic up to the 1990s as falling into three periods: 1961–1969, 1970–1977, and 1978–1989. The peak of the pandemic was during periods 1 and 2 (1967–1974), after which morbidity declined until 1985. Then, from 1985 to 1989, the pandemic seemed to accelerate once again, with 52,000 cases reported in thirty-six countries. In total, between 1961 and 1989, approximately 1.72

million cases of cholera were reported to WHO from 117 countries (see Table 4).[26]

Explanations for the origins of the pandemic were similar to previous ones, namely transmission around the world from an endemic country via travel. As Leonard Bruce-Chwatt observed, the impairment of sanitation on many Indonesian islands because of overpopulation of urban peripheries, military operations, and other disturbances, combined with certain cultural habits (e.g., use of night soil), allowed cholera to reach epidemic proportions.[27] However, the epidemiology of this pandemic has proven different in two fundamental ways: it has been more geographically widespread (spatial dimension) and has lasted longer (temporal dimension). First, the seventh pandemic has encompassed a large number of countries that have either never experienced cholera before, not done so for many decades, or never to such an intensity. In many parts of Africa, in particular, public health officials have experienced difficulty controlling the disease largely because of a lack of adequate surveillance, treatment, or prevention measures. As D. Barua wrote, "All the factors favoring endemicity of cholera exist in present-day Africa, particularly in the populous coastal and riverine areas, where there is little possibility of improving water supply, waste disposal and personal hygiene in the near future. In all probability, cholera is going to become, if it is not already, entrenched in this continent at least temporarily."[28] Barua's predictions have proven correct, and cholera has now become endemic throughout west, east, and southern Africa for the first time.[29]

This unprecedented geographical spread is also observable in the Americas, where the majority of cases have occurred in the 1990s. After disappearing from the Western Hemisphere for almost a century, El Tor cholera was simultaneously reported in two cities in Peru in January 1991. By mid-February, there were 12,000 confirmed cases. WHO described how the epidemic moved with "unexpected speed and intensity," traveling quickly 2,000 kilometers along the coast to Ecuador. By March–April, it had reached Colombia and Chile. By the end of the year, the epidemic had reached a new country every month, resulting in nearly 400,000 cases

Table 4 First Three Periods of the Seventh Cholera Pandemic, 1961–1989

Date	Reported Cases	Countries Reporting
1961–1969	419,968	24, mainly in Asia
1970–1977	706,261	73 (27 Asia, 32 Africa, 12 Europe, 2 Americas)
1978–1989	586,828	83

Source: Adapted from M. Narkevich et al., "The Seventh Pandemic of Cholera in the USSR, 1961–89," *Bulletin of the World Health Organization* 71, no. 2 (1993): 189–196.

224   *Globalization and Cholera*

and more than 4,000 deaths. This was more than the total number of re-ported cases worldwide for the previous five years. The epidemic contin-ued into 1992, with more than 300,000 cases and 2,000 deaths in twenty countries.[30]

The second difference of the seventh pandemic has been its duration so far—thirty-nine years. This has been by far the longest pandemic, and it shows few signs of having run its course. As we discussed earlier, cholera took several months to spread from country to neighboring coun-try during the nineteenth century, transported by land or sea. El Tor cholera has also traveled readily by land and sea. It is believed, for exam-ple, that the disease was imported into Turkey and Lebanon in the early 1970s by workers coming from neighboring affected countries. Similarly, severe outbreaks in Mali, Ghana, Niger, Nigeria, and Chad were traced to the arrival of individuals from infected areas. In India, an outbreak in 1971 was primarily among refugees from the former East Pakistan.[31] Perhaps most dramatically, it is thought that the epidemic in Latin America began after a ship from China emptied its ballast tanks in Peruvian waters. The vibrio then infected local seafood eaten by local people. El Tor is also thought to have arrived on the U.S. Gulf Coast in the hulls of ships from Latin America.[32]

Since the 1960s, however, the reduced cost of transportation and the addition of faster technologies (e.g., high-speed rail, ocean liners, and air travel) have brought unprecedented movement of human populations to and from endemic areas. Since the 1960s, mass travel (growth of 7.5–10 percent per annum) has been growing at a rate faster than global popula-tion growth (growth of 1.5–2.5 percent per annum).[33] This intensification of human mobility has posed new problems for public health officials, in-cluding their capacity to contain serious outbreaks of infectious disease. K. F. Kaferstein, Y. Motarjemi, and Douglas Bettcher note that "over the last two hundred years, the average distance travelled and speed of travel have increased one thousand times, while incubation periods of disease have not."[34] As the average journey time of an airliner or a bulk carrier is much shorter than the incubation period of a disease, these different forms of transportation are believed responsible for the increased spread of dis-ease from one location to another.[35] Air travel, for instance, brings large numbers of people into close contact with each other within an enclosed space. In relation to cholera, the disease has been spread via contaminated food served on airplanes[36] and through global trade in food products (e.g., shellfish, frozen coconut milk).

Furthermore, the epidemiology of the disease has been geographically unpredictable. Whereas in the past cholera could be monitored from coun-try to neighboring country, more recently it has "jumped" continents. In 1973, for instance, forty passengers traveling from London to Australia were infected with cholera from contaminated food taken on board in

Bahrain.[37] Similarly, thirty-one passengers were found to have cholera on a flight bound to Los Angeles from Buenos Aires, Argentina, in 1992.[38] At least seventy-five people contracted cholera by eating cold seafood salad loaded on a flight at Lima, Peru, bound for California.[39] It is estimated that, for air travelers from the United States to India, the reported rate of cholera cases is 3.7 cases per 100,000 travelers.[40] It is this "hypermobility" of the causative agent via worldwide transportation networks that has been a key factor in the continuation of the pandemic.

Technological change, however, does not tell the entire story of cholera in the late twentieth century. Indeed, like previous pandemics, socioeconomic and political structures have also been central. The 1920s to 1960s were perhaps a "boom" period for public health systems. Many countries created national health systems. And the aid to the health sector grew through bilateral aid agencies, multilateral organizations (e.g., WHO, UNICEF), charitable foundations (e.g., Rockefeller Foundation), and other nongovernmental organizations (e.g., Save the Children Fund, Oxfam). Although it was clear that not all benefited equally from this intense period of health development, facilitated by advances in medical knowledge, there was a feeling that progress against many traditional scourges of humankind was being achieved. Eradication campaigns against malaria and (more successfully) smallpox were reflections of this belief in the triumph of science over disease.

The seventh pandemic has been a reminder, however, of the persistent and, in many cases, growing inequalities that remain within and across countries. Life expectancy ranges from forty-three years in the poorest countries to an average of seventy-eight years in higher-income countries. Three-fifths of people in the developing world lack access to safe sanitation, one-third to clean water, and one-fifth to modern health services of any kind.[41] The initial outbreak of cholera in the early 1960s took advantage of these conditions to spread among the have-nots in many different societies. By the early 1970s, the pandemic seemed to peak, and cases gradually decreased over the next decade.

By the 1980s, however, cholera began to benefit from fundamental changes in many public health systems around the world. Despite the launch of the primary health care movement in 1978 by WHO and UNICEF, the 1980s saw a pulling back of the state from the financing and provision of health care. Detailed analysis of this period of health sector reform can be found elsewhere.[42] Briefly, as part of the World Bank's structural adjustment program, many lower-income countries were encouraged to reduce public expenditure on health throughout the 1980s and 1990s.[43] Globally, health sector reform in higher- and lower-income countries included policies to encourage market forces to play a greater role in health systems.[44] There was growing evidence in the late 1990s that these policies have impacted adversely on public health capacity in many countries,[45] and the growing awareness of globalizing forces has led to efforts to redefine public health functions in countries around the world.[46]

It was in this context that cholera opportunistically spread in the early 1990s. In Latin America, the adverse impacts of globalization on health systems have included increased national debt, rapid urbanization, environmental degradation, inequitable access to health services, and reduced public expenditure on public health infrastructure.[47] Cholera then arrived in 1991, spreading rapidly across the continent in an epidemic of 1.4 million cases and more than 10,000 deaths in nineteen countries.[48] This scenario has not, however, been confined to Latin America. In October 1994, El Tor cholera was reported in the former Soviet Union amid economic instability, deteriorating health services, drought, and poor hygiene. The most serious outbreak occurred in ten cities in the Ukraine and threatened a population of 50 million people.[49] As the head of the Ukrainian parliament stated at the time, "The spread of cholera and other infectious diseases is the calling card of an economy in trouble."[50]

Another contributory feature of the global political economy to the seventh pandemic has been the mass migration of people. In the early 1990s, it was estimated that 500 million people crossed international borders on commercial airlines annually. There are 100 million migrants in the world today, with an estimated 70 million people, mostly from low-income countries, working legally or illegally in other countries. In addition, a large proportion (30 million) of total migrants do so involuntarily, including 20 million refugees.[51] Enforced migration has become a particular feature of Africa, where 16 million people have been internally displaced.[52] In many cases, such migration has been a cause and effect of "complex emergencies," which have "a singular ability to erode or destroy the cultural, political, and economic integrity of established societies."[53] Given large numbers of displaced people, resulting in overcrowded living conditions, poor sanitation, unclean water supplies, and malnutrition, cholera has become a familiar feature. For example, the mass population movements as a result of the Pakistani-Indian war in 1971 led to thousands of deaths from cholera and further spread of the disease.[54] Between 1987 and 1991, cholera was diagnosed in Mozambican refugees as they migrated from their home villages to camps in Malawi.[55] In August 1994, El Tor cholera broke out in relief camps in Goma, Zaire, among Rwandan refugees. Within twenty-four hours, 800 people had died; the epidemic eventually caused 70,000 cases and 12,000 deaths.[56]

Finally, globalization in its present form is believed to be contributing to changes in the natural environment that enable infectious diseases such as cholera to thrive.[57] Like the British-built irrigation canals in India, which increased the incidence of malaria and cholera, rapid urbanization and industrialization without sufficient attention to sustainable economic development have led to contamination of drinking water. Historically, the

Ganges River has symbolized purification for Hindus, who believe drinking and bathing in its waters will lead to salvation. Today twenty-nine cities, seventy towns, and countless villages deposit about 345 million gallons of raw sewage a day directly into the river. Factories add another 70 million gallons of industrial waste and farmers another 6 million tons of chemical fertilizers and 9,000 tons of pesticides.[58] Perhaps more worrisome still, it is believed that widespread changes in coastal ecology are generating "hot systems" in which mutations of the cholera organism are being selected and amplified under new environmental pressures and then transferred to human populations through the food chain. This is the explanation for the appearance of *Vibrio cholerae* 0139 Bengal in 1992, a new strain of cholera and the first non 01 strain capable of causing epidemics, signaling the beginning of the eighth pandemic.[59]

In summary, the seventh pandemic is a reflection of the contradictions of globalization in the late twentieth century. As in previous pandemics, cholera and deprivation remain closely linked. Development of national health systems worldwide led to the reduction and to what was hitherto believed to be the eradication of cholera in many parts of the world. The global spread of cholera since the early 1960s, however, has revealed persistence and growing inequalities within and across countries. Other features of globalization, notably mass migration, social instability, and environmental degradation, present the disease with the opportunity to establish itself in new areas of the world. Cholera, in short, is a mirror for understanding the nature of globalization.

At the same time, an understanding of globalization is needed to explain the distinct epidemiological profile of El Tor cholera. Through changes in human interaction spatially, temporally, and cognitively, cholera has become more geographically widespread and persistent over time. That the disease can "jump" across continents within hours, for example, poses new challenges for national health systems. Indeed, the globalization of cholera may require new responses that more closely integrate different levels and types of governance.

Global Governance for Health:
Learning Lessons Once Again from Cholera

The emergence of global governance as a central concept in international relations responds to a perceived change in the nature of world politics. In contrast to international governance, the defining feature of global governance is its comprehensiveness. Global governance views the globe as a single place within which the boundaries of the interstate system and nation-state have been eroded. Although the nation-state remains an important actor, processes and mechanisms of global governance are growing to encompass the structures of international governance that manage the system of nation-states. The emerging processes and mechanisms of global governance can be seen as forms of supraterritorial authority.[60]

The processes and mechanisms of global governance are diverse, as are the actors and structures that participate within them. In addition to nation-states, these actors include international institutions, governmental organizations, various nonstate actors, regimes, values, and rules.[61] These different actors compete with each other to shape the nature of global order, the establishment of which is the main purpose of global governance. Global governance may be used to stabilize and expand market capitalism on a global scale, as sought by the International Monetary Fund (IMF) and World Bank, or to establish an order based on greater social justice and redistribution of global resources.[62]

Although scholars, practitioners, and policymakers in the health field may not explicitly recognize or widely use the term *global governance,* there is growing recognition of the need to establish more effective mechanisms for addressing a range of global health issues. Such issues are wide-ranging and are reviewed elsewhere.[63] Developing responses to them lead to questions concerning scope of activity, distribution of authority, decisionmaking process, institutional structure, and resource mobilization and allocation.

The development of an effective system for the prevention, control, and treatment of infectious diseases is perhaps the classic transborder health issue. It has long been recognized that diseases do not recognize national borders and that states acting alone are unable to prevent their spread. In recent years, this message has been stated with renewed vigor in relation to emerging and reemerging diseases and globalization. As a U.S. report warns, "The modern world is a very small place, where any city in the world is only a plane ride away from any other. Infectious microbes can easily travel across borders with their human and animal hosts. . . . [And] diseases that arise in other parts of the world are repeatedly introduced into the United States, where they may threaten our national health and security."[64] Similarly, Paul Farmer writes that "EIDs [emerging infectious diseases] have often ignored political boundaries, even though their presence may cause a certain degree of turbulence at national borders. The dynamics of emerging infections will not be captured in national analyses, any more than the diseases are contained by national boundaries."[65]

A brief review of the existing institutional framework for international cooperation on infectious diseases shows a strong emphasis on biomedical understanding of human disease and state-based health systems. Since its founding in 1948, WHO has carried out surveillance and monitoring of various infectious diseases. Diseases deemed to pose a particular international threat, however, have been governed since 1951 under the International Health Regulations (IHR), a consolidation of various International

Sanitary Conventions adopted from the nineteenth century onward. Over the years, the IHR have been periodically updated to take account of changing health needs (e.g., removal of smallpox from the list of notifiable diseases after eradication). In their present form, the IHR set out procedures for limiting the transmission of infectious disease via shipping, aircraft, and other modes of transport. The regulations do not control the movement of international traffic directly but concentrate on controlling the spread of disease where transborder conveyance may occur. The IHR also call on states to "report to WHO, within specific periods, cases of these three diseases [i.e., cholera, plague, and yellow fever] within their territories. Second, to facilitate reporting and deter unnecessary interference with international travel and trade, members must limit their responsive health measures (applied to international traffic for the protection of their territories against these diseases) to maximum measures permitted by these regulations."[66]

Responsibility for the IHR and other infectious disease–related activities falls on WHO's Cluster on Communicable Diseases (CDS), formerly the Division of Emerging and Other Communicable Disease Surveillance and Control (EMC) (now referred to as Communicable Disease Surveillance and Response).

Other international agreements concerned with infectious diseases are the WHO and Food and Agriculture Organization's Codex Alimentarius, the World Trade Organization's Agreement on the Application of Sanitary and Phytosanitary Measures, and the International Civil Aviation Organization's Facilitation to the Convention on International Civil Aviation. Supporting international cooperation, in principle, is a network of national health systems led by ministries of health in each member state and extending to national health services, research institutions, public health laboratories, and monitoring and surveillance systems. Together, it is assumed that WHO coordinates top-down guidance and information, provided from the bottom up by national health systems.

In practice, there are gaps at both the international and national levels. Internationally, the IHR cover only three diseases, and WHO does not have the means to enforce compliance with even these limited stipulations. International surveillance and monitoring relies on the goodwill of governments, but fears of adverse effects on trade or tourism can lead to underreporting. India lost an estimated U.S.$1,700 million in exports, tourism, and transportation services because of the outbreak of plague in 1996.[67] Exports of shellfish by Latin American countries were similarly affected by reports of cholera in the region. Although efforts are in play to revise the IHR to stipulate reporting of "syndromes" rather than diseases, the question of authority remains.

Another difficulty lies in the limited resources available to mount rapid responses to major transborder outbreaks. Given the limits of WHO resources, the U.S. Centers for Disease Control (CDC) at times has stepped in more quickly in health emergencies (e.g., the outbreak of Ebola in northern Zaire in 1976 and the refugee camps in Goma, Zaire). At the national level, variation in health capacity is even more acute. Many lower-income countries have less than U.S.$4 per capita to spend on health care annually.[68] Structural adjustment programs place further pressure on public health expenditure, and the World Bank continues to attribute problems, such as the reemergence of cholera, on the failure to privatize rather than on a crisis in resources. As one World Bank study concludes,

> The return of cholera in 1991 to Latin America and [the] Caribbean region was only a symptom of the deep-seated problems and the fragility and inadequacy of publicly operated water supply and sanitation systems. Consequently, the agencies that operate these systems are entering a crucial phase of deciding whether they can greatly improve their operations while remaining in the public sector or whether they should seek increasing private sector financing and participation in both operations.[69]

To address these deficiencies, international efforts have focused on improving surveillance, monitoring, and reporting systems. WHO is now working to create a Global Surveillance Network using electronic links for rapid exchange of information.[70] In 1994, the Program for Monitoring Emerging Diseases (ProMED) was created with the impetus of sixty prominent experts in human, animal, and plant health. Accessed via the Internet, ProMED is intended to be a global system of early detection and timely response to disease outbreaks. Similarly, the Global Health Network was established to monitor the spread of emerging infectious diseases through links with public health organizations, multilateral organizations, NGOs, and independent research centers. Although such technology is clearly a vital feature of a global system of disease control, this emphasis on technical issues highlights two further flaws in the present system of international health governance.

First, underlying these initiatives is a rational model of policymaking, which assumes that lack of information is the key factor in the globalization of infectious disease. However, as we argue in this essay, the seventh cholera pandemic has been shaped by the structural features of the global political economy that have contributed to the vulnerability of certain populations and environments within and across countries. Second, globalization in its present course has created transborder externalities in the form of health risks that increasingly defy state-centric approaches of the past. Although national epidemiological data remain significant, there is also a need for disaggregated data that allow comparisons and analysis within and across countries and regions. Furthermore, focusing on control measures at the national level amid intensified human interaction has so far reinforced a fortress mentality among many governments.[71] Yet effective control of all infectious diseases at national borders is neither practicable nor ethical. Many diseases remain asymptomatic or have long periods of incubation.

It is here that the existing literature on global governance may offer ideas for creating new forms of authority and institutional linkages to address the challenges of global health. To begin with, the global governance literature highlights the need to be more comprehensive in our approach to global health. Needed, for instance, is a greater appreciation of the link between health and the environment. Douglas Bettcher and Derek Yach point out that public health issues are central components of sustainable development programs and should be incorporated into the system of global governance that has emerged from the United Nations Conference on the Environment and Development (1992) around sustainable development.[72] Piggybacking on strategies for global sustainable development may boost the chances of a system of global health governance being established. Similar linkages between health and changing governance of other sectors, such as agriculture, transportation, communications, and trade and finance, need far greater exploration.

Another central theme of the global governance literature is the need to ensure that the processes and mechanisms of global governance have the support of those governed. Various proponents of global governance agree that there is a need to reform the UN's core institutions so that they are more democratic and representative of the global population. WHO, for example, is an organization often described as governed by a "medical mafia" and influenced by the extrabudgetary funding of a small number of donor governments.[73] At the national and subnational levels, as well, there have long been calls for going beyond the traditional focus on ministries of health and government institutions. Civil society, in particular, is identified as requiring a greater role in policymaking at many levels. For example, the influence of certain global social movements, such as the women's health movement, has been recognized as positively contributing to the democratization of certain policy issues (i.e., population policy).

The nation-state and existing institutions of international health governance (e.g., the WHO and IHR) will remain central to any future system of global health governance. The challenge for scholars and policymakers is how to construct processes and mechanisms of global health governance that recognize the interests of nation-states and civil society. This is a massive challenge, yet recent developments in global health governance suggest some optimism about the ability to meet it. For example, plans for a Framework Convention on Tobacco Control bring together shared interests across nation-states, civil society, and the business community (e.g., the pharmaceutical sector) for a more comprehensive effort to control the production and consumption of tobacco. WHO's policy document "Health for All in the 21st Century" adopts a similar approach to deal with persistent inequalities in health within and across countries.[74] These initiatives are directly concerned with strengthening global health governance, proposed by an intergovernmental organization (i.e., WHO) and supported by an amalgam of member states, civil society groups, and individuals.

Finally, there is a need for critical analysis of health determinants that conceptualize social change in the context of long-term and fundamental socioeconomic structures, rather than shorter-term, technically specific change. Such an approach leads to a recognition of the structure-agent links that exist between globalization and health, including the possibility that present forms of globalization are, in fact, incompatible with human health. Importantly, critical theorists see globalization as a historical process constructed not by rationality but by embedded power relations and consequences. Locating cholera and other global health issues within this reflexive starting point therefore seeks to address, and ultimately redress, the underlying causal factors behind ill health.

Conclusion

In summary, we have analyzed cholera from the nineteenth century as a case study of the links between globalization and health. How human populations have lived—population size and distribution, social structure, cultural practices, distribution of resources—has historically been linked to patterns of health and disease. We have also sought to show how globalization is changing the nature of human societies across the world and, consequently, the health of populations. At the same time, cholera has been reflective of particular features of globalization from its earlier stages to the present.

Globalization has shaped the pattern of the disease, the vulnerability of certain populations, and the ability of public health systems to respond effectively. The contributing features of globalization to the epidemiologically distinct seventh pandemic have included socioeconomic instability, intensified human interaction and mobility, environmental degradation, and inequalities within and across countries.

As public health systems have struggled to control the seventh pandemic, reports of an eighth pandemic came in 1993. As we described earlier, the new pandemic involves a new strain of *Vibrio cholerae*, believed hardier than El Tor cholera in terms of environmental adaptation. Its emergence is thought to have resulted from changes to coastal ecologies in South Asia. By 1995, the pandemic spread to Calcutta, India, with 15,000 cases and 230 deaths, and then moved rapidly to Dhaka, Bangladesh, where 600 cases were reported daily. Severe flooding in Bangladesh in 1998 worsened conditions significantly. Reaching 100,000 cases by 1996, the disease has since spread to Pakistan, Thailand, and ten other Southeast

Asian countries. Travel-associated cases have been reported in the United States, Europe, and Japan.[75] Cholera is poised, it seems, to offer yet another opportunity to learn hard lessons. ⊕

Notes

Kelley Lee is senior lecturer in International Health Policy at the London School of Hygiene and Tropical Medicine. She is author of *Historical Dictionary of the World Health Organization* (1998) and chairs the WHO External Advisory Group on Globalization and Health. Richard Dodgson received his doctorate from the University of Newcastle upon Tyne, England. He has taught at the University of Newcastle upon Tyne, the University of Durham, and Sunderland University.

1. Richard Preston, *The Hot Zone* (New York: Corgi, 1994); Leslie Garrett, *The Coming Plague: Newly Emerging Diseases in a World Out of Balance* (New York: Farrar, Straus & Giroux, 1994); Frank Ryan, *Virus X: Understanding the Real Threat of the New Pandemic Plagues* (London: HarperCollins, 1996).

2. Institute of Medicine, *Emerging Infections: Microbial Threats to Health in the United States* (Washington, D.C.: National Academy Press, 1992); U.S. Committee on International Science, Engineering, and Technology Policy (CISET), *Global Microbial Threats in the 1990s* (Washington, D.C.: Working Group on Emerging and Re-emerging Infectious Diseases, 1995); Institute of Medicine, *America's Vital Interest in Global Health* (Washington, D.C.: National Academy Press, 1997).

3. Louise Amoore, Richard Dodgson, Barry Gills, Paul Langley, Don Marshall, and Iain Watson, "Overturning Globalisation: Resisting the Teleological, Reclaiming the Political," *New Political Economy* 2, no. 1 (1997): 179–195.

4. Kelley Lee, "Globalisation and Health Policy: A Review of the Literature and Proposed Research and Policy Agenda," in Pan American Health Organization, *Health and Human Development in the New Global Economy* (Washington, D.C.: Pan American Health Organization, 2000).

5. Roland Robertson, *Globalization: Social Theory and Global Culture* (London: Sage, 1992).

6. F. Cairncross, *The Death of Distance* (Cambridge: Harvard Business School Press, 1997).

7. Alan Rugman and Michael Gestrin, "New Rules for Multilateral Investment," *International Executive* 39, no. 1 (1997): 21–33.

8. Anthony Giddens, *The Consequences of Modernity* (London: Polity Press, 1990); Robertson, *Globalization.*

9. Robert Clark, "Global Life Systems: Biological Dimensions of Globalisation," *Global Society* 11, no. 3 (1997): 280.

10. Mark Nathan Cohen, "The History of Infectious Disease," in Mark Nathan Cohen, *Health and the Rise of Civilization* (New Haven: Yale University Press, 1989); Arno Karlen, *Man and Microbes, Disease and Plagues in History and Modern Times* (New York: Simon & Schuster, 1995).

11. J. N. Hays, "New Diseases and Transatlantic Exchanges," in J. N. Hays, *The Burdens of Disease, Epidemics and Human Response in Western History* (New Brunswick, N.J.: Rutgers University Press, 1998), pp. 62–77, quotation from p. 72.

12. Cohen, "The History of Infectious Disease."

13. There are more than sixty serogroups of *Vibrio cholerae,* but only serogroup 01 causes cholera. Serogroup 01 has two biotypes (classical and El Tor), and each biotype has two serotypes (Ogawa and Inaba).

234   *Globalization and Cholera*

14. World Health Organization, *Guidelines for Cholera Control* (Geneva: WHO, 1993).

15. R. S. Speck, "Cholera," in K. F. Kiple, ed., *The Cambridge World History of Human Diseases* (Cambridge: Cambridge University Press, 1993), p. 647.

16. Eric Hobsbawm, *The Age of Capital: 1848–1875* (London: Weidenfield & Nicolson, 1975), p. 310.

17. Sheldon Watts, "Cholera and Civilization: Great Britain and India, 1817 to 1920," in Sheldon Watts, *Epidemics and History, Disease, Power and Imperialism* (New Haven: Yale University Press, 1997), pp. 167–212.

18. R. S. Bray, *Armies of Pestilence: The Effects of Pandemics on History* (Cambridge: Lutterworth Press, 1996), pp. 180–183.

19. Watts, "Cholera and Civilization," p. 194.

20. Amid a severe cholera outbreak in London, John Snow found a concentration of cases around a pump in Broad Street. Hoping to prove his theory that cholera is a waterborne disease, he removed the pump handle in front of public officials; and the outbreak was contained.

21. David Armstrong, *The Rise of International Organisation: A Short History* (London: Macmillan, 1982), p. 43.

22. Bray, *Armies of Pestilence*.

23. The causative agent is named after the El Tor quarantine camp on the Sinai Peninsula, where it was first isolated in 1905 from the intestines of pilgrims returning from Mecca.

24. World Health Organization, *Guidelines for Cholera Control*.

25. Leonard Bruce-Chwatt, "Global Problems of Imported Disease," *Advances in Parasitology* 11 (1973): 86.

26. M. Narkevich et al., "The Seventh Pandemic of Cholera in the USSR, 1961–89," *Bulletin of the World Health Organization* 71, no. 2 (1993): 189–196.

27. Bruce-Chwatt, "Global Problems of Imported Disease."

28. D. Barua, "The Global Epidemiology of Cholera in Recent Years," *Proceedings of the Royal Society of Medicine* 65 (1972): 423–432.

29. J. van Bergen, "Epidemiology and Health Policy—A World of Difference? A Case-Study of a Cholera Outbreak in Kaputa Distict, Zambia," *Social Science and Medicine* 43, no. 1 (1996): 93–99.

30. Richard Guerrant, "Twelve Messages from Enteric Infections for Science and Society," *American Journal of Tropical Medicine and Hygiene* 51, no. 1 (1994): 27.

31. Barua, "The Global Epidemiology of Cholera in Recent Years," pp. 426–448.

32. S. McCarthy, R. McPhearson, A. Guarino, and J. Gaines, "Toxigenic Vibrio Cholerae 01 and Cargo Ships Entering Gulf of Mexico," *Lancet* 339 (1992): 624–625.

33. Andrew Cliff and Peter Haggett, "Disease Implications of Global Change," in R. J. Johnston, P. J. Taylor, and M. J. Watts, eds., *Geographies of Global Change: Remapping the World in the Late 20th Century* (Oxford, England: Blackwell, 1995), p. 209.

34. K. F. Kaferstein, Y. Motarjemi, and Douglas Bettcher, "Foodborne Disease Control: A Transnational Challenge," *Emerging Infectious Diseases* 3, no. 4 (1997): 8.

35. Bruce Jay Plotkin and Ann Marie Kimball, "Designing an International Policy and Legal Framework for the Control of Emerging Infectious Diseases: First Steps," *Emerging Infectious Diseases* 3, no. 1 (1997): 1–9.

36. David L. Heymann and Guenael R. Rodier, "Global Surveillance of Communicable Diseases," *Emerging Infectious Diseases* 4, no. 3 (1998): 1–5.

37. Bruce-Chwatt, "Global Problems of Imported Disease," p. 87.

38. William Booth, "Cholera's Mysterious Journey North," *Washington Post,* 26 August 1991.

39. Robert Tauxe, Eric Mintz, and Robert Quick, "Epidemic Cholera in the New World: Translating Field Epidemiology into New Prevention Strategies," *Emerging Infectious Diseases* 1, no. 4 (1995): 141–146.

40. J. Todd Weber, William C. Levine, David P. Hopkins, and Robert V. Tauxe, "Cholera in the United States, 1965–1991," *Archives of Internal Medicine* 154 (14 March 1994): 551–556.

41. Barbara Crossette, "Kofi Annan's Astonishing Facts," *New York Times,* 27 September 1998, p. WK16; United Nations Development Programme, *Human Development Report* (New York: UNDP, 1998).

42. Antonio Ugalde and J. Jackson, "The World Bank and International Health Policy: A Critical Review," *Journal of International Development* 7, no. 3 (1995): 525–542.

43. World Bank, *Financing Health Services in Developing Countries: An Agenda for Reform* (Washington, D.C.: IBRD, 1987); World Bank, *World Development Report: Investing in Health* (Washington, D.C.: IBRD, 1993).

44. Mary Ruggie, *Realignments in the Welfare State: Health Policy in the United States, Britain, and Canada* (New York: Columbia University Press, 1996).

45. Ankie Hoogvelt, *Globalisation and the Postcolonial World: The New Political Economy of Development* (London: Macmillan, 1997); Robert Beaglehole and Ruth Bonita, *Public Health at the Crossroads, Achievements and Prospects* (London: Cambridge University Press, 1997).

46. Douglas Bettcher, Steve Sapirie, and Eric Goon, "Essential Public Health Functions: Results of the International Delphi Study," *World Health Statistics Quarterly* 51 (1998): 44–54.

47. Alberto Cardelle, "Health Care in the Time of Reform: Emerging Policies for Private-Public Sector Collaboration in Health, *North-South Issues* 6, no. 1 (1997): 1–8.

48. Jose Sanchez and David Taylor, "Cholera," *Lancet* 349 (21 June 1997): 1825–1830.

49. World Health Organization, *The World Health Report 1996: Fighting Disease, Fostering Development* (Geneva: WHO, 1996).

50. Alexander Moroz, quoted in Ryan, *Virus X,* p. 108.

51. Mary Wilson, "Travel and the Emergence of Infectious Diseases," *Emerging Infectious Diseases* 1, no. 2 (1995): 39–46.

52. "Migration: The Facts," *New Internationalist,* no. 305 (1998): 18.

53. Mark Duffield, "Complex Emergencies and the Crisis of Developmentalism," *IDS Bulletin* 25, no. 4 (1994): 38. Duffield defines complex emergencies as "protracted political crises resulting from sectarian or predatory indigenous responses to socioeconomic stress and marginalisation."

54. A. Zwi, "Cholera in South Africa," *South African Outlook* 11 (1981): 172–177.

55. Susan Cookson et al., "Immigrant and Refugee Health," *Emerging Infectious Diseases* 4, no. 3 (1998): 1–2.

56. Sanchez and Taylor, "Cholera"; Heymann and Rodier, "Global Surveillance of Communicable Diseases," p. 2.

57. A. J. McMichael, B. Bolin, R. Costanza, G. Daily, C. Folke, K. Lindahl-Kiessling, E. Lindgren, and B. Niklasson, "Globalization and the Sustainability of Human Health: An Ecological Perspective," *BioScience* 49, no. 3 (1999): 205–210.

58. Crossette, "Kofi Annan's Astonishing Facts."

236   *Globalization and Cholera*

59. Paul Epstein, "Emerging Diseases and Ecosystem Instability: New Threats to Public Health," *American Journal of Public Health* 85, no. 2 (February 1995): 168–172.

60. Jan Aart Scholte, "The Globalization of World Politics," in John Baylis and Steve Smith, eds., *The Globalization of World Politics: An Introduction to International Relations* (Oxford: Oxford University Press, 1997), pp. 13–30.

61. James Rosenau, "Governance in the Twenty-first Century," *Global Governance* 1, no. 1 (January–April 1995): 13–43.

62. André C. Drainville, "The Fetishism of Global Civil Society," in M. P. Smith and L. E. Guarnizo, eds., *Transnationalism from Below* (London: Transaction Publishers, 1998), p. 37; Richard Falk, *On Humane Governance: Toward a New Global Politics* (Cambridge, England: Polity Press, 1995).

63. Lee, "Globalisation and Health Policy."

64. U.S. Committee on International Science, Engineering, and Technology Policy, *Global Microbial Threats in the 1990s.*

65. Paul Farmer, "Social Inequalities and Emerging Infectious Diseases," *Emerging Infectious Diseases* 2, no. 4 (1996): 259–266.

66. Quoted in Plotkin and Kimball, "Designing an International Policy and Legal Framework," p. 3.

67. Collette Kinnon, "Globalization, World Trade: Bringing Health into the Picture," *World Health Forum* 19 (1998): 397–406.

68. World Health Organization, *The World Health Report, 1995: Bridging the Gaps* (Geneva: WHO, 1995).

69. Emanuel Idelovitch and Klas Ringskog, *Private Sector Participation in Water Supply and Sanitation in Latin America* (Washington, D.C.: World Bank, Directions in Development Series, 1995).

70. World Health Organization, *Global Cholera Update* (Geneva: WHO, 1998).

71. Institute of Medicine, *America's Vital Interest in Global Health.*

72. Douglas Bettcher and Derek Yach, "The Globalisation of Public Health Ethics?" *Millennium: Journal of International Studies* 27, no. 3 (1998): 495.

73. D. Pitt, "Power in the UN Superbureaucracy: A New Byzantium?" in D. Pitt and T. Weiss, *The Nature of United Nations Bureaucracies* (London: Croom Helm, 1992), chap. 2; P. Vaughan, S. Mogedal, S. E. Kruse, K. Lee, G. Walt, and K. de Wilde, *Co-operation for Health Development: Extrabudgetary Funds and the World Health Organisation* (Oslo: Governments of Australia, Norway, and the United Kingdom, 1995).

74. World Health Organization, "Health for All: Policy for the 21st Century," WHO Doc. WHA51/5, May 1998.

75. Sanchez and Taylor, "Cholera."

[27]

Public–private partnerships for health: their main targets, their diversity, and their future directions

Roy Widdus[1]

Abstract The global burden of disease, especially the part attributable to infectious diseases, disproportionately affects populations in developing countries. Inadequate access to pharmaceuticals plays a role in perpetuating this disparity. Drugs and vaccines may not be accessible because of weak distribution infrastructures or because development of the desired products has been neglected. This situation can be tackled with push interventions to lower the costs and risks of product development for industry, with pull interventions providing economic and market incentives, and with the creation of infrastructures allowing products to be put into use. If appropriately motivated, pharmaceutical companies can bring to partnerships expertise in product development, production process development, manufacturing, marketing, and distribution — all of which are lacking in the public sector. A large variety of public–private partnerships, combining the skills and resources of a wide range of collaborators, have arisen for product development, disease control through product donation and distribution, or the general strengthening or coordination of health services. Administratively, such partnerships may either involve affiliation with international organizations, i.e. they are essentially public-sector programmes with private-sector participation, or they may be legally independent not-for-profit bodies. These partnerships should be regarded as social experiments; they show promise but are not a panacea. New ventures should be built on need, appropriateness, and lessons on good practice learnt from experience. Suggestions are made for public, private, and joint activities that could help to improve the access of poor populations to the pharmaceuticals and health services they need.

Keywords Intersectoral cooperation; Public sector; Drug industry; Pharmaceutical preparations/supply and distribution; Social justice; Motivation; Forecasting (*source: MeSH*).

Mots clés Coopération intersectorielle; Secteur public; Industrie pharmaceutique; Préparations pharmaceutiques/ressources et distribution; Justice sociale; Motivation; Prévision (*source: INSERM*).

Palabras clave Cooperación intersectorial; Sector público; Industria farmacéutica; Preparaciones farmacéuticas/provisión y distribución; Justicia social; Motivación; Predicción (*fuente: BIREME*).

Bulletin of the World Health Organization, 2001, **79**: 713–720.

Voir page 719 le résumé en français. En la página 720 figura un resumen en español.

Introduction

The disparities in health between rich and poor populations are, in a significant measure, attributable to a lack of access to drugs and vaccines as well as to differences in the geographical distributions of certain disease agents and sanitation. Historically, drugs and vaccines have become available through an informal division of responsibilities between public entities and private companies, all undertaking activities in accordance with their mandates or motivations. This division of labour constitutes a poorly defined partnership in which the outcomes desired by different parties have never been explicitly negotiated. In the more economically advanced countries it is generally regarded as reasonably successful, having led to the availability of a broad range of effective drugs and vaccines. However, this kind of system is not particularly responsive to the specific health needs of the world's poorest populations.

Substantial differences in health status have probably always existed between rich and poor populations and have certainly been documented for decades. Improved comparative data are now reinforcing the long-standing humanitarian and ethical concerns about inequalities in access to health

[1] Manager, Initiative on Public–Private Partnerships for Health, Global Forum for Health Research, International Centre Cointrin, Block G, Third Floor, 20 route de Pré-Bois, Case postale 1826, 1215 Geneva 15, Switzerland (email: info@ippph.org).

Ref. No. **00-1103**

Global Health

products, health services, and resource allocation. Trends in increased travel, global awareness, information flow, and commerce — collectively termed globalization — have raised the level of interest about the possible causes and consequences of the uneven distribution of disease, particularly of emerging infections. As a result, increasing attention is being directed at the need to reduce global disparities in health.

Globalization has been accompanied by a reassessment of the strengths and limitations of public/governmental, private/commercial, and civil society institutions in grappling with world problems. Particularly in the health arena it seems to be recognized that intractable problems require not just better coordination of traditional roles but also new ways of working together in order to achieve a synergistic combination of the strengths, resources, and expertise of the different sectors.

With the aim of stimulating discussion on the most effective types of future action this paper presents a preliminary examination of experience in public–private partnerships. The focus is on partnerships between international or governmental agencies on the one hand and commercial pharmaceutical companies on the other. Most of these partnerships also include civil society bodies, e.g. nongovernmental organizations. Simple donations of funds or products by pharmaceutical companies, while potentially useful, are not considered here, nor is general corporate philanthropy.

Disparity in health between rich and poor

The health disparity between rich and poor countries results in average life spans of 77 and 52 years respectively (*1*). Deaths attributable to infectious diseases (Table 1) contribute most to the disparity. Deaths associated with diarrhoea and respiratory infection are rare in industrialized countries but are the major killers of children in developing countries. Diseases that do not occur in industrialized countries, e.g. malaria and schistosomiasis, or ones that are comparatively rare in these countries, e.g. tuberculosis and HIV/AIDS, impose a heavy burden on both adults and children in developing countries. The burden of morbidity from a number of untreated, debilitating but rarely fatal diseases in developing countries, including sexually transmitted infections, has a substantial impact on productivity.

An analysis of the differences in the disease burden between the poorest and the richest 20% of the world's population suggested that, in 1990, nearly 80% of the difference between the poor and rich in terms of death and disability-adjusted life years was attributable to communicable diseases (*4*). This is still likely to be true, as the incidences of HIV, malaria, and tuberculosis are increasing. Furthermore, the ageing of the population in the developing world can be expected to bring increases in the absolute burden of noncommunicable diseases (*5*).

Table 1. **Deaths from infectious diseases worldwide, 1998** [a]

Causes [b]	Deaths
No satisfactory vaccine available when data compiled	
AIDS	2 285 000 (27.47) [c]
Tuberculosis	1 498 000 (18.01)
Malaria	1 110 000 (13.34)
Pneumococcus	1 110 000 (13.22)
Rotavirus	800 000 (9.62)
Shigella	600 000 (7.21)
Enterotoxigenic *E. coli*	500 000 (6.02)
Respiratory syncytial virus	160 000 (1.92)
Schistosomiasis [d]	150 000 (1.80)
Leishmaniasis	42 000 (0.50)
Trypanosmiasis	40 000 (0.48)
Chagas disease	17 000 (0.20)
Dengue	15 000 (0.18)
Leprosy	2000 (0.03)
Subtotal	**8 319 000 (100)**
Satisfactory vaccine available	
Hepatitis B	1 000 000 (30.55)
Measles	888 000 (27.12)
Haemophilus influenzae type B	500 000 (15.27)
Tetanus	410 000 (12.52)
Pertussis	346 000 (10.57)
Cholera	120 000 (3.67)
Diphtheria	5000 (0.15)
Japanese encephalitis	3000 (0.09)
Poliomyelitis	2000 (0.06)
Subtotal	**3 274 000 (100)**
Grand total	**11 593 000**

[a] Source: unless otherwise indicated, ref. *2*.

[b] Some pathogens are not included because etiology-specific estimates were not available.

[c] Figures in parentheses are percentages.

[d] Source: ref. *3*.

Gwatkin & Guillot have also analysed the poor–rich health disparity in terms of the fraction of total burden attributable to various diseases (*4*). Pharmaceuticals exist that can treat most and prevent many of the diseases causing the bulk of morbidity and mortality in the poorer countries, with the caveat that for some diseases the available therapies require improvement in respect of ease of administration or length of treatment. Moreover, vaccines need to be improved for tuberculosis and developed for HIV/AIDS, malaria, and some other diseases. The disparity in health status probably results largely from differential access to drugs that are already available as well as to sanitation and safe water, which influence the transmission of some diseases.

Determinants of access to pharmaceuticals

The determinants of appropriate access to pharmaceuticals of acceptable quality can be categorized as in

Box 1. In debates on how to improve access, drug affordability — interpreted as manufacturers' selling prices — is often simplistically singled out because it appears to be especially amenable to control. However, access presents a multifaceted problem and action is required on many fronts.

Each year, WHO compiles estimates from national experts on the percentages of countries' populations thought to have access to the essential drugs on the basic minimum list, most of which are off-patent. Fig. 1 shows that in many countries, large numbers of people still have unacceptably low levels of access to basic drugs.

It is difficult to identify which of the determinants of access should be dealt with in order to achieve the greatest possible benefit. A lack of availability of any useful product is the dominant determinant of access for only a few diseases. In some instances, a better preventive product, such as a vaccine, would lead to improved disease control; in these cases, the product development step is essential. For many diseases, however, access is determined by the systems of pharmaceutical distribution and by economic factors.

An analysis of access to pharmaceuticals in sub-Saharan Africa during the 1980s and early 1990s indicated that there were major losses in therapeutic benefit because of inefficiencies in distribution systems (7). Given the economic problems in sub-

Saharan Africa it is hardly surprising that the situation is similar today, as confirmed by WHO's estimates of the scale of unsatisfactory access to essential drugs (Fig. 1).

It is clear in sub-Saharan Africa, and it is probably also true in other parts of the world, that one of the major areas requiring attention is the inefficiency of pharmaceutical distribution systems. This is principally a responsibility of national governments. Additional analysis is needed so that global efforts can be guided. In this connection it would probably also be useful to assess the fraction of the burden attributable to each disease that might be reduced by access to off-patent drugs and vaccines (comprising 95% of the WHO model list of essential drugs); access to recently licensed/patented drugs and vaccines; and new products, yet to be developed. Different actions are already possible and are needed for each of these categories, but the required analysis has not yet been conducted.

It is important to recognize that the term "developing countries" now covers a wide range of economic well-being, ranging from poverty to relative affluence. In Brazil, China, India, Indonesia, and Mexico, for example, there are moderate to large populations that are comparatively rich. Thus in the developing world there are countries and populations that can afford, much more easily than the poorest, to pay for health products and services either directly or, preferably, through schemes based on the principle of collective health insurance.

Box 1. **Determinants of access to pharmaceuticals**

- **Availability** (i.e. whether a satisfactory product has been developed)
  - basic research
  - discovery
  - development
  - marketing

- **Accessibility**

  Quality, selection, prescribing, and use
  - Assurance of quality
  - Rational selection
  - Appropriate prescribing
  - Appropriate use, including patient compliance

  Effectiveness and efficiency of distribution system
  - reliable sources of supply
  - availability where needed

  Economic factors
  - resources for financing
  - costs
  - pricing policies and controls
  - price at point of use, including distributor mark-ups

  Knowledge and health-seeking behaviour of consumers
  - social norms
  - educational interventions
  - variations with socioeconomic status of potential consumers

---

Interventions to improve access

The prospective market for products needed largely or exclusively in poorer developing countries is commercially unattractive in comparison with, for example, that linked to chronic health problems in affluent populations. In other words there is an unfavourable outlook for return on investment (Fig. 2, segment B relative to segment A). The balance can be moved positively by the reduction of commercial expenditure (segment A) or by increased prospects of revenue (segment B).

Although there is considerable diversity in size, orientation, country location, and motivation among pharmaceutical companies, they consistently pay less attention to poor populations than those that are rich because of the need to provide a return to investors from the worldwide market (Fig. 3).

Various interventions have been considered for stimulating product development and/or reducing infrastructural and economic barriers to access. These are generally grouped into pull and push interventions, as described below.

Pull interventions

An economic incentive is required for industry to address the needs of developing countries in a sustained manner. Pull mechanisms should ideally include more attractive markets in the larger middle-income countries, where individuals themselves or

Special Theme – Public–Private Partnerships

Fig. 1. **Percentage of population with regular access to essential drugs, 1997**

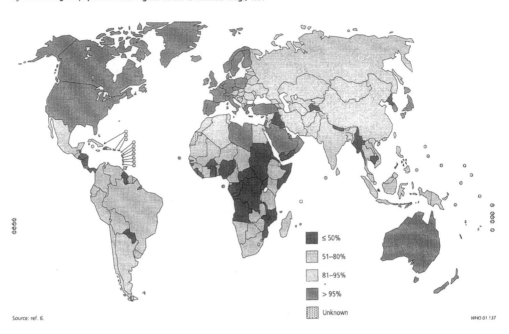

Source: ref. 6.   WHO 01.137

Legend:
- ≤ 50%
- 51–80%
- 81–95%
- > 95%
- Unknown

their governments can afford to purchase products and, in the most impoverished countries, some sort of market-guarantee funding from external aid. Other possible pull interventions include tax credits on sales for priority products and early recommendations for product introduction from international organizations. The creation of health service infrastructures, allowing products and services to reach people in need, is essentially a pull mechanism since it is necessary to achieve a return on investment.

Push interventions

For industry to be attracted to the development of products for neglected diseases there must also be push interventions. These reduce the costs and risks to industry of developing the products. Push mechanisms can take many forms, such as public investment in basic research, sharing the costs of efficacy trials or other aspects of development, sharing the costs of production facilities, harmonizing international regulatory requirements, and introducing tax credits for investment in research and development.

Push and pull interventions typically require legislation or funding appropriations. They are generally created for a category of products, as in the orphan drug legislation in the United States of America. It was concluded at a recent conference that the most effective solution would probably be to create a mix of the two kinds of intervention (*10*).

However, a unique combination of challenges is faced in the progression of each product from research concept to wide utilization. In order to facilitate this progression there has frequently been a joining of forces by public and private sector organizations in new collaborative mechanisms. These public–private partnerships allow the different skills of the two sectors to be focused on the challenges specific to the products and diseases in question.

Although pharmaceutical markets in developing countries may expand, it appears that special arrangements will be necessary to meet the drug and vaccine requirements of some countries for the foreseeable future, including external financial assistance and, perhaps, concessionary or tiered pricing. Concessionary supply to the poorest countries is one of the most promising, although difficult, areas for public–private sector dialogue.

What forms have public–private partnerships taken?

The term "partnership" has recently been used to cover collaboration in general and the emerging forms of collaboration. However, it poorly represents the diversity of new relationships, a wide variety of which have been placed under the umbrella term of "public–private partnerships" (*11*).

Commercial pharmaceutical and other health-related companies have entered into a remarkable number of collaborations with public sector and civil society organizations in order to improve access to health products for poor populations. An initial inventory of over 70 collaborative relationships, mostly at the international level, has been established under the Geneva-based Initiative on Public–Private Partnerships for Health. These ventures involve a diversity of arrangements, varying with regard to participants, legal status, governance, management, policy-setting prerogatives, participants, contributions, and operational roles (*11*). Public–private partnerships for health should be distinguished from the trend to privatization, i.e. the private sector for-profit provision of health services. In the latter case, the public health policy goal and the rules under which for-profit entities operate are set and enforced solely by government agencies. The objectives of health partnerships are outlined in Box 2.

Among the legally independent, not-for-profit, public–private partnerships that have been established to deal with requirements for product development are the Medicines for Malaria Venture (for malaria drug replacements) (*12*), and the International AIDS Vaccine Initiative (for HIV/AIDS vaccines) (*13*). The Global Alliance for TB Drug Development is one of a number of partnerships that have just been launched (*14*).

The best known of the partnerships for disease control are the donation/distribution partnerships involving donations of albendazole (*15*), eflornithine (*16, 17*), leprosy multidrug therapy (MDT) (*18*), Malarone® (*19*), Mectizan® (*20, 21*), and Zithromax® (*22*). The contributions from the companies concerned have gone beyond the provision of products and have included involvement in supporting activities to ensure efficient distribution and effective use. Most of these donation/distribution programmes use products that are curative and relatively easy to administer in that few doses are required. Notwithstanding the health benefits, concerns have been expressed about these partnerships (*23*). When other services are absent, partnerships directed to the distribution and utilization of donated products may not tackle the health problems of highest priority, as perceived

---

Box 2. Objectives of a health partnership

- developing a product
- distributing a donated or subsidized product, to control a specific disease
- disease control through product donation and distribution
- strengthening health services
- educating the public
- improving product quality or regulation
- coordinating multifaceted efforts

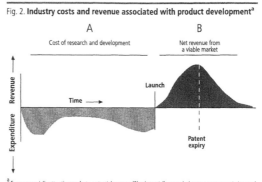

Fig. 2. **Industry costs and revenue associated with product development**[a]

ᵃ For commercially attractive products, potential revenue (B) substantially exceeds the average costs to industry of research and development, including failures (A).

Expenditure on clinical studies, manufacturing, marketing, etc. continues after the launch but in the diagram are deducted from revenue in the interest of simplicity.

Costs to industry for vaccine development are reported to be approximately the same as those for drugs but with lower amounts spent in early development of vaccine concepts (that typically come from publicly funded basic research) and higher costs for production process development and efficacy trials. Many (but not all) vaccines have a relatively long life-cycle but revenue falls as competition increases.

Source: ref. 8.   *WHO 01.138*

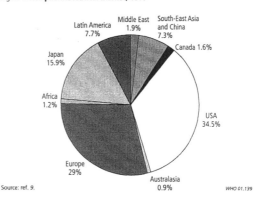

Fig. 3. **World pharmaceutical market, 1997**

Source: ref. 9.   *WHO 01.139*

locally. However, they are likely to be welcomed if they meet a need.

Particularly in relation to HIV/AIDS, partnerships are emerging which aim to strengthen health services. They include the Gates Foundation/Merck Botswana Comprehensive HIV/AIDS Partnership (*24*). Other partnerships, mostly aiming to improve coordination, are managed from within international organizations. The lodging of a partnership within a host organization significantly influences the rules governing its operations. Some so-called public–private partnerships could be more accurately described as public sector programmes with private sector participation. Collaborations in this category include the former Children's Vaccine Initiative, which had a secretariat in WHO, and the current Roll

Back Malaria (*25*), Safe Injection Global Network (*26*), and Stop TB initiatives (*27*), all of which have secretariats in WHO. The successor to the Children's Vaccine Initiative, the Global Alliance for Vaccines and Immunization (*28*) has its secretariat in UNICEF, but the major funding vehicle associated with its work, the Global Fund for Children's Vaccines (*29*), is a legally independent, not-for-profit, private sector body.

Most partnerships have relied on the altruism of pharmaceutical companies and the prospect of good public relations. Few of the identified partnership have explicitly attempted to expand the sale of health products, for example by tapping new market segments. The exceptions include the social marketing of contraceptives and oral rehydration salts, and the creation of an otherwise unserviced market of the poorest countries for new vaccines, proposed by the Children's Vaccine Initiative in conjunction with UNICEF and WHO and subsequently implemented under the Global Fund for Children's Vaccines.

Apparent good practices for public–private partnerships are being analysed by various groups, including the Initiative on Public-Private Partnerships for Health.

Where should individual sector and partnership efforts focus in the future?

Partnerships between public/governmental entities, private/commercial entities, and civil society have a contribution to make in improving the health of the poor by combining the different skills and resources of various organizations in innovative ways. Public agencies clearly benefit from working in collaboration with the private sector in areas where the public sector lacks expertise and experience, e.g. in product development, production process development, manufacturing, marketing, and distribution.

However, there are areas, such as public health policy-making and regulatory approval, where the concept of partnership with for-profit enterprise is not appropriate. The purposes of partnerships should therefore be carefully considered and well articulated.

Partnerships appear to be most justified where: traditional ways of working independently have a limited impact on a problem; the specific desired goals can be agreed by potential collaborators; there is relevant complementary expertise in both sectors; the long-term interests of each sector are fulfilled (i.e. there are benefits to all parties); and the contributions of expertise and resources are reasonably balanced.

Public–private partnerships should not be expected to substitute for action on responsibilities that properly rest elsewhere. In particular, public sector agencies should continue to: fund fundamental research; set standards for product safety, efficacy, and quality; establish systems whereby citizens have adequate access to health products and services; use public resources in an efficient manner; and create environments in which commercial enterprise is appropriately motivated to meet the needs of whole populations.

Constructive analysis of the appropriateness, governance, accountability, operations, and benefits of partnerships is only possible when the subjects of analysis are properly defined. Such analysis requires the variation in arrangements for partnerships, particularly as regards legal status, to be taken into account.

Public–private partnerships should generally be viewed as social experiments that are attempting to learn how to tackle intractable health problems in better ways. There is no formula for constructing them and it is unlikely that a universally applicable one will be found. Criticisms of partnerships have been made (*30*) but it should be borne in mind that, without them, little new would be happening to tackle certain problems.

Public–private partnerships can be helpful but they are not a panacea. In the poorer countries, action is needed to overcome market failure and weak delivery systems that limit the availability and accessibility of pharmaceuticals and result in health disparities.

Certain actions by the public sector alone would mobilize new resources, strengthen demand, and allow market mechanisms to meet health needs in a broader range of countries, and more broadly within countries. Similarly, the for-profit private sector could also take some actions unilaterally to build a better base on which to construct partnerships. Building on these actions, collaborative efforts between the public and private sectors would yield added value. Examples of the contributions each sector could make individually and jointly are given in Box 3. Identifying the components of an appropriate strategy is relatively easy in comparison with the difficulties of implementation. It is necessary for all players, including many who are distrustful of those with whom they need to collaborate, to adopt a long-term view. Implementation requires long-term commitment. The onus of seeking new and more effective ways of working on intractable health problems rests as much — if not more — on the public-sector, governmental and intergovernmental agencies as on the private sector institutions, as the former carry the responsibility for the public's health. ∎

Acknowledgements

Funding for this work was provided to the Initiative on Public–Private Partnerships for Health of the Global Forum for Health Research by the Bill and Melinda Gates Foundation, the Rockefeller Foundation, and the World Bank.

Conflicts of interest: none declared.

Box 3. **Action that could be taken by the public and private sectors**

The **public sector** could:
- mobilize new resources for financing health, both within countries and from external sources, to help the poorest people;
- establish public health priorities for drugs, vaccines, diagnostics, and other health products;
- create fair health care financing systems to cover all people;
- assess the disease burden for major pathogens, country by country;
- assess the economic impact of diseases, country by country;
- conduct cost-effectiveness assessments for existing and anticipated products;
- strengthen research capability, including that associated with clinical trial sites in areas where certain diseases are endemic, through increased funding and training;
- support legislation that provides incentives or lowers the costs and risks of developing new or improved products for neglected diseases;
- support market segmentation for the poorest countries and price-tiering policies by industry;
- support market assurance mechanisms not only politically but also with solid financial appropriations.[a]

The **for-profit private sector** could:
- increase the use of devices such as licensing, tiered royalties, market segmentation, and tiered pricing to make products more accessible to all in need;
- allow wider access, under appropriate legal conditions, to chemical compound libraries in order to facilitate the search for new indications for old drugs;
- broaden personnel exchanges in order to allow public sector programmes to benefit from private sector skills, e.g. market/demand forecasting;

- create information policies in order to permit easier identification of partners for potential collaboration by interested parties.

The **collaborative efforts between the public and private sectors** could:
- agree on a working definition of the neediest countries and on how to target resources and special attention to them;
- estimate the need, demand, and uptake for existing and new products in developing countries collaboratively, since the public sector has the data and the private sector has the expertise;
- manage the challenges of concessionary supply to the poorer countries, including preventing the diversion of products from intended beneficiaries to markets where prices are higher and the potential erosion of revenue from the richer markets necessary to support continued research and development;
- test and pilot new products earlier in developing countries to establish their potential benefits and reduce the delays that occur before the products become widely available;
- review partnerships engaged in donation/distribution and strengthening of health services, for lessons on distribution systems in poorer countries, and devise ways in which future efforts can apply the lessons within the framework of national plans and priorities;
- create additional partnerships, where necessary, in order to develop the products most needed to meet the health needs of the poor. This work should aim for products suitable for use under the conditions prevailing in poorer countries: simple administration and short-course treatment are desirable characteristics. Given the anticipated increase in the burden of noncommunicable diseases, it is advisable to look now at partnerships that would tackle the requirements of developing countries in this area.

[a] In the absence of efforts to make markets function effectively to meet health needs in as many countries as possible, the bilateral development assistance community will be faced with the unmanageable prospect of subsidizing health in many countries for the foreseeable future. In the absence of a prospect of some revenue and effective delivery systems, there is little reason to think that the interest of the pharmaceutical industry in the needs of poorer populations can be markedly increased solely by push interventions for product development.

Résumé

Partenariats public-privé pour la santé : cibles, diversité et orientations futures

La charge mondiale de morbidité, notamment la partie imputable aux maladies infectieuses, touche de manière disproportionnée les populations des pays en développement. L'accès insuffisant aux produits pharmaceutiques contribue à pérenniser cette disparité. Les difficultés d'accès aux médicaments et vaccins peuvent être dues à la faiblesse des infrastructures de distribution ou au fait que le développement des produits voulus a été relégué au second plan. Mais il est possible de remédier à cette situation par des mesures dissuasives (*push* interventions) visant à réduire, pour l'industrie, les coûts et les risques afférents au développement de produits, par des mesures incitatives (*pull* interventions) prévoyant des incitations économiques et commerciales, et par la création des infrastructures nécessaires. Correctement motivées, les sociétés pharmaceutiques peuvent apporter aux partenariats leurs connaissances techniques pour le développement des produits, la mise au point de méthodes de production, la fabrication, la commercialisation et la distribution, autant d'aspects dans lesquels le secteur public n'a guère d'expérience. Un vaste éventail de partenariats public-privé s'est créé, réunis-

sant les compétences et les ressources d'une grande variété de collaborateurs dans les domaines du développement de produits, de la lutte contre la maladie au moyen de dons ou par la distribution de produits, ou encore du renforcement général ou de la coordination des services de santé. Sur le plan administratif, ces partenariats peuvent soit comporter une affiliation à des organisations internationales – c'est-à-dire être essentiellement des programmes du secteur public avec une participation du secteur privé – soit être des organismes à but non lucratif juridiquement indépendants. Ces partenariats doivent être considérés comme des expériences sociales : ils sont prometteurs mais il ne faut pas en attendre des miracles. Les nouveaux projets doivent reposer sur l'appréciation des besoins, être adaptés au contexte et profiter des leçons tirées de l'expérience pour ce qui est des pratiques à adopter. L'article se termine par des suggestions concernant les activités du secteur public, du secteur privé ou des secteurs public et privé, qui puissent contribuer à améliorer l'accès des populations pauvres aux produits pharmaceutiques et aux services de santé dont elles ont besoin.

Resumen

Alianzas de los sectores público y privado en pro de la salud: principales objetivos, diversidad y futuras orientaciones

La carga mundial de morbilidad, en especial la parte atribuible a las enfermedades infecciosas, afecta desproporcionadamente a las poblaciones de los países en desarrollo. El acceso insuficiente a los productos farmacéuticos contribuye a perpetuar esa disparidad. Los problemas de acceso a los medicamentos y vacunas pueden deberse a deficiencias de la infraestructura de distribución o al hecho de haber relegado a segundo término el desarrollo de los productos deseados. Esta situación puede abordarse mediante intervenciones impulsoras encaminadas a reducir los costos y los riesgos del desarrollo de productos para la industria, mediante intervenciones atractoras basadas en incentivos económicos y de mercado, y mediante la creación de infraestructuras que permitan utilizar los productos. Si se las motiva adecuadamente, las empresas farmacéuticas pueden aportar a las alianzas conocimientos técnicos sobre el desarrollo de productos, la puesta a punto de métodos de producción, la fabricación, la comercialización y la distribución, aspectos todos en los que el sector público apenas tiene experiencia. Se han forjado muy diversas alianzas de los sectores público y privado que combinan las competencias y los recursos de una amplia gama de colaboradores en el terreno del desarrollo de productos, la lucha contra las enfermedades mediante la donación y distribución de productos, o el fortalecimiento o la coordinación generales de los servicios de salud. Desde el punto de vista administrativo, esas alianzas entrañan ya sea la asociación a organizaciones internacionales, como los programas fundamentalmente públicos en los que participa el sector privado, o bien la constitución de órganos no lucrativos jurídicamente independientes. Esas alianzas pueden considerarse experimentos sociales: son prometedoras, pero no son una panacea. Las nuevas iniciativas deberían basarse en las necesidades, la idoneidad y las lecciones extraídas de la experiencia en cuanto a las prácticas adecuadas. Se hacen algunas propuestas para el desarrollo de actividades –del sector público, del sector privado o de ambos– que puedan ayudar a mejorar el acceso de las poblaciones pobres a los productos farmacéuticos y a los servicios de salud que necesitan.

References

1. **Sachs J.** Helping the world's poorest. *The Economist*, 14 August 1999: 16–22.
2. Children's Vaccine Initiative, 1999. *CVI Forum*, 1999, **18**: 6.
3. R. Bergquist, personal communication, 1999.
4. **Gwatkin DR, Guillot M.** *The burden of disease among the global poor*. Washington, DC, World Bank, 1999.
5. **Murray JLC, Lopez AD.** *Global burden of disease: a comprehensive assessment of mortality and disability from diseases, injuries and risk factors in 1990 and projected to 2020*. Boston, MA, Harvard School of Public Health, 1996.
6. M. Everard, personal communication, 1999.
7. *Better health in Africa*. Washington, DC, World Bank, 1994.
8. R. Ridley, personal communication, 2000.
9. Market report: 5 year forecast of the global pharmaceutical markets. IMS Health (Internet communication, 13 July 2001 at http://www.ims-global.com/insight/report/global/report.htm).
10. *Creating global markets for neglected drugs and vaccines: a challenge for public-private partnerships*. Report of a meeting held at Quail Lodge, Carmel Valley, CA, 18–21 February 2000. San Francisco, CA, Institute for Global Health, University of California, Berkley, CA.
11. **Widdus R et al.** Towards better defining public-private partnerships for health. Geneva, Global Forum for Health Research, 2001 (in press).
12. *Medicines for Malaria Venture*. Geneva (Internet communication, 4 June 2001 at http://www.mmv.org/).
13. *International AIDS Vaccine Initiative*. New York (Internet communication, 4 June 2001 at http://www.iavi.org/) (4 June 2001).
14. *Global Alliance for TB Drug Development*. Geneva (Internet communication, 4 June 2001 at http://www.tballiance.org).
15. *Lymphatic filariasis*. Geneva, World Health Organization (Internet communication, 4 June 2001 at http://www.filariasis.org/).
16. *Sleeping sickness/eflornithine*. Strasbourg, Aventis (Internet communication, 4 June 2001 at http://www.aventis.com/main/0,1003,EN-XX-10590-42250–,FF.html).
17. *Sleeping sickness/eflornithine*. Geneva, International Federation of Pharmaceutical Associations (Internet communication, 4 June 2001 at http://www.ifpma.org/African.htm#WHO).
18. *Leprosy*. Geneva, World Health Organization (Internet communication, 4 June 2001 at http://www.who.int/lep/).
19. *Malarone*. GlaxoSmithKine (Internet communication, 4 June 2001 at http://www.malaronedonation.org/).
20. *Mectizan*. Atalanta, GA, Task Force for Child Survival and Development (Internet communication, 4 June 2001 at http://www.taskforce.org/MDP/).
21. *Mectizan*. Geneva, World Health Organization (Internet communication, 4 June 2001 at http://www.who.int/ocp/apoc/).
22. *International Trachoma Initiative/Zithromax*. New York, International Trachoma Initiative (Internet communication, 4 June 2001 at http://www.trachoma.org/).
23. **Kale OO.** *Review of disease-specific corporate drug donation programmes for the control of communicable diseases*. Paper presented at conference on Drugs for Communicable Diseases: Stimulating Development and Securing Availability. Paris, Médecins Sans Frontières Foundation, 14–15 October 1999.
24. *Botswana Comprehensive HIV/AIDS Partnership*. Bill and Melinda Gates Foundation, Seattle, WA, (Internet communication, 4 June 2001 at http://www.gatesfoundation.org/pressroom/release.asp?PRindex=243).
25. *Roll Back Malaria*. Geneva, World Health Organization (Internet communication, 4 June 2001 at http://mosquito.who.int/).
26. *Safe Injection Global Network*. Geneva, World Health Organization (Internet communication, 4 June 2001 at http://www.injectionsafety.org/).
27. *Stop TB initiatives*. Geneva, World Health Organization (Internet communication, 4 June 2001 at http://www.stoptb.org/).
28. *Global Alliance for Vaccines and Immunization*. Geneva, UNICEF (Internet communication, 4 June 2001 at http://www.vaccinealliance.org/).
29. *Global Fund for Children's Vaccines*. Lyon, c/o Parteurop (Internet communication, 4 June 2001 at http://www.vaccinealliance.org/reference/globalfund.html).
30. *HAI*. Amsterdam, Health Action International (Internet communication, 4 June 2001 at http://www.haiweb.org/pubs/hailights/mar2001/mar01_lead.html).

[28]

GLOBAL HEALTH GOVERNANCE, A CONCEPTUAL REVIEW

Richard Dodgson, Kelley Lee and Nick Drager

*The solution lies not in turning one's back on globalization, but in
learning how to manage it. In other words, there is a crying need
for better global governance...*

UN Deputy Secretary-General Louise Frechette (1998)

*...global governance cannot replace the need for good governance
in national societies; in fact, in the absence of quality local
governance, global and regional arrangements are bound to fail or
will have only limited effectiveness. In a way, governance has to
be built from the ground up and then linked back to the local
conditions.*

R. Vayrynen, *Globalization and Global Governance* (1999)

1.1 INTRODUCTION

In today's world of changing health risks and opportunities, the capacity to
influence health determinants, status and outcomes cannot be assured
through national actions alone because of the intensification of crossborder
and transborder flows of people, goods and services, and ideas. The need for
more effective collective action by governments, business and civil society to
better manage these risks and opportunities is leading us to reassess the rules
and institutions that govern health policy and practice at the subnational,
national, regional and global levels. This is particularly so as a range of health
determinants are increasingly affected by factors outside of the health sector –
trade and investment flows, collective violence and conflict, illicit and criminal
activity, environmental change and communication technologies. There is an
acute need to broaden the public health agenda to take account of these
globalizing forces, and to ensure that the protection and promotion of human
health is placed higher on other policy agendas (McMichael and Beaglehole
2000). There is a widespread belief that the current system of international
health governance (IHG) does not sufficiently meet these needs and, indeed,
has a number of limitations and gaps. In light of these perceived
shortcomings, the concept of global health governance (GHG) has become a
subject of interest and debate in the field of international health.

This paper seeks to contribute to this emerging discussion by reviewing the
conceptual meaning and defining features of GHG.[1] This paper begins with a
brief discussion of why GHG has become such a subject of discussion and
debate. The particular impacts that globalization may be having on
individuals and societies, and the fundamental challenges that this poses for
promoting and protecting health, are explained. This is followed by a review of
the history of IHG and, in particular, the traditional role of the World Health
Organization (WHO). The purpose of this brief section is to draw out the
distinction between international and global health governance, and the
degree to which there is presently, and should be, a shift to the latter.[2] This is
achieved by defining, in turn, the terms global health and governance from
which the essential elements of GHG can be identified. This leads to an

---

[1] A more detailed analysis of the institutional forms and mechanisms of international and global health
governance is provided in Fidler D. (2002), "Global Health Governance: Overview of the role of
international law in protecting and promoting global public health," Discussion Paper No.3.
[2] A more detailed analysis of the historical dimensions of global health governance is provided in
Loughlin K. and Berridge V. (2002), Historical Dimensions of Global Health Governance, Discussion
Paper No.2.

identification of key challenges faced by the health community in bringing about such a system in future. The paper concludes with suggestions on how the key types of actors and their respective roles in GHG might be defined further.

1.2   HEALTH GOVERNANCE: THE CHALLENGE OF GLOBALIZATION

In broad terms, **governance** can be defined as the actions and means adopted by a society to promote collective action and deliver collective solutions in pursuit of common goals. This a broad term that is encompassing of the many ways in which human beings, as individuals and groups, organize themselves to achieve agreed goals. Such organization requires agreement on a range of matters including membership within the co-operative relationship, obligations and responsibilities of members, the making of decisions, means of communication, resource mobilisation and distribution, dispute settlement, and formal or informal rules and procedures concerning all of these. Defined in this way, governance pertains to highly varied sorts of collective behaviour ranging from local community groups to transnational corporations, from labour unions to the UN Security Council. Governance thus relates to both the public and private sphere of human activity, and sometimes a combination of the two.

Importantly, governance is distinct from *government.* As Rosenau (1990) writes,

> Governance is not synonymous with government. Both refer to purposive behaviour, to goal oriented activities, to systems of rule; but government suggests activities that are backed by formal authority...whereas governance refers to activities backed by shared goals that may or may not derive from legal and formally prescribed responsibilities and that do not necessarily rely on police powers to overcome defiance and attain compliance.

Government, in other words, is a particular and highly formalised form of governance. Where governance is institutionalised within an agreed set of rules and procedures, regular or irregular meeting of relevant parties, or a permanent organizational structure with appropriate decision making and implementing bodies, we can describe these as the means or mechanisms of governance (Finkelstein 1995), of which government is one form. In other cases, however, governance may rely on informal mechanisms (e.g. custom, common law, cultural norms and values) that are not formalised into explicit rules.

Health governance concerns the actions and means adopted by a society to organize itself in the promotion and protection of the health of its population. The rules defining such organization, and its functioning, can again be formal (e.g. Public Health Act, International Health Regulations) or informal (e.g. Hippocratic oath) to prescribe and proscribe behaviour. The governance mechanism, in turn, can be situated at the local/subnational (e.g. district health authority), national (e.g. Ministry of Health), regional (e.g. Pan American Health Organization), international (e.g. World Health Organization) and, as argued in Section 1.5, the global level. Furthermore, health governance can be public (e.g. national health service), private (e.g. International Federation of Pharmaceutical Manufacturers Association), or a combination of the two (e.g. Malaria for Medicines Venture).

Historically, the locus of health governance has been at the national and subnational level as governments of individual countries have assumed primary responsibility for the health of their domestic populations. Their authority and responsibility, in turn, has been delegated/distributed to regional/district/local levels. Where the determinants of health have spilled over national borders to become international (transborder) health issues (e.g. infectious diseases) two or more governments have sought to cooperate together on agreed collective actions. This is discussed in Section 1.3. Growing discussions of the need to strengthen health governance at national, regional, international and, more recently, the global level has, in part, been driven by a concern that a range of globalizing forces (e.g. technological change, increased capital flows, intensifying population mobility) are creating impacts on health that existing forms of governance cannot effectively address. This has led to debates about, for example, the appropriate balance among different levels of governance, what roles public and private actors should play, and what institutional rules and structures are needed to protect and promote human health.

This paper sees **globalization** as an historical process characterised by changes in the nature of human interaction across a range of social spheres including the economic, political, technological, cultural and environmental. These changes are globalizing in the sense that boundaries hitherto separating us from each other are being transformed. These boundaries – spatial, temporal and cognitive - can be described as the dimensions of globalization. Briefly, the spatial dimension concerns changes to how we perceive and experience physical space or geographical territory. The temporal dimension concerns changes to how we perceive and experience time. The cognitive dimension concerns changes to how we think about ourselves and the world around us (Lee 2000b).

Many argue that globalization is reducing the capacity of states to provide for the health of their domestic populations and, by extension, intergovernmental health cooperation is also limited. The impact of globalization upon the capacity of states and other actors to co-operate internationally to protect human health is fourfold. First, globalization has introduced or intensified **transborder health risks** defined as risks to human health that transcend national borders in their origin or impact (Lee 2000a). Such risks may include emerging and reemerging infectious diseases, various noncommunicable diseases (e.g. lung cancer, obesity, hypertension) and environmental degradation (e.g. global climate change). The growth in the geographical scope and speed in which transborder health risks present themselves directly challenge the existing system of IHG that is defined by national borders. The mechanisms of IHG, in other words, may be constrained by its statecentric nature to tackle global health effectively (Zacher 1999b).

Second, as described above, globalization is characterised by a growth in the number, and degree of influence, of nonstate actors in health governance. Many argue that the relative authority and capacity of national governments to protect and promote the health of domestic populations has declined in the face of globalizing forces beyond national borders that affect the basic determinants of health as well as erode national resources for addressing their consequences (Deacon et al. 1997). Nonstate actors, including civil society groups, global social movements, private companies, consultancy firms, think tanks, religious movements and organized crime, in turn, have gained relatively greater power and influence both formally and informally.[3] The

---

[3] The emerging and potential role of civil society and private sector in global health governance are discussed in Discussion Paper Nos. 4 and 5.

emerging picture is becoming more complex, with the distinct roles of state and nonstate actors in governance activities such as agenda setting, resource mobilisation and allocation, and dispute settlement becoming less clear. New combinations of both state and nonstate actors are rapidly forming, in a myriad of forms such as partnerships, alliances, coalitions, networks and joint ventures. This apparent "hybridisation" of governance mechanisms around certain health issues is a reflection of the search for more effective ways of cooperation to promote health in the face of new institutions. At the same time, however, it throws up new challenges for creating appropriate and recognised institutional mechanisms for, *inter alia,* ensuring appropriate representation, participation, accountability and transparency.

Third, current forms of globalization appear to be problematic for sustaining, and even worsening existing socioeconomic, political and environmental problems. UNDP (1999), for example, reports that neoliberal forms of globalization have been accompanied by widening inequalities between rich and poor within and across countries. In a special issue of *Development*[4], authors cite experiences of worsening poverty, marginalisation and health inequity as a consequence of globalization. In some respects, these problems can be seen as "externalities" or "global public bads" (Kaul et al. 1999) that are arising as a result of globalizing processes that are insufficiently managed by effective health governance. As Fidler (1998a) writes, these deeply rooted problems "feed off" the negative consequences of the globalization of health, creating a reciprocal relationship between health and the determinants of health. Although many of these problems are most acute in the developing world, they are of concern to all countries given their transborder nature (i.e. unconfined to national borders).

Fourth, globalization has contributed to a decline in both the political and practical capacity (see reading) of the national governments, acting alone or in cooperation with other states, to deal with global health challenges. While globalization is a set of changes occurring gradually over several centuries, its acceleration and intensification from the late twentieth century has brought attention to the fact that states alone cannot address many of the health challenges arising. Infectious diseases are perhaps the most prominent example of this diminishing capacity, but equally significant are the impacts on noncommunicable diseases (e.g. tobacco-related cancers), food and nutrition, lifestyles and environmental conditions (Lee 2000b). This decapitating of the state has been reinforced by initiatives to further liberalise the global trade of goods and services. The possible health consequences of more open global markets have only begun to be discussed within trade negotiations and remain unaddressed by proposed governance mechanisms for the emerging global economy.

The fourth of the above points is perhaps the most significant because it raises the possibility of the need for a change in the fundamental nature of health governance. As mentioned above, IHG is structured on the belief that governments have primary responsibility for the health of its people and able, in co-operation with other states, to protect its population from health risks. Globalization, however, means that the state may be increasingly undermined in its capacity to fulfil this role alone, that IHG is necessary but insufficient, and that additional or new forms of health governance may be needed. Some scholars and practitioners believe that this new system of health governance needs to be global in scope, so that it can deal effectively with problems caused by the globalization of health (Farmer 1998; Kickbusch 1999).

---

[4] *Development*, Special Issue on Responses to Globalization: Rethinking health and equity, December 1999, 42(4).

Globalization, in short, is an important driving force behind the emergence of GHG.

1.3 THE ORIGINS OF INTERNATIONAL HEALTH GOVERNANCE
1.3.1 The growth of health governance in the nineteenth century

A fuller understanding of the distinction between international and global health governance requires an historical perspective, of which a brief overview is provided here. [5] Historically, we can trace health governance to the most ancient human societies where agreed rules and practices about hygiene and disease were adopted. Early forms of IHG, in the form of cooperation on health matters between two or more countries, span many centuries with the adoption of quarantine practices amidst flourishing trade relations and the creation of regional health organizations. The process of building institutional structures, rules and mechanisms to systematically protect and promote human health across national borders, however, began more concertedly during the nineteenth century. Following the conclusion of the Napoleonic Wars, European states formed a number of international institutions to promote peace, industrial development and address collective concerns including the spread of infectious disease. This process of institutionalisation of IHG, according to Fidler (1997), was a consequence of the intensified globalization of health during this period. [6] Notably, these initiatives enjoyed the support of political and economic elites across European societies who believed that the crossborder spread of disease would hamper industrialisation and the expansion of international trade (Murphy 1995; Fidler 1998a).

The first institution to be created during this period was the International Sanitary Conference, with the first conference held in 1851. The achievements of this meeting, and the ten conferences subsequently held over the next four decades, were limited. In total, four conventions on quarantine and hygiene practices were concluded, along with an agreement to establish an institution for maintaining and reporting epidemiological data, and coordinating responses to outbreaks of infectious diseases (Lee 1998). Importantly, however, the conferences formalised a basic principle that has defined subsequent efforts to build IHG, namely the recognition that acting in cooperation through agreed rules and procedures enable governments to better protect their domestic populations from health risks that cross national borders. As such, the institutions adopted were envisioned as an extension of participating governments' responsibilities in the health field to the international (intergovernmental) level.

Along with this emerging sense of an international health community, constructed of cooperating states, was a growing body of scientific knowledge that was beginning to be shared in a more organized fashion (1998a). Scientific meetings on health-related themes reflected substantial advances during this period in understanding the causes of a number of diseases, such as cholera and tuberculosis. In addition, international meetings were held on social issues that impacted on public health, notably trafficking of liquor and

---

[2] A more detailed analysis of the historical dimensions of global health governance is provided in Loughlin K. and Berridge V. (2002), Historical Dimensions of Global Health Governance, Discussion Paper No.2.

[6] Early regional health organizations include the Conseil Superieur de Sante de Constantinople (c. 1830), European Commission for the Danube (1856) and International Sanitary Bureau of the Americas (1902). For a history of health cooperation in the nineteenth century see Howard-Jones N. (1975), *The Scientific Background of the International Sanitary Conferences, 1851-1938* (Geneva: WHO History of International Public Health Series); and Weindling P. ed. (1995*), International Health Organizations and Movements, 1918-1939* (Cambridge: Cambridge University Press).

opium.   Between 1851-1913, eighteen international conferences on health
were held (Box 1.1), and twelve health-related international institutions[7] had
been established by 1914 (Murphy 1995). Among the most prominent were
the International Sanitary Bureau (later the Pan American Sanitary Bureau) in
1902 and *Office International d'Hygiene Publique* (OIHP) created in Paris in
1907. The OIHP was a milestone in IHG in that it provided a standing (rather
than periodic) forum for countries to exchange ideas and information on
public health (Roemer 1994). This was followed in 1920 with the formation of
the Health Organization of the League of Nations. While a lack of resources
and political support restricted its activities, and inter-organizational
competition with the OIHP hindered the scope of its work, the organization
emerged from the interwar period with a strong reputation for data collection
and public health research.

BOX 1.1: WORLD AND EUROPEAN CONFERENCES ON HEALTH: 1851-1913

1851	First Sanitary Conference, Paris
1859	Second Sanitary Conference, Paris
1866	Third Sanitary Conference, Instanbul
1874	Fourth, Sanitary Conference, Vienna
1881	Fifth Sanitary Conference, Washington
1885	Sixth Sanitary Conference, Rome
1887	Liquor on the North Sea, venue unrecorded
1892	Seventh Sanitary Conference, Venice
1893	Eight Sanitary Conference, Dresden
1894	Ninth Sanitary Conference, Paris
1897	Tenth Sanitary Conference, Venice
1899	Liquor Traffic in Africa, Brussels
1903	Eleventh Sanitary Conference, Paris
1906	Liquor T·affic in Africa, Brussels
1909	Opium, Shanghai
1911	Twelfth Sanitary Conference, Paris
1911	Opium, The Hague
1913	Opium, The Hague

Source: Murphy, C.N. (1994), *International Organization and Industrial Change: Global
Governance since 1850* (Cambridge: Polity Press), p.59.

From the mid nineteenth century, the nongovernmental sector also began to
grow and contribute to IHG, essentially filling gaps or supplementing
government action.   For example, religious missions and The Rockefeller
Foundation's International Health Division (established in 1913) led the way in
supporting health services and disease control programmes in many parts of
the developing world.   The International Committee of the Red Cross
(established in 1863) succeeded in establishing the Geneva Convention, a
precursor of future international health regimes in setting out norms of
behaviour and ethical standards for treating casualties of war. Other notable
NGOs created during this period were the League of Red Cross Societies (1919)
and Save the Children Fund (1919).

By the 1920s, governmental and nongovernmental health organizations were
contributing to a vision of IHG that was increasingly defined by
humanitarianism. Many medical practitioners and public health officials
building national public health systems at the national level (e.g. Margaret
Sanger) became closely involved in designing these early international health
institutions. Many of attended international scientific conferences from the
mid nineteenth century, bringing with them a strong belief that international

---

[7] The twelve health-related international institutions established compares with five on human rights,
three on humanitarian relief and welfare, and ten on education and research (Murphy 1995).

health cooperation should seek to provide health to as many people as possible. To achieve this vision of 'social medicine' required a strong emphasis on universality as a guiding principal, achieved through the inclusion of as many countries as possible in any international system of health governance that was formed.

1.3.2 International Health Governance after the Second World War

The postwar period brought a significant expansion in IHG through the establishment of new institutions and official development assistance for health purposes. Within the UN system, the World Health Organization (WHO) was created in 1948 as the UN specialised agency for health. Other organizations contributing to health were the UN Relief and Rehabilitation Administration (UNRRA) in 1943, UN International Children's Emergency Fund (UNICEF) in 1946 and UN High Commissioner for Refugees (UNHCR) in 1949. WHO was similar in a number of ways to the Health Organization of the League of Nations that preceded it. Above all, the ideal of universality was, and remains, central to its mandate and activities. As stated by the Constitution of WHO (1946), the overall goal of the organization is "the attainment by all peoples of the highest possible level of health". Even in the face of scepticism at the attainability of such a mandate, and challenges to the appropriateness of social medicine (Goodman 1971), WHO was founded with a strong commitment to addressing the health needs of all people. The universalism of WHO has been reaffirmed on a number of occasions since 1948, most clearly during the 1970s with the Health for All strategy and Renewing Health for All Strategy in the 1990s (Antezana et al. 1998).

WHO's pledge to universality, however, has been strongly defined by the sovereignty of its member states. The working assumption of the organization has been that "health for all" can be achieved by working primarily, if not exclusively, through governmental institutions, notably ministries of health. Universality, in this sense, is measured by number of member states. Where a large number of countries participate, such as the World Health Assembly (WHA), it is assumed that the health needs of all peoples are represented. The role of WHO, in turn, is designed as supporting the efforts of governments to promote and protect the health of their populations.

Beyond national governments NGOs have been allowed to apply for permission to enter into official relations with WHO since 1950 if it is concerned with matters that fall within the competence of the organization and pursues (whose aims and purposes are in conformity with those of the Constitution of WHO). In 1998, there were 188 NGOs in official relations (WHO 1998) from such diverse fields as medicine, science, education, law, humanitarian aid and industry. In principle, therefore, NGOs are recognised as important contributors to achieving the goals of WHO. In practice, however, the actual role NGOs have played has been limited. Lucas et al. (1997), for example, found that WHO has engaged with NGOs in its support at country level in contrast with trends within agencies and other UN organizations such as UNDP and UNICEF. At the headquarters and regional levels, officially recognised NGOs have observed proceedings of the World Health Assembly or meetings of the regional committees, and have limited access to programme-related meetings dealing with more specific health issues. However NGOs have not been routinely consulted despite their importance as channels of health sector aid since the 1980s (Hulme and Edwards 1997) increased.

This traditional focus on member states and, in particular, ministries of health has been in a context of greater diversity of policy actors. By the mid 1990s,

11

the map of IHG was one of considerable uncertainty, as Zacher (1999bc) describes, fractured into an "organizational patchwork quilt". Alongside WHO has emerged a multiplicity of players, each accountable to a different constituency and bringing with them different guiding principles, expertise, resources and governance structures. The World Bank maintains a prominent place because of its unrivalled financial resources and policy influence. Regional organizations, such as the European Union, and other UN organizations (e.g. UNICEF, UNDP, UNFPA) retain health as an important component of their work but are more limited in membership and/or scope. The Organization for Economic Cooperation and Development (OECD) and World Trade Organization (WTO) approach health from an economic and trade perspective. Varied civil society groups, such as consumer groups, social movements and research institutions, also make substantial contributions to health development. Finally, the growth of the private sector actors in health, within and across countries, is notable. New fault lines and allegiances had emerged to form an increasingly complex milieu for health cooperation, with interests divided within and across countries and organizations. Undertaking a wide-ranging process of reform, WHO has sought to change some of its traditional governance features, notably its strong focus on ministries of health, by engaging other public and private sector actors, and creating new consultation mechanisms. As discussed in 1.4 below, there have been clear efforts to increase the involvement of the NGO sector in areas of WHO activities, such as tobacco, tuberculosis and HIV/AIDS, since the late 1990s. At the same time, it has reiterated its commitment to universality as the defining principle of its activities. How to define, let alone achieve health for all, remains an enduring challenge.

In summary, IHG has evolved alongside an intensification of human interaction across national borders over a number of centuries, gradually becoming more institutionalised from the mid nineteenth century. During the twentieth century, this institutional framework has grown and spread, encompassing both rich and poor countries, in all regions of the world. The defining feature of IHG has been the primacy given to the state although non-state actors and interests were ever present. By the late twentieth century, however, what Held et al. (1999) calls a "thickening" of the globalization process was challenging this statecentric system of health governance. It is within this context that discussions and debates about global health governance have emerged.

1.4 AN EMERGING SYSTEM OF GLOBAL HEALTH GOVERNANCE?

The precise origins of the term GHG are unclear, although many scholars and practitioners who use the term draw upon a number of different fields. These mixed origins mean that GHG can be difficult to define. This problem of definition is compounded by the fact that the term GHG is used widely in a number of different contexts. We can begin to overcome this problem of definition by breaking GHG into its component parts – global health and governance.

1.4.1 International versus global health

Globalization brings into question how we define the determinants of health and how they can be addressed. In principle, the mandate of WHO is based on a broad understanding of health[8], although in practice its activities have

---

[8] The Constitution of WHO defines health as "a state of complete physical, mental and social well being and not merely the absence of disease or infirmity."

traditionally been biomedical in focus. Since the 1970s, efforts have been made to incorporate a more multisectoral and multidisciplinary approach into the organization's activities. For example, *Health for all in the 21st Century* links the attainment of good health to human rights, equity, gender, sustainable development, education, agriculture, trade, energy, water and sanitation (Antezana et al. 1998). Similarly, the replacement of the Global Programme on AIDS by UNAIDS was in large part due to a desire to go beyond a narrow biomedical approaches to HIV/AIDS (Altman 1999).

Globalization from the late twentieth century has emphasised even more poignantly the need for greater attention to the basic determinants of health including so-called non-health issue areas. In arguing for a reinvigoration of public health, McMichael and Beaglehole (1999) point to the need to address underlying socioeconomic (notably inequalities), demographic and environmental changes that global change is creating. Similarly, Chen et al. (1999) argue that globalization is eroding the boundary between the determinants of public (collective) and private (individual) health. For example, susceptibility to tobacco-related diseases, once strongly linked to, and blamed on, the lifestyle choices of individuals, is increasingly seen as attributable to the worldwide marketing practices of tobacco companies. The distinction between *global* health and *international* health therefore is that the former entails a broadening of our understanding of, and policy responses to, the basic determinants of health to include forces that transcend the territorial boundaries of states. Global health requires a rethinking of how we prioritise and address the basic determinants of health, and engagement with the broad range of sectors that shape those underlying determinants.

The need to address the basic determinants of health leads to the practical question of how to do so. Since at least the early 1990s, there has been a growing confusion of mandates among UN organizations that have substantial involvement in the health sector - WHO, UNICEF, UNDP, UNFPA and the World Bank. In large part, this has been due to efforts to develop multisectoral approaches to both health and development, as well as key areas (e.g. reproductive health, environmental health) that bring together the activities of two or more organizations (Lee et al. 1996). Globalization invites a further widening of the net of relevant organizations, requiring engagement with actors that have little or no formal mandate in the health field. Notable have been efforts to establish greater dialogue between WHO and the WTO. While trade interests have historically defined, and in many ways confined, international health cooperation, officially the two spheres have been addressed by separate institutions. Nonetheless, the multiple links between trade and health policy are well recognised (WHO 2002, Brundtland 1998; Brundtland 1999), resulting in high-level meetings between the two organizations since the late 1990s. At present, WHO holds official observer status on the Council of the WTO, and committees relating to Sanitary and Phytosanitary Measures (SPS) and Technical Barriers to Trade (TBT) agreements. However, the capacity to articulate public health concerns regarding, for example, the agreement on trade-related intellectual property rights (TRIPS), has been hampered by the framing of health among trade officials as a "non-trade issue", and as such the reluctance of certain countries to discuss health within the context of a trade negotiations. Moreover, the ability of WHO to influence the WTO has been hampered by the fact that states (many of which are members of both organizations) have accorded a higher priority to trade issues, rather than those relating to human health. As such, there remain considerable barriers to incorporating health as a legitimate and worthy concern on the global trade agenda.

1.4.2 The different meanings of governance

As described above, the ability of a society to promote collective action and deliver solutions to agreed goals is a central aspect of governance. As shown in Table 1.1 the term governance has been used in a number of different ways, ranging from the relatively narrow scope of corporate and clinical governance, to the broader concept of global governance.

TABLE 1.1: VARIOUS USES OF THE TERM GOVERNANCE

TYPE OF GOVERNANCE	CHARACTERISTICS
governance	• the actions and means to promote collective action and deliver collective solutions • "an exercise in assessing the efficacy of alternative modes (means) of organization. The object is to effect good order through the mechanisms of governance" (Williamson 1996: 11) • "The manner in which power is exercised in the management of a country's economic and social resources for development" (World Bank 1994)
corporate governance	• clear systems of transparency and accountability to investors • mechanisms for meeting social responsibility by corporations • "the framework of laws, regulatory institutions, and reporting requirements that condition the way that the corporate sector is governed" (World Bank 1994)
good governance (World Bank 1994)	• public sector management • accountability of public sector institutions • legal framework for development • transparency and information
good governance (UNDP 1997)	• management of nations affairs • efficiency, effectiveness and economy • liberal democracy • greater use of non-governmental sector
clinical governance	• "a framework through which NHS organizations are accountable for continuously improving the quality of their services and safeguarding high standards of care by creating an environment in which excellence in clinical care will flourish" (UK 1998)
global governance	• "not only the formal institutions and organizations through which the rules and norms governing world order are (or are not) made and sustained - the institutions of the state, inter-governmental co-operation and so on - but also those organizations and pressure groups - from MNCs, transnational social movements to the plethora of non-governmental organizations – which pursue goals and objectives which have a bearing on transnational rule and authority systems" (Held et al. 1999)

Recent interest in governance within the development community can be traced to the late 1980s as part of a desire among aid agencies to address the uneven performance of low and middle-income countries to macro economic reforms (Dia 1993). The term **good governance** was introduced by the World Bank (1994) as an explanation for problems being experienced in many countries, namely the weakness of public sector institutions and management, and as a basis for setting further lending conditionalities. In this context, governance is defined as "the manner in which power is exercised in the management of a country's economic and social resources of development."

For governance to be "good", social and economic resources must be managed by a small efficient state that is representative, accountable, transparent, respectful of the rule of law, and supportive of human rights through programmes of poverty reduction.

The conceptualisation and application of the term good governance by the World Bank is seen by Leftwich (1993) as problematic in a number of ways. First, he argues that it is an extension of neoliberal-based policies, (for example, structural adjustment programmes) that are arguably themselves contributing to the problems experienced by many countries since the 1980s. Second, the World Bank focuses narrowly on the performance of public sector administration and management, while ignoring the importance of good governance for the private sector or donor communicty itself, along with levels of foreign debt, in influencing how countries have fared. Third, the prescriptive element of good governance again focuses on governments, while at the same time adopting a technocratic view of how governments should work.

Other development agencies have since taken up the term good governance as important components of their policies[9]. The UN Development Programme (UNDP) is a notable example. In seeking to go beyond public sector management, UNDP (1997) has incorporated a range of principles into its conceptualisation of good governance including legitimacy (democracy), freedom of association, participation, and freedom of the media. As Deputy Director of the UN Department for Development Support and Management Services A.T.R. Rahman (1996) states, "good governance is an overall process that is essential to economic growth, to sustainable development and to fulfilling UN-identified objectives such as the advancement of women and elimination of poverty".[10]

Another increasingly used term is **corporate governance.** Williamson (1996) defines corporate governance, for example, in terms of recent developments on transaction-cost approaches in economic theory. He writes that governance concerns institutional structures and accompanying practices (e.g. rules) that facilitate economic production and exchange relations. "Good" governance structures are those that effectively "mitigate hazards and facilitate adaptation". These can be simple or complex depending on the degree of hazard faced. Other writers on corporate governance similarly focus on mechanisms that enhance economic transactions. The underlying assumption of such approaches is that good corporate governance, in the form of improved (more democratic) systems of accountability and transparency for investors, will enhance the process of wealth creation and prevent greater regulation by governments (McRitchie 1998).

A broader perspective on corporate governance is more closely related to the definition of good governance put forth within the development community. This approach focuses more directly on the nature of social responsibility by business, rather than the enhancement of profits. There has been a growing movement to encourage the corporate sector to be more responsible, not only to shareholders, but to the wider communities within which they operate. The notion of corporate responsibility and citizenship has thus arisen in relation to such practices as fair trade, ethical investment and activist shareholders,

---

[9] For the UK government's view on good governance see Department for International Development (DfID), *Eliminating World Poverty: A Challenge for the 21ˢᵗ Century* (DfID, 1997). See also UN General Assembly, Resolution 50/225, 1996.

[10] Since completion of this paper, the UNDP Poverty Report 2000, has expanded on the link between "good governance" and poverty relief.

social and environmental impact assessments, improved working conditions for workers in low-income countries, and the social auditing of companies (Cantarella 1996).

The values of management-oriented approaches to corporate governance have entered the health lexicon in the guise of **clinical governance.** In the UK, where the term that has become especially popular, clinical governance refers to "a framework through which NHS [National Health Service] organizations are accountable for continuously improving the quality of their services and safeguarding high standards of care by creating an environment in which excellence in clinical care will flourish." (UK 1998). Initially emerging as part of health sector reform, it has been a response in particular to differences in quality of care in parts of the country, and to public concerns regarding well-publicised cases of poor clinical performance. The focus, therefore, has been improving the quality of patient care through evidence based practice, collecting information to measure performance against agreed standards, providing ongoing education for health care professionals, and managing and learning from complaints (Scally and Donaldson 1998). Institutional mechanisms (e.g. National Institute for Clinical Excellence) and practices have been introduced for these purposes (Paris and McKeown 1999; The King's Fund 1999). Criticisms of clinical governance focus on whether there is anything new about its aims. Some argue that clinical governance offers little more than a confirmation of "the common sense message that we [doctors and health professionals] must all strive after quality in practising medicine" (Goodman 1998).

A further use of the term governance, and the focus of this paper, is **global governance** which can be broadly defined as

> not only the formal institutions and organizations through which the rules and norms governing world order are (or are not) made and sustained – the institutions of the state, inter-governmental co-operation and so on – but also those organizations and pressure groups – from MNCs, transnational social movements to the plethora of non-governmental organizations – which pursue goals and objectives which have a bearing on transnational rule and authority systems.
>
> (Held et al. 1999).

The concept of global governance has come to the health field from the discipline of International Relations (IR) within which a diverse, and theoretically riven, debate has developed on the specific nature of globalization, the emerging global order, key actors, and ultimate goals of global governance (Table 1.2). **Liberal-internationalist** scholars view the purpose of global governance as ultimately moving towards a more liberal democratic global order in which states and IGOs have equal roles. Within such an order it is envisaged that power and influence will flow in a top-down manner, although states and IGOs may be held accountable via a global assembly composed of representatives from national and global civil society (Commission on Global Governance 1995). In contrast, **radical/critical** scholars believe that the direction of global governance should be guided from the bottom-up. Emphasis is placed on the potential of actors from within (global) civil society (in particular social movements) to bring about more 'humane governance' (Gill 1998). **Cosmopolitan democrats** pursue a vision of global governance that embraces the diversity of people across national and other forms of identity within a shared political community. This ideal may be achieved, for instance, through consensus on universal principles (e.g. human rights), increased public scrutiny of existing IGOs, global referendums and an

16

expanded international legal system (Held 1995; McGrew 1997). This is a somewhat simplistic summary of a substantial and intellectually rich literature.[11]

TABLE 1.2: THEORETICAL APPROACHES TO GLOBAL GOVERNANCE

CENTRAL ISSUE OF GLOBAL GOVERNANCE	LIBERAL-INTER NATIONALISM	CRITICAL/RADICAL	COSMOPOLITAN DEMOCRACY
Globalization	Multi-causal process – generates interdependence and 'zones of peace'	Economically driven – subject to contradictions	Multi-causal process with transformative potential
Nature of the current global order	Emerging post-Westphalian order	Global neoliberalism	Post-Westphalian order
Actors in global governance	States, international organizations corporations and NGOs etc.	Transnational capitalist class, elites through states, International organization and civil society.	States, peoples, international organization, corporations and social movements
Key actors in collective problem solving	States and international organization	Transnational capitalist class, international organization, states and civil society.	States, international organization, corporations and social movements
Nature of global governance	Reformist and top-down	Revolutionary and bottom-up	Transformationalist and participatory
Change towards	Liberal democratic consensus politics	Humane governance	Cosmopolitan democracy

Source: Adapted from McGrew A. (1997), "Globalization and Territorial Democracy: an introduction" in McGrew A. ed., *The Transformation of Democracy?* (London: Polity Press), p.20.

To summarise, the concept of governance has generally been used in two broad ways in relation to health. The first defines governance as a problem-solving approach to address the shortfalls of public and private institutions to function efficiently. Strongly influenced by recent developments in management and economic theory, good or better governance is equated with strengthening efficiency and effectiveness within existing institutional structures. The second takes a more transformative approach by finding existing forms of governance falling short in its responsiveness to the needs of society as a whole. Faced with a range of intensifying and/or new risks and opportunities, more effective governance is believed to be needed to respond to social change. This volume is located within this second view in its efforts to encourage wider discussion of the challenges posed by globalization, and the clearer vision needed to address them through global governance.

1.4.3 The essential elements of global health governance

From the above discussion, we can identify some essential elements of GHG and the challenges for achieving them. The first is the "deterritorialisation" of how we think about and promote health, and thus *the need to address factors which cross, and even ignore, the geographical boundaries of the state*. The formation of the international system of states in the sixteenth century, the birth of public health during the nineteenth century, and the creation of national health systems in the twentieth century have contributed to a system of governance that is premised on protecting the integrity of the state. IHG has been historically focused on those health issues that cross national borders, with the aim of protecting domestic populations within certain defined geographical boundaries through such practices as quarantine, cordon

---

[11] For a more detailed discussion see Hewson and Sinclair (1999).

sanitaire, and internationally agreed standards governing the reporting of infectious disease, trade and population mobility. All of these efforts have been focused on the point of contact, the national border of states.

However, forces of global change, in various forms, have intensified crossborder activity to such an extent as to undermine the capacity of states to control them. The increased levels of international trade and movement of people are examples. Moreover, a wide range of others forces render national borders irrelevant. The worldwide flows of information and communication across the Internet; the ecological impacts of global environmental change; the frenzied exchange of capital and finance via electronic media; the illicit trade in drugs, food products and even people; and the global mobility of other life forms (e.g. microbes) through natural (e.g. bird migration) and manmade (e.g. bulk shipping) means render border controls irrelevant. Many of these global changes impact on health and requires forms of cooperation that go beyond IHG.

A second essential element of GHG is *the need to define and address the determinants of health from a multi-sectoral perspective.* Biomedical approaches to health have dominated historically in the form of disease-focused research and policy, the skills mix of international health experts and officials, and the primacy given to working through ministries of health and health professionals. A global system of health governance begins with the recognition that a broad range of determinants impact on population health including social and natural environments. In recent decades, this has been recognised to some extent through the increased involvement of other forms of expertise in health policy making (e.g. economics, anthropology) and links with other social sectors (e.g. education, labour). More recently, ministries of health and inte:national health organizations have sought to engage more directly with sectors traditionally seen as relatively separate from health (e.g. trade, environment, agriculture) in recognition of "cross sectoral" policy issues at play. Informal consultations between WHO and WTO, for example, have been prompted by the importance of multilateral trade agreements to health.

The main challenge to achieving greater cross sectoral collaboration lies in the danger of casting the health "net" so widely that everything becomes subsumed within the global health umbrella. Opening up GHG too indiscriminately can dilute policy focus and impact, and raise questions about feasibility. The linking of traditional health and non-health issues also demands a clear degree of understanding and empirical evidence about cause and effect. Defining the scope of GHG, therefore, remains a balance between recognising the interconnectedness of health with a varied range of globalizing forces, and the need to define clear boundaries of knowledge and action.

The third essential element of GHG is *the need to involve, both formally and informally, a broader range of actors and interests.* As described above, while nonstate actors have long been an important part of the scene, IHG has been firmly state-defined. Health-related regional organizations (e.g. PAHO, European Union), along with major international health organizations such as WHO and the World Bank are formally governed by member states. Their mandates, in turn, are defined by their role in supporting the national health systems of those member states. The universality of their activities is measured by the number of member states participating in them. Defining criteria and measures of progress to address the burden of disease, health determinants and health status are focused on the state or groups of states.

GHG, however, is distinguished by the starting point that globalization is creating health needs and interests that increasingly cut across and, in some cases, are oblivious to state boundaries. To effectively address these global health challenges, there is a need to strengthen, supplement and even replace existing forms of IHG. Importantly, this does not mean that the role of the state or IHG will disappear or become redundant, but that they will rather need to become part of a wider system of GHG. Many existing institutions will be expected to play a significant role in GHG, and states will continue to be key actors. However, states and state-defined governance alone is not enough. Forms of governance that bring together more concertedly state and nonstate actors will be central in a global era (Scholte 2000). As described by the Commission on Global Governance (1995), "[global governance] must...be understood as also involving NGOs, citizen's movements, multinational corporations, and the global capital market," as well as a "global mass media of dramatically enlarged influence."

As described above, state and nonstate actors have long interacted on health governance. The difference for GHG will lie in their degree of involvement and nature of their respective roles, varying with the health issue concerned. Three brief examples illustrate this. First, relations among the diverse NGO community are constantly changing depending on the issue. On certain issues, they may be willing to form strategic networks or alliances with other NGOs, thus representing an important governance mechanism within GHG. Such a mechanism was formed around the global campaign against the marketing of breastmilk substitutes that led to the formation of the International Baby Food Action Network. Cooperation among the International Baby Food Action Network, UNICEF, WHO and selected governments led to the International Code of Marketing on Breast-Milk Substitutes in 1981. Like-minded NGOs also came together to form more permanent, but still highly fluid, global social movements around the environment and women's health. These movements opposed each other at the UN Conference on the Environment and Development (1992), yet worked together to propose an alternative view of development at the World Summit for Social Development in 1995. Close relations among the women's health movement, national governments and UNFPA was also a defining feature of the International Conference on Population and Development (1994). Relations between the women's health movement and some states, in particular the US, were so close that members of the women's health movement served on some of the official government delegations. Parties involved in the conference believed that such close relations played a key role in shaping the resultant commitment to reproductive health (Dodgson 1998).

A second example is the closer relations among state and nonstate actors characterising the emerging global strategy on tobacco control. Under the auspices of WHO, negotiations for a Framework Convention on Tobacco Control (FCTC) have been attended by officially recognised NGOs, along with state delegations. The Tobacco Free Initiative (TFI), WHO maintains that NGO participation is central to the overall success of the FCTC, and has supported the creation of a global NGO network to support the FCTC (i.e. Framework Convention Alliance). Links were also formed with representatives of the women's movement to ensure that tobacco and women's health was discussed during the Beijing Plus 5 process. At the same time, TFI has developed links with the business community, in particular, the pharmaceutical industry, to explore how nicotine replacement treatments can be made more widely available. Other coordination efforts have been focused on bringing together different UN organizations through the formation of a UN Ad Hoc Inter-Agency Task Force on tobacco control, and the holding of public hearings to encourage the submission of a wide range of evidence from different interest groups.[12]

These efforts to build formal links with such a diverse range of stakeholders to support global tobacco control policy is unprecedented for WHO, and a good example of emerging forms of GHG. It represents an important challenge to traditional ways of working for WHO in its efforts to tackle health issues with global dimensions (Collin et al. 2002). Ensuring state and nonstate actors work collectively on different levels of governance (i.e. global, regional, national[13] and subnational), the FCTC is an example of how "behind-the-border" convergence could be promoted in the future. The goal of adopting a legally binding treaty and associated protocols is also a new development in institutionalising global governance in the health sector. The FCTC is based on international regimes that have emerged to promote collective action on global environmental problems. These international regimes can be defined as "sets of implicit or explicit principles, norms, rules and decision-making procedures around which actors expectations converge in a given area of international relations" (Krasner 1983). In addition to the FCTC, other examples of international regimes in the field of health are the International Health Regulations[14] , the International Code for the Marketing of Breast Milk Substitutes and the Codex Alimentarius (Kickbusch 1999). These examples of international health regimes demonstrate that they have played a significant role in IHG. The remit and organizational structure of the FCTC and its implementation suggest that such regimes will be a core feature of GHG in future.

A third example of state-nonstate governance is so-called global public-private partnerships (GPPPs) defined as "a collaborative relationship which transcends national boundaries and brings together at least three parties, among them a corporation (and/or industry association) and inter-governmental organizations, so as to achieve a shared health creating goal on the basis of a mutually agreed division of labour" (Buse and Walt 2001). Among the most prominent GPPPs are the Albendazole Donation Programme, Medicines for Malaria Venture and International AIDS Vaccine Initiative. The idea of building partnerships with business is at the centre of UN-wide views on the governance of globalization (Global Compact). For this reason, and the fact that GPPPs bring much needed resources to major health issues, the number of GPPPs is likely to grow in future. At the same time, like the FCTC process, GPPPs require a period of reflection on a range of governance issues. Buse and Walt (2001), for example, raise questions about accountability, transparency and long-term sustainability of GPPPs. They also ask who benefits, people who seek treatment or the pharmaceutical companies that gain good public relations. Some governments of low-income countries, a number of NGOs and UN institutions have expressed concerns about the viability of building links among actors with fundamentally differing objectives and interests. For example, Carole Bellamy, UNICEF Executive Director comments, "it is dangerous to assume that the goals of the private sector are

---

[12] Interview with Douglas Bettcher, Framework Convention Team, Tobacco Free Initiative, Geneva, 9 December 1999.

[13] Technical documents that have been written as part of the consultation process for the FCTC suggest that all signatory states should adopt an autonomous national tobacco control commission. See for example, A. Halvorssen, "The Role of National Institutions in Developing and Implementing the WHO Framework Convention on Tobacco Control", *Framework Convention on Tobacco Control: Technical Briefing Series*, No.5 (1999).

[14] Following a long process of review, the International Health Regulations (IHRs) are on the brink of being reformed to make them more effective and binding on states. Most significantly, the revised IHRs require the reporting of all "events of urgent international importance related to public health".

somehow synonymous with those of the United Nations, because they most emphatically are not."[15]

Thus, global health emphasises the need for governance that incorporates participation by a broadly defined "global" constituency, and engaging them in collective action through agreed institutions and rules. The challenges of achieving GHG, defined in this way, are considerable. At the heart lies the need to define the core concept of democracy in the context of globalization in terms of political identity and representation. If existing forms of health governance are seen to be undemocratic, alternatives that appropriately balance actors and interests are needed. Systems for ensuring accountability and transparency must be agreed. There requires greater clarity about what contributions different actors make to GHG, and what governance mechanisms can ensure that these roles are fulfilled. The issue of meaningful participation and responsibility remains problematic. For example, the WHA is attended by WHO member states but there are inequities in capacity to follow proceedings and contribute to decision making. This is a challenge for many international organizations including the WTO. Conflicts are also likely to emerge and need to be resolved. The familiar yet enduring problem of coordination of international health cooperation remains unresolved. Overall, the principle of closer state-nonstate cooperation is an increasingly accepted one, but the "nitty gritty" of what this should look like in practice is only beginning to be explored within the health sector. This theme is taken up by discussion papers on the potential role of civil society and the private sector in this series.

1.5 CONCLUSIONS: BEGINNING TO DEFINE AND SHAPE THE ARCHITECTURE FOR GHG

The task of defining and shaping a system of GHG in further detail, both as it appears to be currently evolving and more prospectively, begins with a number of important challenges for research and policy. The first, and perhaps the most fundamental, is the need to agree the normative framework upon which GHG can be built. There is a need to reach some degree of consensus about the underlying moral and ethical principles that define global health cooperation. As discussed in this paper, universalism has been a strong ethos guiding the emergence of social medicine, the Health for All movement from the late 1970s and, more recently, calls for health as a human right. Alongside such communitarian ideas have been approaches informed by principles of entitlement (economic or otherwise) and utilitarianism. Despite recent high-profile initiatives on "global health", an informed discussion about their normative basis remains to be carried out.

A second challenge is the need to define leadership and authority in GHG. As discussed above, health cooperation has evolved into an arena populated by a complex array of actors operating at different levels of policy and constituencies, with varying mandates, resources and authority. Figure 1 is an attempt to identify the key actors potentially concerned with GHG and their possible positions at a given point in time. WHO and the World Bank are shown as central because they represent the main sources of health expertise and development financing respectively. At the same time, they are accompanied by a cluster of institutions, state and nonstate, that fan outwards including, but are not restricted to, the International Monetary Fund (IMF), World Trade Organization (WTO), United Nations Children's Fund

---

[15] Interview with J. Ann Zammit, The South Centre, 9th December 1999. "UNICEF: Bellamy warns against partnership with private sector", *UN Wire*, 23rd April (1999).

(UNICEF), International Labour Organization (ILO), United Nations Development Programme (UNDP), and United Nations Population Fund (UNFPA). Specific regional and bilateral institutions (e.g. USAID) are included as politically and economically influential.[16] GHG also includes the wide variety of actors within the private sector and civil society, the latter defined as "a sphere of social interaction between economy and state, composed above all of the intimate sphere (especially family), the sphere of associations (especially voluntary associations) and forms of public communication" (Jareg and Kaseje 1998). Some of these actors (e.g. Bill and Melinda Gates Foundation) have become highly prominent in recent years. Others, as described above, including NGOs, social movements, epistemic communities, professional associations and the mass media, can be influential on a more policy specific basis.

FIGURE 1: GLOBAL HEALTH GOVERNANCE MAPPED

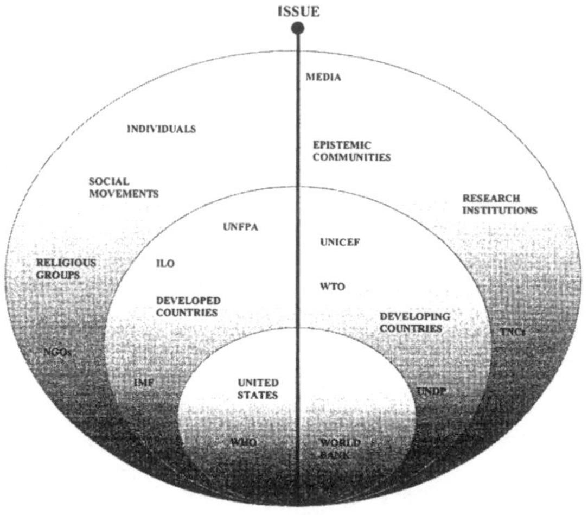

In this complex arena of actors, the issue of leadership and authority is a difficult one. As well as setting the normative framework for global health cooperation, leadership can provide the basis for generating public awareness, mobilising resources, using resources rationally through coordinated action, setting priorities, and bestowing or withdrawing legitimacy from groups and causes. The willingness of states to 'pool' their sovereignty and act collectively through mechanisms of GHG is one historically significant hurdle. The absence of a single institution, with the authority and capacity to act decisively, to address health issues of global concern is another. The panoply of vested interests that characterise global politics represents another clear difficulty. After the Second World War, the agreement to establish the World Health Organization was prompted by a strong collective recognition of the need to improve health worldwide. The global nature of many emerging health issues, including the threat of major threats to humankind (e.g. emerging diseases, antimicrobial resistance) may prompt similar consensus.

---

[16] This is not to suggest of course that these are the only bilateral actors to play a role in international health, United Kingdom's Department for International Development is one many other such institutions.

A third challenge for GHG is the need to generate sufficient resources for global health cooperation and distribute them appropriately according to agreed priorities. The present system is ad hoc in nature, reliant on the annual spending decisions of governments, and the goodwill of private citizens and companies. Efforts to provide debt relief and increase development assistance recognise the inherent inequities of current forms of globalization (UNDP 1999). Recent discussions about the creation of a Tobin Tax or equivalent surcharge, on global activities that rely on a secure and stable world (e.g. financial transactions, air travel), could generate substantial and much needed sums.

Fourth, the sovereignty of states is also a hurdle to giving "teeth" to global health initiatives because of the lack of effective enforcement mechanisms. With the exception of the International Health Regulations, which in itself is highly circumscribed in remit, WHO can recommend rather than command action by member states. The reporting of outbreaks of yellow fever, cholera and plague, for example, is traditionally reliant on governments who may not be willing to report such information for fear of causing adverse economic reactions. By definition, a global health issue is one where the actions of a party in one part of the world can have widespread consequences in other parts of the world. Reliance on voluntary compliance with agreed practices, such as the use of antibiotics and antimicrobials, without sufficient monitoring and enforcement, can lead to serious and even irreversible health impacts.

Finally, the enigma of how to achieve a more pluralist, yet cohesive, system of GHG stands before us. As the globalization of health continues, health governance will have to become broader in participation and scope. The proto forms of GHG that are presently emerging (e.g. FCTC, GPPPs) might be seen as examples of improving practice as they open up participation in health governance to a wider range of actors. Nonetheless, a critical evaluation of these forms of governance is yet to be undertaken, nor is it yet clear whether these emerging forms of GHG will achieve their objectives.

The task of moving forward this complex, yet much needed, debate can be facilitated by a number of further tasks that are the focus of future discussion papers in this series. The purpose of this paper has been to review the conceptual meaning of GHG and, in turn, to highlight the challenges faced in moving towards such a system. A second task is to better understand the historical context of IHG and GHG, and how this can inform the transition from one to the other. Many different types of governance mechanisms for health purposes have been tried and tested since the end of the Second World War, and it would be useful to explore these in relation to the criteria set in this paper. This is the subject of Discussion Paper No. 2.

The next task is to better understand the "nitty gritty" of global governance in terms of what, in concrete terms, it looks like in practice. This moves us into the legal realm where international lawyers have grappled with the formulation and implementation of governance at the global level. An examination of what currently exists within the health field, as well as other fields such as trade and environment, may shed light on future possibilities. While such a review can only be selective in nature, it can point to lessons for building mechanisms for GHG. This is the subject of Discussion Paper No. 3.

Lastly, there is the task of defining more clearly the potential role of nonstate actors within a system of GHG. Relationships, patterns of influence and agreed roles among state and nonstate actors within an emerging system of GHG are still emerging. This myriad of different actors, each with individual spheres of activity, types of expertise, resources, interests and aspirations, cannot yet be described as a "global society". As defined by Fidler (1998b), a global society is "made of individuals and non-state entities all over the world that conceive of themselves as part of a single community and work nationally and transnationally to advance their common interests and values." The ad hoc nature of GHG so far, however, suggests that a more concerted effort to define and describe existing and potential roles would contribute to policy debates on possible future directions. The potential role of civil society in GHG is the subject of Discussion Paper No. 4, and the potential role of the private sector is examined in Discussion Paper No. 5.

References

Altman D. (1999), "Globalization, political economy, and HIV/AIDS," *Theory and Society*, 28: 559-84.

Antezana F., Chollat-Traquet C. and Yach D. (1998), "Health for all in the 21st century", *World Health Statistics Quarterly*, 51(1): 3-4.

Ball C. and Dunn L. (1995), *Non-Governmental Organizations: Guidelines for Good Policy and Practice* (London: The Commonwealth Institute).

Brundtland G. (1998), "Speech of the WHO Director-General", *Ad hoc Working Group on Revised Drug Strategy*, Geneva, 13 October.

Brundtland G. (1999), "International Trade Agreements and Public Health: WHO's Role", *Conference on Increasing Access to Essential Drugs in a Globalized Economy*, Amsterdam, 25-26 November.

Buse K. and Walt G. (2000), ""Global public-private health partnerships: Part I – a new development in health?" *Bulletin of the World Health Organization,* 78(4): 509-561.

Buse K. and Walt G. (2000), "Global public-private health partnerships: Part II - what are the health issues for global governance?" *Bulletin of the World Health Organization,* 78(5): 699-709.

Cantarella F. (1996), "Corporate social solutions," *The Corporate Board: Journal of Corporate Governance,* November 1996.

Chen L., Evans T. and Cash R. (1999), "Health as a Global Public Good" in Kaul I., Grunberg I. and Stern M. eds., *Global Public Goods: International Co-operation in the 21st Century* (Oxford University Press): 285-89.

Collin J., Lee K. and Bissell K., (2002), "The Framework Convention on Tobacco Control: The politics of global health governance, Third World Quarterly, 23(2).

Commission on Global Governance, *Our Global Neighbourhood* (Oxford: Oxford University Press 1995).

Deacon B. (1997), Global Social Policy (London: Sage).

Dia M. (1993), *A Governance Approach to Civil Service Reform in Sub-Saharan Africa*, World Bank Technical Paper, No. 225, Washington D.C.

Dodgson R. (1998), "The Women's Health Movement and the International Conference on Population and Development", *PhD Dissertation*, University of Newcastle upon Tyne, UK.

Farmer P. (1996), "Social Inequalities and Emerging Infectious Diseases." *Emerging Infectious Diseases*, 2(4): 259-66.

Fidler D. (1997), "The Globalization of Public Health: Emerging Infectious Diseases and International Relations," *Indiana Journal of Global Legal Studies*, 5(1): 11-51.

Fidler D. (1998a), "International Law and Global Public Health," International Colloquium on Public Health Law, Durban, South Africa, 22-24 November.

Fidler D. (1998b), "Microbialpolitik: Infectious Diseases and International Relations," *American University International Law Review*, 14(1): 1-53.

Finkelstein L. (1995), "What is global governance?" *Global Governance*, 1(3): 367-72.

Frechette L. (1998), "What do we mean by global governance?" Address by the UN Deputy Secretary-General, Global Governance Autumn Meetings Series, Global Governance and the UN: Beyond Track 2, Overseas Development Institute, London, 8 December.

Gill S. ed. (1997), *Globalization, Democratization and Multilateralism* (London: Macmillan).

Goodman N. (1971), *International Health Organizations and Their Work* (London: Livingstone Churchill).

Goodman N. (1998), "Clinical Governance", *British Medical Journal*, 317 (19 December): 1725-27.

Held D. (1992), "Democracy: From City States to Cosmopolitan Order?" in Held D. ed. *Prospects for Democracy* (London: Blackwell Publishers).

Held D. (1995), *Democracy and the Global Order* (Stanford: Stanford University Press).

Held D., McGrew A., Goldblatt D. and Perraton J. (1999), *Global Transformations: Politics, Economics and Culture* (Stanford: Stanford University Press).

Hewson M. and Sinclair T. (1999), "The Emergence of Global Governance Theory" in Hewson M. and Sinclair T. eds. *Approaches to Global Governance Theory* (New York: SUNY): 3-22.

Hulme D. and Edwards M. (1997), *NGOs, States and Donors, Too Close for Comfort?* (London: Macmillan).

Jareg P. and Kaseje D.C. (1998), "Growth of Civil Society in Developing Countries: Implications for Health", *The Lancet,* 351 (14 March):

Kaul I., Grunberg I. and Stern M. (1999*), Global Public Goods, International Cooperation in the 21st Century* (Oxford: Oxford University Press).

Kickbusch I. (1997), "New players for a new era: responding to the global public health challenges." *Journal of Public Health Medicine,* 19(2): 171-78.

Kickbusch I. (1999), "Global + Local = Global Public Health," *Journal of Epidemiology and Community Health.*

Kickbusch I. (1999), "Global Public Health: Revisiting health public policy at the global level," *Health Promotion International.*

Kickbusch I. (1999), "Shifting global environments for health and development," Keynote Address to 6th Canadian Conference on International Health, Canadian Society for International Health, Ottawa, 14 November.

Krasner (1983) ed., *International Regimes* (Ithaca, NY: Cornell University Press.

The King's Fund (1999), "What is clinical governance?" *Briefings,* London.

Lee K. (1998), *Historical Dictionary of the World Health Organization* (New Jersey: Scarecrow Press).

Lee K. (1998), "Shaping the future of global health co-operation: where can we go from here?" *The Lancet,* 351 (March 21): 899-902.

Lee K. (2000a), "An overview of global health and environmental risks" in Parsons L. and Lister G. eds. Global Health, A Local Issue (London: The Nuffield Trust), pp. 34-46. www.nuffieldtrust.org.uk

Lee K. (2000b), "The impact of globalization on public health: Implications for the UK Faculty of Public Health Medicine," *Journal of Public Health Medicine,* 22(3).

Lee K. (2001), "Globalization - A new agenda for health?" in McKee M., Garner P. and Stott R. eds. *International Co-operation and Health* (Oxford: Oxford University Press), Chapter 2.

Lee K., Collinson S., Walt G. and Gilson L. (1996), "Who should be doing what in international health: a confusion of mandates in the United Nations?" *British Medical Journal,* 312, 3 February: 302-307.

Leftwich A. (1993), "Governance, Democracy and Development in the Third World", *Third World Quarterly,* 14(3): 605-21.

Lucas A., Mogedal S., Walt G., Hodne Steen S., Kruse S.E., Lee K. and Hawken L. (1997), *Cooperation for Health Development, The World Health Organization's support to programmes at country level* (London: Governments of Australia, Canada, Italy, Norway, Sweden and the U.K.).

McGrew A. ed. (1997), *The Transformation of Democracy* (London: Polity Press).

McMichael A.J. and Beaglehole R. (2000), "The changing global context of public health", *The Lancet,* 356: 495-99.

McRitchie J. (1998), "Corporate governance, Enhancing the Return on Capital Through Increased Accountability." http://www.corpgov.net

Murphy C. (1994), *International Organization and Industrial Change, Global governance since 1850* (London: Polity Press).

Paris J.A.G. and McKeown K.M. (1999), "Clinical governance for public health professionals," *Journal of Public Health Medicine,* 21(4): 430-34.

Rahman A.T.R. (1996), *UN Development Update.*

Roemer M. (1994), "Internationalism in Medicine and Public Health" in Porter D. ed., *The History of Public Health and the Modern State* (London: Clio Medica/ Wellcome Institute).

Rosenau J.N. (1995), "Governance in the Twenty-first Century", *Global Governance,* 1(1).

Scally G. and Donaldson J. (1998), "Clinical governance and the drive for quality improvement in the new NHS in England", *British Medical Journal,* 317 (4 July): 61-65.

Scholte J.A. (1997), "The Globalization of World Politics", in: John Baylis and Steve Smith (Eds), *The Globalization of World Politics: An Introduction to International Relations* (Oxford University Press), Chapter 1.

Scholte J.A. (2000), Globalisation: A Critical Introduction (London: Palgrave].

Sikkink K. (1986), "Codes of conduct for transnational corporations: the case of the WHO/UNICEF code," International Organization, 40: 817-40.

UK Department of Health (1998), *The new NHS, a first class service* (London: HMSO).

UNDP (1997), *Reconceptualising Governance* (New York: Management Development and Governance Division).

Vaughan J.P., Mogedal S., Walt G., Kruse S.E., Lee K. and de Wilde K. (1996), "WHO and the effects of extrabudgetary funds: is the Organization donor driven?" *Health Policy and Planning*, 11(3): 253-64.

Vayrynen R. ed. (1999), Globalization and Global Governance (New York: Rowman & Littlefields).

Williamson O. (1996), *The Mechanisms of Governance* (Oxford: Oxford University Press).

World Bank (1994), *Governance: The World Bank's Experience* (Washington D.C.: IBRD).

World Bank (1997), *World Development Report, The State in a Changing World* (Washington D.C.: IBRD).

WHO (1995), "The rise of international co-operation in health." *World Health Forum*, 16(2):

WHO (1998) www.who.int/ina-ngo/ (accessed 22 March 2001)

WHO (2002), Health and Trade: Towards Common Ground (Geneva:WHO/HDE).

Zacher M. (1999a), "Global Epidemiological Surveillance: International Cooperation to Monitor Infectious Diseases" in Kaul I., Grunberg I. and Stern M. (1999*), Global Public Goods, International Cooperation in the 21st Century* (Oxford: Oxford University Press).

Zacher M. (1999b), "Uniting Nations: Global Regimes and the United Nations System" in Vayrynen R. ed. *Globalization and Global Governance* (New York: Rowman and Littlefield Publishers).

[29]

BETWEEN ISOLATIONISM AND MUTUAL VULNERABILITY: A SOUTH-NORTH PERSPECTIVE ON GLOBAL GOVERNANCE OF EPIDEMICS IN AN AGE OF GLOBALIZATION

Obijiofor Aginam[*]

We meet as we fight to defeat SARS, the first new epidemic of the twenty-first century. . . . Globalization of disease and threats to health mean globalization of the fight against them. SARS has been a wake-up call. But the lessons we have learned have implications that go way beyond the fight against this public health threat. . . . The events of the last few weeks also prompt us to look closely at the instruments of national and international law. Are they keeping up with our rapidly changing world?[1]

I. THE CRUX OF THE ARGUMENT

The transnational spread of infectious and non-communicable diseases in an era of globalization constitutes one of the most formidable challenges facing the normative orthodoxy of the Westphalian governance architecture. Exponents of "globalization of public health"[2] have explored the globalized nature of

[*] LL.B. (University of Nigeria); BL (Nigerian Law School); LL.M. (Queen's University); Ph.D. (University of British Columbia); Assistant Professor of Law, Carleton University, Ottawa, Canada; Global Security and Co-operation Research Fellow of the Social Science Research Council (SSRC) of New York, 2003-04; Global Health Leadership Officer, World Health Organization, Geneva, Switzerland, 1999-2001. An earlier version of this article was presented at the "SARS, Public Health and Global Governance" conference hosted by the Institute for International Law and Public Policy, Temple University James E. Beasley School of Law, Philadelphia, PA, March 24-25, 2004. I would like to thank Professors Jeffrey Dunoff and Scott Burris (Temple University School of Law) for inviting me to present aspects of this article at the conference. I would also like to thank Professor Ronald Bayer (Columbia University School of Public Health), Ambassador Hans Corell (formerly of the United Nations), Dr. Mandeep Dhaliwal (International HIV/AIDS Alliance), Charles Weiss (Distinguished Professor, Georgetown University), Dr. Joanne Csete (Human Rights Watch), Professor Susan K. Sell (George Washington University), Professor David P. Fidler (Indiana University), and Sophia Gruskin (Harvard University) for their comments when I presented this paper at Temple University. This article was partly researched and written during my tenure as Global Security and Cooperation Fellow of the Social Science Research Council (SSRC) of New York. I would like to thank the SSRC for generously funding my GSC fellowship.

1. Gro-Harlem Brundtland, Past Director-General, WHO, Address at the 56th World Health Assembly, Geneva, Switzerland (May 18, 2003).

2. For a discussion of "globalization of public health," see generally David P. Fidler, *The Globalization of Public Health: Emerging Infectious Diseases and International Relations*, 5 IND. J. GLOBAL LEGAL STUD. 11 (1997); David Woodward et al., *Globalization and Health: A Framework for Analysis and Action*, in 79 BULL. WORLD HEALTH ORGAN. 875 (2001), *available at* http://www.scielosp.org/pdf/bwho/v79n9/ v79n9a14.pdf; Kelley Lee & Richard Dodgson, *Globalization*

TEMPLE LAW REVIEW [Vol. 77

emerging and reemerging public health threats in an interdependent world. The recent transnational spread of severe acute respiratory syndrome ("SARS") from Asia to North America, as Brundtland observed in the quote above, is not only a wake-up call; it has once· again challenged the legal and regulatory approaches to global health governance. This paper juxtaposes two contending approaches to public health governance: *isolationism* and *mutual vulnerability*, and argues for a reconfiguration of transnational health governance structures based on an inclusive humane globalism. Despite the powerful arguments canvassed by the exponents of globalization of public health, the stark realities of the contemporary South-North health· divide has regrettably popularized isolationism, thereby impeding the emergence and sustenance of humane governance of global public health threats.

Isolationism is premised on the impression that the developing world is a reservoir of disease. In the discourse of hard-nosed realism, isolationism is a conscious effort to create a health sanctuary in the developed world that maximizes the health security of populations in Europe and North America. As SARS and other historical epidemics have infallibly proven, the argument canvassed by scholars of globalization of public health on the obsolescence or anachronism of the distinction between national and international health threats has become less recondite and unassailable in an interdependent world. Using SARS as the subject of analysis, this article explores the challenges of global governance of transnational epidemics in an interdependent world. I argue that global health governance orthodoxy has failed to respond adequately to public health challenges in a world characterized by South-North disparities.[3] ·I offer a reconstructive perspective that goes beyond the normative parameters of state-centric Westphalianism. The reconstruction draws from Richard Falk's ":law of humanity," and David Held's "cosmopolitan social democracy:" a cosmopolitan or quasi-cosmopolitan framework that captures the South-North health divide based on the mutual vulnerability of all of humanity to the menace of disease in an interdependent world.

II. ISOLATIONISM AND THE EVOLUTION OF PUBLIC HEALTH DIPLOMACY

Thus, the eleventh International Sanitary Conference in 53 years had as its essential purpose the protection of Europe against the importation of exotic diseases.[4]

---

and Cholera: Implications for Global Governance, 6 GLOBAL GOVERNANCE 214 (2000); Derek Yach & Douglas Bettcher, *The Globalization of Public Health, I: Threats and Opportunities,* 88 AM. J. PUB. HEALTH 735 (1998); Derek Yach & Douglas Bettcher, *The Globalization of Public Health, II: The Convergence of Self-Interest and Altruism,* 88 AM. J. PUB. HEALTH 738 (1998).

3. I use the term "South-North" throughout this paper as suggested by IVAN L. HEAD in ON A HINGE OF HISTORY: THE MUTUAL VULNERABILITY OF SOUTH AND NORTH 14 (1991). Professor Head expressed a preference for "South-North" as a more accurate reflection of the current international system. *Id.* He argued that "North-South" is misleading because "it lends weight to the impression that the South is the diminutive." *Id.*

.4. NORMAN HOWARD-JONES, THE SCIENTIFIC BACKGROUND OF THE INTERNATIONAL SANITARY CONFERENCES 1851-1938, at 85 (1975).

Isolationism, a conscious effort to insulate populations within the geopolitical boundaries of a nation-state from exotic diseases, is as old as the history of public health diplomacy. Before the European-led international sanitary conferences in the nineteenth century that were driven by the European cholera epidemics in 1830 and 1847, Neville Goodman identified three dominant reactions by nation-states to the trans-boundary spread of disease.[5] The first was the predominant view that disease was a punishment from the gods that could only be cured by prayers and sacrifices.[6] The second reaction was the isolation of a healthy society from an unhealthy one through the practice of *cordon sanitaire* to prevent either importation or exportation of disease.[7] The third reaction was the practice of quarantine that enabled governments to isolate goods or persons coming from places suspected of suffering an outbreak of disease to protect the community from importation of exotic diseases.[8] Between the fourteenth and nineteenth centuries, almost the entire *civilized* world practiced some form of quarantine. This consisted mainly of imposing an arbitrary period of isolation on the ships, crews, passengers, and goods arriving from foreign sea ports and destinations believed to be reservoirs of major epidemic diseases, especially plague, cholera, and yellow fever.[9]

The nineteenth century, within which public health diplomacy evolved in Europe through the International Sanitary Conferences, raises intriguing questions on the transnational governance of infectious diseases. This is because the civilized-uncivilized construct invented in the Age of Columbus had become firmly entrenched in the vocabulary of nineteenth century international law and relations. Peter Malanczuk observed that the international community in the nineteenth century was virtually *Europeanized* on the basis of conquest and domination; the international legal system became an exclusive European club to which non-Europeans would only be admitted if they proved that they were civilized.[10] The *realpolitik* of nineteenth century public health diplomacy driven

---

5. NEVILLE M. GOODMAN, INTERNATIONAL HEALTH ORGANIZATIONS AND THEIR WORK 27-29 (2d ed. 1971).

6. *Id.* at 27.

7. *Id.* at 28.

8. For a history and discussion of the concept of quarantine, see *id.* at 29 (stating that quarantine derived from "forty-day (*quaranta*) isolation period imposed at Venice in 1403 and said to be based on the period during which Jesus and Moses had remained in isolation in the desert"); Paul Slack, *Introduction* to EPIDEMICS AND IDEAS: ESSAYS ON THE HISTORICAL PERCEPTION OF PESTILENCE 15 (Terence Ranger & Paul Slack eds., 1992); B. Mafart & J.L Perret, *History of the Concept of Quarantine*, 58 MED. TROPICALE 14, 14-20 (1998) (French) (defining quarantine as "a concept developed by society to protect against outbreak of contagious diseases") (on file with author).

9. DAVID P. FIDLER, INTERNATIONAL LAW AND INFECTIOUS DISEASES 26 (1999); GOODMAN, *supra* note 5, at 31.

10. PETER MALANCZUK, AKEHURST'S MODERN INTRODUCTION TO INTERNATIONAL LAW 13 (7th ed. 1997). *See also* MOHAMMED BEDJAOUI, TOWARD A NEW INTERNATIONAL ECONOMIC ORDER 51-53 (1979) (discussing idea that international law in nineteenth century was synonymous with European imperialism); Antony Anghie, *Finding the Peripheries: Sovereignty and Colonialism in Nineteenth-Century International Law*, 40 HARV. INT'L L.J. 1, 2 (1999) (stating that virtually all territories in Asia, Africa, and Pacific were governed by European law by end of nineteenth century).

by the international sanitary conferences was the desire to protect civilized Europe from exotic diseases and pathogens that emanated from the uncivilized non-European societies. As Norman Howard-Jones observed, the international sanitary conferences were not motivated by a wish for the general betterment of the health of the world, but by the desire to protect certain favored (especially European) nations from contamination by their less-favoured (especially Eastern fellows).[11] Cholera presents an apt illustration of the European desire to keep exotic diseases far from reaching European territorial boundaries. Goodman observed that for centuries cholera, although terrible in rapidity and high morbidity, was considered a disease largely confined to Central Asia, particularly Bengal. But between 1828 and 1831, it was reported to have passed out of India and spread rapidly to the whole of Europe and to the United States.[12] From Punjab, Afghanistan, and Persia:

> [I]t reached Moscow in 1830 and infected the whole of Europe, including England, by the end of 1831. It reached Canada and the United States of America in the summer of 1832 . . . . Another pandemic followed in 1847 and five others in the next fifty years. This was a new and terrifying disease to the Western world . . . .[13]

The entire gamut of the international sanitary conventions and regulations negotiated at each of the European-led international sanitary conference is replete with conscious efforts to insulate Europeans from exotic diseases. Both the sanitary convention and regulations negotiated at the first International Sanitary Conference in 1851 by eleven European states and Turkey on plague, cholera, and yellow fever were focused on ships "having on board a disease reputed to be importable."[14] According to David Fidler, the objective of protecting Europe from "Asiatic cholera" dominated the European-led international sanitary conferences of 1866, 1874, 1885, 1892, 1893, and 1894 because each of these conferences were convened after another cholera scare in Europe.[15] The four international treaties concluded between 1892 and 1897 followed the trend of European insulation from diseases of the *uncivilized*. While the 1892 International Sanitary Convention focused on the importation of cholera from the Suez Canal by Mecca Muslim pilgrims, the 1893 International Sanitary Convention focused broadly on policing European geopolitical boundaries against the importation of cholera. While the 1894 International Sanitary Convention focused on Mecca pilgrimages and maritime traffic in the Persian Gulf, the 1897 International Sanitary Convention focused on keeping plague out of Europe.[16] At the 1897 international sanitary conference convened specifically on plague, Great Britain, then the colonial overseer of India, was

---

11. Norman Howard-Jones, *Origins of International Health Work*, 6 Brit. Med. J. 1032, 1035 (1950).

12. Goodman, *supra* note 5, at 38.

13. *Id.* (footnote omitted).

14. *Id.* at 46.

15. Fidler, *supra* note 9, at 28-30.

16. *Id.* at 30.

severely criticized by other European states because of a serious and persistent epidemic of plague from Bombay to the north-west littoral of India. Austria-Hungary proposed the 1897 international sanitary conference because it feared that its Muslim subjects from Mecca pilgrimage might bring plague with them after being in contact with pilgrims from India.[17]

Transiting to the twentieth century, public health diplomacy continued to evolve in the complex multilateral terrain of the civilized-uncivilized disease construct. Commenting on the 1903 consolidation of the 1892, 1893, 1894, and 1897 conventions, Howard-Jones observed that the 1903 international sanitary conference "had as its essential purpose the protection of Europe against the importation of the exotic diseases from the East."[18] Today, even in the age of globalization, the isolationist legacy of the nineteenth century public health diplomacy remains one of the dominant characteristics of global health governance. Notwithstanding the expansion of the international society through the establishment of the United Nations in 1945, and the decolonization and political self-determination of most African, Asian, and South Pacific entities in the 1960s and 1970s, contemporary public health Westphalianism is still embedded in a colonial-type relationship. The present South-North health divide conjures images of systematic exclusion of the *uncivilized* from the dividends of global public goods for health in the "emerging global village." Global governance, including global health, oscillates between the paradoxical challenges of what Upendra Baxi has explored as "Global Neighborhood and Universal Otherhood," a disguised or conscious entrenchment of age-old inequalities and structures which banish a sizable part of the developing world to the margins of global governance.[19]

The dominant perception in the developed world that the developing world is a reservoir of disease as a result of collapsed or even nonexistent public health infrastructure has led to isolationist national health policies in most of the global North. In nearly all the industrialized countries of the global North, immigrants from Africa are prohibited from donating blood to national blood banks because of the perception that every African blood is naturally tainted with malaria and other "*African*" diseases. Although the phenomenon of globalization has continued to erode geopolitical boundaries, globalization of public health has paradoxically reinforced the powers of nation-states in the global North to

---

17. HOWARD-JONES, *supra* note 4, at 78.

18. *Id.* at 78. *See also* FIDLER, *supra* note 9, at 31 (observing that "of the 184 articles in the 1903 International Sanitary Convention, 131, or approximately seventy-one percent of the treaty, deal with places (for example, Egypt, and Constantinople) and events (for example, Mecca pilgrimages) located outside Europe").

19. Upendra Baxi, "*Global Neighborhood" and the "Universal Otherhood": Notes on the Report of the Commission on Global Governance, in* 21 ALTERNATIVES 525, 544-45 (1996). I have applied Baxi's paradoxical matrix in the global health context. *See also* Obijiofor Aginam, *The Nineteenth Century Colonial Fingerprints on Public Health Diplomacy: A Postcolonial View*, 1 LAW SOC. JUST. & GLOBAL DEV. J. 1, 7-8 (2003) (discussing paradox between "global neighbourhood" and "universal otherhood"), *available at* http://elj.warwick.ac.uk/global/issue/2003-1/aginam.htm (last visited Sept. 7, 2004).

isolate potential immigrants who are perceived to be carriers of leading communicable diseases.[20] Immigration policies are now constructed around mandatory medical screening and testing of potential immigrants. Disease has emerged as a ground to shut the borders of Europe and North America against immigrants from Africa, Asia, South America, and the Caribbean. As Robert Kaplan observed in his widely cited essay *The Coming Anarchy*:

> As many internal African borders begin to crumble, a more impenetrable boundary is being erected that threatens to isolate the continent as a whole: the wall of disease . . . . Africa may today be more dangerous in this regard than it was in 1862 . . . . As African birth rates soar and slums proliferate, some experts worry that viral mutations and hybridizations might, just conceivably, result in a form of the [acquired immunodeficiency syndrome ("AIDS")] virus that is easier to catch than the present strain.
>
> It is malaria that is most responsible for the disease wall that threatens to separate Africa and other parts of the Third World from more-developed regions of the planet in the twenty-first century. Carried by mosquitoes, malaria, unlike AIDS, is easy to catch.[21]

Although countries often overreact to outbreaks of epidemics in other countries with trade, travel, and economic embargoes ostensibly to protect their populations, these embargoes are always more severe and isolationist when the disease or health threat emanates from a developing country. While science and risk assessment played some role in the ban of British beef by most European Union countries following the United Kingdom mad cow disease/bovine spongiform encephalopathy ("BSE") crisis and the recent United States' ban of Canadian beef as a result of the single BSE case in Alberta, the embargoes that followed the Indian plague outbreak in 1994, and the East African cholera outbreak in 1997, and the Ebola outbreak in Zaire (now Democratic Republic of the Congo) were pure isolationist policies by the developed world. Commenting on the economic embargoes that followed the Indian plague outbreak, David Heymann stated that such excessive measures included closing of airports to aircraft arriving from India, unnecessary barriers to importation of foodstuffs from India, and in many cases the repatriation of Indian guest workers even though many of them had not lived in India for many years.[22] In 1997, the European Community ("EC") imposed a ban on the importation of fresh fish from East Africa following an outbreak of cholera in remote areas in certain

---

20. For an argument that globalization presents a paradox by opening the borders of developing countries to multinational corporations from the North while shutting the borders of developed countries to immigrants, see Obijiofor Aginam, *Global Village, Divided World: South-North Gap and Global Health Challenges at Century's Dawn*, 7 IND. J. GLOBAL LEGAL STUD. 603, 610 (2000).

21. Robert D. Kaplan, *The Coming Anarchy*, *in* GLOBALIZATION AND THE CHALLENGE OF A NEW CENTURY: A READER 34, 40 (Patrick O'Meara et al. eds., 2000).

22. David Heymann, The International Health Regulations: Ensuring Maximum Protection with Minimal Restriction, Annual Meeting of the ABA, Program Materials on Law & Emerging & Re-Emerging Infectious Diseases (1996) (unpublished manuscript, on file with author). *See also* Laurie Garret; *The Return of Infectious Diseases*, FOREIGN AFF., Jan.-Feb. 1996, at 66; 74 (stating that India lost almost two billion dollars as a result of excessive measures following outbreak of plague).

East African countries.[23] At the time of the ban, fish exports from the affected countries, Kenya, Mozambique, Tanzania, and Uganda, to the European countries stood at $230 million.[24] Is isolationism an effective public health strategy in an era of globalized epidemics? Does isolationism offer effective defenses against microbial forces that routinely disrespect geopolitical boundaries? History is in fact repeating itself. If *cordon sanitaire*, the dominant isolationist policy of European states in the nineteenth century was ineffective against the cross-border cholera epidemics of 1830 and 1847, then modern day isolationism would also be futile as globalization erodes national boundaries and renders populations within those boundaries vulnerable to the menace of disease. To gain deeper insights into the tension between isolationism and globalization of public health in the Westphalian system, we must explore the concept of mutual vulnerability in the dynamic of global health governance in an interdependent world.

III. MUTUAL VULNERABILITY TO DISEASE IN A GLOBALIZING WORLD

Today, in an interconnected world, bacteria and viruses travel almost as fast as e-mail and financial flows. Globalization has connected Bujumbura to Bombay and Bangkok to Boston. There are no health sanctuaries. No impregnable walls exist between a world that is healthy, well-fed, and well-off and another that is sick, malnourished, and impoverished. Globalization has shrunk distances, broken down old barriers, and linked people. Problems halfway around the world become everyone's problem.[25]

Because globalization of public health postulates the anachronism of the erstwhile distinction between national and international health threats, it is now infallible that disease pathogens neither carry national passports nor respect the geopolitical boundaries of sovereign states. State sovereignty is an alien concept in the microbial world. With the contemporary globalization of the world's political economy, which is amply evidenced by the huge volumes of goods, services, and people that cross national boundaries, all of humanity is now mutually vulnerable to the emerging and reemerging threats of disease in an interdependent world. Mutual vulnerability, as employed in the global health context, is the accumulation of the vicious threats posed to humans by disease and pathogenic microbes in an interdependent world, the fragility of humans to

---

23. *See* Commission Decision of 23 December 1997 concerning certain protective measures with regard to certain fishery products originating in Uganda, Kenya, Tanzania and Mozambique, 1997 O.J. (L356) 64 (banning importation of "fresh fishery products from, or originating in Kenya, Uganda, Tanzania and Mozambique" because of cholera epidemic); Commission Decision of 16 January 1998 on protective measures with regard to fishery products from, or originating in Uganda, Kenya, Tanzania and Mozambique and repealing Decision 97/878/EC, 1998 O.J. (L15) 43 (mandating testing of all frozen or fresh fishery products from or originating in Uganda, Kenya, Tanzania and Mozambique "to verify that they present no threat to public health").

24. FIDLER, *supra* note 9, at 80 n.158.

25. Gro-Harlem Brundtland, *Global Health and International Security*, 9 GLOBAL GOVERNANCE 417, 417 (2003).

succumb to these threats, and the obsolescence of the distinction between national and international health threats.[26] International trade, travel, intentional and forced migrations fueled by wars, conflicts, and environmental disasters propel the efficacy of mutual vulnerability as a phenomenon of "South-North dangers"[27] and one of the fundamental determinants of the contemporary Westphalian system.

The multiple dimensions of mutual vulnerability, although complex, are not at all new in humanity's encounter with disease. Historical accounts of the Plague of Athens in 430 BC,[28] the fourteenth century European bubonic plague (Black Death),[29] and the microbial consequences of the Columbian exchange between the Old and New Worlds,[30] suggest that one dimension of mutual vulnerability–the permeation of national boundaries by disease–is an entrenched feature of humanity's interaction with the microbial world. In contemporary public health diplomacy, the crisis of emerging and reemerging infectious diseases ("EIDs") reinforces our mutual vulnerability to disease in a globalizing world. The United States' Centers for Disease Control and Prevention ("CDC") defines EIDs as "diseases of infectious origin whose incidence in humans has increased within the past two decades or threatens to increase in the near future."[31] In 1995, the United States' government interagency Working Group on Emerging and Reemerging Infectious Diseases ("CISET") listed twenty-nine

26. I do not claim originality of the use of the concept of mutual vulnerability. For earlier uses of the concept to explore the political economy of South-North relations, development, and under-development, see HEAD, *supra* note 3, at 185-87 (discussing global vulnerability to diseases such as AIDS and malaria); JORGE NEF, HUMAN SECURITY AND MUTUAL VULNERABILITY: THE GLOBAL POLITICAL ECONOMY OF DEVELOPMENT AND UNDERDEVELOPMENT 13-26 (2d ed. 1999) (analyzing global vulnerability).

27. Ivan L. Head, *South-North Dangers*, FOREIGN AFF., Summer 1989, at 71, 84-86.

28. *Thucydides: History Of The Peloponnesian War*, *in* 6 GREAT BOOKS OF THE WESTERN WORLD 345, 399 (Robert Maynard Hutchins et al. eds., Richard Crawley trans., 1952) (suggesting that the plague, which devastated Athens, originated from Ethiopia and spread through Egypt and Libya before it reached Athens following movement of troops during war).

29. J.N. HAYS, THE BURDENS OF DISEASE: EPIDEMICS AND HUMAN RESPONSE IN WESTERN HISTORY 39-40 (1998) (arguing that path of Bubonic Plague originated in Central Asia, spread across Asian steppes in the 1330s, was carried by ship from Crimea to Sicily in 1347, and followed international travel and trading routes before arriving in major European sea ports before the end of 1348).

30. *See generally* ALFRED W. CROSBY JR., ECOLOGICAL IMPERIALISM: THE BIOLOGICAL EXPANSION OF EUROPE, 900-1900 (1986) (arguing that Europeans' successful displacement and replacement of native peoples in world's temperate zones has a biological, ecological origin); ALFRED W. CROSBY JR., THE COLUMBIAN EXCHANGE: BIOLOGICAL AND CULTURAL CONSEQUENCES OF 1492 (1972) (discussing exchange of disease and food supply following Columbus' finding new world); DOROTHY PORTER, HEALTH, CIVILIZATION AND THE STATE: A HISTORY OF PUBLIC HEALTH FROM ANCIENT TO MODERN TIMES (1999) (describing mutual interchange of biological and epidemiological trends of Old and New Worlds).

31. CDC, ADDRESSING EMERGING INFECTIOUS DISEASE THREATS: A PREVENTION STRATEGY FOR THE UNITED STATES 7 (1994). *See also* WHO, WORLD HEALTH REPORT 1996: FIGHTING DISEASE, FOSTERING DEVELOPMENT 15 (1996) [hereinafter WHO, WORLD HEALTH REPORT] (describing emerging infectious diseases).

2004]*A SOUTH-NORTH PERSPECTIVE ON GLOBAL GOVERNANCE* 305

examples of new infectious diseases identified since 1973.[32] Some of the diseases in the list published by .CISET include Ebola hemorrhagic fever (1977), Legionnaire's disease (1977), toxic shock syndrome (1981), Lyme disease (1982), acquired immunodeficiency syndrome ("AIDS") (1983), and Brazilian hemorrhagic fever (1984). The CISET Working Group categorized reemerging infectious diseases into three groups: (i) infectious diseases that have flared up in regions in which they historically appeared; (ii) infectious diseases that have expanded into new regions; and (iii) infectious diseases that have developed resistance to anti-microbial treatments and have spread through traditional and/or new regions because of such resistance.[33] Tuberculosis falls into each of the three categories of emerging and reemerging infectious diseases. It is an old disease that has reemerged in regions where it historically occurred, it has returned as a public health threat in the South and the North, and certain strains of tuberculosis have developed strong resistance to anti-microbial treatments.[34] Arno Karlen, in *Man and Microbes*, published a "partial list of new diseases" that first appeared between 1951 and 1993.[35] In Karlen's analysis, not even the most powerful country in the world, the United States, could insulate its populations from the outbreaks of Lassa fever and Legionnaires' disease suspected to have arrived in the United States from the developing world because "[h]igh-speed travel had created a global village for pathogens."[36] Even with an isolated disease like malaria, widely thought to be confined to Africa, high-speed travel, tourism, migration, and international airline networks have combined to entrench the disease firmly in the discourse of mutual vulnerability. Cases of "imported malaria" and "airport malaria" have reemerged in Europe, North America, and other regions of the world where the mortality and morbidity burdens of malaria constitute little or no threats to public health.[37] The disparities between the South and the North on the burdens of malaria are stark, with overwhelming malaria cases occurring in Africa. Nonetheless, airport and imported malaria can no longer be neglected, especially in Europe, because there have been reports of a surprising number of malaria deaths in countries of

---

32. NATIONAL SCIENCE & TECHNOLOGY COUNCIL COMMITTEE ON INTERNATIONAL SCIENCE, ENGINEERING, & TECHNOLOGY ("CISET"), INTERAGENCY WORKING GROUP ON EMERGING INFECTIOUS DISEASES, INFECTIOUS DISEASES: A GLOBAL THREAT 14 (Sept. 1995).

33. *See id.* (listing factors contributing to re-emergence of infectious diseases).

34. *See generally* JOHN CROFTON, GUIDELINES FOR THE MANAGEMENT OF DRUG-RESISTANT TUBERCULOSIS (1997) (discussing strategies for tuberculosis management); David P. Fidler, *Return of the Fourth Horseman: Emerging Infectious Diseases and International Law*, 81 MINN. L. REV. 771 (1997) (analyzing emerging and re-emerging infectious diseases).

35. ARNO KARLEN, MAN AND MICROBES 6 (1995).

36. *Id.* at 7.

37. For a distinction between "imported malaria" and "airport malaria," see Norman G. Gratz et. al., *Why Aircraft Disinsection?*, *in* 78 BULL. WHO 995, 996-97 (2000) (stating that the "most direct evidence of transmission of disease by mosquitoes imported on aircraft is the occurrence of airport malaria, i.e. cases of malaria in and near international airports, among persons who have not recently traveled to areas where the disease is endemic or who have not recently received blood transfusions. Airport malaria should be distinguished from imported malaria among persons who contract the infection during a stay in an area of endemicity and subsequently fall ill.").

the North following unrecognized infection through a blood transfusion or a one-off mosquito bite near an international airport. Cases in Europe of airport malaria, which mostly occur in the absence of anamnestic signs of any exposure to malaria risk, are often difficult to diagnose.[38] From 1969 to 1999, confirmed cases of airport malaria have been reported in France, Belgium, Switzerland, the United Kingdom, Italy, the United States, Luxembourg, Germany, the Netherlands, Spain, Israel, and Australia.[39] Epidemiological data in Europe suggest that 1,010 cases were imported into the countries of the European Union in 1971; 2,882 in 1981; about 9,200 cases in 1991; and 12,328 cases in 1997.[40] In 1993, some thirty years after the eradication of malaria in the former Soviet Union, some 1,000 cases of malaria were registered in the Russian Federation and in the newly independent states: Belarus, Kazakhstan, Ukraine, Azerbaijan, Tajikistan, Turkmenistan, and Uzbekistan.[41] In the United Kingdom, 8,353 cases of imported malaria were reported between 1987 and 1992. A breakdown of this figure shows that United Kingdom nationals who visited their friends and relations in malaria endemic regions accounted for forty-nine percent of the cases, visitors to the United Kingdom accounted for nineteen percent, tourists accounted for sixteen percent, while immigrants and expatriates accounted for eleven and five percent respectively.[42]

The World Health Organization ("WHO") blames the global crisis of emerging and reemerging infectious diseases on "fatal complacency" as a result of antibiotic discovery, global eradication of smallpox, the progress made in rolling back the mortality burdens of measles, guinea worm, leprosy, poliomyelitis, and neo-natal tetanus.[43] This cautious optimism has turned into a fatal complacency that is costing millions of lives annually.[44] The emergence in the North of West Nile virus, airport and imported malaria, drug-resistant tuberculosis, and SARS through global travel, tourism, trade, and human migrations, provide the premise for an irrefutable conclusion: the distinction between national and international has become obsolete in an interdependent world. Populations within the geopolitical boundaries of Westphalian nation-states have now, more than ever before in recorded history, become mutually vulnerable to pathogenic microbes. Humanity is "on a hinge of history," and the Westphalian governance architecture must devise effective ways to protect humanity from advancing microbial forces.

---

38. WHO REGIONAL OFFICE FOR EUROPE, STRATEGY TO ROLL BACK MALARIA IN THE WHO EUROPEAN REGION 6 (1999), *available at* http://www.euro.who.int/document/e67133.pdf (last visited Sept. 7, 2004). *See also* Gratz et al., *supra* note 37, at 998 (stating that "[a]irport malaria is particularly dangerous in that physicians generally have little reason to suspect it. This is especially true if there has been no recent travel to areas where malaria is endemic.").

39. Gratz, *supra* note 37, at 998.

40. WHO REGIONAL OFFICE FOR EUROPE, *supra* note 38, at 6.

41. *Id.* at 3.

42. WHO, REPORT ON INFECTIOUS DISEASES: REMOVING OBSTACLES TO HEALTHY DEVELOPMENT 52 (1999).

43. WHO, WORLD HEALTH REPORT, *supra* note 31, at 1.

44. *Id.*

IV. SARS AND THE TENSION BETWEEN ISOLATIONISM AND MUTUAL VULNERABILITY

SARS, the first severe infectious disease to emerge in the twenty-first century, has taken advantage of opportunities for rapid international spread made possible by the unprecedented volume and speed of air travel. SARS has also shown how, in a closely interconnected and interdependent world, a new and poorly understood infectious disease can adversely affect economic growth, trade, tourism, business and industrial performance, and social stability as well as public health.[45]

In February 2003, an infectious disease in the form of an atypical pneumonia of unknown cause, SARS, was first recognized in Hanoi, Vietnam. In a few weeks, WHO was informed of similar outbreaks in various hospitals in Hong Kong (China), Singapore, and Toronto (Canada). Subsequent investigations by WHO traced the source of the outbreaks to a hotel in Hong Kong with a visiting physician from the Guangdong Province in China. The physician had treated patients with atypical pneumonia before traveling to Hong Kong and was symptomatic on arrival. The Chinese Ministry of Health, on February 11, 2003, informed WHO of an outbreak of acute respiratory syndrome involving over 300 cases with five deaths in the Guangdong province. On February 14, WHO was informed that the disease had been detected as far back as November 16, 2002, and that the outbreak was coming under control.[46] According to WHO, SARS has several features that constitutes a serious threat to global public health.[47] First, "there is no vaccine or treatment, forcing health authorities to resort to control tools dating back to the earliest days of empirical microbiology: isolation, infection control and contact tracing."[48] Second, the virus has been identified as a previously unknown member of the coronavirus family, and some coronaviruses undergo frequent mutation thereby frustrating the development of effective vaccines.[49] Both the epidemiology and pathogenesis of SARS are poorly understood. Third, SARS had a high case fatality ratio in the range of fourteen to fifteen percent.[50] Between November 2002 and April 2003, over 3,200 SARS cases were reported in twenty-four countries.[51]

SARS implicated the tension between isolationist national responses to goods and people from SARS-afflicted countries, and mutual vulnerability to the

---

45. WHO Secretariat, *Revision of the International Health Regulations: Severe acute respiratory syndrome (SARS)*, 56th World Health Assembly, at 2, WHO Doc. A56/48 (May 17, 2003), *available at* http://www.who.int/gb/ebwha/pdf_files/WHA56/ea5648.pdf.

46. *Id.* at 1.

47. *Id.* at 2.

48. *Id.*

49. *Id.* at 2-3.

50. *Id.*

51. WHO, Cumulative Number of Reported Probable Cases of Severe Acute Respiratory Syndrome (SARS), *at* http://www.who.int/csr/sars/country/2003_04_15/en/print.html (Apr. 15, 2003).

disease as a result of globalization and the speed of travel and trade. In part, this tension is epitomized by the heavy economic damage as a result of the embargoes and boycott of the SARS-afflicted countries, and the WHO's Global Outbreak Alert and Response Network that collaborated well with the United States' CDC and eleven laboratories around the world put together to identify the cause of SARS. In Canada, the economic cost of SARS was estimated at $30 million daily. It is projected that China and South Korea suffered some $2 billion in SARS-related tourism and economic losses. Visitor arrivals in China, South Korea, Singapore, and Canada dropped drastically as a result of the WHO travel advisories, isolationist responses, and overreaction from other countries.[52] In Hong Kong, it was estimated that lost revenue from hotels, restaurants, and shops could amount to 0.5% of its total gross domestic product in 2003. Thailand, whose economy relied on tourism, barred visitors suspected of carrying the virus from entering the country.[53] This modern-day *cordon sanitaire*, when compared with the mutual vulnerability to SARS as a result of its rapid spread across national boundaries - from Asia to North America – underscores why global collaboration is the best way to fight epidemics in an age of globalization. Echoing the central theme of globalization of public health, Ilona Kickbusch observed with respect to the transnational spread of SARS that:

> Countries – small and large – will need to pool both sovereignty and resources based on a new mindset; they will need to acknowledge that while health is a national responsibility, it is also a global public good.... As a global community, we need to stop focusing on the reactive mode that fights disease by disease and outbreak by outbreak. We need to ensure the international legal framework for such a fight and develop sustainable financing of global surveillance, rapid global response and local capacity.[54]

The continued oscillation of public health diplomacy between *isolationism* and *mutual vulnerability* indicts the governance architecture of the Westphalian system and opens new vistas in global efforts to fight transnational epidemics.

V. FIDELITY TO HUMANITY'S HEALTH: A POST-WESTPHALIAN EXPLORATION BETWEEN "LAW OF HUMANITY" AND "COSMPOLITAN SOCIAL DEMOCRACY"

Globalization of public health de-emphasizes the "territorialization" of public health risks simply because the concept of state sovereignty is alien to the

---

52. Michael D. Lemonick & Alice Park, *The Truth about SARS*, TIME, May 5, 2003, at 50-51.

53. CENTER FOR STRATEGIC & INTERNATIONAL STUDIES, SARS'S GLOBAL SPREAD DEMANDS INTERNATIONAL COLLABORATIVE CONTAINMENT EFFORTS, *at* http://www.globalization101.org/news.asp?NEWS_ID=49 (Apr. 14, 2003). For a detailed study on the economic cost of SARS, see Jong-Wha Lee & Warwick J. McKibbin, *Globalization and Disease: The Case of SARS*, AUSTRALIAN NAT'L UNIV. WORKING PAPERS IN TRADE & DEV., Working Paper No. 2003/16 (2003) (revised version of paper presented at the Asian Economic Panel, Tokyo, Japan, May 11-12, 2003), *available at* http://rspas.anu.edu.au/economics/ publish/ papers/wp2003/wp-econ-2003-16.pdf.

54. Ilona Kickbusch, *SARS: Wake-Up Call for a Strong Global Health Policy*, YALE GLOBAL ONLINE (Apr. 25, 2003), *at* http://yaleglobal.yale.edu/article.print?id=1476.

microbial world.[55] Globalized public health requires a global policy universe and humane global health governance framework involving a multiplicity of actors—international organizations, private and corporate actors, and civil society. Exploring the politics of the "domestic-foreign Frontier," James Rosenau identified a policy response that treats the emergent "Frontier" "as becoming more rugged and, thus, as the arena in which domestic and foreign issues converge, intermesh, or otherwise become indistinguishable within a seamless web."[56] Thus:

> While foreign policy still designates the efforts of societies to maintain a modicum of control over their external environments, new global interdependence issues such as pollution, currency crises, AIDS, and the drug trade have so profoundly changed the tasks and goals of foreign policy officials . . . .[57]

Global governance of transnational epidemics like SARS comes within the list of complex global issues that shape Rosenau's "domestic-foreign Frontier." Fashioning effective and humane global health governance accords will be difficult, but as Rosenau put it, "global governance is not so much a label for high degree of integration and order."[58] Governance of globalized public health threats in the 'Frontier' involves critical choices. What is most important is for evolving multilateral governance structures to focus on the "world" as its primary constituency, and humanity (human life) as the endangered species that it seeks to conserve. In an era of globalized epidemics, therefore, an indispensable part of post-Westphalian global governance architecture lies within the normative boundaries of Falk's "law of humanity"[59] and Held's "cosmopolitan social democracy."[60] According to Falk, "[t]he character of the law of humanity is not self-evident. It could mean law that is enacted by and for the peoples of the world, as distinct from the elites who act in law-making settings on behalf of states."[61]

The promise of civil society participation in humane governance is founded on the perceived or actual exclusion, by the state, of a sizable part of humanity

55. In adopting this view of globalization, I am a student of David Held and Anthony McGrew who defined globalization as "a process (or set of processes) which embodies a transformation in the spatial organization of social relations and transactions." DAVID HELD, ET AL., GLOBAL TRANSFORMATIONS: POLITICS, ECONOMICS AND CULTURE 16 (1999). *See also* JAN AART SCHOLTE, GLOBALIZATION: A CRITICAL INTRODUCTION 16 (2000) (characterizing globalization as "a spread of supraterritoriality").

56. JAMES N. ROSENAU, ALONG THE DOMESTIC-FOREIGN FRONTIER: EXPLORING GOVERNANCE IN A TURBULENT WORLD 5 (1997).

57. *Id.* at 20.

58. *Id.* at 10-11.

59. RICHARD FALK, LAW IN AN EMERGING GLOBAL VILLAGE: A POST-WESTPHALIAN PERSPECTIVE 33 (1998).

60. For a concise version of Held's perspective on cosmopolitan social democracy, see DAVID HELD & ANTHONY MCGREW, GLOBALIZATION/ANTI-GLOBALIZATION 118-36 (2002) (discussing reconstruction of world order). In exploring the discourses of Falk and Held, I do not suggest that "law of humanity" and "cosmopolitan social democracy" neatly overlap.

61. FALK, *supra* note 59, at 34.

from its protective structures from the Treaty of Westphalia 1648 to the present day.[62] This has led to vicious tensions between global policies, incubated in multilateral forums exclusively by nation-states acting as repositories of political power within geopolitical boundaries often perceived as not fully protective of human well-being, and an animation of transnational civic society agenda involving human rights, public health, the environment, and other substantive areas where states and market forces are perceived to be endangering public goods.[63] Falk uses "globalization-from-above" and "globalization-from-below" to explore the tension at the two extremes of law of humanity. In his metaphor of "predatory globalization," Falk argues that the governance frameworks of international institutions are now manipulated by market forces.[64] In a capital-driven, non-territorial world order, most states, especially developing countries, are unable to protect their citizens against decisions and policies of the World Bank, the International Monetary Fund, and the World Trade Organization within the colossal edifice of economic globalization.[65] Similar to this, Held's cosmopolitan social democracy postulates that:

> Political communities can no longer be considered ... as simply 'discrete worlds' or as self-enclosed political spaces; they are enmeshed in complex structures of overlapping forces, relations and networks. . . .
> The locus of effective political power can no longer be assumed to be simply national governments – effective power is shared and bartered by diverse forces and agencies at national, regional and international levels.[66]

Reconstructing world order based on cosmopolitan social democracy, according to Held and Anthony McGrew, revolves around respect for international law, greater transparency, accountability, and democracy in global governance, a more equitable distribution of the world's resources and human security, the protection and reinvention of community at diverse levels, the regulation of the global economy through the public management of global financial and trade flows, the provision of global public goods, and the engagement of leading stakeholders in corporate governance.[67] Applied to the global health context, other cosmopolitan scholars like Thomas Pogge argue that the current distribution in national rates of infant mortality, life expectancy, and disease can be accounted for largely by reference to the existing world market system.[68] In contemporary global discourses, it has now been recognized, at least

---

62. *Id.* at 35.

63. *Id.* In using Falk's argument, I do not suggest that nation-states will become completely irrelevant in global governance or that they will automatically cede a significant part of their powers to civil society. Rather, I suggest that nation-states are no longer the only actors in global governance. A genuine dialogue between state and non-state actors is critically needed to review and fill the gap in the Westphalian system.

64. RICHARD FALK, PREDATORY GLOBALIZATION: A CRITIQUE 56 (1999).

65. *Id.*

66. HELD & MCGREW, *supra* note 60, at 123.

67. *Id.* at 131.

68. THOMAS W. POGGE, REALIZING RAWLS 237 (1989).

at the doctrinaire level, that health is a global public good.[69] As well, there now exists some persuasive evidence anchored on solid facts that significant financial and technical resources are urgently needed to address the mortality and morbidity burdens of killer infectious and non-communicable diseases, and the deadly partnership of poverty and ill health, in order to boost disease surveillance capacity in most of the Third World.[70] The pertinent question is whether emerging global health accords like the *Global Fund to Fight AIDS, Tuberculosis and Malaria*, and the *International Health Regulations* are cosmopolitan enough to catalyze a change in the sovereign mindset of poor and wealthy nation-states in the Westphalian system. Do they attract enough attention and resources to address the stark realities of contemporary South-North health divide? Do these accords place humanity as the epicenter of their core framework? Although this article does not provide all, or indeed any of the answers, the fact remains that the promise of global governance as a weapon against advancing microbial forces is uncertain. National, international, and global health regulatory institutions, as presently constructed, look like Michel Foucault's "panopticons," a strict spatial partitioning through which the North can catch every exotic disease from the South before it reaches their borders.[71] Regrettably, this isolationist global health governance policy has betrayed the public health trust that should drive interstate relations in an interdependent world. Deploring the betrayal of trust on which humane global public health architecture is presently constructed, Laurie Garrett observed that:

> The new globalization pushed communities against one another, opening old wounds and historic hatreds, often with genocidal results. It would be up to public health to find ways to bridge the hatreds, bringing the world toward a sense of singular community in which the health of each one member rises or falls with the health of all others.[72]

Leading epidemiologist, John Last reminds us that:

> Dangers to health anywhere on earth are dangers to health everywhere. International health, therefore, means more than just the health problems peculiar to developing countries . . . . There are

---

69. *See* David Woodward & Richard D. Smith, *Global Public Goods and Health: Concepts and Issues, in* GLOBAL PUBLIC GOODS FOR HEALTH: HEALTH, ECONOMIC, AND PUBLIC HEALTH PERSPECTIVES 3-8 (Richard Smith et. al. eds., 2003) (analyzing how global public good for health concept can best be utilized); Inge Kaul, Isabelle Grunberg, & Marc A. Stern, *Defining Global Public Goods, in* GLOBAL PUBLIC GOODS: INTERNATIONAL COOPERATION IN THE 21ST CENTURY 2-20 (Inge Kaul et al. eds., 1999) (introducing idea of global public goods).

70. *See* REPORT OF THE COMMISSION ON MACROECONOMICS & HEALTH (chaired by Jeffrey D. Sachs), MACROECONOMICS AND HEALTH: INVESTING IN HEALTH FOR ECONOMIC DEVELOPMENT 4 (2001) (recommending "that the world's low- and middle-income countries, in partnership with high-income countries, should scale up the access of the world's poor to essential health services."), *available at* http://www.un.org/esa/coordination/ecosoc/docs/RT.K.MacroeconomicsHealth.pdf (last visited Oct. 21, 2004).

71. For a discussion of Foucault's panopticism, see MICHEL FOUCAULT, DISCIPLINE AND PUNISH: THE BIRTH OF THE PRISON 195 (Alan Sheridan trans., 2d ed. 1995).

72. LAURIE GARRETT, BETRAYAL OF TRUST: THE COLLAPSE OF GLOBAL PUBLIC HEALTH 585 (2000).

several good reasons why we should be concerned about world health. The most obvious is self-interest: Some of the world's health problems endanger us all.[73]

While globalization has immersed all of humanity in a single microbial sea, global health governance constructed on South-North dichotomy and isolationist paradigms have left a sizable percentage of humanity, especially in the developing world, multilaterally defenseless in the face of advancing microbial forces. It is up to the future of global governance to humanize emerging and future global health accords to tackle global epidemics like SARS.

---

73. JOHN M. LAST, PUBLIC HEALTH AND HUMAN ECOLOGY 337 (2d ed. 1998).

[30]

Governing the Globalization of Public Health

Allyn L. Taylor

The number and the scale of transboundary public health concerns are increasing. Infectious and non-communicable diseases, international trade in tobacco, alcohol, and other dangerous products as well as the control of the safety of health services, pharmaceuticals, and food are merely a few examples of contemporary transnationalization of health concerns. The rapid development and diffusion of scientific and technological developments across national borders are creating new realms of international health concern, such as aspects of biomedical science, including human reproductive cloning, germ-line therapy, and xenotransplantation, as well as environmental health problems, including climate change, biodiversity loss, and depletion of the ozone layer. Growth in international trade and travel, in combination with population growth, has served to increase the frequency and intensity of health concerns bypassing or spilling over sovereign boundaries.

Although health has traditionally been seen an area of limited multilateral cooperation, there is growing awareness that contemporary globalization has led to the proliferation of cross border determinants of health status and is undermining the capacity of nation states to protect health through domestic action alone. Consequently, globalization is creating a heightened need for new global health governance structures to promote coordinated intergovernmental action.

This emerging need for new mechanisms and models for collective health action is a fundamental force behind the rapid expansion of international health law. Today, the growing field of international health law encompasses treaties and other legal instruments addressing diverse and complex concerns and is increasingly recognized as integrally linked to most other traditionally defined international legal realms.

Despite growing awareness of the capacity of conventional international law to serve as a dynamic tool for multilateral health cooperation in an increasingly interdependent world, little scholarly consideration has been paid to how twenty-first century global health lawmaking should be managed from an international institutional basis.[1] With multiple international organizations sharing lawmaking authority for global health and with other actors engaged in the international legislative process, international lawmaking shows potential for fragmented, uncoordinated, and inefficient sprawl.

This article seeks to contribute to the emerging discussion on global health governance by examining how globalization and the rising need for new global health governance structures is a driving force behind the expansion of conventional international health law. The article considers the complexities associated with using conventional vehicles to advance international cooperation and the inherent limitations of the international legislative process. It examines whether the present institutional framework is adequate and appropriate to meet the emerging global health law governance needs of the world community and whether leadership by the World Health Organization could strengthen global coordination and effective implementation of future developments in this rapidly evolving domain of international legal concern. Conventional international law is the primary international legal vehicle by which international organizations can advance international legal cooperation, so the article focuses on treaty law rather than other sources of international law.

The Evolution of International Law Related to Public Health

Globalization and the Expanding Domain of International Health Law

It has been widely observed that globalization has critical implications for public health and global public health governance.[2] A dominant characteristic of contemporary globalization is that it has introduced or expanded risks to health that transcend national borders in their origin or impact.[3] Such risks may include emerging and re-emerging infectious diseases, global environmental degradation, food safety, and an array of non-communicable diseases as well as trade in harmful commodities such as tobacco.

For example, the magnitude of the global impact of catastrophic appearances of new infectious diseases and the violent worldwide reemergence of old contagions has vividly evidenced the globalization of public health. Over the last two decades nations worldwide have been confronted with outbreaks of virulent strains of many old diseases and over thirty newly recognized pathogens, including, most notably, HIV/AIDS. Most recently, the well-publicized global threats of severe acute respiratory syndrome (SARS) in late 2002 and 2003 and outbreaks of both human (H3N2) and avian (H5N1) influenza less than a year later captured public and media attention. The SARS epidemic spread rapidly from its origins in southern China until it had reached more than 25 other countries within a matter of months. In addition to the number of patients infected with the SARS virus, totaling more than 8000 cases and 774 known deaths, the disease had

Allyn L. Taylor, JD, LLM, JSD, *is currently Adjunct Professor in Residence at the University of Maryland School of Law. From 1998 to 2003 she was a Senior Health Policy Adviser at the World Health Organization. Geneva.*

Allyn L. Taylor

profound economic and political repercussions in many of the affected regions. Reports in early 2004 of isolated new SARS cases and a fear that the disease could reemerge and spread put public health officials on high alert for any indications of possible new outbreaks. Concerns about rapid worldwide transmission of communicable diseases were confounded by epidemic outbreaks of both human (H3N2) and avian (H5N1) influenza in 2003-2004. Although these two recent epidemics have thus far had a limited relative impact on global health, the magnified public attention has promoted a mobilizing vision for coordinated health action and, in some cases, jolted global awareness and appreciation of the interconnectedness between domestic and international health.

The impact of increasing global integration for the globalization of public health is not, of course, an entirely new phenomenon. It has long been recognized that challenges to health are increasingly international[4] and have led to the obsolescence of the traditional distinction between national and international health policy.[5] However, contemporary globalization has had an unprecedented impact on global public health.

As Dodgson, Lee, and Drager have observed, the dramatic growth in geographical scope and speed with which contemporary transborder health risks have emerged has effectively challenged the established system of health governance defined by national boundaries.[6] Contemporary globalization has thus contributed to the rapid decline in the practical capacity of sovereign states to address contemporary health challenges through unilateral action alone and has amplified the need for health governance that transcends traditional and increasingly inadequate unilateral national approaches.

Conventional international law – treaty law – has received new prominence as a tool for multilateral cooperation in the public health field as states increasingly recognize the need to complement domestic action in the health sector with cross-sector and cross-border action to protect the health of their populations. The momentum of globalization is such that governments must turn increasingly to international cooperation to attain national public health objectives. Globalization has increased the need for new, formalized frameworks of international collaboration, including conventional international law, to address emerging global health threats and to improve the health status of poor states that have not benefited from globalization – the so-called "losers" of globalization.[7] Global health governance is, therefore, not about one world government, but about institutions and legal practices that facilitate multilateral cooperation among sovereign nation states.[8]

Globalization has also impacted the development of international health law, because increasing global integration has compounded the impact of other contemporary global developments that are strongly connected with health status and thereby magnified the need for frameworks for international cooperation. For example, the spread of communication and information technologies has dramatically accelerated the rate of scientific progress and its diffusion and application around the globe. This rapid worldwide dissemination of recent advances in scientific knowledge and technology has advanced international agreement and action by providing the evidence base and the technological tools needed for effective national action and international cooperation in a wide range of treaties – including those concerned with the safety of chemicals, pesticides, and food and the disposal of hazardous wastes. At the same time, however, the use of environmentally damaging technologies has also contributed to the codification of international law by propelling global health threats such as biodiversity loss, marine pollution, depletion of the ozone

layer, and climate change. Further, continuing scientific progress and developments are generating ongoing global debate on codifying new international commitments, including global bans on certain novel technologies, such as reproductive human cloning.[9]

Issue Linkage

Globalization has contributed to the expansion of international health by contributing to enhanced appreciation of the interconnectedness of contemporary global concerns and, concomitantly, the "linkage" of health to other international legal issues. International legal scholars have conventionally compartmentalized and treated substantive subject matters such as human rights, environmental protection, health and arms control, as discrete, self-contained areas with limited connections.[10] Students of international law have only recently begun to recognize the nexus among different realms of international law, such as trade and human rights, and human rights and environmental protection.[11]

The evolution of the concept of international security, a realm at the fore of the global community's political agenda, provides an interesting example of this phenomenon. The traditional understanding of international security has come under increasing scrutiny in recent years with growing support for a comprehensive and multisectoral conceptualization of security that addresses the wide-ranging factors that impact on the vulnerability of people. The linkage between health and security sits squarely at the center of this movement. For instance, in May 2003, the Commission on Human Security released a report proposing a new security framework that focuses directly on improving the human condition, including a key public health component.[12]

As a further example, the development agenda has evolved over the past few years from a view focused exclusively on unbridled and "trickle-down" economic growth, towards a more holistic perspective that economic growth should be cased by multidimensional concepts such as sustainable development and human development. The concepts of human development and sustainable development encompass the idea of expanded intersectoral action and coordination of economic, social, and environmental policy to improve the human condition. Health and the relationship between improved health and development are at the core of this development agenda.[13] At the same time as these developments public health policy-makers have expanded intersectoral global public health action to address the increasingly evident intersectoral determinants of health status, including poverty, education, technology, and the environment.

These global public policy developments have important implications for the conceptualization and advancement of international health law.[14] As a consequence of "issue linkage" international health law is increasingly understood to be a key component of other international legal regimes, including labor law, human rights, environmental law, trade, and arms control. For example, the extraordinary growth of international trade means the link between health and trade in a number of the World Trade Organization (WTO)'s treaties is becoming increasingly manifest in a wide range of areas including access to medicines, food security, nutrition, infectious disease control, and biotechnology.[15] In addition, as noted above, health has been linked to international peace and security issues in multiple contexts, including those of HIV/AIDS, and biological and other weapon systems. Overall, health is emerging as a central issue of multilateralism as a consequence of issue linkage in combination with the widespread impact of globalization.

"Issue linkage" is not limited to mere doctrinal debates, but also im-

> Globalization is creating a heightened need for new global health governance structures to promote coordinated intergovernmental action.

pacts contemporary codification efforts. Coordinated action on health and other traditionally distinct substantive concerns has become increasingly commonplace in international legislative projects. For example, as described above, sustainable development encompasses the idea of intersectoral coordination of environmental, economic, and social policy to improve the human condition.[16] The praxis of sustainable development informed the 1992 Rio Declaration on Environment and Development and has been elaborated in a number of international instruments, including the Conventions on Climate Change and Biological Diversity.

As a further example, the evolution of international health law has been very much tied to the protection and promotion of human rights related to physical and mental integrity.[17] The principal international legal basis for the right to health and other human rights relevant to health is found in the core instruments of human rights law: the International Bill of Rights which consists of the Universal Declaration of Human Rights (1948), the International Covenant on Economic, Social and Cultural Rights (1966), and the International Covenant on Civil and Political Rights (1966). However, there has been an emerging global understanding, arising primarily from public health approaches to HIV/AIDS, that human rights and public health are intertwined and interdependent.[18] Consequently, the domain of human rights in relation to health has expanded conspicuously in the last decade or so with bodies of the United Nations system paying increasing attention to the interrelation between health and human rights, and tailored human rights instruments now address the rights of particular populations, such as persons with HIV/AIDS and disabilities, women, children, migrant workers, and refugees[19] and, most recently, the interrelation between the human right to health and access to medicines.

The Promise and Limitations of International Law for Global health Governance

Health has emerged as a key global policy issue as a consequence of the globalization of public health, including the recently enhanced appreciation of the centrality of health to most realms of international relations.

Contemporary international health law includes a wide and growing diversity of international concerns. The scope and depth of contemporary international health law and its nexus with other realms of international legal concern reflects growing multilateral concern with and international cooperation to address the impact of contemporary globalization on public health, including aspects of biomedical science, human reproduction and cloning, organ transplantation and xenotransplantation, infectious and non-communicable diseases, international trade and the control of safety of health services, food and pharmaceuticals, and the control of addictive substances such as tobacco and narcotics.[20] As described above, international health law is also increasingly linked with other realms of multilateral concern. Arms control and the banning of weapons of mass destruction, international human rights and disabilities, international labour law and occupational health and safety, environmental law and the control of toxic pollutants, nuclear safety and radiation protection, and fertility and population growth are all intimately related to the domain of international health law.[21] The current configuration of international health law and the contribution of intergovernmental organizations to its development have recently been examined.[22]

Globalization is creating new and increasingly difficult governance needs. In the realm of public health, enhanced cooperation among nation states is proving increasingly necessary to address the rising number and complexity of transboundary health problems. Global health governance in the twenty-first century, therefore, is likely to include expanded use of international law through the codification of new agreements and the adaptation of existing ones as nations at all levels of development increasingly recognize the need to provide

a framework for coordinated action in an increasingly interdependent world. Global health development strategies, including the codification and implementation of treaty law, will be needed to address increasingly complex, intersectoral, and interrelated global health problems.

The burgeoning literature examining health and international health law as global public goods testifies to the increasing significance of conventional international law as a mechanism for future international collective action in this era of globalization.[23] The interdependence and integration associated with globalization means that providing global public goods such as public health increasingly requires action to be undertaken at the global level through effective international cooperation.

Notably, the ever-expanding sense of global health interdependence and global health vulnerability fostered by contemporary globalization may also, over time, become a powerful factor in overcoming the penchant for isolationism or unilateralism that, at times, has characterized the foreign policy of some powerful states, including, most notably, the United States, and thus contribute to the relevance of international health law by encouraging both the codification and implementation of effective international commitments.

Conventional international law is, of course, an inherently imperfect mechanism for international cooperation and the international legislative process is characterized by numerous and manifest limitations – including challenges to timely commitment and implementation – although considerable advances have been made in the last few decades.[24]

Globalization has also, in some respects, magnified the complexity of using conventional international law as an effective vehicle for intergovernmental cooperation. Increasing global interdependence may, as suggested above, enhance the codification and implementation of effective international health commitments by expanding awareness of global health vulnerability and the need for collective and concerted action. However, while contemporary health challenges are of concern to all countries because of their transborder character, many such problems are particularly acute in the poorest nations that are in the weakest position to negotiate effective and collective international obligations. Further, the deepening of poverty and accentuation of health inequalities among and within countries as well as the expanding numbers of increasingly complex and multifarious transnational health concerns and determinants of health status considerably compounds the challenge of using international legislation as a means to promote global public goods. In addition, as described further herein, the expansion in the number and power of non-state actors in the health domain is impacting on the capacity of traditional modes of state- to- state cooperation, including international law, to address global health concerns.

Despite the conspicuous limitations of the international lawmaking process and the inherent challenges associated with using treaties to promote international collective action in a globalizing world, treaties can be useful for raising public awareness and stimulating international commitment and national action. As an increasing number of health threats are global in scope or have the potential to become so, international treaties and other such legal mechanisms are of vital and ever-increasing importance and are an essential, albeit limited, component of future global health governance.

Global Health Governance and International Law: The Institutional Framework

Contemporary Global Health Governance

In recent years there has been considerable development in the field of international organization with the number of intergovernmental organizations active in the domain of health and other fields of international relations growing dramatically. A diversity of intergovernmental organizations now contribute to the elaboration of the

Allyn L. Taylor

increasingly complex and multivaried field of international health law.[25] These include the United Nations and its agencies, organs, and other bodies, and international and regional organizations outside of the United Nation's system. Within the comprehensive United Nations system, for example, organizations with significant involvement in the health sector include WHO, UNICEF, FAO, UNEP, UNDP, UNFPA and The World Bank. Globalization has also expanded the web of relevant international organizations in the field of global health, including, notably, the WTO. Overall, an increasing number of intergovernmental organizations with express lawmaking authority and relevant mandates have served as platforms for the codification of international law related to health; others have influenced contemporary international law in this field.

More than fifty years after the founding of the United Nations, the world has changed dramatically and there has been a multiplication of non-state actors in international health with the private sector becoming an increasingly important player in health governance. These non-state actors include a wide assortment of foundations, religious groups, nongovernmental agencies and for-profit organizations – such as the pharmaceutical industry – with a powerful influence on international health policy, including global lawmaking. Innovative "international health coalitions" that involve diverse global health actors,[26] such as health research networks and public-private partnerships are also increasingly commonplace and have an important influence on contemporary global health governance.[27]

The growing significance of non-state actors in global health governances combined with widespread criticism of the United Nations and its specialized agencies, including WHO, has led some commentators to suggest a declining and, perhaps, dwindling role for intergovernmental organizations in global health governance. Further, it is argued that globalization is not only reducing the capacity of national governments to address health challenges alone, but also, by extension, collectively through intergovernmental institutions.[28] The rise of innovative health coalitions, which often incorporate international organizations, is considered as a particular challenge to the continued authority of international organizations. Some commentators have emphasized a gradual reallocation of power from intergovernmental organizations to private-sector actors and the innovative health coalitions which have gained increasing power and influence in global health governance.[29] According to this view, the overall growth in the number and degree of influence in non-state actors in health governance has led to blurring of the distinct roles of state and non-state actors in governance activities such as resource mobilization[30] and contributed to a reallocation of authority and, perhaps, legitimacy in health governance.

Although globalization has facilitated the rise and influence of new non-state actors in health, increasing global health interdependence in fact requires that multilateral organizations play a larger role in international health cooperation[31] – at least in the emerging realm of international health lawmaking and implementation. As this article has illustrated, contemporary globalization has brought about profound changes in the international context creating a greater need for meaningful intergovernmental coordination than ever before. At the same time, it is widely recognized that globalization has tended to weaken, diminish, and even fragment the state, but it has not crushed, destroyed, or replaced it. Ultimately, states retain the final authority and responsibility to decide which issues are considered and negotiated at the international level and implemented into domestic law and policy. Hence, while the growing influence of new health actors may have led to the blurring of traditional roles in some aspects

of international health, this is not the case for international health lawmaking.

The vast majority of international legislative projects are conducted under the auspices of international organizations. Public international organizations are institutional mechanisms for multilateral cooperation and collective action. Their organizational structures and formal administrative arrangements provide stable negotiating forums for member states in realms within their relevant legal authority, thereby anchoring and facilitating intergovernmental cooperation.[32] Private-sector actors cannot replace international organizations as institutional focal points for global debate and codification of binding norms by state actors. Consequently, as this article has illustrated, public international organizations with relevant lawmaking authority will provide increasingly important vehicles through which states can develop and implement public policy as global integration progresses.

Institutional Overload

The proliferation and patchwork development of multilateral organizations with overlapping ambitions and legal authority creates the risk that international health law may develop in an inconsistent and suboptimal manner. The experience of international environmental law over the last twenty years provides a cautionary example that demonstrates that uncoordinated lawmaking activity by different intergovernmental organizations may have counterproductive and inconsistent results.[33] Scholars argue that, as a consequence of the absence of an umbrella environmental agency, global environmental governance has suffered from "institutional overload."[34] That is, the plethora of treaties and organizations relating to the environment has exceeded the capacity of states to effectively participate in and comply with them. The inefficient management of global environmental lawmaking has, in part, led some commentators to identify the need for the establishment of a new public international organization – the "World Environment Organization."[35]

There is significant risk that a similar condition of "institutional overload" and inconsistent standard-setting will emerge in international health, a development which will detract from efforts to address the important global risks to health and to manage the new technologies with great potential to advance global public health. For example, dramatic advances in the field of biomedical science – a realm with vast opportunities and risks to global public health – has recently triggered numerous, uncoordinated regional and global initiatives,[36] which have considerably complexified rather than rationalized the global legal framework.

At the global level, UNESCO, WHO, the United Nations Commission for Human Rights, UNEP and the WTO have all contributed to the elaboration of international instruments in this rapidly evolving field without any meaningful institutional consultation, coordination or planning. The first international instrument to address a broad range of human rights and public health implications of biotechnology, the Universal Declaration on the Human Genome and Human Rights was adopted by the UNESCO General Conference in 1997. More recently, in 2003, UNESCO adopted an International Declaration on Human Genetic Data and, at the time of this writing, is in the process of preparing to negotiate a new proposed Declaration on Universal Norms on Bioethics. During this same period of time, the United Nations Commission for Human Rights has adopted resolutions pertaining to human rights and bioethics with implications for public health,[37] while WHO has also adopted resolutions

> Health has emerged as a key global policy issue as a consequence of the globalization of public health, including the recently enhanced appreciation of the centrality of health to most realms of international relations.

and recommended standards on the social, ethical, and scientific implications of biotechnology, including human reproductive cloning.

There is growing evidence of fragmentation, duplication, and inconsistency in this highly complex realm, particularly with respect to binding instruments that have been adopted under the auspices of the assorted international organizations involved in the field. For example, some of the aspects of the biotechnology revolution for biodiversity are addressed in the United Nations Environment Programme's Convention on Biological Diversity and Biosafety Protocol. At the same time, the WTO's Convention on Trade-related Aspects of Intellectual Property establishes standards for protection of intellectual property applicable to biotechnology and several other WTO agreements also apply to biotechnology-related trade disputes. Most recently, in December 2001, the United Nations General Assembly established an Ad Hoc Working Group of the Sixth Committee to consider a proposed new treaty to ban the reproductive cloning of human beings. This negotiation process has been stymied by a split between those states, led by the United States, that favor a broad-based cloning treaty that bans all human cloning, including therapeutic cloning, and those states that favor a treaty with a narrow focus on human reproductive cloning. In the absence of consensus on the scope of the proposed instrument, in late 2003, the United Nations Member States agreed to postpone discussions of the proposed treaty until late 2004.[38] Notably, no consideration has been given to extending the scope of the treaty to comprehensively address critical and timely issues in species altering technology, such as germ line therapy.[39]

These examples illustrate that international law in biotechnology is developing in a splintered and disconnected manner as intergovernmental organizations with overlapping claims to legal jurisdiction are addressing isolated aspects of the genetics revolution in a piecemeal and incomplete manner.[40] Instead of fostering effective interagency coordination and strengthened multilateral cooperation to harness the genetics revolution to advance global public health, the splintered legal process is aggravating uncertainty about the legal regime that governs biotechnology. This is partly because standards adopted under the auspices of different international organizations are being developed in increasingly contradictory ways, including conflicting legal standards related to intellectual property.[41]

This suggests that, similar to the experience of international environmental law, the multiplicity of public international organizations engaged in standard-setting in biotechnology is also likely to lead to "treaty congestion" and overwhelm the capacity of states to participate in the lawmaking enterprise and to implement international commitments. In some respects "institutional overload" in biotechnology appears to be leading to a situation of normative overkill. At the same time, the emerging patchwork of international law in biotechnology may still fail to comprehensively address the most important implications of the genetics field for human health. Despite the extensive international legislative activity in this area, there is no legally binding global instrument even under consideration that addresses the considerable public health implications of the globalization of biotechnology.

Advancing Global Health Law Governance
An International Health Law Mandate for WHO
Lessons from the experience of the last several decades of global environmental governance and recent codification efforts in biotechnology illustrate that the international health law enterprise necessitates more effective collective management. More effective institutional coordination than exists in the current decentralized or-

> The penchant for isolationism or unilateralism, at times, has characterized the foreign policy of some powerful states, including, most notably, the United States

ganizational framework is also needed because the phenomenon of "issue linkage" in contemporary lawmaking confounds the conundrum of contradictory international health law rules developed under the auspices of different organizations with overlapping legal authority. In international law generally, the question of issue linkage is increasingly understood to concern the allocation of legal jurisdiction among international organizations.[42]

The World Health Organization has a unique directive to provide leadership and promote rational and effective development of the evolving field of international health law. As the largest international health organization, WHO has wide-ranging responsibilities to address global public health concerns based on responsibilities assigned by its constitution and its affiliation with the United Nations.[43]

The structure of the relationship between the United Nations and WHO is grounded in the United Nations Charter and, in particular, those sections that describe the objectives of the United Nations. Article 55 of the Charter describes the goals that the United Nations has pledged to promote among its members, including solutions of international, economic, social, health, and related problems. As the specialized agency with the primary constitutional directive to act as the "directing and co-ordinating authority" on international health work, WHO has the cardinal responsibility to implement the aims of the Charter with respect to health. Although the broad idea that WHO should promote coordination throughout the United Nations system is not new to global health governance literature, it deserves more serious consideration in this neglected realm of international health lawmaking because of the implications of the current leadership vacuum.

System-wide coordination does not mean full centralization of all international health lawmaking functions under WHO's auspices. For at least six reasons, consolidation of all international health law making functions under WHO is neither feasible nor desirable. First, as described the field of international health law is growing rapidly encompassing more diverse and complex concerns, in part, as a consequence of issue linkage. Although health is a component of an increasing number of such codification efforts, not all such treaty enterprises fall squarely within WHO's core mandate. Second, as described further herein, WHO currently has highly limited experience in international health lawmaking and management of global legal developments. Therefore, WHO lacks the requisite capacity to undertake full centralization of all lawmaking functions in this rapidly developing field. Third, expanding WHO's mandate to address all aspects of international health law codification could also deplete the organization's existing resources and potentially undermine the ability of the institution to fulfil its well-established and essential international health functions.

Fourth, member states are highly unlikely to limit their autonomy and freedom of action by granting WHO such broad jurisdiction or, given current economic conditions, to provide it with the vast new resources needed to implement such an expansive new mandate. Fifth, other international organizations with overlapping legal jurisdiction would undoubtedly defend against full centralization under the auspices of WHO.[44] WHO has no binding authority over the activities of other autonomous intergovernmental organizations and, regrettably, competition rather than coordination has been a traditional stamp of organizational relations throughout the United Nations system.

Fifth, it is important to recognize that there are some advantageous aspects of the decentralization of the international lawmaking enterprise. In particular, as Doyle and Massey have observed, decentralization generates opportunities for international organizations to

Allyn L. Taylor

specialize and promotes innovation[45] For example, some existing international organizations, such as the Food and Agriculture Organization of the United Nations, have substantial specialized technical expertise and legal experience that will make an important contribution to future lawmaking efforts. The growing complexity and interconnectedness of global health problems suggest that certain situations will require moving beyond the "single instrument and single institution" approach.[46] Notably, in the realm of international environmental law, decentralization of the actual lawmaking enterprise among different institutions has been recognized as a critical factor in the regime's widely recognized dynamism.[47]

While all lawmaking functions should not be consolidated under WHO auspices, WHO leadership in coordinating codification and implementation efforts among the diverse global actors actively engaged in health lawmaking could, in theory, foster the development of a more effective, integrated and rational legal regime and, consequently, better collective management of global health concerns. Expectations of WHO's capacity to manage the international health law enterprise must be reasonable and pragmatic, however. It is important to recognize that effective coordination of international legal efforts cannot be guaranteed by WHO or by any other intergovernmental organization. Efficiency of international standards and consistency among different treaties may not always be a priority among states codifying international commitments or the wide array of global health actors, including other autonomous intergovernmental organizations, that influence the international legislative process. Although effective coordination of the increasingly complex international health law regime cannot be assured, an effort to rationalize the international health law enterprise should pursued with reasonable expectations and awareness of the limitations of organizational action.

Organizational and Political Capacity

A fundamental precept in global governance is that the "the mandate should fit the organization and vice versa."[48] While WHO clearly has the legal capacity to serve as a platform for international health law coordination efforts, a key question that remains is whether or not it has the necessary organizational and political capacity to meet the complex new challenges associated with the international health law leadership mandate proposed in this article.

WHO is unique among United Nations specialized agencies in that the Organization has traditionally neglected the use of international legislative strategies to promote its global public policies. Despite wide-ranging advancements in international lawmaking by numerous intergovernmental organizations since the founding of the United Nations over fifty years ago, until recently, WHO encouraged the formulation of binding international standards in very limited and traditional contexts and never promoted the use of its constitutional authority to serve as a platform for treaty negotiations in any area of public health. A decade ago, I attributed WHO's "traditional conservatism" about the use of legal institutions largely to its cultural predispositions – its organizational culture.[49]

Some observers continue to marginalize the role of WHO in international law, but it is unclear whether and to what extent the conceptualization of WHO's traditional culture is still relevant. Under the leadership of Dr Gro Harlem Brundtland, Director-General of WHO from 1998-2003, there were wide-ranging changes in WHO's traditional organizational behavior. During Brundtland's tenure international law became more widely integrated into WHO's work than at any other time in the Organization's history. Among other things, the Organization initiated efforts to explore practical linkages between health and other realms of international law and develop and influence relevant global public policy. For example, some concrete efforts were made to establish a broader dialogue between WHO and the WTO in order to promote health as a legitimate concern on the global trade agenda and currently WHO holds official observer status on the

Council of the WTO and some of its key committees.[50] As a further example, notable strides were made to address the Organization's historical neglect of the linkage between health and human rights.[51] Among other things, the Organization established its first health and human rights adviser post and sought to strengthen is role in providing technical, intellectual and political leadership in the field.[52]

Two international legislative projects were also effectively launched in the last five years. First, the Organization rejuvenated the process of revising and updating the International Health Regulations, potentially a key international instrument in the area of communicable disease control. Second and, perhaps, most significantly, WHO revived and accelerated the process of negotiating and adopting its first convention – the Framework Convention on Tobacco Control – an idea that had been initiated in the early 1990s[53] and formally proposed in an independent feasibility study for WHO in 1995,[54] but had languished prior to the election of Brundtland. With a strong push from WHO in the late 1990s, the idea of a WHO tobacco convention became a viable international negotiation process involving over 160 countries. A final draft of the Convention was adopted by the World Health Assembly, the legislative organ of WHO, in May 2003, just prior to the end of Brundtland's term as Director-General.

As I have described elsewhere, these legal developments may herald a "turning-point": a new era in international health cooperation and, perhaps, an important step towards a new international health law leadership role for WHO.[55] The Organization's unprecedented consideration of the role of international law and institutions in promoting public health policies in tobacco control and other realms of international health law concerns suggests a rethinking, reformulation and expansion of the organization's traditional scientific, technical approaches to public health.

The question that remains is whether or not the organizational changes initiated under Brundtland, a unique WHO head because of her unconventional background in international lawmaking and diplomacy as well as public health, reflect merely limited and inconsequential deviations from established procedures or key steps towards genuine adaptation or evolution WHO's conservative culture[56] that will be sustained and fostered under WHO's new Director-General, Dr. Jong-wook Lee, and beyond. The process of change in international organizations is stimulated by a variety of factors external and internal to the institution, including organizational leadership. The heads of international organizations typically have considerable agenda-setting power and leadership change and institutional change frequently go hand in hand in international organizations.[57]

At the time of this writing Dr. Lee, a distinguished international health practitioner who had been at WHO for a substantial number of years prior to his election as Director-General, has been in his new office for less than a year. It is, therefore, perhaps too soon to conclude whether or not his administration is committed to expanding WHO's leadership in international health law and whether or not new practices in this realm will be successfully institutionalized and integrated into the regular processes of the Organization. However, in a perhaps noteworthy early signal of Lee's support for international legal approaches for public health, on July 30, 2003 the Organization announced internal structural changes, including the creation of a new department incorporating ethics, trade, human rights and law. Prior to Lee's restructuring of the institution, WHO's work on these areas was conducted by discrete departments with limited connections to one another and substantial overlaps in mandates. The consolidation of these realms under a single department at WHO has the potential to significantly rationalize, coordinate, and advance WHO's work on international health law. More importantly, however, current conditions of increasing financial stringency at WHO, including increased reliance on the private-sector, may serve to limit or inhibit WHO's autonomy to promote the advancement of international health law.

Ultimately, WHO's capacity to fulfill the leadership mandate described depends on political support from its member states, particularly the major powers who provide the majority of the Organization's budget. The willingness of governments to support this mandate will depend on factors external and internal to WHO. For example, consistency of legal regimes may not always be a priority, or even a goal, for states facing competing interests (principally from private-sector actors). Furthermore, the broadened mandate has important implications for WHO's budget and resources, which must be supported by states who may also face conflicting financial priorities. As described, WHO has been operating under the conditions of a declining budget in real terms, limiting its autonomy to effect decisions independent of its Member States and compounding pressure on the Organization to institute reforms and implement programmes that are responsive to the demands of key donors.

Governmental support of an expanded international health law mandate, in the near future, may also depend partly on assessment of the institution's existing strengths and past successes in contributing to the codification and administration of global health law. To this end, the 2003 WHO Framework Convention on Tobacco Control, the first treaty to be adopted under the auspices of the WHO in its fifty plus year history, may serve as a critical test of WHO's organizational and political capacity to provide leadership in future international health law efforts. The treaty will enter into force for state parties if and when it is ratified by forty states.

Much has been written about the effectiveness of the FCTC negotiation process in promoting national and international tobacco control.[58] However, viewed as an international instrument, there are number of aspects of the FCTC that raise the concern that the treaty itself may have limited impact in promoting effective national and international action for tobacco control, including the elaboration of detailed protocol agreements, assuming it ultimately enters into force. The FCTC is modeled upon the framework convention-protocol approach, an approach to international lawmaking made popular in the realm of international environmental law.[59] Although there is no single definition of a framework convention, such treaties tend to establish broad obligations and concrete institutions of global governance that provide a platform to promote negotiation and codification of detailed obligations in future protocol agreements. While the FCTC tends to establish broad obligations, the text is lacking many of the core institutional arrangements found at times in framework conventions, such as a prescribed annual or biannual meeting of the contracting parties, which serve as the bedrock for an ongoing international legislative enterprise.

Despite some of the manifest limitations of the final text of the FCTC, governments' evaluations of WHO's role in the FCTC process are unlikely to depend on the substantive outcome of the FCTC – whether the Convention and its proposed protocols are relatively effective or ineffective at promoting multilateral coordination to counter the tobacco pandemic or even if the FCTC ever enters into force. Intergovernmental organizations have important catalytic functions in treaty development, including the preparation of draft texts of the treaty. Ultimately, however, international organizations have limited capacity to influence the factors that encourage states to adopt, ratify, and implement effective commitments.

Rather, the willingness of states to use WHO as a platform, catalyst, and coordinator for international health law negotiations in the near future may depend on governments' final evaluations of WHO's effectiveness as a coordinator and manager of the FCTC negotiations and, potentially, the treaty regime. That is, governments are

likely to collectively assess whether or not WHO provided the administrative coordination and public health expertise necessary to advance complex, multilateral negotiations in international health. Most importantly, perhaps, governments may evaluate WHO's capacity to address global health law matters in the near future on the basis of their collective assessment of whether or not WHO was able to serve as an honest broker for all states participating in the negotiation exercise. Some degree of tension between international organizations and their member states is commonplace in contemporary treaty negotiations. However, the states' collective judgment about the ability of an international organization to function as a neutral platform for all participating states is a critical element of the organization's ongoing political capacity to serve effectively as a center for international debate and codification.

In any assessment of WHO's performance as platform for the negotiations of the FCTC there are bound to be differences in judgment. Even so, perhaps many would agree that the institution's performance presents a mixed picture with some important successes and some major weaknesses. To this end, it is perhaps notable that in 2001, at the height of the FCTC negotiations, two new international legislative projects with potentially significant public health implications were initiated, the proposed convention banning the reproductive cloning of human beings and, as will be discussed further herein, a proposed Comprehensive and Integral International Convention on Protection and Promotion of the Rights and Dignity of Persons with Disabilities. Although WHO has the legal authority to serve as a platform for the negotiation of these proposed treaties, in both cases states chose an alternative forum.[60] Perhaps notable as well, in the final text of the FCTC adopted in May 2003 Member States included a provision that granted WHO the status of interim treaty secretariat with the permanent secretariat to be designated after the treaty enters into force. For a variety of reasons WHO is ultimately likely to be awarded the permanent secretariat if the treaty enters into force. Nevertheless, the FCTC provision on WHO interim secretariat status is rather unusual since specialized agencies tend to be customarily granted permanent secretariat status without such an interim period in treaties negotiated solely under their auspices.

> These legal developments may herald a "turning-point": a new era in international health cooperation and, perhaps, an important step towards a new international health law leadership role for WHO.

Taking the Agenda Forward: Recommendations for WHO Global Health Governance Leadership

Global health problems pose important legal challenges for the international community. The increasingly globalized nature of public health problems calls for an unprecedented degree of international cooperation and leadership by the World Health Organization.

It is, of course, important that expectations for organizational action in this realm remain realistic. As described herein, WHO has highly limited experience and resources in international health lawmaking and coordination. In other realms of international concern, the capacity of international organizations in international lawmaking and mobilization has developed over a generation. Consequently, it may take years before WHO is able to build the requisite expertise to provide maximum leadership in international health law cooperation, mobilization, and codification. Further, as described above, effective coordination of international legal efforts cannot be guaranteed by WHO or by any other intergovernmental organization in a world of autonomous states. Recognizing these inherent limitations, an effort to rationalize the international health law enterprise is essential and should be advanced.

It should be recognized that concerns about the fragmented nature of the legal system and the absence of a coordinated approach to

Allyn L. Taylor

norm-creating process are not unique, of course, to international health or even international environmental law. Rather, concerns about conflicts among norms and conflicts of legal jurisdiction cut across a variety of international legal disciplines. A variety of commentators have urged that international organizations should forge more effective linkages to promote coherent norm development. To this end, increased attention is being paid to the various institutional and legal mechanisms that can be used to enhance inter-organizational collaboration, including, most notably, organizational leadership and oversight structures. This article cannot fully describe the strategies that WHO could use to promote rational management of international legal developments. However, scholarship in international environmental law suggests some important starting points.[61] In particular, WHO can provide leadership and promote more coherent and effective development of international health law by endeavoring to serve as coordinator, catalyst and, where appropriate, platform for important international health agreements.

Promoting Global Dialogue and Agenda Setting

WHO can catalyze more effective and coordinated international health cooperation by promoting global awareness of international health law concerns and contributing to the "agenda-setting"[62] that is acutely needed in this realm.

One of the major challenges in effective management of public health problems of international legal concern is mobilizing public awareness as well as national political commitment and action. Global health problems battle for political attention against other international issues. At the same time, public health remains low on the priority list for national action or international cooperation in many states.

WHO can establish a key role for itself in catalyzing international agreements and national action by, among other things, establishing a mechanism of educating and informing national policy-makers of critical public health issues ripe for international legal action. Among other things, WHO can institutionalize an open and inclusive process for identifying priority issues for international legal cooperation and promoting them among relevant constituencies. By identifying priorities for international legal action and coordinating relevant public health and legal information, WHO can serve a critical role and meet an essential need by building global dialogue and educating governments, other global health actors, including other intergovernmental organizations, and the public about global health issues of legal concern. Critical to the success of such a process is the establishment of a mechanism to extend the dialogue to national policy-makers beyond ministries of health that form the traditional core of WHO's constituency. Effective coordination of such a process with other relevant intergovernmental organizations may serve to expand the network of national actors involved in the global heath law dialogue, promote national awareness and commitment, and contribute to the rationale development of the international legal regime.

In addition, constructing a more effective dialogue between states and the web of other global health actors will be a critical component of better collective management of international health law in the future. The rise of new global health actors, including civil society, religious groups, foundations, the private sector and broad international health coalitions has considerably complexified health governance and highlighted the limitations of the traditional state-centered focus of international law. Indeed, the complex network of governance structures that are burgeoning around the legal structures being established by the state-centered system indicates the need for an inclusive approach to engagement with new global health actors.

As a highly prominent international organization, WHO has the opportunity to play a pivotal role in building a dialogue among states and other health actors and in setting and launching the international health law agenda. Through these and other measures, WHO may promote global dialogue, build effective partnerships and stimulate

more coordinated and, perhaps, more effective governmental and intergovernmental action.

Monitoring International Health Law Developments and Promoting Coordinated Institutional Action

WHO can also promote effective consideration, better collective management, and development of international legal matters by monitoring and actively participating, where appropriate, in the increasing array of treaty efforts initiated in other forums that have important implications for global public health. For example, in December 2001, the General Assembly of the United Nations established an Ad Hoc Committee to consider proposals on a Comprehensive and Integral International Convention on Protection and Promotion of the Rights and Dignity of Persons with Disabilities. As a specialized agency of the United Nations system, WHO could contribute to this codification effort as an official observer to the negotiation sessions. However, the Organization did not contribute to the early sessions of the Ad Hoc Committee. WHO could make a significant contribution to this codification effort, and the development of international health law generally, by monitoring the legislative process and by informing and educating state delegations participating in negotiations about relevant public health and legal information.

Among other things, WHO could provide details of the global incidence of disabilities, and public health considerations involved in human rights issues of accommodation and access for persons with disabilities. Moreover, WHO may be able to broaden the dialogue and promote a comprehensive public health approach to disability by bringing forth information and stimulating global public debate on aspects of prevention, treatment and rehabilitation that may be ripe for national practice and, potentially, for inclusion in the text of the proposed treaty.

Further, as described above, WHO should incorporate other intergovernmental organizations with relevant mandates in the global dialogue on global health law priorities to promote more coordinated and rational development of the legal regime.

Platform for Treaty Negotiations

WHO can also effectively steer intergovernmental health cooperation by serving, where appropriate, as a platform for the codification and implementation of international legal agreements. The recent experience of biotechnology indicates that unless WHO plays a legislative role critical global public health issues may not be addressed in a timely and effective manner and may be subject to excessive institutional fragmentation and critical gaps. WHO is the only public international organization that brings together the institutional mandate, legal authority, and public health expertise for the codification of treaties that principally address global public health concerns.

Given the problems of legal jurisdiction raised by issue linkage and overlapping legal authority among various international organizations, a thorny question is which types of issues will benefit from codification under WHO's auspices. This needs to be decided on a case-by-case basis and there may always be differences in judgment. However, WHO is the appropriate institutional setting for the elaboration of legal standards encompassing issues, such as tobacco control, that overlap with other realms of international concern (such as human rights, trade, agriculture, customs, and the environment) but are at the heart of the public health mandate of WHO and are beyond the central mission of another public international organization.

Conclusion

International health law can make an important contribution to the framework for global cooperation and coordination on public health matters in an increasingly interdependent world. An essential component of global health governance in the twenty-first century is an effective and politically responsive institution to promote collective supervision as well as the coherent development of this rapidly evolving field. The extent to which WHO can and will be able to provide such leadership in international health law will have an important influence on the collective ability of intergovernmental organizations to promote effective global cooperation to advance global public health.

References

1. A.L. Taylor, "Global Governance, International Law and WHO: Looking Towards the Future," *Bulletin of the World Health Organization* 80 (2002): 975–80.
2. K. Lee, "Shaping the Future of Global Health Cooperation: Where Can We Go From Here?" *Lancet* 351 (1998): 899–902.
3. K. Lee, "An Overview of Global Health and Environmental Risks," in L. Parsons and G. Lister, eds., *Global Health: A Local Issue* (London: The Nuffield Trust, 2000): 34–46,.
4. F. Grad, "Public Health Law: Its Forms, Function, Future and Ethical Parameters," *International Digest of Health Legislation* 49 (1998): 19–40. A.L. Taylor, "Making the World Health Organization Work: A Legal Framework for Universal Access to the Conditions for Health,*American Journal of Law and Medicine* 18 (1992):301- 46.
5. GA Gellart, et. al., "The Obsolescence of Distinct Domestic and International Health Sectors," *Journal of Public Health Policy* 10 (1989): 421-25.
6. R. Dodgson, K. Lee, and N. Drager, *Global Health Governance: A Conceptual Review*, (London: Center on Global Change & Health, London School of Hygiene & Tropical Medicine, 2002).
7. N. Drager and R. Beaglehole, "Globalization: Changing the Public Health Landscape,"*Bulletin of the World Health Organization* 79 (2001): 803–09; D. Woodward, et. al., "Globalization and Health: A Framework for Analysis and Action, "*Bulletin of the World Health Organization*, 79 (2001): 875–81; A. Woodward, et. al., "Protecting Human Health in a Changing World: the Role of Social and Economic Development," *Bulletin of the World Health Organization*, (2000):1148-55; Dodgson, Lee, and Drager, *supra* note 7.
8. D. Nynar, "Towards Global Governance," in *Governing Globalization* (Oxford: Oxford University Press, 2002): 3–18.
9. R. Adorno, "Biomedicine and International Human Rights Law: In Search of a Global Agenda," *Bulletin of the World Health Organization* 80 (2002): 959–63; G.J. Annas, L.B. Andrews, and R.M. Isasi, "Protecting the Endangered Human: Towards and International Treaty Prohibiting Cloning and Inheritable Alterations, *American Journal of Law and Medicine* 28 (2002):151–78; A.L.Taylor, "The Contribution of International Law to a Global Bioethic: The Proposed United Nations Convention Against the Reproductive Cloning of Human Beings," in J. Anderson, ed., *Once in a Lifetime: Interdisciplinary Perspectives on Cloning and Genetic Technologies* (Cambridge: Cambridge University Press [in press]).
10. P. Sands, "Sustainable Development: Treaty, Custom and the Cross-fertilization of International Law," in A. Boyle, and D. Freestone, eds., *Sustainable Development and International Law* (Oxford: Oxford University Press, 1999):39–60.
11. J.E. Alvarez, ed., "Symposium: The Boundaries of the WTO," *American Journal of International Law* 96 (2002): 1 Taylor, infra, note 23. 158.
12. Commission on Human Security, *Human Security Now: Protecting and Empowering People* (2003), at <www.humansecurity-chs.org.>
13. A. Woodward, *supra* note 11; G.H. Brundtland, Address to the World Business Council for Sustainable Development: our Common Future and Rio 10 years after: How far Have We Come and Where Should we be Going? November 4, 1999, Berlin, *available at* <http://www.who.int/directorgeneral/speeches/1999/english/19991104_berlin.html.>
14. Taylor, *supra* note 1.
15. World Health Organization, *WTO Agreements and Public Health*, (Geneva: World Health Organization, 2002).
16. Sands, *supra* note 14.
17. H.D.C. Abbing, "Health, Human Rights, and Health Law: the Move Towards Internationalization, with a Special Emphasis on Europe," *International Digest of Health Legislation*, 49 (1998): 101–12; S. Gruskin and D. Tarantola, "Health and Human Rights," in Detels, *supra* note 4, at 311-57; A.L. Taylor et. al., "International Health Law Instruments: An Overview," in R. Detels, et. al., eds., *Oxford Textbook of Public Health: The Scope of Public Health* (Oxford: Oxford University Press, 2002): 359–86.
18. Gruskin and Tarantola, *supra* note 18.
19. *Id.*
20. Grad, *supra* note 1.
21. *Id.*
22. Taylor, *supra* note 23.
23. L.C. Chen , T.G. Evans, and R.A. Cash, "Health as a Global Public Good," in I. Kaul, I. Grunberg, and M. Stern eds., *Global Public Goods: International Cooperation in the 21st Century* (London: United Nations Development Programme, 1999): 284–305; R. Smith, et. al. eds., *Global Public Goods for Health: Health Economic and Public Health Perspectives* (Oxford, Oxford University Press, 2002).
24. P.C. Szasz, "International Norm-Making,"in E.B. Weiss, ed., *Environmental Change and International Law* (Tokyo: United Nations University Press, 1992): 340–84.
25. Taylor et. al., *supra* note 23.
26. Chen, *supra* note 24.
27. *Id.*; K. Buse and G. Walt, "Global Public-Private Partnerships: Part 1 – a New Development in Health?" *Bulletin of the World Health Organization* 78 (2000): 549–61. M. R. Reich, ed. *Public -Private Partnerships for Public Health* (Cambridge: Harvard University Press, 2002).
28. Dodgson, Lee, and Drager *supra* note 7.
29. Chen, *supra* note 24.
30. Dodgson, Lee, and Drager, *supra* note 7.
31. G. Walt, "Globalisation of International Health," *Lancet* 351 (1998): 434–37.
32. D. Kapur, "Processes of Change in International Organizations," in Nynar, *supra* note 9, at 334–55.
33. S. Charnovitz, "A World Environment Organization," *Columbia Journal of Environmental Law* 27 (2002): 323–62; M.W. Doyle and R.I. Massey, "Intergovernmental Organizations and the Environment: Looking Towards the Future," in P.R. Chasek, ed., *The Global Environment in the Twenty-First Century: Prospects for International Cooperation*, (Tokyo: United Nations University Press, 2000) 411–26; P. Birnie and A. Boyle, *International Law and the Environment*, (Oxford: Oxford University Press 2002).
34. P.M. Haas, R.O. Keohane, and M.A. Levy, *Institutions for the Earth: Sources of Effective International Environmental Protection*, (Cambridge: MIT Press, 1993).
35. Charnovitz, *supra* note 34.
36. A.L. Taylor. "Globalization and Biotechnology: UNESCO and an International Strategy to Advance Human Rights and Public Health," *American Journal of Law and Medicine* 25 (1999): 479–541.
37. See, e.g., United Nations Commission for Human Rights, Resolution 2001/71 on Human Rights and Bioethics, April 25, 2001.
38. U.N. Wire, *Discussion of U.N. Treaty on Human Cloning Delayed Two Years*, November 6, 2003.
39. Taylor, *supra* note 10.
40. S.D.Murphy, "Biotechnology and International Law," *Harvard Journal of International Law* 42 (2001): 47–139; S. Pridan-Frank, "Human Genomics: A Challenge to the Rules of the Game of International Law," *Columbia Journal of Transnational Law* 40 (2001): 619–76.
41. *Id.*
42. J.P. Trachtman, "Institutional Linkage: Transcending 'trade and...'," *American Journal of International Law* 96 (2002): 77–93.
43. Taylor, *supra* note 23; G.L. Burci and C.H. Vignes, "World Health Organization," in *International Encyclopedia of Laws* (Dordrecht: Kluwer [in press]).
44. Doyle and Massey, *supra* note 34.
45. *Id.*
46. P.C. Szasz, "IAEA Safeguards: Sanctions," in P.C. Szasz, *Selected Essays on Understanding International Institutions and the Legislative Process* (New York: Transnational Publishers 2001): 201–20.
47. *Id.*
48. Doyle and Massey, *supra* note 34.
49. Taylor, *supra* note 5.
50. Dodgson, Lee, and Drager, *supra* note 7.
51. Taylor, *supra* note 5.
52. World Health Organization, "The-State-of-the-Art: A Human Rights Based Approach in WHO," Report to the Second Interagency Workshop on Implementing a Human Rights-based Approach in the Context of UN Reform, Stamford, USA, May 5–7, 2003.
53. R. Roemer, J. Larivier, and A. Taylor, "The Origins of the WHO Framework Convention on Tobacco Control," forthcoming in *American Journal of Public Health*.
54. A.L.Taylor and R. Roemer, "An International Strategy for Tobacco Control," (Geneva: World Health Organization: 1996) (WHO document WHO/PSA/96.6).
55. Taylor, *supra* note 1.
56. *Id.*
57. Kapure, *supra* note 33.
58. Roemer, LaRiviere, and Taylor, *supra* note 54.
59. Taylor and Roemer, *supra* note 55.
60. G.L. Burci and C.H. Vignes, *The World Health Organization* (The Hague: Kluwer Law International, 2004).
61. Doyle and Massey, *supra* note 34.
62. *Id.*

[31]

The New International Health Regulations: An Historic Development for International Law and Public Health

David P. Fidler and Lawrence O. Gostin

The World Health Assembly (WHA) adopted the new International Health Regulations (IHR) on May 23, 2005.[1] The new IHR represent the culmination of a decade-long revision process and an historic development for international law and public health. The new IHR appear at a moment when public health, security, and democracy have become intertwined, addressed at the highest levels of government. The United Nations (UN) Secretary-General Kofi Annan, for example, identified IHR revision as a priority for moving humanity toward "larger freedom."[2] This article analyzes the new IHR and their implications for global health and security in the 21st century.

The IHR and the Revision Process

The WHA instructed the WHO Director-General (DG) to revise the IHR in 1995 because the Regulations did not provide an effective framework for addressing the international spread of disease.[3] Doubts about the IHR's effectiveness had, however, been present long before 1995.[4] The critiques identified the narrow scope of the regulations (applying only to a small number of infectious diseases), the lack of compliance by states, and the absence of a strategy for responding to rapid changes in public health's global economic and technological environments.

The resurgence of infectious diseases in the 1980s and 1990s highlighted the IHR's ineffectiveness. Particularly troublesome were the IHR's inapplicability to the spread of endemic diseases, such as tuberculosis and malaria, and new diseases, such as HIV/AIDS and viral hemorrhagic fevers. Concern also existed that some governments lacked the capacity or political will to report and respond to diseases of international importance. By 1995, WHO understood that the revised IHR would have to break with traditional approaches and construct a novel framework for health and security in an era of accelerating globalization. The innovative framework began to emerge with WHO's first proposal in January 1998, which had a broad scope and permitted the use of non-governmental data sources.[5]

The outbreak of Severe Acute Respiratory Syndrome (SARS) in 2003 accelerated the IHR revision process. WHO viewed its response to SARS as a "roll-out" of ideas being crafted in the IHR revision process.[6] In the wake of WHA resolutions on SARS and the IHR revision process in May 2003,[7] WHO issued a complete proposed text in January 2004, which served as the basis for WHO's regional consultations through the spring and summer of 2004.[8] These consultations led to a revised proposed text, issued in September 2004 for the first intergovernmental negotiations held in November 2004.[9] Following the first negotiating session, the Chair of the negotiations promulgated a "Chair's text" for consideration at the second negotiating session in February 2005.[10] The negotiations were completed in May 2005 prior to the WHA's annual meeting,[11] at which the Assembly adopted the new IHR.

David P. Fidler, J.D., *is Professor of Law and Harry T. Ice Faculty Fellow, Indiana University School of Law – Bloomington and Senior Scholar, Center for Law and the Public's Health, Georgetown and Johns Hopkins Universities.* **Lawrence O. Gostin, J.D., L.L.D., (Hon.),** *is Associate Dean and Professor, Georgetown University Law Center; Professor, Johns Hopkins University; and Director, World Health Organization Collaborating Center on Public Health Law and Human Rights. Dean Gostin is Adjunct Professor and Fellow at Oxford University and a lifetime Member of the Institute of Medicine.*

The New IHR: An Important Development in Global Health Governance

The new IHR contain 66 articles organized into ten parts and include nine annexes (see Table). The purpose of the new IHR is "to prevent, protect against, control and provide a public health response to the international spread of disease in ways that are commensurate with and restricted to public health risks, and which avoid unnecessary interference with international traffic and trade" (Article 2). The IHR seek to balance the state's right to protect its people's health with obligations to take health-protecting actions in ways that do not unnecessarily interfere with international trade and travel.

The new IHR capture this balancing task by providing that "States have...the sovereign right to legislate and to implement legislation in pursuance of their health policies. In doing so they should uphold the purpose of these Regulations" (Article 3.4). By calibrating health and trade interests, the IHR resonate with international trade law under the World Trade Organization (WTO), which also recognizes the state's right to restrict trade for health purposes but limits this right to ensure that restrictions are necessary.[12] The synergies between the new IHR and international trade law emphasize that public health is embedded in an international system that facilitates economic activity through globalized markets. Finding effective ways of balancing public health and international economic activity has become critically important to the success of international trade and international health governance.

The new IHR radically depart from the traditional approach informing the old IHR. The new IHR transform the international legal context in which states will exercise their public health sovereignty in the future. As examined below, the new IHR expand the scope of the IHR's application, incorporate international human rights principles, contain more demanding obligations for states parties to conduct surveillance and response, and establish important new powers for WHO.

The transformative nature of the new IHR connects to growing consensus on the importance of public health to global governance in the 21st century. Over the decade during which the IHR revision unfolded, it became apparent that public health had emerged as critical to virtually every major global governance issue, ranging from national and international security, trade, and economic development, to environmental protection and human rights. The new IHR not only transform the traditional approach to international disease spread but they also represent a politically important opportunity for public health to engage expansively with the international community.

Scope of the New IHR: An All-Risks Approach

As indicated above, the old IHR applied only to a short list of infectious diseases whose spread was historically associated with trade and travel (e.g., cholera, plague, and yellow fever). The Regulations now encompass public health risks whatever their origin or source (Article 1.1), including: (1) naturally occurring infectious diseases, whether of known or unknown etiological origin; (2) the potential international spread of non-communicable diseases caused by chemical or radiological agents in products moving in international commerce; and (3) suspected intentional or ac-

Table

Structure and Content of the New IHR

Part	Articles	Substance Matter
Part I	1-3	Definitions, Purpose, and Scope, Principles and Responsible Authorities
Part II	5-14	Information and Public Health Response
Part III	15-18	Recommendations
Part IV	19-22	Points of Entry
Part V	23-34	Public Health Measures
Part VI	35-39	Health Documents
Part VII	40-41	Charges
Part VIII	42-46	General Provisions
Part IX	47-53	The IHR Roster of Experts, the Emergency Committee, and the Review Committee
Part X	54-66	Final Provisions
Annex 1		Core Capacity Requirements for Surveillance and Response and for Designated Airports, Ports, and Ground Crossings
Annex 2		Decision Instrument for the Assessment and Notification of Events that May Constitute a Public Health Emergency of International Concern
Annex 3		Model Ship Sanitation Control Exemption Certificate/Ship Sanitation Control Certificate
Annex 4		Technical Requirements Pertaining to Conveyances and Conveyance Operators
Annex 5		Specific Measures for Vector-Borne Diseases
Annex 6		Vaccination, Prophylaxis, and Related Certificates
Annex 7		Requirements Concerning Vaccination or Prophylaxis for Specific Diseases
Annex 8		Model Maritime Declaration of Health
Annex 9		Health Part of the Aircraft General Declaration

cidental releases of biological, chemical, or radiological substances.

This "all risks" approach embodies an important conceptual shift concerning public health's role in the IHR. Trade calculations determined the old IHR's scope, but risks to human health define the new IHR's scope. The result is a set of rules with more public health legitimacy, flexibility, and adaptability. This expanded public health approach is found throughout the new IHR. Reporting health events, handling epidemiological data, making WHO recommendations, and limiting national health measures apply across the spectrum of health events. The expanded scope creates a more demanding framework than anything that ever appeared in the traditional approach.

Incorporation of Human Rights Principles: Autonomy, Privacy, and Liberty

The traditional approach to international disease spread developed prior to the emergence of international human rights law. The new IHR incorporate human rights principles, recognizing the effects of public health interventions on civil and political rights, such as security of person and freedom of movement.[13]

The New IHR and General Human Rights Principles
The new IHR proclaim that "[t]he implementation of these Regulations shall be with full respect for the dignity, human rights and fundamental freedoms of persons" (Article 3.1). This provision raises the question whether the new IHR conform to existing international human rights principles. For a public health measure to restrict a civil and political right lawfully, the measure must (1) respond to a pressing public or social need; (2) pursue a legitimate aim; (3) be proportionate to the legitimate aim; and (4) be no more restrictive than is required to achieve the purpose sought by restricting the right.[14] The rights-restricting measure must also be implemented in a non-discriminatory manner (International Covenant on Civil and Political Rights (ICCPR), Articles 2.1 and 26). Individuals deprived of liberty must be treated with humanity and respect for the inherent dignity of the human person (ICCPR, Article 10.1).

The new IHR generally reflect the requirements in international human rights law. The Regulations require states parties to identify a public health risk that justifies imposing health measures against persons (Articles 23.2, 31.1, 31.2, and 43.1), apply an appropriate health response to such risk (Articles 23.2, 23.5, 30, 31.2, and 43.2), and implement measures that are no more intrusive or invasive of persons than reasonably available alternatives that would achieve the level of health protection desired (Articles 23.2,

31.2, and 43.1). These disciplines also apply to WHO recommendations made under the new IHR (Article 17). All health measures must be applied in a transparent and non-discriminatory way (Article 42). In addition, states parties must treat travelers with respect for their dignity, human rights and fundamental freedoms and minimize any discomfort or distress associated with health measures, including by treating them with courtesy and respect; taking into consideration their gender, socio-cultural, ethnic, or religious concerns; and providing adequate food, water, accommodation, baggage protection, medical treatment, and means of communication for quarantine or isolated travelers (Article 32).

The extent to which the new IHR incorporate human rights principles means that international human rights law is relevant to the interpretation and implementation of the new IHR.[15] The Regulation's incorporation of human rights will suffer, however, if states parties do not integrate human rights thinking into the operation of their respective public health systems. As human rights problems with HIV/AIDS and other public health concerns suggest, making the new IHR's human rights elements effective will require commitment and vigilance. WHO and states parties should have human rights principles in mind as they build the public health capacities required by the new IHR.

Informed Consent and Privacy
The new IHR also contain provisions on the important human rights areas of informed consent and privacy. States parties cannot apply health measures to travelers without their prior express informed consent, except in situations that warrant compulsory measures (Articles 23.3 and 31.2). The new IHR also reflect the right to privacy by requiring states parties to preserve the confidentiality of personally identifiable information they receive from other states parties or WHO (Article 45.1). States parties and WHO must ensure that disclosure and processing of personal information in order to address a public health risk protects individual privacy (Article 45.2). The Regulations also require WHO to respond to individuals who want to review personally identifiable data WHO possesses about them (Article 45.3).

Although an improvement over the traditional approach in terms of recognizing the importance of informed consent and privacy, problems and questions remain. For example, the new IHR fall short in terms of protecting human rights with regard to compulsory measures applied in the absence of informed consent. The rules relevant to compulsory measures only oblige states parties to apply the least intrusive and invasive measure with respect to medical examinations but not

The new IHR require WHO to share information it receives from non-governmental sources with all states parties and relevant intergovernmental organizations when necessary to enable responses to public health risks.

to vaccinations, other prophylaxis, isolation, or quarantine (Articles 23.2 and 31.2). In addition, the Regulations do not include due process protections necessary when states apply compulsory measures.

In terms of privacy, the new IHR mandate confidential treatment of personal health data by states parties "as required by national law" (Article 45.1). Similarly, the requirement of states parties to protect privacy in addressing public health risks must be fulfilled "in accordance with national law" (Article 45.2). These provisions may make privacy protections under the new IHR relative to disparate levels of national privacy protection rather than subject to internationally recognized privacy standards.

National Public Health Capacities: Surveillance and Response

The new IHR require states parties to develop, strengthen, and maintain core surveillance and response capacities (Articles 5.1 and 13.1 and Annex 1). The old IHR had requirements for public health capabilities only at points of entry and exit. The far-reaching provisions in the new IHR shore up major weaknesses in global strategies created by inadequate national surveillance and response capabilities.

The new IHR reflect, however, states' concerns about sovereignty. States parties do not have to fulfill the capacity obligations until 2012 – five years after the new IHR enter into force in 2007 (Articles 5.1 and 13.1). A state party can obtain a two-year extension by submitting a justified need and an implementation plan to WHO (Articles 5.2 and 13.2); and, in exceptional circumstances, it can request a further two-year extension that the DG has the power to grant or deny (Articles 5.2 and 13.2).

Although the new IHR's provisions on surveillance and response capacities recognize the critical need for capacity building, questions remain about the handling of this issue. The most pressing question concerns the availability of financial and technical resources needed to improve national core capacities, especially in developing and least developed countries. WHO's duties to provide surveillance and response assistance (Articles 5.3, 13.3, and 13.6) do not address its own shortage of funds and personnel. The new IHR also contain no obligations on states parties to provide financial and

technical resources to support capacity-building. Although the new IHR urge states parties to provide financial and technical resources, these provisions are either non-binding (Article 13.5) or weak (Article 44.1). Given the financial demands created by other global health problems, such as increasing access to HIV/AIDS treatment[16] and meeting the health-related Millennium Development Goals,[17] the new IHR's silence on how the economic demands of the core capacity objectives will be met is a serious problem for which the new IHR provide no apparent answers or strategies.

Notification Obligations: Reporting Health Events to WHO

The new IHR require states parties to notify WHO of all events within their territories that may constitute a public health emergency of international concern (Article 6), defined as "an extraordinary event which is determined...(i) to constitute a public health risk to other States through the international spread of disease and (ii) to potentially require a coordinated international response" (Article 1.1). A "decision instrument" is used to guide states parties in determining whether a disease event may constitute a public health emergency of international concern (Annex 2) (See Figure).

In keeping with the new IHR's expanded scope, the notification obligations reflect a radically different, and more demanding, approach to addressing the international spread of disease. The notification provisions place a premium on states parties having sufficient surveillance capacities to detect disease incidents, assess them under the decision instrument, and report disease events that may constitute public health emergencies of international concern. As discussed above, whether many WHO member states have, or can develop, surveillance capacities sufficient to support these notification obligations remains a serious question.

Another problem looms for the new IHR's notification requirements. States parties often violated the old IHR by failing to report cases of diseases subject to the Regulations because they feared other countries would implement economically damaging trade or travel restrictions.[18] Will the more expansive and demanding notification requirements in the new IHR avoid the wide-spread non-compliance that undermined the old IHR? Answering this question requires considering the new IHR's approach to information supply and verification, which constitutes its strategy for countering non-compliance with notification obligations.

Figure

Decision Instrument for the Assessment and Notification of Events that May Constitute a Public Health Emergency of International Concern (New IHR, Annex 2)

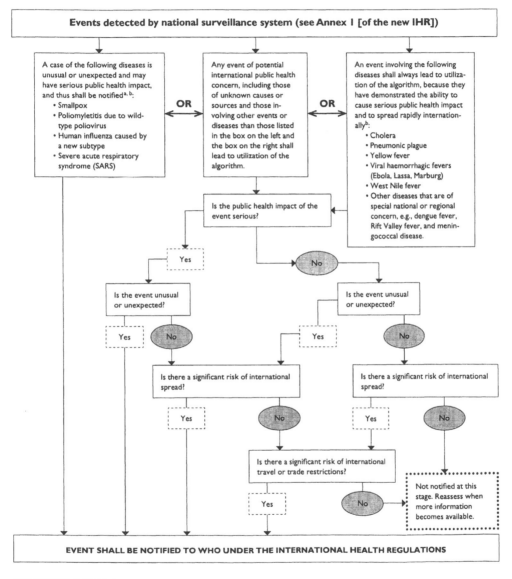

a As per WHO case definitions.
b The disease list shall be used only for purposes of these Regulations.

Data and Verification Provisions: Unofficial Sources of Information

The old IHR limited WHO to officially using information provided by states parties. This limitation handicapped WHO's ability to respond to disease events if a government refused to notify WHO of incidents, supply needed information, or otherwise cooperate. By contrast, the new IHR allow WHO to "take into account reports from sources other than notifications or consultations" from or with governments and to seek verification of such information from states parties in whose territories the events are allegedly occurring (Articles 9.1 and 10.1). States parties must respond to WHO verification requests (Article 10.2). The new IHR require WHO to share information it receives from non-governmental sources with all states parties and relevant intergovernmental organizations when necessary to enable responses to public health risks (Article 11.1).

From the beginning of the IHR revision process, WHO identified access to non-governmental sources of information as critical to constructing an effective global surveillance system.[19] Harnessing new information technologies, such as the Internet, for global surveillance has been at the heart of WHO's Global Outbreak Alert and Response Network (GOARN). GOARN – a collaborative network of institutions and experts that pools human and technical resources for rapid identification, confirmation, and response to outbreaks of international importance – is centrally important to the new IHR's functioning.[20]

WHO demonstrated the power of having access to non-governmental sources of information during the SARS outbreak.[21] Globalization has significantly decreased the state's ability to control the flow of epidemiological information into and out of its territory, and thus its prospects of keeping serious disease events hidden from international scrutiny. The avian influenza outbreaks in Asia also teach this lesson.

WHO's access to non-governmental information, its authority to request verification from states parties, and its power to share such information with the international community increase incentives for states parties to comply with the notification requirements. Further, the new IHR's information and verification provisions mitigate the consequences of non-compliance with notification obligations because WHO will, in all likelihood, learn of disease events through other sources, triggering the information verification and dissemination processes. The best chance states parties have to minimize adverse economic consequences from disease events is to be transparent and cooperate with WHO and other countries in addressing the threats. In short, the information and verification provisions privilege global health governance over state sovereignty.

The new IHR contain, however, a provision that bears watching to see how it affects the flow of non-governmental information. The Regulations require WHO to share non-governmental information with states parties "and only where it is duly justified may WHO maintain the confidentiality of the source" (Article 9.1). The general requirement on WHO to disclose the source of non-governmental information might deter non-state actors from supplying WHO with information, particularly individuals living under authoritarian regimes. In contrast to its protections for confidentiality of health-related personal information, the Regulations generally require WHO to supply information on persons who are non-official sources of information. The new IHR provide no guidance for determining under what circumstances WHO would be justified in maintaining the confidentiality of non-state sources. Such determinations might involve WHO having to assess the likelihood that governments may punish individuals in their jurisdictions for disseminating disease-related information. Thus, decisions to protect confidentiality of non-state sources will likely involve political controversy for WHO.

Declaration and Recommendation Powers

The new IHR grant two other important powers to WHO that never appeared in the old IHR. First, the new IHR accord WHO the authority to determine whether a disease event constitutes a public emergency of international concern (Article 12). States parties have to notify disease events that *may* constitute such emergencies, but the DG determines if disease events are public health emergencies of international concern. Although the DG must consult with states parties in whose territories disease events are occurring, he or she is not bound to follow their views. In other words, a state party's refusal to cooperate does not bar WHO action.

Second, if the DG determines that a public health emergency of international concern is occurring, then he or she shall issue non-binding, temporary recommendations to states parties on the most appropriate ways to respond (Article 15). The DG may also issue non-binding, standing recommendations on routine, periodic application of health measures for specific, ongoing public health risks (Article 16). The new IHR contain criteria for issuing temporary or standing recommendations (Article 17) and examples of the kinds of measures WHO could recommend (Article 18). These powers allow WHO to provide leadership on what health measures are appropriate from scientific and public health perspectives and on the proper ways to balance health protection with respect for human rights and acknowledgement of trade concerns.

Permissible Health Measures: Limits on National Public Health Interventions

States parties to the new IHR are not legally bound to follow WHO temporary or standing recommendations; but the new IHR contain binding limits on the types of health measures states parties can take against public health risks. These limits are designed to ensure adequate health protection with minimal interference with international traffic and respect for human rights. Generally, states parties cannot require an invasive medical examination, vaccination or other prophylaxis as a condition of entry for any traveler (Article 31.1); nor can a state party require any health document for travelers other than those permitted by the new IHR or recommended by WHO (Article 35). The new IHR also regulate measures states parties can apply to ships, aircraft, goods, and containers (Articles 25-29, 33-34, and 41) and harmonize the types of health documents required from ships and aircraft (Articles 37-39).

The new IHR permit states parties to apply health measures that achieve the same or greater level of health protection than WHO recommendations or that are otherwise prohibited by the IHR (Article 43.1). Such health measures must be based on scientific principles, available scientific evidence, relevant guidance or advice from WHO, and cannot be more restrictive of international traffic or more invasive or intrusive to persons than reasonably available alternatives that would achieve the level of health protection sought (Articles 43.1-43.2).

These provisions resemble the approach taken to health-protecting measures in WTO agreements, such as the Agreement on the Application of Sanitary and Phytosanitary Measures (SPS Agreement). Unlike the SPS Agreement, however, the new IHR do not have a strong enforcement mechanism if states parties fail to comply with the obligations on permissible health measures. Enforcement of the SPS Agreement benefits from the mandatory WTO dispute settlement process. Dispute settlement in the new IHR is essentially voluntary (Article 56). Failure by states to comply with the old IHR undermined their effectiveness. The lack of an enforcement mechanism in the new IHR may mean that non-compliance with rules on permissible health measures becomes a problem.

Rejections and Reservations

As a treaty, the new IHR cannot legally bind states unless they consent to be bound. Therefore, states can reject the new IHR (Article 61) or formulate reservations to provisions to which they refuse to be bound (Article 62). The changes made by, and the more demanding nature of, the new IHR may create incentives for states to reject the revised Regulations or formulate reservations. A reservation becomes effective (1) if less than one-third of relevant states object to the reservation (Article 62.5); or (2) if at least one-third of relevant states object to the reservation, and the reserving state does not withdraw the reservation, when the WHO by majority vote approves the reservation as compatible with the IHR's object and purpose (Article 62.9). Rejections and reservations have to be made within 18 months of the date of the new IHR's adoption (Article 59.1). The United States has already indicated that it will submit a "narrowly tailored" reservation providing that it will implement the IHR in a manner consistent with American federalism.[22] The process of making and reviewing reservations bears monitoring because of the potential for reservations to weaken the new IHR's universal application.

Political Controversies in the IHR Reform Process

Three political conflicts emerged during the negotiations to revise the IHR that threatened to stall or even prevent final adoption: conflicts of law with other international regimes; the role of WHO in combating biological, chemical, and nuclear terrorism; and the relationship of Taiwan to the new IHR regime.

Conflicts of International Law

WHO member states expressed concerns that the expanded scope of the new IHR would bring the Regulations into conflict with other international agencies and treaties that addressed cross-border health risks – e.g., the International Atomic Energy Agency (nuclear accidents);[23] the World Trade Organization (health measures that restrict international trade);[24] and the Codex Alimentarius Commission (food standards and guidelines to protect consumer health and promote trade in safe products). WHO addressed these concerns by demonstrating that few conflicts existed; amending the negotiating text to remove the small number of possible conflicts;[25] and adding provisions to facilitate cooperation and coordination between WHO and other international organizations (e.g., Articles 14, 17(f), 57.1).

Biological, Chemical, and Nuclear Terrorism

How the revised IHR would apply to suspected intentional releases of biological, chemical, and radiological agents proved highly controversial. Negotiating drafts required states parties to share information with WHO if they had evidence of a suspected intentional release of a biological, chemical, or radiological agent.

This proposal reflected the belief that appropriate public health responses were needed whether the risk was naturally occurring, accidental, or intentionally caused. However, the proposal was politically charged as it touched on issues of national and international security related to weapons of mass destruction. Concern was expressed that WHO's public health mission could be to, public health risks (Article 2). Provision of information under Article 7 is no different than the provision of information for any disease event or public health risk to which the new IHR apply, meaning that WHO would be focused on the health risk only. "Health measure" is defined to exclude law enforcement or security measures (Article 1.1). Although information WHO gath-

---

Less clear is whether the new IHR might embroil WHO in the politics of national and international security to the detriment of its core public health functions. Although it makes some experts uncomfortable, the potential for terrorism involving weapons of mass destruction connects public health to security concerns.

---

compromised if it had to investigate whether states had violated arms control treaties or UN Security Council resolutions.[26]

The new IHR handle these concerns awkwardly, reflecting difficult negotiations. The new IHR do not contain any specific requirement on information-sharing concerning suspected intentional releases. What remains is a weaker provision: "If a State Party has evidence of an unexpected or unusual public health event within its territory, irrespective of origin or source, which may constitute a public health emergency of international concern, it shall provide WHO with all relevant public health information" (Article 7). However, this article, combined with the expanded scope, makes clear that the new IHR apply to a suspected intentional release of a biological, chemical, and radiological agent. The understanding issued by the United States that the new IHR apply to all "health threats – chemical, biological, and radiological – and all causes and modes of events – regardless whether they are naturally occurring, accidental, or deliberate" is correct.[27]

Less clear is whether the new IHR might embroil WHO in the politics of national and international security to the detriment of its core public health functions. Although it makes some experts uncomfortable, the potential for terrorism involving weapons of mass destruction connects public health to security concerns. The anthrax attacks in the United States in 2001 demonstrated that public health responses to bioterrorism are critical aspects of national and homeland security. The new IHR recognize this unfortunate reality.

At the same time, the new IHR limit WHO's role to public health activities in these security-sensitive contexts. The new IHR's purpose states that the Regulations involve prevention, protection, control, and response activities concerning the international spread of disease in ways commensurate with, and restricted ers and analyzes would be important in assessments of whether a state violated obligations under arms control agreements or Security Council resolutions, the new IHR do not put WHO in the position of making such assessments.

Despite these attempts to contain WHO's role in situations involving possible violations of arms control and other security obligations, the new IHR do not settle the controversies about WHO's relationship to security concerns related to weapons of mass destruction. Following recommendations made by a high-level panel of experts[28] and the UN Secretary-General,[29] the Security Council could decide to intervene in a situation involving naturally occurring diseases or a suspected intentional release of biological, chemical, or radiological agents in a way that involves WHO in politically difficult circumstances. Whether such an intervention by the Security Council would be warranted is not an issue that the new IHR could address.

The Taiwan Problem

The standoff between China and Taiwan entered the politics of the IHR revision process. Following the SARS outbreak in 2003, during which Taiwan required assistance from WHO, Taiwan advocated for being included in the new IHR regime. Taiwan argued that the new IHR should have universal geographical coverage to be effective in the era of globalized disease threats. During the negotiations, China refused to allow Taiwan to participate formally in the new IHR.

What remains of this controversy is found in the principle that "[t]he implementation of these Regulations shall be guided by the goal of their universal application for the protection of all people of the world from the international spread of disease" (Article 3.3). Taiwan interprets this provision as "a basis for Taiwan to make contact with the WHO directly without China's interference."[30] China disagrees and points to a memorandum it negotiated with WHO in May 2005 that requires China's consent before WHO has any direct contact with Taiwan.[31] In short, the new IHR do not resolve the Taiwan-China problem, nor could the IHR revision process be expected to produce *rapprochement* between Taiwan and China.

The New IHR and the Future of Global Health Governance

The new IHR contain an international legal regime unprecedented in the history of the relationship between international law and public health. The revised Regulations promise to become a centerpiece for global health governance in the 21st century. As the UN Secretary-General's support for the IHR revision illustrates,[32] the new IHR have global governance significance far beyond anything contemplated under, or achieved by, the old IHR. Whether the issue involves international security, trade, economic development, environmental degradation, UN reform, or human rights, policy makers and experts have identified public health as a central governance challenge nationally and internationally in the 21st century. The transformational nature of the new IHR create a regime that has the potential to contribute significantly to the general global governance mission of improving national and international health. The Regulations provide a framework that supports not only improved international cooperation on health but also the strengthening of national health systems, producing more robust health governance horizontally among states and vertically within them.

The new IHR's novelty should not, however, obscure hard realities facing its future. WHO was systematically using non-governmental surveillance information from GOARN's establishment in 1998, well before the IHR revision process was completed; and this strategy would have continued whether or not the new IHR had been adopted. More difficult issues arise with producing effective responses to identified public health risks. For decades, WHO has issued recommendations on many public health problems; but the mixed record of state compliance with WHO guidance should temper enthusiasm for the new IHR's recommendation provisions. The political controversies that surrounded WHO's more aggressive actions during SARS may deter WHO from taking similar actions under the new IHR. Laments about the erosion of global and local public health capabilities suggest that WHO's decades-long effort to improve health conditions in developing countries has also met with only qualified success. The new IHR will not change this dynamic overnight, particularly when the Regulations generate no fresh financial resources to support capacity-building. Com-

pliance with international legal restrictions against the implementation of health measures that unnecessarily restrict trade or infringe on human rights has not, in the past, been stellar, as illustrated by how non-compliance helped destroy the old IHR's effectiveness. Whether the quantity and quality of compliance with the new IHR's rules on health measures are better will not depend on any improved enforcement mechanism because the Regulations do not create one.

The new IHR are no "magic bullet" for global health problems. Previous transformations in international law's relationship with public health have, over time, atrophied into insignificance. The history of the old IHR tells just such a story. Further, the new IHR's relevance to some pressing global health problems, such as increasing access to HIV/AIDS treatment in the developing world or stemming the "brain drain" of health workers from developing to developed countries,[33] is not apparent. Controversies and problems surrounding the threat of avian influenza also suggest that the new IHR do not cut through the tangled knot of very hard political, economic, scientific, and public health choices governments must make to address this public health emergency of international concern.

The new IHR are the product of a decade of work by WHO and its member states, and the revised Regulations have been designed to be a robust governance framework far into the future. Harvesting the new IHR's benefits for global health requires understanding not only the difficulties this task faces but also the potential the Regulations represent. At present, this potential exists mainly on paper, which is why the implementation phase is critical. WHO needs to approach implementation with the energy and vision it demonstrated during SARS. The seminal achievement of the new IHR constitutes only the end of the beginning. The hard work of making this transformative revision of global health governance effective for individuals, states, and the international community now begins.

References

1. World Health Assembly, *Revision of the International Health Regulations*, WHA58.3 (May 23, 2005).
2. UN Secretary-General, *In Larger Freedom: Towards Development, Security, and Human Rights for All: Report of the Secretary-General*, A/59/2005 (March 21, 2005).
3. World Health Assembly, *Revision and Updating of the International Health Regulations*, WHA48.7 (May 12, 1995).
4. P. Dorelle, "Old Plagues in the Jet Age: International Aspects of Present and Future Control of Communicable Diseases," *Chronicle of the World Health Organization* 23 (1969): 103-111; E. Roelsgaard, "Health Regulations and International Travel," *Chronicle of the World Health Organization* 28 (1974): 265-268; B. Velimirovic, "Do We Still Need International Health Regulations?" *Journal of Infectious Diseases* 133 (1976): 478-482.
5. World Health Organization, *Provisional Draft of the International Health Regulations* (Geneva, Switzerland: World Health Organization, January 1998).

INDEPENDENT

6. World Health Organization, *Severe Acute Respiratory Syndrome (SARS): Status of the Outbreak and Lessons for the Immediate Future* (Geneva, Switzerland: World Health Organization, 2003).
7. World Health Assembly, *Severe Acute Respiratory Syndrome (SARS)*, WHA56.29 (May 28, 2003); World Health Assembly, *Revision of the International Health Regulations*, WHA56.28 (May 28, 2003).
8. World Health Organization, *International Health Regulations: Working Paper for Regional Consultations*, IGWG/IHR/Working paper/12.2003 (January 12, 2004); L. O. Gostin, "International Infectious Disease Law: Revision of the World Health Organization's International Health Regulations," *JAMA* 291 (2004): 2623-2627.
9. World Health Organization, *Review and Approval of Proposed Amendments to the International Health Regulations: Draft Revision*, A/IHR/IGWG/3 (September 30, 2004).
10. World Health Organization, *Review and Approval of Proposed Amendments to the International Health Regulations: Proposal by the Chair*, A/IHR/IGWG/2/2 (January 24, 2005).
11. World Health Organization, *Revision of the International Health Regulations: Note by the Secretariat*, A58/4 (May 16, 2005).
12. World Health Organization and World Trade Organization, *WTO Agreements & Public Health: A Joint Study by the WHO and the WTO Secretariat* (Geneva, Switzerland: World Health Organization, 2002).
13. International Covenant on Civil and Political Rights, *United Nations Treaty Series* 171 (December 19, 1966): 999.
14. UN Economic and Social Council, UN Sub-Commission on Prevention of Discrimination and Protection of Minorities, *Siracusa Principles on the Limitation and Derogation of Provisions in the International Covenant on Civil and Political Rights*, UN Doc. E/CN.4/1985/4, Annex, 1985.
15. Vienna Convention on the Law of Treaties, *United Nations Treaty Series* 331 (May 23, 1969): 1155.
16. World Health Organization, The 3 by 5 Initiative, *available at* <http://www.who.int/3by5/en/> (last visited December 12, 2005).
17. World Health Organization, *Achievement of Health-Related Millennium Development Goals: Report by the Secretariat*, A58/5 (May 13, 2005).
18. D. P. Fidler, *International Law and Infectious Diseases* (Oxford, England: Clarendon Press, 1999).
19. World Health Organization, *The International Response to Epidemics and Applications of the International Health Regulations: Report of a WHO Informal Consultation*, WHO/EMC/IHR/96.1 (December 11-14, 1995).
20. World Health Organization, *Global Defense Against the Infectious Disease Threat* (Geneva, Switzerland: World Health Organization, 2002).

21. D. P. Fidler, *SARS, Governance, and the Globalization of Disease* (Basingstoke, England: Palgrave Macmillan, 2004).
22. *Statement for the Record by the Government of the United States of America Concerning the World Health Organization's Revised International Health Regulations*, May 23, 2005. Press Release, U.S. Mission to the United Nations in Geneva, *at* <http://www.us-mission.ch/Press2005/0523IHRs.htm> (last visited January 9, 2006).
23. Convention on Assistance in the Case of a Nuclear Accident or Radiological Emergency, September 26, 1986, 1457 *United Nations Treaty Series* 133; Convention on Nuclear Safety, July 5, 1994, 1963 *United Nations Treaty Series* 317.
24. General Agreement on Tariffs and Trade, April 15, 1994, in World Trade Organization, *The Legal Texts: The Results of the Uruguay Round of Multilateral Trade Negotiations* (Cambridge, England: Cambridge University Press, 1999): 424-492; Agreement on the Application of Sanitary and Phytosanitary Measures, April 15, 1994, in World Trade Organization, *The Legal Texts: The Results of the Uruguay Round of Multilateral Trade Negotiations* (Cambridge, England: Cambridge University Press, 1999): 59-72.
25. World Health Organization, *Review and Approval of Proposed Amendments to the International Health Regulations: Relations with Other International Instruments*. A/IHR/IGWG/INF. DOC./1 (September 30, 2004).
26. G. S. Pearson, *The UN Secretary-General's High Level Panel: Biological Weapons Related Issues* (Strengthening the Biological Weapons Convention, Review Conference Paper No. 14) (May 2005).
27. *Supra* note 22.
28. UN Secretary-General's High-Level Panel on Threats, Challenges, and Change, *A More Secure World: Our Shared Responsibility* (New York, New York: United Nations, 2004).
29. *Supra*, note 2.
30. J. Rickards, "Taiwan-WHO Ties Improving, Officials Say," *China Post*, May 26, 2005 *available at* <http://www.chinapost.com.tw/archive/detail.asp?cat=1&id=62934> (last visited January 9, 2006).
31. X. Yen, "Taiwan's WHO Bid Has No Legal Basis," *China Daily*, May 31, 2005, at 4.
32. See UN Secretary-General, Press Release, *World Health Assembly's Revised Regulations "Bold and Necessary Step" to Protect Global Public Health, Says Secretary-General* (May 23, 2005) SG/SM/9886, SAG/365.
33. World Health Assembly, *International Migration of Health Personnel: A Challenge for Health Systems in Developing Countries*, WHA58.17 (May 25, 2005).

[32]

Committed to health for all? How the G7/G8 rate

Ronald Labonte*, Ted Schrecker

Saskatchewan Population Health and Evaluation Research Unit, University of Saskatchewan, 107 Wiggins Road, Saskatoon, Saskatchewan, Canada S7N 5E5

Abstract

The G7/G8 group of nations dominate the world political and economic order. This article reports selected results from an investigation of the health implications of commitments made at the 1999, 2000 and 2001 Summits of the G7/G8, with special reference to the developing world. We emphasize commitments that relate to the socioeconomic determinants of health (primarily to reducing poverty and economic insecurity) and to the ability of national governments to make necessary basic investments in health systems, education and nutrition. We conclude that without a stronger commitment to redistributive policy measures on the part of the G7/G8, historic commitments on the part of the international community to providing health for all are likely not to be fulfilled.

Keywords: International health problems; Political economy; Political systems; Globalization; Structural adjustment; Poverty

Introduction and rationale

In 1978, building on the 1948 *Universal Declaration of Human Rights*, a United Nations conference proposed the goal of health for all by the year 2000 (WHO, 1978). In 2003, only limited progress has been made toward that goal. This article assesses the reasons for that lack of progress, with specific reference to the dominant role played by the G8 (Group of 8) nations in the international economic and political order. In other words, it provides a "report card" on key health impacts and implications of G8 policies, with particular reference to effects in countries outside the industrialized world that account for roughly five-sixths of the world's population.

The G8 was formed in 1975 after the "oil crisis" provided an early warning of the dangers of economic interconnectedness. The six countries originally included were France, the United States, Britain, Germany, Italy and Japan. Canada joined in 1976; the European Community (now the European Union) joined in

*Corresponding author. Tel.: + 1-306-966-2349; fax: + 1-306-966-7920.

E-mail addresses: ronald.labonte@usask.ca (R. Labonte), schrecker@sask.usask.ca (T. Schrecker).

1977, but does not have the same status as national governments. Russia achieved partial membership in the group in 1998, and full membership as of 2003; thus, the G7 is now the G8. The G8 account for 46.6 percent of global GDP and 46.8 percent of global exports (International Monetary Fund, 2003, Table A). Perhaps more importantly, the G7 countries dominate World Bank and IMF decision making, and wield considerable power in the World Trade Organization (WTO) because the size of their markets and access to specialized expertise provide them with formidable bargaining advantages with respect to countries of the developing world.

Access to health care is only one factor amongst many affecting the health status of a population (Evans and Stoddart, 1990; Diderichsen, Evans, & Whitehead, 2001). For much of the world's population, ability to lead a healthy life is limited by direct and indirect effects of poverty. Almost half the world's people live on an income of $2 per day or less (World Bank, 2001, pp. 36–38). This figure has been criticized on methodological grounds as a substantial underestimate of the extent of absolute poverty (Reddy & Pogge, 2003), but clearly it describes complex and health-destructive vulnerabilities (Narayan, Chambers, Shah, & Petesch, 2000; Diderichsen, Evans, & Whitehead, 2001). Ill

1662   *R. Labonte, T. Schrecker / Social Science & Medicine 59 (2004) 1661–1676*

health not only results from poverty, but also can limit the ability of individuals, households and entire societies to escape from poverty. "[F]or the poor their body is often their only asset, and when the body is weakened through hunger, illness and accidents, an entire family can plunge into destitution" (Narayan, 2001, p. 15; see generally Narayan, Chambers, Shah, & Petesch, 2000). The potential contribution to economic development of low-cost interventions to improve health was a central theme of the work of the World Health Organization's Commission on Macroeconomics and Health (2001). Conversely, the impacts of HIV/AIDS and malaria provide especially dramatic, large-scale illustrations of the economic damage that can result from poor health (Haacker, 2002; Sachs & Malaney, 2002).

"Globalization" adds a further dimension to the challenge of providing health for all. The term is a convenient way of describing the growing interconnectedness of the world's economies and societies. Some observers regard globalization as a "process of closer interaction of human activities across a range of spheres including economic, political, social and cultural...[and] occurring along three dimensions: spatial, temporal and cognitive" (Lee, 2000, p. 30). Such broad descriptive definitions, while accurate, fail to take into account the fact that the primary influences of globalization on the social determinants of health are changes in patterns of international trade and investment, along with the underlying technological developments (Labonte & Torgerson, 2003). The economic manifestations of globalization, defined in this way, affect health by changing exposures to health risks, by changing the characteristics of health systems, and by affecting the structure of household, community and national economies (Zielinski Gutiérrez, & Kendall, 2000; Butler, Douglas, & McMichael, 2001; Woodward, Drager, Beaglehole, & Lipson, 2001; Labonte & Torgerson, 2003). Perhaps most dramatically, financial crises arising from the rapid flow of capital across national borders can plunge millions of people into poverty, while health and social service spending decreases (Hotchkiss & Jacobalis, 1999; Chavez & Cordero, 2001; O'Brien, 2002; Kim et al., 2003). Over a longer time scale, technological and institutional change have resulted in the emergence of a genuinely global labour market, within which there are clear winners and losers (World Bank, 1995).

Methodology

In preparing the "report card", we pursued two lines of inquiry. First, we considered the extent to which G7 countries have lived up to their Summit commitments. Second, we considered the adequacy of those commitments when measured against relevant population health challenges. In other words, we were concerned both with the policy effectiveness of the G7, when assessed with reference to their stated intentions, and with the substantive impact of their policies, when assessed with reference to a large and growing body of research on the determinants of health in the developing world (for overviews see Evans, Whitehead, Diderichsen, Bhuiya, & Wirth, 2001; WHO, 2002c).

These lines of inquiry are analytically distinct, but also related. Notably, in 2000 the G7 committed themselves "to the agreed international development goals (IDGs), including the overarching objective of reducing the share of the world's population living in extreme poverty to half its 1990 level by 2015" (G8, 2000, p. 13). These IDGs were published in 2000 as a joint effort of the UN, the OECD, the World Bank and the International Monetary Fund (2001), with the comment that: "Each of the seven goals addresses an aspect of poverty. They should be viewed together because they are mutually reinforcing" (International Monetary Fund, OECD, United Nations & World Bank Group, 2000, p. 4). A resolution (A/RES/55/2) of the UN General Assembly in 2000 incorporated several of the IDGs, as well as other objectives that are equally ambitious, and also directly related to health (Table 1), to generate a list that is now widely referred to as the Millennium Development Goals (MDGs). Because the G7 countries, both individually (the MDGs) and collectively (the IDGs), have committed themselves to support a range of goals that are related to improving global health, it is appropriate to assess their Summit undertakings in light of that position.

We analysed commitments made at the three Summits preceding the start of our research: Cologne (1999), Okinawa (2000) and Genoa (2001). In addition, we limited our focus to the G7 countries, given Russia's newer membership and transitional situation. Early on, we confronted a fundamental choice. We could restrict our assessment of G7 performance to a few narrowly specific commitments, ideally involving dichotomous end points. Alternatively, we could err on the side of inclusiveness, starting from an inventory of statements many of which were not readily amenable to quantitative assessment of subsequent performance. We followed the latter course, for two reasons. First, the complexity of the determinants of health and the long period of time that sometimes elapses between policy change and health impact mean that it is necessary to assess *patterns* of policy commitment and implementation over time. Second, as we have noted, the fact that the G7 countries have lived up to the specific terms of a commitment made at the Summits says nothing about the adequacy of the response described in that commitment, or about its consistency with other policy objectives such as those embodied in the IDGs/MDGs.

R. Labonte, T. Schrecker / Social Science & Medicine 59 (2004) 1661–1676 1663

Table 1
The international development goals and the millennium development goals compared

International development goals	Millennium development goals (Goals 1–7)
1 Reduce the proportion of people living in extreme poverty (less than US $1/day) by 2015	Goal 1: Eradicate extreme poverty and hunger
	Target 1: Halve, between 1990 and 2015, the proportion of people whose income is less than 1$ a day
	Target 2: Halve, between 1990 and 2015, the proportion of people who suffer from hunger
2 Enrol all children in primary school by 2015	Goal 2: Achieve universal primary education
	Target 3: Ensure that, by 2015, children everywhere, boys and girls alike, will be able to complete a full course of primary education
3 Eliminate gender disparities in primary and secondary education by 2005	Goal 3: Promote gender equality and empower women
	Target 4: Eliminate gender disparity in primary and secondary education preferably by 2005 and to all levels of education no later than 2015
4 Reduce infant and child (under-5) mortality rates by two-thirds between 1990 and 2015	Goal 4: Reduce child mortality
	Target 5: Reduce by two-thirds, between 1990 and 2015, the under-5 mortality rate
5 Reduce maternal mortality ratios by three-quarters between 1990 and 2015	Goal 5: Improve maternal health
	Target 6: Reduce by three-quarters, between 1990 and 2015, the maternal mortality ratio
6 Provide access for all who need reproductive health services by 2015	Goal 6: Combat HIV/AIDS, malaria and other diseases
	Target 7: Have halted by 2015, and begun to reverse, the spread of HIV/AIDS
	Target 8: Have halted by 2015, and begun to reverse, the incidence of malaria and other major diseases
7 Implement national strategies for sustainable development by 2005 so as to reverse the loss of environmental resources by 2015	Goal 7: Ensure environmental sustainability
	Target 9: Integrate the principles of sustainable development into country policies and programs and reverse the loss of environmental resources
	Target 10: Halve, by 2015, the proportion of people without sustainable access to safe drinking water
	Target 11: By 2020, to have achieved a significant improvement in the lives of at least 100 million slum dwellers

Sources: International Monetary Fund, OECD, United Nations and World Bank Group (2000) for International Development Goals; Devarajan, Miller and Swanson (2002, pp. 34-35) for Millennium Development Goals.

We began with key texts from the 1999–2001 Summits, primarily the formal statements issued at the start of Summits and the Communiqués issued at their conclusion.[1] Three individuals, each familiar with

[1] An electronic archive of these texts is maintained by the University of Toronto G8 Research Centre at http://www.g8.u-

(footnote continued)
toronto.ca. It must be emphasized that the commitments made at Summits represent the carefully choreographed end points of a long process of networking and negotiation by officials of member governments; by no stretch of the imagination can they be considered "off the cuff" utterances.

1664   R. Labonte, T. Schrecker / Social Science & Medicine 59 (2004) 1661–1676

population health determinants (the two social scientist authors of this article and a post-doctoral researcher with training in health sociology) read these texts and independently identified statements with potential significance for population health using 13 subject matter headings. Summit commitments were then classified into one (or, sometimes, more) of three columns in a matrix:

1. Commitments that could be assessed in quantitative or dichotomous terms (e.g. expenditure figures, actions taken or not).
2. Commitments about which data exist, but where assessment would be primarily qualitative or narrative (e.g. commitments using language such as "improve" or "increase").
3. Commitments reflecting a pre-existing, but contestable or problematic position on appropriate social and economic policies (e.g. the presumption that integrating developing countries into the global economy represents the only appropriate development strategy).

The matrix is available in full on the Internet (http://www.spheru.ca/www/html/Research/ Research_globalization.htm). Many commitments spanned more than one column; some also related to more than one subject matter heading. This article summarizes our findings with respect to health systems and to three other areas that are especially important influences on determinants of health: macroeconomic policy, nutrition, and education.

We then surveyed what turned out to be a massive literature in order to assess G7 performance with respect to Summit commitments, and the health implications of the policies reflected by those commitments. The literature comprised: quantitative data assembled by organizations including the World Bank, OECD, and several United Nations agencies; an extensive body of research by civil society organizations (CSOs) such as Oxfam and Jubilee Research; and an expanding research literature on determinants of population health in the developing world. These categories tend to overlap, in particular as the work of key CSO-affiliated researchers is published by "mainstream" agencies (Third World Network, 2001; Pettifor & Greenhill, 2002; Watkins, 2003). We carried out our own calculations and policy evaluations using these data, but did not check on their accuracy beyond the identification of clear inadequacies in the data as published. It must be noted that at least as many questions have been raised about the accuracy of data generated by agencies such as the World Bank and the World Health Organization (e.g. Musgrove, 2003; Reddy & Pogge, 2003) as about the research and policy recommendations of CSOs.

Table 2 shows in extremely condensed form our inventory of "promises kept, promises broken" with respect to the subject areas included in this article, along with a one-sentence commentary. We explain these findings in the sections that follow, after which we discuss the links between the policies that they document and a more general conception of the development process that appears to underpin and unify the positions taken by the G7. That development model incorporates a powerful presumption against substantial international redistribution of resources, but our findings indicate that genuinely redistributive policies are imperative in order to improve the health of populations in the developing world.

Macroeconomic policy, structural adjustment and debt relief

Because of the numerous causal pathways and feedback loops linking poverty and ill health (Narayan, Chambers, Shah, & Petesch, 2000; Commission on Macroeconomics and Health, 2001; Diderichsen, Evans, & Whitehead, 2001), we emphasize in this article the impacts of G7 commitments that operate on domestic macroeconomic and social policy. Those commitments, in turn, must be analysed with reference to the issue of developing country debt because, "despite repeated rescheduling of debt by creditor countries, developing countries continue[d] to pay out more each year in debt service than the actual amounts they receive in official development assistance—ODA" between 1986 and 1996 (Cheru, 1999, ¶ 10). The net outflow of funds became even more significant in the years that followed, as a result of the financial crisis in south Asia (Pettifor & Greenhill, 2002; United Nations, 2002). Debt service obligations represent the most fundamental constraint on many developing countries' ability to meet basic health-related needs—a constraint the significance of which has been recognized at least since the mid-1980s (World Commission on Environment and Development, 1987, pp. 67–75; Ramphal, 1999).

The Heavily Indebted Poor Countries (HIPC) initiative, announced by the World Bank and IMF in 1996 and "enhanced" in 1999, has become the centrepiece of G7 debt relief efforts (G8, 2001, ¶ 7,15). This is true even though the 41 HIPC-eligible countries, 33 of which are in sub-Saharan Africa, account for only 10 percent of the developing world's debt (UNRISD, 2000, p. 22), and HIPC's value in terms of poverty reduction is limited because a clear majority of the world's poor people live in countries that are not eligible for HIPC (Table 3). As of January 2003, 26 countries had reached their "decision point"—the point at which debt relief is approved—and were receiving debt service relief that will amount to $40.4 billion (World Bank, 2003a, Table 2). This is more than 70 percent of the total debt relief anticipated under the Initiative (World Bank, 2002b,

Table 2
'Promises kept (✔), promises broken (×)

Commitment		Assessment
Support for international development goals, "including the overarching objective of reducing the share of the world's population living in extreme poverty to half its 1990 level by 2015"	×	Many IDG targets for 2015 will almost certainly not be achieved
Provision of debt relief under Heavily Indebted Poor Countries (HIPC) initiative	✔	Debt relief now being provided, but amount is often inadequate; Poverty Reduction Strategy Paper process seriously flawed; many heavily indebted countries not covered
Create the Global Fund to Fight AIDS, Tuberculosis and Malaria	✔	Current financial pledges far below need identified by Commission on Macroeconomics and Health
By 2010: reducing the number of HIV/AIDS-infected young people by 25 percent, reducing TB deaths and prevalence of the disease by 50 percent, and reducing the burden of disease associated with malaria by 50 percent	×	Resources almost certainly inadequate
Non-specific commitment to strong national health systems	×	Official development assistance (ODA) for health from all industrialized countries: $6 billion/year (less than one-quarter the needed amount as identified by Commission on Macroeconomics and Health); during three Summit years of study, ODA from G7 countries actually declined slightly
Recognize need for "flexibility" with respect to intellectual property protection in order to ensure availability of essential drugs	✔	Agreement now reached on interpretation of intellectual property provisions of WTO Agreement, but its significance remains uncertain
Non-specific commitments to supporting agriculture through ODA as an element of poverty reduction, to "target the most food-insecure regions, particularly Sub-Saharan Africa and South Asia"	×	Few specifics, and no clear commitment to IDG of reducing underweight among children; recent slow progress in reducing undernutrition now reversed
Heavy emphasis on promoting biotechnology to increase agricultural productivity	✔	Appropriateness of such 'solutions' questionable
Clear support for Dakar Framework goals re: improving access to education by 2015	×	Strong evidence that these goals will not be achieved

p. 1). The G7, in other words, have lived up to their debt relief commitments as stated at the Summits.

However, such commitments may not be adequate when measured against the resources that will be required to achieve such objectives as the IDGs. Oxfam (2001, Fig. 1) has calculated that in 14 HIPC countries, annual debt servicing costs will exceed combined public spending on health and primary education even *after* the maximum debt relief available under HIPC is obtained. This is because the value of debt relief available under HIPC is currently determined based on a ratio of debt service costs to anticipated future export revenues; a country's debt load is considered "sustainable" if its net present value is less than 150 percent of annual export revenues. A more appropriate criterion for assessing sustainability would ensure that debt service costs did not compromise a country's ability to meet such objectives as the IDGs/MDGs (Greenhill, 2002; Greenhill & Sisti, 2003). Hanlon (2000), working backward from estimates of the expenditure that would be required to meet a list of targets similar to the MDGs,

estimated that approximately US$600 billion (at current value) in debt cancellation would be necessary to ensure that debt repayment did not occur at the expense of essential social spending. This is an order of magnitude greater than the value of all debt relief to be provided under enhanced HIPC. Hanlon's estimates consider not only the HIPC countries, which he estimates will require debt relief worth $180 billion, but also many others. His calculations imply, for instance, debt relief of $24 billion for now-beleaguered Argentina (for which national poverty data are not even available), $116 billion for Indonesia, and $98 billion for India. A more cautious set of calculations, restricted to the HIPC countries, nevertheless reached the conclusion that meeting the MDGs in many countries would require not only *complete* cancellation of external debt but also substantial increases in revenues from ODA (Greenhill & Sisti, 2003).

Further problems arise because eligibility for HIPC is contingent on the recipient government's completion of a Poverty Reduction Strategy Paper (PRSP). PRSPs

1666   R. Labonte, T. Schrecker / Social Science & Medicine 59 (2004) 1661–1676

Table 3
Poverty in non-HIPC countries

	Population (million)	Number of people living on <$1/day (million)	Number of people living on <$2/day (million)
Bangladesh	133.4	38.8	103.8
Brazil	172.6	20.0	45.7
China	1271.9	239.1	669.0
India	1033.4	456.8	890.7
Indonesia	213.6	27.6	139.9
Mexico	99.4	15.8	37.5
Nigeria	129.9	91.2	117.9
Pakistan	141.5	43.9	119.9
These 8 (non-HIPC) countries		933.2	2124.4
Entire world		1198.9	2801.0

Sources: World Bank, 2001; World Bank, 2003b.

were launched by the World Bank and IMF in December 1999, as "a new approach to the challenge of reducing poverty in low-income countries based on country-owned poverty reduction strategies that would serve as a framework for development assistance" (International Development Association/IMF, 2002, p. 5). Although PRSPs ostensibly place poverty reduction at the centre of their analysis, direct parallels exist between the process of qualifying for debt relief through the preparation of a PRSP and earlier forms of conditionality (Cheru, 2001; International Monetary Fund, 2001, pp. 50–52; UNCTAD, 2002a, p. 191). In order to understand the significance of these parallels, some historical background is needed. In 1980, the World Bank initiated structural adjustment loans to help heavily indebted poor countries cope with the impact of the 1979–80 recession on their ability to service external debt. Structural adjustment became far more important after 1982, when the government of Mexico announced that it was prepared to default on billions of dollars in loans, primarily made by major US banks. The result was the first of a series of "debt crises". Apprehensions about the stability of major banks in the industrialized world in the event of coordinated default led industrialized country governments, bilaterally and through the World Bank and the IMF, to provide new money for debt rescheduling.

However, the new money came with strings attached (conditionality): funds were made available only if the debtor country agreed to a relatively standard package of macroeconomic policies including reduced subsidies for basic items of consumption, the removal of trade and investment controls, and privatization of state-owned enterprises (Sparr, 1994; Dixon, Simon, & Närman, 1995; Milward, 2000). As early as 1987, a UNICEF-

sponsored study indicated that a combination of global recession and the austerity measures adopted by national governments as the price of debt relief had the effect of reducing such basic indicators of child welfare as nutrition, immunization levels and education (Cornia, Jolly, & Stewart, 1987, 1988; see also Stewart, 1991). By the end of the 1980s, "cross-conditionality" that involved both the World Bank and the IMF (Walton, Sedden et al., 1994, p. 19) further ensured subordination of domestic policy goals to the imperative of fiscal restraint and the generation of export revenues sufficient to meet debt obligations. Among the consequences was reduced access to such services as health care and education as public expenditures were cut and user charges introduced (see e.g. Cheru, 1999; Cornia, Jolly, & Stewart, 1987, 1988; Schoepf, Schoepf, & Millen, 2000; Walton, Sedden et al., 1994; Yong Kim, Shakow, Bayona, Rhatigan, & Rubín de Celis, 2000).

The United Nations Development Program, in its assessment of the PRSP process, notes that advice on the requirement for a macroeconomic framework identifying fiscal and financing policies for poverty reduction is weak, contains many unexamined assumptions and does not adequately emphasize distributional impacts of macroeconomic policies (UNDP, 2002). The United Nations Conference on Trade and Development (UNCTAD, 2002b, p. 197) links the PRSP process with the inadequacy of overall levels of debt relief, noting that in order to ensure that a PRSP is perceived as "realistic", countries like Uganda and Tanzania are still investing far less than the minimum amounts required for health and social programs. The World Health Organization goes further in analysing serious gaps in existing PRSPs with respect to health (WHO, 2002a). Among its major criticisms: PRSPs deal with ill health as a *consequence* of poverty, but do not reflect an understanding of its role as a *cause* of poverty, and thus are too willing to recommend cost recovery as a way of financing health care services for the poor. In addition, PRSPs do not deal with such important health system issues as expenditure levels well below the minimum needed to provide basic primary health care. As the next section of the article shows, this has been another neglected area in terms of G7 commitments.

Health and health systems

In 2000, the G7 committed themselves to an "ambitious agenda" of "deliver[ing] three critical UN targets" by 2010: reducing the number of HIV/AIDS-infected young people by 25 percent, reducing TB deaths and prevalence of the disease by 50 percent, and reducing the burden of disease associated with malaria by 50 percent (G8, 2000, ¶ 29). However, without major increases in the resources available for health care

R. Labonte, T. Schrecker / Social Science & Medicine 59 (2004) 1661–1676 1667

expenditure, it is unlikely that these targets can be met. Much the same is true for the health-related components of the IDGs and MDGs, even though major improvements in health could be achieved by way of relatively low-cost, low-technology interventions to prevent the spread of infectious disease and reduce the toll from diarrheal disease and childbirth (Spinaci & Heymann, 2001). The World Bank recently concluded, based on a scenario of 3.6 percent annual per capita income growth in the developing countries between 2005 and 2015 (which may well be optimistic) that South Asia was the only region likely to achieve the infant and child mortality reduction target specified in the IDGs (World Bank, 2002a, pp. 31–33).

The world's Least Developed Countries (LDCs)[2] spend an average of just $11 per capita annually on health, including both public and private expenditures. For other low-income countries, average per capita expenditure on health is $25 (Global Forum on Health, 2002, p. 5). The Commission on Macroeconomics and Health (2001, p. 11) estimated the cost of a "set of essential interventions", which would not need to be the same for each country, at $34 per capita per year. The report warned that: "If anything, we are on the low end of the range of estimates of the cost of such essential interventions." As if to corroborate this observation, according to the former Director-General of the World Health Organization: "It is becoming clear that health systems which spend less than $60 or so per capita are not able to even deliver a reasonable minimum of services, even through extensive internal reform" (Brundtland, 2000).

The Commission on Macroeconomics and Health identified the need for "an additional $22 billion per year by 2007 and $31 billion per year by 2015" in grant financing for country-specific interventions against infectious diseases and nutritional deficiencies. Above and beyond these country-specific interventions, it called for additional grant funding of $5 billion by 2007 and $7 billion by 2015 for research and development on diseases of the poor and other public goods like epidemiological surveillance, for a total of $27 billion in 2007, rising to $38 billion in 2015. This estimate must be compared with total ODA for health that is now "on the order of

$6 billion" (Commission on Macroeconomics and Health, 2001, p. 11).

In 2001, the G7 addressed three infectious diseases that are major killers in the developing world by establishing the Global Fund to Fight AIDS, Tuberculosis and Malaria (GFATM). They described its creation as fulfilling a pledge from the preceding year "to make a quantum leap in the fight against infectious diseases and to break the vicious cycle between disease and poverty" (G8, 2001, ¶ 15). Financial commitments from governments to date amount to $4.68 billion, with $1.6 billion paid to date and the balance payable at various dates as far away as 2008 (http://www.theglobalfund.org/en/funds_raised/pledges/, accessed November 27, 2003). Since pledges do not all cover the same period, direct comparisons must be made with caution. However, the gap between the lowest per capita contribution among the G7 ($1.57, from Japan) and the highest ($10.80 from France) indicates varying levels of enthusiasm for the Fund's activities.[3] More importantly, financial commitments made to date are far below the amounts recommended by the Commission on Macroeconomics and Health (2001), which argued that GFATM will require $8 billion per year by 2007, and $12 billion per year by 2015, in order to provide adequate support for prevention and treatment. To put these amounts into perspective, $8 billion is about as much as Americans spend per year on cosmetics or bathroom renovations, and about one-sixth as much as Europeans spend on cigarettes (Scott, 2002; UNDP, 1998, p. 37). It is easy to dismiss such comparisons as polemical, but they serve a critically important purpose in comparing the discretionary consumption of the global few with the low cost of health improvements for the many.

The Commission on Macroeconomics and Health estimates assume that developing countries have functioning health care systems. However, in many countries, the more immediate problem is how to avoid collapse of existing health infrastructure because of such factors as constraints on government expenditure, the impact of HIV/AIDS and the emigration of health professionals (see e.g. Sanders, Dovlo, Meeus, & Lehmann, 2003) . Although the G8 stated in 2001 that "[s]trong national health systems will continue to play a key role in the delivery of effective prevention, treatment and care and in improving access to essential health services and commodities without discrimination" ([24]G8, 2001, ¶ 17), aid for all aspects of health system development accounts for just over 4 percent of total G7 ODA expenditure. To the extent that available data permit the calculation of trends, this proportion was

---

[2] The United Nations Economic and Social Council classifies countries with fewer than 75 million people as LDCs if they are characterized by low GDP (currently US $900 or less per capita), weak human assets, and a high level of vulnerability. Forty-nine countries are now classified as LDCs (UNCTAD, 2002b). The upper population threshold means the LDC category excludes countries that may actually have larger number of people than the entire population of "official" LDCs living in comparable privation and insecurity, and only 450 million of the more than 2.5 billion people worldwide estimated to be living on $2 per day or less live in LDCs (UNCTAD, 2002b, p. 59).

[3] Calculated from contribution figures posted on the Global Fund web site ⟨http://www.globalfundatm.org⟩ (last visited November 27, 2003) and national population figures from UNDP (2003).

1668 *R. Labonte, T. Schrecker / Social Science & Medicine 59 (2004) 1661–1676*

Table 4
Trends in aid to health as percentage of total G7 ODA

	1990/92 average[a]	1996/98 average[a]	1999[b]	2000[b]	2001[b]
Canada	3	3	1.8	2.6	4.3
France	3	4	4.5	4.4	6.0
Germany	1	5	4.0	3.2	3.3
Italy	5	4	7.2	7.7	4.7
Japan	1	2	2.7	2.9	2.8
UK	9	10	6.8	9.6	5.9
US	5	17	4.4	4.1	4.7
G7 average				4.3	4.3

Source: OECD, 2001, Table 2 (1990/92 and 1996/98 data); OECD, 2002, Tables 14 and 19 (2000 data); OECD, 2003, Tables 13, 15 and 19 (2001 data).

[a] Because of data limitations, includes only bilateral aid.

[b] Includes both bilateral and multilateral aid (contributions made by donor countries to the European Commission, the World Bank and regional development banks). Published data on the sectoral distribution of individual countries' multilateral aid contributions are not available. Instead, we attributed multilateral aid contributions to specific sectors based on the following calculation: country specific percentage of total aid contributed through each of the three multilateral agencies (Regional Development Banks, World Bank, European Commission) × the percentage of aid provided to the specific sector by each of the multilateral agencies. The sum of these calculations was then added to that country's sector-specific bilateral contribution. There may be small margins of error; the OECD report from which our data were drawn (OECD, 2002) itself cautions that figures for the European Commission are "approximate." Total 2001 ODA contributions are based on the same calculations, using data from OECD (2003). An even greater note of caution is expressed for 1999 multilateral estimates. We applied the same formula as for 2000 and 2001, but the percentage of European Commission aid contributions by sector is not available for 1999. We therefore used the percentages for 2000 as a rough approximation, but calculated G7 averages only in years for which data are more reliable (2000, 2001).

stable or even declined during the 1990s (Table 4), albeit with wide variations between years and countries.[4] Declining child vaccination coverage in all developing areas during the 1990s may illustrate the consequences. The decline in Africa is particularly troubling since almost 50 percent of African children are now not adequately vaccinated (Simms, Rowson, & Peattie, 2001; UNICEF, 2001, p. 89; WHO, 2002b). In addition, when governments lack the funds for minimally adequate health infrastructure, privatization of health services and the adoption of cost recovery measures tend to emerge as a superficially attractive, but highly inequitable alternative (Arhin-Tenkorang, 2000; Melgar, 1999; Schoepf, Schoepf, & Millen, 2000; Whitehead, Dahlgren, & Evans, 2001; Yong Kim, Shakow, Bayona, Rhatigan, & Rubín de Celis, 2000). The resulting "medical poverty trap" (Whitehead, Dahlgren, & Evans, 2001) may actually undermine the potential for future economic growth.

---

[4] The precipitous increase in US health ODA in 1996–98 may be an artifact of changes in how the US categorized its development assistance (OECD, 2000: 6). This only underscores its subsequent dramatic declines in 1999 and 2000, although we note that in 2001 the US portioned more of its health aid to "basic health" (primary health care) than did other G7 countries and provides more development assistance to "population and reproductive health" programs than it does to health systems ([49]OECD, 2003, Tables 13, 15 and 19).

By 2001, controversy over the pricing of antiretroviral drugs for HIV/AIDS in southern Africa had demonstrated the potential constraint on health services in developing countries created by harmonized patent protection under the Trade-Related Intellectual Property Rights (TRIPs) component of the WTO Agreement ('t Hoen, 1999; Médecins sans Frontières, 2001). The authors of the year 2000 United Nations *Human Development Report* took the problem seriously enough to warn that TRIPs may conflict with international human rights agreements that recognize the right to share in scientific progress, because it "dramatically reduces the possibilities for local companies to produce cheaper versions of important life-saving drugs" (UNDP, 2000, p. 84; see also Mayne & Bailey, 2002; Médecins sans Frontières, 2001; Watkins 2002, pp. 208–224). Although patents are only part of the problem, since effective administration of antiretrovirals is among many therapeutic interventions that require adequate health care infrastructure (Attaran and Gillespie-White, 2001; see also Attaran & Sachs, 2001), they are not irrelevant.

In 2001, the G7 stated: "We welcome ongoing discussion in the WTO on the use of relevant provisions in the TRIPs Rights agreement. We recognize the appropriateness of affected countries using the flexibility afforded by that agreement to ensure that drugs are available to their citizens who need them, particularly those who are unable to afford basic medical care." (G8,

R. Labonte, T. Schrecker / Social Science & Medicine 59 (2004) 1661–1676 1669

2001, ¶ 17). Subsequently, the November 2001 WTO Ministerial Conference at Doha acknowledged the need for "flexibility" when public health is at issue (WTO, 2001), and stated that TRIPs "does not and should not prevent Members from taking measures to protect public health". It took until August, 2003, however, for the General Council of the WTO to agree on an interpretation of TRIPs that reflected this position (WTO, 2003),[5] and concern persists about its true effectiveness because of the limited circumstances under which a "public health emergency" can be invoked by developing country governments (Pollock & Price, 2003).

Nutrition and education

The pairing of nutrition and education may at first seem surprising, but is logical because each is an indispensable prerequisite for protecting and enhancing health; access to each is closely related to economic variables, and in particular adversely affected by poverty; and each has been the focus of commitments by the G7 nations either as members of the Group or as part of the broader international community. Nutritional deficiencies represent an adverse health outcome in themselves, and increase vulnerability to other stressors such as infectious disease (see e.g. Rice, Sacco, Hyder, & Black, 2000). The World Health Organization (2002c, pp. 49–56) has estimated that 15.8 percent of the global burden of disease (GBD) is attributable to childhood and maternal undernutrition—an underestimate of the full significance of nutritional factors, since it does not take into account, e.g. the relation between adult nonmaternal undernutrition and infectious disease. A strong correlation exists between poverty and childhood underweight, which alone accounts for 9.5 percent of the GBD.

At the 2001 Summit, G7 leaders made vague commitments to supporting agriculture through ODA as an element of poverty reduction (G8, 2001, ¶ 20) and to "target the most food-insecure regions, particularly Sub-Saharan Africa and South Asia"—apparently, given the context of the statement, for food relief. In addition, one of the key IDGs involves reducing the proportion of children under five who are underweight, but the G7 made no specific commitments related to achieving this goal. Notably absent at the Summits we studied was any commitment to the goal endorsed by the

World Food Summit (WFS) in 1996[6] of halving the number of undernourished people in developing countries by 2015, with "a mid-term review to ascertain whether it is possible to achieve this target by 2010" (World Food Summit, 1996).

Instead, the 1999–2001 Summits addressed issues of nutrition primarily by emphasizing the need to promote applications of biotechnology. The biotechnology industry is actively supported by some G7 governments as an element of their strategies for the knowledge economy, but its relevance to nutrition and food security is highly controversial (Crouch, 2001; Persley & Lantin, 2000; Serageldin, 1999; Tilman et al., 2001). Part of the dispute is about whether the problem should be defined with reference to resource scarcity (with the corollary being that it can be "solved" by improving agricultural productivity through, e.g. the diffusion of genetically modified crops) or resource distribution. Amartya Sen (1981, 1982, 1989)'s path-breaking work on the political economy of famine showed that famines are not "natural" phenomena, and that access to nutrition and food security are directly related either to purchasing power or to the availability of some other entitlement to food. This may explain the absence of specific G7 commitments on the topic. It could be argued that they are addressing the issues instead by way of economic development and poverty reduction, but the adequacy of their commitments in this area is itself open to question. So, too—as we note later in the article—is the appropriateness of the underlying presumptions about economic development.

What is beyond dispute is the slow pace of worldwide progress toward improving nutrition, perhaps because of the marginal political status of food security issues and the associated international institutions (Amalric et al., 2001; UNFAO, 2001). According to the UN Food and Agriculture Organization (UNFAO, 2003, p. 30), "[t]he number of undernourished people in the developing world decreased by less than 20 million since the 1990–1992 period used as the baseline at the WFS. Worse yet, over the most recent 4 years for which data are available, the number of chronically hungry people actually increased at a rate of almost 5 million a year." These figures actually understate the extent of undernutrition, and its potential health consequences, since they refer only to insufficient caloric intake and not to

---

[5] This delay was caused by several G7 countries (notably the United States but also, initially, Canada), which objected to proposals to the WTO TRIPs Council from developing countries to operationalize this "flexibility" and attempted to restrict interpretation of the agreement reached at the WTO Doha ministerial (Inside US Trade, 2002).

[6] With some reservations, notably the United States' insistence that the reference to a right to food in the Declaration issued by the Summit "is a goal or aspiration to be realized progressively that does not give rise to any international obligations" (United Nations Food and Agriculture Organization (UNFAO), 1996, Annex II). The United States was the only industrialized country to declare such a reservation—which it repeated at the successor World Food Summit in 2002.

micronutrient deficiencies that affect much larger numbers of people.

Connections between education and health are harder to quantify than those involving nutrition, but it is known that education operates to reduce health risk both directly and through such intervening variables as economic growth and gender equity. Income and health gains are more dramatic as education levels for women rise, and "societies that limit girls' access to education pay a price in poorer health, and thereby in poorer economic growth" (WHO, 2001, p. 75). Education also reduces HIV risk (World Bank, 2002c), particularly for girls and women. Those countries showing the greatest lack of knowledge about HIV/AIDS (primarily in Sub-Saharan Africa and several of the former Soviet republics) are also ones with very low and in some cases rapidly declining rates of education spending and participation (Canadian International Development Agency, 2002; World Bank, 2002c).

In contrast to the situation with respect to nutrition, the G7 have clearly stated support for numerical targets in the field of education. The Dakar Framework for Action, which emerged from multilateral meetings in 2000, identified several goals for the developing world, including "ensuring that by 2015 all children, particularly girls, children in difficult circumstances and those belonging to ethnic minorities, have access to and complete free and compulsory primary education of good quality" and "eliminating gender disparities in primary and secondary education by 2005, and achieving gender equality in education by 2015" (UNESCO 2000). Support for the Dakar Framework was clearly expressed at the 2000 Summit, and restated in 2001 (G8, 2000, ¶ 33–34; G8, 2001, ¶ 18), although without identifying the resources that would be made available. Enrolling all children in primary school by 2015 and eliminating gender disparities in primary and secondary education by 2005 are also among the IDGs.

UNESCO's 2002 *Monitoring Report* on progress toward the Dakar goals warned that 37 countries will probably not meet the universal primary education (UPE) target by 2015, with another 20 countries noted as requiring "renewed efforts" (UNESCO, 2002b, p. 17). Only 21 countries remained on target. Estimating progress toward the Dakar goals using school completion figures, rather than enrolment figures, the World Bank has arrived at an even more pessimistic assessment: this technique "raises the number [unlikely to meet the UPE goal] to 88 countries, out of the total 155 for which data were established. Some 35 countries are unlikely to meet the goal of eliminating gender disparities at the primary level by 2005, even when the goal is simply universal primary education and not universal primary completion" (World Bank, 2002d, p. 3).

As with health systems, the amounts of additional financing that would be needed to achieve major improvements are small in the global scheme of things. UNESCO (2002b, p. 75), noting that documentation from G7 bilateral aid agencies makes it difficult to sum up their new education commitments, estimates them at about US $1billion annually, of which US $0.3 billion will probably go to basic education—less than 10 percent of UNESCO's estimate of the new annual contributions that will be needed to meet the goals of universal primary education and eliminating gender disparity. Further, although in 2001 the G7 committed its members to "support UNESCO in its key role for universal education" (G8, 2001, ¶ 18), UNESCO's Director-General subsequently warned that budget constraints mean "the Organization cannot afford to remain on such a path of continuous belt-tightening lest it be depleted of its vitality and ability to respond to new challenges" (UNESCO, 2002a, p. ix). Here, again, we see the theme of rhetoric unmatched by necessary financial commitments.

Discussion: health, development and redistribution

Other things being equal, richer is healthier. Over the long term, the evidence for this proposition is overwhelming, both within and among nations (World Bank, 1992, pp. 10–12, 50–55; World Bank, 1993, pp. 7, 34, 39–42; Sieswerda, Soskolne, Newman, Schopflocher, & Smoyer, 2001), but how long is the long term? And how much longer may the poor be asked to wait for improvements in access to health care and in the basic determinants of health? The question is not just a rhetorical one, because contemporary development policy appears implicitly to accept a trade-off of short-term health deterioration for the prospect of eventual improvement. That acceptance was made explicit by a team of World Bank researchers studying dramatic declines in health status in Central Europe and the former Soviet Union: "In the long run, the transition towards a market economy and adoption of democratic forms of government should ultimately lead to improvements in health status.... In the short run, however, one could expect that health status would deteriorate" as incomes drop, inequalities widen, stress increases, basic health services break down and already inadequate regulation of environmental and workplace hazards deteriorate (Adeyi, Chellaraj, Goldstein, Preker, & Ringold, 1997, p. 133). The G7 have not directly addressed this issue, but analysis of the health implications of commitments made at the 1999–2001 G7 Summits, informed by the history of the last few decades of development policy and by an expanding literature on the connections between social and economic policy and population health, leads us to question the seriousness

R. Labonte, T. Schrecker / Social Science & Medicine 59 (2004) 1661–1676   1671

of the G7 commitment "to make globalization work for all [their] citizens and especially the world's poor" (G8, 2001, ¶ 3).

This conclusion is strengthened by observations of G7 policies in two other policy fields: ODA and trade. In *Agenda 21*, the document that emerged from the Earth Summit, developed countries as a whole "reaffirm[ed] their commitments to reach the accepted United Nations target of 0.7 percent of GDP for ODA", first proposed in 1969, and "to augment their aid programmes in order to reach that target as soon as possible" (United Nations, 1992, p. 33). In 1999, the G7 committed themselves gradually to increase the volume of ODA, and to put special emphasis on countries best positioned to use it effectively (G8, 1999, ¶ 27). At the 2000 and 2001 Summits, emphasis shifted instead to the "effectiveness" of ODA (G8, 2000, ¶ 20; G8, 2001, ¶ 14). Today, none of the G7 countries approaches the 0.7 percent target and, in contrast to the performance of some industrialized countries outside the G7, the trend has been one of declining G7 commitments to ODA over the past 15 years (Table 5), during the very period of growth that has produced, for those countries, unprecedented prosperity. Table 5 shows that some other industrialized countries have met and exceeded the target, so it is not inherently implausible. Table 6 breaks down the costs for each G7 country of moving to the 0.7 percent figure, in terms of one of the most familiar international commodities: the Big Mac.

As for market access, Oxfam (Watkins, 2002) and the World Bank (2002a) alike have noted that the industrialized world continues to restrict access to its markets to the products of the developing world, even though unrestricted market access might generate more

Table 5
Trends in G7 ODA as a percentage of gross national income (GNI)

	1984–85	1989–90	2001
Canada	0.50	0.44	0.22
France	0.62	0.60	0.32
Germany	0.46	0.42	0.27
Italy	0.27	0.36	0.15
Japan	0.31	0.31	0.23
United Kingdom	0.33	0.29	0.32
United States	0.24	0.18	0.11
And for comparison …			
Denmark	0.83	0.94	1.03
Netherlands	0.97	0.93	0.82
Norway	1.02	1.11	0.83
Sweden	0.83	0.93	0.81

Includes both bilateral aid and commitments to multilateral institutions.
Source: OECD, 2002, Table 4; OECD, 2003, Table 4.

Table 6
G7 aid commitments, 2001

Country	Value of ODA 2001 $ million	ODA as percentage of GNI 2001	Additional resources that would be made available by meeting the 0.7 percent target $ million	Population million	Value per capita of additional resources needed to meet the 0.7 percent target $	Cost of a Big Mac 2001, $	Additional annual cost of meeting the 0.7 percent target, in Big Macs per capita
Canada	1533	0.22	3345	31.08	107.63	2.14	49
France	4198	0.32	4985	59.19	84.22	2.49	34
Germany	4990	0.27	7947	82.31	96.55	2.30	42
Italy	1627	0.15	5965	57.35	104.01	1.96	54
Japan	9847	0.23	20,122	127.21	158.18	2.38	65
United Kingdom	4579	0.32	5438	58.79	92.50	2.85	33
United States	11,429	0.11	61,301	285.02	215.08	2.54	85
Total		0.18	109,103				

Source: OECD, 2003, Tables 4, 19, 37 except Big Macs/capita calculation, based on national cost figures (for the Big Mac) from "Big Mac Currencies Index," *The Economist*, April 19, 2001.

substantial benefits to developing economies than the current combined value of ODA and debt relief. Agricultural subsidies in the industrialized world, which simultaneously limit developing countries' market access and offer domestic producers an incentive to generate surpluses that are dumped on international markets, represent an especially intractable problem. It is difficult to disagree with economist Ha-Joon Chang (2002) description of the growth strategy now being urged on the developing world by the G7, the World Bank and the IMF as "kicking the ladder away": the strategy is one that no G7 country followed on its own path to industrialization and wealth creation—with the partial exception of England after the repeal of the Corn Laws, which had the advantage of empire as a captive market as well as a source of raw materials. Thus, not only the ethical defensibility of contemporary neoliberal prescriptions for health through wealth through growth, but also their empirical plausibility, is called into question.

Population health measures, including infection control and some forms of environmental protection, may represent genuine "public goods" that the rich world cannot feasibly purchase for itself while excluding others (Chen, Evans, & Cash, 1999). On this line of reasoning, population health represents an investment in global security, and the economic costs associated with the recent outbreak of Severe Acute Respiratory Syndrome show the value of infection control as a public good. A more expansive economic argument is exemplified by the work of the Commission on Macroeconomics and Health, for which "investment in health" represented an investment in future development, because it can initiate virtuous cycles of human capital formation and growth. The approach is empirically well grounded, yet without further elaboration it invites a form of triage in which the countries, regions and populations that receive investments in health will primarily be those where "development" offers the greatest promise of economic returns, e.g. because of the availability of expanding consumer markets or the availability of healthy and relatively skilled, yet low-cost labour.

John Williamson, who coined the term "Washington consensus" to describe official wisdom on development policy circa 1989 (Williamson, 1990), has noted that in codifying the consensus he "deliberately excluded from the list anything which was primarily redistributive, as opposed to having equitable consequences as a byproduct of seeking efficiency objectives, because [he] felt the Washington of the 1980s to be a city that was essentially contemptuous of equity concerns" (Williamson, 1993, p. 1329). Our analysis suggests that with some important exceptions, the attitude to which Williamson referred appears to have diffused throughout the official levels of the G7. It is stronger than ever in today's Washington. Our analysis also suggests that in the absence of more extensive redistribution of wealth across national borders, progress toward improving health for all will be slow at best, and may not be possible at all in some situations. Future research must not only investigate in greater detail the health consequences of contemporary development policy as promoted by the G7 and the international financial institutions, but also undertake explicit ethical analysis of the health consequences of current G7 development policies.

Acknowledgements

Research for this article was funded by the International Development Research Centre (Canada). We are grateful for the research assistance of Jennifer Cushon and Renée Torgerson, and for the comments of two referees. All views expressed are exclusively those of the authors.

References

Adeyi, O., Chellaraj, G., Goldstein, E., Preker, A., & Ringold, D. (1997). Health status during the transition in central and eastern Europe: Development in reverse? *Health Policy and Planning, 12*, 132–145.

Amalric, F. (2001). Strategically speaking: The World Food Summit, five years later (with responses by commentators). *Development, 44* (no. 4, December), 6–16.

Arhin-Tenkorang, D. (2000). *Mobilizing resources for health: The case for user fees revisited.* Cambridge, MA: WHO commission on macroeconomics and health (CMH) working paper series, paper no. WG3: 6, November, http://www.cmhealth.org/docs/wg3_paper6.pdf, last visited May 27, 2003.

Attaran, A., & Gillespie-White, L. (2001,). Do patents for antiretroviral drugs constrain access to AIDS treatment in Africa? *JAMA, 286*, 1886–1892.

Attaran, A., & Sachs, J. (2001,). Defining and refining international donor support for combating the AIDS pandemic. *Lancet, 357*, 57–61.

Brundtland, G. (2000). *[Speech to] Winterthur massive effort advocacy meeting.* Geneva: World Health Organization, 3 October, http://www.who.int/directorgeneral/speeches/2000/english/20001003_massive_effort.html, last visited February 1, 2003.

Butler, C., Douglas, R., & McMichael, A. J. (2001). Globalisation and environmental change: Implications for health and health inequalities. In R. Eckersley, J. Dixon, & R. Douglas (Eds.), *The social origins of health and well-being* (pp. 34–50). Melbourne: Cambridge University Press.

Canadian International Development Agency (2002). *CIDA's Action Plan on Basic Education.* Ottawa: CIDA; http://www.acdi-cida.gc.ca/cida_ind.nsf/b2a5f300880e7192852567450078b4cb/e4fc8a9ac2b9b129852569ba005550bc/$FILE/ATT14SUO/BEActionPlan.pdf, last visited May 27, 2003.

R. Labonte, T. Schrecker / Social Science & Medicine 59 (2004) 1661–1676   1673

Chang, H-J. (2002). *Kicking away the ladder: Development strategy in historical perspective.* London: Anthem Press.

Chavez, J. J., & Cordero, R. D. (2001). *The Asian financial crisis and Filipino households: Impacts on women and children.* London: Focus on the Global South/Save the Children UK, http://www.focusweb.org/publications/Books/women%20and%20children.pdf.

Chen, L., Evans, T., & Cash, R. (1999). Health as a global public good. In I. Kaul, I. Grunberg, & M. Stern (Eds.), *Global public goods: International cooperation in the 21st century* (pp. 184–204). New York: Oxford University Press (for the United Nations Development Programme).

Cheru, F. (1999). *Effects of structural adjustment policies on the full enjoyment of human rights: Report by the independent expert submitted in accordance with commission decisions 1998/102 and 1997/103,* E/CN.4/1999/50. New York: Economic and Social Council, United Nations Commission on Human Rights, February 24, ⟨http://www.unhchr.ch/Huridocda/Huridoca.nsf/TestFrame/f991c6c62457a2858025675100348aef?Opendocument⟩, last visited May 27, 2003.

Cheru, F. (2001). *The highly indebted poor countries (HIPC) initiative: A human rights assessment of the Poverty Reduction Strategy Papers (PRSP),* Report submitted to the United Nations Economic and Social Council, E/CN.4/2001/56. New York: United Nations, 18 January, http://www.hri.ca/fortherecord2001/documentation/commission/e-cn4-2001-56.htm, last visited May 27, 2003.

Commission on Macroeconomics and Health (CMH). (2001). *Macroeconomics and health: Investing in health for economic development.* Geneva: WHO, December, http://www3.who.int/whosis/cmh/cmh_report/report.cfm?path=cmh,cmh_report&language=english, last visited May 27, 2003.

Cornia, G., Jolly, R., & Stewart, F. (Eds.). (1987). *Adjustment with a human face: Protecting the vulnerable and promoting growth,* Vol. 1. Oxford: Clarendon Press.

Cornia, G., Jolly, R., & Stewart, F. (Eds.). (1988). *Adjustment with a human face: Ten country case studies,* Vol. 2. Oxford: Claredon Press.

Crouch, M. L. (2001). From golden rice to terminator technology: Agricultural technology will not feed the world or save the environment. In B. Tokar (Ed.), *Redesigning life? The worldwide challenge to genetic engineering* (pp. 22–39). Montreal: McGill-Queen's University Press.

Devarajan, S., Miller, M., & Swanson, E. (2002). *Goals for development: History, prospects and costs.* Washington, DC: World Bank, http://econ.worldbank.org/files/13269_wps2819.pdf, last visited May 30, 2002.

Diderichsen, F., Evans, T., & Whitehead, M. (2001). The social basis of disparities in health. In T. Evans, M. Whitehead, F. Diderichsen, A. Bhuiya, & M. Wirth (Eds.), *Challenging inequities in health: From ethics to action* (pp. 12–23). Oxford: Oxford University Press.

Dixon, C., Simon, D., & Närman, A. (1995). Introduction: The nature of structural adjustment. In D. Simon, W. van Spengen, C. Dixon, & A. Närman (Eds.), *Structurally adjusted Africa* (pp. 1–14). London: Pluto Press.

Evans, R., & Stoddart, G. (1990). Producing health, consuming health care. *Social Science & Medicine, 31,* 1347–1363.

Evans, T., Whitehead, M., Diderichsen, F., Bhuiya, A., & Wirth, M. (Eds.). (2001). *Challenging inequities in health: From ethics to action.* Oxford: Oxford University Press.

G8 (Group of 8 Nations). (1999). *G8 Communiqué Köln 1999.* Cologne, June 20, http://www.g8.utoronto.ca/summit/1999koln/finalcom.htm, last visited December 17, 2003.

G8 (Group of 8 Nations). (2000). *G8 Communiqué Okinawa 2000.* Okinawa, July 23, http://www.g8.utoronto.ca/summit/2000okinawa/finalcom.htm, last visited December 17, 2003.

G8 (Group of 8 Nations). (2001). *Communiqué.* Genoa, July 22, http://www.library.utoronto.ca/g7/summit/2001genoa/finalcommunique.html, last visited December 17, 2003.

Global Forum on Health. (2002). *The 10/90 report on health research 2001–2002.* Geneva: Global Forum on Health, April, ⟨http://www.globalforumhealth.org/pages/index.asp⟩, last visited December 17, 2003.

Greenhill, R. (2002). *The unbreakable link: Debt relief and the millennium development goals.* London: Jubilee Research, February, http://www.jubilee2000uk.org/analysis/reports/unbreakable_link.pdf, last visited May 27, 2003.

Greenhill, R., & Sisti, E. (2003). *Real progress report on HIPC.* London: Jubilee Research at the New Economics Foundation, September, http://www.jubileeplus.org/analysis/reports/realprogressHIPC.pdf, last visited December 17, 2003.

Haacker, M. (2002). *The economic consequences of HIV/AIDS in Southern Africa,* WP02/38. Washington, DC: International Monetary Fund, February, http://ideas.repec.org/p/imf/imfwpa/0238.html, last visited December 22, 2002.

Hanlon, M. (2000). How much debt must be cancelled? *Journal of International Development, 12,* 877–901.

Hotchkiss, D. R., & Jacobalis, S. (1999,). Indonesian heath care and the economic crisis: Is managed care the needed reform? *Health Policy, 46,* 195–216.

Inside US Trade. (2002). *EU and US split over scope of TRIPS exception for public health.* March 8, http://lists.essential.org/pipermail/ip-health/2002-March/002756.html, last visited May 27, 2003.

International Development Association, International Monetary Fund. (2002). *Review of the Poverty Reduction Strategy Paper (PRSP) approach: Early experience with interim PRSPs and full PRSPs.* Washington, DC: World Bank, March 26, http://www.imf.org/External/NP/prspgen/review/2002/032602a.pdf, last visited July 9, 2003.

International Monetary Fund (IMF). (2001). *Structural conditionality in fund-supported programs.* Washington, DC: Policy Development and Review Department, IMF, February 16, http://www.imf.org/External/NP/prspgen/review/2002/031502a.pdf, last visited March 15, 2003.

International Monetary Fund (IMF). (2003). *World economic outlook, September 2003.* Washington, DC: Author.

International Monetary Fund (IMF), OECD, United Nations, World Bank Group. (2000). *2000—A better world for all: Progress towards the international development goals.* Paris: OECD, http://www.paris21.org/betterworld, last visited January 12, 2003.

Kim, H., Chung, W. J., Song, Y. J., Kang, D. R., Yi, J. J., & Nam, C. M. (2003,). Changes in morbidity and medical care utilization after the recent economic crisis in the Republic of Korea. *Bulletin of the World Health Organization, 81,* 567–572.

Labonte, R., Torgerson, R. (2003). *Frameworks for analyzing the links between globalization and health*, STU/H&T/ 2003.2. Geneva: World Health Organization.

Lee, K. (2000). Globalization and health policy: A review of the literature and proposed research and policy agenda. In A. Bambas, J. A. Casas, H. A. Drayton, & A. Valdés (Eds.), *Health human development in the new global economy: The contributions and perspectives of civil society in the Americas* (pp. 15–41). Washington: Pan American Health Organization.

Mayne, R., & Bailey, M. (2002). *TRIPs and public health: The next battle*. Briefing Paper 15. Washington, DC: Oxfam International, March 2002, http://www.oxfam.org.uk/ what_we_do/issues/health/downloads/bp15_trips.rtf, last visited December 17, 2003.

Médecins sans Frontières. (2001). *A matter of life and death: The role of patents in access to essential medicines*. Geneva: Campaign for Access to Essential Medicines, MSF, November, http://www.msf.org/countries/page.cfm?articleid=47871B51-83A7-4960-BDD40D60958FC49F, last visited May 27, 2003.

Melgar, J. (1999). Ailing Philippine health: Proof of market failings. *Development, 42* (no. 4, December), 138–141.

Milward, B. (2000). What is structural adjustment? In G. Mohan, E. Brown, B. Milward, & A. B. Zack-Williams (Eds.), *Structural adjustment: Theory, practice and impacts* (pp. 24–38). London: Routledge.

Musgrove, P. (2003). Judging health systems: Reflections on WHO's methods. *The Lancet, 361*, 1817–1820.

Narayan, D. (2001). 'Consultations with the poor' from a health perspective. *Development, 44*(no. 1, March), 15–21.

Narayan, D., Chambers, R., Shah, M., & Petesch, P. (2000). *Voices of the poor: Crying out for change*. New York: Oxford University Press for the World Bank.

O'Brien, R. (2002,). Organizational politics, multilateral economic organizations and social policy. *Global Social Policy, 2*, 141–162.

Organization for Economic Cooperation and Development (OECD). (2001). Development co-operation: 2000 report. *DAC Journal, 2*(1) (entire issue). Paris: Author.

Organization for Economic Cooperation and Development (OECD). (2002). Development co-operation: 2001 report. *DAC Journal, 3*(1) (entire issue). Paris: Author.

Organization for Economic Cooperation and Development (OECD). (2003). Development co-operation: 2002 report. *DAC Journal, 4*(1) (entire issue). Paris: Author.

Oxfam (2001). *G8: Failing the World's Children*. Washington DC: Oxfam International, July; www.oxfam.org/pdfs/ pp0107_G8_Failing_the_worlds_children.pdf, last visited May 27, 2003.

Persley, G. J., & Lantin, M. M. (Eds.). (2000). *Agricultural biotechnology and the poor: Proceedings of an international conference*, Washington, DC, 21–22 October 1999. Washington, DC: Consultative Group on International Agricultural Research, http://www.cgiar.org/biotech/rep0100/ contents.htm, last visited May 27, 2003.

Pettifor, A., & Greenhill, R. (2002). *Debt relief and the millennium development goals, background paper for human development report 2003*. New York: Human Development Report Office, United Nations Human Development Programme, December.

Pollock, A., & Price, D. (2003). New deal from the World Trade Organisation: May not provide essential medicines for poor countries. *British Medical Journal, 327*, 571–572.

Ramphal, S. (1999). Debt has a child's face. In UNICEF, *The progress of nations 1999* (pp. 27–29). New York: UNICEF, http://www.unicef.org/pon99/pdf.htm, last visited December 2, 2003.

Reddy, S. G., & Pogge, T. W. (2003). *How not to count the poor*. New York: Columbia University, March 26, http://www.columbia.edu/~sr793/count.pdf, accessed December 2, 2003.

Rice, A., Sacco, L., Hyder, A., & Black, R. (2000,). Malnutrition as an underlying cause of childhood deaths associated with infectious diseases in developing countries. *Bulletin of the World Health Organization, 78*, 1207–1221.

Sachs, J., & Malaney, P. (2002,). The economic and social burden of malaria. *Nature, 415*, 680–685.

Sanders, D., Dovlo, D., Meeus, W., & Lehmann, U. (2003). Public health in Africa. In R. Beaglehole (Ed.), *Global public health: A new era* (pp. 135–155). Oxford: Oxford University Press.

Schoepf, B., Schoepf, C., & Millen, J. (2000). Theoretical therapies, remote remedies: SAPS and the political ecology of poverty and health in Africa. In J. Yong Kim, et al. (Ed.), *Dying for growth: Global inequality and the health of the poor* (pp. 91–126). Monroe, ME: Common Courage Press.

Scott, A. (2002). Interior Life. *The New York Times Magazine*, December 1, 19–20.

Sen, A. (1981). *Poverty and famines: An essay on entitlement and deprivation*. New York: Oxford University Press.

Sen, A. (1982,). The food problem: Theory and policy. *Third World Quarterly, 4*, 447–459.

Sen, A. (1989,). Food and freedom. *World Development, 17*, 769–781.

Serageldin, I. (1999,). Biotechnology and food security in the 21st century. *Science, 285*, 386–388.

Sieswerda, L., Soskolne, C., Newman, S., Schopflocher, D., & Smoyer, K. (2001). Toward measuring the impact of ecological disintegrity on human health. *Epidemiology, 12*, 28–32.

Simms, C., Rowson, M., & Peattie, S. (2001). *The bitterest pill of all: The collapse of Africa's health systems*. London: Medact/Save the Children, http://193.129.255.93/pressrels/ PDFS/Bitterpill.pdf, last visited November 23, 2002.

Sparr, P. (1994). What is structural adjustment? In P. Sparr (Ed.), *Mortgaging women's lives: Feminist critiques of structural adjustment* (pp. 1–12). London: Zed Books.

Spinaci, S., & Heymann, D. (2001). Communicable disease and disability of the poor. *Development, 44*(no. 1, March), 66–72.

Stewart, F. (1991). The many faces of adjustment. *World Development, 19*, 1847–1864.

Third World Network. (2001). *The multilateral trading system: A development perspective*. New York: Bureau for Development Policy, United Nations Development Programme, December, http://www.undp.org/mainundp/propoor/docs/ multitradesystem.pdf, accessed May 27, 2003.

't Hoen, E. (1999). Access to essential drugs and globalization. *Development, 42*(no. 4, December), 87–91.

Tilman, D., Fargione, J., Wolff, B., D'Antonio, C., Dobson, A., Howarth, R., Schindler, D., Schlesinger, W. H., Simberloff, D., & Swackhamer, D. (2001). Forecasting

R. Labonte, T. Schrecker / Social Science & Medicine 59 (2004) 1661–1676 1675

agriculturally driven global environmental change. *Science*, 292, 281–284.

UNESCO. (2000). *The Dakar framework for action*. Paris: World Education Forum, http://www2.unesco.org/wef/en-conf/dakframeng.shtm, last visited May 27, 2003.

UNESCO. (2002a). *Approved programme and budget, 2002–2003*, 31C/5. Paris: Author, March, http://unesdoc.unes-co.org/images/0012/001253/125343e.pdf, last visited May 27, 2003.

UNESCO. (2002b). *EFA global monitoring report, 2002: Is the world on track?* Paris: Author, November, http://www.unesco.org/education/efa/global_co/policy_group/hlg_2002_monitoring_complete.pdf, last visited May 27, 2003.

UNICEF. (2001). *The state of the world's children 2001*. Oxford: Oxford University Press.

United Nations. (1992). *Agenda 21*. New York: United Nations Division for Sustainable Development, http://www.un.org/esa/sustdev/documents/agenda21/english/agenda21toc.htm, last visited November 28, 2002.

United Nations. (2002). *International financial system and development: Report of the Secretary-General*, A/57/151. New York: Author, http://ods-dds-ny.un.org/doc/UN-DOC/GEN/N02/469/61/PDF/N0246961.pdf?OpenElement, last visited May 27, 2003.

United Nations Conference on Trade and Development (UNCTAD). (2002a). The PRSP approach and poverty reduction in the least developed countries. In IMF, World Bank, *External comments and contributions on the joint bank/ fund staff review of the PRSP approach, Vol. I: Bilateral agencies and multilateral institutions* (pp. 187–196). Washington, DC: IMF, February, http://www.imf.org/exter-nal/np/prspgen/review/2002/comm/v1.pdf.

United Nations Conference on Trade and Development (UNCTAD). (2002b). *Escaping the poverty trap: The least developed countries report 2002*. New York: United Nations, http://www.unctad.org/Templates/webflyer.asp?do-cid = 2026&intItemID = 1397&lang = 1&mode = downloads.

United Nations Development Programme (UNDP). (1998). *Human development report 1998*. New York: Oxford University Press.

United Nations Development Programme (UNDP). (2000). *Human development report 2000: Human rights and human development*. New York: Oxford University Press.

United Nations Development Programme (UNDP). (2002). UNDP review of the poverty reduction strategy paper. Iin IMF, World Bank, *External comments and contributions on the joint bank/fund staff review of the PRSP approach, Vol. I: Bilateral agencies and multilateral institutions* (pp. 201–216). Washington, DC: IMF, February, http://www.imf.org/external/np/prspgen/review/2002/comm/v1.pdf, last visited May 27, 2003.

United Nations Food and Agriculture Organization (UNFAO). (1996). *Report of the world food summit, WFS 96/REP*. Geneva: UNFAO, http://www.fao.org/wfs/index_en.htm, last visited December 2, 2003.

United Nations Food and Agriculture Organization (UNFAO). (2001). *The state of food insecurity in the world 2001*. Rome: UNFAO, http://www.fao.org/docrep/003/y1500e/y1500e00.htm, last visited May 27, 2003.

United Nations Food and Agriculture Organization (UNFAO). (2003). *The state of food insecurity in the world 2003*. Rome: UNFAO, ftp://ftp.fao.org/docrep/fao/006/j0083e/j0083e00.pdf, last visited December 17, 2003.

United Nations Research Institute for Social Development (UNRISD). (2000). *Visible hands: Taking responsibility for social development*. Geneva: Author, http://www.unrisd.org/80256B3C005BCCF9/(httpPublications)/FE9C9439D82 B525480256B670065EFA1?OpenDocument&panel = addi-8panel = additional, lastvisitedMay27, 2003.

Walton, J., Seddon, D. et al. (1994). *Free markets and food riots: The politics of global adjustment*. Cambridge, Massachusetts: Blackwell.

Watkins, K. (2002). *Rigged rules and double standards: Trade, globalisation, and the fight against poverty*. Washington, DC: Oxfam International, http://www.maketradefair.com/style-sheet.asp?file = 03042002121618&cat = 2&subcat = 6&select = 1, last visited January 12, 2003.

Watkins, K. (2003). Northern agricultural policies and world poverty: Will the Doha 'development round' make a difference? *Presented at the annual world bank conference of development economics*, May 15–16, London: Oxfam, http://wbln0018.worldbank.org/eurvp/web.nsf/Pages/Pa-per + by + Watkins/$File/WATKINS.PDF, last visited January 9, 2004.

Whitehead, M., Dahlgren, G., & Evans, T. (2001,). Equity and health sector reforms: Can low-income countries escape the medical poverty trap? *Lancet, 358*, 833–836.

Williamson, J. (1990). What Washington means by policy reform. In J. Williamson (Ed.), *Latin American adjustment: How much has happened?* (pp. 7–38). Washington, DC: Institute for International Economics.

Williamson, J. (1993). Democracy and the 'Washington consensus'. *World Development, 21*, 1329–1336.

Woodward, D., Drager, N., Beaglehole, R., & Lipson, D. (2001,). Globalization and health: A framework for analysis and action. *Bulletin of the World Health Organization, 79*, 875–881.

World Bank. (1992). *World development report 1992: Development and the environment*. New York: Oxford University Press.

World Bank. (1993). *World development report 1993: Investing in health*. New York: Oxford University Press.

World Bank. (1995). *World development report 1995: Workers in an integrating world*. New York: Oxford University Press.

World Bank. (2001). *Global economic prospects and the developing countries 2001*. Washington, DC: World Bank.

World Bank. (2002a). *Global economic prospects and the developing countries 2002: Making trade work for the world's poor*. Washington, DC: World Bank.

World Bank. (2002b). *Financial impact of the HIPC initiative: First 25 country cases*. Washington, DC: HIPC Unit, World Bank, March.

World Bank. (2002c). *Education and HIV/AIDS: A window of hope*. Washington, DC: World Bank, http://www1.world-bank.org/education/pdf/Ed%20&%20HIV_AIDS%20 cover%20print.pdf, last visited July 9, 2003.

World Bank. (2002d). *Education for dynamic economies: Action plan to accelerate progress towards education for all,*

DC2002-0005/Rev1. Prepared for joint ministerial committee of the boards of governors of the world bank and the international monetary fund on the transfer of real resources to developing countries. Washington, DC: Author, April 9, http://lnweb18.worldbank.org/DCS/devcom.nsf/9dfe2a10d8acb5df852567ec00544e90/b90050b78fbc831685256b8f00729cde/$FILE/DC2002-0005-1.pdf, last visited May 27, 2003.

World Bank. (2003a). *Heavily indebted poor countries (HIPC) initiative—Statistical update*, IDA/R2003-0042/2. Washington, DC: Author, April 11, www.worldbank.org/hipc/progress-to-date/StatUpdate_April03.pdf, last visited November 27, 2003.

World Bank. (2003b). *World development report 2003: Sustainable development in a dynamic world*. New York: Oxford University Press.

World Commission on Environment and Development. (1987) *Our common future*. New York: Oxford University Press.

World Food Summit. (1996). *World food summit plan of action*. Rome: UNFAO, http://www.fao.org/docrep/003//w3613e/w3613e00.htm, last visited December 2, 2003.

World Health Organization. (1978). Declaration of Alma-Ata. *International conference on primary health care*, Alma-Ata, USSR, 6–12 September, Geneva: Author, http://www.who.int/hpr/archive/docs/almaata.html, last visited January 12, 2003.

World Health Organization. (2002a). *Health in PRSPs: WHO submission to world bank/IMF review of PRSPs*. Geneva: Author, http://www.worldbank.org./poverty/strategies/review/index.htm, last visited January 25th, 2002; also in IMF, World Bank, *External comments and contributions on the joint bank/fund staff review of the PRSP approach, Vol. I: Bilateral agencies and multilateral institutions* (pp. 217–246).

Washington, DC: IMF, February, http://www.imf.org/external/np/prspgen/review/2002/comm/v1.pdf, last visited January 12, 2003.

World Health Organization. (2002b). *State of the world's vaccines and immunization*. Geneva: Department of Vaccines and Biologicals, WHO, October, http://lnweb18.worldbank.org/DCS/devcom.nsf/9dfe2a10d8acb5d-f852567ec00544e90/b90050b78fbc831685256b8f00729cde/$FILE/DC2002-0005-1.pdf, last visited May 27, 2003.

World Health Organization. (2002c). *World health report 2002: Reducing risks, promoting healthy life*. Geneva: Author.

World Trade Organization. (2001). *Declaration on the TRIPs agreement and public health*, WT/MIN(01)/DEC/2. Geneva: WTO, November 20, 〈http://www.wto.org/english/thewto_e/minist_e/min01_e/mindecl_trips_e.htm〉, last visited September 18, 2002.

World Trade Organization. (2003) *Implementation of paragraph 6 of the Doha declaration on the TRIPS agreement and public health*, Decision of the General Council of 30 August 2003, WT/L/540. Geneva: Author, September, http://www.wto.org/english/tratop_e/trips_e/implem_para6_e.htm, last visited October 27, 2003.

Yong Kim, J., Shakow, A., Bayona, J., Rhatigan, J., & Rubin de Celis, E. (2000). Sickness amidst recovery: public debt and private suffering in Peru. In J. Yong Kim, J. Millen, A. Irwin, & J. Gershman (Eds.), *Dying for growth: Global inequality and the health of the poor* (pp. 127–154). Monroe, Maine: Common Courage Press.

Zielinski Gutiérrez, E., & Kendall, C. (2000). The globalization of health and disease: The health transition and global change. In G. Albrecht, R. Fitzpatrick, & S. Scrimshaw (Eds.), *The handbook of social studies in health & medicine* (pp. 84–99). London: Sage.

[33]

Making G8 leaders deliver: an analysis of compliance and health commitments, 1996–2006

John J Kirton,[a] Nikolai Roudev[a] & Laura Sunderland[a]

Abstract International health policy-makers now have a variety of institutional instruments with which to pursue their global and national health goals. These instruments range from the established formal multilateral organizations of the United Nations to the newer restricted-membership institutions of the Group of Eight (G8). To decide where best to deploy scarce resources, we must systematically examine the G8's contributions to global health governance. This assessment explores the contributions made by multilateral institutions such as the World Health Organization, and whether Member States comply with their commitments. We assessed whether G8 health governance assists its member governments in managing domestic politics and policy, in defining dominant normative directions, in developing and complying with collective commitments and in developing new G8-centred institutions. We found that the G8's performance improved substantially during the past decade. The G8 Member States function equally well, and each is able to combat diseases. Compliance varied among G8 Member States with respect to their health commitments, and there is scope for improvement. G8 leaders should better define their health commitments and set a one-year deadline for their delivery. In addition, Member States must seek WHO's support and set up an institution for G8 health ministers.

Bulletin of the World Health Organization 2007;85:192-199 .

Une traduction en français de ce résumé figure à la fin de l'article. Al final del articulo se facilita una traducción al español. الترجمة العربية لهذه الخلاصة في نهاية النص الكامل لهذه المقالة.

Introduction

How can international institutions encourage their member governments to commit to and comply with actions to improve global public health? This question is important for health policy-makers, who now have a diverse array of institutional instruments to choose from when allotting scarce resources to achieve their goals. At the international level, governments still use long-established, functionally focused, ministerial-guided multilateral organizations such as the World Health Organization and other organizations of the United Nations system.[1] However, governments increasingly have access to newer, informal, summit-delivered plurilateral institutions, most notably those of the Group of Eight (G8).[2]

Since 1996 the G8 has given particular attention to health issues, for example at its annual summit in St Petersburg in 2006.[3] Health policy-makers need to know which international institutions to rely upon. In addition, these organizations need to work together more effectively, as mutual reinforcers rather than rivals, in order to meet global health needs. For the purposes of this paper, health encompasses all references to public health, human health and well-being, ageing, infectious disease, health-related international organizations and initiatives, drug use, drug conventions, pharmaceuticals, medications, potable water, biotechnology and the impact of bio-terrorism on human health.

To assess the contribution of the newer G8 summit-centred system, it is important to ask whether attention from the leaders of the most powerful countries actually makes a difference to the health of people around the world. This question has given rise to a broad debate.[4] Critics argue that the G8 has failed in terms of fundraising, and has been unable to raise the large amounts of money needed to combat human immunodeficiency virus/acquired immunodeficiency syndrome (HIV/AIDS) and other diseases. In addition, the old UN system organizations have been unable to induce their own members to provide the necessary funds.[5,6] Other critics argue that the G8 has done too much of the wrong thing. They claim that its members remain attached to neo-liberal principles that are vital to improving health, and thus display "fatal indifference" to

new patterns of disease.[7–10] Still different critics claim that the G8 fails to deliver on health because it is easily distracted by other issues, has a narrow audience and places a premium on short-term public relations success.[11–13]

Those who are supportive of the G8, however, argue that the G8 is emerging as the global-health governor. This is not out of choice, but as a consequence of the poor performance of the old multilateral organizations and the high technical and economic capacity of G8 members.[14,15] Other supporters view the G8 as a potential leader in the health field as a whole, and claim that the G8 is already forging a new path for global health governance in an era in which globalized markets threaten to overwhelm Member States.[16] Commentators have described the G8 as the emerging centre of 21st century global health governance.[17–22] This is because of the inclusive, multi-stakeholder model on which the G8 is now based, and stems from the identified need for task-oriented collaboration between the private and public sectors as the model for future global health governance.[17–22]

To advance this debate, we car-

[a] G8 Research Group, Munk Centre for International Studies, 6 Hoskin Ave., Toronto, Ontario M5S 1H8, Canada. Correspondence to John J Kirton (email: john.kirton@utoronto.ca).

Ref. no. **06-039917**

(Submitted: 4 October 2006 – Final revised version received: 19 December 2006 – Accepted: 26 December 2006)

ried out an evidence-based assessment of G8 health governance and explored its impact on foreign policy and the domestic behaviour of G8 Member States. These include Canada, France, Germany, Italy, Japan, the Russian Federation, the United Kingdom, the United States and the European Union (EU).[2] Drawing on the concert equality model that uses six governance functions to explain institutional performance, we will first assess the G8's performance with respect to its health commitments. These six functions are: supporting the domestic management of policies and politics; deliberating on key issues; defining new directions and future commitments; taking collective decisions about specific commitments; delivering these decisions through members' compliance with their commitments; and developing global governance by creating new and directing existing international institutions. We examine whether G8 members comply with their collective commitments, and why. We explore whether G8 leaders, through their active use of compliance catalysts, plurilateral institutions and multilateral organizations, can work to ensure greater compliance with global health goals.

G8 global health governance

Since the onset of rapid globalization in 1996, the G8 has emerged as a more effective leader of global health governance than other existing institutions (see Table 1).[23–27] In relation to its first function of domestic political management, the Group of Seven (G7), then without the Russian Federation, initially took up health issues that concerned the Member States at that time, such as cancer. The G7's concerns subsequently gravitated towards diseases, such as malaria, that primarily affect countries outside of the G7. When the Russian Federation became a full member in 1998, the G8 began to focus on HIV/AIDS, which was becoming increasingly prevalent within that country. As hosts of the 2006 St Petersburg Summit, the Russian Federation's choice of infectious disease as one of three priority themes was driven by concern that the epicentre of HIV/AIDS was migrating from Africa to Eurasia, and it sought to address the issue of HIV/AIDS within its own borders. A poll taken on the summit's eve identified infectious dis-

ease as a key issue, voted for by 84% of Russian respondents and 86% of those in the G8, and giving the topic second priority after terrorism.[28]

The second function of the G8 is deliberation, in which outcomes are measured by the number of paragraphs devoted to health topics in summit declarations issued in the leaders' names. Health became a major agenda item in 1996 and 1997 under French and American leadership and continued to grow as an issue. At the 2006 summit a record 84 paragraphs were devoted to health. In relation to the third function of setting new normative directions, the G8 in 2002 began to place priority on health by dealing with the subject in the Chair's Summary document, which highlights the leaders' top priorities. At the St Petersburg Summit in 2006, the Chair's Summary devoted a record eight paragraphs to infectious disease. In reference to health, documents generated from the summit emphasized democratic principles and civil society participation.

Collective decision-making is the fourth function of G8 Member States, whereby future commitments are documented and published in the leaders' names. In relation to this function, the first inclusion of health issues occurred in 2002. During this time, under Canadian leadership, 25 commitments were made. The St Petersburg Summit in 2006 set a record high of 64 health commitments, double the number made by any previous summit. Increased commitment to mobilizing new money for global health began under French leadership in 2003. At the British-hosted Gleneagles Summit in 2005, a record of US$ 24 billion was committed to global health.

Compliance with these commitments, the fifth function of G8 Member States, involves the actual implementation of these collective decisions. In this respect, however, performances by G8 Member States have varied. On this issue the best systematic evidence comes from the G8 Research Group's annual assessment of members' compliance with critical commitments in the year following the summit. The role of the G8 Research Group is to assess the actions taken by member governments, including verbal reaffirmations, assigning personnel and resources, initiating new programmes and documenting whether the commitments result in their intended effect.[29]

First-order compliance is measured on a scale from −100% to +100%. Minus 100% represents no action or a Member State acting against fulfilling the commitment; +100% represents complete compliance with it. Compliance with the critical health commitments made at the Summits hosted by Japan in 2000 and France in 2003 was very high, but it has been considerably lower in other years.

Finally, in relation to the sixth function of G8 members, to ensure the development of global governance, there has been steady action in relation to health since 2001. This function is measured by the number of G8-centred health institutions created at the ministerial and official level, during the Summit hosting year. Prior to 2001 results were poor, with only one or two institutions created each year and none created in 2005. Only in 2006 was this issue addressed at the ministerial level, with the first-ever meeting of G8 health ministers.

Thus with respect to its first four functions the G8 has increased its outputs relating health, with virtually all of its members contributing to this rise during their leadership. This pattern suggests that the G8 is indeed a concert of equals, driven to govern in health as elsewhere in accordance with the concert equality model of G8 governance.[26,30–32] This change has come about because of the increasingly equal vulnerability of citizens from each G8 Member State to a new generation of infectious diseases, including HIV/AIDS. Older organizations within the UN system, led by WHO, have proven increasingly ineffective in mobilizing their members' resources on the scale required and in meeting targets and timetables.[5,14,15] By contrast, the G8 Member States possess the globally predominant and specialized capabilities needed to combat these new diseases worldwide. Their core, common, G8-grounded principles of open democracy and social advance bring G8 leaders close to their newly democratic African partners, who are more comfortable with the multi-stakeholder approaches required to combat a new generation of diseases. From 2001 to 2005, seven of the same leaders came to an unprecedented five summits in a row, to meet the same four core democratic African partners in the G8 club. At these summits they discussed global health in the inclusive, interlinked and innovative way the world needs.

Table 1. **Overview of G8 health performance**

	Deliberative[a]	Directional[b]	Decisional: total commitment[c]	Decisional: money (US$)[c]	Delivering commitments[d]	Development of global governance[e]
1975	0	0	0	0	NA	0
1976	0	0	0	0	NA	0
1977	0	0	0	0	NA	0
1978	0	0	0	0	NA	0
1979	1	0	0	0	NA	0
1980	1	0	0	0	NA	0
1981	0	0	0	0	NA	0
1982	4	0	0	0	NA	0
1983	1	0	1	0	NA	0
1984	1	0	0	0	NA	0
1985	2	0	0	0	NA	0
1986	2	0	1	0	NA	0
1987	7	0	0	0	NA	1
1988	2	0	0	0	NA	0
1989	3	0	0	0	NA	0
1990	7	0	0	0	NA	0
1991	9	0	1	0	NA	0
1992	3	0	0	0	NA	1
1993	3	0	1	0	NA	0
1994	2	0	0	0	NA	0
1995	2	0	0	0	NA	0
1996	14	0	5	0	+43%[f]	0
1997	17	0	10	0	0.0%[f]	0
1998	6	0	5	0	+26%[f]	0
1999	11	0	4	0	+32%[f]	0
2000	30	0	17	0	**+84%[f]**	0
2001	15	0	5	1.3 billion	+38%[f]	1
2002	19	2	25	0	+17%[f]	1
2003	50	6	32	500 million	+80%[f]	**2**
2004	36	5	14	3.3 billion	+33%[f]	1
2005	22	1	14	**24 billion**	+24%[f]	0
2006	**84**	**8**	**64**	4.4 billion		1

NA, not available; US$, United States Dollars. Bold type indicates peak scores.
[a] Annual assessment of G8 leaders' references to health in annual documentation, including Chair's Summary. Each paragraph containing a mention of health is counted as 1.
[b] Annual assessment of G8 leaders' references to health in the communiqué chapeau, introduction or Chair's Summary. Each paragraph containing a mention of health is counted as 1.
[c] Annual assessment of G8 leaders' specific future-oriented commitments in the leaders' name. Each commitment is counted as 1.
[d] Annual assessment of member's compliance with critical commitments in the year after the Summit, measured on a scale from −100% to +100%.
[e] The number of G8-centred health institutions created at the official and ministerial level during the Summit hosting year.
[f] Data supplied by the University of Toronto G8 Research Group and Jenevieve Mannell.

Compliance with G8 health commitments

Of the six G8 global governance functions, compliance stands out as not corresponding to the G8's improved commitment to global health issues. From 1996 to 2005, compliance as the G8's fifth function scored on average only +35%. Although health compliance has scored positively every year, scores vary widely, with very high compliance noted in both 2000 and 2003.

Variations in compliance are also seen across Member States. From 1996

to 2005, the average scores in decreasing order were as follows: European Union (EU) +81%, United Kingdom +64%, Canada +63%, United States +57%, France +43%, Germany +34%, Japan +31%, Italy +22% and the Russian Federation +10% (see Table 2). This pattern is similar to that for compliance with commitments from other areas aside from health. These data suggest that highly organized institutions such as the EU may reinforce the G8's health compliance task rather than serving to rival or replace the G8.

With respect to health, compliance varies even more widely by component issue area. For example, from 1996 to 2005 the average scores were in decreasing order: severe acute respiratory syndrome (SARS) +78%, ageing +67%, biotechnology +66%, the Global Fund to fight AIDS, Tuberculosis and Malaria +56%, drugs and medicine +49%, HIV/AIDS +33%, polio +31%, training +29% and development 0%. This pattern suggests that the G8 performs better when the health issue in question most directly affects citizens in G8 countries,

John J Kirton et al.

Special theme — Health and foreign policy |
Compliance and the G8 |

Table 2. **G8 health compliance by country and health issue**

Health commitments by year[a]	Average score	Canada	France	Germany	Italy	Japan	Russian Federation	United Kingdom	United States	European Union
Polio	**+31%**	**+60%**	**−20%**	**+60%**	**−20%**	**0%**	**+20%**	**+60%**	**+60%**	**+67%**
2002	0.00	0	0	0	0	0	0	0	0	NA
2003	+1.00	+1	+1	+1	+1	+1	+1	+1	+1	NA
2004	+0.44	+1	−1	+1	−1	0	+1	+1	+1	+1
2004	0.00	0	0	0	0	0	0	0	0	0
2005	+0.11	+1	−1	+1	−1	−1	−1	+1	+1	+1
HIV/AIDS	**+33%**	**+80%**	**+100%**	**−20%**	**00%**	**−20%**	**−75%**	**+80%**	**+80%**	**+75%**
1998	+0.33	+1	+1	0	−1	0	−1	+1	+1	+1
1998	+0.11	+1	+1	−1	−1	−1	−1	+1	+1	+1
1999	+0.63	+1	+1	−1	+1	+1	0	+1	+1	NA
2002	0.00	0	NA	0	NA	0	NA	0	0	0
2004	+0.56	+1	+1	+1	+1	−1	−1	+1	+1	+1
Drugs/medicines	**+49%**	**+75%**	**+25%**	**+50%**	**+33%**	**+75%**	**+50%**	**+75%**	**+25%**	**+50%**
1996	+0.43	0	0	+1	NA	+1	NA	+1	0	NA
2000	+1.00	+1	+1	+1	+1	+1	+1	+1	+1	+1
2002	+0.38	+1	0	0	0	+1	0	+1	0	NA
2003	+0.13	+1	0	0	0	0	NA	0	0	0
Diseases: HIV, polio, malaria, tuberculosis	**+65%**	**+75%**	**+67%**	**+67%**	**+67%**	**+75%**	**00%**	**+67%**	**+50%**	**+100%**
1999	0.00	0	0	0	0	0	0	0	0	NA
2000	+0.60	+1	NA	NA	NA	+1	0	NA	0	+1
2000	+1.00	+1	+1	+1	+1	+1	NA	+1	+1	+1
2003	+1.00	+1	+1	+1	+1	+1	NA	+1	+1	NA
The Global Fund	**+56%**	**+75%**	**+50%**	**+25%**	**+50%**	**+50%**	**+75%**	**+50%**	**+50%**	**+100%**
2001	+0.75	+1	+1	+1	+1	0	+1	+1	0	NA
2002	+0.25	+1	0	0	+1	0	0	0	0	NA
2003	+0.89	+1	+1	0	+1	+1	+1	+1	+1	+1
2005	+0.33	0	0	0	−1	+1	+1	0	+1	+1
Development	**0%**	**−50%**	**−50%**	**+50%**	**−50%**	**0%**	**0%**	**+50%**	**+50%**	**NA**
1997	0.00	−1	−1	+1	−1	0	NA	+1	+1	NA
2001	0.00	0	0	0	0	0	0	0	0	NA
Biotechnology	**+66%**	**+100%**	**+100%**	**+50%**	**+50%**	**+100%**	**−100%**	**+100%**	**+50%**	**NA**
2000	+0.75	+1	+1	+1	+1	+1	−1	+1	+1	NA
2002	+0.57	+1	+1	0	0	+1	NA	+1	0	NA
Ageing	**+67%**	**+100%**	**+100%**	**+50%**	**+100%**	**+100%**	**+100%**	**+100%**	**+100%**	**+100%**
1998	+0.33	0	NA	0	NA	NA	NA	NA	+1	NA
2003	+1.00	+1	+1	+1	+1	+1	+1	+1	+1	+1
Training	**+29%**	**0%**	**+100%**	**0%**	**NA**	**+100%**	**NA**	**−100%**	**0%**	**+100%**
2005	+0.29	0	+1	0	NA	+1	NA	−1	0	+1
SARS	**+78%**	**+100%**	**+100%**	**0%**	**+100%**	**+100%**	**0%**	**+100%**	**+100%**	**+100%**
2003	+0.78	+1	+1	0	+1	+1	0	+1	+1	+1
Average scores	**35%**	**63%**	**43%**	**34%**	**22%**	**31%**	**10%**	**64%**	**57%**	**81%**

AIDS, acquired immunodeficiency syndrome; the Global Fund, the Global Fund to fight AIDS, Tuberculosis and Malaria; NA, not available; SARS, severe acute respiratory syndrome.

[a] For which G8 Research Group compliance data exists.

or involves instruments directly controlled by the G8 Member States. The G8 performs better within a biomedical model aimed at responding to acute outbreaks of diseases such as SARS, not at proactively addressing health's socioeconomic determinants and underdevelopment's root causes. This finding supports concerns that the G8 fails to adequately address a new generation of diseases because of its neo-liberal approach to economic and social policy.[7,8]

Compliance: explaining variations

What explains these patterns of compliance in relation to health? Although the concert equality model explains G8 performance on the other five functions of G8 governance, variation in performance on compliance is difficult to explain.[3,30,33] Recent research exploring G8 finance and development commitments suggests that compliance is linked to three factors:

- the conscious action of the G8 leaders as active agents at summits,
- the reinforcing action of the G8 ministerial institution, and
- the vulnerabilities and relative capabilities that constitute the structure of the international system.[48]

Is the same true in the field of health? Health is a much newer focus of the G8, and at present no G8 ministerial-level institution deals exclusively with health issues.

As active agents, G8 leaders at times consciously embed within their commitments expressions of their political will. Particular catalysts provide specific guidance about how to deliver their commitments. A recent analysis of compliance with 46 of the G8's finance and development commitments from 1996 to 2005 found that two catalysts improved compliance. These were priority placement, whereby reference is made to health in the communiqué chapeau, introduction, preamble or Chair's Summary, and timetable, where a specific target date or year is set. However, no improvements were seen from the other catalysts, which included:

- targets (specific, numerical, measurable goals);
- remit mandates (requirements to report back at the next summit);
- money mobilized (new money promised at the summit);

- specified agents (national or intergovernmental groups, institutions or individuals nominated to take charge of the commitment);
- G8 body (a named G8-centred or G8-created institution, its ministers, or members who take charge of the commitment);
- international institutions (whose named ministers or members take charge of the commitment).[25]

To explore the impact of these compliance catalysts in the field of health, some refinements were made. The timetable catalyst was divided into one-year variants and multiyear variants. International institutions were divided into WHO, the most functionally relevant multilateral organization, and "other". The commitment was coded as WHO when it contained a specific reference to this organization. All referenced multilateral institutional initiatives not exclusively directed by WHO, including references to the UN, the Joint UN Programme on HIV/AIDS (UNAIDS), the Codex Alimentarius Commission, the Global Polio Eradication Initiative and the Stop TB Partnership, were coded as other because they are partly directed by other organizations. The category "past promise", a reaffirmation of a commitment made in a previous year, was added to capture the important impact of iteration and continuity.[49]

Between 1996 and 2006 a health commitment contained up to four such catalysts and as few as none (see Table 3; available at http://www.who.int/bulletin). The most frequently employed catalysts across the 30 measured health commitments were, in decreasing order: priority placement (12 commitments), specified agent (10), other international institution (8), money mobilized (7), past promise (7), multiyear timetable (6), one-year timetable (4) and G8 body (4).

WHO was explicitly invoked in only two commitments: one in 2000 on HIV/AIDS, malaria and tuberculosis, for which the compliance score was +100%, and one in 2005 on polio, for which the compliance score was +11%. From 2003 onwards, priority placement and money mobilized have been the catalysts of choice.

The effect of the catalyst variables on commitment compliance was formally tested in a multivariate ordinary least squares (OLS) model.[52] In this

model, which uses a subset of catalyst variables deemed to best balance the trade-off between predictive power and parsimony, two catalysts had highly significant positive effects on compliance. The presence of a specific timetable of one year or less tended to increase compliance with that commitment by an average of +0.65 compliance points, over and above the baseline value of average compliance with commitments without such a timetable (p-value=0.03; t-value=2.219). Similarly, delegating some responsibility for implementation to WHO tended to improve compliance with that commitment by +0.55 compliance points, in comparison to compliance with commitments not delegated to WHO (p-value=0.06; t-value=1.93). Although significant only at the 94% confidence interval level, the estimate is considered to be admissible given the small sample size.[53]

To identify more specifically why compliance differs from the overall level of compliance across all commitments in a given year, we calculated a mean-adjusted compliance variable from each individual commitment compliance score. In this analysis the only significant variables that emerged were international institution and "other". However, by delegating some responsibility for implementation to an international organization other than WHO, compliance tended to reduce by 5.9 compliance points relative to the baseline average compliance with commitments where this catalyst variable was absent (p-value=0.07; t-value=1.83).

A second potential cause of compliance is the conscious collective action of the ministers involved in G8 governance, who may autonomously seek to support their leaders even when solicited. In the field of finance and development, compliance increases when the G8 finance ministers act supportively.[25,54] Specifically, the G7/G8 finance ministers are coded as supportive of the health agenda if the ministers mention the issue-area of the commitment in their ministerial communiqué; for example, active ageing, polio eradication and supporting the Global Fund.

The G7/G8 finance ministers have been active on the issue of health almost continuously since 1998, and were particularly engaged in 2000 and 2003. In 2000, three of the six G7/8 finance ministers meeting dealt with health issues, and in 2003 this increased to

Global Health

three of the four ministries. In addition, both 2000 and 2003 had a higher than average number of compliance catalysts embedded by the leaders in their health commitments. In addition, 2000 and 2003 are the same years in which there was a peak of health compliance. Yet regression analysis highlights that when the G8 finance ministers addressed the same issue as that contained in their leaders' health commitments, it had no effect on compliance before, during or after the summit year. In conclusion, G8 leaders must look outside their current G8 institutional system if they are to improve compliance.

The efforts of G8 leaders and finance ministers to improve compliance with health commitments will likely be driven by changes in the structure of the international system. This is because the relevant vulnerabilities and capabilities among G8 members will change over time. In the field of finance and development, a combination of increasingly equal vulnerability and capability

among the G8 members has in the past inspired finance ministers to remember and repeat such commitments, but this did not directly increase compliance.[25] However, with respect to health no indirect or direct impact has been identified. There have been no impacts noted on the demand side, even when G8 Member States have shown increased vulnerability to pandemics such as HIV/AIDS. Nor have there been impacts on the supply side, despite the fact that the ability of G8 members to respond to health issues has become more internally equal and globally predominant.

Conclusion

Our analysis indicates that G8 leaders can improve compliance with the health commitments that they make at annual summits. We conclude that health ministers and other health-policy stakeholders can do three things to ensure health commitments are addressed during the first year. First, they can encourage G8

leaders to make health commitments at the summit and to set a one-year timetable for action. This timetable should correspond with the period within which compliance is measured, and the interval between this and the next summit. Second, they should advise G8 leaders to seek the support of WHO, especially on issues that relate to HIV/AIDS, malaria and tuberculosis.[4] Third, they should work to create a G8 health ministers institution by building on the success of the first meeting of G8 health ministers that took place in 2006.

Both the UN and the G8 systems can assist the powerful countries assembled in the G8 to comply with the rising number of health commitments that they make. In both cases it will be institutions that are fully focused on health, rather than those with more diffuse responsibilities, that can be counted on to ensure improved compliance. ∎

Competing interests: None declared.

Résumé

Comment les dirigeants du G8 ont honoré leurs engagements dans le domaine sanitaire de 1996 à 2006

Les responsables de l'élaboration des politiques internationales en matière de santé disposent désormais d'un éventail d'instruments institutionnels pour les aider à atteindre leurs objectifs sanitaires mondiaux et nationaux. Il s'agit aussi bien d'organisations multilatérales bien établies du système des Nations Unies, que d'institutions plus récentes et à composition plus restreinte, mises sur pied dans le cadre du G8. Pour déployer au mieux les ressources limitées dont on dispose, il importe d'examiner systématiquement la contribution apportée par le G8 à la gouvernance sanitaire mondiale. Cette évaluation examine les contributions des organisations multilatérales comme l'Organisation mondiale de la Santé et détermine si les Etats Membres respectent leurs engagements. L'étude a cherché à vérifier dans quelle mesure la gouvernance sanitaire du G8 aide les gouvernements des pays membres à gérer

les politiques au plan interne, à définir les principales orientations normatives, à développer et à respecter des engagements pris à titre collectif et à mettre sur pied de nouvelles institutions rattachées au G8. L'étude a permis de constater que les résultats obtenus par le G8 s'étaient sensiblement améliorés au cours des dix dernières années. Les résultats sont également satisfaisants au niveau des différents Etats Membres du G8, chacun se révélant en mesure de lutter contre les maladies. Le respect des engagements dans le domaine sanitaire varie cependant d'un Etat à l'autre, et des améliorations encore être apportées. Ainsi, les dirigeants du G8 devraient mieux définir leurs engagements en matière de santé et se fixer un délai d'une année pour les honorer. En outre, les Etats Membres devraient demander l'appui de l'OMS et créer un organisme regroupant les ministres de la santé des pays du G8.

Resumen

Análisis del cumplimiento de los compromisos de los líderes del G8 en materia de salud (1996–2006)

Los planificadores de las políticas internacionales de salud disponen en la actualidad de diferentes instrumentos institucionales para alcanzar sus objetivos sanitarios mundiales y nacionales. Esos instrumentos van desde las organizaciones multilaterales oficiales de las Naciones Unidas hasta instituciones más recientes y restringidas del Grupo de los Ocho (G8). Para decidir la mejor forma de emplear recursos escasos, debemos examinar de forma sistemática las contribuciones del G8 a la gobernanza de la salud mundial. En este estudio exploramos las contribuciones hechas por las instituciones multilaterales, tales como la Organización Mundial de la Salud (OMS) e investigamos si los Estados Miembros cumplen sus compromisos. Hemos analizado si la gobernanza sanitaria del G8 ayuda a sus gobiernos miembros a gestionar la política y las

políticas nacionales, a definir las principales direcciones normativas, a desarrollar y cumplir los compromisos colectivos y a crear nuevas instituciones centradas en el G8. Hemos verificado que el desempeño del G8 ha mejorado considerablemente en el último decenio. Los Estados Miembros del G8 funcionan igualmente bien, y todos ellos son capaces de luchar contra las enfermedades. El cumplimiento de sus compromisos sanitarios fue variable entre los Estados Miembros del G8, y este aspecto es mejorable. Los líderes del G8 deben definir mejor sus compromisos sanitarios y fijar plazos anuales para su cumplimiento. Además, los Estados Miembros deben buscar el apoyo de la OMS y crear una institución formada por los ministros de salud del G8).

| Special theme — Health and foreign policy | |
| Compliance and the G8 | John J Kirton et al. |

ملخص

تمكين قادة البلدان الثمانية الكبرى من العطاء: تحليل للامتثال وللالتزامات الصحية، 1996 – 2006

إن لدى أصحاب القرار السياسي في الصحة الدولية مجموعة من الأدوات المؤسساتية تمكّنهم من تحقيق المرامي الصحية الوطنية والعالمية. وتتراوح هذه الأدوات من المنظمات الرسمية المتعدّدة الأطراف للأمم المتحدة إلى المؤسسات المحدودة العضوية لمجموعة البلدان الثمانية الكبرى، وللوصول إلى قرار حول أفضل مكان لتوظيف الموارد الشحيحة كان من الواجب علينا أن نقوم بدراسة منهجية للمساهمات التي قدّمتها الدول الثمانية الكبرى للجهات القائمة على حَوْكمة الصحة في العالم. ويستقصي هذا التقييم المساهمات التي قدّمتها مؤسسات متعدّدة الأطراف مثل منظمة الصحة العالمية، وفيما إذا كانت الدول الأعضاء قد التزمت بأداء ما عليها من التزامات. كما قيّمنا ما إذا كانت الجهات القائمة على الحكومة الصحية في البلدان الثمانية الكبرى، قد ساعدت الحكومات في دولها الأعضاء في إدارة السياسات الوطنية وفي أدائها

السياسي، وفي تعريف الاتجاهات المعيارية السائدة، وفي إعداد الالتزامات الجماعية والامتثال لها، وفي إعداد مؤسسات جديدة تتركز في البلدان الثمانية الكبرى. وقد وجدنا أن أداء البلدان الثمانية الكبرى قد تحسّن تحسُّناً واضحاً خلال العقد المنصرم، وأن أداء البلدان الأعضاء في مجموعة البلدان الثمانية الكبرى متساوٍ في جودته، وأن كلاً منها يستطيع مكافحة المرض. ويتفاوت الامتثال بين الدول الثمانية الكبرى بقدر ما لدى كل منها من التزامات صحية، مع وجود مجال للتحسُّن. وعلى قادة البلدان الثمانية الكبرى أن يحدّدوا التزاماتهم بشكل أفضل، وأن يحدّدوا الزمن الأقصى للعطاء خلال عام واحد؛ وبالإضافة إلى ذلك ينبغي على الدول الأعضاء أن تلتمس المعونة من منظمة الصحة العالمية في إعداد مؤسسة لوزراء الصحة في الدول الثمانية الكبرى.

References

1. Abbott W, Keohane R, Moravcsik A, Slaughter A-M, Snidal D. The concept of legalization. *Int Organ* 2000;54:401-20.
2. Kirton JJ, Trebilcock MJ, eds. *Hard choices, soft law: voluntary standards in global trade, environment, and social governance.* Aldershot: Ashgate; 2004.
3. Hajnal PI. *The G7/G8 system: evolution, role, and documentation.* Aldershot: Ashgate; 1999.
4. Cooper AF, Kirton JJ, Schrecker T, eds. *Governing global health: challenge, response, innovation.* Aldershot: Ashgate; 2007.
5. Lewis S. *Race against time: searching for hope in AIDS-ravaged Africa.* Toronto: House of Anansi; 2005.
6. Drohan M. Broken promises. *Lit Rev Canada* 2005;13:11-2.
7. Labonté R, Schrecker T, Sanders D, Mieeus W. *Fatal indifference: the G8, Africa, and global health.* Ottawa: International Development Research Centre; 2004.
8. Labonté R, Schrecker T. Committed to health for all? How the G7/8 rate. *Soc Sci Med* 2004;59:1661-76.
9. Labonté R, Schrecker T. *The G8, Africa, and global health: a platform for global health equity for the 2005 summit.* London: Nuffield Trust; 2005.
10. Labonte R, Sanders D, Schrecker T. Health and development: how are the G7/G8 doing? *J Epidemiol Community Health* 2002;56:322-322.
11. Foster JW. Canada and international health: a time of testing on AIDS. In: Hillmer N, Molot MA, eds. *Canada among nations 2002: a fading power.* Toronto: Oxford University Press; 2002. pp. 191-208.
12. Foster JW. *Canada's foreign policy in health: signs and signals from HIV/AIDS.* Canadian Foreign Policy and Global Health Conference, 5 December, 2003 Available from: http:// www.nsi-ins.ca/english/pdf/Cdn_policy_global_ health.pdf
13. Kwayera J. G8 failed to tackle the toxic politics of drug making and selling. *East African,* 9 June 2003. Available from: http://www.nationaudio.com/ News/EastAfrican/09062003/Business/Business_Opinion090620033.html
14. Price-Smith A. *Plagues and politics: infectious disease and international policy.* New York: Palgrave; 2001.
15. Price-Smith A. *The health of nations: infectious disease, environmental change, and their effects on national security and development.* Cambridge MA: Massachusetts Institute of Technology Press; 2002.
16. Savona P, Oldani C. Globalisation: the private sector perspective. In: Fratianni M, Savona P, Kirton JJ, eds. *Sustaining global growth and development.* Aldershot: Ashgate; 2003. pp. 99-112.
17. Bayne N. *Hanging in there: the G7 and G8 summit in maturity and renewal.* Aldershot: Ashgate; 2000.
18. Bayne N. Managing globalisation and the new economy: the contribution of the G8 summit. In: Kirton JJ, von Furstenberg GM, eds. *New directions in global economic governance: managing globalisation in the twenty-first century.* Aldershot: Ashgate; 2001. pp. 171-188.
19. Bayne N. *Staying together: the G8 summit confronts the 21st century.* Aldershot: Ashgate; 2005.

20. Aginam O. Salvaging our global neighbourhood: critical reflections on the G8 summit and global health governance in an interdependent world. *Law, Social Justice, and Global Development* 2004;1. Available from: http:// www2.warwick.ac.uk/fac/soc/law/elj/lgd/2004_1/aginam/
21. Aginam O. *Global health governance: international law and public health in a divided world.* Toronto: University of Toronto Press; 2005.
22. Orbinski J. AIDS, Médecins Sans Frontières, and access to essential medicines. In: Hajnal PI, ed. *Civil society in the information age.* Aldershot: Ashgate; 2002. pp. 127-135.
23. Kirton JJ, Mannell J. The G8 and global health governance. In: Cooper AF, Kirton JJ, Schrecker T, eds. *Governing global health: challenge, response, innovation.* Aldershot: Ashgate; 2007. pp. 115-146.
24. Kirton JJ, Kokotsis E. Keeping faith with Africa's health: catalysing G8 compliance. In: Cooper AF, Kirton JJ, Schrecker T, eds. *Governing global health: challenge, response, innovation.* Aldershot: Ashgate; 2007. pp. 157-180.
25. Kirton JJ. *The G8 and global health governance: the case for a 2006 Eurasian HIV/AIDS initiative.* The International Parliamentary Conference, 6 June 2006, Moscow. Available from: http://www.g8.utoronto.ca/scholar/ kirton2006/kirton_health_060609.pdf
26. Kirton JJ. America at the G8: from vulnerability to victory at the Sea Island summit. In: Fratianni M, Kirton JJ, Rugman AM, Savona P, eds. *New perspectives on global governance: why America needs the G8.* Aldershot: Ashgate; 2005. pp. 31-50.
27. Kirton JJ. *Gleneagles G8 boosts Blair at home.* Toronto: G8 Research Group; 2005. Available from: http://www.g8.utoronto.ca/evaluations/ 2005gleneagles/coverage.html
28. Global Markets Institute. *G8 summit in St Petersburg.* New York: Goldman Sachs; 2006.
29. Kokotsis E. *Keeping international commitments: compliance, credibility, and the G7, 1988-1995.* New York: Garland; 1999.
30. Kirton JJ. *Explaining G8 effectiveness: a concert of vulnerable equals in a globalizing world.* International Studies Association, 17-20 March 2004. Available from: http://www.g8.utoronto.ca/scholar/kirton2004/kirton_isa_ 040304.pdf
31. Kirton JJ. The seven power summits as a new security institution. In: Dewitt D, Haglund D, Kirton JJ, eds. *Building a new global order: emerging trends in international security.* Toronto: Oxford University Press; 1993. pp. 335-357.
32. Kirton JJ. *Contemporary concert diplomacy: the seven-power summit and the management of international order.* International Studies Association, 29 March to 1 April 1989, London.
33. Kirton JJ, Kokotsis E. *Producing international commitments and compliance without legalization: the G7/8's trade performance from 1975 to 2002.* International Studies Association, 23 February to 3 March 2003, Portland. Available from: http://www.g8.utoronto.ca/scholar/kirton2003/ KirtonPortland2003.pdf

John J Kirton et al.

Special theme — Health and foreign policy
Compliance and the G8

34. Li Q. Commitment compliance in G-7 summit macroeconomic policy coordination. *Polit Res Q* 2001;54:355-78. Available from: http://links.jstor.org/sici?sici=1065-9129(200106)54%3A2%3C355%3ACCIGSM%3E2.0.CO%3B2-M

35. Baliamoune M. Economics of summitry: an empirical assessment of the economic effects of summits. *Empirica* 2000;27:295-315.

36. Daniels JP. *The meaning and reliability of economic summit undertakings.* New York: Garland Publishing; 1993.

37. von Furstenberg GM, Daniels JP. Can you trust G-7 promises? *Int Econ Insights* 1992;3:24-7. Available from: http://www.g7.utoronto.ca/scholar/furstenberg1992/document.html

38. von Furstenberg GM, Daniels JP. Economic summit declarations, 1975-1989: examining the written record of international cooperation. In: *Princeton Studies in International Finance* 72. Princeton: Princeton University Press; 1992.

39. von Furstenberg GM, Daniels JP. *Policy undertakings by the seven "summit" countries: ascertaining the degree of compliance.* Carnegie-Rochester Conference Series on Public Policy 1991;35:267-308.

40. Kirton JJ, Kokotsis E. Keeping faith with Africa: assessing compliance with the G8's commitments at Kananaskis and Evian. In: Atwood JB, Brown RS, Lyman P, eds. *Freedom, prosperity, and security: G8 partnership with Africa, Sea Island 2004 and beyond.* Washington DC: Council on Foreign Relations; 2005. pp. 11-33.

41. Kirton JJ, Kokotsis E, Stephens G, Juricevic D. The G8 and conflict prevention: commitment, compliance, and systemic contribution. In: Kirton JJ, Stefanova R, eds. *The G8, the United Nations, and conflict prevention.* Aldershot: Ashgate; 2004. pp. 59-84.

42. Kirton JJ, Kokotsis E, Juricevic D. G7/8 commitments and their significance, 1975-2001. In: Fratianni M, Savona P, Kirton JJ, eds. *Governing global finance: new challenges, G7 and IMF contributions.* Aldershot: Ashgate; 2002. pp. 227-228.

43. Kirton JJ, Kokotsis E, Juricevic D. Okinawa's promises kept: the 2001 G8 compliance report. In: Kirton JJ, Takase J, eds. *New directions in global political governance: the G8 and international order in the twenty-first century.* Aldershot: Ashgate; 2002. pp. 269-280.

44. Kokotsis E. *Explaining G8 effectiveness: the democratic institutionalist and concert equality models compared.* International Studies Association, 17-20 March 2004, Montreal. Available from: http://www.g8.utoronto.ca/scholar/kokotsis_isa2004.pdf

45. Kokotsis E. *Keeping sustainable development commitments: the recent G7 record.* Toronto: G8 Research Group, 1995. Available from: http://www.g8.utoronto.ca/scholar/kirton199503/kokotsis

46. Kokotsis E, Daniels JP. G8 summits and compliance. In: Hodges MR, Kirton JJ, Daniels JP, eds. *The G8's role in the new millennium.* Aldershot: Ashgate; 1999. pp. 75-91.

47. Kokotsis E, Kirton JJ. *National compliance with environmental regimes: the case of the G7, 1988-1995.* International Studies Association, 18-22 March 1997, Toronto.

48. Kirton JJ. Explaining compliance with G8 finance commitments: agency, institutionalization, and structure. *Open Econ Rev* 2006;17:459-475.

49. Bayne N. Continuity and leadership in an age of globalisation. In: Hodges MR, Kirton JJ, Daniels JP, eds. *The G8's role in the new millennium.* Aldershot: Ashgate; 1999. pp. 21-44.

50. G8 Research Group. *All G7/8 commitments, 1975-2006.* Toronto: G8 Research Group; 2006. Available from: http://www.g8.utoronto.ca/evaluations/G8_commitments.pdf

51. Kirton JJ, Roudev N, Sunderland L, Kunz C. *Count on the WHO: explaining compliance with G8 leaders' health commitments, 1996-2006.* Moscow: WHO; 2006.

52. Weisberg, S. *Applied linear regression, third edition.* Hoboken NJ: John Wiley; 2005.

53. Long JS. *Regression models for categorical and limited dependent variables.* Thousand Oaks CA: Sage Publications; 1997.

54. Bergsten CF, Henning CR. *Global economic leadership and the group of seven.* Washington DC: Institute for International Economics; 1996.

Special theme — Health and foreign policy
Compliance and the G8

John J Kirton et al.

Table 3. **G8 health commitments with compliance catalysts**

Commitment	Individual commitment score	Overall summit score	Overall health summit score	Number of catalysts	Priority placement [a]	Timetable (1 year) [b]	Timetable (multiyear) [c]	Remit mandate [d]	Money mobilized [e]	Specified agents [f]	International institution: WHO [g]	International institution: other [h]	G8 body [i]	Past promise [j]
1996 drugs	+0.43	+36.0	+0.43	1	0	0	0	0	0	0	0	1	0	0
1997 development	0.00	+12.8	0.00	1	0	0	0	0	0	1	0	0	0	0
1998 HIV	+0.33	+0.32	+0.26	2	0	0	0	0	0	0	0	1	0	1
1998 HIV	+0.11	+0.32	+0.26	1	0	0	0	0	0	0	0	0	1	0
1998 ageing	+0.33	+0.32	+0.26	0	0	0	0	0	0	0	0	0	0	0
1999 HIV	+0.63	+0.44	+0.32	1	0	0	0	0	0	0	0	0	0	1
1999 HIV, polio, tuberculosis	0.00	+0.44	+0.32	1	0	0	0	0	0	0	0	0	0	1
2000 HIV, malaria, tuberculosis	+0.60	+0.81	+0.84	0	0	0	0	0	0	0	0	0	0	0
2000 HIV, malaria, tuberculosis	+1.00	+0.81	+0.84	3	0	0	1	0	0	1	1	1	0	0
2000 drugs	+1.00	+0.81	+0.84	4	0	1	0	0	0	1	0	1	0	1
2000 biotechnology	+0.75	+0.81	+0.84	2	0	0	1	0	0	0	0	1	0	0
2001 Global Fund	+0.75	+0.46	+0.38	4	0	1	0	0	1	0	0	1	0	1
2001 development	0.00	+0.46	+0.38	1	0	0	0	0	0	1	0	0	0	0
2002 polio	0.00	+0.36	+0.17	2	1	0	1	0	1	0	0	0	0	0
2002 HIV	0.00	+0.36	+0.17	0	0	0	0	0	0	0	0	0	0	0
2002 medicines	+0.38	+0.36	+0.17	2	0	0	0	0	0	1	0	0	0	1
2002 Global Fund	+0.25	+0.36	+0.17	3	1	0	0	0	0	0	0	0	1	1
2002 biotechnology	+0.57	+0.36	+0.17	0	0	0	0	0	0	0	0	0	0	0
2003 ageing	+1.00	+0.51	+0.80	1	1	0	0	0	0	0	0	0	0	0
2003 Global Fund	+0.89	+0.51	+0.80	4	1	1	0	0	1	1	0	0	0	0
2003 polio	+1.00	+0.51	+0.80	2	1	0	1	0	1	0	1	0	1	0
2003 SARS	+0.78	+0.51	+0.80	1	1	0	0	0	0	0	0	0	0	0
2003 medicines	+0.13	+0.51	+0.80	2	1	0	0	0	0	1	0	0	0	0
2003 HIV, malaria, tuberculosis	+1.00	+0.51	+0.80	1	1	0	0	0	0	0	0	0	0	0
2004 HIV	+0.56	+0.55	+0.33	1	1	0	0	0	0	0	0	0	0	0

John J Kirton et al.

(Table 3, cont.)

Commitment	Individual commitment score	Overall summit score	Overall health summit score	Number of catalysts	Priority placement[a]	Timetable (1 year)[b]	Timetable (multiyear)[c]	Remit mandate[e]	Money mobilized[d]	Specified agents[f]	International institution: WHO[g]	International institution: other[h]	G8 body[i]	Past promise[j]
2004 polio	+0.44	+0.55	+0.33	3	1	1	0	0	1	1	0	0	0	0
2004 polio	0.00	+0.55	+0.33	2	1	0	1	0	0	0	0	0	0	0
2005 training	+0.29	+0.65	+0.24	1	0	0	0	0	0	1	1	0	0	0
2005 Global Fund	+0.33	+0.65	+0.24	4	1	0	0	0	1	1	0	1	1	1
2005 polio	+0.11	+0.65	+0.24	3	0	0	1	0	1	1	1	1	0	0
Total scores	**NA**	**NA**	**NA**	**53**	**12/30**	**4/30**	**6/30**	**0/30**	**7/30**	**10/30**	**2/30**	**8/30**	**4/30**	**7/30**

Global Fund, the Global Fund to fight AIDS, Tuberculosis and Malaria; HIV, human immunodeficiency virus; NA, not available; SARS, severe acute respiratory syndrome.

[a] The presence (1) or absence (0) of the issue in the communiqué chapeau, introduction, preamble or Chair's Summary.
[b] The presence (1) or absence (0) of a one-year timetable in the text of the commitment.
[c] The presence (1) or absence (0) of a more than one-year timetable in the text of the commitment.
[d] The presence (1) or absence (0) of a requirement to report back at the next Summit in the text of the commitment.
[e] The presence (1) or absence (0) of new money promised in the text of the commitment.
[f] The presence (1) or absence (0) of a national or intergovernmental group, institution or individual to take charge of the commitment in the text of the commitment.
[g] The presence (1) or absence (0) of a reference to WHO or its initiatives in the text of the commitment. Although this analysis of compliance with 30 health commitments contains only two cases where the WHO compliance catalysts is used, a parallel analysis of 35 cases of compliance with G8 health commitments from 1996 to 2006 confirms these results.[50,51]
[h] The presence (1) or absence (0) of a reference to any multilateral institutions or initiatives not exclusively directed by WHO in the text of the commitment.
[i] The presence (1) or absence (0) of a reference to a G8-centred or G8-created institution, its ministers or members named to take charge of the commitment in the text of the commitment.
[j] The presence (1) or absence (0) of the reaffirmation of a commitment made in a previous year, within the text of the commitment.

[34]

The Challenge of Global Health

Laurie Garrett

BEWARE WHAT YOU WISH FOR

LESS THAN a decade ago, the biggest problem in global health seemed to be the lack of resources available to combat the multiple scourges ravaging the world's poor and sick. Today, thanks to a recent extraordinary and unprecedented rise in public and private giving, more money is being directed toward pressing heath challenges than ever before. But because the efforts this money is paying for are largely uncoordinated and directed mostly at specific high-profile diseases—rather than at public health in general—there is a grave danger that the current age of generosity could not only fall short of expectations but actually make things worse on the ground.

This danger exists despite the fact that today, for the first time in history, the world is poised to spend enormous resources to conquer the diseases of the poor. Tackling the developing world's diseases has become a key feature of many nations' foreign policies over the last five years, for a variety of reasons. Some see stopping the spread of HIV, tuberculosis (TB), malaria, avian influenza, and other major killers as a moral duty. Some see it as a form of public diplomacy. And some see it as an investment in self-protection, given that microbes know no borders. Governments have been joined by a long list of private donors, topped by Bill and Melinda Gates and Warren Buffett, whose contributions to today's war on disease are mind-boggling.

LAURIE GARRETT is Senior Fellow for Global Health at the Council on Foreign Relations and the author of *Betrayal of Trust: The Collapse of Global Public Health.*

The Challenge of Global Health

Thanks to their efforts, there are now billions of dollars being made available for health spending—and thousands of nongovernmental organizations (NGOS) and humanitarian groups vying to spend it. But much more than money is required. It takes states, health-care systems, and at least passable local infrastructure to improve public health in the developing world. And because decades of neglect there have rendered local hospitals, clinics, laboratories, medical schools, and health talent dangerously deficient, much of the cash now flooding the field is leaking away without result.

Moreover, in all too many cases, aid is tied to short-term numerical targets such as increasing the number of people receiving specific drugs, decreasing the number of pregnant women diagnosed with HIV (the virus that causes AIDS), or increasing the quantity of bed nets handed out to children to block disease-carrying mosquitoes. Few donors seem to understand that it will take at least a full generation (if not two or three) to substantially improve public health—and that efforts should focus less on particular diseases than on broad measures that affect populations' general well-being.

The fact that the world is now short well over four million health-care workers, moreover, is all too often ignored. As the populations of the developed countries are aging and coming to require ever more medical attention, they are sucking away local health talent from developing countries. Already, one out of five practicing physicians in the United States is foreign-trained, and a study recently published in *JAMA: The Journal of the American Medical Association* estimated that if current trends continue, by 2020 the United States could face a shortage of up to 800,000 nurses and 200,000 doctors. Unless it and other wealthy nations radically increase salaries and domestic training programs for physicians and nurses, it is likely that within 15 years the majority of workers staffing their hospitals will have been born and trained in poor and middle-income countries. As such workers flood to the West, the developing world will grow even more desperate.

Yet the visionary leadership required to tackle such problems is sadly lacking. Over the last year, every major leadership position on the global health landscape has turned over, creating an unprecedented moment of strategic uncertainty. The untimely death last May of Dr. Lee Jong-wook, director general of the World Health Organization

Laurie Garrett

(WHO), forced a novel election process for his successor, prompting
health advocates worldwide to ask critical, long-ignored questions,
such as, Who should lead the fight against disease? Who should pay
for it? And what are the best strategies and tactics to adopt?

The answers have not been easy to come by. In November, China's
Dr. Margaret Chan was elected as Lee's successor. As Hong Kong's
health director, Chan had led her territory's responses to SARS and
bird flu; later she took the helm of the
WHO's communicable diseases division.
But in statements following her election,
Chan acknowledged that her organization
now faces serious competition and novel
challenges. And as of this writing, the Global
Fund to Fight AIDS, Tuberculosis, and
Malaria remained without a new leader
following a months-long selection process that saw more than 300
candidates vie for the post and the organization's board get mired
in squabbles over the fund's mission and future direction.

> Much of the cash now
> flooding the global
> health field is leaking
> away without result.

Few of the newly funded global health projects, meanwhile, have
built-in methods of assessing their efficacy or sustainability. Fewer
still have ever scaled up beyond initial pilot stages. And nearly all have
been designed, managed, and executed by residents of the wealthy
world (albeit in cooperation with local personnel and agencies). Many
of the most successful programs are executed by foreign NGOs and
academic groups, operating with almost no government interference
inside weak or failed states. Virtually no provisions exist to allow the
world's poor to say what they want, decide which projects serve their
needs, or adopt local innovations. And nearly all programs lack exit
strategies or safeguards against the dependency of local governments.

As a result, the health world is fast approaching a fork in the road.
The years ahead could witness spectacular improvements in the
health of billions of people, driven by a grand public and private effort
comparable to the Marshall Plan—or they could see poor societies
pushed into even deeper trouble, in yet another tale of well-intended
foreign meddling gone awry. Which outcome will emerge depends
on whether it is possible to expand the developing world's local talent
pool of health workers, restore and improve crumbling national and

The Challenge of Global Health

global health infrastructures, and devise effective local and international systems for disease prevention and treatment.

SHOW ME THE MONEY

THE RECENT surge in funding started as a direct consequence of the HIV/AIDS pandemic. For decades, public health experts had been confronted with the profound disparities in care that separated the developed world from the developing one. Health workers hated that inequity but tended to accept it as a fact of life, given that health concerns were nested in larger issues of poverty and development. Western AIDS activists, doctors, and scientists, however, tended to have little experience with the developing world and were thus shocked when they discovered these inequities. And they reacted with vocal outrage.

The revolution started at an international AIDS meeting in Vancouver, Canada, in 1996. Scientists presented exhilarating evidence that a combination of anti-HIV drugs (known as antiretrovirals, or ARVs) could dramatically reduce the spread of the virus inside the bodies of infected people and make it possible for them to live long lives. Practically overnight, tens of thousands of infected men and women in wealthy countries started the new treatments, and by mid-1997, the visible horrors of AIDS had almost disappeared from the United States and Europe.

But the drugs, then priced at about $14,000 per year and requiring an additional $5,000 a year for tests and medical visits, were unaffordable for most of the world's HIV-positive population. So between 1997 and 2000, a worldwide activist movement slowly developed to address this problem by putting pressure on drug companies to lower their prices or allow the generic manufacture of the new medicines. The activists demanded that the Clinton administration and its counterparts in the G-8, the group of advanced industrial nations, pony up money to buy ARVs and donate them to poor countries. And by 1999, total donations for health-related programs (including HIV/AIDS treatment) in sub-Saharan Africa hit $865 million—up more than tenfold in just three years.

In 2000, some 20,000 activists, scientists, doctors, and patients gathered in Durban, South Africa, for another international AIDS conference. There, South Africa's former president, Nelson Mandela,

Laurie Garrett

defined the issue of ARV access in moral terms, making it clear that the world should not permit the poor of Harare, Lagos, or Hanoi to die for lack of treatments that were keeping the rich of London, New York, and Paris alive. The World Bank economist Mead Over told the gathering that donations to developing countries for dealing with HIV/AIDS had reached $300 million in 1999—0.5 percent of all development assistance. But he characterized that sum as "pathetic," claiming that the HIV/AIDS pandemic was costing African countries roughly $5 billion annually in direct medical care and indirect losses in labor and productivity.

In 2001, a group of 128 Harvard University faculty members led by the economist Jeffrey Sachs estimated that fewer than 40,000 sub-Saharan Africans were receiving ARVs, even though some 25 million in the region were infected with HIV and perhaps 600,000 of them needed the drugs immediately. Andrew Natsios, then director of the U.S. Agency for International Development (USAID), dismissed the idea of distributing such drugs, telling the House International Relations Committee that Africans could not take the proper combinations of drugs in the proper sequences because they did not have clocks or watches and lacked a proper concept of time. The Harvard faculty group labeled Natsios' comments racist and insisted that, as Sachs put it, all the alleged obstacles to widespread HIV/AIDS treatment in poor countries "either don't exist or can be overcome," and that three million people in Africa could be put on ARVs by the end of 2005 at "a cost of $1.1 billion per year for the first two to three years, then $3.3 billion to $5.5 billion per year by Year Five."

Sachs added that the appropriate annual foreign-aid budget for malaria, TB, and pediatric respiratory and diarrheal diseases was about $11 billion; support for AIDS orphans ought to top $1 billion per year; and HIV/AIDS prevention could be tackled for $3 billion per year. In other words, for well under $20 billion a year, most of it targeting sub-Saharan Africa, the world could mount a serious global health drive.

What seemed a brazen request then has now, just five years later, actually been eclipsed. HIV/AIDS assistance has effectively spearheaded a larger global public health agenda. The Harvard group's claim that three million Africans could easily be put on ARVs by the end of 2005 proved overoptimistic: the WHO's "3 by 5 Initiative" failed to meet half of the three million target, even combining all poor and middle-income

The Challenge of Global Health

nations and not just those in Africa. Nevertheless, driven by the HIV/AIDS pandemic, a marvelous momentum for health assistance has been built and shows no signs of abating.

MORE, MORE, MORE

IN RECENT YEARS, the generosity of individuals, corporations, and foundations in the United States has grown by staggering proportions. As of August 2006, in its six years of existence, the Bill and Melinda Gates Foundation had given away $6.6 billion for global health programs. Of that total, nearly $2 billion had been spent on programs aimed at TB and HIV/AIDS and other sexually transmitted diseases. Between 1995 and 2005, total giving by all U.S. charitable foundations tripled, and the portion of money dedicated to international projects soared 80 percent, with global health representing more than a third of that sum. Independent of their government, Americans donated $7.4 billion for disaster relief in 2005 and $22.4 billion for domestic and foreign health programs and research.

Meanwhile, the Bush administration increased its overseas development assistance from $11.4 billion in 2001 to $27.5 billion in 2005, with support for HIV/AIDS and other health programs representing the lion's share of support unrelated to Iraq or Afghanistan. And in his 2003 State of the Union address, President George W. Bush called for the creation of a $15 billion, five-year program to tackle HIV/AIDS, TB, and malaria. Approved by Congress that May, the President's Emergency Plan for AIDS Relief (PEPFAR) involves assistance from the United States to 16 nations, aimed primarily at providing ARVs for people infected with HIV. Roughly $8.5 billion has been spent to date. PEPFAR's goals are ambitious and include placing two million people on ARVs and ten million more in some form of care by early 2008. As of March 2006, an estimated 561,000 people were receiving ARVs through PEPFAR-funded programs.

The surge in giving has not just come from the United States, however. Overseas development assistance from every one of the nations in the Organization for Economic Cooperation and Development (OECD) skyrocketed between 2001 and 2005, with health making up the largest portion of the increase. And in 2002, a unique funding-dispersal

Laurie Garrett

mechanism was created, independent of both the UN system and any government: the Global Fund to Fight AIDS, Tuberculosis, and Malaria. The fund receives support from governments, philanthropies, and a variety of corporate-donation schemes. Since its birth, it has approved $6.6 billion in proposals and dispersed $2.9 billion toward them. More than a fifth of those funds have gone to four nations: China, Ethiopia, Tanzania, and Zambia. The fund estimates that it now provides 20 percent of all global support for HIV/AIDS programs and 66 percent of the funding for efforts to combat TB and malaria.

The World Bank, for its part, took little interest in health issues in its early decades, thinking that health would improve in tandem with general economic development, which it was the bank's mission to promote. Under the leadership of Robert McNamara (which ran from 1968 to 1981), however, the bank slowly increased direct investment in targeted health projects, such as the attempted elimination of river blindness in West Africa. By the end of the 1980s, many economists were beginning to recognize that disease in tropical and desperately poor countries was itself a critical impediment to development and prosperity, and in 1993 the bank formally announced its change of heart in its annual *World Development Report*. The bank steadily increased its health spending in the following decade, reaching $3.4 billion in 2003 before falling back to $2.1 billion in 2006, with $87 million of that spent on HIV/AIDS, TB, and malaria programs and $250 million on child and maternal health. The bank, along with the International Monetary Fund (IMF), the OECD, and the G-8, has also recently forgiven the debts of many poor nations hard-hit by AIDS and other diseases, with the proviso that the governments in question spend what would otherwise have gone for debt payments on key public services, including health, instead.

When the Asian tsunami struck in December 2004, the world witnessed a profound level of globalized generosity, with an estimated $7 billion being donated to NGOs, churches, and governments, largely by individuals. Although health programs garnered only a small percentage of that largess, many of the organizations that are key global health players were significantly bolstered by the funds.

In January 2006, as the threat of avian influenza spread, 35 nations pledged $1.9 billion toward research and control efforts in hopes of

The Challenge of Global Health

staving off a global pandemic. Since then, several G-8 nations, particularly the United States, have made additional funding available to bolster epidemiological surveillance and disease-control activities in Southeast Asia and elsewhere.

And poor nations themselves, finally, have stepped up their own health spending, partly in response to criticism that they were under-allocating public funds for social services. In the 1990s, for example, sub-Saharan African countries typically spent less than 3 percent of their budgets on health. By 2003, in contrast, Tanzania spent nearly 13 percent of its national budget on health-related goods and services; the Central African Republic, Namibia, and Zambia each spent around 12 percent of their budgets on health; and in Mozambique, Swaziland, and Uganda, the figure was around 11 percent.

For most humanitarian and health-related NGOs, in turn, the surge in global health spending has been a huge boon, driving expansion in both the number of organizations and the scope and depth of their operations. By one reliable estimate, there are now more than 60,000 AIDS-related NGOs alone, and there are even more for global health more generally. In fact, ministers of health in poor countries now express frustration over their inability to track the operations of foreign organizations operating on their soil, ensure those organizations are delivering services in sync with government policies and priorities, and avoid duplication in resource-scarce areas.

PIPE DREAMS

ONE MIGHT think that with all this money on the table, the solutions to many global health problems would at least now be in sight. But one would be wrong. Most funds come with strings attached and must be spent according to donors' priorities, politics, and values. And the largest levels of donations are propelled by mass emotional responses, such as to the Asian tsunami. Still more money is needed, on a regular basis and without restrictions on the uses to which it is put. But even if such resources were to materialize, major obstacles would still stand in the way of their doing much lasting good.

One problem is that not all the funds appropriated end up being spent effectively. In an analysis prepared for the second annual meeting

Laurie Garrett

of the Clinton Global Initiative, in September 2006, Dalberg Global Development Advisors concluded that much current aid spending is trapped in bureaucracies and multilateral banks. Simply stripping layers of financing bureaucracy and improving health-delivery systems, the firm argued, could effectively release an additional 15–30 percent of the capital provided for HIV/AIDS, TB, and malaria programs.

A 2006 World Bank report, meanwhile, estimated that about half of all funds donated for health efforts in sub-Saharan Africa never reach the clinics and hospitals at the end of the line. According to the bank, money leaks out in the form of payments to ghost employees, padded prices for transport and warehousing, the siphoning off of drugs to the black market, and the sale of counterfeit—often dangerous—medications. In Ghana, for example, where such corruption is particularly rampant, an amazing 80 percent of donor funds get diverted from their intended purposes.

> One might think that with all this money on the table, the solutions to many global health problems would be in sight—but one would be wrong.

Another problem is the lack of coordination of donor activities. Improving global health will take more funds than any single donor can provide, and oversight and guidance require the skills of the many, not the talents of a few compartmentalized in the offices of various groups and agencies. In practice, moreover, donors often function as competitors, and the only organization with the political credibility to compel cooperative thinking is the WHO. Yet, as Harvard University's Christopher Murray points out, the WHO itself is dependent on donors, who give it much more for disease-specific programs than they do for its core budget. If the WHO stopped chasing such funds, Murray argues, it could go back to concentrating on its true mission of providing objective expert advice and strategic guidance.

This points to yet another problem, which is that aid is almost always "stovepiped" down narrow channels relating to a particular program or disease. From an operational perspective, this means that a government may receive considerable funds to support, for example, an ARV-distribution program for mothers and children living in the nation's capital. But the same government may have no financial capacity to

The Challenge of Global Health

support basic maternal and infant health programs, either in the same capital or in the country as a whole. So HIV-positive mothers are given drugs to hold their infection at bay and prevent passage of the virus to their babies but still cannot obtain even the most rudimentary of obstetric and gynecological care or infant immunizations.

Stovepiping tends to reflect the interests and concerns of the donors, not the recipients. Diseases and health conditions that enjoy a temporary spotlight in rich countries garner the most attention and money. This means that advocacy, the whims of foundations, and the particular concerns of wealthy individuals and governments drive practically the entire global public health effort. Today the top three killers in most poor countries are maternal death around childbirth and pediatric respiratory and intestinal infections leading to death from pulmonary failure or uncontrolled diarrhea. But few women's rights groups put safe pregnancy near the top of their list of priorities, and there is no dysentery lobby or celebrity attention given to coughing babies.

The HIV/AIDS pandemic, meanwhile, continues to be the primary driver of global concern and action about health. At the 2006 International AIDS Conference, former U.S. President Bill Clinton suggested that HIV/AIDS programs would end up helping all other health initiatives. "If you first develop the health infrastructure throughout the whole country, particularly in Africa, to deal with AIDS," Clinton argued, "you will increase the infrastructure of dealing with maternal and child health, malaria, and TB. Then I think you have to look at nutrition, water, and sanitation. All these things, when you build it up, you'll be helping to promote economic development and alleviate poverty."

But the experience of bringing ARV treatment to Haiti argues against Clinton's analysis. The past several years have witnessed the successful provision of antiretroviral treatment to more than 5,000 needy Haitians, and between 2002 and 2006, the prevalence of HIV in the country plummeted from six percent to three percent. But during the same period, Haiti actually went backward on every other health indicator.

Part of the problem is that most of global HIV/AIDS-related funding goes to stand-alone programs: HIV testing sites, hospices and orphanages for people affected by AIDS, ARV-dispersal stations, HIV/AIDS education projects, and the like. Because of discrimination against people infected

Laurie Garrett

with HIV, public health systems have been reluctant to incorporate HIV/AIDS-related programs into general care. The resulting segregation has reinforced the anti-HIV stigma and helped create cadres of health-care workers who function largely independently from countries' other health-related systems. Far from lifting all boats, as Clinton claims, efforts to combat HIV/AIDS have so far managed to bring more money to the field but have not always had much beneficial impact on public health outside their own niche.

DIAMONDS IN THE ROUGH

ARGUABLY THE best example of what is possible when forces align properly can be found in the tiny African nation of Botswana. In August 2000, the Gates Foundation, the pharmaceutical companies Merck and Bristol-Myers Squibb, and the Harvard AIDS Initiative announced the launching of an HIV/AIDS treatment program in collaboration with the government of Botswana. At the time, Botswana had the highest HIV infection rate in the world, estimated to exceed 37 percent of the population between the ages of 15 and 40. The goal of the new program was to put every single one of Botswana's infected citizens in treatment and to give ARVs to all who were at an advanced stage of the disease. Merck donated its anti-HIV drugs, Bristol-Myers Squibb discounted its, Merck and the Gates Foundation subsidized the effort to the tune of $100 million, and Harvard helped the Botswanan government design its program.

When the collaboration was announced, the target looked easily attainable, thanks to its top-level political support in Botswana, the plentiful money that would come both from the donors and the country's diamond wealth, the free medicine, and the sage guidance of Merck and Harvard. Unlike most of its neighbors, Botswana had an excellent highway system, sound general infrastructure, and a growing middle class. Furthermore, Botswana's population of 1.5 million was concentrated in the capital city of Gaborone. The national unemployment rate was 24 percent—high by Western standards but the lowest in sub-Saharan Africa. The conditions looked so propitious, in fact, that some activists charged that the parties involved had picked an overly easy target and that the entire scheme was little more than a publicity stunt, concocted

The Challenge of Global Health

by the drug companies in the hopes of deflecting criticism over their global pricing policies for AIDS drugs.

But it soon became apparent that even comparatively wealthy Botswana lacked sufficient health-care workers or a sound enough medical infrastructure to implement the program. The country had no medical school: all its physicians were foreign trained or immigrants. And although Botswana did have a nursing school, it still suffered an acute nursing shortage because South Africa and the United Kingdom were actively recruiting its English-speaking graduates. By 2005, the country was losing 60 percent of its newly trained health-care workers annually to emigration. (In the most egregious case, in 2004 a British-based company set up shop in a fancy Gaborone hotel and, in a single day, recruited 50 nurses to work in the United Kingdom.)

By 2002, the once-starry-eyed foreigners and their counterparts in Botswana's government had realized that before they could start handing out ARVs, they would have to build laboratories and clinics, recruit doctors from abroad, and train other health-care personnel. President Festus Mogae asked the U.S. Peace Corps to send doctors and nurses. Late in the game, in 2004, the PEPFAR program got involved and started working to keep HIV out of local hospitals' blood supplies and to build a network of HIV testing sites.

After five years of preparation, in 2005 the rollout of HIV treatment commenced. By early 2006, the program had reached its goal of treating 55,000 people (out of an estimated HIV-positive population of 280,000) with ARVs. The program is now the largest such chronic-care operation—at least per capita—in the world. And if it works, Botswana's government will be saddled with the care of these patients for decades to come—something that might be sustainable if the soil there continues to yield diamonds and the number of people newly infected with HIV drops dramatically.

But Kwame Ampomah, a Ghana-born official for the Joint UN Programme on HIV/AIDS, based in Gaborone, now frets that prevention efforts are not having much success. As of 2005, the incidence of new cases was rising eight percent annually. Many patients on ARVs may develop liver problems and fall prey to drug-resistant HIV strains. Ndwapi Ndwapi, a U.S.-trained doctor who works at Princess Marina Hospital, in Gaborone, and handles more of the government's HIV/AIDS

Laurie Garrett

patients than anyone else, also frets about the lack of effective prevention efforts. In slums such as Naledi, he points out, there are more bars than churches and schools combined. The community shares latrines, water pumps, alcohol—and HIV. Ndawpi says Botswana's future rests on its ability to fully integrate HIV/AIDS care into the general health-care system, so that it no longer draws away scarce doctors and nurses for HIV/AIDS-only care. If this cannot be accomplished, he warns, the country's entire health-care system could collapse.

Botswana is still clearly somewhat of a success story, but it is also a precariously balanced one and an effort that will be difficult to replicate elsewhere. Ampomah says that other countries might be able to achieve good results by following a similar model, but "it requires transparency, and a strong sense of nationalism by leaders, not tribalism. You need leaders who don't build palaces on the Riviera. You need a clear health system with equity that is not donor-driven. Everything is unique to Botswana: there is a sane leadership system in Gaborone. So in Kenya today maybe the elite can get ARVs with their illicit funds, but not the rest of the country. You need a complete package. If the government is corrupt, if everyone is stealing money, then it will not work. So there is a very limited number of African countries that could replicate the Botswana experience." And despite the country's HIV/AIDS achievements and the nation's diamond wealth, life expectancy for children born in Botswana today is still less than 34 years, according to CIA estimates.

BRAIN DRAIN

As IN HAITI, even as money has poured into Ghana for HIV/AIDS and malaria programs, the country has moved backward on other health markers. Prenatal care, maternal health programs, the treatment of guinea worm, measles vaccination efforts—all have declined as the country has shifted its health-care workers to the better-funded projects and lost physicians to jobs in the wealthy world. A survey of Ghana's health-care facilities in 2002 found that 72 percent of all clinics and hospitals were unable to provide the full range of expected services due to a lack of sufficient personnel. Forty-three percent were unable to provide full child immunizations; 77 percent were unable to provide

The Challenge of Global Health

24-hour emergency services and round-the-clock safe deliveries for women in childbirth. According to Dr. Ken Sagoe, of the Ghana Health Service, these statistics represent a severe deterioration in Ghana's health capacity. Sagoe also points out that 604 out of 871 medical officers trained in the country between 1993 and 2002 now practice overseas.

Zimbabwe, similarly, trained 1,200 doctors during the 1990s, but only 360 remain in the country today. In Kadoma, eight years ago there was one nurse for every 700 residents; today there is one for every 7,500. In 1980, the country was able to fill 90 percent of its nursing positions nationwide; today only 30 percent are filled. Guinea-Bissau has plenty of donated ARV supplies for its people, but the drugs are cooking in a hot dockside warehouse because the country lacks doctors to distribute them. In Zambia, only 50 of the 600 doctors trained over the last 40 years remain today. Mozambique's health minister says that AIDS is killing the country's health-care workers faster than they can be recruited and trained: by 2010, the country will have lost 6,000 lab technicians to the pandemic. A study by the International Labor Organization estimates that 18–41 percent of the health-care labor force in Africa is infected with HIV. If they do not receive ARV therapy, these doctors, nurses, and technicians will die, ushering in a rapid collapse of the very health systems on which HIV/AIDS programs depend.

> Even comparatively wealthy Botswana lacks sufficient health-care workers; the country has no medical school.

Erik Schouten, HIV coordinator for the Malawi Ministry of Health, notes that of the country's 12 million people, 90,000 have already died from AIDS and 930,000 people are now infected with HIV. Over the last five years, the government has lost 53 percent of its health administrators, 64 percent of its nurses, and 85 percent of its physicians—mostly to foreign NGOs, largely funded by the U.S. or the British government or the Gates Foundation, which can easily outbid the ministry for the services of local health talent. Schouten is now steering a $270 million plan, supported by PEPFAR, to use financial incentives and training to bring back half of the lost health-care workers within five years; nearly all of these professionals will be put to use distributing ARVs. But nothing is being done to replace the health-care workers

Laurie Garrett

who once dealt with malaria, dysentery, vaccination programs, maternal health, and other issues that lack activist constituencies.

Ibrahim Mohammed, who heads an effort similar to Schouten's in Kenya, says his nation lost 15 percent of its health work force in the years between 1994 and 2001 but has only found donor support to rebuild personnel for HIV/AIDS efforts; all other disease programs in the country continue to deteriorate. Kenya's minister of health, Charity Kaluki Ngilu, says that life expectancy has dropped in her country, from a 1963 level of 63 years to a mere 47 years today for men and 43 years for women. In most of the world, male life expectancy is lower than female, but in Kenya women suffer a terrible risk of dying in childbirth, giving men an edge in survival. Although AIDS has certainly taken a toll in Kenya, Ngilu primarily blames plummeting life expectancy on former President Daniel arap Moi, who kept Kenyan spending on health down to a mere $6.50 per capita annually. Today, Kenya spends $14.20 per capita on health annually—still an appallingly low number. The country's public health and medical systems are a shambles. Over the last ten years, the country has lost 1,670 physicians and 3,900 nurses to emigration, and thousands more nurses have retired from their profession.

Data from international migration-tracking organizations show that health professionals from poor countries worldwide are increasingly abandoning their homes and their professions to take menial jobs in wealthy countries. Morale is low all over the developing world, where doctors and nurses have the knowledge to save lives but lack the tools. Where AIDS and drug-resistant TB now burn through populations like forest fires, health-care workers say that the absence of medicines and other supplies leaves them feeling more like hospice and mortuary workers than healers.

Compounding the problem are the recruitment activities of Western NGOS and OECD-supported programs inside poor countries, which poach local talent. To help comply with financial and reporting require-ments imposed by the IMF, the World Bank, and other donors, these programs are also soaking up the pool of local economists, accountants, and translators. The U.S. Congress imposed a number of limitations on PEPFAR spending, including a ceiling for health-care-worker training of $1 million per country. PEPFAR is prohibited from directly topping

The Challenge of Global Health

off salaries to match government pay levels. But PEPFAR-funded programs, UN agencies, other rich-country government agencies, and NGOs routinely augment the base salaries of local staff with benefits such as housing and education subsidies, frequently bringing their employees' effective wages to a hundred times what they could earn at government-run clinics.

USAID's Kent Hill says that this trend is "a horrendous dilemma" that causes "immense pain" in poor countries. But without tough guidelines or some sort of moral consensus among UN agencies, NGOs, and donors, it is hard to see what will slow the drain of talent from already-stressed ministries of health.

GOING DUTCH?

THE MOST commonly suggested solution to the problematic pay differential between the wages offered by local governments and those offered by international programs is to bolster the salaries of local officials. But this move would be enormously expensive (perhaps totaling $2 billion over the next five years, according to one estimate) and might not work, because of the problems that stem from injecting too much outside capital into local economies.

In a recent macroeconomic analysis, the UN Development Program (UNDP) noted that international spending on HIV/AIDS programs in poor countries doubled between 2002 and 2004. Soon it will have doubled again. For poor countries, this escalation means that by the end of 2007, HIV/AIDS spending could command up to ten percent of their GDPs. And that is before donors even begin to address the health-care-worker crisis or provide subsidies to offset NGO salaries.

There are three concerns regarding such dramatic escalations in external funding: the so-called Dutch disease, inflation and other economic problems, and the deterioration of national control. The UNDP is at great pains to dismiss the potential of Dutch disease, a term used by economists to describe situations in which the spending of externally derived funds so exceeds domestic private-sector and manufacturing investment that a country's economy is destabilized. UNDP officials argue that these risks can be controlled through careful monetary management, but not all observers are as sanguine.

Laurie Garrett

Some analysts, meanwhile, insist that massive infusions of foreign cash into the public sector undermine local manufacturing and economic development. Thus, Arvind Subramanian, of the IMF, points out that all the best talent in Mozambique and Uganda is tied up in what he calls "the aid industry," and Steven Radelet, of the Center for Global Development, says that foreign-aid efforts suck all the air out of local innovation and entrepreneurship. A more immediate concern is that raising salaries for health-care workers and managers directly involved in HIV/AIDS and other health programs will lead to salary boosts in other public sectors and spawn inflation in the countries in question. This would widen the gap between the rich and the poor, pushing the costs of staples beyond the reach of many citizens. If not carefully managed, the influx of cash could exacerbate such conditions as malnutrition and homelessness while undermining any possibility that local industries could eventually grow and support themselves through competitive exports.

> Preventing brain drain by bolstering the salaries of local officials would be enormously expensive—and it might not work.

Regardless of whether these problems proliferate, it is curious that even the most ardent capitalist nations funnel few if any resources toward local industries and profit centers related to health. Ministries of health in poor countries face increasing competition from NGOs and relief agencies, but almost none from their local private sectors. This should be troubling, because if no locals can profit legitimately from any aspect of health care, it is unlikely that poor countries will ever be able to escape dependency on foreign aid.

Finally, major influxes of foreign funding can raise important questions about national control and the skewing of health-care policies toward foreign rather than domestic priorities. Many governments and activists complain that the U.S. government, in particular, already exerts too much control over the design and emphasis of local HIV/AIDS programs. This objection is especially strong regarding HIV-prevention programs, with claims that the Bush administration has pushed abstinence, fidelity, and faith-based programs at the expense of locally generated condom- and needle-distribution efforts.

The Challenge of Global Health

Donor states need to find ways not only to solve the human resource crisis inside poor countries but also to decrease their own dependency on foreign health-care workers. In 2002, stinging from the harsh criticism leveled against the recruitment practices of the NHS (the United Kingdom's National Health Service) in Africa, the United Kingdom passed the Commonwealth Code of Practice for the International Recruitment of Health Workers, designed to encourage increased domestic health-care training and eliminate recruitment in poor countries without the full approval of host governments. British officials argue that although the code has limited efficacy, it makes a contribution by setting out guidelines for best practices regarding the recruitment and migration of health-care personnel. No such code exists in the United States, in the EU more generally, or in Asia—but it should.

Unfortunately, the U.S. Congress has gone in the opposite direction, acceding to pressure from the private health-care sector and inserting immigration-control exemptions for health-care personnel into recent legislation. In 2005, Congress set aside 50,000 special immigration visas for nurses willing to work in U.S. hospitals. The set-aside was used up by early 2006, and Senator Sam Brownback (R-Kans.) then sponsored legislation eliminating all caps on the immigration of nurses. The legislation offers no compensation to the countries from which the nurses would come—countries such as China, India, Kenya, Nigeria, the Philippines, and the English-speaking Caribbean nations.

American nursing schools reject more than 150,000 applicants every year, due less to the applicants' poor qualifications than to a lack of openings. If it fixed this problem, the United States could be entirely self-sufficient in nursing. So why is it failing to do so? Because too few people want to be nursing professors, given that the salaries for full-time nurses are higher. Yet every year Congress has refused to pass bills that would provide federal support to underfunded public nursing schools, which would augment professors' salaries and allow the colleges to accept more applicants. Similar (although more complex) forms of federal support could lead to dramatic increases in the domestic training of doctors and other health-care personnel.

Jim Leach, an outgoing Republican member of the House of Representatives from Iowa, has proposed something called the Global

Laurie Garrett

Health Services Corps, which would allocate roughly $250 million per year to support 500 American physicians working abroad in poor countries. And outgoing Senator Bill Frist (R-Tenn.), who volunteers his services as a cardiologist to poor countries for two weeks each year, has proposed federal support for sending American doctors to poor countries for short trips, during which they might serve as surgeons or medical consultants.

Although it is laudable that some American medical professionals are willing to volunteer their time abroad, the personnel crisis in the developing world will not be dealt with until the United States and other wealthy nations clean up their own houses. OECD nations should offer enough support for their domestic health-care training programs to ensure that their countries' future medical needs can be filled with indigenous personnel. And all donor programs in the developing world, whether from OECD governments or NGOs and foundations, should have built into their funding parameters ample money to cover the training and salaries of enough new local health-care personnel to carry out the projects in question, so that they do not drain talent from other local needs in both the public and the private sectors.

WOMEN AND CHILDREN FIRST

INSTEAD OF setting a hodgepodge of targets aimed at fighting single diseases, the world health community should focus on achieving two basic goals: increased maternal survival and increased overall life expectancy. Why? Because if these two markers rise, it means a population's other health problems are also improving. And if these two markers do not rise, improvements in disease-specific areas will ultimately mean little for a population's general health and well-being.

Dr. Francis Omaswa, leader of the Global Health Workforce Alliance—a WHO-affiliated coalition—argues that in his home country of Zambia, which has lost half of its physicians to emigration over recent years, "maternal mortality is just unspeakable." When doctors and nurses leave a health system, he notes, the first death marker to skyrocket is the number of women who die in childbirth. "Maternal death is the biggest challenge in strengthening health systems," Omaswa says. "If

The Challenge of Global Health

we can get maternal health services to perform, then we are very nearly perfecting the entire health system."

Maternal mortality data is a very sensitive surrogate for the overall status of health-care systems since pregnant women survive where safe, clean, round-the-clock surgical facilities are staffed with well-trained personnel and supplied with ample sterile equipment and antibiotics. If new mothers thrive, it means that the health-care system is working, and the opposite is also true.

Life expectancy, meanwhile, is a good surrogate for child survival and essential public health services. Where the water is safe to drink, mosquito populations are under control, immunization is routinely available and delivered with sterile syringes, and food is nutritional and affordable, children thrive. If any one of those factors is absent, large percentages of children perish before their fifth birthdays. Although adult deaths from AIDS and TB are pushing life expectancies down in some African countries, the major driver of life expectancy is child survival. And global gaps in life expectancy have widened over the last ten years. In the longest-lived society, Japan, a girl who was born in 2004 has a life expectancy of 86 years, a boy 79 years. But in Zimbabwe, that girl would have a life expectancy of 34 years, the boy 37.

The OECD and the G-8 should thus shift their targets, recognizing that vanquishing AIDS, TB, and malaria are best understood not simply as tasks in themselves but also as essential components of these two larger goals. No health program should be funded without considering whether it could, as managed, end up worsening the targeted life expectancy and maternal health goals, no matter what its impacts on the incidence or mortality rate of particular diseases.

Focusing on maternal health and life expectancy would also broaden the potential impact of foreign aid on public diplomacy. For example, seven Islamic nations (Afghanistan, Egypt, Iraq, Pakistan, Somalia, Sudan, and Yemen) lose a combined 1.4 million children under the age of five every year to entirely preventable diseases. These countries also have some of the highest maternal mortality rates in the world. The global focus on HIV/AIDS offers little to these nations, where the disease is not prevalent. By setting more encompassing goals, government agencies such as USAID and its British counterpart could both save lives in these nations and give

Laurie Garrett

them a legitimate reason to believe that they are welcome members of the global health movement.

Legislatures in the major donor nations should consider how the current targeting requirements they place on their funding may have adverse outcomes. For example, the U.S. Congress and its counterparts in Europe and Canada have mandated HIV/AIDS programs that set specific targets for the number of people who should receive ARVs, be placed in orphan-care centers, obtain condoms, and the like. If these targets are achievable only by robbing local health-care workers from pediatric and general health programs, they may well do more harm than good, and should be changed or eliminated.

In the philanthropic world, targeting is often even narrower, and the demand for immediate empirical evidence of success is now the norm. From the Gates Foundation on down to small family foundations and individual donors, there is an urgent need to rethink the concept of accountability. Funders have a duty to establish the efficacy of the programs they support, and that may require use of very specific data to monitor success or failure. But it is essential that philanthropic donors review the relationship between the pressure they place on recipients to achieve their narrow targets and the possible deleterious outcomes for life expectancy and maternal health due to the diversion of local health-care personnel and research talent.

SYSTEMS AND SUSTAINABILITY

PERCHED ALONG the verdant hillsides of South Africa's KwaZulu-Natal Province are tin-roofed mud-and-wood houses, so minimal that they almost seem to shiver in the winter winds. An observant eye will spot bits of carved stone laying flat among the weeds a few steps from the round houses, under which lay the deceased. The stones are visible evidence of a terrifying death toll, as this Zulu region may well have the highest HIV prevalence rate in the world.

At the top of one hill in the Vulindlela area resides Chief Inkosi Zondi. A quiet man in his early 40s, Zondi shakes his head over the AIDS horror. "We can say there are 40,000 people in my 18 subdistricts," he says. "Ten thousand have died. So about 25 percent of the population has died." In this rugged area, only about ten percent of the adults have

The Challenge of Global Health

formal employment, and few young people have much hope of a reasonable future. Funerals are the most commonplace form of social gathering. Law and order are unraveling, despite Chief Zondi's best efforts, because the police and the soldiers are also dying of AIDS.

In such a setting, it seems obvious that pouring funds into local clinics and hospitals to prevent and treat HIV/AIDS should be the top priority. For what could be more important that stopping the carnage?

But HIV does not spread in a vacuum. In the very South African communities in which it flourishes, another deadly scourge has emerged: XDR-TB, a strain of TB so horribly mutated as to be resistant to all available antibiotics. Spreading most rapidly among people whose bodies are weakened by HIV, this form of TB, which is currently almost always lethal, endangers communities all over the world. In August 2006, researchers first announced the discovery of XDR-TB in KwaZulu-Natal, and since then outbreaks have been identified in nine other South African provinces and across the southern part of the continent more generally. The emergence of XDR-TB in KwaZulu-Natal was no doubt linked to the sorry state of the region's general health system, where TB treatment was so poorly handled that only a third of those treated for regular TB completed the antibiotic therapy. Failed therapy often promotes the emergence of drug-resistant strains.

There is also an intimate relationship between HIV and malaria, particularly for pregnant women: being infected with one exacerbates cases of the other. Physicians administering ARVs in West Africa have noticed a resurgence of clinical leprosy and hepatitis C, as latent infections paradoxically surge in patients whose HIV is controlled by medicine. HIV-positive children face a greater risk of dying from vaccine-preventable diseases, such as measles, polio, and typhoid fever, if they have not been immunized than do those nonimmunized children without HIV. But if financial constraints force health-care workers to reuse syringes for a mass vaccination campaign in a community with a Vulindlela-like HIV prevalence, they will almost certainly spread HIV among the patients they vaccinate. And if the surgical instruments in clinics and hospitals are inadequately sterilized or the blood-bank system lacks proper testing, HIV can easily spread to the general population (as has happened in Canada, France, Japan, Kazakhstan, Libya, Romania, and elsewhere).

Laurie Garrett

As concern regarding the threat of pandemic influenza has risen worldwide over the last two years, so has spending to bolster the capacities of poor countries to control infected animal populations, spot and rapidly identify human flu cases, and isolate and treat the people infected. It has become increasingly obvious to the donor nations that these tasks are nearly impossible to perform reliably in countries that lack adequate numbers of veterinarians, public health experts, laboratory scientists and health-care workers. Moreover, countries need the capacity to coordinate the efforts of all these players, which requires the existence of a public health infrastructure.

At a minimum, therefore, donors and UN agencies should strive to integrate their infectious-disease programs into general public health systems. Some smaller NGOs have had success with community-based models, but this needs to become the norm. Stovepiping should yield to a far more generalized effort to raise the ability of the entire world to prevent, recognize, control, and treat infectious diseases—and then move on to do the same for chronic killers such as diabetes and heart disease in the long term. Tactically, all aspects of prevention and treatment should be part of an integrated effort, drawing from countries' finite pools of health talent to tackle all monsters at once, rather than dueling separately with individual dragons.

David de Ferranti, of the Brookings Institution, reckons that meeting serious health goals—such as getting eight million more people on ARVs while bringing life expectancies in poor countries up to at least the level of middle-income nations and reducing maternal mortality by 15–20 percent—will cost about $70 billion a year, or more than triple the current spending.

Even if such funds could be raised and deployed, however, for the increased spending to be effective, the structures of global public health provision would have to undergo a transformation. As Tore Godal, who used to run the neglected-diseases program at the WHO, recently wrote in *Nature*, "There is currently no systemic approach that is designed to match essential needs with the resources that are actually available." He called for a strategic framework that could guide both donations and actions, with donors thinking from the start about how to build up the capabilities in poor countries in order to eventually transfer operations to local control—to develop exit

Laurie Garrett

strategies, in other words, so as to avoid either abrupt abandonment of worthwhile programs or perpetual hemorrhaging of foreign aid.

In the current framework, such as it is, improving global health means putting nations on the dole—a $20 billion annual charity program. But that must change. Donors and those working on the ground must figure out how to build not only effective local health infrastructures but also local industries, franchises, and other profit centers that can sustain and thrive from increased health-related spending. For the day will come in every country when the charity eases off and programs collapse, and unless workable local institutions have already been established, little will remain to show for all of the current frenzied activity.⊕

Name Index